# MOON HANDBOOKS

# MICHIGAN

## SECOND EDITION

### TINA LASSEN

AVALON
TRAVEL

**Moon Handbooks: Michigan**
**Second Edition**

Tina Lassen

Published by
Avalon Travel Publishing
5855 Beaudry St.
Emeryville, CA 94608, USA

Please send all comments, corrections,
additions, amendments, and critiques to:

**Moon Handbooks: Michigan**
AVALON TRAVEL PUBLISHING
5855 BEAUDRY ST.
EMERYVILLE, CA 94608, USA
email: atpfeedback@avalonpub.com
website: www.moon.com

Printing History
1st edition—March 1999
2nd edition—April 2002
5 4 3 2 1

ISBN: 1-56691-391-8
ISSN: 1099-8780

Editor and Series Manager: Erin Van Rheenen
Copy Editor: Jeannie Trizzino
Graphics Coordinator: Melissa Sherowski
Production Coordinator: Jacob Goolkasian
Map Editor: Naomi Alder Dancis
Cartographers: Mike Morgenfeld, Kat Kalamaras, Chris Folks, Landis Bennett
Proofreader: Mia Lipman
Indexer: Leslie Miller

Front cover photo: © 2002 Laurence Parent Photography, Inc.

Distributed by Publishers Group West

Printed in the USA by R. R. Donnelley

# ABOUT THE AUTHOR
## Tina Lassen

When Tina Lassen was nine years old, hunting for greenstones on a rocky Isle Royale beach, she watched a moose trundle out of the balsams and slip into a wild Lake Superior bay—and she's been smitten with northern Michigan ever since.

A native of the Great Lakes region, Tina has lived in Madison, Wisconsin, since 1979. After obtaining a B.A. in Journalism from the University of Wisconsin, she worked in corporate communications for five years (certainly enough for one lifetime) before founding her freelance writing studio, Pen & Inc Business Communications, Ltd.

Today, Tina writes for a variety of corporate clients throughout the United States, and also writes about travel, outdoor sports, and recreation for several national magazines, including *National Geographic Adventure, Northwest Airlines World Traveler, Better Homes and Gardens* and *Midwest Living*.

Researching *Moon Handbooks: Michigan* was an arduous job, requiring Tina to wander around some of the most beautiful wilderness areas in the Midwest, while avoiding getting her Subaru stuck in the mud on an abandoned logging road 11 miles from the nearest telephone. (Hey, it only happened once.) As part of her research, Tina paddled a sea kayak everywhere from the Keweenaw Peninsula to Drummond Island, mountain biked through the better part of three national forests, hiked in the company of more black bears than she can count, and ate far more blueberries than should be legal. Tina continues to conduct quality testing on red wines from Paw Paw to the Mission Peninsula.

In her free time, Tina enjoys windsurfing, hiking, kayaking, downhill skiing, escaping to the Upper Peninsula, and not getting stuck in Detroit's airport.

*To my parents, who raised me
on national parks and* National Geographic.

# Contents

## Introduction

## The Lower Peninsula

# Keeping Current

Details, details, details. Guidebooks are filled with them—good when they're helpful, very bad when they're out-of-date or misleading. Two years of research went into this book, and every effort was made to make sure information contained herein is correct. But let's face it: places open and close, phone numbers change, prices go up and, yes, writers sometimes screw up. If you know of something special we've missed—or worse, something we've done in error—please let us know so we can make the appropriate additions or corrections in subsequent editions of *Moon Handbooks: Michigan*. Your input will be greatly appreciated. (We welcome nice comments, too.) Please send your comments to:

*Moon Handbooks: Michigan*
Avalon Travel Publishing
5855 Beaudry Street
Emeryville, California 94608
atpfeedback@avalonpub.com

# Maps

## The Lower Peninsula

## The Upper Peninsula

| | | |
|---|---|---|
| ═══ Divided Highway | ☐ County Road | ⸙ Ranger Station |
| ─── Primary Road | ★ Point of Interest | ⚑ Ski Resort |
| ─── Secondary Road | • Accommodation | ✗ Airfield/Airstrip |
| - - - - - Trail | ▾ Restaurant/Bar | ▲ State Park |
| ═ ═ ═ Tunnel | ▪ Other Location | ⋏ Campground |
| ·········· Ferry | ◉ State Capital | ☈ Waterfall |
| ⬡ U.S. Interstate | ○ City | ▲ Mountain |

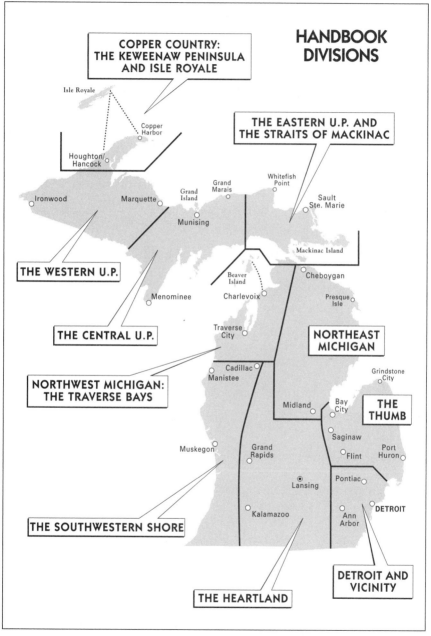

**HANDBOOK DIVISIONS**

COPPER COUNTRY:
THE KEWEENAW PENINSULA
AND ISLE ROYALE

THE EASTERN U.P. AND
THE STRAITS OF MACKINAC

THE WESTERN U.P.

THE CENTRAL U.P.

NORTHWEST MICHIGAN:
THE TRAVERSE BAYS

NORTHEAST
MICHIGAN

THE THUMB

THE SOUTHWESTERN SHORE

THE HEARTLAND

DETROIT AND
VICINITY

Isle Royale

Copper
Harbor

Houghton/
Hancock

Ironwood

Marquette

Grand
Island

Grand
Marais

Whitefish
Point

Sault
Ste. Marie

Munising

Mackinac Island

Cheboygan

Menominee

Beaver
Island

Charlevoix

Presque
Isle

Traverse
City

Grindstone
City

Cadillac

Manistee

Midland

Bay
City

Saginaw

Muskegon

Grand
Rapids

Flint

Port
Huron

Lansing

Pontiac

DETROIT

Kalamazoo

Ann
Arbor

© AVALON TRAVEL PUBLISHING, INC.

# Introduction

# Introduction

## A Tale of Two Peninsulas

*"Si Quæris Peninsulam Amœnam Circumspice."* Translated, the state's somewhat ponderous official motto means, "If you seek a pleasant peninsula, look about you." Hmm. Not the most exciting description. But this watery, wooded state is indeed pleasant, especially if you tend toward understatement.

Surrounded by the wide horizons of four Great Lakes, Michigan's borders stretch along 3,288 miles of shoreline, more than the entire Atlantic seaboard of the United States. That's more freshwater coast than any other state, and more coastline, period, than any state except Alaska. Michigan also claims some of the Midwest's most dramatic topography, including awe-inspiring waterfalls, the nation's highest sand dunes, lofty virgin pine forests, and miles and miles of wild, desolate beach. Those who expect the Midwest to consist only of table-flat cornfields… well, they'll be pleasantly surprised.

Michigan is among the most unusual of the nation's contiguous states. Split in two, it consists of two enormous peninsulas, each surrounded largely by Great Lakes shoreline. Most people associate the state with the mitten-shaped Lower Peninsula, though the Upper Peninsula looms plenty large—big enough to hold the combined states of New Jersey, Connecticut, Rhode Island, and Delaware within its scalloped borders.

There are, in fact, three Michigans. The first is urban Michigan, including the industrial centers of Detroit, Flint, and, to a lesser extent, Grand Rapids. Here are the souvenirs of boom and bust, a fascinating if sobering cycle of American industrialization that has left behind both rags and riches. Not surprisingly, Detroit and southeast Michigan command most of the state's

Old Presque Isle Lighthouse, Rogers City

© VITO PALMISANO

## TWO STATES IN ONE

Is it a case of simple sibling rivalry or a marriage of irreconcilable differences? The Upper and Lower Peninsulas of Michigan are a five-mile bridge and a world apart. Lower Peninsula residents—non-outdoorsy ones, anyway—dismiss the Upper Peninsula as a bug-infested backwoods filled with yokels. U.P. residents (who proudly call themselves "Yoopers") find the generalizations insulting, especially when those same Lower Peninsula folk seem to enjoy the U.P.'s woods and wildlife and beaches while on vacation, thank you very much.

The fact the two are joined as a single state is a bit of a lark in the first place. The Michigan Territory actually wound up with the Upper Peninsula as a consolation prize, part of a deal struck with Ohio in 1837. Both Michigan and Ohio had fought over who controlled the "Toledo Strip," a valuable port on Lake Erie. For Michigan to earn admission to the Union, Congress demanded that the Michigan Territory relinquish all rights to the Toledo Strip in exchange for the "barren wasteland" of the Upper Peninsula. Michigan got the last laugh, though, when priceless quantities of iron ore and copper were discovered in its bedrock just a few years later.

Much of the rivalry is good-natured; Yoopers joke about blowing up the Mackinac Bridge, and like to display a bumper sticker portraying a giant U.P. with a tiny Lower Peninsula dangling from its eastern end. Yet there is a kernel of truth to the squabble. Upper Peninsula residents feel they pay state taxes to a very distant state capital and receive very little in return—except for some government-protected land or wildlife program, which they think they have plenty of, anyway. From time to time, residents launch pseudo-serious drives to declare sovereignty from the rest of Michigan and create the state of Superior. As a musical group from Ishpeming, Da Yoopers, sings, "Dear Mr. Governor, you better turn us loose/We asked you for some rest stops, instead you sent us moose/The honeymoon is over, the declaration's written/We'll take what's above the bridge, and you can keep the mitten."

population and its share of urban problems. Balancing that, though, are the world-class symphonies, art museums, one of the world's finest research universities (the University of Michigan in Ann Arbor), and the state's intellectual hub.

Secondly, there's rural Michigan. The Lower Peninsula still has plenty of idyllic little communities, slower-paced places that existed before the automobile, where neighbors chat at the corner drugstore and participate earnestly in county politics. It also has seen many of these out-of-the-way spots—especially in its northern reaches—evolve into summer vacation towns. No longer out of the way at all, they brim with simple northern "camps" in some places, million-dollar vacation homes, and tony resorts in others. It's a trend that began more than a century ago, changing many of Michigan's small towns forever. Traverse City has grown so popular, some think of it as the state's northern capital.

Finally, there's the Upper Peninsula. Like Mr. Dangerfield, the "U.P." just can't get its share of respect. Treated like a backwoods second-class citizen by many Michiganders, the U.P. is usually completely overlooked by the rest of the nation. Many can't even place it on a map, and more than one cartographer has been known to erroneously deed the giant landmass to Wisconsin, Canada, or the blue boundaries of Lake Superior. Both emotionally and physically, the U.P. is unlike any other part of Michigan, and those who overlook the stereotypes will discover a magnificent land. Filled with vast tracts of wilderness and a wild beauty, the U.P. is a rare find for anyone searching for unspoiled America.

Pleasant? You could say that. Hopefully, after a visit to Michigan, you'll be more likely to add a few stronger adjectives of your own.

# The Land

## Geology and Geography

A combination of cataclysmic volcanic eruptions and soupy tropical seas initially formed what we know now as Michigan. In the northern part of the state, around Lake Superior and northern Lake Huron, erupting volcanoes billions of years ago laid down thick layers of basalt, which later tilted and faulted, forming the area's rugged, rocky topography of ancient mountain ranges and steep, saw-toothed shorelines.

Farther south, a shallow sea covered the vast Michigan Basin, an area that now encompasses the lower four Great Lakes. Over millions of years, sand, shells, and other detritus compacted into thick layers of sedimentary rock, the limestone, dolomite, sandstone, and shale now found from the shores of northern Lake Michigan to the state's southern border and beyond.

Much later, powerful glaciers added their indelible touch to the Michigan landscape, the last one as recently as 12,000 years ago. Four separate ice sheets scraped across the region, scouring out depressions that became lakes, lowlands, and ragged shorelines. When the ice melted and glaciers retreated, the meltwater filled vast basins and created the modern-day Great Lakes.

Michigan comprises three distinct land regions, the Superior Uplands, Northern Highlands, and Great Lakes Plains. The Superior Uplands spans the western two-thirds of the Upper Peninsula, the region formed by that ancient volcanic activity. It is a landscape of dramatic beauty, characterized by rugged basalt cliffs and thick boreal forest of fir, spruce and birch, all of it part of the vast Canadian Shield that dips down from the Canadian arctic, across portions of the northern Great Lakes region, and back up the west side of Hudson Bay in a giant horseshoe. Much of the region rises more than 1,000 feet above sea level, including the state's highest point, Mt. Arvon, which tops out at

*The Great Lakes State, Water Wonderland, Land of Hiawatha. . . many of Michigan's nicknames accurately describe this most beautiful of Midwestern states.*

1,979 feet. The Superior Uplands harbors some of the nation's richest sources of minerals, especially copper and iron ore deposits.

South of the Superior Uplands lies the Northern Highlands, covering the eastern Upper Peninsula and the northern half of the Lower Peninsula. Here basalt bedrock gives way to sandstone and limestone, and boreal forests segue into pine and hardwoods. Once heavily logged for its vast, valuable stands of white and red pine, today the Northern Highlands area is prized largely for the recreation provided by its woods, water, and wildlife.

The Great Lakes Plains stretches across southern Michigan (as well as southern Wisconsin and northern Ohio). This region received the full brunt of the Ice Age and its powerful glaciers, leaving behind a flattened landscape of sandy glacial lakebeds, grasslands, prairie, and wetlands. It also left behind fertile topsoil in many areas, making this Michigan's primary farming region for a variety of vegetable and fruit crops.

Geographically, no other state is so distinctly cut in two. The state consists of two separate landmasses, the Lower Peninsula and the Upper Peninsula, circled by Lakes Michigan, Superior, Huron, and Erie. The two peninsulas are connected solely by the manmade Mackinac Bridge, which spans five miles across the Straits of Mackinac.

Ask Michiganders to give you directions in the Lower Peninsula, and odds are they will immediately hold up a right hand and use their palm to pinpoint within the state. Shaped like a mitten, the Lower Peninsula is 286 miles long and 195 miles wide, with the landmass jutting out into Lake Huron universally dubbed "the Thumb."

The Upper Peninsula shares a border with northeastern Wisconsin, then stretches east for 334 miles between Lakes Superior and Michigan. It reaches a third Great Lake, Huron, where it terminates at Drummond Island. Also considered part of the U.P. is 45-mile-long Isle Royale, the largest island in Lake Superior, and several smaller surrounding islands. The entire Isle Royale archipelago is a national park, one of the most remote and least-visited in the national park system.

Altogether, Michigan's landmass covers 58,527 square miles, making it the 23rd largest state and the largest one east of the Mississippi. But it is water that defines Michigan. Along with its 3,288-mile shoreline—second only to Alaska—

Michigan encompasses more than 11,000 lakes, 36,000 miles of rivers, and more than 150 waterfalls. It boasts 16 federally designated wild and scenic rivers, and another half dozen are under consideration. Both the Upper and Lower Peninsulas are home to a national lakeshore—Pictured Rocks and Sleeping Bear Dunes, respectively.

The Great Lakes State, Water Wonderland, Land of Hiawatha. . . many of Michigan's nicknames accurately describe this most beautiful of Midwestern states.

# Climate

It's difficult to make too many generalities about Michigan's weather, since its two peninsulas cover a lot of latitude, and the Great Lakes tend to complicate weather patterns a whole lot.

Michigan's weather is probably more moderate than you think, since the ever-looming Great Lakes cool the hot air of summer and warm the cold winds of winter. Michigan has four distinct seasons. Summers are shorts–and–T- shirt weather pretty much everywhere (except near Lake Superior, where you just never want a sweatshirt too far away). July and August temperatures average in the 80s in the Lower Peninsula and the 70s in the Upper Peninsula. Come December through February, they drop to the 30s in the Lower Peninsula and the 20s in the U.P. Temperatures listed in the book are in degrees Fahrenheit.

But don't take any of this too seriously. You can enjoy spring-like skiing conditions in the U.P. in February, or freeze to death at Thanksgiving. You may swelter on a summer hike through the woods, then grab for your Polarfleece on a Great Lakes beach. Boring it ain't.

## The Lake Effect

The Great Lakes act like big insulators—slow to warm up, slow to cool down. That's what allows for Michigan's valuable fruit harvest: Lake Michigan moderates springtime temperatures, so fruit trees and vines aren't usually tempted to bud until the threat of frost has passed.

The Great Lakes also have a dramatic effect on snowfall. Dry winter air travels over the Great Lakes on the prevailing western winds, absorbing moisture. When this air hits land, it dumps its load of precipitation in the form of snow. Weather people refer to this phenomenon as **lake effect snows.** They can be surprisingly localized, which is why, for example, you'll find most of Michigan's most successful ski resorts clustered along the western edge of the state.

The prevailing western breezes also affect Great Lakes water temperatures, most noticeably on Lake Michigan. In summer, the warm surface waters tend to blow right into those nice, sandy eastern Lake Michigan beaches. While Lake Michigan is rarely warm enough to do much swimming on the Wisconsin side, it can be downright pleasant in Michigan—as evidenced by the hundreds of popular swimming beaches lining the state.

Lake Superior is another story. Temperatures on this deep, huge, northern lake never climb out of the 40s, save for the occasional shallow bay. "No one's ever drowned in Lake Superior," the saying goes. "They all die of hypothermia first."

Freshwater freezes faster than saltwater, and the Great Lakes will often freeze over from land to several miles out. The ice gets thick enough that brave souls snowmobile to the islands, especially nearby ones like Mackinac. The commercial ship-

## AVERAGE TEMPERATURES

| | (High/Low °F) | |
|---|---|---|
| | **Detroit** | **Escanaba** |
| January | 32/19 | 25/10 |
| February | 34/19 | 29/9 |
| March | 44/27 | 34/18 |
| April | 57/36 | 46/31 |
| May | 70/57 | 58/42 |
| June | 80/58 | 69/52 |
| July | 84/63 | 75/58 |
| August | 81/61 | 73/57 |
| September | 74/55 | 65/50 |
| October | 62/43 | 54/40 |
| November | 46/33 | 40/28 |
| December | 35/23 | 29/16 |

ping season shuts down from January 15 to March 25, but bad weather often hampers it for much longer. Commercial ships regularly pound through ice up to a foot thick; more than that, and they rely on the Coast Guard's *Mackinaw*, a 290-foot heavily reinforced ship specifically designed for ramming a passage through ice. The *Mackinaw* can "back and ram" its way through walls of ice as high as 12 feet.

### A Few Words about Winter

Yes, Michigan has winter. You can usually count on snow and cold temperatures in northern Michigan from about Thanksgiving to Easter. If you want reliable snow, head to the Upper Peninsula. While the Detroit area averages less than 40 inches of snow a year, the U.P. gets blanketed with more than 160 inches annually.

That's an average. U.P. snows are legendary, especially in the Keweenaw Peninsula, where 300-inch winters aren't that unusual. (Sticking far out into Lake Superior, it *really* gets nailed with lake effect snows.) In summer, you'll often notice curious pier-like contraptions sprouting

from front doors and leading to sidewalks on Keweenaw homes, usually a couple feet off the ground. They're to cut down on shoveling—no need to shovel that front walk clear until there's at least 24 inches on the ground. Ladders nailed to roofs are there for a reason, too. When accumulated snows threaten to collapse the roof, the ladders give a foothold from which to clear the stuff off.

You should be aware of a dangerous little thing called the **windchill factor,** the threat that comes when cold temperatures are coupled with biting winds. When it's 5° F outside, a 15-mph wind will make it feel like -25°. Not only is this exceedingly uncomfortable, it means you're at an even greater risk for frostbite or hypothermia. Weather forecasts tend to warn you about the windchill factor, but not always; remember to take into consideration both the temperature and the wind speed when dressing for the outdoors.

Having said all this, many people welcome Michigan's winter, and it's a huge piece of the state's tourism pie. Few other areas in the Midwest can offer as reliable a season for skiing, snowboarding, snowmobiling, ice fishing, and snowshoeing. Of course, sitting around a fire or soaking in a hot tub is acceptable behavior, too.

### When to Go

When to visit Michigan depends on your interests. For traditional warm-weather pursuits, count on summer arriving sometime in early June and lasting until early September. July is the warmest month. (In the U.P., it's also the buggiest.) Try to time a camping trip before the mosquito/black fly hatch—*usually* in mid-June or after mid-August.)

Autumn may be the best month to visit, when days are warm, nights are cool, bugs are gone, and Michigan's hardwoods put on a color show to rival Vermont's. September and October are fine months in Michigan, though be aware that late October can become quite winterish in the Upper Peninsula. For peak color, figure on the first or second week of September for the U.P., and the second week of October for the most southern portions of the Lower Peninsula. Then figure that this will not be accurate the year you plan to visit.

Winter kicks in pretty reliably in December in the U.P., in January in the L.P., and sticks around through March most years. For snow sports, February is probably your safest bet to ensure good cover.

If you can, avoid November and April, both characterized by gray skies and rain/snow/sleet mixtures. Ugh. Spring begins showing up in southern Michigan in early May, working its way northward. The shady pine forests of the U.P. can easily hold snow until Memorial Day. Like autumn, spring in Michigan can be wonderful, with moderate temperatures and blossoming trees.

# Flora and Fauna

## Animals

Though it's called the Wolverine State, there's no evidence wolverines ever lived in Michigan—just a lot of highly suspect tall tales about how it acquired the nickname. (Most likely, early fur traders brought wolverine pelts to the numerous trading posts here.) With more than half the state forested, Michigan harbors lots of red foxes, skunks, squirrels, badgers, minks, muskrats, and other small **mammals.** The state has a huge—and problematic—population of white-tailed deer throughout, and a very healthy number of black bears in its northern reaches. Elk can be found in the northeastern portion of the L.P., part of a successful reintroduction program. Wolves, moose, bobcats, and cougars live in secluded areas of the U.P.

Some 300 kinds of **birds** live in the state, including such notable species as bald eagles, peregrine falcons, loons, swans, herons, and dozens of songbirds. Hunting is popular for game birds such as ducks, geese, grouse, and pheasant. Michigan lies on a major migratory pathway, so it offers excellent birdwatching in spring and fall. Of special note is the hawk migration, as thousands fly between the southern Lower Peninsula and Canada.

With so much water, **fish** thrive here, too, of course, in both the Great Lakes and inland waters. Though commercial fishing has decreased dramatically in the last few decades (the result of overfishing, and the accidental introduction of the lamprey eel and zebra mussel), sportfishing remains popular on the Great Lakes, for chinook salmon, coho, steelhead, lake trout, and brown trout. On inland waters, the walleye and yellow perch are prized for flavor, while the muskie and northern pike are considered top sport fish. Bass, trout, and panfish can also be found on inland waters. Michigan has several blue-ribbon streams, especially near Traverse City and Grayling in the Lower Peninsula, and in the eastern U.P.

The robin is the state bird.

## Insects

And yes, Michigan has its share of pesky insects. There's a reason you spot those corny T-shirts proclaiming the **mosquito** as the Michigan state bird. The first hatch of mosquitoes usually occurs in early June (depending on local weather conditions), and the little buggers immediately discover their love for humans. They won't hurt you, but their sting will cause a small lump and an itchy reaction. Mosquitoes can persist all summer, but tend to be less of a problem as summer wears on, especially if conditions are dry. Mosquitoes are most populous in low-lying wet areas and woods. They tend to be most active at dusk. Your best way to avoid them is to stay in a breeze, and wear long pants and long sleeves. Many people swear by repellent; the stuff with DEET is most effective, but studies have linked it with various health risks. If you choose to use repellent, be sure to wash your hands carefully before eating, and read the label warnings, especially before applying it on small children. Some people

BOB RACE

swear that eating a lot of garlic makes one less attractive to mosquitoes. (Probably to your hiking partners, too, but hey, this is about survival.)

**Black flies** can be an equally obnoxious travel companion. Like mosquitoes, black flies don't pose any health risk but have a nasty bite—somewhere between a mosquito bite and a bee sting on the pain scale. Black flies look like houseflies on steroids. They tend to be worst in the deep woods and in early summer. U.P. black flies can be the stuff of legend; anyone planning time in the backcountry there would be wise to carry the nastiest repellent they can find, and pack a head net, too.

### Reintroduction Programs

Michigan has had great success reintroducing two large mammals to the state. The eastern elk was once common in Michigan, though it had disappeared from the state by 1870. In 1918, state officials relocated seven **Rocky Mountain elk** to Cheboygan County in the northeastern Lower Peninsula. Today, more than 1,000 Rocky Mountain elk roam the woods and meadows of a four-county area. The largest concentration lies within the Pigeon River Country Forest Area near Vanderbilt.

In the 1980s, **moose** were reintroduced to a remote area south of the U.P.'s Huron Mountains, where officials released a total of 59 moose from Ontario in two separate operations. Most interesting was the method of reintroduction: wildlife biologists airlifted the moose one by one in a sling dangling beneath a helicopter to a base camp where they were trucked 600 miles to the Huron Mountains. Van Riper State Park in Michigamme has an interesting display with photos of the infamous "moose lifts." It worked—today, 200 to 300 roam the central U.P.

### Endangered Species

At last count, Michigan was home to 35 threatened or endangered animals, and a whopping 197 plant species. One of the ones that didn't make it was the passenger pigeon. Michigan was one of the premier places in the world to watch the passenger pigeon migration, which would

© BOB BRODBECK

**Elk have been successfully reintroduced to the northeastern part of the state.**

literally blacken the skies as hundreds of thousands of birds took flight. Unfortunately, their meat became a delicacy and they were easy to hunt, a combination that wiped out the species nationwide by 1914.

One hopes a happier ending will result for the gray wolf. With plenty of deer to eat and few roads and people to disturb them, **wolves** have begun to repopulate the Upper Peninsula without help from humans, strolling over from perhaps Minnesota, or across the ice from Ontario. (The wolves that originally populated Isle

Royale came across on the ice in the late 1940s.) The wolf is doing so well, in fact, that it will probably be removed from the state endangered species lists in both Wisconsin and Michigan. With all the controversy surrounding the wolf reintroduction to Yellowstone, Michigan's wolves are indeed a success story.

## Trees and Plants

There's a reason the **white pine** is the state tree—vast stands of the magnificent tree once covered the northern portions of the state, making Michigan the nation's leading lumber center. Michigan pine largely rebuilt Chicago after the Great Fire and supplied a hungry nation as it expanded westward across the treeless plains.

Today, a few tracts of virgin white pine, red pine, hemlock, and cedar remain in Michigan, magnificent species scraping the sky several stories above. Much of Michigan's original prime logging land is now second-growth pines, many growing tall again. Today's logging operations still clear-cut, but in much smaller sections, and are increasingly going to selective-cutting methods.

Along with pines in the north, much of the state is covered in hardwoods, especially oak, maple, aspen, and birch. Michigan had few native prairies, except in the southwestern corner of the state. Therefore, many of its plant species are woodland varieties, including columbine, lilies, iris, various berries, shooting star, violet, trillium, and several species of orchids.

# History

## Michigan's Native Peoples

Buried under layers of glacial ice until about 10,000 years ago, the land that is now Michigan was inhospitable to many of the native cultures that thrived in much of the Midwest, like the Paleo and Archaic Indians. Some of the first signs of civilization can be found in the Upper Peninsula's Keweenaw Peninsula, where the Copper Culture Indians of about 5000–500 B.C. left evidence of their skill as prehistoric miners, devising ways to extract copper from bedrock and fashioning it into tools. Archaeologists believe they may be the earliest toolmakers in all the world.

Later, the **Algonquin** Indians migrated to the Great Lakes region from the banks of the St. Lawrence Seaway, probably sometime after A.D. 1000. The Algonquins were divided into three tribes: the **Ottawa** (or Odawa), the **Ojibwa** (or Chippewa), and the **Potawatomi.** Together, they called themselves the **Anishinabe,** or "First People." They named their new land Michi Gami, meaning "Large Lake." In and around that lake they found the state's abundant wildlife—including white-tailed deer, great schools of fish, moose, elk, and black bear—and rich natural resources that nourished the tribes physically and mentally for centuries before the arrival of Europeans.

The three tribes coexisted peacefully, each moving to a different area. The Ottawa settled around the Straits of Mackinac, Sault Ste. Marie, and the Leelanau Peninsula; the Ojibwa moved west, along the shores of Lake Superior; and the Potawatomi headed south, to the southern half of the Lower Peninsula. They communicated regularly, and their peaceable relationship proved valuable when others came to their lands. Together, they successfully fought off the warring Iroquois who came from the east in the 1600s, and presented themselves as a strong, unified people when the white people arrived.

## The French

Étienne Brulé, the first European to arrive on the state's soil (in 1615), was more interested in exploiting the land than worshipping it. Brulé was sent by Samuel de Champlain, lieutenant governor of New France, who hoped to find copper and a shortcut to the Far East. Brulé sent back reports recounting the land's untamed beauty and strange new flora and fauna.

Other opportunists soon followed. Some were after Michigan's rich supply of furs, others after the souls of what they saw as a godless land. Among the most famous of these early explorers

© DOVER PUBLICATIONS

**Ottawa porcupine quill basket**

was Father Jacques Marquette, who established the state's first permanent settlement at Sault Ste. Marie in 1668, and a second outpost at the straits of Michilimackinac in 1671. The French *coureurs de bois,* a loose term for unlicensed traders, provided a sharp contrast to the priests and nobility. Rugged individualists, they lived among the Native Americans, respected their customs, and hunted and trapped the region's rich stores of game.

Marquette's 17th-century writings brought even more settlers, mostly fur traders such as John Jacob Astor. In the early 1800s, Astor's American Fur Company, headquartered on Mackinac Island, made him the richest man in the United States. Few efforts were made to establish a permanent settlement until 1696, when Antoine de la Mothe Cadillac convinced France's King Louis XIV that the area was under threat from the British, who were forming alliances with the Native Americans, and that it would be a strategic stronghold for the French crown.

The king sent Cadillac and a 100-men-strong passel of priests, soldiers, and settlers to found Fort Pontchartrain in 1701. Cadillac, in turn, persuaded several Native American tribes to form a sort of coalition and settle near the fort. Within a short time, several thousands of Native Americans and several hundred French families lived nearby, many establishing narrow "ribbon farms" along the Detroit River. Known as the village at the strait, *la ville détroit,* it soon became an important trading post and a strategic base for the area's continued settlement. Detroit remains the oldest city in the state and, surprisingly, is among the oldest in the Midwest.

## The British

The area wasn't peaceful for long. As the fur trade became more lucrative, the intensity of the British and French animosity reached its peak, resulting in the French and Indian Wars in the mid-1700s. The war effectively ended the century-and-a-half-long French era and, in 1759, ushered in British rule. Skirmishes continued, though, especially around the Straits of Mackinac. Today, museums and historic state parks in the area chronicle the events.

The British ruled the colony with an iron fist. While the French had treated the Native Americans with a certain amount of respect, the British allied themselves with tribes that were traditional enemies of those native to the area. The British actively discouraged settlement of the state's interior to protect their rich fur empire. In 1783, the Treaty of Paris gave the lands to the newly independent United States.

## On to Statehood

In 1825, New York's Erie Canal, which connected Albany on the Hudson River to Buffalo on Lake Erie, opened. This new water route enabled more and more whites to move westward and settle in the Michigan Territory. From 1820 to 1830, the population more than tripled, to just over 31,000. In 1837, the burgeoning territory was awarded statehood, making Michigan the 26th state in the Union.

By 1840, more than 200,000 people had moved to Michigan. Early industry revolved around farming and agriculture, with lumber becoming a hugely successful enterprise in the later part of the century. Altogether, more than 160 billion board feet of pine were cut and hauled from Michigan's northwoods by the 1890s—enough to build 10 million six-room houses. While the southern part of the state grew increasingly civilized, the northwoods were filled with wild and rollicking logging camps.

## Indian Removal

In one of the saddest chapters in our nation's

# HENRY FORD AND THE HORSELESS CARRIAGE

Henry Ford has been called many things, including industrialist, billionaire, folk hero, preservationist and social engineer. These labels and the many others he amassed support the fact that Henry Ford remains one of the most influential, complex, and puzzling Americans of the 20th century.

Many schoolchildren are taught the story of Ford's pioneering assembly line and the affordably priced Model T it spawned. (No, Ford didn't actually *invent* the automobile.) But most know little else of the automaker who rose from rural southeastern Michigan to become one of the world's richest and most powerful men.

Ford was born in 1863 on a prosperous farm in what is now Dearborn, a Detroit suburb. He enjoyed a typical rural 19th-century childhood, including endless farm chores and long lessons in a one-room schoolhouse. Mechanical things fascinated Ford at an early age. He loved tinkering with watches, and saw his first steam engine at age 12. "From the beginning," he later wrote, "I never could work up much interest for farming. I wanted to have something to do with machinery."

At 16, Ford left the farm and moved to Detroit to serve as a machinist's apprentice. Two years later he was offered an engineer position at the Edison Illuminating Company. By 1893, he had been promoted to chief engineer and began tinkering with a crude iron contraption in his spare time—the first gasoline engine.

In 1894, Ford began his first automobile, which he called the Quadricycle, in a small workshop behind his Detroit home. Two years later, he took it for its first test run. He sold it for $200 in 1896 but later bought it back as a souvenir. By 1898, Ford had quit his job at Edison to devote himself full-time to his dream of producing automobiles.

His first business venture, the Detroit Automobile Company, lasted just a year and was dissolved in 1901. His next effort fared just a little better, with Ford resigning as president of the Henry Ford Company in 1902 after a little more than a year. The company developed into the Cadillac Motor Company under the leadership of Henry Leland.

Ford finally hit pay dirt with the Ford Motor Company, which he established in 1903 at age 40.

The inexpensive, two-cylinder Model A and Model C sold so fast that by 1905 the company was forced to move out of its original factory into larger quarters.

Ford succeeded in part because he viewed the automobile not as a luxury or a toy, but as a tool that could ease the burden of everyday men such as workers and farmers. He believed in making his products as inexpensive as possible, feeling that a low price tag and prompt service would please his customers more than frills and flashy trim.

The car that put America on wheels was Ford's legendary Model T, which became the nation's workhorse. By 1925, the price had dropped to just $260, and sales climbed. More than 15 million were bought and sold. A major factor contributing to the car's low cost was the rise of the assembly line—also pioneered by Ford. Workstations were positioned waist high to minimize the effort expended and the line moved at the exact speed needed to mount a carburetor or lubricate a chassis. The assembly line cut production costs tremendously.

In 1914, Ford made yet another contribution: a profit-sharing plan that more than doubled the salaries of his workers to the then-unheard-of $5 per day. This reduced Ford's turnover and training costs and made Ford a national hero. Workers flocked to Detroit from around the country and the world to work in Ford's plants.

By 1918, Ford had become bored with cars and the company. He increasingly turned to other interests, including a failed attempt to end World War I and an unsuccessful bid for the U.S. Senate.

While his engineering skills were untouchable, others of Ford's habits were less sound. Ford Motor Company's "Sociological Department" was established to monitor the conduct of his workers, but also invaded the privacy of their homes. Ford was also known and condemned for his anti-Semitic beliefs and practices.

Ford grew increasingly rigid in his views as he aged. Despite the fact that his $5-a-day plan made him a working-class hero, he continued to voice violent opposition to the formation of labor unions during the 1920s. This caused widespread unrest in his factories. Ford Motor Company, in fact, was the last of the major auto companies to sign with the United Auto Workers in 1941. Ford died in 1947.

Because Ford amassed an enormous amount of fame and wealth, it has been incorrectly assumed that he was the first to build a gas-powered car. That title, in truth, belongs to George B. Selden of Rochester, N.Y., who applied for the first patent in 1879, the same year that Ford left the family farm. Problems with patents caused some of Ford's largest frustrations long after his original competitors were out of business.

While Ford is perhaps the best known of Michigan's motoring men, others also played key roles. Charles B. King, an engineer, drove the first gas-powered horseless carriage through the streets of Detroit in 1896, six months before Ford. That same year, Ransom Olds of Oldsmobile fame drove a gas-powered vehicle through downtown Lansing. A successful industrialist, Olds developed a steam-powered experimental vehicle as early as 1887. He made his greatest mark, however, in 1900 when he invented a tiny, motorized buggy with a curved dash known as a "Runabout." The $695 price tag brought it within reach of a much wider audience. Olds later left the company to start the REO Motor Car Company, named for his initials. Other key names throughout the automobile's early history were Dodge, Leland, Durant, and others, all of whom played key, if often forgotten, parts in the history of the car.

Today's "Big Three" includes Ford Motors, General Motors, and the Chrysler Corporation. Of the three, Ford is the only one still owned in part by the original family. Henry Ford was always at the center of his company, and his descendants remain involved today. William Clay Ford, Jr., one of his great-grandsons, was named chairman of the board in 1998, the first Ford to hold the title in more than 15 years.

history, President Andrew Jackson signed the Indian Removal Act in 1830, giving the U.S. government permission to "trade" Native American lands east of the Mississippi for unspecified lands out west. The federal government claimed it was for the tribes' own protection, reporting—and correctly so—that whites would continue to surge into their homelands in the name of frontier expansion.

The Indians, of course, had no interest in leaving what had been their homeland for centuries. For unknown reasons, tribes in the northern Michigan and Wisconsin regions were largely ignored by the federal Indian Bureau at first. Most likely, this was only because the government found their lands undesirable at the time; the Potawatomi, who lived on desirable farmland in southern Michigan, were forcibly removed from their lands.

Unfortunately, the federal government didn't leave the Indians alone for long. By the mid-1800s, treaties "legally" took away more and more Indian land in both the Upper and Lower Peninsulas and established many of the reservations that exist today.

The new state government, however, did treat the tribes with a modicum of decency. In 1850, Indians were given the right to vote and even run for office in counties where the population was predominantly Indian—a concession unheard of elsewhere for many years.

## The Copper Rush

In 1840, State Geologist Douglass Houghton confirmed the presence of copper in the Upper Peninsula's Keweenaw Peninsula—vast deposits of pure, native copper, much of it right near the surface, there for the taking. The U.S. acquired the western half of the U.P.—and its mineral rights—from the Ojibwa in 1842, as prospectors began flooding toward the wild and remote Keweenaw. The young United States had an insatiable appetite for the metal, first for new industrial machinery, and later, for Civil War hardware, electrical wiring, and other innovations. Houghton's find was nearly as good as gold.

The Copper Rush began almost overnight, first with prospectors, then large mining enterprises swarming the Keweenaw. Lucky prospectors secured deck space on Great Lakes vessels, sailing up Lakes Huron and Michigan, then along the southern shore of Superior. But hundreds of others straggled through the roadless wilderness, trudging overland through northern Wisconsin by snowshoe, or following rivers through thick forests to reach the fabled riches. It was the nation's first mineral rush. Copper employed thousands of immigrant laborers, built cities, made millionaires, and prompted extravagant luxuries like opera houses and "copper baron" mansions. Before it was over, King Copper generated more than $9.6 billion—10 times more money than the California Gold Rush.

The entire nation turned to the Keweenaw for its copper. From 1845 to 1895, the Keweenaw Peninsula produced 75 percent of U.S. copper; during the Civil War, it produced 90 percent. More than 400 mining companies operated in the Keweenaw over the course of the 19th century, and the resulting demand for labor drew immigrants from more than 30 countries—most notably, the British Isles and the Scandinavian countries. With multiple cultures sharing the same mine shafts and communities, the Copper Country served as one of the nation's first true melting pots.

But virtually all the big mines disappeared one by one in the mid-1900s, sealed up by economic conditions, leaving behind tattered houses and empty streets. They had extracted the easiest-to-reach copper; soon newer mines in the southwestern U.S. and South America proved more cost-effective.

## The 20th Century and the Rise of the Mighty Automobile

In the early 1900s, industrial giants such as Kellogg, Upjohn, and Dow Chemical were getting their start, giving rise to industries that flourish even today. Yet few innovations had as much influence on the state—or on the nation—as the "horseless carriage." Shortly after the turn of the century, it gave birth to the state's largest corporate citizens: Ford Motor Co., General Motors, and Chrysler Motors. As the entire nation quickly grew dependent on their products, the pow-

erful Big Three automakers would soon change the face of the state forever.

With the auto industry came thousands of well-paying jobs and, for most, an improved standard of living. Henry Ford's revolutionary $5-a-day wage attracted workers from across the country and around the world, making Detroit among the country's richest melting pots. Agricultural workers from the Deep South, looking for a better wage, came north to work in the gleaming new factories. Many were African American, an influx that created the Detroit area's largest ethnic group.

As time passed, changing working conditions and a lack of employee representation in the auto factories spurred another American invention: the creation of the labor movement and the rise of unions.

## The 1930s–1950s

While labor unions have existed in Michigan since statehood, few were organized until the 1930s. A number of factors combined to contribute to their growth, including auto industry automation, the uncertainties of the Great Depression, and the pro-labor New Deal environment. The most famous confrontation between labor and management was the December 30, 1936, sit-down strike in Flint, which led to General Motors accepting the United Auto Workers as the sole bargaining agent for its workers.

In contrast to the Depression, the 1950s were an era of great growth and prosperity. Only Florida and California attracted more people during the decade. The rise of the number of school-age children led, in part, to the greatest expansion of the state's educational system and the founding of new community colleges and other facilities of higher education. While plans to build a bridge connecting the state's two peninsulas had existed as early as 1884, it wasn't until the 1950s that the Mackinac Bridge Authority was founded and funds were raised. Work on the bridge began in 1954, one of the largest and most innovative engineering projects in the country. "Mighty Mac" (also called "Big Mac" by some pundits) opened to the public on November 1, 1957, at last linking the two disparate halves of the state—physically, anyway.

## The Civil Rights Era through Today

Racial tensions have erupted into violence on occasion throughout Michigan's history, but few eras were as turbulent as the 1960s. The national struggle for social justice and equality came to a head in Michigan, in some of the state's worst race riots. Before state and federal troops restored a semblance of order in Detroit on July 23, 1967, 43 people had been killed, more than 1,000 injured, and more than 7,000 arrested. Damage to property topped $50 million. This tragic event, one of several urban race riots throughout the country, was just one of a number of violent episodes that marked (and marred) the era.

In some ways, the city of Detroit and the state of Michigan are still digging out from those indelible events. While the makeshift yellow fences that bordered riot sites have long been replaced by new development in many parts of the city, the psychological scars have proven significantly harder to heal. Race relations are an ongoing, front-burner issue in Detroit, one of the most racially divided cities in the country. Always described as the metro area's largest "minority" group, African Americans are, in fact, no longer the minority at all, at least in a demographic sense: projections show that by 2005, Detroit will be almost four-fifths black.

Along with healing racial wounds, Michigan faces a number of other challenges in the coming millennium, according to a study prepared for the Michigan Senate, *Michigan Beyond 2000.* The state must wrestle with a declining and increasingly poor urban population, increasing concern with quality of life, and an overdependence on the ever-fluctuating fortunes of the automobile industry.

On the positive side, one of Michigan's enduring strengths is its abundant natural resources, including one of the nation's largest forest areas and a staggering supply of freshwater—a commodity that, in the long run, will probably prove more valuable than oil. With a 19th-century history of land scarred from clear-cutting virgin forests and lackadaisical mining practices, one hopes Michigan has learned some lessons. Only history will tell if the state chooses to protect or exploit its vast cache of natural riches.

# Economy and Government

## ECONOMY

Despite its patchwork of farm and field, Michigan remains a highly industrialized state. Heavy manufacturing leads the state's list of income-producing industries, followed by tourism and agriculture.

For almost two centuries, Michigan has been a mirror of the country's great industrial transition. As the state's economy has evolved from agriculture and fur trading to metals, logging, and, finally, automobile manufacturing, the state has ridden a roller coaster that shows no signs of stopping.

Ironically, the ups and downs that sometimes curse the state's economic fortunes are nothing new. Just as today's auto industry has experienced both wild success and dismal failure, so it was with the mining era in the Upper Peninsula, which left a legacy of fantastic wealth juxtaposed with depressed towns huddled around played-out mines. In the 1880s, just before the birth of

## MADE IN MICHIGAN

Yep, Henry Ford invented the autombile in Michigan, which in turn prompted the nation's first mile of concrete highway in 1909, and its first freeway in 1942. A few other notable Michiganders and their inventions:

- Mel and Anna Bissell's carpet sweeper
- Dan Gerber's prepared baby food
- John Kellogg's ready-made breakfast cereal
- Dr. William Upjohn's dissolvable pill

the automobile, one reporter noted that "many thoughtful Detroiters have made up their minds that the city had probably seen its greatest growth." Little did they know that in the city's workshops and laboratories, inventors were talking about a revolution.

## Industry

Most Americans today need only look in their garages or on their kitchen tables to find evidence of Michigan's diversified economy. While a variety of businesses—including 22 Fortune 500 companies—call Michigan home, the state will always be associated with the **automobile industry.** Nicknamed "Motor City" and "Motown," the state's largest city and most of its economy are driven by the most enduring of American inventions.

With $5-a-day wages and innovative automated assembly lines, Henry Ford revolutionized the industrial world with his "horseless carriage." To this day, the "Big Three"—Ford, Chrysler, and General Motors—maintain world headquarters in metropolitan Detroit. Those corporations in turn spawned dozens upon dozens of auto-related businesses and legions of millionaires.

Outside of Detroit, industries are a bit more varied. Battle Creek, west of Detroit, is the **cereal** capital of the country, a place where the Kellogg brothers pioneered their new breakfast food at the Battle Creek Sanitarium. Grand Rapids has long been associated with the furniture industry. Midland is the home of Dow Chemical Company. Tiny Fremont claims Gerber, one of the world's best-known baby-food companies. Other Michigan exports include nonelectric machinery, appliances, chemicals, and lumber.

## Agriculture

Beyond the larger cities, however, agriculture dominates. Farming remains an important presence in the state, with approximately 54,000 farms occupying a total of 10,800,000 acres. Crops vary from corn to cherries. The state ranks first in the nation in the production of red tart cherries, dry beans, blueberries, picking cucumbers, and potted geraniums.

Other principal field crops include hay, oats, corn, rye, potatoes, soybeans, wheat, and sugar beets. The western side of the state, which enjoys warmer temperatures modified by Lake Michigan, is known as the "Fruit Belt," and has made the state a leading producer of apples, plums, peaches, and sweet cherries. It also has proved surprisingly tolerant for growing wine grapes, and Michigan's **winemaking** industry continues to surprise people with its award-winning and ever-improving vintages. Rounding out the state's wide-ranging agricultural products are fresh market and processing vegetables, mushrooms, potted Eastern lilies, and spearmint.

## Logging and Mining

Farther north, the Upper Peninsula's economy was long based on logging and mining. Great fortunes were made in logging in the late 1800s, as Michigan's vast stands of virgin timber produced enough wood to lay an inch-thick plank across the state—with enough left over to cover Rhode Island, too. Few can even grasp the riches of Michigan's copper and iron mining industries, which each dwarfed the Gold Rush taking place in California. Michigan produced more than $9.6 billion in **copper** and a staggering $48 billion in **iron,** compared with $955 million from the Gold Rush. The riches and the miners disappeared as the most accessible deposits were exhausted and global economics began to play a role. Nearly all the U.P.'s mines shut down by the mid-1900s.

Since then, the area has relied largely on tourism to keep its sputtering economy going, attracting visitors with its unsurpassed rugged beauty. But **tourism** certainly isn't limited to the U.P. It has become one of the state's largest income producers, accounting for some $7 billion in annual revenues.

## Shipping

Just as semis rumble down the interstate, commercial ships transport commodities across the Great Lakes. Officially designated as the nation's "Fourth Seacoast" by Congress in 1970, the Great Lakes serve as a vital transportation artery for the nation's commerce. Nearly 200 million tons of cargo—worth about $13 billion—travel across

© TRAVEL MICHIGAN

**Michigan is a leading producer of the country's peaches.**

lakes each year. Without them, many of the country's largest industries couldn't survive.

With its hundreds of miles of Great Lakes shoreline and dozens of deepwater ports, Michigan is a key player in the Great Lakes transportation network. What's more, the Soo Locks that link Lakes Superior and Huron at Sault Ste. Marie rank as the largest and busiest lock system in the world.

Iron ore forms the foundation of the Great Lakes trade. In Upper Peninsula ports like Escanaba and Marquette, huge lake carriers as long as 1,000 feet load iron ore from nearby mines, then transport it to steelmaking centers in the southern Great Lakes, where the steel is, in turn, used by heavy manufacturers like Detroit's auto industry. The Great Lakes fleet hauls more than 58 million tons of iron ore every year—nearly twice the "float" of any other commodity. Shipping is an economical way to transport a heavy and bulky commodity like ore; without the Great Lakes, the auto industry and other Michigan manufacturers probably could not survive.

Heavy manufacturing also drives much of the demand for the second-largest cargo, limestone, which is used as a purifying agent in steelmaking. The construction, chemical, and paper industries rely on limestone, too, resulting in annual shipments of about 23 million tons. Michigan has a good corner on the market: the limestone quarry in Rogers City, north of Alpena, ranks as the largest in the world.

Great Lakes shipping does face its share of competition. Much of it comes from overseas, in the form of imported finished products ranging from refrigerators to automobiles. That translates to a decrease in steel production here, which in turn reduces the need for iron ore shipments. Secondly, other transportation networks like trains and trucks compete with shipping for certain commodities. But overall, shipping has proved to be a steady industry, and total cargo shipments have remained pretty even over the last decade.

## GOVERNMENT

Politically, the state has traditionally been a stronghold of the Republican party. One of the major developments of the post–World War II years in Michigan, however, was the emergence of a competitive two-party political arena. Starting during the Depression, the Democratic Party made major inroads into a state that had traditionally been Republican.

Labor union leadership, including the powerful United Auto Workers, became much more active in postwar politics, reflecting the union's interest in larger social issues and quality of life outside the workplace. The electoral support of blacks, whose population had more than doubled between 1940 and 1950, also helped strengthen the Democratic Party in the state. In 1948, Democrat G. Mennen Williams won the first of what would be six terms as Michigan's governor.

Beginning in the 1950s and continuing through today, Michigan politics reflect a highly competitive two-party state. Among the current Michigan politicians in the spotlight is Governor **John Engler,** a farm boy made good who has run the state since 1990. Frequent rumors have him tapped for the Republican nominee for pres-

ident sometime in the future. While he is well-loved by many around the state, others in Michigan—especially liberals, nature lovers, and arts supporters—wouldn't be sorry to see him go.

Also worth watching is Detroit mayor **Dennis Archer,** whose term expired in November 2001. The former Michigan Supreme Court judge took over from controversial mayor Coleman Young in 1992. While Young was best known for antagonizing the suburbs and championing the rights of urban African Americans, Archer proved much more of a peacemaker who has worked hard to mend the sometimes seemingly insurmountable rift between the predominantly black city and its predominantly white suburbs. *Newsweek* magazine has listed Archer as one of the 25 most dynamic mayors in America.

## The People

While the Algonquins were the land's first inhabitants, the residents of Michigan today reflect a much more diverse population. The French "empire builders" were the first Europeans to come, and in due time the British replaced the French. Early American settlers included a large group of Yankees from western New York and New England. From Europe came immigrants seeking a better life, including Finns, Cornish, Swedes, and Italians who worked in the Upper Peninsula mines and lumber camps. Germans, Irish, and Dutch settled in the cities and the rich agricultural lands to the south. Later, the automobile industry attracted large numbers of immigrants from southern and eastern Europe and, later, a large influx of southerners. Between 1850 and 1900, the state's population increased by more than 600 percent.

Today, Michigan's residents number 9.3 million, making it the eighth most populous state in the United States. The vast majority of the state's residents live in the southern third of the Lower Peninsula, mostly near major cities. Just three counties—Wayne, Oakland, and Macomb, near Detroit—contain 43 percent of Michigan's entire population.

### Native Americans

In most books of Michigan history, the land's first inhabitants are given little more than a cursory nod, a line or two that identifies the approximately 100,000 early Native Americans as belonging to the tribes of the "Three Fires," the **Ojibwa, Ottawa,** and **Potawatomi.** The three tribes collectively called themselves the *Anishinabe,* or "First People." Other tribes with a presence in the state during the 1700s included the **Huron,** also known as the Wyandotte, who came to southeastern Michigan from Ontario; the **Sauk,** who lived in the Saginaw River Valley; the **Miami,** who lived along the St. Joseph River; and the **Menominee,** who lived in northern Wisconsin and parts of the U.P.

The fact that Native Americans get little more than a footnote in most history books reflects a larger cultural ignorance both in Michigan and across the country. One of the few state museums to devote any energy or space to the subject is the excellent Van Andel Museum Center of the Public Museum of Grand Rapids, where the fine permanent exhibit, "Anishinabek: The People of This Place," traces the story of the Native Americans of western Michigan. While many American Indian tribes were being removed from their

## PONTIAC: HERO OF THE OTTAWA

A chief of the Ottawa tribe, Pontiac (1720?–1769) was a key Native American leader in the 1750s and 1760s. The son of an Ojibwa mother and Ottawa father, he eventually became the chief of the Ottawa, Ojibwa, and Potawatomi people in the Great Lakes region. Pontiac is best known for organizing the most powerful coalition in Indian history, which successfully fought off invading British soldiers in the 1750s and 1760s.

During the French and Indian War (1754–1763), Native Americans joined the French in their battles against the British over land claims in North America. Nonetheless, the British successfully drove the French out of their most lucrative fur-trading areas. In early 1763, Pontiac organized a conference near Detroit. He brought together the many tribes of the Great Lakes and Ohio Valley and convinced them to join together to fend off the British. The far-reaching alliance was a remarkable achievement, considering how widespread and disparate the tribes were at the time.

Pontiac's diplomacy skills were matched by his military ones. In 1763, Pontiac's forces seized every British post between the Straits of Mackinac and western New York except for two. The fort at Detroit proved their downfall. While some accounts say Pontiac's plan to capture Detroit were exposed by a "half-breed" girl, Pontiac's men did besiege the fort for five months, withdrawing only when the French cut off their supplies. Pontiac and his people retreated to their hunting grounds and eventually signed a peace treaty with the British at Detroit in 1765.

Despite pressure from the French to renew warfare, Pontiac lived among the British in peace until 1769, when he was mysteriously killed by an Indian in Illinois, who was reportedly bribed by a British trader.

---

lands to reservations in Kansas and Oklahoma during the 1880s, Michigan's Anishinabe used skillful negotiation and hard work to remain in their homeland. Through video, hundreds of objects of decorative arts, clothing and tools, and photographs borrowed from local families, the exhibition tells of the high price the tribe paid to remain citizens of the state, and of its ongoing struggle to preserve and protect this heritage in a swiftly changing modern society.

Today, Michigan is home to one of the largest Native American populations in the country, estimated at 50,000. Surprisingly, no one can name an exact figure, since the label of "Native American" or "Indian" can be defined in more than one way—by political (tribal membership), ethnic (genealogy), or cultural (were you "raised Indian?") criteria. Depending on how you count, Michigan may have the largest Indian population east of the Mississippi.

Whatever the accurate number, only a small percentage live on reservations. As with the state's population in general, the majority of the state's Native American population resides in Wayne County, near Detroit, and near Grand Rapids in Kent County.

There are a number of reservations in the state, including federally recognized tribes in Brimley, Suttons Bay, Wilson, Fulton, Baraga, Grand Rapids, Watersmeet, Manistee, Petoskey, Dowagiac, Mt. Pleasant, Brutus, Grand Ledge, and Sault Ste. Marie. Of these tribes, seven are authorized to operate their own tribal courts, which exercise exclusive jurisdiction over certain laws involving Indians and events that occur on their reservations. Tribal courts have broad powers in matters involving child welfare and in a variety of civil matters involving Indians and non-Indians when the activities in question occur on their reservations. In addition, Native American tribal councils throughout the state provide a variety of outreach services, economic development initiatives, and cultural activities.

Many reservations have cultural centers with museums, or at least displays, open to the public. Many tribes also host powwows (native dance ceremonies) and festivals. Check with local convention and visitors bureaus, or inquire at tribal headquarters, which are prominent and well-marked buildings on most reservations.

## The Immigrants

Traveling Michigan's numerous rivers as early as the 1600s, the French fur traders, missionaries, and voyageurs were the area's first white settlers, establishing posts in far-flung areas across the state. The majority of white immigrants, however, didn't arrive until more than a century later, arriving in great waves in the early 1800s. Expatriate New Englanders were the first in the 1830s, grabbing up vast tracts of land in the state's southern counties. More and more settlers followed them in the next two decades, in response to a European food shortage.

During the remaining 19th and early 20th centuries, refugees from at least 40 countries arrived in record numbers. Among them were the **Germans,** still the largest ethnic group in Michigan. In the early 1830s, the first families settled the Ann Arbor area and the Saginaw River valley town of Frankenmuth—today a major tourist destination, famous for its all-you-can-eat chicken dinners more than anything else.

Other early immigrants included **Dutch, Irish,** and **Poles,** who continue to make up large chunks of the state's ethnic population. Concentrations of Dutch can still be found in Holland, a western city along Lake Michigan, where the tulip festival is one of the state's largest tourist attractions. Poles can be found throughout the state, but most notably in Detroit's Hamtramck neighborhood, which has such a large Polish population that it was a stop on Pope John Paul II's American visit in the 1980s. Not far away, the Irish settled Detroit's charming Corktown, the city's oldest neighborhood, better known now as the soon-to-be former site of Tiger Stadium.

By the beginning of the 20th century, a new wave of immigrants poured into the state from southern and eastern Europe, including Austria, Hungary, Italy, and the Balkan States. Their arrival coincided perfectly with Detroit's newest industry, and thousands of them went to work in the auto factories. More recent migrations included Africans, Asians, Latinos, and Middle Eastern immigrants.

**African Americans** today make up one of the most influential ethnic groups in 20th-century Michigan and are the dominant ethnic group in the city of Detroit. While the majority of blacks came from the south to work in the auto industry, there has been an African-American presence in the state since Jean de Sable traded furs in the 1600s.

From the 1830s to 1860s, Michigan played an important role in the Underground Railroad, helping slaves escape to the north and relative freedom. Many escaped slaves went on to Canada, but many stayed in Michigan. The Lower Peninsula's southwest corner attracted a large number of escapees, who started their own farms in towns such as Benton Harbor and Cassopolis. Still, the largest number of African Americans came to Michigan after 1910, leaving farms and families in the south to find better jobs in Detroit's factories.

One of the state's newest waves of immigrants has been from the **Arab** world, including Iraq, Jordan, Lebanon, and Syria. Michigan today has one of the largest groups of Arabic people living in cities such as Dearborn and Southfield near Detroit. Drive through these cities and it's not unusual to see storefront signs in Arabic and women on the streets in full headdress.

The immigrants of the Upper Peninsula vary from the Lower Peninsula's as much as its topography does. The iron and copper mines lured many immigrants—from Sweden, Finland, Italy, and Cornwall, England—with promises of steady work and decent wages. (It came, however, at a price: job conditions were extremely difficult and unhealthy.) **Swedes** and **Finns** in particular took to the U.P., at home with the area's woods and rushing rivers. Finnish names, foods, and the ubiquitous sauna can be found throughout the Keweenaw Peninsula, and Hancock remains largely Finnish, down to its street signs. Farther south, in Detroit, the Finnish Saarinen family helped develop Cranbrook Academy, a well-known private school and arts community near Detroit that was designed by Eliel Saarinen.

# On the Road

This being the birthplace of the automobile, getting out "on the road" is still viewed as the most stalwart of American traditions in Michigan. While other transportation options certainly exist, the auto is the preferred method of travel, a truth never more apparent than on Friday afternoons from about May through October. That's when it seems about half the state's southern residents load up the car and head out on the highway—to hotels, resorts, cabins, camps, and campgrounds "up north."

Though it's best to avoid northbound highways on Friday afternoons (southbound ones on Sunday afternoons aren't much better), you should take a cue from those Michiganders.

Michigan is highly worthy of a road trip—no matter which way you choose to travel. Yes, it sounds like travel-book babble, but this really is a state of remarkable diversity, much more so than anyone expects.

This book begins with Michigan's largest city, Detroit. If you're beginning your travels in Detroit, understand that nothing outside the metro area looks anything like Detroit. And that Muskegon looks nothing like Marquette, and Beaver Island looks nothing like Mackinac, and that the beaches along Lake Huron look nothing like the Lake Superior shore.

Get out on the road and see it for yourself.

© RAYMOND J. MALACE

Dearborn

M

# Recreation

## National Parks and Forests

Michigan is home to four national forests, two national lakeshores, a national park, a national historic park, and a national wildlife area. The federal land is rather evenly divided between the two peninsulas—the Lower and Upper Peninsulas can each claim two national forests and a national lakeshore. **Seney National Wildlife Refuge** occupies 95,000 acres of cutover logging land in the eastern Upper Peninsula, while **Isle Royale National Park** is in a world of its own, a 45-mile long wilderness surrounded by the waters of Lake Superior.

For whatever reason, national forests are often overlooked as visitor destinations—except for maybe a few key attractions like particular waterfalls or beaches—yet they offer a remarkable quantity and quality of activities for anyone interested in the outdoors. **Hiking** trails tend to be little-used. **Campsites** are more secluded, more rustic, and usually lightly used. **Mountain biking** is permitted on miles and miles of federal forest land, and much of it is terrific (mountain biking, however, is often forbidden in state or national parks). Inland lakes can be a little difficult to reach with a boat trailer, so they tend to be ideal for those looking for a quiet **paddling** experience. You get the idea.

The national forests also cover an astounding amount of real estate. The **Ottawa National Forest** in the western Upper Peninsula covers 982,895 acres; the **Hiawatha National Forest** in the eastern U.P. adds another 860,000 acres. In the Lower Peninsula, the **Manistee National Forest** stretches from Lake Superior inland to Cadillac, an area of 500,000 acres. The **Huron National Forest** covers 415,000 acres over on the east side, encompassing lightly developed rivers like the Au Sable. Contact the national forest headquarters to receive information on hiking, camping, paddling, and other activities: Ottawa National Forest, Ironwood, 906/932-1330; Hiawatha National Forest, Escanaba, 906/786-4062; Huron-Manistee National Forest, Cadillac, 231/775-2421.

## State Forests

Like national forests, state forests are a bit of a hidden gem for anyone looking for a quiet corner of woods or water. Much of the state's forest land was actually acquired by default, picked up after the Depression when its owners couldn't pay the property taxes. Their loss was the public's gain—much of the property is exceptional, comprising rivers, waterfalls, lakes, beaches, and, naturally, forest. Altogether, it encompasses 3.9 million acres of land, the largest state forest holding in any state east of the Rocky Mountains.

Visit the Department of Natural Resources website at www.dnr.state.mi.us or contact the following headquarters offices to receive maps and information on Michigan state forest camping, hiking, etc.: Au Sable State Forest, Mio, 517/826-3211; Copper Country State Forest, Baraga, 906/353-6651; Escanaba River State Forest, Escanaba, 906/786-2351; Lake Superior State Forest, Newberry, 906/293-5131; Mackinaw State Forest, Gaylord, 517/732-3541; Pere Marquette State Forest, Cadillac, 231/775-9727.

## State Parks

You'll see it written probably a dozen times in this book: Michigan has an outstanding state park system. They're well-planned, well-maintained and showcase some of the state's most diverse and most beautiful land. Some state parks were clearly set aside for public access—the state park beaches along the Lake Michigan shore come to mind—while others preserve historic sites and state jewels like the Porcupine Mountains and Mackinac Island.

Michigan has 96 state parks, with three more currently under development near Detroit, Traverse City, and Alpena. The Michigan Department of Natural Resources Parks and Recreation Division, 517/373-9900, publishes a handy *State Parks Guide* that includes a map, a short profile of each park, and a chart that lists each park's amenities. You can get much of the same information from its website, www.dnr.state.mi.us.

# SIGHTSEEING HIGHLIGHTS

We love to rank things in America. Still, taking into account varied interests and the wealth of things to see and do in Michigan, a "Top 10" list of attractions seems like a ridiculous, not to mention futile, effort. So how about this instead? Here's a list of 10 sightseeing highlights—in no particular order, for no particular reason except that they're interesting, appealing, only-in-Michigan kind of places.

**Lighthouses:** More than 100 lighthouses pepper the shoreline of Michigan, and 35 of them are open to the public—more than any other state. Many are now operated by local historical societies and include small museums. Better yet, several still let you climb the light tower for guaranteed great views.

**Henry Ford Museum and Greenfield Village:** Not only a place to learn about one of Michigan's most famous sons, this complex outside of Detroit began as Ford's personal collection of inventions that he felt represented the ingenuity of Americans. It has grown to include an exhaustive array of displays and interactive exhibits, including Thomas Edison's actual laboratory, the world's first helicopter, a working 1880s farm, and, oh yes, Henry Ford's birthplace.

**Mackinac Island:** This charming spot off the northern tip of the Lower Peninsula has been celebrated in film and enjoyed by generations of Michiganders. Once you visit, you'll understand why. Free of autos and filled with Victorian mansions and grand hotels, it is a remarkable step back in time.

**Isle Royale:** About as different from Mackinac as you can get, Isle Royale National Park is a wild, rocky archipelago in the northern reaches of Lake Superior. More people visit Yellowstone in a day than visit Isle Royale in a whole season, giving it the distinction of being the least-visited property in the National Park System. Backpackers shouldn't miss it.

**Automaking Tour:** Get a firsthand glimpse of the industry that singlehandedly changed Michigan and the nation. In Lansing, you can tour the General Motors body and chassis plants, where Chevrolets, Oldsmobiles, Pontiacs, and Buicks roll off the assembly line to dealers all over the United States.

**Soo Locks:** Hop on the bleachers in downtown Sault Ste. Marie for a front-row view of the busiest waterway in the world. Mammoth 1,000-foot freighters squeeze through these locks between Lakes Huron and Superior as they navigate the Great Lakes. It's an enjoyable and educational way to spend an hour or an afternoon.

**Sleeping Bear Dunes:** Sleeping Bear Dunes National Lakeshore preserves the largest freshwater dunes in the world, rising more than 450 feet above Lake Michigan. You can hike the dunes, or swim and beachcomb along miles and miles of soft sand beach.

**Tahquamenon Falls:** If waterfalls are your thing, look no farther than the Upper Peninsula, where you can barely turn around without seeing one. The granddaddy of them all is "Taq" Falls near Paradise, the second-largest waterfall east of the Mississippi. Yep, only Niagara Falls is bigger.

**Keweenaw National Historic Park:** With sites spread throughout the Keweenaw Peninsula, this national park helps preserve Michigan's copper mining heritage and educates visitors about a fading, yet fascinating, chapter in the state's history.

**Grand Traverse Bay:** This immense bay in the Lower Peninsula's northwest corner, one of the state's most beautiful and popular vacation areas, is lined with resort towns. The water itself is the key attraction, sparkling in brilliant and ever-changing shades of blue and green usually seen only in the Caribbean.

All state parks charge an entry fee per motor vehicle of $4 per day or $20 per year, no matter how many passengers are in the car. The $20 annual sticker is good for all Michigan state parks. The price is the same for in-state and out-of-state residents. The exception is senior citizens, who may obtain an annual pass for $5, but only with a vehicle registered in Michigan.

There is an additional fee for **camping,** which costs $6–9 per night for rustic campsites, $12–18 per night for modern campsites (flush toilets, showers and electricity), depending on location. Some parks also rent "mini cabins" for $32 a night, tiny shelters that offer you a roof and walls to protect you from the elements, but little more. These book up fast, so reserve yours well ahead of time. A few parks, including Porcupine Mountain Wilderness State Park and Craig Lake State Park, rent rustic cabins, equipped with bunks and stove or other cooking facility, for $25–65 per night. They're great if you have a group or if you're visiting when bugs are particularly fierce. These are *extremely* popular; if you hope to get one, call in January.

> *For whatever reason, national forests are often overlooked as visitor destinations, yet they offer a remarkable quantity and quality of activities for anyone interested in the outdoors.*

For a $2 fee, you can make a camping reservation at any park in advance by calling 800/44-PARKS, or reserving online at www.dnr.state.mi.us. You can request a specific site, but it is not guaranteed. Camping reservations are highly recommended in summer months at many state parks; this book indicates if a park is particularly popular.

## Hiking

With its bounty of national parks, state parks, national forests, state forests, national lakeshores, and whatever various counties set aside for public use, Michigan has almost unlimited offerings for hikers, especially in the Upper Peninsula. Where you go depends certainly on your taste; this book will give you plenty of ideas.

For backpackers, Isle Royale National Park in Lake Superior is an outstanding choice, free of roads and other development. Rustic campsites along the way allow you to hoof your way across the 40-mile-long island; water-taxi services can get you back to your starting point. A little less remote, Porcupine Mountains Wilderness State Park in the western Upper Peninsula also offers great backpacking in a rugged backcountry environment one doesn't normally associate with state parks.

Michigan also has lots of linear hiking trails, like the Bay de Noc to Grand Island Trail, which bisects the U.P., and the Shore to Shore riding/hiking trail, which stretches from Empire on Lake Michigan to Au Sable on Lake Huron. And for those really looking for an adventure, the North Country Trail traverses both the Upper and Lower Peninsulas as part of a national trail that, when complete, will stretch from North Dakota to New York. Many long segments of the trail crossing national forest land are already open to hikers in Michigan. Check with national forest officials for more information.

## Bicycling

With its rolling topography, shorelines, and ample country roads, Michigan makes for a great bicycling destination. Some favorite areas for road riding include the wine country region in the southwest corner of the state around Saugatuck and South Haven, the farmland around historic Marshall, and the lovely Leelanau Peninsula. Check with local visitors bureaus for suggested routes. **Michigan Bicycle Touring,** 231/263-5885, website: www.bikembt.com, offers organized trips throughout the state.

Michigan leads the nation in the number of rails-to-trails, with 55 old railroad beds converted into multi-use trails. Some, like the Bill Nichols trail in the U.P.'s Keweenaw Peninsula, are very rough—they essentially removed the rails and left everything else, including railroad ties and sharp old mining rock. Some of these more primitive trails are appropriate only for snowmobiles and all-terrain vehicles, but most are great for mountain bikes passing through wonderful wilderness terrain. (The Bill Nichols, by the way, is a gem.) At the other end of the spectrum, the 22-mile Hart-Montague state park trail is paved, making it especially popular with families (not to mention in-line skaters).

Unlike much of the Midwest, Michigan is kind to mountain bikers. Good technical mountain biking can be found in many state and national forests, and ski resorts in the Lower Peninsula have wisely courted mountain bikers by maintaining their cross-country trail networks for biking in the off season. Shanty Creek in Bellaire even hosts a pro National Off-Road Bicycle Association (NORBA) event each year.

As for the Upper Peninsula, well, you can pretty much look at it as a giant mountain bike park. Between the national and state forests, you probably have more miles than you could ever ride; then throw in hundreds of miles of old logging roads. Off-road riding in places like the Keweenaw and the Huron Mountains is the best you'll find between the Rockies and the Appalachians—and Michigan adds a little extra perk—some stunning Great Lakes views.

## Skiing

The Great Lakes churn out plentiful lake effect snows, which drop onto some of the Midwest's hilliest terrain. That convenient marriage has made Michigan the top ski destination in the Midwest. While you can't really call anything here mountainous, resorts do an admirable job of working with the terrain they've got, carving out 600-foot vertical drops and runs that wind through the pines or give you jaw-dropping views of the Great Lakes.

Though downhill ski areas can be found throughout the state, they're concentrated in two primary areas: in the western Upper Peninsula from Ironwood to the Porcupine Mountains, and in the northwest corner of the Lower Peninsula from south of Traverse City to just north of Petoskey.

Cross-country skiers have even more to choose from. Garland, near Lewiston, pampers guests with a beautiful log lodge hidden away in the northeastern Lower Peninsula, surrounded by miles and miles of groomed Nordic trails. Though they don't all offer lodging, Michigan has several privately run Nordic trail systems. Many of the downhill resorts, such as Crystal Mountain in Thompsonville and Shanty Creek in Bellaire, also have notable Nordic trails. The national lakeshores and many state parks groom trails for skiing, and the state and national forests offer virtually limitless opportunity for backcountry skiing.

For information on both downhill and cross-country skiing, contact Travel Michigan, 888/78-GREAT, website: www.michigan.org/skiing.

## Golfing

Turns out, northern Michigan has both the perfect climate for turf-growing and a diverse terrain of hills and water views that makes for great golf courses. Golf course architects have noticed. Michigan is home to all kinds of nationally ranked courses, including several with "designer" names like Arnold Palmer, Robert Trent Jones, and Jack Nicklaus attached.

Traverse Bay, Mackinac Island, and the city of Oscoda on Lake Huron form sort of a golden triangle of golf courses. Here, you'll find award-winners like The Bear at the Grand Traverse Resort near Traverse City, Bay Harbor near Petoskey, The Signature near Gaylord, The Fountains in Lewiston, and Scottish-style The Gailes and Lakewood Shores near Oscoda. You'll find plenty of well-kept and challenging courses outside this "triangle" throughout the state, too. For more information, contact Travel Michigan, 888/78-GREAT, website: www.michigan.org/golf.

## Boating and Fishing

Michigan leads the nation in boat registrations—a whopping 874,000. Boaters cruise from port to port on the Great Lakes; sail around large bays like Grand Traverse and along island chains like the one extending off the tip of Wisconsin's Door County; water-ski on thousands of inland lakes; paddle its whitewater rivers and quiet waters; cruise the inland waterway through Cheboygan County; and fish just about everywhere.

Small watercraft like daysailers, fishing boats, and canoes are readily available in many Michi-

© BOB BRODBECK

canoeing on the Au Sable river

gan communities. Contact the local chamber of commerce or visitors bureau in the area you plan to visit for more information. For larger sail- or powerboats, contact the **Michigan Charter Boat Association,** 800/MCBA-971, website: www.micharterboats.com. The Travel Michigan website, www.michigan.org, also has an interactive travel planner that can provide you with a list of charter operations in a given region.

If you'll be trailering your own boat, the Department of Natural Resources, 517/373-9900, website: www.dnr.state.mi.us, publishes a list of public launch sites. (If you'll be arriving by water, see the Getting There section later in this chapter for information on Great Lakes public mooring facilities.) A Coast Guard–approved lifejacket—known as a PFD, or personal flotation device—is required for each person on any kind of boat.

Michigan is a paddler's dream. You can **canoe** down several national wild and scenic rivers, **surf** waves along Lake Michigan's shoreline, **sea kayak** along Pictured Rocks or Isle Royale National Park, or run whitewater. For mellow paddling, the Au Sable is a perennial favorite, stretching from Grayling to Lake Huron. It's the site of the

popular 120-mile Au Sable River Canoe Marathon held every July. Also in the northeastern Lower Peninsula, the Rifle River is less crowded and is a designated wild and scenic river. Other popular paddling rivers include the Platte and Betsie Rivers south of Traverse City, and the Sturgeon River in the Upper Peninsula. The U.P. also has several notable whitewater rivers, including the beautiful Presque Isle River and the Ontonagon. For more information on paddling destinations and liveries, contact the **Michigan Association of Paddle Sports Providers,** P. O. Box 270, Wellston, MI 49689, 231/862-3227, website: www.michigancanoe.com.

Fishing is extremely popular in Michigan, deeply imbedded in the state's psyche. It comes in all seasons and styles, too, from fly-fishing along a pristine stream to hanging out in an ice-fishing shanty, watching the Lions-Packers game. The quantity of blue-ribbon trout streams is unrivaled this side of Montana—enough clear, swift, and rocky waters to make you weep on your Orvis vest. The Fox, the Jordan, the Boardman. . . you'll find most of the best ones in the eastern U.P. and the north-central to northwestern part of the Lower Peninsula.

"Deep-sea" charters on the Great Lakes go

after the big chinook salmon, coho, and lake trout. Lake Michigan's Bay de Noc arguably offers the finest walleye fishing in the state, if not all the Great Lakes. Inland, literally thousands of lakes harbor walleye, northern pike, muskie, bass, and panfish. Some of the most popular spots are the lakes around Cadillac and Indian River in the Lower Peninsula, and Manistique Lakes chain and huge Lake Gogebic in the U.P.

But to avoid the people and the whine of outboards, you really should head for the dozens of small lakes in the Ottawa and Hiawatha National Forests, which are peaceful, harder to get to, not heavily used, and teeming with fish. Some, like the Sylvania Wilderness, have special fishing regulations, so check with authorities. All Michigan waters require a valid Michigan fishing license. For fishing information, contact the Department of Natural Resources Fisheries Division, 517/373-1204, or visit the Department of Natural Resources website at www.dnr.state.mi.us. For current fishing conditions, call 800/ASK-FISH.

## Beaches

For a state nearly surrounded by water, Michigan does not disappoint with its beaches. It offers beaches, in fact, for almost any mood. Public access is excellent. State parks alone provide 142 miles of Great Lakes frontage; county and local parks provide countless more.

The western shore of the Lower Peninsula gets most of the attention; along this Gold Coast, a wide, soft ribbon of sand stretches along Lake Michigan from the Indiana state line nearly 200 miles north to the tip of the Leelanau Peninsula, the longest freshwater beach in the world. With the prevailing western winds carrying warm surface water to these shores, Gold Coast beaches are comfortable for summertime bathing, too. Favorite spots include the immensely popular **Warren Dunes State Park,** near the southern border, and **Ludington State Park,** a six-mile-long sandy point wedged between Lake Michigan and inland Hamlin Lake. High dunes rise along stretches of the Gold Coast, including **Nordhouse Dunes,** between Ludington and Manistee, and **Sleeping Bear Dunes National Lakeshore,**

on the Leelanau Peninsula.

The eastern side of the Lower Peninsula, bordered by Lake Huron, also has fine sand beaches curving along the "Sunrise Shore." **Tawas Point State Park,** near Tawas City, is noted for its pure white sand; **Port Crescent State Park,** at the tip of the Thumb, offers three miles of sandy beach and dunes. The Huron shore, though, is most famous for its many **lighthouses,** which were needed to signal mariners traveling near this low-lying shore.

The beaches of the Upper Peninsula have a completely different mood—often wild and windswept, rocky and remote. Striped cliffs rise directly from Lake Superior at **Pictured Rocks National Lakeshore;** nearby, the **Grand Sable Dunes** and **Twelvemile Beach** provide enough sand to thrill even the most devoted beachcomber. You probably won't see many people along Twelvemile Beach, but you may glimpse a deer, or even a black bear, headed to the water's edge for a drink. While perfect for long, sandy walks, only a hardy (or foolhardy?) few actually swim in Superior—the water temperatures rarely climb out of the 40s.

The U.P. shares its southern shore with Lake Michigan, a winding border filled with bays and inlets. A favorite of anglers, it also has some good beaches—if you know where to look. Public access is a little more difficult here. The best spots are along US-2 from Naubinway to the Straits of Mackinac, where rest stops and county parks point you toward nice sandy beaches hidden behind the pines. You'll find another good sandy stretch along Green Bay between Menominee and Escanaba, where **J.W. Wells State Park** and several county parks offer good swimming beaches.

## Diving

A century ago, the Great Lakes were like today's interstates—the fastest and most efficient way to get around. Commodities like lumber and iron ore were hauled from the forests and mines to Great Lakes ports; passengers traveled on steamships from urban areas around the southern Great Lakes to imbibe the fresh, cool air of northern resorts.

Of course, the Great Lakes also were known

for shallow reefs and violent storms, which led to hundreds of shipwrecks. What's more, the fresh, cold, barnacle- and worm-free waters kept those shipwrecks from decaying. Many of them sit on the lake floor, undisturbed and almost unchanged.

A century later, all of this comes at the delight of divers. Michigan has set aside nine areas where shipwrecks were particularly prevalent as **underwater preserves,** protecting their historic significance, and mapping and marking them for divers. Together, they cover 1,900 square miles of Great Lakes bottomland—an area the size of Delaware. Underwater preserves are located off the Keweenaw Peninsula, Marquette, Munising, and Whitefish Point on Lake Superior; around the Straits of Mackinac, off Thun-

der Bay, the tip of the Thumb and the Sanilac Shores on Lake Huron; and along the Manitou Passage on Lake Michigan.

Most of the popular dive sites are marked with buoys in summer by volunteers of the Michigan Underwater Preserve Council. All the preserves are served by dive charters. For more information, request the booklet that describes each preserve and provides a list of dive charters and other services from the **Michigan Underwater Preserve Council,** 11 S. State St., St. Ignace, MI 49781, 906/643-8717. You can also contact the chamber of commerce or visitors bureau near the preserve you wish to visit, and consult the appropriate chapters in this book.

## Arts and Entertainment

## MUSEUMS AND THE ARTS

### Fine Arts

While the state's tourism boosters have long sung the praises of the state's legendary sand and surf, they've only recently begun promoting Michigan's considerable cultural riches. The majority of the arts scene in Michigan is concentrated in its larger cities, including Detroit, Grand Rapids, and the "northern capital" of Traverse City. Yet the arts thrive from Kalamazoo to Kalkaska, too, both mainstream and underground cultures that plug along without an overwhelming amount of state government support.

When discussing museums, the **Detroit Institute of Arts,** is considered among the top five art museums in the country and is the site of the groundbreaking Detroit Film Theatre.

Also in Detroit, the **Cranbrook Academy of Art and Science** is a huge educational community that pioneered the Finnish Modern school. A tiny treasure worth mention is Detroit's **Pewabic Pottery,** a leading manufacturer of arts and crafts tile, which is enjoying a renaissance among homeowners and history lovers.

in the collection of the Henry Ford Museum

# THE HEIDELBERG PROJECT

Tour buses full of Japanese tourists are a strange sight in this run-down neighborhood on Detroit's near east side, a part of the city better known for its crack houses than its tourist attractions. But then artist Tyree Guyton, who grew up on Heidelberg Street, began what he calls the "Heidelberg Project," a remarkable piece of inner-city environmental art.

As a child, Guyton lived here in poverty, neglected, abused, and harassed for a growing interest in art. Only his grandfather encouraged him. Despite the odds, Guyton went on to study at Detroit's respected Center for Creative Studies (CCS), but he never forgot his roots on Heidelberg. His first work was "Fun House," which he created from an abandoned house next door to his grandfather's duplex. He transformed the dilapidated frame structure with bright patches of color and covered it with old toys, dollhouses, picture frames, shoes, signs, and other urban cast-offs.

The Heidelberg Project grew to encompass most of Heidelberg Street between Mt. Elliott and Emery (to get there from downtown, take Gratiot northeast to Mt. Elliot and turn right). It went on to draw acclaim from newspapers and art journals as well as curators at the nearby Detroit Institute of Arts, but failed to win over neighbors and then-mayor Coleman Young, who regularly demolished Guyton's work along with vacant houses. It takes pride in its reputation as Detroit's most controversial art project.

Recent mayor Dennis Archer was more enlightened, and though he didn't openly encourage Guyton's work, he didn't discourage it either. Guyton's grandfather, who served as an unofficial tour guide, died not long ago. His neat duplex is now part of the project, known as the "Dotty Wotty House" and dedicated to the memory of the grandfather and Martin Luther King, Jr. Other recent additions include the incorporation of trees and elements of the landscape, the "OJ House" (a scathing comment on the famous trial), and Guyton's recent series using mismatched shoes—symbolizing unemployment lines, the homeless, and other "lost soles." Admission is free if you visit on your own. To schedule tours and learn more, contact 313/537-8037 or visit the website: www.heidelberg.org.

---

Outside Detroit, notable art museums include the **University of Michigan Museum of Art** in Ann Arbor, a city known for its galleries and excellent summer art festival; the **Flint Institute of Arts,** which ranks second in size and scope only to the Detroit Institute of Arts; and the **Kresge Art Museum** at Michigan State University in East Lansing, noted for its collections spanning more than 5,000 years of art and local history. The **Marshall M. Fredericks Sculpture Gallery,** part of Saginaw State University, contains one of the state's finest sculpture collections.

## Historical Museums

Henry Ford Museum and Greenfield Village, near Detroit, ranks among the state's top tourism draws, with a funky collection that ranges from vintage washing machines to the Oscar Meyer Wienermobile. Adjacent Greenfield Village is a patchwork quilt of historic buildings, including Thomas Edison's Menlo Park laboratory and the Wright brothers' shop, moved to metro Detroit from around the country. Detroit's new Museum of African American History is the largest of its kind in the world, filled with dramatic visual arts and historic artifacts, including a full-size 19th-century slave ship.

Not surprisingly, many of the state's museums cover the lore and legends of the Great Lakes and the state's maritime industry. Belle Isle, Detroit's 1,000-acre urban park, is home to the **Dossin Great Lakes Museum,** which includes a full-size freighter pilothouse and an anchor from the *Edmund Fitzgerald,* the Great Lakes ship that sank mysteriously in 1975 and later became the subject of a hit song by Gordon Lightfoot.

In South Haven, the **Michigan Maritime Museum** traces the state's history from Native Americans to the 19th century, when huge freighters crossed Lake Michigan, the start of the state's tourism era. In the Upper Peninsula, more stories can be found at Whitefish Point's **Great Lakes**

## FESTIVALS AND EVENTS

**North American Snowmobile Festival:** Cadillac, early February, 800/22-LAKES. More than 10,000 snowmobilers gather on frozen Lake Cadillac for a variety of theme races, then take to the woods on guided safaris. A torchlight parade tops off the weekend.

**UP 200 Sled Dog Championship:** Marquette, mid-February, 800/544-4321. Mushers and their sled dogs race 240 miles from the Lake Superior port of Marquette to the Lake Michigan port of Escanaba and back. An estimated 15,000 gather at the starting line, then celebrate at snowball dances, ice-fishing tournaments, and pancake feeds.

**Blossomtime Festival:** St. Joseph and Benton Harbor, late April/early May, 616/926-7397. Michigan's oldest festival celebrates the blossoming of area fruit orchards with an arts-and-crafts fair, carnival, and Grand Floral Parade.

**Tulip Time Festival:** Holland, mid-May, 800/822-2770. Nothing can top the view of millions of tulips in bloom in this Dutch town, but the festival also hosts *klompen* dancing, traditional "street scrubbing," and wooden shoe making demonstrations.

**National Morel Mushroom Hunting Festival,** Boyne City, mid-May, 231/582-6222. Buses ferry participants to "secret" hunting grounds to search for this gourmet mushroom, while local restaurants feature morel-inspired dishes.

**Summer Arts Festival:** Interlochen Center for the Arts (14 miles southwest of Traverse City), June–Aug., 231/276-6230. The lineup of musicians and entertainers for Interlochen's nightly summer concerts ranges from Yo Yo Ma, Itzhak Perlman, and the Manhattan String Quartet to Ray Charles, the Neville Brothers, Judy Collins, and Vince Gill.

**Straits Area Antique Auto Show:** St. Ignace, late June, 906/643-8087. Auto buffs from around the nation come for this gathering of more than 3,000 classic, hot rod, and custom cars. Events include a vintage car parade and outdoor sock hop.

**National Cherry Festival:** Traverse City, early July, 231/947-4230. Celebrate the area's beloved cherry crop with pie-eating contests, orchard tours, parades, fireworks, and nightly concerts on the shores of Grand Traverse Bay.

**Au Sable Canoe Marathon and River Festival:** Grayling to Oscoda, late July, 800/235-4625 or 937-8837. Dozens of two-person paddling teams run through the streets of Grayling, then launch in the Au Sable for a furious, all-night paddle to Oscoda. Pre-race festivities include a parade, street dance, and ice-cream social.

**National Blueberry Festival:** South Haven, mid-August, 616/637-5171. This four-day celebration honors the fruit with a variety of blueberry foods, a pie-eating contest, five-kilometer run, parade, street dance, and more.

**Ford Montreux Detroit Jazz Festival:** Detroit, Labor Day weekend, 313/963-7622. At Detroit's riverfront Hart Plaza, more than 100 jazz acts perform on four stages, the largest free jazz fest in the nation.

**Mackinac Bridge Walk:** Mackinaw City and St. Ignace, Labor Day, 906/643-7600. Here's your once-a-year opportunity to walk across the five-mile span that connects the Upper and Lower Peninsulas of Michigan. Local restaurants offer special "power" breakfasts to fuel up the estimated 75,000 who take part in this popular event.

**Festival of Native American Culture:** St. Ignace, Labor Day weekend, 906/643-9161. One of the most elaborate powwows, this festival celebrates the Ojibwa tribe's heritage through colorful dancing, feasting, ancient stories, and ceremonies.

© MARJI SILK

the restored Fox Theater

**Shipwreck Museum,** which tells the haunting tale of the hundreds of ships who met their match in the area's frigid, turbulent waters. Also in the U.P., the **National Ski Hall of Fame** in Ishpeming chronicles the downhill and cross-country versions of the sport, while neighboring Negaunee is home to the **Michigan Iron Industry Museum,** an excellent state-run facility on the site of one of the state's first iron forges.

## ENTERTAINMENT

The home of Motown. Need we say more? American music has never been the same since Berry Gordy started a small recording studio, giving birth to the Motown Sound. Soon this fresh, exciting American creation was known worldwide, made famous by local talents like Smokey Robinson, Mary Wells, Diana Ross, Marvin Gaye, Gladys Knight, The Temptations… the list seems almost endless.

But other entertainers make their mark here,

too. Jeff Daniels may be a Hollywood type, but he prefers tiny Chelsea, near Ann Arbor. Daniels, founder of the city's acclaimed **Purple Rose Theatre** (named after the Woody Allen film in which he starred), is just one of the many successful artists and performers who call Michigan home. Others include actors Robin Williams, Sandra Bernhard, and Tom Selleck; the queen of soul, Aretha Franklin, and the queen of pop, Madonna.

Though they hardly fall in the same category as pop entertainers, the world has also been entertained by the words of several notable Michigan writers and poets, including Ernest Hemingway, Bruce Catton, Elmore Leonard, Robert Traver, Theodore Rothke, and Joyce Carol Oates.

### All of Michigan's a Stage

In Motown, the restored Theater District is second only to Broadway in its number of available seats, with performances ranging from cutting edge productions to the classics. Queen of the venues is the 5,000-seat **Fox Theater,** a gloriously gaudy 1920s-era theater that defied the odds to survive until its 1988 restoration by Little Caesars magnate Mike Ilitch. Other Theater District highlights include the **Music Hall,** a favorite venue of traveling dance troupes and home to the Detroit Youtheatre; the intimate 450-seat **Gem Theater;** and the newly restored **Michigan Opera Theatre,** housed in yet another beautifully restored vintage venue. Farther north, the historic **Cheboygan Opera House** was once a stop for luminaries such as Mary Pickford and Annie Oakley.

## Music

As the birthplace of the Motown Sound, it's hardly surprising that Detroit has a long tradition of dance and music. One of the state's most famous exports is the Motor City's piano-playing Little Stevie Wonder (as he was then known), who, along with Diana Ross and the Supremes, Smokey Robinson and the Miracles, The Temptations, and other Motown legends, went on to change the face of American music in the 1950s and 1960s.

Their stories are told in the **Motown Museum,** also known as "Hitsville USA," where displays include everything from the legendary Studio A to original records and flashy Supremes and Temptations costumes. (While Michael Jackson's popularity may have slipped, his white glove remains a popular exhibit.)

Classical fans flock to the acoustically perfect 80-year-old Detroit Orchestra Hall, home to the **Detroit Symphony Orchestra.** Almost as old is the **Grand Rapids Symphony,** founded in 1929. Today this award-winning orchestra stages classical concerts as well as jam sessions by the Grand Rapids Youth Symphony. Farther north, the Traverse City Orchestra is one of the region's premier ensembles.

The lands around Traverse City and the Lake Michigan shore also provide plenty of inspiration for the 1,200-acre **Interlochen Center for the Arts,** which has been described as equal parts music academy, arts camp, and festival. Students from around the world come to practice and perform in a variety of open-air concerts, most of

which are open to the public. Each June, the camp hosts a festival featuring renowned conductors and soloists.

Other summer events include the **International Theatre Festival,** held annually in St. Joseph, and the **Michigan Festival** in East Lansing, which features music and performing arts from around the state.

Alternative music fan? Plenty of options exist in lower Michigan. In Detroit, bands favor St. Andrews Hall and the Royal Oak Music Theater, both known for their warm receptions to cutting-edge artists. Lelli's, in Hamtramck, is also a frequent host of many new wave bands. Kalamazoo's historic State Theater has a regular series that features both local and national touring acts.

Well-known folk artists usually add the Hill Auditorium in Ann Arbor to their list of dates, or the city's legendary Ark, where a variety of names have played through the years. Fans of blues and jazz can find plenty of places to hang out in downtown Detroit, including the Soup Kitchen Saloon and the Rhinoceros, both with long-standing ties to Detroit's music community.

## Dance

Detroit is one of the few large cities without a resident dance company. Companies have started up through the years, but failed, due to mismanagement and a lack of clear vision rather than a lack of audience. Ballets from around the world stop at the city's restored Opera Theater, which sells out regularly. You'll have a better chance of finding modern dance performances at university venues in Ann Arbor and East Lansing. Elsewhere in the state, dance events tend to be held sporadically throughout the summer season.

## Nightlife

Michigan's larger cities have a full plate of nightlife options. On most nights and every weekend, you can choose from blues, jazz, alternative, rock, country, and everything in between. In Detroit, check out the free *Metro Times,* an alternative weekly that provides a comprehensive entertainment listing (and is also known for its colorful personal ads). Another good bet is the Friday "Weekend" section of the *Detroit Free Press,* which lists city events as well as dates throughout the state. Outside of Detroit, nightlife varies, but almost universally gears up in the summer season. From gay bars in Saugatuck to Nugent-lovers in Jackson, there's something for everyone.

## Professional Sports

When it comes to professional team sports, all the biggies are represented in Detroit. For schedule and ticket information, contact: Detroit Lions (football), 800/616-ROAR, website: www.detroitlions.com; Detroit Pistons (basketball), 248/377-0100, website: www.nba.com/pistons; Detroit Red Wings (hockey), 313/396-7575, website: www.detroitredwings.com; and Detroit Tigers (baseball), 313/962-4000, website: www.detroittigers.com.

## Indian Gaming and Detroit Casinos

As sovereign lands, Indian reservations often are able to offer high-stakes gambling that isn't legal elsewhere in the state. Michigan's first Indian-run casino opened in 1984. The Bay Mills Blackjack Casino had just 15 blackjack tables and one dice table in a 2,400-square-foot room in the tribal center. While it wasn't Las Vegas or Atlantic City, visitors quickly displayed their love of gambling, pouring tens of millions of dollars into casino coffers. It started a gambling tradition that has escalated ever since.

There are currently 17 Indian casinos in Michigan. They range from small, simple gambling halls to glitzy showplaces rivaling Las Vegas, such as Leelanau Sands in Suttons Bay. Many are open seven days a week, 24 hours a day, and have become enormous tourism draws.

By the early 1990s, the state wanted in on the deal. In September 1993, Governor John Engler passed the Tribal-State Gaming Compact, giving the state eight percent of net win income derived from games of chance. Contributions total hundreds of millions of dollars. While providing the state government with easy cash, the success of Indian gaming has also given new power and influence to tribal governments.

Now non-Indian groups are eager to seize a piece of this fat cash cow. In 1997, voters in the city of Detroit approved a controversial referendum permitting non-Indian casino gambling within the city limits. Years later, city leaders and residents continue to argue over sites. Three casinos were originally planned for the riverfront; those plans now have been scrapped. In the meantime, three quite permanent-looking "temporary" casinos (see the Detroit chapter for specifics) are busy raking in the cash. Most Detroiters have tired of the controversy—and those still pushing for casino development are advised not to look too closely across the river at Windsor, Canada, where casinos have brought in thousands for their operators but have done little for that city's struggling economy.

With competition from Detroit on the horizon, many of the Indian-owned facilities are expanding. Soaring Eagle, in Mount Pleasant, recently added a 518-room luxury hotel. The Vegas Kewadin complex in Sault Ste. Marie has added an interesting art gallery, which displays paintings, jewelry, and crafts by Native Americans. Not surprisingly, more and more tribes, many of whom live at or near the poverty level, are seeking to open casinos.

While the pros and cons of gambling remain an ethical debate, there's no arguing the positive effect gaming has on the reservations' economies. Within the Indian community, gambling provides jobs and funds schools, health-care facilities, cultural centers, and all sorts of other resources. Many overlook that it provides loads of economic benefits to those outside the Indian community, too, providing jobs especially for the building trades and neighboring tourism industry. Michigan residents and visitors, it seems, just can't spend enough on Lady Luck.

## Accommodations and Food

### LODGING OPTIONS

Yes, from Holiday Inns to Super 8s to Hiltons, Michigan is well represented by all the big chains. If you prefer staying in a tried-and-true chain establishment, pick up a copy of its national directory to find current locations, rates, and services for its properties in Michigan. There's nothing inherently wrong with chains, but you've got plenty of other alternatives, too. All Michigan lodgings charge a 6-percent "use tax," similar to a sales tax. Many counties also have additional room taxes, ranging from 2 to 5 percent, to fund their visitors bureaus and other tourism-related services.

### Independent Motels

The combination of interstate highways and chain motels dealt a fatal one-two punch to hundreds of independently owned motels in the last few decades, as Americans proved their love for efficiency and predictability. The pendulum seems to be swinging the other way these days—interesting inns and distinctive lodges seem to be cropping up in the most unlikely places.

But we're not talking fancy here. We're talking about those good old "mom-and-pop" motels, places with a neon vacancy sign and a couple of lawn chairs out front, the kind of places now romanticized along Route 66.

Well, the happy news is that they never went away in northern Michigan, especially the Upper Peninsula. Too out-of-the-way to attract the big chains, perhaps, many U.P. towns have several independent motels. They're still not fancy, and in some cases, those folks seeking predictability had a point—some *can* be kind of beat up and grungy. But on the other hand, many mom-and-pop motels are clean, tidy, remarkably inexpensive, and offer perks most chains don't—allowing pets, for example. Additionally, they're often pedestrian-friendly, located in town or along a waterfront, rather than stranded out along a highway. (One caveat: Some don't take credit cards, but if they don't, will almost always ac-

cept a personal check.) Many are listed in this book, and you may discover many more. Don't be afraid to try.

### Bed-and-Breakfast Inns

Michigan has hundreds of bed-and-breakfast inns. Some are the traditional, old-fashioned variety—a spare room or two in someone's quaint old farmhouse—but those have become the exception rather than the rule. Today's B&Bs run the gamut from large inns with amenities like pools and tennis courts to renovated lighthouses and other neat historic buildings. For a Michigan Bed and Breakfast directory, send $6 to B&B Directory, 444 Oak St., Holland, MI 49424, or visit the website: www.laketolake.com.

### Ski/Golf Resorts

Many of Michigan's ski resorts double as golf resorts in summer, ringed with lodging that ranges from motel-style rooms to condo units and townhouses with kitchens (which allow you to save considerable money by eating some meals in). Many also offer a number of other amenities like pools, game rooms, fitness centers, and such, so they can be a particularly good choice for families with active kids. While golf resorts tend to be pricey, ski resorts that *don't* have the summer golf draw can be great bargains. For information on golf resorts, and ski resorts with lodging open in the off-season, contact Travel Michigan, 888/78-GREAT.

### Camping

How exactly does one sum up camping in Michigan in a paragraph or two? You can park an RV next to a pool with a waterslide, or you can pitch a tent in backcountry so remote you could go weeks without seeing another soul. Most of us, of course, seek out something in between. With tens of thousands of campsites in the state, you can probably find it, too.

This book lists many campgrounds, though admittedly does shy away from highly developed RV-type properties. Many of the state park campgrounds are included, because they are almost universally good—usually the nicest campgrounds in a particular area. Some can get busy in summer months, though. You can reserve one ahead of time (and even request a specific site, though that's not guaranteed) by calling 800/44-PARKS; website: dnr.state.mi.us.

State and national forests also tend to have nice camping facilities, often more rustic but in appealing, out-of-the-way locations. Backcountry camping is permitted on many forests and commercial land owned by paper and mining companies.

For a complete list of private campgrounds, request a *Michigan Campground Directory* ($3) from the Association of RV Parks and Campgrounds of Michigan, 9700 M-37 South, Buckley, MI 49620, 231/269-CAMP, website: www.michcampgrounds.com; or a free *RV and Campsite Guide* from the Michigan Association of Recreational Vehicles and Campgrounds, 2222 Association Dr., Okemos, MI 48864, 800/422-6478, website: www.marvac.org.

For help in selecting public or private campgrounds geared to tastes and destination, check out the interactive Travel Planner on the state tourism website at www.michigan.org.

## FOOD AND DRINK

Most of the "Indian" food featured in Michigan these days is the kind flavored with curry, not the wild fish and game enjoyed by the state's Native Americans. Short of the few annual powwows held around the state, there's no place to sample the staples of the region's original inhabitants. Michigan's immigrant ethnic heritage is well represented, however. From Hamtramck to Frankenmuth, Dearborn to Detroit, the state's diversity has found its way to the dinner plate.

In Detroit, you can feast on *saganaki* in Greektown and soul food in Bricktown. In the waterfront area known as Mexican Town, busy eateries stay open until 4 A.M. to serve the hungry mole and margarita fans who wait for up to two hours for a table at one of a dozen restaurants. Not far away is Hamtramck, a Polish enclave within the Detroit city limits known for traditional Polish

---

## PASTIES

Prepare your favorite pastry-crust recipe, making enough for four nine-inch pies.

Then mix together:
2 lbs. cooked pork and/or beef, cut into half-inch cubes
2 cups onion, diced
1 cup rutabagas, diced
1 cup potatoes, diced
Salt and pepper to taste

Roll pastry out and cut four circles, using a nine-inch plate as a pattern. On one half of dough, layer meat, then onion, rutabaga, potatoes, and more meat. Fold pastry in half, then roll and crimp edges tightly together. Prick with fork three times. Bake on cookie sheet for one hour at 400°F. Makes four large pasties.

---

kielbasa and pierogi; once a year on Fat Tuesday, Detroiters of all nationalities jam the glass-fronted bakeries to buy up *paczki* (POONCH-key), freshly baked jelly doughnuts. T-shirts for sale claim "I Survived Paczki Day." A little farther west, Dearborn is home to one of the largest groups of Arab peoples in the United States, where restaurants on almost every corner sport signs in English and Arabic and serve up lentil soup, smoothies, tabbouleh, and *fattoush.*

In Frankenmuth, a village near Saginaw settled by Germans in the mid-1800s, buses and cars come from miles around for the all-you-can-eat chicken and strudel in two cavernous restaurants owned by the Zehnder family. Made popular by traveling salesmen and Detroit families "out for a drive" in the 1950s, the Bavarian-inspired town has become a phenomenon and one of the state's top tourist attractions. In Holland, Dutch food reigns of course, with flaky pastries the specialty at the popular Queen's Inn at Dutch Village.

Throughout the Upper Peninsula, many main street cafés and bakeries serve up the pasty, a potpie creation of beef, potatoes, onions, rutabagas, and other vegetables. (Pronounce it "PASS-tee," not "PACE-tee," like the stripper accessory!) Brought to the U.P. by Cornish miners, the pasty made for a hearty and filling meal, one that was easy to transport deep into the mine and warm up later with their candles. The same concept works well today if you're headed from town to your campfire.

Another Michigan food well worth tasting is its abundant fresh fish, from brook trout to Great Lakes whitefish. In Great Lakes ports, you'll often be able to find a commercial fishery operating a small retail store, usually down by the docks. They often sell both fresh catch and smoked fish. The latter is absolutely superb with a bottle of wine and a Great Lakes sunset.

## Wine-tasting

With temperature extremes moderated by prevailing western winds and Lake Michigan, two areas of the state have developed into bona fide wine-producing regions. Both in the southwestern corner of the Lower Peninsula and around Grand Traverse Bay, local wineries have won international acclaim producing wines from Michigan grapes. White wines like rieslings and chardonnays tend to be their best offerings, but vintners like Larry Mawby have had success with reds, too.

Many Michigan wineries offer free tours and tastings. A few to try: Warner Vineyards, Paw Paw, 616/657-3165; Tabor Hill Winery, Buchanan, 800/283-3363; L. Mawby Vineyards, Suttons Bay,

The proprietor of Drier's Meat Market stands behind his wares.

231/271-3522; and Chateau Grand Traverse, Traverse City, 231/223-7355. For more information on Michigan wineries, contact the **Michigan Grape and Wine Industry Council,** 517/373-1104, website: www.michiganwines.com.

## Transportation

### GETTING THERE

#### By Car

About a half dozen major interstates and highways make it mighty efficient zipping around Michigan. I-75 stretches from the southern border at Toledo through Detroit, and all the way north across the Mackinac Bridge to Sault Ste. Marie. I-94 comes over from Chicago, then traverses the southern tier of the state to Detroit. I-69 cruises up the middle, from Indianapolis up through Lansing, then east to Flint and Port Huron. Major state highways include US-27, which heads north from Lansing and links up

with I-75 near Grayling; US-131 from Kalamazoo to Petoskey; and US-31, which follows the Lake Michigan shore as a major four-lane from Benton Harbor to Ludington, then becomes a smaller two-lane to Traverse City and on to Petoskey.

In the Upper Peninsula, two routes pretty much traverse the peninsula east to west: M-28 is the northern route, passing through Marquette; US-2 is the southern route, passing through Escanaba. Several state (and a couple of federal) highways running north-south link the two. If you're traveling all the way from the eastern end of the U.P. to Ironwood, M-28 is usually faster.

## By Bus

**Greyhound,** 800/231-2222, website: www.greyhound.com, operates in all major Michigan cities. It can be a very inexpensive way to travel if you've got the time. Traveling from Kalamazoo to the Keweenaw Peninsula, for example, takes 16 hours—but costs only about $60.

## By Train

**Amtrak,** 800/USA-RAIL, runs a handful of regular routes through Michigan, with plenty of bus and train connections possible. (Chicago is an Amtrak hub, so most westbound travel routes through there.) One Michigan route travels from Chicago through Benton Harbor and Holland to Grand Rapids. A second travels from Chicago through Battle Creek to Port Huron. A third Chicago train splits at Battle Creek and heads for Detroit. A fourth runs between Detroit and Toledo, Ohio. From Detroit and Port Huron, Canada's **VIA Rail** offers service to Toronto.

## By Plane

No surprise here: the **Detroit Metropolitan Airport (DTW),** 800/642-1978, is the state's biggest and busiest. It's also a hub for Northwest Airlines, 800/225-2525, and its sister airline KLM, so you can fly direct from Detroit to pretty much anywhere in the United States and Canada, and to a surprising number of cities around the globe, from Amsterdam to Osaka. Northwest also offers the most comprehensive service elsewhere in the state. It flies into most of the state's commercial airports, including Benton Harbor, Escanaba, Grand Rapids, Hancock, Kalamazoo/Battle Creek, Lansing, Marquette, Muskegon, Pellston/Mackinac Island, Saginaw/Bay City/Midland, and Traverse City.

Of course, Northwest's muscle means other airlines don't offer as many flights in and out of the state. Check with American Airlines/American Eagle, 800/433-7300; Delta, 800/221-1212; Southwest, 800/435-9792; TWA, 800/221-2000; United/United Express, 800/241-6522; and US Airways, 800/428-4322. Northwest, United, and American are your only options to the Upper Peninsula. Since routes and carriers seem to

change with the weather, your best bet is to call a travel agent.

## By Water

Surrounded by zillions of miles of shoreline, many visitors do enter Michigan via the Great Lakes, and they'll find plenty of places to tie up the boat when they get here. The state's Parks and Recreation Division has established a network of 73 protected **public mooring facilities** along the Great Lakes, a "marine highway" that ensures boaters are never far from a safe harbor. More are being added every year, with the goal of locating them so a boater is never more than 15 shoreline miles away from a protected public mooring. Mooring fees vary. For more information or a free *Michigan Harbors Guide,* contact Department of Natural Resources, Parks and Recreation Division, P. O. Box 30257, Lansing, MI 48909, 517/373-9900.

Nonboaters, too, can arrive by water via the SS *Badger,* the only passenger steamship on the Great Lakes. The 410-foot-long ship ferries up to 620 passengers and 130 autos across the middle of

ON THE ROAD

**Port Huron**

© BOB BRODBECK

Lake Michigan, from Manitowoc, Wisconsin, to Ludington, Michigan. For travelers to and from Wisconsin, the four-hour passage saves an ugly, congested auto trip through Chicago, or a pretty but lengthy jaunt up across the Upper Peninsula. Plus it saves gas and is great fun.

Built in 1952, the SS *Badger* was one of seven railroad and passenger ferries crossing Lake Michigan; you can still see the railroad tracks that lead into the car deck. The *Badger* marked the end of an era; ferries were to the Great Lakes what steamboats were to the Mississippi. Today, it's the only ferry of its kind that remains and has been quite inventive about making a go at it. It does some commercial business (transporting loaded trucks) and does get occasional business travelers, but tourism is its bread and butter. The ship is comfortably outfitted with tables and chairs, lounge seating, a theater showing free movies, a cafeteria, gift shop, and small staterooms that you can rent for $29 extra each way. Equipped with twin berths, these are well worth it if you hope to catch some sleep. There's ample deck space and chaise lounges, if it's warm enough. The crew even hosts kids' games, a sing-along, and bingo, if you're so inclined.

The *Badger* sails daily from mid-May through mid-October. It departs Ludington at 8:30 A.M. from the beginning of the season to mid-June and from late August to the end of the season. From mid-June through late August it offers two passages daily, at 7:30 A.M. and 7:45 P.M. Rates in high season (spring and fall are a few bucks less) are $42 one-way, $69 roundtrip for adults, $18 and $31 for children 5–15, $39 and $64 for seniors 65 and older, $45 each way for autos, and $5 each way for bicycles. Pets must remain in your auto or in a kennel (which you must provide) on the car deck, which can get extremely hot in summer months and is not recommended. You cannot access your vehicle during the crossing.

For information and reservations (strongly recommended), contact **Lake Michigan Car Ferry**, 888/337-7948, website: www.ssbadger.com.

## GETTING AROUND

For information on getting around by bus, train, or plane, see the companies listed in Getting There, above.

### The Road

Roads in Michigan are plentiful and good. Along with interstates and federal highways, the state is crisscrossed with numerous state highways, marked on road maps by a number with a circle or oval around it. In conversion, they are often preceded by an "M," as in, "Follow M-28 west to Marquette." County roads are marked with squares on most road maps. In this book, county road numbers are preceded by "CR."

When planning a route in the Upper Peninsula, consult your map legend regarding road surfaces. Roads you simply might assume are paved may be gravel or dirt, which can make for very slow going. All state and federal highways are paved and well-maintained, as are most county roads and many more secondary roads. But just be aware. For road construction updates, the Michigan Department of Transportation has a road construction hotline, 800/641-6368.

Interstate speed limits in Michigan are 70 miles per hour, unless otherwise posted. Most four-lane highways, and many two-lanes, have increased their limits to 65 mph.

Finally, there's a myth that driving a foreign car is a thoughtless or even dangerous practice in the birthplace of the American automobile. While that may have been somewhat true in the 1970s when the Japanese were doing serious damage to the U.S. auto industry, it's not the case today.

> *There's a myth that driving a foreign car is a thoughtless or even dangerous practice in the birthplace of the American automobile. These days, many "foreign" cars are made in the United States, and U.S. plants supply parts to foreign automakers, so it's pretty much a moot point.*

## HOW FAR IS IT?

Comprising two large peninsulas, Michigan is a bigger place than it appears on many maps. It can be deceptively far from Point A to Point B, especially if Point A is, say, Kalamazoo and Point B is Copper Harbor. Would you believe 584 miles? To put it in perspective, traveling the same distance from Kalamazoo would take you to St. Louis or Washington, D.C.

### Distance from Detroit to:

Alpena: 233 miles
Benton Harbor/St. Joseph: 183 miles
Copper Harbor: 595 miles
Escanaba: 429 miles
Ironwood: 593 miles
Mackinaw City: 281 miles
Marquette: 448 miles
Traverse City: 242 miles

### Distance from Marquette to:

Benton Harbor/St. Joseph: 469 miles
Copper Harbor: 147 miles
Ironwood: 145 miles
Menominee: 120 miles
Munising: 43 miles
Port Austin: 413 miles
St. Ignace: 165 miles
Traverse City: 269 miles

These days, many "foreign" cars are made in the United States, and U.S. plants supply parts to foreign automakers, so it's pretty much a moot point. But don't push it too far. You might not feel comfortable parking your Toyota, say, in front of a tavern near the Flint GM plant.

### Winter Driving

Michigan roads are generally very well-maintained in winter, plowed free of snow, then salted or sanded. (Salt does a better job of melting, sand is less destructive to the environment.) During or immediately after a storm, though, don't expect smooth sailing; it's often hard for road crews to keep up with conditions. County and city crews have a well-established hierarchy, first

taking care of interstates, state highways, major thoroughfares, roads to schools and hospitals and such, then addressing less-vital routes. Smaller roads are a little different, especially in the Upper Peninsula. If a sign reads Seasonal Road: Not Maintained In Winter, that means it is not plowed or patrolled. To check winter driving conditions before you travel, call the AAA road conditions number, 800/337-1334.

If you're not used to driving in snow, don't learn on the road in a Michigan snowstorm. Drive slowly, allow lots of extra room between you and the car in front of you, and remember it may take a lot longer to stop. Tap your brakes lightly in succession to come to a stop; never stomp on them, or you'll send your car reeling into what high-school kids call a "doughnut." If you have the newer ABS anti-lock brakes, apply steady pressure instead, and let the system's computer do the work. Remember, too, that four-wheel-drive may get you going better than the next guy, but it won't help you stop.

Chains or studded snow tires are not permitted on Michigan roads. Many residents do switch to snow tires, which have a heavier tread. If you have a rear-wheel-drive car, adding weight to the back end can greatly improve traction. Bags of sand or water-softener salt work well, and sand can be used if you get stuck.

Snow isn't the only hazard. Ice is considerably more dangerous, since it provides even less traction and stopping ability than snow. Especially be aware of "black ice," pavement that looks wet but is actually glare ice. Watch for icy roads as rain turns to snow (called "freezing rain"), especially on bridges, where the cold air circulating above and below the road will cause it to freeze first. Ice also forms when lots of cars travel over a snowy surface, packing it down to a super-slick hardpack. This often happens on heavily traveled interstates and state highways. On four-lane roads, the less-used left lane usually looks snowier but may actually be less icy and less slippery.

Equip your vehicle with a shovel, sand (kitty litter works even better), and boots, in case you get stuck. Throw the sand/kitty litter under the front tires for a front-wheel-drive car, the rear tires on a rear-wheel-drive car. Keep the tires straight and *slowly* apply the gas. Flooring it will only spin you deeper. Gently rocking the car forward and back, especially if you have someone who can push, works best.

Keep a flashlight, flares, blankets, and extra clothing in your vehicle in case you have to spend the night in your car. It could save your life. Especially in rural areas, help may not always be on the way. If you see a car hung up on a snowbank or in a ditch, by all means offer a push or a ride to town.

## Driving and Deer

Several million deer inhabit Michigan, posing a significant threat to drivers. Hundreds of thousands contribute to automobile accidents each year, some of them fatal. Deer behave erratically and will dart in front of your car with no warning. Be particularly alert at dawn and dusk, when deer are most active, and during hunting season in November, when they're really nuts. Yellow-and-black "leaping deer" signs warn motorists of roadways where crossings are common, but they can occur virtually anywhere.

Deer may come from the woods or from an open field, almost out of nowhere. If you see deer by the side of the road, slow down and get ready to stop. If you see a deer cross ahead of you, also slow down—where there's one deer, there are usually several. If you do hit a deer, notify the nearest law enforcement office immediately.

## Car Rentals

Rental cars are available at most commercial airports around the state. Especially in smaller cities, you'll be limited to the big players like National, 800/227-7368; Budget, 800/527-0700; Hertz, 800/654-3131; and Avis, 800/831-2847. Any good local operators are mentioned in the appropriate travel section. It is highly recommended to reserve a car in advance; big cities do a huge volume, and small locales don't keep many on the lot. If you plan to do any exploration in the Upper Peninsula, ask about the rental company's policies regarding off-road driving. Many forbid you to leave pavement, which can curtail your access to a lot of U.P. sights.

## Entering Canada

U.S. citizens entering Canada are usually given little more than a perfunctory glance. You won't need a passport, but do need photo identification. A driver's license is sufficient. Unless you happen to be transporting plants or animals, you'll probably be asked a question or two about why you're visiting and then will be waved right through. Pets require proof of proper vaccinations; plants will be confiscated.

Non-U.S. citizens must have a valid passport. If you're a citizen of a non-European country, you may need a visa (obtained in advance from the Canadian Consulate) as well. U.S. resident aliens may be asked to show a green card.

Unless you travel from Michigan to Canada by boat, you'll do so by bridge or tunnel. There are four toll bridges connecting Michigan and Ontario: the Ambassador Bridge from Detroit to Windsor ($2.25), the Windsor Tunnel from Detroit to Windsor ($2.50), the Blue Water Bridge from Port Huron to Sarnia ($1.50), and the International Bridge from Sault Ste. Marie to Sault Ste. Marie ($1.50). If you do arrive by boat, you're required to check in at the nearest customs station immediately upon arrival.

# Information and Services

## VISITOR INFORMATION

For general information on traveling in Michigan, your best source is the state-run **Travel Michigan,** P. O. Box 3393, Livonia, MI 48151-3393, 888/78-GREAT. It also has a TDD number, 800/722-8191. Your call is answered by a real person who can send or fax brochures and consult a vast database to field your questions about festivals, lodgings, and all kinds of other stuff. It's a much more helpful service than many tourism hotlines and is staffed seven days a week. Call Mon.–Fri. 8 A.M.–11 P.M., Sat.–Sun. 8 A.M.–5 P.M.

You may find it even more convenient to surf the state tourism database yourself, at **www.michigan.org.** This is a terrific website, with an interactive travel planner that gives you specific information tailored to the parameters you set. Tell it you want to go charter fishing on Lake Superior in fall, and it will print a list of appropriate charters; click on each for a detailed description, rates, directions, and more. Currently, the travel planner has categories for accommodations, attractions, camping, charter boats, communities, events, golf, restaurants, shopping, and skiing.

For information specific to the Upper Peninsula, you'll find the folks at the **Upper Peninsula Travel and Recreation Association** particularly helpful, too. Contact UPTRA at 618 Stephenson Ave., P. O. Box 400, Iron Mountain, MI 49801, 800/562-7134.

The Michigan Department of Transportation operates 13 **Welcome Centers** throughout the state. These facilities are stocked with travel literature and staffed with "travel counselors" who are quite knowledgeable about the state in general and their region in particular. The Welcome Centers are open year-round.

You'll find Welcome Centers at major gateways to the state (except Detroit) and at a couple other "interior" locations. They're marked on the state highway map and with signs on the nearest highway. Hours vary.

## MAPS

Michigan's official state road map is one of the few maps of the state that doesn't parcel the Upper Peninsula into infuriating and impossible-to-follow pieces. (No, the Keweenaw Peninsula really isn't part of eastern Ontario.) Pick one up at a Michigan Welcome Center or request one from Travel Michigan (see above).

For more detail, the DeLorme *Michigan Atlas and Gazetteer* provides great detail, with the state portrayed in 102 large-scale maps. Though the 15-inch-long format is unwieldy for hikers, it's a great resource for planning your trip, and even identifies lighthouses, historic sites, waterfalls, industrial tours, and other points of interest. You can find it at many Midwestern bookstores for $15.95, or contact DeLorme Mapping Co., P. O. Box 298, Freeport, ME 04032, 207/865-4171, website: www.delorme.com.

If you'll be exploring the backcountry, you're best off with an official topographical map produced by the U.S. Geological Survey. Michigan's national forests and lakeshores have topographical maps for sale at their visitors centers/ranger stations. Outside federal lands, you may find them (or other good detailed maps) in local outfitter shops, but don't count on it. If the shop you visit is out of the map you need, you may be a hundred miles from the next store that has it in stock. If you can, buy one ahead of time at an outfitter or map specialty store that carries topo maps; even if they don't have the one you need, they can help you figure out its number and can probably order it for you. You also can contact the U.S. Geological Survey yourself at 800/872-6277 for a free map index and order form.

## TIME AND MONEY

Michigan is located in the eastern time zone, with the exception of the four Upper Peninsula counties that border Wisconsin. Gogebic, Iron, Dickinson, and Menominee Counties are in the central time zone.

ON THE ROAD

Visa and MasterCard are accepted statewide, even in the smallest towns. ATMs also are becoming more and more prevalent, tied into the national Cirrus network. Having said that, there still are mom-and-pop motels that balk at charge-card fees and accept only cash or checks. (You might be surprised at how many small establishments are willing to take an out-of-town check and, in fact, prefer them over credit cards.) Cash, too, is needed at self-registration campgrounds. As any wise traveler knows, never count on getting by with only plastic.

If you're traveling to or from Canada, you'll find currency exchanges at the border and at nearby banks in both countries. Used to be, you could use Canadian and U.S. money almost interchangeably near the border, especially coins. In recent years, though, the exchange rate has changed dramatically, with the Canadian dollar worth roughly 65 cents in U.S. dollars. Plan to exchange currencies when coming or going.

If you're a U.S. resident with Canadian money "left over" at the end of a trip, try to end up with bills, not coins. Many banks (especially away from border towns) will exchange only paper money, and with $1 and $2 Canadian coins, you can easily find yourself with $10 or $20 worth of heavy souvenirs.

## EMERGENCIES

All of Michigan is tied into the 911 emergency system. Dial 911 free from any telephone (including pay phones) to reach an operator who can quickly dispatch local police, fire, or ambulance services. This service also works from cellular phones. Be aware, however, that cell towers can be few and far between in rural areas. Much of the Upper Peninsula remains without reliable cellular service, not to mention digital wireless service, at the time of this writing.

## HEALTH RISKS

### Contaminated Water

There are a couple of critters in Michigan worth mentioning. That crystal-clear stream may look inviting for a drink, but don't do it. Even many of the most pristine Michigan waters may be tainted with *Giardia lamblia,* a nasty little organism that is most commonly transmitted in the feces of beavers, moose, and other mammals. It is present in many lakes and streams in Michigan. **Giardiasis** can result in severe stomach cramps, vomiting, and/or diarrhea. As one Isle Royale ranger once said, "It won't kill you, but it may make you wish you were dead." Neither chemical treatment with Halizone nor a water filter will make water safe from giardia. You need a water purifier filtering down to 0.4 microns or less. Boiling is also effective, but make sure to get your water to a full, rolling boil for five minutes. Isle Royale waters also may be infected with the **hydatid tapeworm,** which also requires purifying and/or boiling.

### Ticks

**Wood ticks** and **deer ticks** are found in Michigan woods and grasslands. The larger wood tick, about a quarter-inch long, attaches itself to your skin and gorges on your blood. Gross, yes, but relatively harmless. If you find a wood tick on yourself, your companion, or your pet, grasp it as close to the head as possible and yank. Don't leave a piece of the animal imbedded, or it might cause an infection. Ticks aren't super particular, but they prefer warm areas—scalp, neck, armpits, genitals. Ditto for your dog. On Fido, check under the collar and all around the ears, too.

Deer ticks are the more dangerous beast. They may be transmitters of **Lyme disease,** a potentially debilitating disease. Lyme disease shows up as a temporary red rash that often resembles a ring that slowly expands outward. Other symptoms as the disease progresses are sore joints, fatigue, and nausea; if left untreated, it can lead to arthritis and severe neurological and cardiac problems. Caught early, antibiotics treat it effectively.

To complicate matters, deer ticks are tiny—often hardly larger than the head of a pin. Like wood ticks, they burrow into the skin, especially in warm places. After hiking, check yourself and hiking partners carefully. If it's large enough, grasp the tick and pull it like you would a wood tick, or use tweezers. If you've been in a tick-infested area, watch for a developing rash within the next week and have anything suspicious looked at by a doctor promptly. Your best defense against ticks is to wear long pants and long sleeves, and spray yourself liberally with a hard-core repellent like those containing DEET.

Dogs are also highly susceptible to Lyme disease. Check your dog carefully and thoroughly for deer ticks by slowly running your fingers or a comb through his coat to get a look at the skin—a task that requires a lot of patience on the part of you and your dog. Again, ears, necks, bellies, and genitals are favorite tick hiding places. Signs that your dog may have acquired Lyme disease include nausea, fatigue, and lameness that may come and go from different joints. If you see potential symptoms, get to a vet right away. Like humans, dogs respond well to antibiotics if the disease is caught early enough.

There is a canine vaccine for Lyme disease, but veterinarians are divided on how effective it is. There are some very good tick repellent sprays on the market. Use them.

## Animals

When it comes to bigger animals, deer are by far your biggest danger—they cause thousands of accidents a year on Michigan roads. (See Getting Around, above.) But **black bears** certainly seem more frightening, especially when you're deep in the woods. Black bears are found throughout northern Michigan; the Upper Peninsula has an especially large population. They usually live in areas of heavy forest, but will routinely wander into open areas, especially for berries and other food sources. They're beautiful animals, and you should consider yourself lucky to observe one.

Black bears are generally shy creatures that would prefer to have nothing to do with you. If they hear you coming down the trail, they'll likely run the other way. If you happen to see one before it sees you, make sure you've left it an "escape route," then clap, yell, or bang pans. Give especially wide berth to a mother and cubs. There are very, very few documented cases of black bear aggression against humans, and theories vary on what to do if you should ever find yourself in such a sorry position, anyway. Most behaviorists believe that, unlike grizzlies, black bears will be intimidated by dominance behavior like shouting and waving your arms.

The biggest problems come when bears are lured into populated areas by human carelessness. It's always sad to see a bear relocated away from its home territory, but it happens frequently in campgrounds, where humans don't properly store food or do away with garbage. If you're car camping, keep all foodstuffs in your car (with doors and windows closed!). If you're tent camping, keep everything in airtight storage containers if possible, and suspend the containers on a line between two trees, high enough off the ground and far enough apart to be out of a bear's reach. Latched coolers shoved under a picnic table are not only *not* sufficient to keep out bears, they're hardly even a challenge.

Clean pans and utensils right away, dumping the water well away from camp, and store them with the food. Never, ever keep any food (even gum) in your tent. Bears have an extremely good sense of smell and may be tempted to join you. Some say cosmetics also can attract them, so play it safe and store your soap and toothpaste with the food. You might want to leave your tent unzipped during the day while you're gone. Bears are curious, and if they want to check out your tent, they'll make their own entrance if they can't find one.

If you're at a campground, deposit garbage in the animal-proof refuse containers provided. If you're backcountry camping, pack it out. Never, ever attempt to feed a bear, no matter how "tame" it may seem. That goes without saying, right?

# The Lower
# Peninsula

Mention Michigan, and the Lower Peninsula is likely the place most people picture, that mitten-shaped landmass very nearly surrounded by Lakes Michigan, Huron, and Erie. The Lower Peninsula lies in stark contrast to the state's "other half," the wild, wooded Upper Peninsula that looms above it.

But the Lower Peninsula offers plenty of contrasts of its own. Detroit, the largest city in Michigan and the seventh largest in the nation, defines Michigan to many people—unfortunately, since this urban, industrial center is much maligned and misunderstood. The birthplace of the automobile, Detroit's auto plants and related industries lured workers from all over the United States and all over the world in the early- to mid-1900s, resulting in a metropolitan area of incredible diversity.

Detroit is, in many ways, a city that has risen from the ashes. Its history of high crime and urban decay is well chronicled, a reputation that endures even as things improve. Meanwhile, the culture and color that come from so many ethnicities living within the boundaries of a single city get overlooked. Detroit is really a concentration of neighborhoods, each with residents, restaurants, shops, festivals, and museums that can give you a view nearly as worldly as the United Nations.

Beyond Detroit and the densely populated southeast corner comes the Michigan many don't expect: agrarian towns dotted with roadside fruit stands, Great Lakes ports guarded by staunch lighthouses. Get north of about Saginaw, and the tempo really changes. Now, you're officially "Up North," where, with apologies to Jimmy Buffett, the change in latitude also brings a distinct change in attitude.

Northern Michigan is one of the most popular tourist destinations in Middle America, a largely wooded, rolling landscape dotted with thousands of clean lakes and clear rivers. Its Great Lakes shoreline can be absolutely breathtaking, like the islands, sand dunes, and turquoise bays that surround the Traverse Bays region. Some communities are characterized by small cottages on fishing lakes, others by grand summer estates on yacht-filled harbors. Travelers who delight in surprises and shattering stereotypes will heartily enjoy themselves in the Lower Peninsula—where the next county can seem a world away.

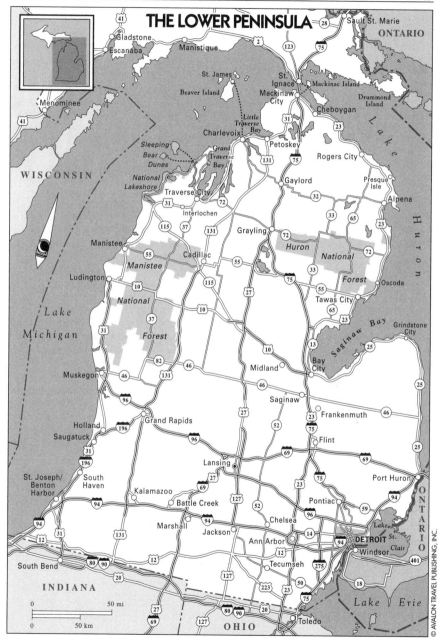

THE LOWER PENINSULA

# Detroit and Vicinity

*The grayness and the grit,*
*the dirty, funky, hardheavy city,*
*home of greasecake hands*
*and the baddest right hook you've*
*ever seen.*

—*B.P. Flanigan,* **Freeway Series**

Some say it's appropriate that a relatively recent work of public sculpture in Detroit is a huge, 1,300-pound fist cast in bronze by American sculptor Robert Graham. Controversial even before it was unveiled in 1986, it was seen by some as a symbol of the city's almost legendary violence, and by others as a powerful—if not exactly pretty—tribute to the toughness and tenacity of heavyweight boxer Joe Louis and the city where he was born.

Toughness and tenacity are what Detroit is all about. Long a one-horse town dependent on the cycles of the auto industry, Detroit has

known great periods of boom and bust. Like the "Brown Bomber" Louis, it often has been down for the count and given up for dead. Like Louis, each time it has struggled to get on its feet again and come back fighting.

While there's no doubt that Detroit could use a good spin doctor, much of the city's problems are exaggerated in the national media. While crime remains an ongoing problem, it no longer is the losing battle it once was. And despite its lingering national reputation, Detroit has always been a city willing to take a chance. From the first hardy (some said foolhardy) pioneers who settled the area, undeterred by reports of "one huge uninhabitable swamp," to the scores of hopeful immigrants who followed their American dream to the numbing rhythm of the assembly line, the Motor City has long

**Detroit River**

stood for imagination, innovation, and the desire for something better. The diversity of its people, gathered from the far corners of the world, has long been one of the city's greatest strengths and its heart. It's these same people who have begun to turn the city around. Detroit is—at last—a city on the rebound. Recent articles in the national media have touted the city's theater district (the largest outside of Manhattan), General Motors' purchase of the Renaissance Center, and the prodigal decision by the Detroit Lions football team to eschew the city's northern suburbs for a new home downtown, a glitzy stadium that incorporates some historic warehouses, opening in 2002.

Much of the credit for this long-in-coming renaissance goes to former mayor Dennis Archer, who left office in November 2001 and who has done what for years seemed impossible: mended fences between the city and its often-hostile suburbs. There's a new spirit of cooperation and a new sense of optimism that can be felt on both sides of 8 Mile Road, the city's physical and philosophical dividing line.

That's not to say the city doesn't have its share of growing pains. It does, and will continue to have them. But it appears at last that Detroit, dubbed the Renaissance City in the 1970s, is working hard to deserve the name.

## The Making of the Motor City

Few think of Detroit as an old city. It is, in fact, the Midwest's oldest, founded in 1701 by Antoine de la Mothe Cadillac for Louis XIV of France.

Early Detroit was alternately ruled by the British and the French. In 1763, Pontiac, the Ottawa war chief, ordered an attack on British posts all over Michigan, an attempt to drive the growing British population out of the area. Tired of the abuse under the British army, Pontiac united the many Indian nations living around Detroit in a determined effort to capture the fort and restore a French rule. A secret war council was attended by chiefs of the Ottawa, Huron, Potawatomi, and Lake Superior Chippewa Indians. Unfortunately, legend has it that a squaw tipped off the British and Pontiac's men were met by a waiting British army. Rebuffed and defeated, Pontiac was later assassinated in 1769. Today, Pontiac's Rebellion is still regarded as one of the most formidable Indian uprisings in American history.

In 1783, Britain yielded the area to the United States. in the Treaty of Paris. However, because the area's Indians disputed the U.S. claim, it wasn't until 1796 that Detroit finally unfurled the stars and stripes. The city fell again during the War of 1812 but was recaptured by the Americans a year later. Despite discouraging reports from initial settlers, people continued to pour in from the east. Between 1830 and 1860, the population doubled with every decade, and the city became best known as a nucleus of beer brewing and stove making.

All that changed by the turn of the century, when the auto industry took off and Detroit exploded into America's fifth-largest city. The state's first self-propelled vehicle was probably a steam-powered car built by John and Thomas Clegg of Memphis, Michigan, in 1884. Later, Ransom Olds of Lansing developed a gasoline-powered auto and founded the Olds Motor Vehicle Company. Two important milestones occurred in 1896: Charles C. King, an engineer and auto designer, drove the first car through the streets of Detroit, and Henry Ford tested his Quadricycle, which chugged along fairly well despite no brakes and no reverse gear (Ford's Quadricycle can still be seen in Dearborn's Henry Ford Museum).

It was Ford and his later perfection of the assembly line that changed the face of the city—and America—seemingly overnight. Between 1905 and 1924 thousands of immigrants poured in from all over the world, attracted by Henry Ford's then-unheard-of wage of $5 per day. By 1917, 23 companies were busy in Detroit and its suburbs assembling vehicles for an ever-eager public. The Motor City had arrived.

By the 1930s and 1940s, Detroit was the place to be. Lively and full of energy, it was home to

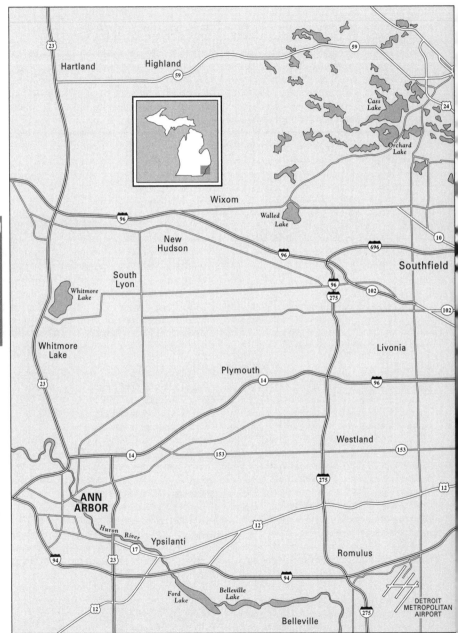

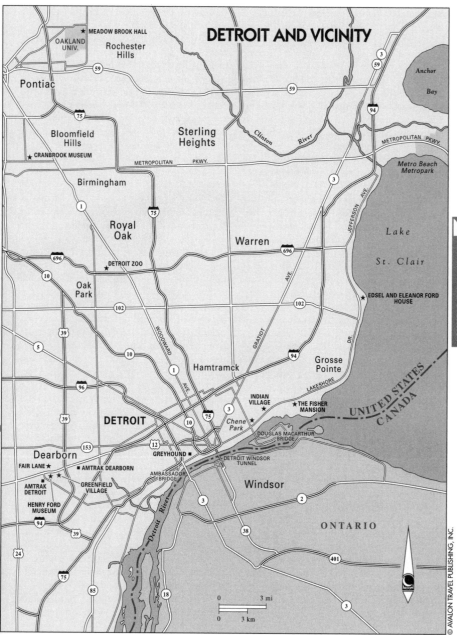

DETROIT AND VICINITY

★ MEADOW BROOK HALL

OAKLAND UNIV.

Rochester Hills

Pontiac

Anchor Bay

Bloomfield Hills

★ CRANBROOK MUSEUM

Sterling Heights

Clinton River

METROPOLITAN PKWY.

METROPOLITAN PKWY.

Metro Beach Metropark

Birmingham

Royal Oak

Warren

Lake St. Clair

★ DETROIT ZOO

Oak Park

★ EDSEL AND ELEANOR FORD HOUSE

WOODWARD AVE.

GRATIOT AVE.

JEFFERSON AVE.

Hamtramck

Grosse Pointe

INDIAN VILLAGE

LAKESHORE

★ THE FISHER MANSION

DETROIT

Chene Park

DOUGLAS MACARTHUR BRIDGE

Dearborn

FAIR LANE ★

■ AMTRAK DEARBORN

GREYHOUND ■

DETROIT WINDSOR TUNNEL

AMTRAK DETROIT

GREENFIELD VILLAGE

AMBASSADOR BRIDGE

Windsor

HENRY FORD MUSEUM

Detroit River

ONTARIO

UNITED STATES

CANADA

0    3 mi

0    3 km

DETROIT AND VICINITY

© AVALON TRAVEL PUBLISHING, INC.

after-hours bars known as "blind pigs" (police—"pigs"—turned a "blind eye" to Prohibition-era hideouts that served liquor) and "black and tan" clubs where people of all races mingled. But things began to sour after World War II. As in other U.S. metropolises, the middle class began to head for the suburbs. Bigger and better freeways took people farther and farther away from the heart of the city, leaving behind vacant storefronts, vacant houses, empty streets, and empty lives too soon filled by poverty and crime.

The 1960s were difficult years. One bright spot was the birth of the Motown Sound, which was derived from the city's early nickname, Motor Town, and began in Berry Gordy, Jr.'s tiny basement studio. Like the city, Motown had a hard-driving beat, and it quickly took over airwaves across the country. Detroit became known for producing more than cars, with Hitsville U.S.A. churning out rhythmic Top 10 tunes by artists such as Marvin Gaye, Smokey Robinson and the Miracles, Little Stevie Wonder, The Temptations, and the Supremes.

The late 1960s brought massive unrest to the country and the worst race riot in Detroit's history. In 1967, Detroit was the site of one of 59 racial "disturbances" around the country, a tragedy in which more than 43 people were killed. The nightly news in cities throughout the world showed a Detroit in flames, leaving a lasting impression on the country and a deep scar on the city's psyche.

The riots touched off an even greater exodus, the infamous "white flight" that left Detroit with a black majority in less than five years. By the 1970s, downtown had become a virtual desert after business hours. Controversial mayor Coleman Young, who ruled for more than 20 years, once said you could shoot a cannon down Woodward in those years without hitting a soul.

Today, some 4.5 million people call Detroit and its suburbs home. They comprise myriad ethnic groups, with more than 900,000 African Americans in the metropolitan area. Not surprisingly, Detroit is also home to the largest branch of the NAACP. Detroit also has the country's largest population of Bulgarians,

Chaldeans, Belgians, and Arabs (the most outside the Middle East).

While the city has courted big business almost since the first horseless carriage jounced awkwardly off the assembly line, Detroit has never been a major tourist destination. An active convention and visitors bureau (the first in the country, formed more than a century ago) is attempting to change that, with frequent fetes for national and international media and an aggressive campaign to attract visitors from other parts of the country as well as Europe and Japan.

In 1996, the much-celebrated anniversary of the "birth" of the car turned an international spotlight on the city, with favorable reports in both the *New York Times* and *USA Today.* Detroit responded with a centennial bash and invited the entire world. More recently, in 2001, the city celebrated its third century with exhibitions, events and a month-long riverfront party with visits that included both tall ships and the Temptations. Stevie Wonder led the homecoming concert, which attracted approximately one million people (ironically, more than city's current population). While city boosters don't expect flashy events such as these to erase the memories of Detroit in flames during the 1967 riots, they hope they will help scab over the open wounds that have too long plagued the city. "The only way to erase powerful images of the past is to lay equally powerful images over them," says Renee Monforton of the city's convention and visitors bureau.

Today more than 2,000 square miles make up the metropolitan area known as Detroit; the city itself measures 136 square miles. Most of the terrain of southeast Michigan shares more with neighboring Ohio than the state's rumpled lands to the north. Almost monotonously flat, it's crossed by a frightening—though usually efficient—series of freeways that allows you to zip easily between the city, its numerous suburbs, and other parts of the state.

Not surprisingly, you'll need a car to explore Detroit. The city's forefathers wouldn't have wanted it any other way.

# Sights: The City

Almost prophetically, early Detroit was laid out like spokes of a wheel. The plan—laid down by Judge Augustus Woodward, the first chief justice of the new Michigan territory—foreshadowed the city's major industry by more than a century.

Woodward arrived in 1805 to find no more than a burned-out trading post on the narrow straits of the river—hence the name, *"Détroit,"* which means "Straits." While little else remains of Woodward's grandiose plans to make Detroit the "Paris of the Midwest," the city's main streets—Woodward Avenue, Gratiot Avenue, Grand Avenue, and Fort Street—still echo that early hexagonal grid, shooting off at often confusing diagonal angles from a central axis. Woodward serves as the city's main dividing line, splitting the landmass and its residents into east and west.

## ON THE WATERFRONT

Motown's earliest history was made on its waterfront, so a tour is a fitting start to any exploration of the city. If it's a sunny day (regardless of the season), stroll the boardwalk near **Hart Plaza** and watch for one of the thousands of hulking freighters that pass annually. Some bear flags from as far away as Eastern Europe.

Once the waterfront was the city's livelihood, with an active port and hundreds of freighters passing annually. During the 20th century, however, the city turned its back on its former front door, choosing instead to erect faceless factories and anonymous office towers along its riverbanks instead of the more gracious green-spaces popular during the century before. For an eye-opening education in the essential difference between the American and Canadian psyches, head across the way to Windsor, where the waterfront is reserved for civic parks.

There are a few exceptions. The 11-acre Hart Plaza is site of the breathtaking Dodge Fountain, designed in 1973 by Isamu Noguchi. It sends more than one million gallons of water per hour into the air via more than 300 streaming

*(continued on page 56)*

DETROIT AND VICINITY

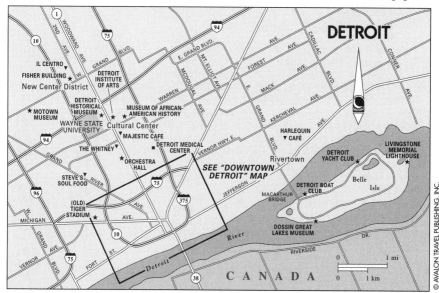

© AVALON TRAVEL PUBLISHING, INC.

# HOMES OF THE AUTO BARONS

As Detroit grew to become the Motor Capital of the world, opportunities to amass great fortunes grew with it. The automobile "royalty" that emerged took on a pampered lifestyle befitting their status and built great estates full of art and intricate workmanship. Now open for tours, these four estates offer visitors the chance to see firsthand the way the auto pioneers lived during the heyday of the auto industry.

## The Fisher Mansion

The only estate within the city limits, the Fisher Mansion, 383 Lenox, 313/331-6740, inspired by William Randolph Hearst's San Simeon, was built by Lawrence P. Fisher of the Fisher Body Company, a talented playboy who once courted actress Jean Harlow and who spent millions of his huge fortune constructing this magnificent riverfront estate. It has been described as "glitz bordering on garish." Completed in 1927, it's most noted for its ornate stone and marble work, exquisite European handcrafted stained glass windows, doors, and arches carved from woods imported from India and Africa, and its rare black walnut and rosewood parquet floors. More than 200 ounces of gold and silver leaf highlight the decorative ceilings and moldings.

The mansion was neglected after Fisher's death and was purchased for just $80,000 in the early 1960s by Alfred Brush Ford, great-grandson of Henry Ford, and Elisabeth Reuther Dickmeyer, daughter of legendary United Auto Workers chief Walter Reuther. They restored the mansion and donated it to the International Society for Krishna Consciousness, of which they are members. Today the mansion is one of 300 Krishna centers worldwide and is also the location of the excellent **Govinda's** vegetarian restaurant on the second floor. Tours are offered Fri.–Sun. at 12:30, 2, 3:30, and 6 P.M., or by appointment. Admission is $6 adults.

## Edsel & Eleanor Ford House

Farther up Jefferson Avenue where it becomes Lake Shore Road is the Edsel & Eleanor Ford House, 1100 Lake Shore Rd., Grosse Pointe Shores, 313/884-4222. The Ford House represents a style of living and quality of craftsmanship that is rapidly vanishing, if not completely gone.

The Cotswold-style mansion designed by noted local architect Albert Kahn was built in 1929 for Henry Ford's only son, who raised his four children in this house. Much of the interior paneling and furniture was lifted from distinguished old English manors; even the roof is of imported English stones expertly laid by imported Cotswold roofers. What makes the house especially interesting is that it remains much as it did when the Fords lived here. Edsel died in 1943, but his wife, Eleanor Clay Ford, left the estate virtually untouched after that. Throughout is evidence of the Fords' love of art, with copies of masterpieces now replacing the originals hanging in the downtown Detroit Institute of Arts.

Tour-goers can take in a 15-minute video about the Fords and a two-hour guided tour that leads them through the distinctive dwelling. Highlights include two stylish and sophisticated Art Deco rooms by famed industrial designer Walter Dorwin Teague; Edsel's personal study, lined with framed family photos and photos of luminaries such as Charles Lindbergh and Thomas Edison; and the playhouse created for daughter Josephine's sixth birthday, crafted in the same Cotswold style. Open year-round (except for the last two weeks of January); tour times vary depending on season. Contact the number above, or visit www.fordhouse.org for a current schedule. Admission is $6 adults, $4 children 6–12.

## Fair Lane

Of the four auto baron estates, Henry Ford's Fair Lane, 4901 Evergreen Rd., Dearborn, 313/593-5590, is, surprisingly, the least baro-

© TRAVEL MICHIGAN

**Fair Lane Mansion**

nial. By the time it was completed in 1914, Ford had become active in World War I politics and spent a lot of time helping the war effort in Europe. Nonetheless, it is justly listed as a National Historic Landmark.

Fair Lane encompasses more than 1,600 acres (to help with navigating, pick up a copy of the $1 grounds map at the reception desk). For some, the natural landscape by Jens Jensen is the highlight of a visit; for others, it's the estate's many technical feats, including the extensive six-level hydroelectric power plant created by Ford and his good buddy Thomas Edison. In this house Ford entertained some of the world's most influential people, including Charles Lindbergh (also a Detroit native), President Herbert Hoover, and the Duke of Windsor. It's an unusual combination of a Scottish baronial structure and the Prairie style developed by

Frank Lloyd Wright. Daily tours uncover quirky details such as Henry's basement bowling alley and his penchant for birds (he once had eight heated birdhouses) as well as Clara's passion for roses. A small but choice gift shop stocks a wide selection of books on related subjects; a charming restaurant staffed by students in University of Michigan—Dearborn's hotel and restaurant management program—is located in the spot that once housed the estate's indoor pool. Ninety-minute tours are conducted year-round; times vary with the season. Admission is $8 adults, $5 children 5–12.

### Meadow Brook Hall

Last but not least is Rochester's Meadow Brook Hall, Adams Rd. and Walton Blvd., 248/370-3140. John Dodge and his brother Horace were among the car makers responsible for Detroit's sudden catapult into big business. John died suddenly in 1920, leaving behind a vast fortune and a widow, Matilda (his former secretary), who remarried a wealthy lumberman, Alfred Wilson, in 1925. Together, Alfred and Matilda toured Europe and dreamed of a grand estate north of the city. They built Meadow Brook Hall in the late 1920s for the then-astonishing sum of $4 million. Interiors were copied from drawings of English estates.

More than 70 years later, Meadow Brook is still largely intact, in part because Mrs. Wilson left the estate to Oakland University, which still administers the property at a cost of $3,000 per day. Rooms—including a two-story ballroom, game rooms copied from old English pubs, and Matilda's bathroom accented with locally made Pewabic tile—still house original family collections and furnishings. A walk in the surrounding woods reveals a six-room playhouse known as Knole Cottage, built for Frances Wilson, Matilda's daughter. Tours of the estate are offered Mon.–Sat. year-round at 1:30 P.M., and Sun. at 1:30, 2:30, and 3:30 P.M. (Extra tours are added in July and August.) Admission is $8 adults, $4 children 5–12.

DETROIT AND VICINITY

nozzles and jets. Those not prone to art appreciation call it the steel doughnut. Plans call for a new three-mile long ribbon park to highlight the city's skyline and Detroit River waterfront.

Hart Plaza is also the site of the **Ford Montreux Detroit Jazz Festival,** held each Labor Day weekend. More than 85 free, open-air concerts and a world-class selection of music masters make it the largest free jam in the world. The popular "Meet the Artists" series and free clinics in improvisation for students are designed to support the city's vital jazz community and ensure its survival. Concerts are held all over the city in conjunction with the festival, including at Chene Park, home of well-attended events and open-air summer concerts.

## Renaissance Center

Next to Hart Plaza is the towering Renaissance Center, known to Detroiters as the decidedly less melodic "RenCen." Soaring an eighth of a mile into the sky, this fortress-like hotel/office/retail complex dominates the Detroit skyline, with four 39-story steel towers containing more than two million square feet of office space, the 73-story Marriott Hotel (the tallest hotel in the world), and more than 80 restaurants and stores.

At least, that's the "official" version put out by the convention and visitors bureau. The truth behind the gleaming center is a little more tarnished. The project originally was proposed by Henry Ford II in part as a response to the 1967 riots. Ford—always a powerful name in Detroit—used his considerable influence to convince friends and foes alike to invest in the riverside complex. With big-name retailers such as Gucci and Cartier, it was intended to draw suburbanites back downtown.

It didn't work. The RenCen was a huge white elephant from the moment it opened in 1977. Designed by John Portman, who was best known for building hotel atriums, it was a confusing maze of circles and elevators that ultimately led nowhere. By 1983, many of the original retailers had pulled out and most of the investors had defaulted on their loans.

The center received a much-needed facelift and helpful new directional signs in the mid-1980s, but

it never became the city's much-heralded savior. Through the 1980s and much of the 1990s the RenCen has been supported mainly by the 140 businesses—including Ford, ANR Pipeline, and others—who maintain offices here. In 1996, however, it received a huge shot in the arm with General Motors' announcement that it had purchased the landmark to use as its new world headquarters. In a major boost for the city, GM moved the majority of its workers—many now spread out across the metro Detroit area—into the RenCen in 1999. A major internal reorganization followed, leaving the space a bit less confusing.

Whatever you think about the center and its architectural merits (or lack of them), this fact remains: the RenCen is still the largest privately financed development in U.S. history, with more than $380 million contributed by private investors. Although misguided, it represents a huge investment in the city's future. It's worth seeing on that basis alone.

Once inside, you'll need a map to navigate. Skip the food at the overrated Summit Restau-

You'll need a map to navigate downtown's Renaissance Center.

rant, but don't miss the observation deck on top of the Marriott. For just $5 you'll have the lights of the city and the metal expanse of the Ambassador Bridge laid out at your feet like a twinkly magic carpet. Bird's-eye views—although not quite as high—are also available from any of the tower's glass elevators.

## Belle Isle

At one time, 30 million tons of cargo were transported along the Detroit River, linking the city with more than 200 overseas ports. The city may have turned its back on the river, but you can still feel the water's tug on Belle Isle, East Jefferson Ave. and East Grand Blvd., three miles from downtown via East Jefferson Ave. and the MacArthur Bridge, 313/267-7115. This 1,000-acre urban sanctuary stranded a half mile out in the river has been a public park since 1879, when the city purchased it for a now paltry $200,000 from the heirs of a wealthy local family.

Named after the then-governor's daughter, Isabelle Cass, it was designed in 1883 by Frederick Law Olmsted, of New York's Central Park fame. One of the city's most underrated (and often neglected) jewels, the park gets a little rowdy on summer weekends, when teenagers from surrounding neighborhoods cruise the narrow streets and pathways looking for action. Although patrolled by both mounted police and squad cars, it's not a safe place to be at night.

On weekdays, however, it's peaceful, especially off season. Belle Isle is a haven for birdwatchers and for families who flock here to fish or tour the nation's oldest freshwater aquarium, the vintage glass conservatory, a small zoo, or the intriguing **Dossin Great Lakes Museum.** The museum traces the development of Great Lakes shipping from sailing vessels to modern freighters, many of which can still be seen from the riverfront or Grosse Pointe. The "Gothic Room" has more than 7.5 tons of handcarved oak arches and decorative work taken from a 1912 steamer, the *City of Detroit III*. The anchor from the ill-fated *Edmund Fitzgerald* is also found here, as is a working pilothouse where kids can take the wheel. Hours are Wed.–Sun. 10 A.M.–5 P.M.; admission is $2.

Others come to circle the island by bicycle or in-line skates (it's strictly BYOB however: Bring Your Own Blades), jog, or just set up a picnic lunch under one of the gazebos and watch passing freighters. Boating enthusiasts wander around the **Belle Isle lighthouse,** which operated from 1882 to 1930 but is now largely neglected, or check out the pleasure craft docked at the 1922 **Detroit Yacht Club** or the 1891 **Detroit Boat Club,** the oldest river club in the United States, also sadly neglected and a reported demolition target. Admission to the island is free, although there has been ongoing heated discussion debating charging a nominal admission to help defray maintenance costs.

It isn't the island's first controversy. Native Americans called Belle Isle "Rattlesnake Island" because of the number of snakes. Later, hogs were brought in by 18th-century settlers to destroy the rattlers, giving rise to the name Isle au Cochon ("Hog Island" in French) until 1845, when it was rechristened Belle Isle. Throughout its long history the island has been used both as a dueling ground and as a place of quarantine for troops, most recently during the cholera epidemic of 1932.

Belle Isle is also the site of the **Detroit Grand Prix,** a fact that causes great chagrin to naturalists and other nature lovers but which brings big bucks to city coffers. For three days in June the birds and bees are drowned out by the drone of a couple dozen roaring Indy cars, which take over the western tip of the island on a 2.1-mile, 14-turn course, considered one of the most challenging in the world. More than 170,000 screaming fans stream onto the island for the annual Free Prix Day and to ogle some of the world's top racing talents, including the Andrettis and Al Unser, Jr. Noise from the event can be heard throughout downtown and as far away as the Grosse Pointes, about 10 miles northeast. Check first before heading here for the event, as the location is reevaluated every year and recent reports have the organizers scouting a new site.

## Pewabic Pottery

Farther along Jefferson Avenue, not far from Belle Isle, is another oasis, Pewabic Pottery, 10125

E. Jefferson Ave., 313/822-0954. Founded by Mary Chase Perry Stratton at the turn of the century, the arts and crafts pottery is housed in a picturesque Tudor Revival building. Best known for its innovative and iridescent glazes, shown to great advantage in the tiles commissioned for many of the city's civic and residential structures, Pewabic tiles can be found in four of the 13 downtown People Mover stations, the stunning 1929 Art Deco Guardian Building, and the Shrine of the Immaculate Conception in Washington, D.C.

*Best known for its innovative and iridescent glazes, Pewabic tiles can be found in four of the 13 downtown People Mover stations, the stunning 1929 Art Deco Guardian Building, and the Shrine of the Immaculate Conception in Washington, D.C.*

After years of mismanagement, threats of closure and a stint as part of Michigan State University, Pewabic is once again a working pottery. Now a nonprofit ceramic arts center and a living museum, it continues to produce the handcrafted vessels and architectural tiles that brought it initial fame. Visitors peer into huge, fiery kilns on a self-guided tour during business hours. A landmark of Detroit's arts community, the pottery is a pilgrimage for potters and ceramic artists from around the country as well as the site of popular workshops for all ages. There's also an interesting on-site museum and archives. But don't look for the secret to the pottery's lustrous glaze—Stratton took it to the grave, leaving her successors to carry on with only an approximation of the original formula.

## DOWNTOWN DETROIT

Tours of Pewabic will whet your appetite for the city's other vintage architecture. Backtrack along Jefferson to Woodward Avenue, which marks your entrance to the city's official downtown business district. While this area is still quiet after business hours (two exceptions are the legendary Coney Island restaurants, which dish up dogs 24 hours a day year-round), it hops during the day with office workers who toil in the banks, insurance companies, and other corporations.

First stop on any architectural tour is the **Wayne County Building** on the east end of Cadillac Square, an early example of the Italian Renaissance style in Michigan. Built 1895–1902, it's one of the oldest buildings in the city. Look up to see its ornamental cornices—they depict "Mad Anthony Wayne" conferring with the Indians.

A few blocks away, on Griswold, is the Art Deco **Guardian Building,** an Aztec-inspired, 32-story local landmark. Friendly guards in the 1929 superstructure serve as mini tour guides and usually are pleased to share tidbits about the breathtaking building or point you in the right direction for a self-guided tour of its Pewabic-accented interior.

Just one block north, the main shopping district along Woodward Avenue is a forlorn reminder of the suburban exodus and the malling of America. Until recently, it was anchored by the huge J.L. Hudson Department Store, which closed its flagship store in 1983 and was razed—despite community outcry—in 1997. The site will be occupied by the Campus Martius project, with Compuware's national headquarters as well as office, loft and retail space.

The buildings of Woodward Avenue cast a long shadow over **Harmonie Park,** just a block away. If Woodward's desolation threatens to overwhelm you, this elegant enclave will restore your hope in the city's future. New restaurants (including the lively **Intermezzo**) and new energy have transformed a formerly deserted area into the city's hottest nightspot. Much of the credit goes to local architectural firm Shervish Vogel Merz, who believed in the area long before anyone else saw a future in its warehouse-style buildings and vintage storefronts. Today, SVM's stylish headquarters in the Harmonie Club building are surrounded by restaurants, galleries, and airy artists' lofts.

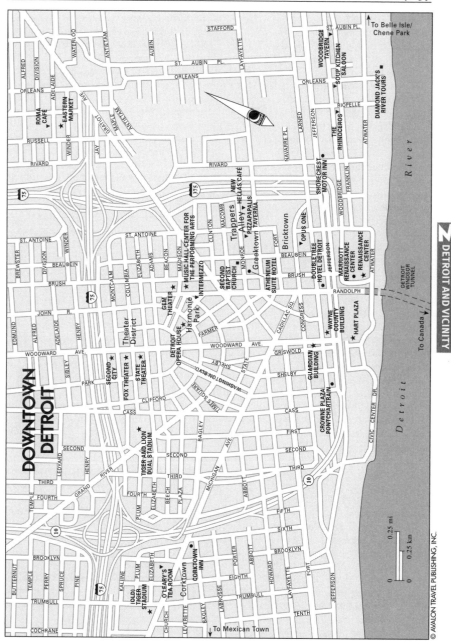

DETROIT AND VICINITY

DOWNTOWN DETROIT

To Belle Isle/
Chene Park

To Canada

To Mexican Town

0    0.25 mi

0    0.25 km

© AVALON TRAVEL PUBLISHING, INC.

## Theater District

Not far from Harmonie Park lies the official entrance to the city's Theater District. Once the city's most exclusive address, the neighborhood known as Brush Park had deteriorated almost to the point of no return before local boy Mike Ilitch—owner of nationwide Little Caesars Pizza chain as well as the Detroit Tigers baseball and Detroit Red Wings hockey teams—stepped in and bought the aging **Fox Theatre,** 2211 Woodward Ave., 313/983-6611, in 1988.

What followed was a painstaking and often slow $8 million restoration that eventually returned the gaudy yet glamorous structure to its original glory. The 5,000-seat Fox is truly a marvel of 1920s architecture. Built in 1928 by William Fox, it was designed in the style of an Arabian tent. The exotic Thai Byzantine style borrows motifs from a range of cultures, including Persian, Burmese, Indian, Thai, and Chinese. There are gold-leafed, hand-stenciled walls, marble-finish pillars, gold-tusked elephants, winged lions, a sunburst ceiling, and dreamlike decorative figures throughout. The lobby is six stories high, with 300,000 sparkling glass jewels, loads of brass, and a 13-foot, two-ton stained-glass chandelier.

The restoration was remarkably successful. Today, the Fox is the nation's most successful theater operation of its kind, with almost nightly presentations, including touring Broadway musicals, big-name concerts, restored film epics, and other special events. You can't miss the 125-foot multicolored neon marquee, which stretches to the 10th floor of the Fox office building. And here's a bit of trivia: during the 1920s, the Fox was the first theater in the United States to sell candy on site.

Spurred by the resounding success of the Fox, other theaters and restaurants soon followed. One contrast to the cavernous Fox is the intimate **Gem and Century Theatres,** 333 Madison, across from the Music Hall, 313/963-9800, a joint cabaret-style venue with 450 seats. Founded in 1928 by a women's group hoping to have an "uplifting influence on the community," the Gem degenerated into a vaudeville house and a sleazy strip joint before foresighted businessman

Chuck Forbes, owner of most of the city's vintage theaters, restored it as a complement to the Fox and a stop for national comedy acts, small plays, and musical revues. It reopened in 1992. Threatened by the new Comerica Park ballpark—home to the Detroit Tigers—it was moved to its present location in 1998. It was the largest commercial building to be moved in the world and made the pages of *Guinness World Records.*

Luciano Pavarotti and Dame Joan Sutherland were just a few of the big names who jetted into Motown in 1996 to attend the opening of the restored **Detroit Opera House,** 1526 Broadway, 313/237-SING. Designed in 1922 by C. Howard Crane as a vaudeville stage, the 7,000-square-foot theater served as a parking garage for most of the 1970s. David Di Chiera, the former university professor who founded the Michigan Opera Theatre in 1971 as a way to bring opera to kids, did the seemingly impossible when he raised $36 million for the opera's 2,700-seat new home. Today it acts as an important cultural resource, attracting productions of everything from opera to ballet.

Other area theaters include the **Music Hall Center for the Performing Arts,** 350 Madison, 313/963-2366, built in 1928 by the widow of auto baron John Dodge for the production of "legitimate" theatrical productions. Its stage has been graced by luminaries such as Lucille Ball, W. C. Fields, Martha Graham, Ella Fitzgerald, Lillian Hellman, and others. The acoustically perfect 1919 **Orchestra Hall,** 3711 Woodward, 313/576-5111, is home to the acclaimed Detroit Symphony. **Orchestra Place,** an adjacent $80-million development, opened in late 1997 with a retail and office center, the gourmet restaurant Duet, and a new public high school for the performing arts.

## Eastern Market

There is one place in the city where old and young, Eastsider and Westsider, black and white meet. Bring your wagon or your grocery bag to Eastern Market, 2934 Russell St. between Mack and Gratiot Avenues, 313/833-1560, on a Saturday morning and you'll find a fragment of old Detroit, a colorful cornucopia of smells, sights,

© MDCVB

the Eastern Market

and sounds. In a city that's known great cycles of boom and bust, Eastern Market is as perennial as the fruit and flowers it sells.

Built on the site of an early hay and wood market, Detroiters have come to this bustling area near Greektown since the 1890s to buy meat, cheese, produce, fruit, and flowers from large, open-air stalls and wholesale/retail specialty shops. Many wholesalers are the descendants of the Belgian, German, and Polish farmers who frequented the market generations ago, or the Italian and Lebanese merchants who began catering to the booming city in the 1920s.

Saturdays are busiest, when thousands of shoppers pour into the area to browse, bargain, and buy among goods that range from fresh chitlins to fresh cilantro. Highlights include the flower stalls (the market is the largest bedding center in the world); the aromas at **Germack's,** the oldest pistachio importer in the United States; and **Rafal's Spice Company,** which has more than 400 herbs and spices, 85 kinds of coffee, and a large assortment of hot sauces and perfume oils filling its narrow shelves.

Another don't-miss stop includes **R. Hirt & Co.,** a century-old grocery in an attractive vintage brick building, for staples and gourmet goodies. An old walk-in wood refrigerator holds cheeses, with chunks cut to order. (Ask for samples!) Irishman Tim McCarthy dispenses free advice along with fine vintages at **Cost Plus Wine Warehouse.** Looking for fresh veggies? Try **Ciarmitaro Brothers** produce, housed in a former 1840s tavern that once hid slaves bound for Canada.

## The Cultural Center

Head north along Woodward Avenue from downtown and you'll run right into the Cultural Center. Bordered by bustling Wayne State University to the west and the Detroit Medical Center to the east, here's where you'll find most of the city's arts and civic museums.

Wander the streets of "Old Detroit" (or at least an idealized version of them) in the basement of the 78,000 square foot **Detroit Historical Museum,** 5401 Woodward, 313/833-1805. You'll trudge along irregular cobblestones that once lined city streets past re-creations of barber shops, grocery stores, and other vintage businesses. The display, which opened in 1951 and has been among the museum's most popular, traces three periods of Detroit history (albeit a decidedly Eurocentric version of it). Admission is by voluntary donation. Hours are Wed.–Fri 9:30 A.M.–5 P.M., Sat.–Sun. 10 A.M.–5 P.M.

The permanent exhibit "From Furs to Factories" traces the city's history from a trading post to an industrial giant, with a walk-in diorama from the 1750s, a railway station, and a mock, turn-of-the-century exposition. Other highlights of the collection include the Glancy Train display, one of the world's largest; the Booth-Wilkinson Costume Gallery; and the ongoing special exhibit tracing African-American businesses in the city.

The museum's newest exhibition, the simply named "Motor City," traces the history of the car, the city, and the people who changed their lives and their world when they came to work here. The exhibit's highlight is the "body drop," a segment of a 1953 assembly line in which the outer shell of a later-model Cadillac is lowered from the ceiling onto an engine body set up on an eye-level platform. It was taken from the assembly line at the old Clark Street Cadillac plant, now demolished.

Detroit has always been a blue-collar town, yet city founders amassed enough green during the heyday of the auto industry to fund what eventually became one of the country's finest art museums. The **Detroit Institute of Arts,** across from the historical museum at 5200 Woodward, 313/833-7900, ranks fifth among the nation's fine arts museums and attracts more than 500,000 visitors each year. The sometimes-confusing 100-plus galleries contain some of the great art treasures of the world, including works by Van Gogh, Rodin, Rembrandt, Brueghel, and other masters. Donations are voluntary; suggested admission for adults is $4. Hours are Wed.–Fri. 11 A.M.–4 P.M., Sat.–Sun. 11 A.M.–5 P.M.

The museum strives to present an encyclopedic collection, with a multicultural scope that traces creativity in all its forms from prehistory through the present. Important collections include the French Impressionist, Italian (the largest outside Italy), German Expressionist, African, Asian, Native American, and 20th-century. It's worth hunting for the museum's generally accepted best works, including Rodin's pensive *Thinker,* Brueghel's *Wedding Dance* (look closely

and you may see some remnants of paint on the bulging codpieces; they were once painted over), Van Eyck's tiny treasure, *St. Jerome in His Study,* Romare Bearden's colorful *Quilting Time,* and Rembrandt's enlightened *Visitation.*

While the building may seem to be full of art made by and for the ruling class, the city's workers have the last laugh in the breathtaking *Detroit Industry* frescoes. Mexican muralist Diego Rivera captured the droning monotony of the assembly line in 27 huge panels surrounding the museum's central courtyard. Rivera spent nine months in Detroit in 1933 before unveiling the series to great controversy. A visionary Edsel Ford stood up to virulent criticism of the Mexican socialist's frescoes, which were damning in their innate criticism of capitalism. Many city leaders wanted the walls whitewashed as soon as the scaffolding came down, but Ford stood firm, defending the murals, which, unlike another series in New York's Rockefeller Center, were saved.

Relax and rest your feet with a cup of java or something stronger in the Kresge Court Café, a soaring green and light-filled space modeled after Florence's Bargello Palace. If you're visiting on a weekend, stick around long enough to take in a movie at the museum's acclaimed **Detroit Film Theatre.** Now in its 28th year, it offers important premieres by new and established directors and is one of the few venues in the city to show restored, rarely seen classics in their correct aspect ratios. *Variety* called it "the best buy for cineastes in America." For a schedule, call 313/833-3237.

Behind the Detroit Institute of Arts is the **Charles H. Wright Museum of African American History,** 315 E. Warren, 313/494-5800, which opened in 1997. Formerly the fledgling Afro-American Museum of Detroit, it was founded in 1965 by 34 local citizens looking to honor the many accomplishments and contributions of African Americans.

Today the 120,000 square-foot museum ranks as the largest African-American museum in the country, with a rotunda-topped $38.4 million building that houses both touring and permanent exhibitions as well as an intriguing shop, a restaurant, and a theater. And you can't miss the museum's centerpiece—a 70-foot slave ship that offers a dramatic introduction to the African-American experience. Suggested admission for adults is $5. Hours are Tues.–Sat. 9:30 A.M.–5 P.M., Sun. 1–5 P.M.

The latest addition to the city's Cultural Center is the new and improved **Detroit Science Center** 5020 John R, 313/577-8400, which reopened to the public in July of 2001. The recently renovated center includes a digital dome planetarium, two science stages, the city's only IMAX theater and areas devoted to motion, life sciences, matter, energy, waves, and vibration. Admission is $7. Hours are Mon.–Thurs. 9:30 A.M.–5 P.M. Fri. 9–9, Sat. 10–9, Sun. 11–5.

## New Center District

The neighborhood known as "New Center" (named in part as an optimistic effort to replace the city's ailing downtown) was once best known for its most famous resident, General Motors. The twin towers of GM's corporate headquarters housed thousands of workers; for decades, its lavish first-floor showrooms were filled year-round with the latest models, hot off the drawing boards located in the upstairs offices.

Much to the chagrin of GM's employees and executives, the corporate headquarters was surrounded by a once-fine neighborhood that had become seedy and derelict. With the clout and bankroll to pull off what few other companies in the world could, GM spent millions upon millions buying, rehabbing, and reselling the old homes in the surrounding neighborhood—redubbed "New Center." The idea was to spruce up the company's surroundings, draw its employees and other middle- and upper-income families back downtown and, hopefully, spur more area redevelopment.

The New Center neighborhood looks pretty good, though GM ended up leaving New Center and moving downtown to the RenCen in 1999. Since then, the GM building (as it's still known by most Detroiters) has struggled to attract tenants. Among those who have moved in are local health care offices and the state of Michigan.

Of the New Center's two main attractions, the **Fisher Building,** 3011 W. Grand Blvd., 313/874-4444, is the most interesting. Even if you're not an architecture fan, it's worth seeing for the dazzling ceiling mosaics alone. The Architectural League of New York recognized the Fisher Building as the world's most beautiful commercial structure when it was built in 1928. Albert Kahn, one of the city's best-known ar-

"Hitsville U.S.A.," the Motown Museum

# HAMTRAMCK

"**A** Touch of Europe in America," reads the sign approaching Hamtramck. A Polish stronghold since World War I, its residents have stubbornly withstood annexation. Thus Hamtramck survives as a "city within a city," 2.5 square miles completely within Detroit city limits. Well known locally, it can be hard to find for the visitor. To get there, take I-75 to the Caniff exit, Exit 55, about 1.5 miles north of I-94.

Named for a German-French Canadian colonel who served during the post-Revolutionary Indian Wars, the strange-sounding hamlet was settled as a village of mostly German farms in 1901, but a new Dodge auto factory and its promise of jobs swelled the population from 3,589 to 45,615 between 1910 and 1920—the largest increase anywhere in the United States. Many were Polish immigrants, earning Hamtramck the nickname

"Little Poland." Today, the auto plant is closed and the Polish population has dropped from 90 percent to about 40 percent (the slack is taken up by Albanians and African Americans), but the nickname and culture remain.

Drive along Joseph Campau, Hamtramck's main street, and you'll find Polish bakeries, Polish bookstores, shops hawking spicy-sweet Polish sausage, and Polish clubs. There's even a tribute at the corner of Belmont St. and Joseph Campau to the Polish pope, John Paul II, who visited this ethnic enclave in the mid-1980s. Stop at the Polish Art Center for unusual goods such as folk art rugs, leaded glass, Ukrainian decorated eggs, and *szopkas,* intricate nativity scenes made of tinfoil.

Detroiters have long known about the old-world charms of Hamtramck. Joseph Campau's

chitects, made lavish use of expensive materials, including 420 tons of bronze, marble, Minnesota granite, and 24-karat gold. Today the building's 28-story central tower and two 11-story wings house the Fisher Theater, shops, restaurants, and office space.

Dwarfed by the Fisher Building and the GM Building is the diminutive **Motown Historical Museum,** 2648 W. Grand Blvd., 313/875-2264. Known to many across the country as "Hitsville U.S.A.," this is where the Motown Sound exploded from the now-legendary Studio A and soon had teenagers around the country "Dancin' in the Streets."

Berry Gordy, Jr. bought the unremarkable two-story house in 1959 as a fledgling songwriter with a dream of managing singers. Today, the state historic site looks much as it would have in the early 1960s, with an office and tape library filled with reel-to-reel tape machines, company manuals, and newspaper clippings. The second floor re-creates Gordy's 1959–60 apartment, where he and his staff would spend nights packing records to ship to radio stations around the country. The museum's most prized display, however, is the original Studio A, where top tunes such as "Stop in the Name of Love" and "My

Girl" were recorded. Diana Ross and the Supremes, Smokey Robinson and the Miracles, Martha and the Vandellas, The Temptations, The Four Tops, Marvin Gaye, Little Stevie Wonder, and the Jackson Five all recorded in this studio during their early careers.

Other artifacts on display in the two museum buildings (at its zenith, the company owned seven buildings along West Grand Blvd.) include rare photos, gold records, flashy costumes, and other memorabilia. Admission is $6 for adults. Hours are Tues.–Sat. 10 A.M.–5 P.M., Sun.–Mon. noon–5 P.M.

## NAVIGATING THE NEIGHBORHOODS

Detroit has long been known as a city of neighborhoods. In his book *Devil's Night and Other True Tales of Detroit,* author Ze'ev Chafets described his hometown as "less a big city than a federation of ethnic villages bound together by auto plants, a place with more basements and bowling alleys than any other metropolis in the country." Although simplistic, his criticism wasn't far off. Split into eastern and western factions by Woodward Avenue, it's still not

glass storefronts have a vintage 1930s feel, full of Polish imports, discount clothing, and baked goods and meats. Many Polish suburbanites return with their families on weekends to sip *czarnina* (duck's blood soup), linger over *nalesniki* (crepes), and consume *pierogi* (filled dumplings) before heading home with loaves of fresh pumpernickel or rye and a few Polish pastries such as *paczki* (plump jelly doughnuts) to enjoy later.

Highlights of Polish Hamtramck include the **New Palace Bakery,** 9833 Joseph Campau, the most popular of the many bakeries; **Polonia-Jaworowka,** 2934 Yemens, 313/873-8432, housed in a former 1930s food co-op; and **Under the Eagle,** 9000 Joseph Campau, 313/875-5905, two restaurants that locals consider the best places to indulge in the chewy rye

bread, heaping helpings of roast pork loin, tangy sauerkraut, and out-of-the-ordinary dill pickle soup that are the cuisine's strongholds. Afterward, walk it all off with a tour of **St. Florian's,** 2626 Poland, one of the last of the old Polish churches. Completed in 1926, it holds more than 1,800 faithful and is the site of a popular Strawberry Fest in the spring.

More recently, Hamtramck's quirky 1930s flair and cheap rents have attracted artists such as potter/jeweler Marcia Hovland and filmmakers Chuck Cirgenski and Janine Menlove. Hollywood-backed *Polish Wedding,* a movie starring Lena Olin, was filmed here in late 1996. With the new wave of artists and filmmakers have come urbane coffeehouses, late-night alternative-music cafés, and colorful studios and shops that add a new hipness to this old-world enclave.

uncommon for people to be born, grow up, work, raise families, and eventually die in their own neighborhoods.

## Greektown

The city's best-known ethnic area, Greektown has long been a bright spot downtown and one of the few districts that jumps after midnight. With its many lively Greek restaurants and the Trappers Alley shopping and entertainment complex, this restored stretch of Monroe Street attracts both natives and visitors. (It also attracts meter maids, so if you park at one of the plentiful metered spots around Monroe, be sure to bring plenty of change. Better yet, opt for the parking structure on Monroe across from St. Mary's church.)

At the core of it all is a Greek neighborhood that dates back to 1915. Although most of the original residents have moved to the suburbs and the majority of restaurants and bakeries have gone upscale, you'll still find a few coffeehouses where old-timers gather to drink strong coffee or sip sweet retsina and play cards. One original grocery remains: open the rusty screen door of the **Athens Grocery/Bakery,** 527 Monroe, and you'll walk past windows full of neatly arranged

and just-baked loaves of bread, sinfully sweet Greek pastries, and shiny tins of pungent imported olives.

Most Detroiters have their favorite Greektown restaurant. Top choices include **The Laikon,** 569 Monroe, 313/963-7058; **New Hellas,** 583 Monroe, 313/961-5544, where the lines wrap around the corner on weekends; **New Parthenon,** 547 Monroe, 313/961-5111; and the upscale **Pegasus Taverna,** 558 Monroe, 313/964-6800. All serve specialties that include a tart *avgolemono* (chicken lemon soup), flaky spinach pie, *pastitsio* (a kind of Greek lasagna), and flaming **saganaki** cheese, lit with a flourish and a cry of *"Opa!"* from the waiter. Afterward, many diners wander over to the popular **Astoria Pastry Shop,** 541 Monroe, for the baklava and other Greek pastries laid out neatly behind gleaming glass countertops.

Not everything worth seeing in Greektown is Greek. **Fishbone's Rhythm Kitchen,** 400 Monroe, 313/965-4600, is a New Orleans–inspired eatery that opened in the mid-1980s and has been jammed ever since. It serves up a surprisingly authentic (read: spicy) gumbo ya ya and jambalaya. Like the adjacent **Atheneum Suite Hotel,** 313/962-2323, the restaurant is a product of area developers Ted Gatzaros and Jim Pappas, two local boys who never forgot their Greektown roots. They lobbied long and hard to bring casinos to the area, a plan that succeeded (despite both fans and foes) in 2000, when the long-awaited Greektown Casino opened (for more, see the casino section).

Other highlights include exotic Ethiopian cuisine at the **Blue Nile,** 508 Monroe, 313/964-6699; Chicago-style pizza at **PizzaPapalis,** 553 Monroe, 313/961-8020; authentic Irish jigs and jams at the **Old Shillelagh,** 349 Monroe; and one of the city's most beautiful Roman Catholic churches, **St. Mary's,** 646 Monroe, which dates to 1835 and is Detroit's third oldest parish. Greektown is also home to the **Second Baptist Church,** 441 Monroe, founded by 13 former slaves in 1836 and a former stop on the state's active Underground Railroad.

### Mexican Town

The smell of fresh tortillas baking at two factories—La Michuacana and La Jalisciense—lead hungry diners and curious visitors to Bagley Street, the main thoroughfare of the city's Mexican district. Located about five miles from downtown on the city's southwest side, the neighborhood is divided by I-75, so there's an eastern and western side, with shops, restaurants, and homes on both. Here's where you'll find colorful Mexican *mercados* and see old Mexican women, heads covered with an old-fashioned lace mantilla, praying the rosary in the one of the historic churches, including **St. Anne's,** the city's oldest. In summer, the area hosts a popular outdoor market on Sunday where you can pick up fresh chili peppers and other spicy souvenirs.

The Mexican restaurants grouped along streets around Bagley provide the area's main income and job base. Forget Taco Bell; this is the real thing. Salt-rimmed margaritas, soft-shell tacos full of spicy meat and onions, and soft, flaky sopaipillas rival the best south of the border. Queen of them all is **Xochimilco,** 3409 Bagley, 313/843-0179, where Mexican art and eyes of God cover the walls and weekend waits can stretch to over an hour. Other fans of Mexican fare prefer Xochi's (Soh-chi) often-less-crowded competitors, such as **Mexican Village,** 2600 Bagley, 313/237-0333, or **Armando's,** 4242 W. Vernor, 313/554-0666. Another good bet is tiny but tasty **Evie's Tamales,** 3454 Bagley, 313/843-5056, known for its chicken enchiladas, its cozy atmosphere and its quick take-out.

## Sights: The Suburbs

*We got a fast car,*
*fast enough that we can fly away.*
*We gotta make a decision,*
*leave today or live and die this way.*

—*Tracy Chapman, "Fast Car"*

Ironically, the same fast cars that made Motown what it was in its heyday are also what crippled it. Bigger and better cars, and more and more efficient freeways only served to take Detroiters farther and farther away from the core city. Many suburbs, like the neighborhoods that preceded them, can still be classified largely by ethnic group. Warren and Sterling Heights to the northeast are full of Poles and Italians; Oak Park and Southfield have large Jewish and African-American populations; Birmingham and Grosse Pointe are still, despite some inroads by other groups, well-heeled havens of WASPish elitism. Most are bedroom communities that bear little interest for the visitor. Exceptions include Royal Oak, the city's bastion of the avant-garde; Birmingham, home to chic boutiques and fine art galleries; Grosse Pointe, where Lakeshore Drive still boasts some of the area's finest homes; and Dearborn, where Henry Ford was born and later founded what became one of the state's largest tourist attractions.

### DEARBORN

Home to Ford international headquarters and the largest collection of Arabic-speaking peoples in the United States, Dearborn is rightly known

## WINDSOR, CANADA

In a strange quirk of geography, Detroiters have the dubious honor of being located north of Canada. Windsor, Ontario, a city of 200,000 (large by Canadian standards) sits along the southern banks of the Detroit River just across from the Motor City.

"Civilized" is the word that comes to mind when Detroiters talk about Windsor. Although separated only by a river, this Canadian city has a virtually nonexistent crime rate, a full plate of excellent restaurants (made even more palatable by a favorable exchange rate, about C$1.35 to every US$1), and a friendly and civic-minded populace who are happy to welcome Yanks. Detroiters have long shuttled back and forth to enjoy Windsor's restaurants. More recently, they've crossed the water for a different reason—gambling. In 1994, the province of Ontario opened Casino Windsor, which was followed in 1996 by its sister, the riverboat *Northern Belle*. While Michiganders are divided on the subject of gambling in their backyard, they seem to have no problem joining in when it belongs to someone else.

There are plenty of other reasons to make a crossing. Chief among them is the city of Windsor itself, with a surprisingly cosmopolitan downtown, great restaurants, and European-style shopping. Wander Ouellette, the main drag, and the narrow streets surrounding it. Shops are full of imported clothing, books (both new and used, many with British publishers), and the T-shirt stands are ubiquitous. Standouts are: **Shanfields-Meyers,** 188 Ouellette, with a sparkling array of crystal, including a whole room devoted to Waterford, and a wide selection of discounted china and gifts, and **McCance English Shop,** 325 Ouellette, with imported woolens and other British-made wares. There's also a **Columbia Sportswear Outlet** at 527 Ouellette, which sells a full range of outdoor apparel at great prices.

While the shopping is good, it doesn't compare to the eating. Top restaurants include **Cook's Shop,** 683 Ouellette, 519/254-3377, a tiny basement eatery where everything is homemade, including the melt-in-your-mouth polenta and pastas prepared tableside on a rolling cart; **La Cuisine,** 417 Pelissier, 519/253-6432, a surprisingly authentic French bistro that has been recognized by the authoritative *Where to Eat in Canada* for many years; and **The Mini,** 475 University Ave. W, 519/254-2221, which started out with one tiny room (hence the name) but expanded as the restaurant's Vietnamese cuisine and fruit slushes caught on with diners from Windsor and across the way. The atmosphere's not much at **Wah Court,** 2037 Wyandotte W in the University district, 519/254-1388, but the more than 30 dim sum selections (available only before 3 P.M.) are first-rate.

There are two transportation options connecting Detroit and Windsor: the Ambassador Bridge ($2.25) and the Windsor Tunnel ($2.25). Claustrophobics tend to opt for the bridge over the tunnel, although the latter is faster and more direct.

**DETROIT AND VICINITY**

as "the town that Ford built." There was little here but farmland when Henry Ford was born in a small white farmhouse at the corner of Ford Road and Mercury Drive.

Today, Dearborn is best known to tourists as the location of the **Henry Ford Museum and Greenfield Village,** 20900 Oakwood Blvd., 313/271-1620, a favorite field trip for local schoolchildren and one of the state's big tourism draws. In the village Henry gathered buildings and other structures in an attempt to show how America grew from an agrarian to an industrial society. It's a charming—if disconcerting—time machine, a patchwork quilt of unrelated people and places, where a 16th-century English Cotswold cottage sits a few hundred yards away from an 18th-century New England saltbox. Admission to the village (closed in winter) is $14.

Ford sent his pickers across the Midwest and New England to assemble enough artifacts to fill the 12-acre museum next to the village. Inside is one vast collection after another, including the world's greatest holdings of 19th-century farm and kitchen tools (the old washing machines are a stitch), a fine grouping of American furniture, and many artifacts that trace the evolution of the electric light bulb (Edison was a great friend of Ford's; the complex was originally called the Edison Institute).

Worth the $12.50 museum admission (the museum and village have separate admissions; there's also a more economical package price if you're going to both) is the excellent exhibit known as "The Automobile in American Life," which nostalgically shows the car's effect on the American landscape. There's a 1950s McDonald's sign, complete with oversized golden arches; a 1946 diner from Marlboro, Massachusetts, where an egg salad sandwich cost 15 cents; and a Holiday Inn guest room, circa 1960. The evolution of the auto industry is explained using TV monitors and restored automobiles from each period (to see the cars in chronological order, start at the ramp in front of the Oscar Meyer Wienermobile).

Also worth a peek is the permanent "Made in America" exhibit, which traces the evolution of American manufacturing. Far from dull, it explains technology in an entertaining manner, accented by film clips, including one from the *I Love Lucy* show in which Lucy joins a candy-making assembly line with disastrous results. With thousands of items and the adjacent village, the entire complex is more than a bit overwhelming. A good idea is to split a visit into two days, with one day earmarked to explore each half.

While in Dearborn, also make time for at least a taste of its Arab culture. Most of Dearborn's Arab citizens live in the neighborhoods that line Warren and Dix. (The Dix neighborhood lies in the shadow of the Ford Rouge Plant, one of the largest factories in the world.) Its working-class residents are more than 90 percent Arab, primarily from Yemen. The south end boasts signs that are in both English and Arabic, headscarves are common on women, and many men wear traditional skullcaps. The restaurants and shops along Dix offer sights and sounds heard in the Arabian peninsula, including a call to prayer broadcast five times daily from a local mosque.

This heavy concentration of immigrant families (many newly arrived) supports two thriving business districts, each with a character uniquely its own. Most well-known restaurants are located around Michigan Avenue and Ford Road, including two of the best, **La Shish East,** 12918 Michigan Ave., 313/584-4477, and **La Shish West,** 22039-41 Michigan Ave., 313/562-7200. La Shish also has an outpost in Warren, on the city's east side.

For a guide to the city's many Arab restaurants, bakeries, and shops, contact the Arab Community Center for Economic and Social Services (ACCESS) at 2651 Saulino Court, Dearborn, MI 48120, 313/842-7010.

## ROYAL OAK

Heading north on Woodward, Royal Oak is one of the first suburbs you'll encounter after you cross 8 Mile Road. It's the only suburb in the Detroit area where you'll find green hair, unusual pierced body parts, and whips and chains in the window at a boutique called **Noir Leather.** Nowhere else in Michigan will you find a store sign that reads "Absolutely no return on bondage items for sanitary reasons."

Royal Oak was a sleepy (some said dying) suburb in the 1970s, known only by its nickname—Royal Joke—and as the site of the respected 125-acre **Detroit Zoo,** 8450 W. 10 Mile Rd., 248/398-0900. The zoo, long a popular city attraction, is home to more than 1,300 animals, including the newer $8.2 Wildlife Interpretive Gallery, site of a popular hummingbird/butterfly garden and the just-opened Arctic Ring of Fire, which features Arctic species. Admission is $8 adults, $6 kids 2–18; hours are daily 10 A.M.–5 P.M. April–Oct., daily 10 A.M.–4 P.M. the rest of the year and 9–8 summer weekends.

In the mid-1980s, the city's gay population was concentrated in Royal Oak, filling the two

> *Royal Oak is the only suburb in the Detroit area where you'll find green hair, unusual pierced body parts, and whips and chains in the window at a boutique called* Noir Leather.

main commercial streets with vintage clothing and record shops, antique emporiums, and funky coffeehouses. While a few of the original boutiques remain (check out Patti Smith for 1960s duds and inexpensive original designs), others have been replaced by high-rent glitzy home furnishings shops and restaurants that now characterize much of the area. Despite this, Royal Oak is still a lively area, where the streets are filled with a pleasing variety of families and punks, gays and straights. Main Street and Washington Avenue, the two main drags, are great places for window-shopping and people-watching. And it seems as if a new eatery opens almost every day here, giving it one of the best and most extensive restaurant scenes in metro Detroit.

Worthwhile stops include the sinful **Gayle's Chocolates,** 417 S. Washington, the first in the city to offer cappuccino and espresso (now found on just about every corner). A more recent addition is the popular juice bar (try the carrot-apple-ginger), but Gayle's heart remains in the chocolate-making facility located upstairs, which churns out some of the best truffles in the country. Also worth a peek is **Lotus Imports,** 419 S. Washington, for ethnic jewelry, clothing, and accessories from all over the world; **Vertu,** 511 S. Washington, known for its 20th-century designs, including furniture by Eames, Nelson, and Herman Miller from the 1930–1950s; **Dos Manos,** 106 W. 4th, for Latin American handicrafts; and **Chosen Books,** 120 W. 4th, metro Detroit's only gay bookstore. **Borders Outlet,** on Main St., is a good place to troll for bargains on a wide variety of titles.

When it's time to eat, you'll be hard-pressed to choose. In the mood for seafood? **Tom's Oyster Bar,** 318 S. Main, 248/541-1186, is a branch of the popular East Side eatery that has the area's most extensive selection of—surprise!—oysters, as well as always innovative fresh seafood. **BD's Mongolian Barbecue,** 108 E. 5th, 248/398-2560, lets you watch as chefs whip up your stir-fry creation on a huge, central grill. It's been so popular, it's opened outposts in other metro Detroit suburbs. If you're interested in something lighter or just a snack, check out **Pronto!,** 608 S. Washington, 248/544-7900, the best of the city's fresh fast-food emporiums, with a snazzy new video bar and gift shop.

## BIRMINGHAM

Naysayers were concerned that downtown Birmingham—a chic enclave of expensive shops and galleries—would shrivel and die when the even more chic Somerset North Shopping Complex (mall is too pedestrian) opened on nearby Big Beaver Road late in 1996. Birmingham has proven remarkably resilient, however, and remains a tony 'burb with one of the few thriving downtowns in surrounding Oakland County. Shoppers from all over the metro area come here to see and be seen, to linger in cafés and restaurants and to exercise their credit cards in the unusual, mostly independent boutiques.

Even if you're not a shopper, Birmingham is worth a trip for its art galleries, one of the most impressive concentrations in the Midwest. Here you'll find everything from cutting edge contemporary at **Robert Kidd,** 107 Townsend, 248/642-3909, to children's book illustrators at **Elizabeth Stone Gallery,** 536 N. Old Woodward, 248/647-7040. More than a dozen influential art outlets are grouped along a section of Woodward north of downtown known as "Gallery Row."

Other highlights include **Halsted,** 560 N. Woodward, 248/644-8284, known for its 19th- and 20th-century photography and out-of-print books on the art; **David Klein,** 163 Townsend, 248/433-3700, a large airy space that works hard to promote local and regional artists; and **Sandra Collins,** 470 N. Old Woodward, 248/642-4795, where a former curator at the Detroit Institute of Arts features the best of contemporary American decorative arts. Afterward, stop at one of the many excellent restaurants in the area or splurge on a night at the Townsend Hotel, the hostelry of choice for visiting rich and famous.

## BLOOMFIELD HILLS

For a look at how the other half (actually, the other one percent) lives, turn the wheel north to Bloomfield Hills. Long the suburb of choice for CEOs, Big Three bigwigs, and other members of the city's power brokers, it ranks as the state's richest town as well as the second-wealthiest in the country. Past and present residents have included Detroit Piston captain Isaiah Thomas and the queen of soul, Aretha Franklin. Unlike Grosse Pointe, which still struggles with the remains of its WASPish heritage, it doesn't matter if you're black or white in Bloomfield Hills. Money is the great equalizer.

If Grosse Pointe epitomizes "old" money, Bloomfield Hills attracts its newer, shinier counterpart. Huge houses are spread throughout its rolling hills—a geographic anomaly in southeastern Michigan. Most are late-20th-century, although older models can be found clustered around Cranbrook, former home of newspaper magnate **George Booth,** who founded the *Detroit News.* Drive the winding lanes and you'll find Old Tudor, Georgian, and other 1920s-era mansions. One notable exception is the house at 5045 Pon Valley Rd., which was designed by Frank Lloyd Wright in 1951.

### Cranbrook

Despite its celebrities, Bloomfield Hills remains best known as home to Cranbrook, a renowned, 315-acre arts and educational complex. Here famed Finnish architect **Eliel Saarinen** created a lush and lovely refuge for artists and students.

Cranbrook is known throughout the world for the integrated aesthetics of its environment. All buildings, gardens, sculpture, and interiors are treated as an integral and important part of a whole. This creative cohesion is the result of two men, patron newspaper magnate George Booth and artist Eliel Saarinen. Booth, one of the early city expatriates, bought a run-down farm in Bloomfield Hills in 1904 and commissioned noted Detroit architect Albert Kahn to build him a large, Tudor-style mansion there. Grandson of an English coppersmith, Booth was a noted proponent of the arts and crafts movement, which preached a reunification of life and art. After a 1922 trip to Rome, where he visited the American Academy, he decided to create a

school of architecture and design.

While the school is still known throughout the world, equal acclaim is drawn by Cranbrook's **Academy of Art Museum,** 39221 N. Woodward, 248/645-3323, with exhibits by prominent faculty and students; and the recently expanded **Institute of Science,** 248/645-3200, a family science and anthropology museum with a fascinating Physics Hall, an extensive mineral collection, a hall of Native American culture, and an observatory that's open to the public Saturday evenings, weather permitting. Hours for the art museum are Wed.–Sun. 1–5 P.M.; the science museum is open Mon.–Thurs. 10 A.M.–5 P.M., Fri.–Sat. 10 A.M.–10 P.M., and Sun. 1–5 P.M. Admission is $7.

## THE GROSSE POINTES

Five cities actually make up the area collectively known as Grosse Pointe on Detroit's far east side. Taken as a whole, Grosse Pointe Shores, Grosse Pointe Farms, Grosse Pointe Woods, the city of Grosse Pointe, and Grosse Pointe Park make up one of the metro area's wealthiest suburbs, a land of landscaped estates, big trees, big homes, and even bigger money.

A summer community in the 1840s, Grosse Pointe began to change about 1910, when wealthy Detroiters sought to separate themselves from the immigrants who crowded the growing city. The wealthiest built mansions that imitated the elegant country houses of England, France, and Italy, importing stone fireplaces and entire rooms that were later incorporated into new construction.

This is where the city's prominent old families settled; many descendants of this founding aristocracy still live here. For years (through roughly the 1950s), prospective home buyers were screened by a Grosse Pointe real estate broker's infamous point system designed to perpetuate WASP homogeneity. Today you'll find a much more diverse population, although, like most of Detroit's suburbs, it's still predominantly white. Grosse Pointe Park is the most liberal and Democratic, with a number of smaller homes and modest, middle-class 1920s housing. One area, now known as the Cabbage Patch because its early Belgian residents grew the vegetable in their yards, was developed to house servants from the nearby estates.

Many of the largest mansions have been razed, although a few remain along Lakeshore. It's a beautiful drive in any season, with the Detroit River attracting joggers, freighter-watchers, and others who come just to ogle the architecture. To get a peek at the inside of one of the area's original estates, stop at the former **Alger House,** 32 Lakeshore, now known as the **Grosse Pointe War Memorial.** It was originally the home of a founder of the Packard Motor Company and now serves as a community center.

Shopping along the area's main drag, Kercheval Avenue, reveals the expected Talbot's and stores hawking Topsiders. There's a Brooks Brothers store—though surprisingly, it was converted to an outlet store a few years ago. More interesting offerings are found between Wayburn and Beaconsfield, an area known as **Kercheval in the Park,** where you'll find a coffeehouse, **Cup-A-Cino,** a couple of antique stores, and the historic **Rustic Cabins,** a one-time blind pig (aka speakeasy) that still sports its original booths, knotty-pine walls, and Art Deco bar.

## Sports and Recreation

### SPECTATOR SPORTS

Detroiters are among the country's most loyal sports fans, with thousands cheering on the home boys at Lions football, Red Wings hockey, Pistons basketball, and Tigers baseball games. Most are played at sparkling modern suburban stadiums that are comfortable, if not distinct from their counterparts across the country.

Historic **Tiger Stadium,** Michigan at Trumbull south of I-75, is still standing—for now. Legendary and long-time home to the Detroit Tigers, it was replaced in April, 2000, by the glitzy new Comerica Park (nicknamed the obnoxious "Copa" by some). Tiger Stadium's future is uncertain, despite ongoing efforts by Save the Stadium preservationists who have suggested a number of reuse plans, including a Little League Stadium and a concert venue.

While it will never be Tiger Stadium, Comerica Park, 2100 Woodward, has its fans. With a family-friendly philosophy that includes a Tiger-themed carousel, huge Tiger sculpture—popular city meeting spots—and on-site restaurants, it has attracted city and national attention as one of the best of the new breed of ballparks. The location in the heart of Foxtown (near the Fox Theatre) is also prime, with the city's vintage buildings rising around you. For ticket information, call 313/962-4000.

For ticket information on the other sports teams, call the following box offices: Detroit Pistons, 248/377-0100; Detroit Lions, 248/335-4131; Detroit Red Wings, 313/396-7444.

### RECREATION

If you'd rather participate than watch, metro Detroit is home to a number of parks and nature areas where you can roller blade, toss a frisbee, or just wander through the woods and escape the urban jungle. Between them, the Detroit-area's Wayne, Macomb, and Oakland Counties boast 13 such areas, ranging from the tiny **Lake Erie Metropark** a quiet place to hike or bike along the southern shores of Lake Erie, near Monroe, to the bustling **Metro Beach Metropark** in Mount Clemens, which despite its summer crush remains one of the best birding spots in the state. For more information on the Metroparks, call 800/47-PARKS.

Experienced bikers head for **Highland Recreation Area,** 5200 E. Highland Rd., White Lake, 810/889-3750, where 17 miles of trails make up some of the area's most challenging biking, or **Pinckney Recreation Area,** 8555 Silver Hill Rd., Dexter Township, 734/426-4913, home to the 17.5 mile Potawatomi Trail, ranked in the nation's top 10 routes.

# Entertainment and Events

**DETROIT AND VICINITY**

## NIGHTLIFE

When the sun goes down, the lights come on around the city. No matter what your style, Detroit has plenty of places where you can party. The city holds a number of options, from alternative bands at **St. Andrews Hall,** 431 E. Congress, 313/961-MELT, to smooth jazz at the long-standing **Baker's Keyboard Lounge,** 20510 Livernois, 313/345-6300. Other popular hangouts include **Bea's Comedy Kitchen,** 541 E. Larned, 313/961-2581, which serves up soul food as well as regional humor, **Floods Bar & Grill,** 731 Ste. Antoine, 313/963-1090, with sweet soul nightly.

Outside the city limits there are even more choices. Hamtramck's **Motor Lounge,** 3515 Caniff, 313/369-0090, is known for its jukebox, more than 100 beers, and fine cigars. Live blues music is offered every Monday; Thursday is earmarked for the bar's nine-piece band, the Motor Power Train. Also in Hamtown is the slick **Lush,** 10241 Joseph Campau, 313/872-6220, where you can close your eyes and pretend you're in New York's East Village or maybe San Francisco. Another good spot for letting your hair down is the **Magic Bag Blues Club** in Ferndale, 22920 Woodward, 248/544-3030, where nationally recognized blues performers jam each weekend and "Brew and View" movies are offered on Wed. and Thurs. "Sonic therapy" is the focus at Ferndale's **Xhedros Cafe,** 240 W. Nine Mile, 248/399-3946, which has an acoustic open mike on Mon., Wed. and Thurs. and live bands on weekends.

## CASINOS

In 1997, city voters approved a controversial referendum permitting casino gambling within city limits. Four years later, three temporary casinos are now open—and remain controversial. Whether gambling is the struggling inner city's angel or devil is still being decided not only at the craps tables, but in the hearts of residents. Most recently, long-term plans to locate permanent casinos on the city's riverfront were abandoned after long-term opposition. Their ultimate sites are still being determined, and may be for some time to come.

In the meantime, for those who enjoy rolling the dice, current options include **MGM Grand Casino,** 1300 John C. Lodge, 877/888-2121, a flashy, Art Deco palace that draws its inspiration from the Hollywood of yesteryear. Motown in all its glory provides the theme for Detroit's own **MotorCity Casino,** 2901 Grand River, 877/777-0711, housed in a former Wonder Bread warehouse and connected by skywalks to downtown restaurants and parking. Most recent is the **Greektown Casino,** 555

---

## DETROIT FESTIVALS

**North American International Auto Show:** Cobo Hall, January, 313/886-6750

**Detroit Hoedown:** Hart Plaza, May, 8–10, 313/399-7000

**Detroit Grand Prix:** Belle Isle, June, 313/393-7749

**International Freedom Festival:** Hart Plaza and riverfront, June–July, 313/923-7400

**Thunderfest Boat Races:** July, 313/331-7770

**Michigan Taste Fest:** Detroit New Center, July 4 weekend, 313/872-0188

**African World Festival:** Hart Plaza, August, 313/833-9800

**Michigan State Fair:** State Fairgrounds, August, 313/369-8250

**Concours D'Elegance Car Show:** Meadowbrook Hall, Rochester, August, 248/370-3148

**Ford Montreux Detroit Jazz Festival:** Hart Plaza, September, 313/963-7622

**Detroit Festival of the Arts:** University Cultural Center, September, 313/577-5088

**Detroit Agrow:** downtown, Monday before Thanksgiving, 313/961-1403

**Thanksgiving Day Parade:** Woodward Ave., November, 313/923-7400

E. Lafayette, 313/223-2999, the city's most spacious, with Las Vegas–style gaming and easy access to the city's liveliest neighborhood. All have on-site restaurants and varying degrees of entertainment.

## THEATER AND MUSIC

Productions at the 5,000-seat **Fox Theater,** 2211 Woodward Ave., 313/983-6611, include touring Broadway musicals, big-name concerts, restored film epics, and other special events. One contrast to the cavernous Fox are the tiny and jewel-like **Gem and Century Theatres,** 333 Madison, 313/963-9800, a cabaret-style venue for national comedy acts, small plays, and musical revues. The restored **Detroit Opera House,** 1526 Broadway, 313/237-SING, attracts full-scale productions of everything from opera to ballet.

Other area theaters include the **Music Hall Center for the Performing Arts,** 350 Madison, 313/963-2366, whose stage has been graced by luminaries such as Lucille Ball, W. C. Fields, Martha Graham, Ella Fitzgerald, Lillian Hellman, and others. The acoustically perfect 1919 **Orchestra Hall,** 3711 Woodward, 313/576-5111, is home to the acclaimed Detroit Symphony.

# Practicalities

## ACCOMMODATIONS

### Downtown

**Atheneum Suite Hotel,** 1000 Brush, 313/962-2323, is downtown's newest accommodation and the city's only all-suite hotel. Located in the heart of Greektown, it borrows classical motifs from the surrounding neighborhood in its 174 regular and 23 luxury suites, all with separate living rooms, minibars, hair dryers, and other convenient amenities. $175–350.

**Crowne Plaza Detroit Pontchartrain,** 2 Washington Blvd., 313/965-0200 or 800/517-3333, was a well-loved 412-room city hotel better known as "The Pontch" before it was bought and spiffed up by Holiday Inn. Chief among its strengths is its location across from Hart Plaza and Cobo Center. $75–150.

**Courtyard by Marriott,** 333 E. Jefferson, 313/222-7770 or 800/222-TREE, is part of the Millender Center development, with 250 oversized room, an extensive health club and an outdoor above-ground tennis court/running track that offers great views of the city's surrounding vintage architecture. $150–175.

**Omni River Place,** 1000 River Place, 313/259-9500 or 800/THE-OMNI, is part of the restored Stroh RiverPlace complex. This small and elegant hotel has 108 rooms decorated in a soothing English Country style. It also has Detroit's only sanctioned croquet court. $175–225.

**Shorecrest Motor Inn,** 1316 E. Jefferson, 313/568-3000 or 800/992-9616, is popular with execs looking to save a buck. The 54-room budget motel in the shadow of the RenCen is family owned and operated and includes a decent short-order restaurant (the Clique), business services, and city tours. $75–125.

GM execs may soon outnumber other guests at the **Marriott Renaissance Center,** 313/568-8000, a huge, 1,392-room hotel, part of the towering Renaissance Center. Formerly a Westin, it was renovated in 2000 and remains the tallest hotel in the world, with three restaurants, a health club, and access to the center's shops, restaurants, and services. $75–125.

### Suburbs

**Hampton Inn,** 20061 Michigan Ave., Dearborn, 313/436-9600, has a great location overlooking Greenfield Village and 119 simple but comfortable guest rooms that make this chain a good bet for the budget minded. Amenities include an indoor pool, free local calls, continental breakfast, and in-room coffeemakers. $75–100.

**Hyatt Regency** Fairlane Town Center, Dearborn, 313/593-1234 or 800/233-1234, is a large steel-and-glass monolith with more than 771 rooms. It's one of the largest in the Hyatt chain. The hotel restaurant, Giulio & Sons, has a lavish Italian-style buffet that's a real bargain. $175–200.

**Kingsley Hotel & Suites,** 39475 N. Woodward, Bloomfield Hills, 248/644-1400 or 800/544-6835, was once a tavern on the old mud road to Pontiac. Today's Kingsley is a bit more refined, with 160 traditional-style rooms, an on-site art gallery, and a pleasant piano bar. $100–175.

**Westin Southfield,** 1500 Town Center, Southfield, 248/827-4000 or 800/WESTIN, is a sleek and shiny recently revamped hotel that attracts business types bound for offices in the north. $75–125.

The **Ritz-Carlton Hotel,** 300 Town Center Dr., Dearborn, 313/441-2000, was built by Ford money, which still drives this understated 308-room hotel. It attracts power brokers from across the country as well as a few understated rock stars and visiting celebrities. The clubby Grille is known for its excellent, if pricey, continental cuisine. $175–425

The **Townsend Hotel,** 100 Townsend St., Birmingham, 248/642-7900, is the posh—if pretentious—European-style hostelry where Paul McCartney stayed when he performed in Detroit on his last tour. Nothing but the best is good enough here—Belgian linens, pillows of the fluffiest down, yards of marble in the baths, and a restaurant staffed with world-class chefs who cater to guests' every whim. You'll feel as if you've stepped into a Ralph Lauren ad. Located near Birmingham's fashionable shops and galleries, it's also a favorite stop for afternoon tea, served every afternoon. $300–425.

# FOOD

## City Restaurants

**Fishbone's Rhythm Kitchen Café,** 400 Monroe St., 313/965-4600, Greektown's only Cajun restaurant, spices up downtown with fare such as whiskey ribs, smoked Cajun salmon, jambalaya, and a fiery gumbo. Expect a wait. Entrees about $15. There are also locations in suburban Southfield and St. Clair Shores.

**Govinda's,** 383 Lenox, 313/331-6740, was once the palatial home of Lawrence P. Fisher of Fisher Body fame. Today it's one of the city's most unusual restaurants, with gourmet vegetarian meals made with ingredients and hard-to-find spices imported from around the world. Renovated in 2001, the restaurant is worth a visit just for the homemade breads and desserts and for the can't-be-beat atmosphere. If you're lucky, you'll be there during a house tour. Entrees average $10.

**Harlequin Café,** 8047 Agnes, 313/331-0922, is a romantic eatery set in the vintage Indian Village neighborhood. The menu includes familiar fare such as steak or chicken Caesar as well as more imaginative items such as Wilshire sweetbreads and tandoori Cornish hen. Entrees average $17.

**Intermezzo,** 1435 Randolph, Harmonie Park, 313/961-0707. A great place for people-watching, this contemporary, glass-fronted eatery specializes in Italian with a twist. Try the veal scallopine with pancetta pan gravy and olives, or the shrimp with green apples. Entrees average $19.

**Majestic Café,** 4124 Woodward, 313/833-9700, is downtown's home of *baba gannoujh,* hummus, and tabbouleh. It packs in the Wayne State and downtown Medical Center crowd at lunch. At dinner, the menu's a bit more varied, with surprises such as gorgonzola wrapped in phyllo and roasted pork loin with Swiss chard, raisins, and apples among the offerings. Average entree $11.

**Milt's Gourmet Bar "B" Que,** 19143 Kelly Rd., 313/521-5959, is one of the east side's many surprises. The walls are plain, the atmosphere bustling, but inexpensive Milt's joint turns out some of the city's best barbecue. The ribs, chicken, and turkey are smothered in a spicy yet sweet sauce that gives Memphis a run for its money. The dessert case showcases a sumptuous homemade sweet potato pie that makes forgetting the diet worth the guilt. Entrees average $6.

**New Hellas Café,** 583 Monroe St., 313/961-5544, attracts long lines on weekends. Worth waiting for are the *saganaki, moussaka,* and *pastit-*

*sio,* all served with the hallmark Greek flair and friendliness. Entrees average $10.

**Old Shillelagh,** 349 Monroe, 313/964-0007, is the place to go when the Greek theme wears a bit thin. On weekends, this authentic Irish pub brims with bands and brews. The bar menu isn't bad either. Entrees average $6.

**Opus One,** 565 E. Larned, 313/961-7766, ranks as the city's most expensive eatery, with a sophisticated menu that reflects both continental and regional influences. Top off your visit with the chocolate gateau with fine nuts, accompanied by freshly brewed Jamaican blue java. Entrees average $30.

**Pizza Papalis,** 553 Monroe, 313/961-8020, is where Motown meets the Windy City. Only the name is Greek: deep-dish pies are the specialty. Entrees average $8.

**Roma Café,** 3401 Riopelle, 313/831-5940, is Detroit's oldest restaurant. It looks a bit dark and dated these days, but it's still a favorite of suburban Italians and the city's old guard. The restaurant takes its reputation seriously, too, with a huge array of Italian specialties, including what many consider the city's best pastas and friendly tuxedoed waiters. Entrees average $15.

The **Whitney,** 4421 Woodward, 313/832-5700, is one of the city's most elegant restaurants. Sheathed in pink Colorado granite, the Whitney is the last of the elaborate mansions that once lined Woodward Avenue. Built for fur trader and financier David Whitney, today it's known as one of the places Detroiters go for special occasions. Don't miss the breathtaking Tiffany window. The food's first-rate, too. Entrees average $25.

**Xochimilco,** 3409 Bagley, 313/843-0179, is a place where no matter how much you try, it's hard to spend more than $20. This is Mexican Town's busiest and best-known restaurant, and the weekend crowds prove it. The place closes at 4 A.M., so any time you visit you'll find a lively crowd of urbanites and suburbanites munching nachos and sipping margaritas. Parking is adjacent to the restaurant. Entrees average $7.

**Note:** For more on city restaurants, see the sections on **Greektown** and **Mexican Town.**

## CONEY CUISINE

Philly may have the cheese steak and Chicago its deep-dish pie, but Detroit has *the* Coney Island. No amusement park, Detroiters take their coneys very seriously and down thousands of the hot dogs topped with chili, cheese, and onions annually. The name "Coney Island" serves simultaneously as both a destination and a dish—strangely enough, a coney is both a restaurant and what you eat when you get there.

Coney Islands exist on virtually every corner in Detroit, both urban and suburban. King of the coneys, however, are two adjacent spots on Lafayette Street in downtown Detroit. Owned by a pair of brothers, the two are unofficial rivals, each with his own quirky and fiercely loyal clientele.

This is where a wiener with skin, beanless chili, onions, and mustard was first called "one with everything." Although American Coney Island, 114 W. Lafayette, 313/961-7758, now serves soups and salads, it's the dogs that bring in a clientele that ranges from cops on the beat to fur-clad suburbanites grabbing a bite after a show at the Fox Theater or the Detroit Opera House. Next door, the Lafayette Coney Island, 118 W. Lafayette, 313/964-8198, remains the favorite of most Detroiters, with a purist-minded menu and a gossipy, gum-chewing waitstaff. Both are open 24 hours; no credit cards accepted.

## Suburban Restaurants

**Beans & Cornbread,** 29508 Northwestern Hwy., Southfield, 248/208-1680, is known for its "gourmet soul food." Located in trendy Southfield, it's a sophisticated spot filled with vintage magazine covers featuring notable African Americans. Despite its uptown style, it has plenty of downtown food, with savory treats that includes greens, catfish, wings and gravy as well as continental bistro fare. Average entree $12.

**B. D.'s Mongolian Barbecue,** 310 S. Main St., Royal Oak, 248/398-7755, is where the theater is part of the fun. You watch as a team of chefs whips up your stir-fry creation on a huge, flat-top grill. Diners enjoy unlimited trips to the stir-fry buffet. One of Royal Oak's most unusual and popular restaurants. Expect a wait on weekends. There are also locations in Ann Arbor, Novi, and Dearborn. Entrees $8–16.

**Big Fish,** 700 Town Center Dr., Dearborn, 313/336-6350, and 111 W. 14 Mile, Troy, 248/585-9533, are popular lunch spots that are also pretty crowded during dinner. Some say the unusual name is a reference to the Big Three execs who power lunch at the original location in Dearborn. Others say it's a reference to the menu, which is mainly seafood. The atmosphere is dark and clubby, accented with fishing and nautical motifs. Specialties include the tangy Martha's Vineyard salad, potato-encrusted whitefish, and any of the excellent daily specials. Average entree $15.

**Morton's of Chicago,** 1 Town Square, Southfield, 248/354-6006, is a well-known steakhouse and Windy City outpost where even the broccoli looks pumped up. When you tire of the massive steaks (Porterhouse is the specialty), check out the gargantuan lobsters and blimp-size spuds. Average entree $18.

**Golden Mushroom,** 18100 W. 10 Mile, Southfield, 248/559-4230, is still home to the United States' first master chef, Milos Cihelka. The elegant and expensive Mushroom serves dishes such as tournedos with foie gras, sautéed Dover sole, and daily game specials with a mélange of—what else?—wild mushrooms. Entrees average $26.

The **Lark,** 6430 Farmington Rd., West Bloomfield, 248/661-4466, once was called "America's finest restaurant" by *Condé Nast Traveler.* It's certainly one of the hardest to get into, with reservations needed well in advance for this five-star restaurant. It features the superb offerings of chef Marcus Haight, from standard entrees such as rack of lamb Genghis Khan to *cataplana,* a Portuguese seafood casserole. Dinners are $59 for a prix fixe meal, including appetizer, soup, and entree.

**Speedboat Bar & Grill,** 749 Biddle Ave., Wyandotte, 734/282-5750), is the home of the masterpiece swine burger, maybe the perfect bar burger. It's thick and juicy and served with spicy rings of jalapeño, pepper cheese, chili, and onions fried golden brown. Or you can opt for a brimming bowl of the spicy red chili, a consistent award-winner. Worth a special trip downriver. Entrees average $6.

**Note:** For more on restaurants in the suburbs, see the sections on **Royal Oak** and **Dearborn.**

# TRANSPORTATION
## By Air
**Detroit Metropolitan Airport (DTW),** 734/942-3550, spreads out over some 6,000 acres 21 miles south of the city in Romulus, just off I-94 and Merriman Road. The new McNamara Midfield Terminal-adding 74 jet gates, 25 commuter aircraft gates, and a 11,000-stall parking garage-is slated to open in 2002, providing much-needed relief to this over-burdened airport. It's a joint project of Wayne County and Northwest Airlines, the airport's major tenant.

American Airlines/American Eagle, 800/433-7300; Delta, 800/221-1212; Southwest, 800/435-9792; TWA, 800/221-2000; United/United Express, 800/241-6522; and US Air, 800/428-4322, all have service here, but the majority of arrivals and departures belong to Northwest, 800/225-2525, which operates a bustling hub. Coach service from downtown hotels to the airport is available by reservation. The one-way cost is $13. For information, call Commuter Express, 800/351-5466 in Michigan, or 800/488-7433 outside. MetroCars, 734/946-5700, offers similar service.

## By Car
Detroit, not surprisingly, is full of freeways. I-75 is the major north-south thoroughfare, with I-96, I-696, and I-94 heading east-west. Avoid traveling any of these routes during rush hours (generally 6–10 A.M. and 3–7 P.M.) or allow plenty of extra time. It's wise to seek out alternate routes such as I-275, which splits off from I-696 or M-59 in Oakland County, and to pick up a map of the area before setting off to ensure you don't get lost (an easy thing to do). Seat belts are required by Michigan law. Rental car companies—including Hertz, Avis, Budget, National and more—may be found at the airport. Check

The elevated People Mover offers a certain perspective on the city.

the local telephone directory for listings. Taxis operate on a meter system; the basic charge is $1.40, plus $1.40 per mile. Additional riders free. **Checker Cab,** 313/963-7000, and **City Cab,** 313/833-7060 are the city's largest. Others are listed in the local telephone directory.

## By Train

**Amtrak,** 800/873-3442 or 800/USA-RAIL, offers convenient daily service to six metro area stops: Ann Arbor, Dearborn, Detroit, Royal Oak, Birmingham, and Pontiac. Downtown, the station is located at 11 W. Baltimore Avenue in the New Center and in suburban Dearborn.

## By Bus

**Greyhound,** 1001 Howard St., 313/961-8011, serves downtown Detroit. Be extra careful at the station—it's not located in the best part of town. Daytime arrivals and departures are always a good idea. Get national information on fares and schedules at 800/231-2222, or website: www.greyhound.com.

## Mass Transit

Most would agree that mass transit in Detroit is a joke. (This is the city that invented the car,

after all). The Detroit Department of Transportation (DDOT) is the state's largest transit system; it serves Detroit and 25 suburban communities. DDOT buses and bus stops are recognizable by their trademark green and yellow colors.

Buses operate on 50 routes during the day and evenings from 6 A.M. until approximately 1 A.M.; 14 of the most popular routes operate 24 hours. Schedules are available by calling 888/336-8287. Fares are $1.25. Southeast Michigan Area Rapid Transit (SMART) offers service in Oakland, Macomb, and some parts of Wayne County. For information, call 313/962-5515.

Two other options offer downtown service: the **trolley,** 888/336-8287, and the **People Mover,** 313/224-2160. The red and brass antique trolleys offer limited service along Jefferson Avenue and Washington Boulevard and are used mostly by tourists. The fare is 50 cents. While the People Mover never lived up to high expectations, it's a handy way to travel while downtown, with a bird's-eye view of the city from its elevated track. For 50 cents, you'll get a 15-minute ride along a three-mile track that circles the heart of the business district. Even if you don't ride, it's worth a visit to check out the 13 People Mover stations, which boast works by local artists. The People Mover operates through the central business district, including the Civic Center, Mon.–Thurs. 7 A.M.–11 P.M., Fri. 7 A.M.–midnight, Sun. noon–8 P.M. Hours are extended during special events. For more information, call 313/224-2160.

## INFORMATION AND SERVICES
### Tourist Offices
The **Detroit Metropolitan Convention and Visitors Bureau,** 211 W. Fort St., Suite 1000, 313/202-1800 or 800/338-7648, distributes free information through the mail or its website (www.visitdetroit.com) and from the lobby at Greenfield Village in Dearborn. Information is also available from the **Michigan Travel Bureau,** 888/78-GREAT, website: www.michigan.org.

### Telephone
Dial 911 for emergency assistance (police, ambulance, or fire). In nonemergency situations, call the police at 313/267-4600 or 311 in the city limits. For weather, call 313/252-2200, ext. 2222.

The area code for Detroit and Dearborn telephone numbers is 313. The area code for Oakland County (including Birmingham, Royal Oak, and most of the northern suburbs) is 248. Ann Arbor's area code is 734. North and east of Detroit, suburbs in Macomb County use an 810 area code.

### Publications
The two daily newspapers, the *Detroit News* and the *Detroit Free Press,* are supplemented by a wide variety of suburban dailies and weeklies, and by the alternative weekly the *Detroit MetroTimes.* The *MetroTimes* is the city's first—and most successful—alternative rag, with thoughtful reporting on a variety of civil and social issues, extensive entertainment listings (a great place to check out what there is to do on any given night) and consciousness- (if not eyebrow-) raising classifieds and want ads. It's distributed free at bins throughout the city and suburbs. Another good read is *Hour Magazine,* a tabloid-size, full-color magazine that's a recent addition to the city's literary scene and is full of thought-provoking and entertaining editorials.

### Security
Unfortunately, crime is a major concern in most American cities, and Detroit is no exception. Tourist areas, however, are well patrolled. For added protection, hide money and cards securely in a money belt or under clothing, and leave valuable jewelry home. Some seasoned urban travelers carry a spare money clip with a $10- or $20-bill wrapped around a wad of ones, so if they're ever accosted they can throw this mad money out and run.

## Ann Arbor

Few would dispute the claim that Ann Arbor, population 114,000 is one of the most interesting cities in the state—if not the country. Home to the University of Michigan, it has become much more than just a typical college town. Located about 40 miles west of Detroit, Ann Arbor is now a regional research center as well as the suburb of choice for Detroit intelligentsia. Popular with all demographic groups, the city was recently named fifth in a survey by *Money* magazine on quality of life, awarded the title "quintessentially cool college

town" by *Seventeen,* and rated the second most "Woman Friendly City in America" by *Ladies Home Journal.*

The media continues to heap accolades on the city, in part because of its appealing blend of big city vitality and small-town Midwestern friendliness. This is Michigan, after all. While there's plenty of typical college-town angst, folks are genuinely helpful when you ask directions and are always ready to recommend a favorite restaurant.

The city is dominated by the well-known uni-

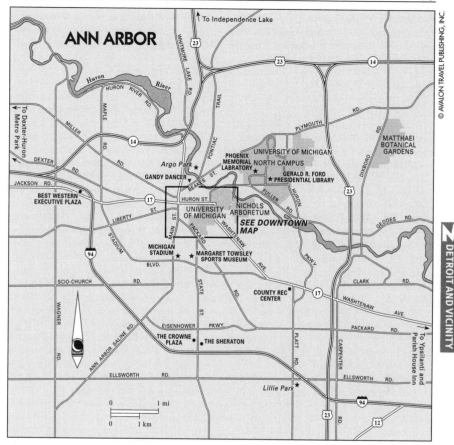

versity, which occupies most of the area just east of downtown. Historic U of M, founded in 1823, is one of the nation's great public institutions, with a long reputation for excellence in academics and athletics. The university is proud of its statistics, including having the largest pre-law and pre-med programs in the country (no other school produces more entrants to medical schools); graduates that include seven NASA astronauts, three Supreme Court justices, one president, and several Pulitzer Prize winners; and a diverse student body that represents all 50 states and more than 100 foreign countries.

For more information on Ann Arbor, contact the **Ann Arbor Convention and Visitors Bu-**reau, 120 W. Huron St., 800/888-9487, website: www.annarbor.org.

## CENTRAL CAMPUS

A campus tour reveals the expected and the less expected—both backpacked and Birkenstocked students and a quirky collection of 1,400 rare musical instruments. The heart of it all is the **"Diag,"** the diagonal walkway crossing the original 40-acre campus between the retail districts on State and North University and on South University at East University. (Luckily, it's much less confusing than it sounds and there's plenty of parking.) Many of the buildings house classrooms, and on most days this is the site of student protest signs and demonstrations. Ann Arbor, while still politically correct, is not the hotbed of activism it was in the 1960s, when an ongoing campaign began here to legalize marijuana and when President Kennedy announced plans to form the Peace Corps on the steps of the Student Union.

For a great view, climb the eight floors to the map room in the Graduate Library. Afterward, cross State Street, where you'll find the venerable **Michigan Union,** built in the 1920s. For many years, women were allowed entry only through a side door, and even then, only for special events. Women were barred from some rooms, including the paneled second-floor billiards room, as late as the 1960s. In response, women alumni built the smaller Michigan League in 1929, still known for its well-stocked newsstand, its basement grill, and its 700-seat theater. The student-staffed first-floor information desk is a handy place for visitors.

Across from the League is the **Burton Tower,** a campus landmark that's capped by the Baird Carillon. It has 53 bells that range in weight from 12 pounds to 12 tons and holds concerts weekdays at noon while school is in session.

Another campus favorite is the **Law Quadrangle,** home of U of M's respected law school. Built 1923–1933, the picturesque quad was modeled after Britain's Cambridge University. The level of workmanship in the Gothic building was rare even in the arts-and-crafts inspired 1920s. Rest your feet in the library's hushed reading room, where blue and gold plaster medallions decorate the ceiling.

U of M has long been a leading research institution, and has developed extensive collections through the years. Most are housed in three exceptional museums, all of which have broadened their focus in the recent past to appeal to a wider audience. The **University of Michigan Exhibit Museum of Natural History,** 1109 Geddes at N. University, 734/764-0478, is one of the best natural science museums in the country, with displays on prehistoric life and dinosaurs, anthropology, Native Americans, Michigan wildlife, biology, and astronomy. Kid-friendly docents

with simple explanations and ready smiles are a plus. Most of the highlights—especially the seven dinosaur dioramas—are on the second floor. Unlike many museums in the Detroit area, it's even open Monday; hours are daily 9 A.M.–5 P.M., Sun. 1–5 P.M. Admission is $2.

Among the top 10 U.S. university art museums, the **University of Michigan Museum of Art,** 525 S. State St., 734/764-0395, has a permanent collection of more than 13,000 regularly rotated pieces. That includes big names such as Picasso, Rembrandt, Monet, Miro, Cézanne, and more. Masterpieces include Max Beckman's *Begin the Beguine,* Monet's *The Breakup of the Ice,* and the especially strong collection of Whistler prints, given to the museum by a Detroit friend of connoisseur Charles Lang Freer, who later founded Washington, D.C.'s Freer Gallery. The knowledgeable staff works hard to make art more accessible and relevant to the general public, with a high-caliber museum shop, enthusiastic docents, and a weekly series of gallery talks, art videos, and slide lectures known as "Midweek and the Museum." If you're especially lucky (or really organized) you may be able to time your visit for 3 P.M. on the last Sunday of the month, when a Japanese tea ceremony is held in the Japanese galleries. The museum is open Tues.–Sat. 10 A.M.–5 P.M., Sun. noon–5 P.M. Donation.

Also on State is the **Kelsey Museum of Archaeology,** 434 S. State across from Angell Hall, 734/764-9304. Contained in a beautiful Richardsonian Romanesque structure built of local fieldstone, it boasts a large Tiffany window as well as Greek, Egyptian, Roman, and Near Eastern antiquities. The total holdings number more than 100,000 pieces, including Egyptian mummy masks, fragile vessels of Roman glass and dramatic Greek vases. Admission is free; hours are Mon.–Fri. 9 A.M.–4 P.M., Sat.–Sun. 1–4 P.M. Donations.

North Campus, an 800-acre area northeast of central campus, was planned in the 1940s by Finnish architect Eero Saarinen, son of Eliel Saarinen of Cranbrook fame. Not as well known (or as interesting) as Central Campus, it's home to the school of art and architecture as well as to the **Gerald R. Ford Presidential Library** (Ford was a 1935 grad), the **Phoenix Memorial Laboratory,** one of the first university nuclear reactors (built in 1954), and the fascinatingly quirky collection of musical instruments collected by drug manufacturer Fred Stearns (check out the first Moog synthesizer, part of an effort to amass 20th-century equipment). The school of music offers free frequent and worthwhile recitals and concerts by students and staff. Once in the area, you can't miss *The Wave Field,* a powerful 70-by-70-foot sculpture created by Maya Lin, who won acclaim for the Washington, D.C., Vietnam Memorial. Just east of the Francois Xavier Bagnoud Building, it was designed to enable visitors to lie down in the troughs of the earth's waves.

No visit to Wolverine territory would be complete without a stop at **Michigan Stadium,** on Stadium Street and Main. The largest collegiate stadium in the United States, it draws more than 105,000 screaming fans for home games and post-game tailgating marathons. An average of 100,000 people visit the U of M Museum of Art each year—the same number who attend just *one* U of M home game.

Great moments in Wolverine football can be found in the **Margaret Towsley Sports Museum** 734/647-2583, at Schembechler Hall on South State Street and McKinley. Devoted to glorifying (some say deifying) Wolverine athletes, it has a long visual timeline (note that no woman appears until the 1970s) accented by related objects such as a vintage football uniform, a computerized program that lets you reenact past plays, trophies, and numerous Go Blue memorabilia. It's generally open 11 A.M.–5 P.M. during the week and on football weekends. Admission is free.

## DISCOVERING DOWNTOWN

The area along State Street remains the main campus commercial strip, with a funky mix of coffeehouses, bookstores, and urbane boutiques. A standout is the historic 1915 Nickels Arcade, a small, European-style arcade filled with ever-changing boutiques and galleries between State and Maynard. Two long-time standouts include

the **Chris Triola Gallery,** 734/996-9955, with chic handmade sweaters inspired by African, Celtic, and Jazz Age motifs, and **Bivouac,** 734/761-7206, the resource for Ann Arbor campers, hikers, climbers, and skiers.

More shopping is concentrated off and on Main Street in the city's vintage downtown. Once a mainstay of longtime German businesses, it has since become a stylish place for browsing, people-watching, and noshing. **Selo/Shevel Gallery,** 301 and 335 S. Main, has one of the state's best collections of handmade contemporary jewelry as well as a nice selection of art glass. Try **Wilderness Outfitters,** 333 S. Main, for classic outdoor wear and the city's best selection of backpacking boots. City kids can often be found squandering their allowances at **Peaceable Kingdom,** 210 S. Main, a local institution with small, inexpensive toys as well as compelling folk art. Adults, on the other hand, prefer the feel-good **Falling Water Books,** 213 S. Main, for arty gifts, journals, jewelry, and other New Age goodies. And if you're in a mind for something really novel (er, navel), former art teacher Suzanne Fauser will oblige with one of her intricately rendered and award-winning creations at **Creative Tattoo,** 612 W. Liberty.

## KERRYTOWN

Once forlorn and forgotten, this old commercial strip north of downtown is enjoying its second go-round as a retail district, with the impressive **Peoples Food Co-op; Wooden Spoon** used books; **Crazy Wisdom,** southeastern Michigan's center for metaphysics and Eastern religions; and a colorful (if a bit expensive) open-air **farmers market.** Flowers and produce are featured on Wednesday and Saturday; on Sunday, the space is taken over by artisans and craftspeople. As is true with most markets, early risers get the cream of the crop. Hours are 7 A.M.–3 P.M. (10 A.M.–4 P.M. for the artists' market).

Top restaurants and interesting indoor shopping bring visitors too, who wander in the Kerrytown complex, browsing and buying in boutiques such as **Vintage To Vogue** (where you can pick up "clothing for the body, mind,

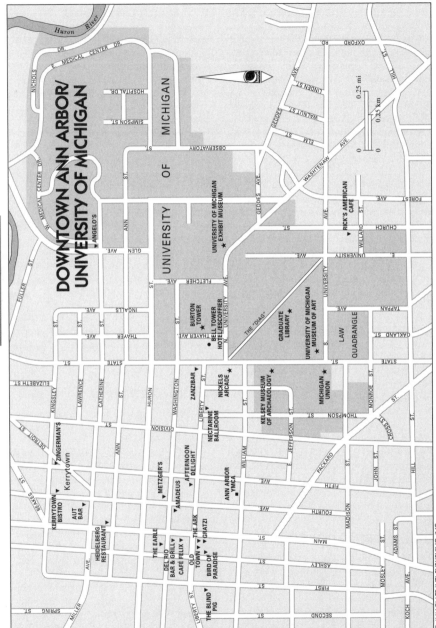

DETROIT AND VICINITY

DOWNTOWN ANN ARBOR/
UNIVERSITY OF MICHIGAN

UNIVERSITY OF MICHIGAN

Huron River

Huron River

© AVALON TRAVEL PUBLISHING, INC.

0.25 mi

0.25 km

and soul"); gourmet-inspired **Kitchen Port;** or the almost-legendary **Treasure Mart,** 529 Detroit St., the city's premier resale shop, which is well known for its collectibles and other fun "recycled" stuff.

Don't miss a stop at **Zingerman's,** 422 Detroit St., 734/663-3354, is a story in itself. Gastronomes and food critics alike consider this New York-style deli the best deli in the Midwest—maybe the nation. Most head for the deli counter offering more than 100 sandwiches (the corned beef Reuben, at $10.99, is the best seller), side salads, and fragrant imported cheeses. The grocery side of the store has fresh breads and surrounding shelves stocked with the best in everything, from jams to jalapeños. The grocery counter is busiest 9–11 A.M., after work, and all day on weekends; the sandwich area is mobbed 11 A.M.–2:30 P.M. and again 5–7 P.M. Consider calling ahead, 734/663-DELI, to have your order waiting and plan on eating at the relaxed Zingerman's Next Door, where you can linger as long as you want over a meal.

## PARKS AND RECREATION

Like most urbanites, Ann Arbor residents cultivate their parks and green-spaces. More than 20 parks are scattered within a few miles of downtown, many with hiking, horseback riding, cross-country skiing, golf, and more.

Not exactly a park but a great place for a nature walk is **Matthaei Botanical Gardens,** 1800 N. Dixboro Rd., 734/998-7060. This expansive conservatory of tropical, warm-temperate, and desert plants seven miles northeast of downtown is open 10 A.M.–4:30 P.M. daily, but is best known for its picturesque gardens, nature trail, and re-created prairie, which are open 8 A.M.–sunset daily. Conservatory admission is $3; grounds are free. Free Mon. until 1 P.M.

**Nichols Arboretum,** 1610 Washington Heights Rd., 734/998-9540, offers some of the area's best hiking and a natural area that serves as an education and research facility for the university and Ann Arbor schools. It's located next to the central campus and offers more than 400 identified tree species as well as a lush peony garden, which blooms in early summer. Trails wind through the 123 acres and a variety of plant collections. Paddlers should head for **Argo Park,** 1055 Longshore Dr., 734/668-7411, a 32-acre park along the Huron River. Reasonable canoe rentals available at the on-site livery.

Environmentalists prefer **Independence Lake County Park,** 3200 Jennings Rd., one mile west of US-23, 734/449-4437, for its observation tower and natural areas, which include managed prairie grass. It is open Memorial Day–Labor Day, weekends in May and September, closed to cars at all other times.

**Lillie Park,** Platt Rd. south of Ellsworth Rd., 734/996-3056, is an 87-acre undeveloped park in nearby Pittsfield Township with two lakes, wetlands, and hiking trails. Kids always enjoy **Rolling Hills County Park,** 7660 Stoney Creek Rd. in nearby Ypsilanti, a 145-acre park with a wet 'n' wild water park, disc golf, fishing in summer, and tobogganing, cross-country skiing, and ice skating in winter.

If you're looking to fit in some in-town fitness, check out the **Ann Arbor YMCA,** 350 S. 5th St., 734/663-0536, or the **County Recreation Center,** 2960 Washtenaw, 734/971-6337. Day passes range $3–5. **Planet Rock,** 82 Aprill Dr., 734/827-2680, offers a climbing gym for rockhounds.

## PRACTICALITIES

### Accommodations

Accommodations in Ann Arbor aren't as varied as the entertainment or the dining. Most are chain hotels grouped near the State Street exit (No. 177) off I-94. You can't miss them on your way into town. **The Crowne Plaza,** 734/761-7800, has an indoor pool, Jacuzzi, and fitness center as well as convenient in-room coffeemakers, hair dryers, and irons. Rates $125–175.

**Sheraton,** 734/996-0600, has spacious rooms and suites as well as a pool, sauna, and restaurant. Rates $100–125. If you opt to stay here, and would rather skip breakfast in the hotel restaurant, consider one of the quick bites at adjacent Briarwood Mall, including a Coney Island and other fast-food options, and the restaurant in Marshall Field's (formerly J. L. Hudson's) department store.

Another reliable hotel is the **Best Western Executive Plaza,** 734/665-4444, the largest hotel in the city, with a ballroom, 10,000-square-foot meeting area, and comfortable lounge. $75–250.

For something out of the ordinary, consider the intimate **Bell Tower Hotel,** 300 S. Thayer, 734/769-3010, which has just 52 rooms and 14 suites on S. Thayer, right in the middle of campus. It's a surprisingly elegant place, with accommodations decorated in a crisp, traditional style as well as the on-site Escoffier, one of the city's best restaurants. $150–200.

If you prefer the coziness of a bed and breakfast, the well-run **Parish House Inn,** 103 S. Huron in nearby Ypsilanti, 734/480-4800, is a good bet, with eight comfortable rooms in the city's historic district. $75–125.

## Food

Ann Arbor and surrounding Washtenaw County is home to more than 250 restaurants, a number seldom found in comparably sized cities. Reliable choices include **Afternoon Delight,** 251 E. Liberty, 734/665-7513, voted Ann Arbor's best lunch for three years in a row; **Amadeus,** 122 E. Washington, 734/665-8767, a cozy European-inspired spot that features hearty Polish, central European, and vegetarian entrees (average entree $12); and **Gratzi,** 326 S. Main, 734/663-5555, a few doors away, a Mediterranean-style spot with Italian fare served up in a vintage 1920s theater. Average entree $16. (For the best view of the large, Bacchalian murals, sit in the balcony.) If you'd like a taste of old-time Ann Arbor, **Metzger's,** 305 N. Zeeb Rd., 734/668-8987, still offers the traditional German specials such as bratwurst and sauerbraten they've been known for since 1928. Entrees average $13.

Other favorites include the splashy **Zanzibar,** 216 S. State, 734/994-7777, which looks like a drug-induced dream of the tropics—lots of bright, neon colors and fake palm trees. Equally colorful food choices include spicy salsa, fizzy Polynesian cocktails, and loads of vegetarian options. For the best historic atmosphere, the **Gandy Dancer,** 401 Depot, 734/769-0592, rates with beautiful surroundings and fresh seafood and homemade pasta in the former 1886 Michigan Central Railroad Station. Entrees average $18. The brunch is one of the area's best, a gluttonous feast for the senses. Another good spot for breakfast is **Angelo's,** 1100 E. Catherine, 734/761-8996, considered the hands-down favorite for their famous deep-fried French toast made with housemade raisin bread and loaded with fresh fruit. Entrees average $6. For great coffee and pastries in a pleasant European-café ambience, head for the reader-recommended **Cafe Felix,** 204 S. Main, 734/662-8650.

Good bets in Kerrytown include the charming **Kerrytown Bistro,** 415 N. 5th (entrance off 4th St.), 734/994-6424, an intimate eatery with French flair. If money is no object, shoot the wad at the **Earle,** 121 W. Washington., 734/994-0211, a long-time favorite with 800 bottles on its wine list and live jazz on weekends. Entrees $15–26. See also **Kerrytown,** above, for information on the New York-style deli Zingerman's and other eateries.

## Nightlife

Like many college towns, Ann Arbor offers up some eclectic nightlife. Top spots include **Bird of Paradise,** 312 S. Main St., 734/662-8310, a pleasant jazz club featuring beboppin' artists every night starting at 9:30, and the **Del Rio Bar & Grill,** 122 W. Washington, 734/761-2530, with local jazz Sun. 5–9:30 P.M. The **Blind Pig,** 208 S. 1st, 734/996-8555, was one of the first clubs outside of Seattle to give Nirvana a boost; besides rock 'n' roll, the club features reggae and blues artists. The city's gay community convenes at the **Aut Bar,** 315 Braun Ct. (entrance off 4th St.), 734/994-3677; or the New York-style **Nectarine Ballroom,** 516 E. Liberty, 734/994-5436, a dance club that features a different theme each night of the week, including Eurobeat, alternative, disco, and gay.

One of the best known of Ann Arbor's clubs is **The Ark,** 316 S. Main, 734/761-1451, which has been hosting local, national, and international performers for decades. The club moved to larger digs on S. Main in the former Kline's Department Store a few years back, but the philosophy is the same: book everything. Tues.–Sat. 7:30–11:30 P.M., the entertainment roster includes folk, bluegrass, women's music, jazz, blues, zydeco, African gospel, and acoustic music. Remnants of Ann Arbor's once-lively counterculture live on at the **Del Rio Bar** (see above); the **Old Town,** 120 W. Liberty, 734/662-9291 and upstairs over the **Heidelberg Restaurant,** 215 N. Main, 734/663-7758, where monthly poetry slams are held.

## Transportation

Ann Arbor is a walking town. Those who don't have cars (and the majority of the students) use foot power or zip around town on roller blades or bikes. There is a reliable public bus system, the Ann Arbor Transportation Authority, 734/973-6500, which delivers passengers around the main campus as well as farther afield. If you've brought your car, watch for the easy-access parking garages spread out throughout the city. There's also plenty of parking on the street, but beware that the city has a very thorough meter maid population. Bring plenty of change.

# The Heartland

By the 1830s, Michigan fever had become an epidemic. Pioneer families from all over the East Coast headed west via the newly completed Erie Canal, passed through Detroit, and continued along the new Detroit-Chicago Road, which cut across the southern half of the state's Lower Peninsula. Their final destination: Michigan's rolling prairies, with rich soil and fertile land that the federal government was selling for the bargain-basement price of $1.25 an acre.

Many of the early settlers were Easterners, leaving an already-overwhelming city to seek better opportunities for themselves and their families. The onrush between 1825 and 1855 spurred the settlement of some of Michi-gan's largest cities, including Lansing, Battle Creek, and Jackson. That early growth was soon augmented by the railroad; by 1849, Michigan Central began making regular state crossings, disgorging thousands of optimistic settlers along the way.

In the region known as Michigan's heartland, the most visible evidence of these early settlers can be found in the Greek Revival homes and clean-lined architecture of the cities and villages they built. They also founded a number of eastern-style private colleges (including Adrian, Albion, Olivet, and the precursor to Eastern Michigan University), a concentration unmatched elsewhere in the state.

© TRAVEL MICHIGAN

near Lansing

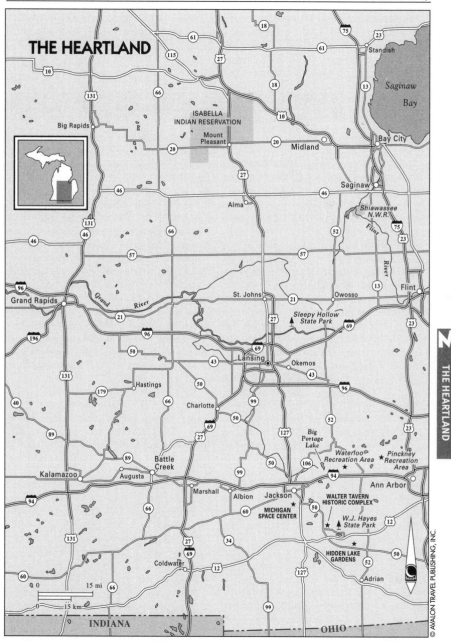

THE HEARTLAND

ISABELLA
INDIAN RESERVATION

Saginaw
Bay

Big Rapids

Mount
Pleasant

Midland

Bay City

Saginaw

Alma

Shiawassee
N.W.R.

Flint

River

Grand Rapids

Grand

River

St. Johns

Owosso

Flint

Sleepy Hollow
State Park

Lansing

Okemos

Hastings

Charlotte

Big
Portage
Lake

Battle
Creek

Kalamazoo

Augusta

Waterloo
Recreation Area

Pinckney
Recreation
Area

Ann Arbor

Marshall

Albion

Jackson

MICHIGAN
SPACE CENTER

WALTER TAVERN
HISTORIC COMPLEX

W.J. Hayes
State Park

Coldwater

HIDDEN LAKE
GARDENS

Adrian

0        15 mi

0      15 km

INDIANA

OHIO

Standish

Yet for all its academic attributes, the state's central region is the only area with no direct link to one of the Great Lakes. (This is the Great Lakes State, after all.) Travelers, therefore, often overlook it, heading for the Huron or Michigan shores, or the forests of the north. But the heartland hides its own quiet beauty, characterized by spring-fed lakes, faded red barns, and rolling oat fields.

# I-94 Corridor

## CHELSEA

Considered by many to be little more than a trendy suburb of neighboring Ann Arbor, Chelsea has begun to make a name for itself, thanks to a big-name Hollywood star who still resides in this picturesque little town, and a big swath of public land just west of town.

When he's not off making movies, actor Jeff Daniels eschews the Tinseltown glitz for his hometown of Chelsea. Daniels keeps busy running the **Purple Rose Theatre,** a critically acclaimed regional company he founded in the late 1980s. The other big-name attraction in town is the **Common Grill,** 112 S. Main St., 734/475-0681, a great restaurant founded by former employees of Detroit's popular Chuck Muer restaurant chain. The Grill has helped put sleepy Chelsea on the map, and waits easily reach two hours on weekends. Folks come for the restaurant's signature fish dishes and the chic yet comfortable atmosphere, which includes painted Hopperesque scenes of old Chelsea (including the Jiffy Baking Company's tower) on the exposed brick walls. Pass the time at the gleaming, stainless steel U-shaped bar.

Sprawling across two counties and some 20,000 acres, the **Waterloo Recreation Area,** 16345 McClure Rd., 734/475-8307, counts as the largest park in the Lower Peninsula. The park's landscape clearly shows evidence of the glaciers that once blanketed this part of the state. Waterloo is located at the intersection of the Kalamazoo and the Missaukee moraine systems, where two glaciers collided thousands of years ago. The ice sheets ripped apart massive mountains of rock from the Canadian shield to the north, carrying fragments with them as the ice moved across this part of the state—a journey one park interpreter describes like "the movement of pancake batter on a hot griddle."

The area is a pleasing patchwork of field, forest, and lake. To navigate your way around, pick up a map at park headquarters to guide you to the **Gerald E. Eddy Geology Center,** with its excellent Walkway of Michigan Rocks, the park's excellent **birdwatching** area, and the 900-acre **Haehnle Memorial Sanctuary,** a favorite fall hangout of sandhill cranes. The map also marks hiking trails, including a 48-mile route that winds from Big Portage Lake Campground, on the west side of the Waterloo Recreation Area, to Silver Lake, on the east side of the adjacent **Pinckney Recreation Area.** It passes through some of the most beautiful southern Michigan countryside, taking in 13 lakes, verdant pine plantations, open meadows, hardwood forests, and wetlands. Bring bug dope in summer.

Waterloo is a great park for horse lovers, with several miles of dedicated **horse trails** and even a campground dedicated to riders, Horsemen's. If you don't have your own horse, **Riding Stable and Dude Ranch,** 12891 Trist Rd., Grass Lake, 517/522-8930, offers guided rides of the area's trails.

Waterloo maintains four campgrounds in all. Horsemen's (open to those with or without horses) and Green Lake are rustic areas, with nice wooded sites. Portage Lake and Sugarloaf Lake are large, modern campgrounds, with sites near (but not on) their namesake lakes. The park admission fee is $4 per car, $20 per year, camping extra.

## JACKSON

If you're looking for Michigan's liberal stronghold, don't look in Jackson. The Republican

Party was founded in this small city of 37,000 back in 1854. More than a thousand Free Soilers, Whigs, and Democrats gathered here, where they adopted the Republican name, issued a platform, and nominated candidates for state office. A tablet still marks the site at the corner of Franklin and 2nd Streets. According to billboards outside of town, Jackson also claims fame as "Nuge Country," a nod to Ted Nugent, rocker and bow hunter extraordinaire, who lives nearby. As if that isn't enough, Jackson holds the state's largest Civil War muster each August, attracting more than 2,000 costumed reenactors from across the country who gather here for battle, balls, and ballistics.

Like many once-booming industrial cities in mid-Michigan, downtown Jackson was hit hard by unemployment and the malling of America. Few shops still occupy the city's stately Victorian and Art Deco storefronts. Even Jacobson's—the posh department store chain founded in Jackson, with stores as far away as Florida—closed its downtown store here (corporate headquarters remain).

But even a flat economy can't affect the wealth of wonderful lakes surrounding Jackson in Jackson County. More than 600 natural lakes dot the countryside, keeping the Jackson area near the top of the list for those in southern Michigan and northern Illinois and Indiana looking for an easy weekend getaway.

## Sights

Trace the development of the Jackson area at the **Ella Sharp Museum,** 3225 4th St., 517/787-2320. Sharp's mother was a rich expatriate who had invested in western Michigan land in the 1800s and later came to live on it—a rarity, since most investors were absentee landlords. Ella, born in Jackson, grew into a successful reformer who worked to improve rural life through good government, women's associations, and conservation. She also was a pack

sandhill crane

BOB RACE

rat, so plenty of 19th-century artifacts and memorabilia fill this museum complex, which includes an 1857 farmhouse, 1840 log cabin, and schoolhouse. Hours are Tues.–Fri. 10 A.M.–4 P.M., Sat.–Sun. 11 A.M.–4 P.M.

The Jackson area is home to four astronauts, more than any other city in the country—a claim to fame celebrated at the **Michigan Space Center,** part of the Jackson Community College, 211 Emmons Rd., 517/787-4425. The four Jackson astronauts (Jim McDevitt, commander of the Apollo 9 mission and Gemini programs; Jack Lousma, Skylabs commander in the early 1970s; Allen Bean, the fourth man to walk on the moon; and Al Worden, who flew to the moon as part of the Apollo 15 mission) all have donated personal effects from their travels. A striking gold geodesic dome houses the Apollo 9 command module, and the center's $35 million collection includes one of the 20 moon rock samples brought back to earth. Other displays deal with past and future space voyages, black holes, the Hubbell telescope, and more. Kids stay interested with interactive exhibits that let them climb inside a space capsule, don a space suit, and explore a simulated lunar landscape. Call for hours, which change seasonally. Admission $3.50 adults, $10 per family; open Tues.–Sat. 10 A.M.–5 P.M., Sun. noon–5 P.M.

While Michigan's Lower Peninsula may lack the awe-inspiring waterfalls that grace the Upper Peninsula, Jackson attempts to make up for that geographical oversight with the largest manmade waterfalls in North America, at Sparks Foundation County Park. Better known as **The Cascades,** 517/788-4320, they were a creation of "Captain" William Sparks, a well-known area industrialist, philanthropist, and former mayor. This is truly an amazing slice of Americana: 18 separate falls up to 500 feet high, six fountains of various heights and patterns, 1,200 colored lights and choreographed show tunes. Kids love it. The falls and surrounding 465-acre Cascades Falls Park date back to the early 1930s, when Sparks, a three-time mayor and chamber of commerce president, developed the whole shebang and presented it as a gift to his beloved city. You can make a day of it here, since the falls are augmented by an 18-hole golf course, driving range, horseshoe pits, fishing ponds, tennis courts, and paddle boat rentals. Get there by taking I-94 to Exit 138 and heading south three miles until you see the signs. Open daily Memorial Day–Labor Day. Lights and music operate 7:30–11 P.M.; $3 admission.

Not far from the Cascades, **The Parlour,** 1401 Daniel Rd., 517/782-7141, is an area institution, an ice-cream emporium that has been dishing it out for more than 50 years. Choose from more than 33 flavors and 50 dishes, including the always-popular Tin Roof and the towering Banana Split, nearly a foot high. All the ice cream is made with natural ingredients at the dairy plant next door.

Ted Nugent's love of big-game adventure and head-bangin' rock 'n' roll is well represented by customers of **Ted Nugent Bowhunters World,** 4133 W. Michigan Ave., 517/750-9060, a popular shop with Nugent groupies and devoted bow hunters. Nugent is a staunchly conservative and outspoken hunter/"sportsman" who often travels the state speaking to groups.

The Jackson area is nuts for **golf** and hides a number of high quality public courses. The **Sparrow Hawk Golf Course,** 2618 Seymour Rd., 517/787-1366, has been recognized by the National Golf Foundation as one of the top ninehole courses in the northeast-central United States. *Michigan Golfer Magazine* considers **Concord Hills,** in nearby Concord, 517/524-8337, "one of the country's most beautiful courses." Its 18 holes feature tall hills with rolling greens, water, and wildlife. For more information, ask the Jackson Chamber of Commerce, 517/783-3330, for its *Golf Guide.*

## The Irish Hills

Just a few miles southeast of Jackson via M-127,

the lovely Irish Hills have long been a popular family getaway, dotted with summer cottages owned by residents of Michigan, Indiana, and Ohio. The area was formed during the last Ice Age, when huge ice chunks swept across the land, leaving behind a varied landscape of round kettlehole lakes, steep valleys, and picturesque sweeping meadows. It got its name from Irish settlers who thought it looked like home.

Development and cheesy attractions have taken their toll on the area, but you can enjoy its natural state at **W. J. Hayes State Park,** 1220 Wampler's Lake Rd., Onsted, MI 49265, 517/467-7401. The 650-acre park features two popular fishing/swimming lakes tucked amid the gentle rolling hills. Facilities include a sandy swimming beach, boat launch, a few short hiking trails, and modern and semimodern campsites. The entrance to the park is just off the intersection of US-12 and M-124.

Endowed as a public garden and given to Michigan State University in 1945, **Hidden Lake Gardens,** seven miles west of Tecumseh on M-50, 517/431-2060, encompasses more than 750 acres of the region's characteristic rolling glacial hills. The visitors center explains more about how the glaciers traveled through the area, leaving behind hills and moraines. From the entrance, a six-mile developed roadway passes through various plantings, including hawthorn, mountain ash, oak, crabapple, and other flowering varieties. (It makes for a pleasant bike ride, but note that bikes are prohibited on Sunday.) Five miles of hilly foot trails take you away from the road. The gardens and an indoor conservatory are open yearround; call for hours.

The 1832 **Walker Tavern Historic Complex,** 13220 M-50 north of US-12, 517/467-4414, tells the story of the spine-crunching Chicago Road, the chief route of settlement during the 1830s pioneer boom. Now a fine small state historical museum, travelers once piled into the tavern's few sleeping rooms, shared beds, and passed much of their time in the tavern's first-floor bar. Daniel Webster and James Fenimore Cooper stayed here on expeditions west. Call ahead to check hours.

Kids seem to like the cheesy **Stage Coach Stop USA,** 7203 US-12, 517/467-2300, although it certainly takes a lot of liberties with history. Billed as "Michigan's Village of the 1800s," it offers daily gunfight shows, kiddie rides, a petting zoo, shops, a restaurant, and an "authentic" Wild West Saloon, despite the decidedly Midwestern location. Open Memorial Day through Labor Day.

## Accommodations

You'll find a range of chain hotels cluster near the I-94 interchange in Jackson, with rates averaging between $75–100, including the **Hampton Inn,** 2225 Shirley Dr., 517/789-5151; the **Fairfield Inn,** 2395 Shirley Dr., 517/784-7877; and the **Super 8,** 2001 Shirley Dr., 517/788-8780.

## Camping

Along with the campgrounds at W. J. Hayes State Park (see above), two county parks offer camping: **Pleasant Lake County Park,** Styles Rd., 517/796-6401, with 69 sites, and developed attractions like swimming, fishing, and mini-golf; and **Swains Lake County Park,** M-60, Concord, 517/524-7666, with 60 sites on 26 acres.

## Food

This is meat-and-potatoes country, and you're going to have a tough time beating it. If you're happy to join it, try long-time area favorite **Gilberts Steak House,** 2323 Shirley Dr., 517/782-7135. Entrees $10–18. Hearty sandwiches, soups and other pub fare complement the homemade brews at the **Jackson Brewing Company Brew Pub and Eatery,** 6020 Ann Arbor Rd., 517/764-7177.

# MARSHALL AND VICINITY

When Lansing was chosen as the seat of the state government in 1847, no city was more surprised and more disappointed than Marshall, current population 7,000, located 31 miles west of Jackson. The State Senate originally passed a bill designating Marshall the capital, a measure defeated by just one vote in the House. Marshall was so sure of its upcoming role as the capital city that it set aside a site known as Capitol Hill. It even built a governor's mansion, which still exists today.

Being spurned by the Legislature, though, gave Marshall a reprieve from rampant development, and today it ranks as one of the country's best preserved 19th-century towns. Lined with large shade trees and an outstanding collection of 1840s and 1850s Greek and Gothic Revival homes, houseproud Marshall has become a poster child for historic preservation, an example of what can be done when businesses and homeowners work together. It has been featured in dozens of travel articles and architectural magazines. "Marshall's small-town pride is a genteel descendant of the boosterism that Sinclair Lewis savaged in Main Street and Babbitt," declared the *New York Times.*

Before Marshall was old enough to turn heads for its architecture, it was carving out a niche as a center of the patent medicine boom in the early 1900s, producer of such classic tonics as Lydia Pinkham's Pink Pills for Pale People. It wasn't until the 1920s that a savvy mayor, Harold Brooks, first recognized the city's fine architecture and led a crusade to maintain it. The first home tour was held in 1964 and remains a large and popular annual event more than 30 years later. Marshall's designated National Historic Landmark District includes 867 homes and businesses, the country's largest district in the "small urban" category. One National Park Service manager called Marshall "a textbook of 19th-century small-town architecture."

There's a rich and controversial history hiding behind those pretty 19th-century facades, too. Marshall drew nationwide attention in 1846 when Adam Crosswhite, a slave who had escaped from Kentucky and lived in Marshall for two years, was seized by slavehunters. The whole town rose up in his support. Local abolitionists helped Crosswhite and his family escape to Canada, arrested the slavehunters, and tried them in Federal District Court. Although the Marshall abolitionists lost in court, the Crosswhite case was instrumental in the creation of the 1850 Fugitive Slave Act, which in turn contributed to the tensions that later caused the Civil War.

## Exploring Marshall's Architecture

The best way to see the area's historic homes is on the annual home tour held the weekend after Labor Day. Other times, you can still enjoy the city's architecture with the help of an excellent (and free) walking-tour brochure available at the chamber of commerce, 109 E. Michigan Ave., 616/781-5163, as well as at a number of local shops and inns.

One of the first stops should be the lavishly quirky **Honolulu House,** 107 N. Kalamazoo St., 800/877-5163, described by the *New York Times* as "the architectural equivalent of a four-rum cocktail served in a coconut." Featuring a pagoda-shaped tower and decorative pineapple trim, the Polynesian-style home was built in 1860 by State Supreme Court Judge Abner Pratt, who served as U.S. consul to the Sandwich Islands (now Hawaii) 1857–1859. His wife's poor health forced the couple to return to Marshall, where they brought back their love of the tropics. Pratt's wife died shortly upon their return, and Pratt himself succumbed to pneumonia soon after—perhaps because of his stubborn habit of wearing tropical-weight clothing during the long and cold Midwestern winters.

Inside, the house features 1880s replicas of Pratt's original tropical murals, a riot of purples, pinks, and dozens of other rich colors, and several exquisite fireplaces. Many of the other furnishings did not belong to the Pratts, but represent Marshall history, such as the Marshall Folding Bathtub in the basement. Disguised as a cabinet, it's a rare remainder of the city's patent medicine boom. The house is open daily mid-May through October and is maintained by the local historical society. Admission is $3. For an additional 25 cents, pick up the informative tour brochure.

Other fine examples of early Marshall architecture can be found two blocks north of the Honolulu House on Kalamazoo Street. They include the home of Mayor Harold Brooks, who spurred the city's revival; the 1857 Italianate Adams-Schuyler-Umphrey House, built on land once owned by James Fenimore Cooper; the 1907 Sears-Osborne House, ordered from the Sears catalog at the turn of the century for just $1,995; the 1886 Queen Anne-style Cronin-Lapietra House, one of the city's most ornate, designed by the Detroit firm best known for the city's Michigan Central Railroad Terminal; and the 1843 Greek Revival Camp-Vernor-Riser House, one-time home of the founder of Vernor's Ginger Ale. The city's walking tour brochure provides addresses and more information.

## Antiquing and Other Attractions

Modern Marshall, with a downtown full of lacy Victorian homes and storefronts, has become an immensely popular weekend getaway for Detroit and Chicago metro area residents. They come to ogle the architecture, shop at a number of well-stocked (if somewhat expensive) antique stores and malls, and stay in one of the town's historic bed and breakfast inns.

You'll find most of the best shops along several blocks of Michigan Avenue and its cross streets. For antiques, try the **Marshall House Antique Center,** 100 Exchange, 616/781-2112, which houses quality dealers in a historic home, the **J. H. Cronin Antique Center,** 101 W. Michigan, 616/789-0077, with an outstanding collection of early advertising art and vintage oak furniture offered by more than 20 local dealers, and the newer **Keystone Architectural and General Antiques,** 110 E. Michigan, 616/789-1355, which specializes in larger pieces and garden ephemera.

Renowned magician David Copperfield has called the **American Museum of Magic,** 107 E. Michigan, 616/781-7674, one of his "favorite places on earth" and, if you believe the local rumor mill, wants to purchase the museum and move it to Las Vegas. For now, anyway, this fascinating attraction remains in Marshall, housed in an 1868 building with a cast iron front.

The late Robert Lund, a retired automotive writer, and his wife, Elaine, opened the American Museum of Magic in 1978, after spending years collecting "notional whimsies, cabalistic surprises, phantasmagorical bewilderments, and unparalleled splendors." Roughly translated, that means anything and everything remotely related to the practice of magic. The extensive collection of artifacts spans four centuries and six continents, and includes antique props (including the milk can used by Harry Houdini for a popular escape stunt, a carrying case once used by Harry Blackstone, and posters celebrating the career of Marjorie Waddell, one of the few successful women magicians). This one-of-a-kind museum has no set hours; call ahead to set up an appointment ($3 admission).

## Magical Colon

Magic buffs should also detour about 40 miles southwest of Marshall to Colon, a sleepy farm community now home to the world's largest magic company. Colon is the former home of Harry Blackstone, one of the most famous American magicians in the 1920s. Blackstone toured the country throughout the winter, returning to Colon every summer to create new acts and rehearse his show. Blackstone was later visited by an Australian magician named Percy Abbott, who fell in love with the charms of the small town and one of its native daughters. Together, Abbott and Blackstone came up with a plan to form a magic manufacturing company.

The pair split after just eight months, but Abbott went ahead with their plans and founded **Abbott's Magic Manufacturing Company,** 124 St. Joseph St., Colon, 616/432-3235, in 1933. As with the American Museum of Magic, even those not particularly interested in magic will likely enjoy a stop here. Photos of famous magicians who have done business with Abbott's, from Doug Henning to David Copperfield, cover the interior walls, and a display room filled with cases and shelves holds just a portion of the 2,000 tricks and gadgets the company makes. There's always a magician around to teach you a few of the tricks of the trade, too.

In 1934, Abbott started an annual open house for magicians as a sales incentive. It evolved into Colon's largest annual event, the **Magical Get-Together.** Held every August, it attracts more than 1,000 amateur and professional magicians, who come to stock up on magic supplies and view the original Blackstone and Abbott memorabilia at the **Colon Community Museum,** 219 N. Blackstone Road.

## Accommodations

**McCarthy's Bear Creek Inn,** 15230 C Drive N, 616/781-8383, is an anomaly in Victorian Marshall. A mile from the city's downtown, this renovated Cape Cod-style house once belonged to an area industrialist. Ask for one of the more spacious rooms in the restored barn overlooking meandering Bear Creek and original fieldstone fencing. Rates $75–100. Established in 1835, the **National House Inn,** 102 S. Parkview, 616/781-7374, is the oldest operating inn in the state. This former stagecoach stop along the Chicago Road once served as a stop on the Underground Railroad. Guest rooms range from the elegant Victorian-style Ketchum Suite to smaller, pleasant country-style rooms with folk art portraits on the walls. A tip: The old road in front of the inn is now a busy intersection. Ask for a room overlooking the garden if you desire peace and quiet. Rates $75–100. Your best budget bet is the **Arbor Inn,** 15435 W. Michigan, 800/424-0807, a budget-minded chain hotel with outdoor pool located along a strip of fast-food restaurants outside of the historic downtown. Rates $50–75.

## Camping

The privately owned **Tri-Lake Trails Campground,** 219 Perrett Rd., 616/781-2297, has 272 open and partially shaded sites on 300 acres in a pleasant, rural setting with three small lakes, a swimming beach, and nature trails.

## Food

**Louie's Bakery,** 144 W. Michigan, 616/781-3542, is the kind of old-fashioned bakery you remember from childhood, with gooey cakes, pies, and sweet rolls—a good spot for an inexpensive (if not particularly nutritious) breakfast. Housed in a renovated storefront with original tin ceilings, **Malia,** 130 W. Michigan, 616/781-2171, features nouvelle Italian cuisine and delectable homemade pastas in a Tuscan-inspired setting. Try the grilled portobello sandwich, the pesto linguine, or the refreshingly light orecchiette primavera. Entrees $8–17. Some folks say The King lives on in nearby Kalamazoo, so it's only natural that Elvis sightings frequently occur at the **Hi-Lite Drive In,** 1005 E. Michigan Ave., 616/781-6571, where the servers will still hook a tray onto your car window and serve you in the comfort of your T-Bird. Even if Elvis doesn't show, the classic burgers, fries, and super-thick shakes are worth a stop. Entrees $4–8.

A sign in the main dining room of **Schuler's,** 115 S. Eagle St., 616/781-0600, reads "The difference between good and great is a little extra effort." Extra effort is a specialty here, where the Schuler family has been serving up comforting fare such as Swiss onion soup, barbecue meatballs, and prime rib for more than 85 years. The restaurant recently added lighter cuisine to the menu, including Sicilian grilled chicken pizza, wood-grilled Texas bay shrimp with black bean quesadillas, and almond-crusted orange roughy. Entrees $12–20.

Wayne and Marjorie Cornwell introduced their first turkey sandwich at a county fair 30 years ago. Today their campy, country-style restaurant and turkey farm just north of Marshall is known as **Cornwell's Turkeyville,** 18935 15-mile Rd., 616/781-4293. The menu includes everything from a classic buttered turkey sandwich to a piled high turkey Reuben or a turkey stir-fry. An adjacent 170-seat dinner theater gives afternoon and evening performances of family favorites. Entrees $5–12.

# BATTLE CREEK

To generations of American youngsters, Battle Creek was the home of Tony the Tiger, that g-r-r-r-e-a-t and magical place where they sent their cereal box tops in exchange for free gifts and toys. For decades before that, however, Battle Creek was known as the home of the Church of Seventh-Day Adventists and for the work done at the church's sanitarium, the Western Health Reform Institute, which opened in 1866. John Harvey Kellogg joined the founders in 1876 and spent the next 25 years developing the sanitarium into an institution recognized around the world for its regimen of hydrotherapy, exercise, and vegetarian diet.

Part of that regimen was a new, healthy grain-based flaked breakfast that Kellogg cooked up in 1894. An alternative to traditional breakfasts such as grits and bacon and eggs, Kellogg's creation went on to revolutionize the breakfast foods industry and to fuel the economy of this former settlement. From 1901 to 1905, more than 1,500 new homes cropped up to house the workers and others who converged on Battle Creek, hoping to capitalize on its renown as the "Health City." (This bizarre tale was the basis for *The Road to Wellville,* a 1995 Hollywood film starring Anthony Hopkins that painted a not-too-positive portrait of the Kellogg family and phenomenon.)

Today, Battle Creek is still home to the Kellogg Company, the Post Cereals division of General Foods, and the Ralston Purina Company. It's also home to the World's Longest Breakfast Table, a downtown PR event held as part of the annual **Cereal City Festival** the second Saturday in June.

For more information on Battle Creek, contact the **Greater Battle Creek/Calhoun County Convention and Visitors Bureau,** 77 E. Michigan Ave., Suite 100, Battle Creek, 800/397-2240, website: www.battlecreekvisitors.org.

## Sights and Recreation

If you're curious about the Kelloggs, you can visit the sanitarium, now the **Battle Creek Federal Center,** 74 N. Washington, 616/961-7015. Recognized on the National Register of Historic Places, the building now houses governmental and military offices, but has artifacts and other items on display about the Kellogg era. Infamous brothers W. K. and John Harvey Kellogg are buried in the **Oak Hill Cemetery,** 255 South St., 616/964-7321, as well as C. W. Post and Sojourner Truth, the famous female Civil War–era freedom crusader. Scores of pilgrimages are made to Truth's humble grave, which rests in the shadow of the ostentatious C. W. Post marble mausoleum. The grounds are open 7:30 A.M.–dusk daily.

The Kelloggs preached plenty of fresh air as part of their health regimen. Battle Creek therefore excels in its number of parks and recreational opportunities. Among the most unusual is the **Battle Creek Linear Park,** 616/966-

BOB RACE

preservationist Will Keith Kellogg (brother to John Harvey Kellogg of cereal fame)

3431, an 11-mile system that links natural waterways and parks with a continuous paved pathway. It's a favorite of local cyclists, skaters, and runners. Walkers and other nature lovers in particular head to the **Leila Arboretum,** Michigan Ave. at 20th St., 616/969-0270, part of Linear Park. This excellent 720-acre botanical garden is one of the best reasons to visit Battle Creek. The gift of Mrs. Leila Post Montgomery, it contains more than 3,000 species of trees and shrubs (many dating back to the 1920s) laid out in the manner of famous European gardens. Highlights include a rhododendron garden, a shade garden featuring hundreds of varieties of hostas, and a breathtaking flowering tree collection.

Also on the arboretum grounds is the **Kingman Museum of Natural History,** 616/965-5117. The museum has all kinds of fun hands-on displays—you can grind corn, "race" in an au-

thentic dugout canoe, and touch dinosaur bones that date back more than 65 million years.

More modern species can be found at the **Binder Park Zoo,** 7400 Division Dr., 616/979-1351, a small but choice zoo that houses exotic and domestic animals in natural settings. A highlight is the new **Michigan Wetlands Encounter Trail,** which takes you over bogs, marshes, and swamps. Coming in 1998: "The Wilds of Africa," a 15-acre savannah with giraffes, zebras, ostriches, antelope, and other animals of the region.

Ornithologists and other bird lovers flock to the experimental **Kellogg Bird Sanctuary,** two miles north of M-89 on C Avenue, 616/671-2510. W. K. Kellogg started the sanctuary in 1928 as a refuge for Canada geese, who were then threatened by a loss of habitat to agriculture and urbanization. Today Canada geese thrive at the sanctuary, now owned by MSU, along with more than 20 species of ducks and seven kinds of swans who stay year-round, and many other species that migrate through the region in spring and fall. The sanctuary also hosts several birds of prey, which you can view from several observation areas on the grounds. A bookstore on-site includes information on how to transform your backyard into a bird sanctuary following the same principles and planting guidelines used in the refuge.

A few miles away from the Kellogg Bird Sanctuary, W. K. Kellogg also began the **Kellogg Forest,** 7060 N. 42nd St. near Augusta, 616/731-4597, as a demonstration project in reforesting abandoned farms. Michigan State University maintains the 716-acre property, which includes more than 200 species of trees, two miles of road, and 35 miles of hiking trails. Hikers and skiers also use the forest's 25 miles of ungroomed firebreaks separating experimental stands of trees. Pick up a free map and brochure at the forest's entrance off 42nd Street.

## Accommodations

**Greencrest Manor,** 6174 Halbert Rd., 616/962-8633, is an unlikely find—a French chateau in the middle of the Midwestern prairie. Eight rooms, including six suites, are decorated with lots of chintz and antiques and cost around

THE HEARTLAND

$100–175. In the $50–75 category, try the **Battle Creek Inn,** 5050 Beckley Rd., 616/979-1100, with spotless rooms, an indoor/outdoor pool, and nicely landscaped grounds, or the cheap but charming **Appletree Inn,** 4786 Beckley Rd., 616/979-3561, with good-sized rooms and free coffee in the lobby.

### Food

In nearby Athens, **Sam's Joint,** 1600 M-66, 616/729-5010, is a popular local hangout that specializes in barbecue and open-flame prime rib. Entrees $6–9. A vintage downtown train depot houses **Clara's On the River,** 44 N. McCamly St., 616/963-0966, with a 16-page menu including everything from simple pizzas and burgers to elaborate pastas and steaks, as well as an extensive Sunday brunch. Entrees $8–19.

The nautical-themed **Gangplank,** 1749 E. Columbia Ave., 616/962-7814, specializes in sandwiches and soups. Live entertainment and dancing Mon.–Sat. Entrees $6–12. The **Waterfront Seafood Restaurant,** 315 W. Columbia Ave., 616/962-7622, is known for its relaxed lakefront dining as well as its salad bar and extensive kids menu. Entrees $10–21. Housed in the city's fanciest hotel, the McCamly Plaza, the **McCamley's Roof Restaurant,** 50 Capital Ave. SW, 616/963-7050, is the place to go for elegant events, with a top-notch view and cuisine that changes regularly but maintains an emphasis on fresh ingredients. Entrees $10–15.

## Kalamazoo and Vicinity

*Kalamazoo, you ain't in a class by yourself; I seen you before in a lot of places.*

—*Carl Sandburg, "The Sins of Kalamazoo"*

Yes, there really is a city named Kalamazoo. In reference to the area's bubbling natural springs, the name is derived from an Indian word meaning "place where the water boils." Its notoriety came later, when it inspired the Big Band–era song, "I Gotta Gal in Kalamazoo," as well as Sandburg's poem.

From Grand Rapids, Kalamazoo is a straight shot south on US-131. Produce from the nearby vegetable growing region, pharmaceutical industries, and several papermaking plants form the foundation of the city's diverse economy. Academia provides steady employment, too: Kalamazoo is home to Western Michigan University and a number of respected private schools, including the academically renowned Kalamazoo College, site of a popular annual Bach festival and internationally known for its "K" Plan, which includes international study and required internships.

Kalamazoo's population of 80,300 comprises a sizable gay community, a substantial African-American community, a burgeoning alternative music scene, a number of big-city refugees, and an almost even split between liberals and conservatives. Kalamazoo's balanced economy and population represent such a slice of the American pie that the *Wall Street Journal* featured the city as a focus group during the 1992 presidential election.

While Sandburg didn't think Kalamazoo offered anything special, its downtown streets reveal many of the vanishing pleasures of small-town life: great streets perfect for walking, a gracious downtown park, vintage architecture, interesting shops (including a number of funky resale and antique outlets), and several top-of-the-line bed and breakfasts. There's a great sense of civic pride and an active population that truly gets involved in city affairs (a recent hot topic: whether or not to reopen the downtown "mall," closed to cars since the 1950s). While not really a final destination, Kalamazoo makes a great stop en route to Harbor Country to the south or Lake Michigan's well-known resort communities in the north.

For more information on the Kalamazoo area, contact the **Kalamazoo County Convention and Visitors Bureau,** 346 W. Michigan, Kalamazoo, 616/381-4003, website: www.kazoofun.com.

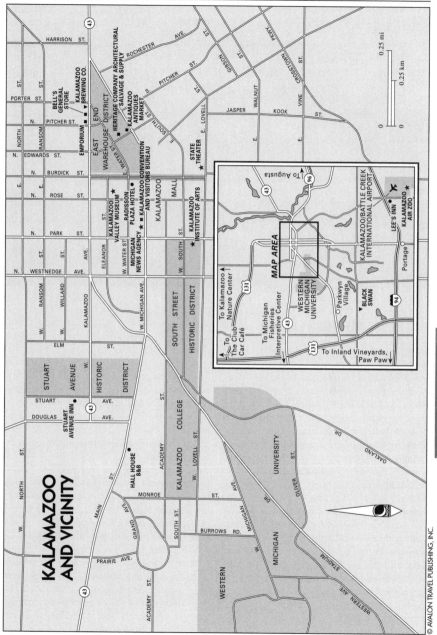

THE HEARTLAND

© AVALON TRAVEL PUBLISHING, INC.

Kalamazoo Air Zoo Museum

## SIGHTS AND RECREATION

### Downtown

Built in 1927, the opulent Spanish-style **State Theater,** 404 S. Burdick St., 616/344-9670, now showcases mostly rock, blues, and folk concerts. The interior is a rare example of the work of famed architect John Eberson, who recreated an exotic Mediterranean town with a working cloud machine and stars that really twinkle. The streets around the theater, known as the **Kalamazoo Mall,** are home to coffeehouses and galleries, restaurants and bakeries, and an unusually diverse selection of resale and vintage clothing shops. Stretching from Lovell to Eleanor Streets, it was the first open-air downtown pedestrian mall created by blocking a city street to car traffic. Like many downtowns, it's suffered from the encroachment of suburban malls, but still offers a fine local department store, funky stores that cater to the college crowd, restaurants, even an indoor climbing center housed in a former shoe store.

Two blocks north of the Kalamazoo Mall, the vintage newsstand **Michigan News Agency,** 308 W. Michigan, 616/343-5958, dates to the 1940s. Inside you'll find everything from the everyday to the truly eclectic: the usual maps, tobaccos, comics, and newspapers, as well as more than 2,500 magazine titles. The friendly and knowledgeable owners don't seem to mind if you spend the better half of the day perusing their publications. There's also a small selection of books by local writers. Open daily 6 A.M.–9 P.M.

The **Kalamazoo Institute of Arts,** 314 S. Park St., 616/349-7775, features a small but choice collection of 20th-century American art, including works by Alexander Calder, Ed Pashke, and Helen Frankenthaler. A tiny museum shop stocks a nice collection of art-related gifts and gewgaws, including some unusual children's books. Free admission; open Tues.–Sat. 10 A.M.–5 P.M., Sun. 1–5 P.M.

New in 1996, the long-planned and eclectic **Kalamazoo Valley Museum,** 230 North Rose St., 616/373-7990, sometimes suffers from trying to be everything to everyone, with a schizophrenic mix of science, technology, history, nature, and cultural exhibits. Highlights include a friendly robot named OPUS, a state-of-the-art Digistar Theater and Planetarium, an exhibit on the Challenger space shuttle (some victims were from the area) that lets visitors plan a 45-minute journey from Earth to deep space, a 2,500-year-old mummy, and nostalgic displays on products formerly and currently made in Kalamazoo: Gibson guitars, Upjohn vitamins, Milady corsets, even the classic yellow Checker Cab (still found in New York and Chicago, although the last one rolled off the assembly line here in 1992). Free admission. Open Mon., Tues., Thurs., Fri., and Sat. 10 A.M.–6 P.M., Weds. 10 A.M.–9 P.M., and Sun. 1–5 P.M.

## Historic Neighborhoods

Unlike many other Michigan towns, Kalamazoo experienced few boom and bust cycles in the last century, thanks to its plentiful and diversified industry. Houses were well maintained, and many stayed in families for generations. You can see the results of that care in the **South Street Historic District.** Impressive houses went up here between 1847 and World War I, in architectural styles ranging from Greek and Gothic Revival to Georgian and Tudor. Just north of Kalamazoo College, along Stuart and Woodward between West Michigan and North, business owners built large suburban homes in what is now known as the **Stuart Avenue Historic District** to display the wealth they amassed after the Civil War. You'll find a variety of elaborate Queen Anne, Italianate, and Eastlake homes here, including the meticulously restored **Stuart Avenue Inn** bed and breakfast.

If you appreciate Frank Lloyd Wright architecture, the city's **Parkwyn Village,** at Taliesin Dr. and Parkwyn Dr. in southwest Kalamazoo, was designed as a cooperative neighborhood by the famed architect in the late 1940s and includes examples of his Usonian style. You can view more Wright homes in the 11000 block of Hawthorne, south of the city of Galesburg.

Kalamazoo's downtown industrial area has morphed (you might say fermented) into the **East End Warehouse District.** Located east of Burdick behind the Radisson Hotel, this reenergized area is home to the acclaimed **Kalamazoo Brewing Company,** a forerunner of the brewpub craze. Owner Larry Bell's acclaimed brews, including Bell's Amber Ale and Bell's Kalamazoo Stout, have won a loyal following in Chicago, where half of his output is sold.

Also in the Warehouse District, **Heritage Company Architectural Salvage & Supply,** 130 N. Edwards, 616/385-1004, caters to the city's active preservation movement, with a cache of salvaged hardware, doors, windows, fixtures, and other goods that some consider trash, others treasure. Upstairs is a bargain section with everything including the kitchen sink (less than $20) and a tempting area stocked with mission-style and arts-and-crafts-inspired furniture. Next door, the **Kalamazoo Antiques Market** represents more than 30 quality dealers selling vintage jewelry, pottery, and lots of household stuff. Speaking of antiques, the **Emporium,** 734 E. Kalamazoo, is worth seeking out for its vintage furniture despite a curmudgeonly owner and weird hours (2–6 P.M. on weekends, 7–9 P.M. weekdays).

## In the Area

How do you tell a fish's age? You can feed fish and your curiosity at **Michigan Fisheries Interpretive Center** and the adjacent **Wolf Lake State Fish Hatchery,** M-43 at Fish Hatchery Rd., 616/668-2876. Each year millions of fish are grown at this facility just outside of Kalamazoo, to stock Michigan's public lakes and streams for the sportfishing so important to the state's tourist trade.

This is one of the nation's most automated hatcheries, with huge tanks, 14 outdoor ponds, an excellent 11-minute slide show, and historical photos that tell the story of the state's fish-hatching program. It's fun to watch the fish being fed, ogle the big ones that didn't get away (including a mammoth 193-pound lake sturgeon), and learn how to determine a fish's age by counting the rings in its scales or bones. Free admission; call for hours, which vary over the year.

After a visit to the **Celery Flats Interpretive Center,** 7335 Garden Lane, Portage, 616/329-4522, you'll know that Kalamazoo used to be known as the "Celery City." The city's once-huge celery industry got its start in the 1860s, when a Dutch farmer developed and marketed a sweeter, yellow variety. Before long, celery was an ingredient in sodas, tonics, and patent medicine, touted as a relaxant. Young boys sold bunches of the vegetable at the city's train station and on street corners, with the slogan "Fresh as the dew from Kalamazoo." The industry died off after World War II, when California became the preferred growing grounds.

Everything you ever wanted to know about celery but were afraid to ask can be found in this funky but fascinating museum. It tells the celery story through tonic bottles, gardening paraphernalia, historical photos, greenhouse tours, and especially the retired celery farmers who serve as guides. Don't miss the collection of campy old postcards, many with King Kong-esque celery stalks towering over the city. The center is open May–Aug. Fri.–Sun. noon–7 P.M.; September hours are Sat.–Sun. noon–5 P.M. Admission is $2.50 adults, $2 seniors, $1.50 children.

Though officially known as Kalamazoo Aviation History Museum, everyone knows this excellent facility near the Kalamazoo/Battle Creek International Airport at 3101 E. Milham Rd., Portage, 616/382-6555, as the **Kalamazoo Air Zoo.** Considered the nation's premier museum of military aircraft and listed among the top 10 U.S. air museums, the air zoo stands out because of its emphasis on education. Not only can visitors examine the vintage planes, they can sit at the controls of seven cockpits in the Simulation Station, take a trip in a Flight Simulator (so realistic that even airsickness bags are provided), and enjoy the daily flight of one of the planes as it takes off and circles the museum's flight decks. For $35, reserve a spot for a 30-minute flight on the 1929 Tin Goose, Henry Ford's contribution to commercial aviation.

Classic craft range from the Tin Goose, Flying Tiger, and Gooney Bird to a collection of the famous Grumman Cats-the Wildcat, Hellcat,

> *Kalamazoo used to be known as the "Celery City." The city's once-huge celery industry got its start in the 1860s with the slogan "Fresh as the dew from Kalamazoo." The industry died off after World War II, when California became the preferred growing grounds.*

Tigercat, and Bearcat. Many of the museum's docents are WW II vets (both male and female), adding a fresh perspective and firsthand glimpse of this classic era. Hours are Mon.–Sat. 9 A.M.–6 P.M., Sun. noon–6 P.M.

## Natural Attractions
A recent $1.2 million overhaul brings even more appeal to the **Kalamazoo Nature Center** 7000 N. Westnedge, 616/381-1574. At 800 acres, it ranks as the largest nature center in the Midwest, with 11 miles of trails, an arboretum, herb garden, a restored 1858 homestead housing crafts and local history artifacts, and a peaceful glen that was the favorite stomping ground of author James Fenimore Cooper. The new "Nature Up Close" area features hands-on, minds-on exhibits where the curious can perform experiments, walk through tree trunks, and view magnified trees, leaves, and insects. Other new-and-improved exhibits include a free-flying butterfly zone, an indoor bird-watching area that looks out over the trees and grounds, and a re-created 1830s settlers' farm. Open Mon.–Sat. 9 A.M.–6 P.M., Sun. 1–6 P.M. Admission $3.

Donated by cereal king W.K. Kellogg, the **Kellogg Bird Sanctuary,** C Ave. off 40th St., Augusta, 616/671-2510, offers protected land for native waterfowl and birds of prey. Innovative wildlife conservationists here have been instrumental in efforts to return the trumpeter swan to the state. Situated along the waterfront of Wintergreen Lake, you can explore the grounds year-round on self-guided trails. The facility is now part of the Michigan State University Kellogg Biological Station. Hours are daily 9 A.M.–8 P.M. (shorter hours in winter-call for information); admission is $2 adults, $1.50 seniors, 50 cents children over four, free for children under four. Two streets away, on

42nd St., is the entrance to the **Kellogg Forest,** 616/731-4597, also run by MSU as an experimental forest with hundreds of tree varieties and acres of deep, dense forests open to hiking, cross-country skiing, or picnicking. Hours are 8 A.M.–8 P.M. in summer, 8 A.M.–sunset in winter. Free admission.

### Kal-Haven Trail

The former Penn Central railroad line now serves as the Kal-Haven Trail, 616/637-2788, an immensely popular 34-mile **bike path** that stretches from Kalamazoo to South Haven on the Lake Michigan shore. The predominantly flat crushed-limestone path meanders along well away from major highways, offering a pleasantly pastoral ride through varied terrain that ranges from fragrant mint and radish farms to small, backwater towns where you can stop for a chocolate soda at an old-fashioned fountain. From Kalamazoo, cyclists pass what remains of the state's mint-growing crop at the former mint plantation owned by A.M. Todd, once known as Kalamazoo's Peppermint King. The company called Mentha operated 1900–54. Farther along, Grand Junction is home to the Michigan Blueberry Growers, a large co-op that markets blueberries grown by its 800 members. Nearing South Haven, the route passes blueberry and peach orchards. You can stop for a dip in the 31-foot deep Saddle Lake near Berlamont, or continue on to South Haven's hot sand beaches and take a big lake break. The trail ends at the Blue Star Highway, a.k.a. A2, just east of South Haven.

The Kalamazoo trailhead is in Oshtemo township, west of US-131 on 10th St. between West Main and H Avenue. Trail fees are $2 per day individual, $5 family (annual pass $10 individual, $25 per family). Rent bikes for approximately $8–16 per day at **True Value Hardware** in Gobles, 616/628-2584, or **Northside Memories** in South Haven near the Dyckman Street Bridge, 616/637-8319. The Kal-Haven Trail is open to snowmobilers and cross-country skiers in winter. For information, contact Van Buren State Park, 23960 Ruggles Rd., South Haven, 616/637-4984.

# PRACTICALITIES

## Accommodations

Kalamazoo's premier hotel is probably the **Radisson Plaza Hotel,** 100 W. Michigan Ave., 616/343-3333 or 800/333-3333, centrally located within walking distance of most downtown attractions. A spacious lobby and arcade of better-than-most shops lead to more than 280 large and well-appointed rooms. Rates $150–175. The hotel's restaurant, **Webster's,** is named after the man who penned the dictionary. Even if you choose not to eat at this decent but rather pricey spot (entrees $17–30), pop in to check out the original dictionary pages on display.

**Lee's Inn,** 2615 Fairfield Rd., Kalamazoo, 616/382-6100, is the best of the area's independent hotels, with rates in the $75–100 range and a bright, airy breakfast room. For economy deals, Kalamazoo offers the usual assortment of chain motels.

The **Stuart Avenue Inn,** 237 Stuart Ave., 616/342-0230, is widely regarded as the city's best B&B. It comprises three adjacent 19th-century homes (including the Bartlett-Upjohn House of pharmaceutical fame) and lovely perennial gardens. The present owners furnished the inn's 17 rooms with many of their own antiques as well as goodies collected on shopping sprees around the state. Rates average $75–100; some larger rooms include whirlpools. The **Hall House B&B,** 106 Thompson St., 616/343-2500, offers six rooms in a restored 1923 home. Just steps away from private Kalamazoo College, it's popular with families of students and visiting professors. Rates $75–150.

## Camping

In nearby Augusta, camp at the 3,000-acre **Fort Custer Recreation Area,** 5163 W. Fort Custer Dr., Augusta, MI 49012, 616/731-4200. Along with 219 rustic sites, you also can rent one of three mini-cabins or rustic cabins, including one on the banks of the Kalamazoo River. Open year-round.

## Food

Take a "Beer 101" tour (on weekends or by appointment) at the highly touted **Kalamazoo Brewing Company** 355 E. Kalamazoo, 616/382-2338, or simply down a few pints and nibble munchies in the brewery's smoke-free **Eccentric Cafe**. This appealing spot has board games scattered around the tables, ping-pong, and live acoustic music on Friday and Saturday nights. In warm weather, casual crowds congregate on the outdoor "beer garden" patio. If you yearn to try your own hand at beermaking, head next door to **Bell's General Store,** 616/382-5712, where you can pick up home-brew supplies, beer-related magazines and T-shirts, and other specialty items.

One of the city's newest restaurants, **The Club Car Cafe,** 6187 W. D Ave., is housed in a retired Denver Rio Grande railroad car. Manufactured by Pullman in 1910, the coach served the Colorado railways until the 1960s, when it became part of a Canadian excursion service. It later served parts of Michigan before being remodeled as a dining car, with original ceiling light fixtures, brass windows pulls, and luggage racks. The menu includes a wide range of dishes, including seafood, sandwiches, and more. Entrees $6–19.

Just a few minutes from downtown, **The Black Swan** is tucked away in a condominium complex at 3501 Greenleaf Blvd., 616/375-2105. The large, airy restaurant overlooks manicured grounds and a pretty fountain. The unusual menu features specialties like Amish duck served with Michigan chutney, venison and morels in black currant sauce, and coconut shrimp. Entrees $15–22.

# Lansing and Vicinity

In the 1940s, the WPA *Guide to Michigan* described Lansing as a place where "the political activity of a State capital, the rumbling tempo of an industrial city, and the even temper of a farming community are curiously blended." A half-century later, it's still an apt description.

Curiously, Lansing was developed by a legislative prank. Until 1847, Detroit was the state's capital, as mandated in a provision in the 1835 constitution. When the provision expired, legislators (two of whom had been burned in effigy by Detroit rowdies) decided that the Detroit border was in constant danger of invasion and voted to move the capital. Where to put it, however, posed a problem. After months of wrangling and debating just about every settlement in lower Michigan, someone jokingly suggested Lansing, a wide spot in the road that consisted of one log house and a sawmill. Amid laughs and for want of a better solution, it won the vote. The state's seat of government was moved in 1847.

Even the name was a lark. The original settlement was named after Lansing, New York, and a New York chancellor. When it became the new capital, many wanted to rename the tiny town Michigan or Michigamme. But the legislature once again became bogged down in political infighting. Lansing it remained.

Once the decision was made and the place had a name, it began to grow. By the time the city was incorporated in 1859, it had 4,000 residents, a number of small businesses, a new capitol building, and two newspapers to cover it all. The city received another economic boost in the early 1900s, when R.E. Olds began making his "merry Oldsmobile" here.

Today, Lansing is the state's governmental seat, headquarters for many trade and professional associations, and home to heavy industry. East Lansing, a neighboring community that is part of the capital city in all respects except government, is the home of Michigan State University, part of the Big Ten conference. Ironically, the powers-that-be also selected the university site by default.

Urban decay and rampant freeway construction have bruised downtown Lansing, and the city is often all but empty after five o'clock. While it has been described as a city in search of a center, it has a surprising amount to offer once you find it: good museums, a full plate of MSU events, some of the state's loveliest and most ac-

© BOB BRODBECK

the Capitol Dome

cessible gardens, even a new minor league baseball team, the Lansing Lugnuts.

For more information, contact the **Greater Lansing Convention and Visitors Bureau,** 1223 Turner St., Lansing, 888/252-6746, website: www.lansing.org.

## SIGHTS

To understand what really drives the city, sign on for a **State Capitol** tour. When the building was dedicated in 1879, it was one of the first state capitols to emulate the dome and wings of the capitol building in Washington, D.C. It took six years to construct the design of Elijah E. Myers, one of the foremost architects of public buildings during the Gilded Age, which lasted from 1865 to 1914. Today, Michigan's governmental heart is considered an outstanding example of Victorian craftsmanship. A major renovation of the building's stunning interior was completed in 1992 at a cost of more than $45 million.

Tours begin in the Rotunda, where visitors

stand on glass tiles imported from England and take in governors' portraits, the restored State Senate and House of Representatives chambers, as well as other bits and pieces of the state's history. Tours last about 45 minutes and include an overview of Michigan history, insights into the many decorative paintings, and a primer on the legislative process. If you have the interest (and the patience), you can stay and watch government in action. The ground-floor tour guide desk in the front wing offers maps, a printed journal of legislative proceedings, and a report of the day's agenda. Free tours, 517/335-1483, are offered every half hour Mon.–Fri. 9 A.M.–4 P.M., Sat. 10 A.M.–4 P.M., Sun. noon–4 P.M.

The **J & K Steamboat Line,** P. O. Box C, Grand Ledge, 517/627-2154, offers another kind of tour of the capital city: old-fashioned riverboat cruises along the Red Cedar and Grand Rivers. The company operates three vintage paddlewheelers, including the *Spirit of Lansing,* the *Princess Laura,* and the lavish *Michigan Princess,* outfitted with oak staircases and crystal chandeliers. Cruises run in spring and summer months on the *Spirit of Lansing* and the *Princess Laura,* and late Feb.–Dec. on the *Michigan Princess.*

For a pleasant walking tour, start at the north end of the Brenke Dam and head toward the city center. Lansing's impressive skyline, dominated by the famous capitol dome, will be ahead of you. Along the way you'll see two distinctive Art Deco structures: the landmark stack of Lansing's city-owned utility, the Board of Water and Light, and one of the city's most historic homes, the Turner-Dodge House, 106 E. North St., built in 1858.

Farther along at the North Lansing dam, you can usually count on at least a few anglers vying for the catfish, bass, bluegill, and perch that run here naturally along with the stocked walleye, coho, and steelhead. The fish ladder here is particularly interesting from late September to late October, when crowds gather to get a glimpse of the big fish who heroically struggle upstream to deposit their eggs. Coho and chinook salmon run as large as 25 pounds.

If it's a Tuesday, Thursday, or Saturday, head for the nearby **Lansing City Market,** 333 N. Cedar

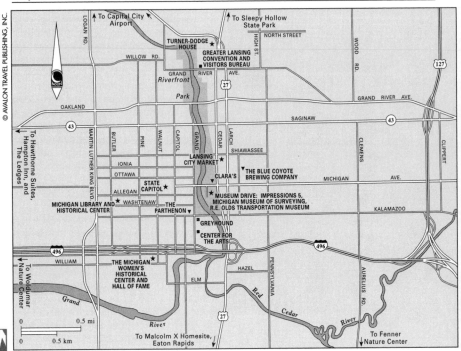

St., 517/483-4300. Built in 1938 by the Works Progress Administration, the market operates year-round and attracts vendors selling fruit, vegetables, sandwiches, baked goods, and more. Eat at indoor tables or at a picnic area near the river.

## The Arts

Lansing and East Lansing suffer in comparison with the more cosmopolitan Ann Arbor, home to the rival University of Michigan, which has always been known for its rich cultural community. But dismissing the capital city altogether would be a mistake, for there are a number of galleries, theaters, and museums worth seeking out, many in the Old Town district and East Lansing. The first Sunday of the month, **gallery walks** of East Lansing and Old Town take in 18 museums, galleries, and restaurants. For more information, call 517/351-2211.

Worth special note are the **Lansing Art Gallery**, 425 S. Grand Ave., 517/374-6400, founded by a handful of dedicated local arts sup-

porters and still the city's only independent non-profit gallery, and **Mackerel Sky Gallery of Contemporary Crafts,** 217 Ann St., East Lansing, 517/351-2211, which features a full range of crafts and rotating shows by area artists. For more on area arts events, contact the Lansing Arts Council's 24-hour hotline at 517/372-4636.

The northern part of Lansing known as Old Town bubbles with signs of renewal and a long-awaited transformation into a lively urban arts center. Check out galleries like the **Otherwise Gallery,** a showcase for local artists; the colorful **Creole Gallery,** featuring mostly African art; and the **Real World Emporium,** a gallery and performance space that caters to the area's small gay community.

Mid-Michigan's only Actor's Equity professional resident theater, known as **BoarsHead,** offers a season of dynamic productions at the city's Center for the Arts, 425 S. Grand Ave., 517/484-7805. This talented troupe performs Thurs.–Sun. from October through early May,

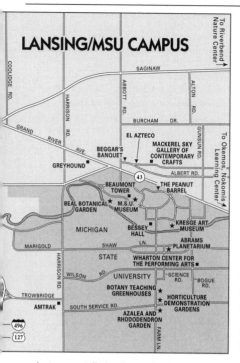

## LANSING/MSU CAMPUS

COOLIDGE RD.

SAGINAW

ABBOTT RD.

HARRISON RD.

BURCHAM DR.

GRAND RIVER AVE.

ALTON RD.

GUNSUN RD.

EL AZTECO

BEGGAR'S BANQUET

MACKEREL SKY GALLERY OF CONTEMPORARY CRAFTS

GREYHOUND ■

ALBERT RD.

43

To Okemos, Nokomis Learning Center

To Riverbend Nature Center

THE PEANUT BARREL

BEAUMONT TOWER

BEAL BOTANICAL ★ M.S.U. GARDEN MUSEUM

MICHIGAN

BESSEY HALL

KRESGE ART MUSEUM

MARIGOLD

SHAW LN.

ABRAMS PLANETARIUM

STATE

WHARTON CENTER FOR THE PERFORMING ARTS ■

HARRISON RD.

WILSON RD.

UNIVERSITY

SCIENCE RD.

BOGUE RD.

TROWBRIDGE

BOTANY TEACHING GREENHOUSES

HORTICULTURE DEMONSTRATION GARDENS

AMTRAK ■

SOUTH SERVICE RD.

AZALEA AND RHODODENDRON GARDEN

FARM LN.

496

127

and tries especially hard to make theater accessible to everyone, with a special pay-what-you-can night once a week.

Lansing has its own opera, known as the **Opera Company of Mid-Michigan,** 517/482-1431. The company lacks a permanent home but performs at various locations throughout the area. Lovers of Broadway musicals, dance, and other special events get their fill at the Wharton Center for the Performing Arts on the MSU campus, 800/WHARTON or 517/432-2000, which seats 2,500 for large productions and also has a more intimate, 600-seat festival stage for smaller dramatic productions. The Greater Lansing Symphony also performs here.

## Michigan Historical Museum

Part of the huge Michigan Library and Historical Center, the free Michigan Historical Museum, 717 W. Allegan St., 517/373-3559, has become a pilgrimage for many history buffs. With four

floors and more than 25 permanent galleries, it tells a detailed story of Michigan's rise from wilderness to industrial powerhouse. Unlike many self-serving state museums, however, the narrative here is frank and intelligent. Placards explain how within a few generations of contact with European settlers, the state's Native American cultures transformed from self-sufficient lifestyles to those with a dependence on manufactured goods. The museum also contains an excellent and detailed copper mining exhibit that's probably better than any found in the U.P. today. It features a walk-through copper mine and videos on life in the mining camps.

The third floor chronicles more recent history, including the dawn of the automobile age, the Depression, and World Wars I and II. Check out the exhibits on stamp collecting and redemption at the S&H Redemption Center, classic radio broadcasts of the 1930s, and an exhibit honoring Michigan's own "Brown Bomber," prizefighter Joe Louis. On the lower level, a small but choice museum store offers one of the best selections in the state of books relating to the history of African Americans. The Michigan Library and Historical Center complex also houses the state archives and state library, a popular pilgrimage spot for genealogists from around the country. The building itself is of interest, too, designed by prominent Detroit architect William Kessler, who relied largely on native building materials. A 70-foot white pine, the state tree, dominates a center courtyard. Hours are Mon.–Fri. 9 A.M.–4:30 P.M., Sat.–Sun. 1–5 P.M.

## Museum Drive

Just east of the State Capitol along the Grand River, enough museums have opened in an old warehouse district to earn it the moniker "Museum Drive." Once storage space for grains and other goods being shipped east and west, today the roomy old mill buildings provide attractive and light-filled alternative museum spaces.

**Impressions 5,** 200 Museum Dr., 517/485-8116, is considered one of the top 10 hands-on science museums in the country. Though aimed at children in grades four through six, kids of all ages find something to interest them here, from a giant soap bubble maker to a walk-through heart exhibit, to an impressive hands-on chemistry lab where kids can create things that ooze, slime, and seep. Other highlights include a realistic model of a spaceship, a giant mouth, and the new area for toddlers known as Kids Space (perhaps a poor name choice when the entire place is geared to kids). A decent deli on the ground floor is a good place to fuel up for the other museums ahead. Admission is $4.50 adults, $3 children 4–18; open Mon.–Sat. 10 A.M.–5 P.M., Sun. noon–5 P.M.

Little kids may be the target audience at Impressions 5, but it's the big kids who rush from exhibit to exhibit at the **R. E. Olds Transportation Museum,** 240 Museum Dr., 517/372-0422. The museum honors Lansing native Ransom E. Olds, who was one of the early pioneers of the auto industry. Olds produced the world's first mass-produced car, the Oldsmobile curved-dash Runabout, which sold more models than all others combined during 1901–1907. Olds is responsible for Oldsmobile's headquarters being in Lansing to this day, although he left in 1904 to form the REO Motor Car Company, named after his initials. While successful during the early years, that company closed during the Depression. The museum traces Oldsmobile from 1883 to the present. Car buffs ooh and aah over the streamlined Oldsmobiles, REOs, and less well-known autos built in Lansing. More than 50 cars are on display, including the first production Olds created in 1897 and one of those famous 1904 models with a curved dash. Admission is $2.50 adults. Hours are Mon.–Sat. 10 A.M.–5 P.M., Sun. noon–5 P.M.

Along Museum Drive, you'll also discover the nation's only surveying museum. While it may seem like an impossibly dull subject, the **Michigan Museum of Surveying,** 220 Museum Dr., 517/484-6605, shows what a daunting task it was to survey the state by foot in the 19th century. Artifacts include the rock that marked the spot southeast of Lansing from which all other state measurements were taken. Despite the job's many hardships, 19th-century surveyors were paid just $3 per day, with which they were required to buy equipment and supplies and pay

up to five workers. Admission is free, but donations are always welcome. Hours are Mon.–Fri. 8 A.M.–5 P.M.

## Other Museums

Not far from downtown, the **Michigan Women's Historical Center and Hall of Fame,** 213 W. Main St., 517/484-1880, honors the mostly unlauded achievements of the state's native daughters through changing and permanent exhibitions. It celebrates the lives and contributions of Michigan women such as Sojourner Truth, a former slave and crusader for human rights; Laura Smith Haviland, an organizer of one of the state's first Underground Railroad stations; and Anne Howard Shaw, minister and physician whose dynamic leadership resulted in the passage of the 19th Amendment. Works of

## SOJOURNER TRUTH

Described by one biographer as a "riveting preacher and spellbinding singer who dazzled listeners with her wit and originality," Sojourner Truth was born sometime around 1790. Towering more than six feet, she gained her freedom in New York state in the early 1820s, dropped her given name, and moved west on a "sojourn to preach truth." Her antislavery crusade took her into both small rural churches and the office of President Abraham Lincoln.

She settled in Battle Creek, an abolitionist stronghold, in 1858 and continued to help her people along the Underground Railroad to Canada. While revisionist history has claimed she never physically assisted runaway slaves, she no doubt inspired many of them with her fiery oratories, which preached economic competence, self-improvement, and social tolerance. A few days before she died in 1883, she said, "I isn't goin' to die, honey, I'se goin' home like a shootin' star." Her funeral was described as the biggest that Battle Creek had ever seen. She is buried in Oak Hill Cemetery by a simple old-fashioned square monument—still a popular pilgrimage spot—just steps away from the ornate marble mausoleum of C. W. Post, founder of Kellogg's.

outstanding Michigan artists and photographers are also featured. Admission is $2.50 for adults; hours are Wed.–Fri. noon–5 P.M., Sat. noon–4 pm., Sun. 2–4 P.M.

Native Americans—specifically the woodland Indians of the Great Lakes—are the focus at **Nokomis Learning Center,** 5153 Marsh Rd. in nearby Okemos, 517/349-5777. The cultures of the Ojibwa, Ottawa, and Potawatomi tribes, known collectively as the People of the Three Fires, are honored through displays of art crafts and artifacts. A small gift shop features beaded jewelry and other handicrafts by local American Indian artists. Hours are Tues.–Fri. 10 A.M.–5 P.M., Sat. noon–5 P.M.; admission is free, but donations are greatly appreciated.

Another influential minority is recognized at the **Malcolm X Homesite** at the corner of Vincent Court and Martin Luther King Jr. Boulevard. The eloquent spokesman for civil rights lived in Lansing in the 1930s on a site that is now a registered historical landmark. After he converted to the Nation of Islam, Malcolm X became one of the first African-American leaders to openly articulate the extent of racial discontent in our society.

# MICHIGAN STATE UNIVERSITY

Dubbed "Moo U," Michigan State University was established in 1855 as the country's first agricultural college and was the forerunner of the nationwide land-grant university system. Despite its nicknames and rather well-known reputation as a party school, the campus has a long, rich history and an excellent reputation in many fields of study—especially agricultural ones, of course. Credit for its founding goes to a group of enlightened Michigan farmers who began lobbying in 1849 for a state college to promote modern agriculture. They chose the 677 acres of forest five miles east of the new state capital, in part because they wanted the school to be autonomous and not tied to an existing university.

Today the MSU campus has grown to more than 5,000 beautifully landscaped acres, home to more than 7,000 different species and varieties of trees, shrubs, and vines. In the older part of the campus, curving drives and Gothic buildings create a parklike setting, shaded by huge beeches and some gnarled white oaks that date back more than 200 years. Students walk to class through what has become a true arboretum with the passing of time, home to more than 5,000 varieties of woodsy plants and trees.

The campus has long been regarded as one giant outdoor laboratory. Very few planted environments in the Midwest have enjoyed such sustained commitment for more than 150 years. At one point, a school policy expected three hours per day of manual labor from all students, part of the hands-on laboratory approach that helped the university maintain the campus and also enabled poor students to afford a college education. Today, both students and professional landscapers maintain the university's impressive collection of gardens.

## Campus Gardens

Newest among MSU's extensive plantings are the **Horticulture Demonstration Gardens,** which opened in 1993. The new gardens are responsible for transforming a bleak-looking, post-1960 section of campus into a dramatic environment. Once as flat and bare as the newest subdivision, the area is now full of pergolas, gazebos, arbors, and topiary. The entrance is off Bogue Road south of Wilson. Before venturing into the gardens, pick up a map at the Visitors Information Center just inside the Plant and Soil Sciences Building. Here you'll also find **Sparty's Flowers & Garden Barn,** 517/353-3770, a colorful garden store run during the week by horticulture students. Midwestern gardeners find lots of ideas to take home on Demonstration Garden tours that last about an hour and are offered June–September. Cost is just $1.

As part of the tour or own your own, don't miss the popular **4-H Children's Garden,** 517/355-0348. Plant themes—62 in all—are designed with young interests in mind. It includes the spicy-smelling Pizza Garden, the Sense-a-tional Garden (with plants like aromatic ginger), an African-American garden featuring hibiscus, okra, black-eyed peas, and other plants brought to the United States from Africa. When they're done

THE HEARTLAND

exploring the garden, kids can wind through a maze, dance on chimes, or marvel at topiary teddy bears designed by the same person who worked on the film *Edward Scissorhands.* The gardens are open April–Oct. and are free.

Also check out the **Idea Gardens,** west of the children's garden, where volunteer master gardeners tend themed plots containing vegetables, cacti, herbs, companion planting, even plants for special-needs children. Green thumbs and wannabes will find more than 1,800 varieties in the **DeLapa Perennial Garden,** a rose garden that features the latest All-American rose selections, and the **Carter Annual Trial Garden,** home to more than a thousand varieties of bedding plants. (They're at their best in July and August.) Visitors are also welcome in the teaching greenhouses.

Founded in 1873, the **Beal Botanical Garden** is believed to be the oldest continuously operated garden of its type in the country. This outdoor museum of living plants includes more than 2,000 species arranged by family and economic use, as well as exotic flowering landscape specimens and an enlightening section on invasive weeds. Other campus areas worth a special stop include the **azalea and rhododendron garden,** most spectacular from late April into early June, and the **Botany Teaching Greenhouses,** full of labeled plants used in botany classes as well as a tropical rainforest room (complete with waterfall), a subtropical room, a desert house, and a butterfly house that flutters with activity year-round.

For a map of MSU plantings and more information on the outstanding campus landscape, contact Campus Park and Planning, 412 Olds Hall, Michigan State University, East Lansing, 517/355-9582, website: www.cpp.msu.edu/beal.

### Other Campus Attractions

With a collection of more than two million items, the 140-year-old **Michigan State University Museum,** West Circle Dr. near the Beaumont Tower, 517/355-2370, has been called one of the Midwest's best-kept secrets. Three floors of exhibits concentrate on the natural and cultural history of the Great Lakes region. Popular stops include the fur-trader's cabin and the life-sized Native American dioramas. Free admission.

Also on campus, the intimate **Kresge Art Museum,** at the corner of Auditorium and Physics Roads, 517/355-7631, houses a permanent collection that spans the centuries from the prehistoric to the contemporary. Wide-ranging highlights include a dramatic *Vision of St. Anthony* by Zurburan, Andy Warhol's *Marilyn,* and a solid collection of art from the 1960s and 1970s, an era often overlooked by other museums.

Another highlight of the MSU campus is the excellent **Abrams Planetarium** at the corner of Shaw Lane and Science Rd., 517/355-4672. The sky theater features fantastic star shows produced by a newly installed state-of-the-art computer graphics star projector. The planetarium also serves as an astronomy research and resource center.

## NATURE CENTERS

Perhaps inspired by MSU, the Lansing area features three appealing nature centers perfect for a little study or just a quiet stroll. The **Fenner Nature Center,** 2020 E. Mount Hope Rd., 517/483-4224, is an excellent learning center that features a replica of a pioneer log cabin, self-guided nature trails, and a year-round visitors center. The **Riverbend Nature Area,** Nichols Rd., 517/322-0030, includes 88 acres of field and forest along the Grand River, with five miles of hiking trails through a range of plant and animal habitats. Come back in winter for the groomed cross-country ski trails. The **Woldumar Nature Center,** 5539 Lansing Rd., 517/322-0030, also along the Grand River, comprises 188 acres of field and forest.

## SPORTS AND RECREATION

Known locally as "the RFP," Lansing's **Riverfront Park and Trail** ranks as one of the finest urban greenspaces in the state. This mostly hidden greenbelt stretches on both sides of the Grand River from Kalamazoo Avenue just north of I-496 to North Street, three miles downstream. A riverwalk runs along the entire east side of the park and is popular with joggers and in-line skaters.

Experienced rock climbers know the Lansing area as home to **The Ledges** in nearby Grand Ledge, 10 miles west via M-43, 517/627-7351. Climbing up from the Grand River just 12 miles from the State Capitol, these quartz sandstone cliffs reach 40 or 50 feet high. Even if you're not a climber, it's interesting to watch from nearby Oak Park, or from along the Ledges Trail, which follows the bank of the river and ends in town at the foot of Harrison Street.

Even beginning paddlers can navigate the usually calm and shallow waters of Lansing's Red Cedar and Grand Rivers. Rent canoes at the Potter Park Canoe Livery, 517/374-1022, or the MSU canoe livery (also known as the Red Cedar Yacht Club), behind Bessey Hall at Farm Lane, 517/355-3397.

If you build it, will they come? Lansing civic boosters hope that the minor league baseball **Lugnuts,** introduced in 1996, will bring the field of dreams to the city's Oldsmobile Park. A Lugnuts game is pure Bull Durham–style ball, with lots of local color, a hokey team mascot known as the Big Lug, and plenty of homemade signs in the stands that read Go Nuts. The quality of the baseball itself may be questionable, but the fun is a sure thing. For tickets and schedule information, call 517/485-4500 or 800/945-NUTS.

Sports are also a big ticket at MSU, of course. For scheduling and ticket information on Big Ten sports events, contact the MSU Athletic Department, 517/355-1610.

## PRACTICALITIES

### Accommodations

No lack of lodging in the Lansing area, thanks to Big Ten fans and business travelers. You'll find a long list of reliable franchise options. A couple of the best are the **Hawthorne Suites,** 901 Delta Commerce Drive, 517/886-0600, with a four-story atrium, rates $100–150; and the **Hampton Inn,** 525 N. Canal Rd., 517/627-8381, with recently renovated rooms, a free breakfast bar, and rates $75–100.

In nearby Eaton Rapids, **Dusty's English Inn,** 728 S. Michigan Rd., 517/663-2500 or 800/858-0598, is a former auto baron's Tudor estate built in 1927, with a great setting on 15 acres near the Grand River. Gardens and greenspace surround the inn, including two miles of nature and cross-country trails. Choose from six bedrooms in the inn, or spring for the three-room master suite in an adjacent cottage with its own pool and a sitting room with fireplace. An intimate on-site restaurant serves up a full English breakfast for guests (included in rates) as well as romantic dinners. Rates $75–175.

### Camping

Just a half hour from Lansing, **Sleepy Hollow State Park,** US-27, 616/527-3750 (Sept.–April) or 517/651-6217 (May–Aug.), has a modern campground within a short walk of the park's Lake Ovid. Pack a fishing rod—the lake is considered one of the best fisheries in this part of the state.

### Food

Decorated with original artwork by area sculptors, painters, and photographers, **Beggar's Banquet,** 218 Abbott Rd., East Lansing, 517/351-4540, is a favorite of everyone from MSU students to the governor of Michigan. Dinners range from the "vegomatic" sandwich to salmon chardonnay. Reservations recommended. Entrees $11–18.

In the heart of downtown, the state's movers and shakers convene for breakfast meetings and power lunches at **The Parthenon,** 227 S. Washington, 517/484-0573, but you should still go for the Greek specialties like moussaka and souvlaki. Reservations recommended. Entrees $6–12.

Housed in a restored Victorian train station, **Clara's,** 637 E. Michigan, 517/372-7120, is chock-full of vintage memorabilia, from train schedules to antique sheet music. The 16-page menu is equally eclectic, with a full range of salads, sandwiches, and dinner entrees. Entrees $6–15.

The **Blue Coyote Brewing Company,** 113 Pere Marquette, 517/487-1687, tops the city's list of newest hotspots, with huge copper vats and a trendy clientele pulled from the city's political scene and MSU's student body. Food ranges from creative salads and sandwiches to pastas and gourmet pizza. Entrees $8–17. You can't beat the combination of good burgers, good service, good prices, and cold beer at the **Peanut Barrel,** 521 E. Grand River, in downtown East

Lansing, 517/351-0608. Entrees $3–6. For Mexican, try **El Azteco,** 225 Ann, 517/351-9111 (entrees $5–9), or **Ramon's,** 718 E. Grand River, 517/482-6690, in Old Town, for great guacamole and fiery, "I can't feel my tongue" homemade red and green salsas.

## Grand Rapids and Vicinity

Grand Rapids—the state's second largest city with a population of 189,100—owes its development and name to the rapids of the freeflowing Grand River, a place of gathering and exchange since Louis Campau established a trading post here in 1826. The power and transportation afforded by the river, coupled with the abundance of wood from the neighboring forests, made the growth of the city's furniture industry a natural.

By 1854, logging had become an important industry, and Grand Rapids entered the most vigorous phase of its development. Huge quantities of logs were floated down the Grand to Grand Rapids' mills. Upstream mill owners, seeing the valuable timber floating unattended past their mills, often stole the logs and cut them into lumber. This practice, known as "hogging," precipitated fierce brawls along the Flat, Rogue, Grand, and other area rivers and caused the birth of the river driver, a colorful character who rode the logs downstream to ensure they reached their final destination safely.

Grand Rapids was not always the Calvinist stronghold it is today. During the 1860s, Campau Square was notorious for its brothels, gambling houses, and basement bars. It became better known for its furniture making after 1881, when the city's first factory, the Wolverine Chair Company, was erected. In 1876, a display of the city's wares at the centennial celebration in Philadelphia helped solidify that reputation; by 1900, Grand Rapids was nicknamed "Furniture City." The moniker that still sticks today, since city serves as headquarters for Herman Miller and Steelcase, two of the largest office furniture companies in the country.

Grand Rapids went through a decline in the

early 1980s, but somehow managed to reinvent itself as a thriving showcase for the arts, local history, and business. Today the downtown sparkles with busy hotels, shopping areas, pedestrian malls, and public artworks. One of the most striking downtown sights is Alexander Calder's dramatic sculpture, *La Grand Vitesse,* a 42-ton strawberry-red sculpture that pays homage to the rapids that built the city. Controversial at first, it has since become a symbol of Grand Rapids. Other city improvements recently completed or in the works include new cultural, recreational, and sports facilities and a new children's museum that opened in mid-1998.

Much of the redevelopment can be attributed to the area's loyal and exceedingly generous business community, a group that includes the headquarters for the Meijer Corporation (pioneers of the dual grocery/discount store phenomenon) and Amway, that genius of direct marketing, which racks up annual sales in the billions. The names DeVos and Van Andel—the founding families of Amway—seem to top the list of every charitable cause in town. Most of the business and civic leaders are alumni of nearby Holland's Hope College (part of the Reformed Church of America) or of Grand Rapids' Calvin College, run by the Christian Reformed Church. Grand Rapids, by the way, is the epicenter of religious publishing in the United States.

Hardworking Grand Rapids may be known for its Protestant work ethic, but a surprising amount of diversity hides beneath the city's Calvinist veneer. Yes, it's a Republican stronghold, but Grand Rapids also is home to an active alternative press and the state's largest Native American population. The city's older neighborhoods celebrate a mix of cultures, comprising Asian, Mexican-American, African-American, Lithuanian, Ukrainian, German, and Polish communities.

For more information on the Grand Rapids area, contact the **Grand Rapids/Kent County Convention and Visitors Bureau,** 140 Monroe Center NW, Suite 300, Grand Rapids, 800/678-9859, website: www.visitgrandrapids.org.

## SIGHTS AND RECREATION
### Heritage Hill Historic District

As a manufacturing city with many locally owned businesses, Grand Rapids residents earned considerable riches and weren't shy about displaying them. Prominent families, including those who owned the city's famed furniture factories, built their mansions on the city's hillside where they could overlook their domain, from far above the smoke and soot their factories generated. **Heritage Hill** was their neighborhood of choice from roughly 1840 through 1920. Located just east of downtown, it displays the wealth of Grand Rapids' lumber boom, with more than 60 architectural styles reflected in its 1,300 residences.

As in most urban areas across the country, today's Heritage Hill residents are more economically and racially diverse. The neighborhood is overseen by the Heritage Hill Association, an active group of organizers who work hard at maintaining both their property and the area's sense of community. Among the most spectacular homes are those built by the city's one-time lumber barons and two designed by Frank Lloyd Wright.

Highlights include the three-story Victorian-style **Voigt House,** 115 College St., 616/456-4600, built in the late 19th century, one of the few open to the public. It contains original family furnishings, even down to the original contents of the family's medicine chest. Not surprisingly, most of the heavy, overstylized furniture was created in Grand Rapids. Tours are offered Tues. 11 A.M.–3 P.M., and the second and fourth Sunday of the month 1–3 P.M. Admission is $3 adults, $2 seniors and children.

At the other extreme is the simple, serene **Meyer May House,** 450 Madison SE, 616/246-4821, an anomaly in this predominantly Victorian neighborhood. It was designed in 1908 by Frank Lloyd Wright for a prominent local clothier during the same year that the famous Robie House in Chicago was designed. Vincent Scully, an architectural historian, has called the Meyer May house the most beautifully and completely restored of Wright's Prairie houses. "To come suddenly into that interior...is to be wholly caught up and carried along by something rarely experienced: absolute peace, integral order, deep quiet grandeur and calm—all of it achieved in a house of no more than moderate size," he says. Through the generous funding of Steelcase, the nationally famous Grand Rapids office furniture maker, the house has since been restored to reflect Wright's original organic building concept, with custom-made furniture, art glass, carpets, light fixtures, even linens. Open Tues. and Thurs. 10 A.M.–1 P.M., Sun. 1–4 P.M.; free.

Wandering Heritage Hill is a great way to spend the afternoon even if you're not an architectural historian. Self-guided walking tour maps can be picked up at the Heritage Hill Association office, 126 College St. SE, 616/459-8950. If you visit in October, many of the residences open their doors to tours during the annual home tour. Call the association for the specific date and more information.

### Museums and Other Attractions

The **Gerald R. Ford Museum,** 303 Pearl St. NW, 616/451-9263, honors Michigan's only native-born president in this triangular building on the west bank of the Grand River. The nation's 38th president—named to the post on August 9, 1974, after the infamous resignation of Richard Nixon—Ford grew up in Grand Rapids and represented the Fifth Congressional District in Michigan from 1948 to 1973, when he became the nation's vice president.

Renovated in 1997, the museum portrays both the private life and public challenges of Ford, president for just two years. The most popular attraction is the full-size replica of the Oval Office as it looked while Ford was president and the holographic tour of the White House. Other exhibits include a surprisingly moving section on Nixon's resignation and Ford's subsequent pardon, the events surrounding the fall of Saigon,

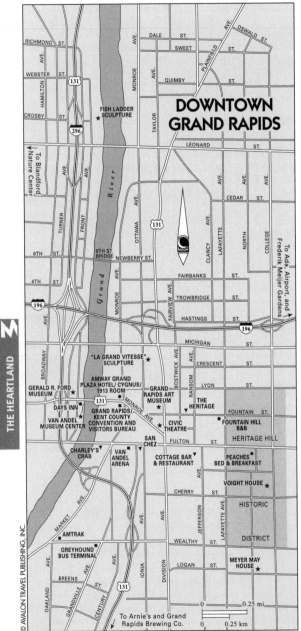

**DOWNTOWN GRAND RAPIDS**

Ford's loss to a soft-spoken Georgia peanut farmer, and a profile of pro-choice and pro-ERA Betty Ford, the controversial first lady who was among the first to express opinions that differed from her husband's. Hours are daily 9 A.M.–5 P.M.; admission $3.

The **Grand Rapids Art Museum,** 155 Division St. NE, 616/459-4677, occupies a renovated 1903 Federal Building that once served as a post office and courthouse. Inside, collections include fine 19th- and 20th-century prints, paintings, photographs, sculptures, and decorative arts with an emphasis on—surprise!—furniture. More than 10 traveling exhibitions are featured each year. Open Tues.–Sun. 11 A.M.–6 P.M. (Fri. till 9 P.M.). Admission is $3.

The art museum's major competition for the dollars and time of museum-goers is the **Van Andel Museum Center of the Public Museum of Grand Rapids,** 272 Pearl St. NW, 616/456-3966. Arguably the city's best museum, the Van Andel is housed in a spectacular structure and ranks as the largest general museum in the state. It cost $35 million to build in 1995, much of it a gift from Amway co-founder Jay Van Andel.

The 76-foot whale skeleton suspended from the three-story main galleria serves as an appropriate metaphor for the Van Andel museum, which holds an outstanding permanent collection of incredible size and scope. You can witness the massive flywheel of a 1905 Corliss-type steam engine that once powered the city's furniture factories in the "Furniture City" exhibit, walk through a recreation of 1890s Grand Rapids, take a turn aboard a

**sculpture of Da Vinci's horse at Meijer Gardens**

restored 1928 Spillman carousel, or see stars at the Roger B. Chaffee Planetarium. The groundbreaking exhibit "Anishinabek: The People of This Place" sensitively explores the culture and artifacts of the Anishinabe people, western Michigan's Native Americans. An illuminating explanation of the state's indigenous Ottawa, Ojibwa, and Potawatomi peoples, it includes video interviews that trace the modern challenges of Native Americans and the stereotypes that continue to haunt them. It also explores in detail traditional crafts such as beadwork, basketmaking, and quillwork. Open daily 9 A.M.–5 P.M. Museum admission is $5 adult, $4 senior, $2 ages 3–17.

Another local benefactor—Fred Meijer, owner and founder of the Meijer grocery/discount stores—has given back to his hometown with the spectacular **Frederik Meijer Gardens,** 3411 Bradford NE, 616/957-1580, which opened its doors in 1995. Its 70 acres encompass a 15,000-square-foot tropical conservatory (the state's largest), an outdoor area of colorful flower gardens complemented by ponds, woods, and wetlands, and an extensive collection of sculpture—including works by noted sculptor Marshall Fredericks, best known for the allegorical *Spirit of Detroit.* Quotations throughout the gardens by Michigan poets such as Theodore Roethke and Jim Harrison connect people to the plants. The gardens are open Mon.–Sat. 9 A.M.–5 P.M., Sun. noon–5 P.M.; admission is $3.50.

The **Civic Theater,** 30 Division Ave. NE, 616/222-6650, represents a grand piece of Grand Rapids architecture. The largest community theater in Michigan and the second largest in the United States, this impressive landmark offers six main-stage and two children's productions annually in a restored 1903 theater.

The *Fish Ladder Sculpture,* on the Grand River at Leonard and Front Streets, is a popular downtown meeting place. This concrete, five-step ladder was built by a local artist to assist salmon in jumping over a six-foot dam to reach their spawning grounds. While the leaping fish can be seen any time of year, they're especially active from late September through late October. Crossing the Grand River just north of downtown, the **Sixth Street Bridge** spans 525 feet, the longest and oldest remaining wrought-iron and steel-truss bridge in the state.

Within the city limits the **Blandford Nature Center,** 1715 Hillburn Ave. NW, 616/453-6192, preserves 143 acres of field and forest. More than four miles of trails—1,000 feet of which are barrier free—wind among the grounds, which contain a variety of restored 19th-century buildings including a log cabin, one-room schoolhouse, barn, and blacksmith shop. Staff and volunteers also take in and rehabilitate injured local wildlife and are happy to share a glimpse of their work with visitors. Free admission. Open Mon.–Fri. 9 A.M.–5 P.M., Sat.–Sun. 1–5 P.M.

For some, modern Grand Rapids and adjacent Ada are known as the towns that Amway built. Today, the **Amway Corporation,** 7575 Fulton St. E, Ada, 616/676-6701, is one of the nation's most successful marketers of beauty and household cleaning products, all sold through the company's direct marketing network. If you're curious about what goes on behind the scenes of this distinctly American powerhouse, sign on for one of the free tours. A one-hour exploration takes visitors behind the scenes in the company's research and development area, printing department, the corporate museum (where you can see past and current products and other merchandising memorabilia), and the promotional video units. Don't expect to uncover any company secrets, however; they're well-guarded. Tours are offered at 9 and 11 A.M., 1 and 3 P.M. weekdays.

## Sports and Recreation

Two events captured the headlines in 1997: the opening of the new, 12,000-seat Van Andel Arena and the formation of the new Grand Rapids Griffins professional hockey team that will call it home. Besides hockey, Grand Rapids is also home to the minor-league Hoops (basketball) and the minor league Whitecaps (baseball), a Detroit Tigers affiliate.

For those who would rather do than watch, get out on the local waters at the **Grand Rogue Campground, Canoe and Tube Livery,** 10 minutes from Grand Rapids in nearby Belmont, 6400 W. River Dr., 616/361-1053. It offers two- and four-hour canoe trips as well as one- and two-hour tubing expeditions. **AAA Canoe Rentals** in Rockford, 616/866-9264, is just 20 minutes from Grand Rapids and offers canoeing, tubing, and kayaking trips down the Rogue River, where you're likely to spot deer, great blue herons, and other bird life on the densely wooded banks.

Climbers head for **Higher Ground Rock Climbing Center,** 616/774-3100, home to a 23-foot artificial rock and instruction for all levels. No one would debate the fact that northern Michigan has better skiing, but for those who can't wait to hit the slopes, the **Cannonsburg Ski Area,** 6800 Cannonsburg Rd. NE, 616/874-6711, is a full-service ski resort with both downhill and cross-country skiing.

# PRACTICALITIES
## Accommodations

The **Amway Grand Plaza Hotel,** Pearl and Monroe St., 187 Monroe NW, 616/774-2000, ranks as the finest accommodations in Grand Rapids and one of Michigan's top hotels. Two hotels actually make up the complex: the original 1913 Paintlind, and the newer Grand Plaza West, completed in 1983. Depending on your mood, you can choose from a lush traditional or cool contemporary room. In all, the two house more than 600 rooms, 10 restaurants, and a state-of-the-art fitness center. Rates $125–225.

**Fountain Hill B&B,** 222 Fountain NE, 616/458-6621, website: www.fountainhill-bandb.com, gives visitors and voyeurs the chance to stay inside one of Heritage Hills' distinctive homes. The 1874 classic Italianate with high ceilings, elaborate plasterwork, and a huge circular staircase manages to be both elegant and relaxed at the same time, no mean feat. Rates $100–125. Housed in a Georgian Country Manor home built in 1916, **Peaches Bed & Breakfast,** 29 Gay Street SE, Grand Rapids, 616/454-8000, features cathedral glass skylights, five fireplaces, an extensive library, and a game room with original wall murals. Unlike most B&Bs, it contains a small exercise room with a weight machine, stair stepper, and free weights. Rates $75–100.

The best downtown value is the **Days Inn,** 310 Pearl St. NW, 616/361-1053, centrally located near the Gerald Ford and other public museums, with clean and attractive rooms. Rates $50–100.

## Camping

Ten minutes from Grand Rapids, the **Grand Rogue Campground** 6400 W. River Dr., Belmont, MI 49306, 616/361-1053, offers 75 wooded modern sites on the Grand and Rogue Rivers, as well as float tubes, canoes, and kayak rental (May–Oct.). The closest state-run campground to Grand Rapids, **Yankee Springs Recreation Area,** 2104 Gun Lake Rd., Middleville, MI 49333, 616/795-9081, has four rustic campgrounds; one, Deep Lake, is open year-round.

## Food

The city's oldest bar and restaurant, **Cottage Bar & Restaurant,** Fulton St. and LaGrave Ave., 616/454-9088, concocts Grand Rapids' best burgers and three different styles of chili. The outside café is a popular meeting place in good weather. Entrees $3.5–6. "To drink is human, to brew divine" is the motto of the **Grand Rapids Brewing Co.,** 3689 28th St. SE, 616/285-5970, a cozy brewpub. It's hard to say what's better, the food or the handcrafted beer. Entrees $4–9.

Tapas, paella, and other specialties of the Iberian peninsula draw crowds tired of the all-too-common prime rib and pasta to the sunny **San Chez,** 38 W. Fulton, Grand Rapids, 616/774-8272. Lively and fun, it draws an eclectic crowd with entrees such as raspberry-guava lamb ribs with chili sauce, grilled chicken mole with five-onion relish, and vegetable saffron rice with scallions and habañero coulis. Entrees $6–18. Sup in style at the **Heritage,** 151 Fountain NE, Grand Rapids, 616/771-3700, while supporting the culinary students at the Grand Rapids Community College. The restaurant is open weekdays for lunch and dinner but is closed during summer. Entrees $5–15.

An area legend, **Arnie's Bakery,** 3561 28th St.

© BOB BRODBECK

the Amway Grand Plaza Hotel

SE, 616/956-7901, is well known for its award-winning breakfasts, overstuffed sandwiches, and kids' menu. Entrees $3–9. **Charley's Crab,** 63 Market St. SE, 616/459-2500, is part of the state's well-loved Chuck Muer chain of seafood restaurants. Try one of the fresh catches or one of the always tasty pastas. . . or carbo load at the Sunday brunch. The signature rolls have been copied by a number of restaurants across the state. In good weather, ask for an outside table overlooking the Grand River. Entrees $14–25.

The elegant **Cygnus,** one of several restaurants in the Amway Grand Plaza, makes all the area's "best of" lists and is well known for its stunning night views of the river and city below. Dishes include veal chops with lobster brioche, seared rack of baby boar in red currant sauce, and roasted free-range chicken with Swiss chard, black-eyed peas, and roasted garlic juice. Also in the hotel, the award-winning **1913 Room** (named for the year the original hotel was built) echoes the opulence of the city's timber era with rich wood and Victorian-style furnishings. Reservations recommended in both restaurants. Entrees $20–30.

THE HEARTLAND

# The Southwestern Shore

The southwest corner of the state bordering Lake Michigan is perhaps best known for its two bumper crops: fruit and "fudgies," the area's nickname for tourists. Lake Michigan bestows upon the region a moderate climate just right for a bounty of fruit crops, including apples, strawberries, cherries, blueberries, plums, and wine grapes. (It ranks as one of the Midwest's best wine-growing regions.) As for the "fudgies" part, the big lake serves as the main attraction for thousands of tourists (who tend to consume huge amounts of the Michigan chocolate treat). This corner of Lake Michigan washes onto a 200-mile-long stretch of sunny, sandy shoreline, in places billowing high into immense freshwater dunes.

The glaciers left behind an ideal setting for building sand beaches and dunes. During the Ice Age, continental glaciers spread southward from Canada, repeatedly burying this area under sheets of ice. When the ice sheets retreated and melted for the last time, about 12,000 years ago,

Tabor Hill Winery and Restaurant

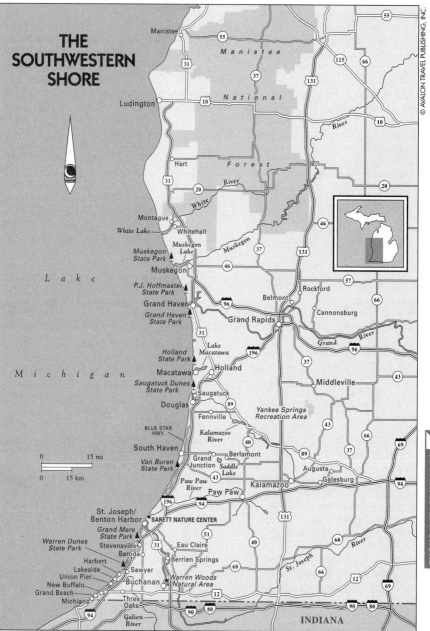

# THE SOUTHWESTERN SHORE

Manistee

*Manistee*

Ludington

*National*

Hart

*Forest*

Montague
White Lake
Whitehall
Muskegon State Park
*Muskegon Lake*
*White*
*River*
Muskegon

*Muskegon*

Rockford
Belmont
Cannonsburg

P.J. Hoffmaster State Park
Grand Haven
Grand Haven State Park

Grand Rapids

*Lake Macatawa*

Holland State Park
Macatawa
Saugatuck Dunes State Park
Saugatuck
Douglas
Fennville

*Grand*
*River*

Middleville

*Yankee Springs Recreation Area*

BLUE STAR HWY.

*Kalamazoo River*

South Haven
Van Buren State Park

Grand Junction
*Saddle Lake*
*Paw Paw River*

Berlamont

Paw Paw

Augusta

Kalamazoo
Galesburg

St. Joseph/ Benton Harbor
SARETT NATURE CENTER
Grand Mere State Park
Warren Dunes State Park
Stevensville
Baroda
Harbert
Lakeside
Union Pier
New Buffalo
Grand Beach
Michiana
Three Oaks
Sawyer
Buchanan

Eau Claire
Berrien Springs

Warren Woods Natural Area

*St. Joseph*
*River*

*Galien River*

INDIANA

*Lake*

*Michigan*

0        15 mi
0        15 km

**SOUTHWESTERN SHORE**

© AVALON TRAVEL PUBLISHING, INC.

they ground bedrock into powder and deposited huge piles of sand and rock debris. The prevailing westerly winds blowing across the lake take over from there, building up the sand on the lake's leeward shore.

Much of Michigan's beachfront is protected, undeveloped, and accessible to public as a string of state parks, national forests, and other preserves. You can explore their trails for a lesson in dune ecology or simply enjoy a classic day at the beach: The same prevailing winds that created the dunes also push Lake Michigan's surface water toward the eastern shore. While temperatures on the Wisconsin side may be in the chilly 50s, the sun-warmed surface waters licking at Michigan's beaches can be almost 20 degrees warmer.

The area's history is steeped in stories of Indians, French explorers, lumber, and agriculture. Many southwestern Michigan towns still bear Indian names: Paw Paw, Muskegon, Man-istee. With dozens of rivers emptying into Lake Michigan—the perfect transportation system for logs—southwestern Michigan prospered during the logging era. After the Civil War, a growing number of sawmills buzzed along its shorelines, and the state soon became one of the leading lumber-producing regions in the country. Most of the lumber used to rebuild Chicago after the Great Fire in 1871 was felled in the forests of southwest Michigan.

The emphasis later shifted from rivers to railroads, and then to roads built for automobiles. With the car came the tourists and southwest Michigan's nickname, "Michigan's Gold Coast." Today a string of resort towns stretch north from the Indiana border, serving as base camps for exploring the region's wealth of bike trails, antique shops, wineries, and, of course, the omnipresent lake—with its bountiful beaches, lovely dunes, and golden sunsets melting into endless blue.

# The State Line to South Haven

## HARBOR COUNTRY

Eight lakefront resort communities cluster north of the Indiana border: Michiana, Grand Beach, New Buffalo, Union Pier, Lakeside, Harbert, Sawyer, and Three Oaks, just a few miles inland. Known collectively as "Harbor Country," they've also been dubbed the "Riviera on Lake Michigan" and the "Hamptons of the Midwest." That's a bit over the top, perhaps, but with a kernel of truth. Just an hour from Chicago's Loop, Harbor Country has indeed become the summer escape of choice for well-heeled Windy City expatriates—including film critic Roger Ebert, novelist Andrew Greeley, architect Stanley Tigerman, and scores of others. The well-to-do weekend at a chorus line of glass-fronted luxury homes and condos lining Lake Michigan, shopping, dining, and driving from town to town. (A few words to the wise: Skip the area in summer if you hate crowds and hate to shop.)

Behind the area's silver-spoon facade, however, are vestiges of the area's original sleepy charm. Tony shops may line the main streets, but the legendary sand, surf, and sunsets are still famous, and, for the most part anyway, still free. Hotels and restaurants exist in all price ranges. While travelers can easily drop $100 for dinner for two at one of the swanky restaurants, they can just as easily chow down on a huge breakfast of thick French toast, two eggs, and two slices of bacon at Rosie's in downtown New Buffalo for less than $5.

For more information on Harbor Country, contact the **Harbor Country Chamber of Commerce,** 530 S. Whittaker St. in New Buffalo, 616/469-5409, website: www.harbor-country.org.

### Shopping

Bypass the pretentious downtown shops (many list store locations like "Newport/Carmel/Harbor Country") and head out on the highway. The offbeat galleries and antique shops that have sprouted up along the **Red Arrow Highway,** from Grand Beach to Harbert (about eight miles north), are one of the area's chief charms. Everything from "serious" art and antiques to campy Popsicle stick lamps can be found here, and it's easy to spend the day wandering, stopping to rest and re-fuel along the way. In between shops, the highway passes old cottage compounds, ramshackle resorts, and elegant lakefront estates that grew like weeds in the 1910s and 1920s.

Galleries seem to dominate at the southern end of Harbor Country, especially in New Buffalo and Lakeside. **Courtyard Gallery,** 813 E. Buffalo St., New Buffalo, 616/469-4110, showcases a broad array of oils, watercolors, bronzes, and sculptured glass. Local artists dominate at **Local Color,** 16187 Red Arrow Hwy., Union Pier, 616/469-5332. Visitors can tour the studios at the internationally renowned **Lakeside Center for the Arts,** 15251 Lakeshore Rd., 616/469-1377, and buy works to take home at the adjacent **Lakeside Gallery,** 15486 Red Arrow Hwy., 616/469-3022. Also in Lakeside, check out the rustic furniture made of tree trunks, branches, and twigs at **Hearthwoods,** 15310 Red Arrow Hwy., 616/469-5551.

In Sawyer and Harbert roadside antiquing haunts fill former cottages, old brick storefronts, and cavernous warehouses. In Sawyer, hunt away at Timeless Treasures, 12908 Red Arrow Highway, 616/426-3636; Dunes Antique Center, 12825 Red Arrow Highway, 616/426-4043. In Harbert, try Harbert Antique Mall, 13887 Red Arrow Highway, 616/469-0977. There are as many shops as you and your Visa card can handle.

## Natural Attractions

If all this conspicuous consumption wears you out, you can find plenty of simpler pleasures in Harbor Country, too. The **Warren Woods Natural Area,** 616/426-4013, protects 311 acres, including one of the state's few remaining vir-

the northern mockingbird

BOB RACE

gin beech-maple forests. Along the banks of the twisting Galien River, beeches, maples, and hemlocks grow so large that two people can't link their arms around them. A 3.5-mile trail circles through the woods and along the Galien. Warren Woods is known far and wide among **birdwatchers,** due partly to its location on the Lake Michigan shoreline and the forest's abundant deadwood, perfect for nesting. Warbler sightings can be particularly good here.

E. K. Warren, a Three Oaks shopkeeper who made his fortune by inventing an affordable corset made of turkey feathers, bought the property in 1879, determined to preserve the land at a time when other businessmen were looking only to exploit it. The area is designated a national natural landmark. The only concessions to human visitors are pit toilets, a wooden footbridge spanning the Galien River, a small parking lot, and one picnic table. In spring, you may notice an abundance of morel mushrooms, but keep in mind all plants are protected in this area. To reach Warren Woods, take the Red Arrow Highway to Union Pier, turn east on Elm Valley Road (marked with a blinking light) and follow it five miles. A state park sticker is required.

The more well-known legacy of E. K. Warren's fortitude and foresight is nearby **Warren Dunes State Park,** 12032 Red Arrow Hwy., Sawyer, 616/426-4013. On hot summer weekends an exodus from Chicago descends on the southern end of the park, jamming a stretch of beach and crunching up the 240-foot Tower Hill dune, with views all the way to the Chicago skyline. It's also a favorite of weekend hang gliders. To get away from the crowds, explore the back dunes farther from the water (stay off fragile dune grasses) or head for the northern two-thirds of

SOUTHWESTERN SHORE

the park—ignored by the weekend crowds and undeveloped except for six miles of hiking and ski trails. The Yellow Birch nature trail includes a birdwatching boardwalk at the trail's north end (wheelchair accessible), frequented by more than 100 bird species.

The ecology of the dunes is a fascinating study in biodiversity. Because of the way dunes form, plant communities can change drastically as you move from the waterfront inland. Closest to the water are the newest "active" dunes, still forming and ever-changing piles of windswept sand. Moving inland, vegetation like marram grass takes hold and begins to stabilize the dunes. Even farther back from the water, older dunes have established larger plant communities that include jack pine, black oak, and a variety of shrubs. In between the dunes, swales filled with bogs and fens harbor water-loving plants like leatherleaf and carnivorous pitcher plants. The result is a staggering array of plants, including many not often seen in northern climates.

For years, **Grand Mere State Park** near Stevensville, 616/426-4013 (the Warren Dunes number), was the well-kept secret of locals and summer residents who wanted to keep it to themselves. Alas, the area has been discovered but remains remarkably natural (though within earshot of the interstate). The 1,000-acre park preserves an interesting and valuable habitat of three interdunal lakes. Glaciers scooped out these depressions, once part of a larger bay. Shoreline currents carrying sediments build sandbars and spits across the bay mouth, damming it, and creating the small inland lakes. Two more lakes once existed south of the current three, now filled in as wooded swamps and remnant bogs. The diverse ecological community supports a distinctive array of birds, including yellow-throated warblers, dickcissels, mockingbirds, summer tanagers, and Bell's vireos. Grand Mere is one of only a dozen Michigan areas listed as national natural landmarks. Four miles of trails wind among the open dunes, and it's a half-mile walk to reach the park's two miles of Lake Michigan shoreline—happily, a far enough distance to deter many beachgoers.

Located 10 miles inland from Lake Michigan and five miles from the Indiana border, the town of Three Oaks has just under 2,000 residents most of the year. In September, however, three or four times that number converge on the area for the **Apple Cider Century,** a one-day cycling event that winds through orchards, woods, vineyards, the Lake Michigan shoreline, and a handful of area towns. Since it began in 1974, the event has grown into the nation's largest one-day, 100-mile ride. It's sponsored by the Three Oaks Spokes Bicycle Club, a group of enthusiasts from Michigan, Indiana, and Illinois that supports the state's only bicycle museum. The delightful **Three Oaks Spokes Bicycle Museum** on Elm Street in Three Oaks, 616/756-3361, houses a collection of bikes from the 1860s through the present, including a spine-crunching 1870s model known as the Boneshaker and an unusual chainless bike from 1890s. While there, ask about the **Backroads Bikeway,** a lovely trail system that follows gurgling streams, open farm country, and two state parks before looping back to the museum. Routes range from eight to 31 miles.

In the 1930s, a Chicago schoolteacher bought up some property between Berrien Springs and Buchanan, and began experimenting and planting gardens. Over the next 30 years, she created perennial gardens, lilac gardens, a boxwood garden, a fern trail, and an enchanting rock garden, gradually building her land into a respected 105-acre preserve and nature center known as **Fernwood**, 13988 Range Line Rd., 616/695-6491.

Today, highlights include the arboretum added in the 1960s, a reconstructed tallgrass prairie (in bloom May–Aug.), and the extensive visitors center, which houses a gift shop, a fern conservatory, and a gallery of changing nature-oriented art exhibits. Near the visitors center is a charming herb and sensory garden grouped by use, including culinary, medicinal, dye, and pest repellent qualities. Admission is $4 adults, $2 ages 13–19, $1 ages 6–12.

## Accommodations

The eight communities of Harbor Country offer as many lodging choices as a mid-sized city, with prices to match. Though you won't find any bargains among the bunch, it would be a shame to visit Harbor Country and not stay at one of its distinctive small inns. The following one-of-a-kind establishments all fall in the $100–200 range, depending on the season. For budget accommodations, your best bet is to stick with franchises along I-94.

The fun and funky **Bauhaus on Barton,** 33 N. Barton St., New Buffalo, 616/469-6419, is a jazzy place with three suites and a single room decorated in 1950s' style, right down to vintage magazines. Full breakfast and terry cloth robes are included in the price, as is its great location—less than two blocks to the beach and shops of New Buffalo. Fifty acres of spring-fed lakes, wildflower meadows, and whispering pines stretch behind the gates of **Sans Souci** in New Buffalo, 616/756-3141. Choose from a suite or the charming English cottage for two, all featuring European-style decor.

*Chicago* magazine voted the **Inn at Union Pier,** 9708 Berrien St., Union Pier, 616/469-4700, one of the region's "best small inns." With a primo location just "200 steps" from Lake Michigan, this inn features 16 large rooms, many decorated with antique Swedish ceramic fireplaces—according to the owners, the largest private collection in the country. The **Pine Garth Inn,** 15790 Lakeshore Rd., Union Pier, 888/390-0909, was built in 1905 as a private summer home. It opened its doors to guests in 1989 and has been a favorite ever since. The unique building is constructed so that the lake and its often-magnificent sunsets can be seen from every room.

Lovers of Mission furniture and decorative arts should opt for Lakeside's **Pebble House,** 15093 Lake Shore, 616/469-1416. The 1912 inn has seven rooms and suites, along with generous Swedish-style breakfasts.

For more lodging options, check out the **Harbor Country Chamber of Commerce** website at website: www.harborcountry.org.

## Camping

Camping may be your best bet if you're looking

to travel cheaply through pricey Harbor Country. **Warren Dunes State Park,** 12032 Red Arrow Hwy., Sawyer, 616/426-4013, offers 180 modern and 122 semimodern (no electricity or showers) sites for $14 per night ($8 in winter), as well as three compact mini-cabins with a woodstove and bunks for $30 a night. Reservations recommended mid-May–Sept., especially on weekends. For reservations at any Michigan state park, call 800/44-PARKS; website: dnr.state.mi.us. Two private lakes and hiking trails add to the ambience at **Bob-A-Ron Campground** in Three Oaks, 616/469-4303, with more than 300 modern sites.

## Food

In New Buffalo, **Hannah's Restaurant,** 115 S. Whittaker, 616/469-1440, features old-world specialties such as pot roast, along with award-winning nouvelle cuisine as well as a children's menu. Entrees $8–20. Also in New Buffalo, **Redamak's,** 616 E. Buffalo St., 616/469-4522, is known for the "hamburger that made New Buffalo famous," as well as its casual, friendly dining. Entrees $4.50–12. The **Retro Cafe,** 616/469-1800, is the place for breakfast in New Buffalo, with homemade muffins, eggs benedict and specialties like cinnamon bun French toast.

An area institution, **Miller's Country House,** on the Red Arrow Highway, Union Pier, 616/469-5950, gives diners two options: casual dining in the rustic grill room where chefs prepare food in the exhibition kitchen, or the dressier dining room overlooking a pretty woodland garden. Entrees range from gourmet pizza and steakburgers to New Zealand rack of lamb. Entrees $6–18. Also in Union Pier, **Red Arrow Roadhouse,** 616/469-3939, offers good value homestyle fare in a casual, lodge-style atmosphere. Enclosed patio. Entrees $3–11.

Up the Red Arrow Highway in Harbert, the delectable, old-fashioned **Harbert Swedish Bakery,** 616/469-1777, has been here since poet Carl

> *The delectable, old-fashioned Harbert Swedish Bakery has been here since poet Carl Sandburg ran a goat farm nearby.*

Sandburg ran a goat farm nearby. It still specializes in traditional Swedish breads and cakes.

## ST. JOSEPH/BENTON HARBOR

Once called Newberryport, the area now known as St. Joseph grew as a rest stop for travelers between Detroit and Chicago. Set on a bluff overlooking Lake Michigan, "St. Joe" is a pleasant city of 9,000 with attractive historic buildings, good shopping, a beautiful beach, and an excellent nature center. Ship captains and lumber barons built many of the town's 19th-century Victorians; today vacationers and second-home owners enjoy the blufftop views of the area's beaches and parks. In contrast, neighboring Benton Harbor, its one-time rival just to the north, is almost a ghost town, with little besides a well-attended Blossomtime Festival in spring to recommend it to travelers.

Home to the Whirlpool world headquarters, St. Joseph, like the rest of southwest Michigan, has seen an influx of second-home buyers from Chicago in recent years. This shift has brought about a change in the downtown, with more and more galleries and coffeehouses and fewer old-time clothiers and newsstands lining its brick streets. While some may balk at the gentrification, St. Joseph has succeeded where many small cities have failed, keeping its downtown vibrant and healthy.

For more information on the area, contact the **Southwest Michigan Tourist Council,** 2300 Pipestone Road in Benton Harbor, 616/925-6301, website: www.swmichigan.org.

### Sights and Recreation

Many visitors need no more entertainment than **Silver Beach,** the lovely municipal beach that skirts downtown St. Joe. A pair of long cement breakwaters juts 1,000 feet into the lake, leading to twin lighthouses guarding the harbor. It's a favorite spot of anglers and anyone wishing for a front-row seat of the sunset

Housed in an old brick four-square house above Lake Michigan, St. Joe's clever **Curious Kids Museum,** 415 Lake Blvd., 616/983-2543,

ranks as one of the best museums of its kind in the state. From the minute they walk in the door, kids (and adults) are treated to bright, colorful displays—including the lobby murals by eccentric Niles cartoonist/artist Nancy Drew—that are both engaging and playful. Excellent exhibits teach but don't preach: Kids can serve adult customers in their own diner, follow an apple crop through autumn processing and sell the results at a farm stand, operate a hot air balloon, or experience what it's like to be handicapped. Down the street at the **Krasl Art Center,** 707 Lake, 616/983-0271, visitors find both energetic volunteers and a schedule of well-chosen changing exhibits. Three galleries display folk art, works by regional artists, and occasional traveling exhibitions. A recently expanded gallery shop offers art-related gifts and other goodies.

Those who seek sanctuary find it at the **Sarett Nature Center,** 2300 Benton Center Rd., Benton Township, 616/927-4832, run by the Michigan Audubon Society. The 350 acres along the Paw Paw River northeast of Benton Harbor include a number of natural habitats, including upland meadows, swamp forests, and lowland marshes. As a nod to birdwatchers, the property includes many benches, elevated towers, and five miles of trails. A naturalist is usually on hand to answer questions. Ask about the full schedule of demonstrations, nature walks, workshops, and classes. The Michigan Audubon Society also operates 15 other sanctuaries, two nature centers, and an observatory. For a list and more information on **birding** in the state, write 6011 W. St. Joseph #403, Lansing, MI 48917, or call 517/886-9144.

Nature's fruits can be enjoyed at two of the area's largest growers: **Tree-Mendus Fruit** and **Crane Orchards.** Tree-Mendus, 9351 Eureka Rd., Eau Claire, 616/782-7101, is one of the area's best U-pick farms, with acres upon acres of apples, pears, cherries, apricots, peaches, plums, and more. Don't miss the chance to bite into one of the special antique apples, a hobby of the Tree-Mendus's owner. Besides the full fields, there's also a full roster of special events such as the International Cherry Pit Spitting Championship (now in its 24th year), pony rides, harvest time activities, and "fruit safaris." Call them or check their website, www.tree-mendus.com, for fruit availability and their calendar of special events from cherry-spitting contests to apple-picking.

In nearby Fennville, Crane Orchards, 6054 124th Ave. (M-89), 616/561-2297, has been in the Crane family for six generations. Almost better known than its U-pick orchard is its country-style **Pie Pantry Restaurant,** which serves up thick sandwiches on homemade bread and Lue Crane's signature pies. If you find yourself growing attached to the charms of farm life, the original farmstead now operates as a five-room bed and breakfast.

Near the intersection of I-94 and I-96, **Lake Michigan Hills,** 800/BIRDIES, has been voted the best public **golf** course in southwestern Michigan by *Michigan Golfer* magazine. It's also the annual qualifying site for both the Western and the United States Amateur golf tournaments.

## Festivals

Among southwestern Michigan's many warm-weather events, two highlights are the Blossomtime Festival, held the last weekend in April, and the Venetian Festival, held the third weekend in July. The **Blossomtime Festival** celebrates the coming of spring with a Grand Floral Parade featuring more than 30 community participants, more than 100 floats, bands, antique cars, food tents, children's events, and more. The **Venetian Festival** is held on the St. Joseph River channel and Silver Beach, with big-name entertainment, fireworks, food vendors, and the famous lighted boat parade.

## Accommodations

The **Boulevard Hotel,** 521 Lake Blvd., St. Joseph, 616/983-6600, overlooks Lake Michigan, with spacious suites and a genteel, old-world decor. Along with its terrific lake views, the Boulevard's downtown location is within easy walking distance to shops, restaurants, and beaches. Rates include a better-than-most continental breakfast of fresh juices, fruit, and pastries. $150–200. The **South Cliff Inn,** 1900 Lakeshore

Dr., St. Joseph, 616/983-4881, is a gracious English-inspired bed and breakfast with seven sun-filled rooms that also overlook the big lake. It's run by charming Bill Swisher, who left behind a 10-year career as director of a probate court to open the inn. Rates $75–125.

## Food

**Schu's Grill and Bar,** 501 Pleasant St., 616/983-7248, is quickly becoming a St. Joe institution, with great sandwiches, soups, and brews in a pub-style setting downtown above the waterfront. Enjoy sandwiches or a dinner menu that includes steaks and whitefish on the lovely outdoor terrace overlooking Lake Michigan at **Bistro on the Boulevard,** in the Boulevard Inn 616/983-6600. For morning coffee and baked goods, head for **Caffé Tosi,** 616/983-3354.

South of town, the **Grand Mère Inn,** 5800 Red Arrow Hwy., in Stevensville, 616/429-3591, is the place for an elegant (but expensive) dinner. The warm dining room overlooks a garden, a wide lawn, and the shore of Lake Michigan. Specialties include lake perch (it's becoming increasingly difficult to find this sweet, tender fish) and barbecued back ribs, a local favorite. Reservations recommended. Entrees $8–20.

## INLAND VINEYARDS

Thanks to the moderating effects of nearby Lake Michigan, a pocket of southwestern Michigan near Berrien Springs and Paw Paw basks in a microclimate surprisingly good for growing grapes. With its sandy soils, gently rolling terrain, and dependable snow cover needed to protect the fragile vines, it has been compared to the wine-producing regions of northern Europe, including France's renowned Champagne region.

While that may be wishful thinking, the state is indeed becoming more and more recognized for its winemaking. (Southwest Michigan is one of two recognized wine regions in the state; the other is farther north, in the Traverse City area.) Early on, wineries experimented with hardy but overly sweet grapes such as concord and catawba. As tastes grew more sophisticated and drier wines became the vogue, French hybrids were introduced, including vidal blanc, from white grapes, and chancellor and chambourcin, from red. Noteworthy successes include St. Julian's popular Simply Red and Lemon Creek's excellent chambourcin, which won a National Gold Medal from the American Wine Society.

"We're seeing a coming of age in Michigan wines," says Christopher Cook, former wine critic for the *Detroit Free Press.* "After a long struggle, Michigan wines are genuinely competitive with those of California and elsewhere." Now Michigan winemakers are attempting to build on their growing success, developing not only their grapes but their marketing sense. Like California, Michigan is working aggressively to promote the picturesque vineyards as a tourist attraction. On weekends, busloads of tourists pour into the St. Julian vineyards in Paw Paw for tours. Tabor Hill has a restaurant overlooking its gorgeous vineyards. Warner Vineyards has an elegant tasting room and a charming patio.

Each of the six vineyards in this part of the state indeed makes a pleasant warm-weather pilgrimage (most are open May–Oct.). You may wish to plan your visit for the weekend after Labor Day, when Paw Paw and Kalamazoo host a five-day **Michigan Wine & Harvest Festival,** featuring winetastings for a fee that benefits local charities. For more on Michigan wines, pick up a copy of the free *Michigan Wine Country* newspaper, available at vineyards, or contact the Michigan Grape and Wine Industry Council, 517/373-1104, website: www.michiganwines.com.

## Tabor Hill Winery

Today's Tabor Hill, 185 Mt. Tabor Rd., Buchanan, 616/422-1161, is a far cry from the winery's early commune-like days under visionary founder and salesman Len Olson. David Upton, an heir to the Whirlpool fortune, rescued the ailing operation in the late 1970s, eventually turning it into the state's second largest producing winery. If you're lucky, you'll catch winemaker Michael Merchant giving a tour. Winetastings and tours are offered May–early Oct., other times by appointment. The winery is best known for its mid-priced wines that use French hybrid grapes,

BOB RACE

including the classic demi-sec, known as the "President's Wine" because it has been served at the White House, the late harvest riesling, and the grand marque, all award-winners. Also recommended are the 1992–1996 chardonnays, the rieslings, and the proprietary blush made of vidal and other hybrid grapes.

After a tour or tasting, consider a stop at Tabor Hill's glass-walled restaurant, where you can watch workers tending the vines and songbirds crowding the feeders. Views sometimes stretch to the distant Lake Michigan dunes. Entrees such as mesquite-grilled shrimp and fresh Maryland soft-shell crabs are always first-rate and feature homemade breads and fresh-from-the-field ingredients. The restaurant is open year-round, Wed.–Sat. for lunch and dinner, Sun. for dinner only. Tabor Hill also has tasting centers in Bridgman and Saugatuck.

## Lemon Creek Vineyards

Lemon Creek, 533 Lemon Creek Rd., Berrien Springs, 616/471-1321, is six miles east of Lake Michigan near Berrien Springs. The young vineyards are part of a 150-year-old, 225-acre fruit farm that has been in the Lemon family (yes, it's their real name) for more than a century. At Lemon Creek tours, you can pick fresh fruit, savor award-winning wines, and follow the phases of wine production, from grape growing through bottling. The farm began growing grapes in the early 1980s as a way of diversifying crops. The winery opened in 1984, eventually drawing more than 100 awards. Well-known varietals include ruby rose, their vidal wines (dry, demi-sec, and semi-sweet), and the full-bodied red chancellor.

Visitors are welcome to wander among the neatly labeled vines outside the tasting room and picnic at the nearby tables. Afterward, sign on for one of the informal tours that give an overview of the winemaking process. If the tour inspires you to try your hand at winemaking at home, you can purchase pre-picked grapes or head out to the fields to pick your own. U-pick options also include raspberries, sweet and tart cherries, nectarines, pears, plums, peaches, and a variety of apples. The winery and farm is open year-round, daily May–Oct., weekends only Nov.–April.

### Heart of the Vineyard

Rick Moersch, formerly a winemaker at the Tabor Hill, began this 30-acre boutique winery, which is located at 10981 Hills Rd., between Berrien Springs and Baroda, 800/716-9463, in 1981. An 1880s post-and-beam farmhouse serves as the tasting room, where you can learn about the winery's unique winemaking style, which incorporates some new techniques pioneered at Michigan State University. A former science teacher, Moersch is more than willing to explain the winery's unique characteristics, including its choice of the French-influenced Alsatian style of winemaking, the unusual vine trellising system introduced by Michigan State University, and the necessity of yeast in making complex wines. The winery hosts several popular events, including a popular fall harvest festival, a free nouveau release party in December, and cross-country skiing in winter. The winery also has a tasting room in the Riviera Gardens in Union Pier. Open daily May–Oct., weekends only off-season.

### St. Julian Wine Company

Family-owned St. Julian, 716 S. Kalamazoo St., Paw Paw, 616/657-5568, has always prided itself on making good wines that are accessible to a wide variety of tastes and budgets. The winery is located on a busy commercial strip and is heavily marketed to tour buses and groups, so it isn't exactly on par with the personalized attention given by smaller boutique wineries. What the largest winery in the state does well is wine education and wine-related tourism: Its tours include an informative audiovisual show, and a visit to the bottling line and fermenting room. Visitors in late August and September can watch grapes being delivered and crushed. Attached to the winery is a tasting room and the Apollo café, which serves St. Julian varietals and Italian cuisine. The winery and its Union Pier tasting center are open year-round.

### Warner Vineyards

Next to St. Julian's, Warner Vineyards, 706 S. Kalamazoo, Paw Paw, 616/657-3165, operates out of an appealing 1898 waterworks building. It boasts the Midwest's only champagne cellar, which realistically simulates the chalk storage vaults of the Champagne region of France. Visitors can take a short, self-guided tour, then relax afterward over a glass of bubbly (or any of the 27 other Warner wines) on the charming wine deck. Warner's specialties include their award-winning dry champagne, a celebrated solera cream sherry, and the popular liebestrauben and holiberry. Open year-round.

## SOUTH HAVEN

Once the center of Michigan's "fruit belt," the South Haven area is still a leading producer of blueberries and peaches. Lake Michigan can take credit for the area's well-drained soil and the moderating temperature effects of the prevailing west winds. Southwest Michigan's fruit belt had its origins in the 1850s, when St. Joseph and Benton Harbor farmers noticed that their peaches survived the severe winters that killed off other crops in the rest of the state. Fresh fruit was in high demand in bustling Chicago, and by the 1860s, crops were being shipped across the lake almost as fast as they could be picked.

Eventually, fruit farming and fruit-related industries spread throughout much of Van Buren and Berrien Counties. South Haven became famous for its peach crop; at the turn of the century, some 144,000 acres were devoted to peaches, more than all the other fruit crops combined. But freezes during the 1920s led many farmers to abandon peach growing in favor of heartier apples. More recently, blueberries have gained popularity, with the area around South Haven emerging as the world's leading blueberry producer. Michigan has grown and sold up to 87 million pounds of blueberries in recent years. In July, you'll spot blueberry stands along rural roadsides. For blueberry products—some nice, some kitschy—check out the **Blueberry Store,** 525 Phoenix Rd., in downtown South Haven, 616/637-6322.

For more information on South Haven, contact the **South Haven/Van Buren County Lakeshore Convention and Visitors Bureau,** 415 Phoenix St., 800/764-2836.

## Sights and Recreation

South Haven proper is known for its beautiful beaches and scenic fishing port, prompting the *London Financial Times* to call it "one of the most picturesque and charming small fishing ports you could hope to find." In summer, the population of this lakeside town swells from 6,000 to nearly 20,000, as visitors fill the historic inns that line North Shore Drive, stroll along the walks and shops that parallel the Black River near its mouth, and sun on the long arc of sand beach that rims the town's northwestern edge.

The **Michigan Maritime Museum,** 260 Dyckman Ave., 616/637-8078, features a variety of maritime displays, chronicling Potawatomi who paddled in birchbark canoes and commercial fishermen who plied the local waters for lake trout. Hours are Tues.–Sat. 10 A.M.–5 P.M., Sun. noon–5 P.M.; admission is $2.50 adults, $1.50 ages 5–12.

**Van Buren State Park,** 23960 Ruggles Rd., South Haven, 616/637-2788, boasts some of the best water views in the this part of the state.

The park's high, wooded sand dunes hide a narrow opening leading to the 350-acre park's main attraction: the limitless blue waters of Lake Michigan edged by a broad sweep of fine, black-speckled sand. No Trespassing signs on the huge barrier dunes hope to prevent human erosion from adding to the natural wear of the fragile sand mountains.

The **Kal-Haven Trail,** open to hiking and biking, stretches from South Haven to Kalamazoo, with several access points along the 43-mile route. For information, contact Van Buren State Park (616/637-2788). Trail fees are $2 per person or $10 per family. Trail passes available at Van Buren State Park, the Lakeshore Convention and Visitors Bureau at 415 Phoenix St., and several area businesses.

## Accommodations

The **Old Harbor Inn,** 515 Williams St., 616/637-8480, is part of a New England–style waterfront shopping village downtown, on the banks of the Black River—a great location, with extras like an indoor pool. Rates $100–200. The **Last Resort B&B,** 86 North Shore Dr., 616/637-8943, was one of South Haven's first resorts. A few rooms have been updated with whirlpool suites, but the place has a funky, laid-back feel to it, largely due to its artist/owner Mary Hammer. All rooms offer views of Lake Michigan or the garden. It's open from late April through October. Rates $75–125. **Lake Bluff Motel,** 76648 11th Ave., 616/637-8531, is a mom-and-pop-style motel that has been well-kept and expanded, on a lovely bluff-top site south of South Haven, with outdoor pool and indoor hot tub. Rates $75–100.

## Camping

Like the area's other waterfront state parks, **Van Buren State Park** draws visitors because it offers a beach as well as the wooded dunes of Lake Michigan. Its 220 modern sites are a five-minute walk from the beach and frequently fill on summer weekends. Reservations highly recommended; contact 800/44-PARKS; website: dnr.state.mi.us.

## Food

**Clementine's Saloon,** at Phoenix and Center Streets, 616/637-4755, was originally a bank and is now a favorite restaurant. Don't miss the old pictures of Lake Michigan steamers and their captains and crews on the walls. The magnificently carved bar spent its first life on one of the many steamboats that once frequented the city. Specialties include the Claim Jumper (spinach, mushrooms, and crab on sautéed chicken breast with alfredo sauce). The **Magnolia Grille,** 515 Williams St., 616/637-8435, serves Cajun specialties, seafood, and prime rib on an authentic 1897 Mississippi riverboat moored in the Black River. The bow houses the kitchen and each of the staterooms serves as a private dining room, with (naturally) great views of the Black River harbor and marina. Try the Great Lakes perch or the Maui-Wowie sandwich, a juicy grilled teriyaki chicken breast.

# Saugatuck to Muskegon

## SAUGATUCK

Some claim success has spoiled Saugatuck. Visit on a summer weekend, and you may be inclined to agree, when the city's narrow streets fill with much of what urban refugees are looking to escape: long lines in restaurants, shops overstuffed with designer threads, and beaches clogged with humanity. But come in any other season—or even midweek in summer—and Saugatuck reveals its real charm. The streets quiet down; you can linger over, not rush through, the excellent local cuisine and rich arts scene. And the folks who run the village's many fine B&Bs kick back and remember why they got into the business to begin with.

Saugatuck ("River's Mouth" in the parlance of the Potawatomi tribe that settled the area), grew up in a fine natural setting—near the mouth of the wide Kalamazoo River, tucked between steep, rolling Lake Michigan dunes immediately west and lush, green orchards immediately east. Lumber interests discovered the region in the mid-1800s. Soon it was home to a thriving mix of sawmills, factories, and the people to support them. Saugatuck, in fact, produced the majority of the lumber used the rebuild Chicago after the Great Fire in 1871.

When the trees inevitably disappeared, so did much of the city. The lack of trees proved especially fateful to a neighboring village known as Singapore. Without the windbreak the trees provided, blowing sand carried by the prevailing western winds eventually buried the city. Today, this ghost town lives on in local lore and in stories told by area tour guides.

While Singapore became the stuff of legend, Saugatuck survived and found new life as an art colony. In 1914, the Art Institute of Chicago, less than two hours away, began sponsoring a summer camp. Lured by the warm breezes and picturesque location, other creative types soon followed, earning Saugatuck an early reputation as Michigan's "art coast." Today, the **Oxbow School of Art and Gallery** is still open to the public from mid-June through mid-August and includes galleries, demonstrations, and changing exhibitions. It's located at 1241 Park Street, near the foot of Mt. Baldhead. Call 616/857-5811 for more information.

Today's Saugatuck is one of the state's premier resort towns. Art continues to be one of the main draws. You can even see it in the public restrooms, its walls painted with scenes from Seurat's *A Sunday Afternoon on the Island of Grande Jatte.* For more information, contact the **Saugatuck/Douglas Convention and Visitors Bureau,** 2902 Blue Star Highway, 616/857-1701.

### Gallery Hopping and Shopping

Saugatuck offers some of the best shopping in West Michigan, with an eclectic mix of more than 50 stores and 25 art galleries, most housed in well-kept 19th-century storefronts. The stylish merchandise ranges from high-brow antiques and trendy housewares to a campy boutique that lures browsers and buyers with a pair of female mannequin legs dangling from a second-story window.

Most of the shops are clustered along Butler, the main street. A few highlights include **American Spoon Foods,** 308 Butler, a Petoskey-based operation that specializes in fruit spreads and other gourmet foodstuffs; the **Old Post Office Shop,** 238 Butler, with elegant imported papers and stationery; the **Singapore Bank Bookstore,** 317 Butler, saved from the sands when it was moved here; and **East of the Sun,** 252 Butler, a large and eclectic gift shop focusing on home accessories. Incense, jewelry, and metaphysical books are the specialty at **Mother Moon,** 127 Hoffman Street. If trendiness threatens to overwhelm you, head for a breather at **Wilkin's,** 439 Butler, the town's old-fashioned hardware store. Here you'll find reassuring necessities such as fertilizer, mailboxes, and garden gloves, as well as wicker and windsocks. It's been in business since 1864. Another old-timer is the long-popular **Saugatuck Drug Store Soda Fountain,** 201 Butler, which has attracted parched tourists and locals since 1913 with phosphates and other authentic soda fountain treats.

The area's reputation as an art coast initially attracted galleries, and they're still coming. Notable stops include the **Button Gallery,** 955 Center, 616/857-2175, with its spectacular outdoor sculpture garden; the **Cain Gallery,** 322 Butler, 616/857-4353, specializing in Midwestern artists; and the eclectic **Good Goods,** 106 Mason St., 616/857-1557, housed in a restored Victorian boardinghouse. Good Goods is the only place in town where you can pick up a one-of-a-kind piece by one of the area's founding artists, Sylvia Randolph Bekker, amazingly prolific into her 90s. The **Joyce Petter Gallery,** 161 Blue Star Hwy., 616/857-7861, has been western Michigan's largest fine art marketplace for more than 20 years. It's housed in a landmark building in nearby Douglas.

## Other Attractions

The SS *Kewatin,* 616/857-2107, is hard to miss. Docked near the bridge that separates Saugatuck from neighboring Douglas, the 350-foot-long cruise ship had to be cut in half to fit through the narrow channel linking Lake Michigan and the Kalamazoo River. Now reassembled as a tourist attraction, it's a fascinating tribute to a lost era. The *Kewatin* was built in 1907, one of the last of the steamships that plied the Great Lakes. Informative tours show off its ornate mahogany interior, and relive the elegant era when passengers toured the lakes to revel in their beauty, fresh air, and fine beaches.

The two-level sternwheeler docked on the riverfront, the ***Queen of Saugatuck,*** offers cruises along the Kalamazoo River. Along the way, she passes beautiful homes, including one that once belonged to gangster Al Capone. (Keep in mind that in the Midwest, Capone apparently lived in as many places as Lincoln slept.) It operates May through October. For trip times and rates, call Saugatuck Boat Cruises, 616/857-4261.

If you're seeking a little more solitude, head instead for 1,100-acre **Saugatuck Dunes State Park** north of town. Despite two miles of undeveloped beach and dunes, and 14 miles of well-marked trails (some winding to the top of the dunes for fantastic views), only about 40,000 visit annually—the least-visited park along this popular shoreline. Just three miles from downtown, the park offers easy-to-reach serenity in stark contrast to downtown Saugatuck. No camping or park office here; for information, contact Holland State Park, 616/399-9390.

Just a few steps from the shop-lined streets, the frilly gingerbread **Chain Ferry,** 616/857-4243 shuttles visitors across the Kalamazoo River to the sandy Lake Michigan shore at **Oval Beach.** Families flock to this popular beach, filling the broad ribbon of sand and scaling Mt. Baldhead, the steep dune that rises between downtown and the beach.

## Accommodations

With more than 30 bed and breakfasts and no large hotels or chains in the downtown, Saugatuck is fast becoming one of the B&B capitals of the Midwest. The **Twin Oaks Inn,** 227 Griffith St., 616/857-1600, is among the friendliest of the inns, with spacious rooms in an 1860 English-style inn that also have portable cribs and pull-out beds for families.

There's even a resident "grandma"—owner Nancy Horney's mother, Kay, who oversees the property (but unfortunately doesn't baby-sit!). Rates $100–150.

An 1860s Greek Revival building adjacent to the village square has served as a luxury resort hotel for more than 130 years. Today it does business as the **Maplewood Hotel,** 428 Butler St., 616/857-1771, with 15 antique-filled bedrooms in the heart of the city's shops, galleries, and restaurants. The hotel includes five suites with double whirlpool tubs; some have fireplaces. Breakfast is served in the Burr Tillstrom Dining Room, named for former Saugatuck resident and the creator of Kukla, Fran, and Ollie (a once-popular children's puppet show). Rates $125–250.

The **Wickwood Country Inn,** 510 Butler St., Saugatuck, 800/385-1174, is owned by Julee Rosso Miller, co-author of the *Silver Palate* cookbook series, who treats guests at her B&B with seasonal menus she created herself. But that's not the only special touch at this art-filled inn, recognized by magazines ranging from *Country Inns* and *Bon Appétit* to *Midwest Living.* The 11 guest rooms are lavishly decorated with English and French country antiques, featherbeds, and antique linens. Rates $125–225.

The **Bayside Inn,** 618 Water St., 616/857-4321, once a boathouse, is a lovely inn with fireplace suites and rooms right on the Kalamazoo River waterfront, steps from downtown. Rates $100–175. Across the river, the family-friendly **Beach Way Resort,** 106 Perryman, 616/857-3331, sits at the foot of the dunes near Oval Beach, with an outdoor pool. Rates $75–175.

If you're looking for more economical options, head away from the water and toward the Blue Star Highway, where you'll find simple motels like the **Captain's Quarters Motel,** 3242 Blue Star Hwy., 616/857-2525. Rates $50–125.

## Camping

Located on Goshorn Lake just west of I-196, **Saugatuck Campground,** 800/336-9724, has grassy, shady sites and a stretch of private beach. Paddleboats, kayaks, and canoes are available for rent.

## Food

**Loaf and Mug,** 236 Culver St., 616/857-2974, is a comfortable, casual eatery/winery/bakery that serves breakfast and lunch daily. The restaurant's signature dish is a hollowed out round loaf of bread filled with the steaming soup du jour. An airy backyard terrace opens up for dining in season. Entrees $8–15. Locals know **Ida Red's Cottage,** 645 Water St., 616/857-5803, for the best breakfast in town, served all day. Specialties include dishes with a Greek or Italian flair, like the delectable Italian sausage omelets. Entrees $5–9.

Pick up an overstuffed sandwich for a carryout picnic at **Pumpernickel's Eatery,** 202 Butler, 616/857-1196, though you may want to eat there when you spot the restaurant's great patio and sun deck. Entrees $4–9. **Chequers,** 220 Culver St., 616/857-1868, is a bit of London in western Michigan, with a pubby atmosphere of dark paneled walls, stained glass, and lots of leather. Classic Brit-inspired grub includes shepherd's pie, fish and chips, and bangers and mash. There's also a good variety of ales and beer. Note: Reservations are not accepted, so expect a wait at peak hours. Entrees $10–18.

The **Global Bar and Grill,** 215 Butler, 616/857-1555, is a rustic-style bistro and one of the those rare restaurants popular with both families and singles. It has Kraft-papered tables with crayons and an avant-garde menu with many Southwestern-inspired specialties such as grilled shrimp with mango salsa. Entrees $6–17. The **Restaurant Toulouse,** 248 Culver St., 616/857-1561, features French country cuisine in a Provençal-inspired setting, complete with tableside fireplaces. Specialties include cassoulet, rack of lamb, veal scaloppine, and a killer chocolate fondue. Entrees $15–25.

## HOLLAND

For years, people of Dutch ancestry dominated the city of Holland, just north of Saugatuck on I-196. In fact, the city remained 90 percent Dutch for more than a century—an impressive demographic in today's melting-pot world. While the ethnic makeup is a bit more

© VITO PALMISANO

**De Zwaan Windmill**

varied today (Holland is also home to the state's largest Hispanic community, a fact that gets noticeably less press), many local families can still trace their roots back to the 1840s, when Dutch separatists settled in this part of the Midwest. Whatever their original heritage, however, Holland's residents know it's the Dutch touch that brings thousands of visitors each year, and they are quick to roll out the "welkom" mat for visitors.

The city hits its stride in mid-May, when the annual **Tulip Time Festival** is in full bloom. Then, the almost-too-quaint downtown streets are a rainbow of flowers (and a jam of tour buses) as well as costumed *klompen* dancers, local bands, and parades. For a schedule of events, call 800/822-2770.

For more information on Holland, contact the **Holland Area Convention and Visitors Bureau,** 76 East 8th St., 800/506-1299, website: www.holland.org.

## Sights

Holland clings proudly to its Dutch heritage at

spots like **Veldheer Tulip Gardens,** 12755 Quincy St., 616/399-1900 (along US-31). Even if you find parts of town overly commercial, you'll be charmed by the sheer spectacle of this rainbow of blooms that take center stage in the spring, followed by more perennials such as lilies and peonies, then annuals from June through October. Beds are numbered to correspond with mail-order catalogs, so visitors can place orders for bulbs and flowering plants after seeing the real thing. Locals recommend visiting the gardens at dusk, when the tour buses are gone and sunset casts a warm glow on the thousands of beautiful blooms.

Adjacent to the gardens, the **De Klomp Wooden Shoe & Delft Factory** remains the only working Delft production factory in the United States. Strategically placed windows allow visitors to watch the crisp blue and white china being made by hand and see craftsmen carve wooden shoes on well-worn Dutch machinery. A gift shop sells the stuff to take home, of course.

Holland's treasure presides over Windmill Island on the east end of town. The 230-year old

**De Zwaan** ("The Swan") was shipped to Michigan in 1964, the last authentic windmill the Dutch government allowed to leave the Netherlands. Guides today give careful and thorough tours of the wooden windmill, lovingly reconstructed and still operating, its massive 40-foot blades spinning in the wind and grinding wheat into flour. "And when it's running, it barely makes a sound," the tour guide notes proudly. "It's quite a marvel of machinery."

De Zwaan serves as the centerpiece of a variety of Dutch displays in **Windmill Island Municipal Park** at 7th St. and Lincoln Ave., 616/396-5433, including reconstructed buildings like the tile-roofed 14th-century Posthouse, an authentic Dutch carousel, and **Little Netherlands,** a 50-foot-long model village, complete with canals, farms, a cheese market, and, naturally, windmills.

City residents are justly proud of two neat-as-a-pin local museums, the **Holland Museum,** 31 W. 10th St., 616/392-9084, and the **Cappon House,** 228 W. 9th St., 616/392-6740. Together they contain more than 400 years of Dutch and American heritage, with displays that cover the city's 150-year history. Both are open year-round; call for hours and admission fees.

The long, broad beach at **Holland State Park,** 2215 Ottawa Beach Rd., 616/399-9390, is one of the most accessible and beautiful in the Lower Peninsula, with a staunch red lighthouse to boot. Like the other state parks along this stretch of the Lake Michigan shore, it attracts sunbathers by the hundreds on weekends. Facilities include a bathhouse, a dozen or so well-used sand volleyball courts, and two large campgrounds. Lake Michigan fishing can be quite good from shore. Nearby **Holland Water Sports,** 2212 Ottawa Beach Rd., 616/786-2628, rents boats and offers parasail rides. **Papa Donn's Bike Rental,** 2250 Ottawa Beach Rd., rents from Memorial Day weekend through Labor Day.

## Accommodations

The **Dutch Colonial Inn,** 560 Central Ave., 616/396-3664, has five nonsmoking rooms and a complimentary full breakfast in a restored 1928 home. Whirlpools, full breakfasts, and warm Dutch hospitality make this inn a safe bet. Rates $75–150. What's in a name? **Parsonage 1908,** 6 E. 24th St., 616/396-1316, is housed in a former Dutch parsonage built in 1908. It offers four guest rooms, a conservatory/porch, and an outdoor patio. Rates $100–125. Away from downtown but near Dutch Village, try the reliable and affordable **Country Inn by Carlson,** 12260 James St., 616/396-6677. Like many places in town, it's decorated with Delft tiles and country decor. Of its 116 guest rooms, 24 have in-room whirlpools. Rates $75–100. **Fairfield Inn,** 2854 W. Shore Dr., 616/786-9700, is another economical choice, with clean rooms, some with microwaves and fridges. Rates $75–100.

## Camping

**Holland State Park,** 2215 Ottawa Beach Rd., 616/399-9390, has 368 sites in two units, one near Lake Michigan, the other near inland Lake Macatawa. Most sites are quite close together with little shade. Chances are you'll be spending most of your time by the water anyway, right?

## Food

Housed in a gray batten-board structure, **Piper Restaurant,** 2225 S. Shore Dr., Macatawa, 616/335-5866, overlooks Lake Macatawa and is known for its extensive seafood selection and bountiful Sunday brunch. Save room for the signature dessert, a rum vanilla custard. Reservations recommended. Entrees $13–18. It's hard to believe, but the **Queen's Inn at Dutch Village,** US-31 at James St., 616/393-0310, claims to be the only area restaurant with Dutch cuisine. Order strudel. Entrees $8–15.

In downtown Holland on 8th Street, **Butch's,** 616/396-8227, serves up great New York–style deli sandwiches to eat on site or pack for a picnic, along with specialty cheeses, wines, and more. The **Alpen Rose Restaurant and Cafe,** 4 E. 8th St., 616/393-2111, specializes in Wienerschnitzel, chicken shortcake, and other Austrian dishes in an authentic old-world atmosphere complete with carvings by master German woodworkers adorning the ceilings and paneling. European pastries are a popular menu item, also available for carryout. Entrees $7–16.

# MUSKEGON AND VICINITY

The largest town along this stretch of Lake Michigan shoreline with more than 40,000 year-round residents, Muskegon has its roots in white pine. The deep Muskegon River that flows through town, into Lake Muskegon, and on to Lake Michigan proved the perfect route for transporting timber from the rich inland pine forests to the city's sawmills.

Muskegon's first sawmill went up in 1837. In the following 50 years, the frontier town grew at a feverish pace: By the 1880s, it was known throughout the world as a lumber metropolis, home to 47 sawmills and at least as many saloons, dance halls, and gambling joints—earning the city nicknames that ranged from "Lumber Queen of the North," to the more unsavory "Red Light Queen."

Muskegon was unprepared for the day just a decade or so later when the area's timber was tapped. Mills soon closed or were mysteriously torched. By the 1890s, the region's lumber industry and population declined steadily. By the 1950s, the city teetered on the brink of ruin—until tourists took over where timber left. After decades of decline in industry and self-image, Muskegon is finally rising from the sawdust. While many parts of the city still have a tattered feel, Muskegon is focusing on its positives, which include more than 26 miles of Lake Michigan shoreline, West Michigan's most extensive lakeshore park system, outstanding cultural and historical resources, and a lively multiethnic population—refreshing in a part of the state so dominated by the Dutch.

For more information, contact the **Muskegon County Convention and Visitors Bureau,** 610 W. Western Ave., 800/250-WAVE, website: www.visitmuskegon.org.

## Sights

The lumber barons in Muskegon left behind grand homes—since lovingly restored—that preservationists point to as some of the finest Queen Annes in North America. The **Hackley & Hume Historic Site,** West Webster at 6th St., 231/722-0278, includes two mansions built by lumber magnates Charles Hackley and Thomas

Hume in the late 1800s. These flamboyant homes feature some 28 shades of paint, lavish woodcarving, stained glass, and high Victorian furnishings. Call for tour times.

Charles Hackley also donated to Muskegon one of the finest art museums in the state. The **Muskegon Museum of Art,** 296 West Webster, 231/720-2570, is a surprise for a city of this size, with a permanent collection that includes the well-known *Tornado Over Kansas* by John Stuart Curry, Whistler's *Study in Rose and Brown, Tea Time* by William Merritt Chase, and works by Winslow Homer, Edward Hopper, and Andrew Wyeth. Another surprise is the largest collection of works by painter Françoise Gilot, best known as Picasso's mistress and mother to their daughter, Paloma. Open Tues.–Fri. 10 A.M.–5 P.M.; free.

**Muskegon County Museum,** 430 W. Clay at 4th, 231/722-0278, recounts the city's colorful logging past, including details about the dangerous life in the city's lumber camps. Don't miss the murals of Muskegon's history in the basement, done for the Lumberman's Bank in 1929. Other exhibits explore the area's geology, early Native Americans, and the now-extinct passenger pigeons that were once common in this region.

The USS *Silversides,* 1346 Bluff, near Pere Marquette Park, 231/755-1230, commemorates life at sea during World War II. Completed just after the attack on Pearl Harbor in 1942, the *Silversides* went on to sink 23 ships, the third highest total of all U.S. warships that served in the second World War. Now a National Historic Landmark, the *Silversides* remains in excellent condition, with original furnishings including bunks, sonar equipment, radios, and furniture. The tour gives a good feel of what it was like to go out on a 45-day tour deep into enemy territory. Tours offered daily June–Aug., less frequently in April, May, September, and October.

Almost a half million swimmers, beachcombers, surfers, sailboarders, boaters, campers, and picnickers descend each year on **Muskegon State Park,** 3560 Memorial Dr., North Muskegon, 231/744-3480. Despite the large numbers, most visitors head for the beach, leaving the rest of the park rather uncrowded. Its 1,357 acres actually feel more like several small parks, divided into swimming, fishing, and hiking areas. In winter, the park is best known for its **Muskegon Winter Sports Complex,** 231/774-9629, which includes one of just two luge runs in the nation. (The other is in Lake Placid, New York). On winter weekends, you can sign up for a quick lesson and give it a try yourself. Speeds reach up to 40 miles per hour, careening down the ice-covered wooden chute—and seem terribly faster on a sled made of wood, metal, and canvas. The luge is open on weekends only; a day's pass includes a sled, helmet, and coach. First-timers are fully supervised. Fees are $20–30 per adult; $15–25 children 12 and under (fees depend on whether you choose the upper or lower luge track). The park is also a favorite of cross-country skiers, who find some of the longest lighted trails in the state. The area enjoys a long season, thanks to reliable lake effect snows.

The **Gillette Sand Dunes Visitors Center** at **P. J. Hoffmaster State Park,** 6585 Lake Harbor Rd., Muskegon, 231/798-3711, gives an excellent introduction to dune history and ecology. Slide shows, dioramas, and colorful displays demonstrate the natural forces that shaped and continue to shape the face of these majestic mountains of sand. Besides the center, the 1,150-acre park contains two miles of shoreline, towering dunes that stand guard over a sandy beach, deep forest, interdunal valleys, 10 miles of hiking and cross-country trails (also popular with snowshoers in winter), and a very good campground.

Muskegon also has plenty to offer for those looking for more commercial amusements. Together, **Michigan's Adventure Amusement Park** and **Wild Water Adventure Water Park,** 4750 Whitehall Rd., 231/766-3377, make up the state's largest amusement and water park, with more than 20 rides (including the state's only two roller coasters), as well as 11 water slides, a wave pool, children's activity pool, and more. Open Memorial Day–Labor Day.

## Accommodations

Overlooking Muskegon Lake, the **Port City Victorian Inn,** 1259 Lakeshore Dr., 231/759-0205, built in 1877, has five guest rooms and a rooftop balcony with great views of the lake. Rates $75–150. The **Holiday Inn Muskegon Harbor,** 939 3rd St., 800/846-5253, has a good location in the heart of Muskegon. Amenities include an indoor pool and health club. Rates $100–125. Another franchise choice: The **AmeriHost Inn,** 4677 Harvey St., 800/434-5800, a new and attractive chain motel with indoor pool on US-31. Rates $75–125.

## Camping

**Muskegon State Park,** 3560 Muskegon Dr. in North Muskegon, 231/744-3480, has three campgrounds with a total of 350 sites. If you're tent camping, opt for the Lake Michigan Campground, since many sites aren't appropriate for RVs. While not on the water, the campground is protected by tall maples and beaches and tucked behind dunes, with an easy walk to the beach. At the south of town, **Hoffmaster State Park,** 6585 Lake Harbor Rd., Muskegon, MI 49441, 231/798-3711, has 348 modern sites in a sandy grove of white pines. Reservations recommended for both parks in summer, 800/44-PARKS; website: dnr.state.mi.us.

## Food

The **Doo Drop Inn,** 2410 Henry St., 231/755-3791, has been a Muskegon favorite for more than 60 years, known as a place with good, solid food. Unfussy fare includes baby back ribs, huge 22-ounce Porterhouses, beef kabobs, and a stuffed cabbage roll dinner. Entrees $6–17. Also try **Tony's,** 785 W. Broadway, 231/739-7196, for steaks, pasta, and Greek specialties.

## Grand Haven

Just a few miles south of Muskegon, the lakeside town of Grand Haven focuses its attention on the waterfront—in particular, the boardwalk that traces the Grand River's south bank from downtown to the river's mouth at Lake Michigan. The 2.5-mile waterfront boardwalk is full of places to shop, eat, and stroll. The walk wanders past the city's vintage railroad station, now the **Tri-Cities Historical Museum,** where a "puffer belly" steam locomotive and three rail cars sit idle. It ends at **Chinook Pier,** where many of the area's Great Lakes fishing boats dock and display the day's catch. Across the street, shops fill the **Harbourfront Place,** a renovated Story & Clark Piano Company factory. Hang around the harbor at dusk, and you'll be treated to a burst of music and a revolving blast of colored lights, as Grand Haven's **musical fountain** begins to spray and dance in a choreographed half-hour show. The fountain is a beloved tradition in this resort town and plays every summer evening.

Connected to downtown by the city's popular boardwalk, you won't find solitude at **Grand Haven State Park,** 231/798-3711, but you will find a sandy swimming beach and convenient campground. The campground has 187 modern sites, mostly in an open area near the water. Reservations highly recommended, 800/44-PARKS; website: dnr.state.mi.us. The park is located one mile southwest of US-31 on Harbor Avenue.

Grand Haven and surrounding Ottawa County claim more than 100 miles of **bicycle paths.** (Most are also open to in-line skates, roller skis and other recreational uses.) The 15-mile Lakeside Trail circles inland Spring Lake, a lovely ride. The Lakeshore Connector Path links Grand Haven to Holland, 30 miles south, utilizing some sidewalks but mostly a paved off-road route near the Lake Michigan shore. The 26-mile-long Musketawa Trail runs from Marne in east Ottawa County toward Muskegon. For more information on bike trails, contact the Grand Haven/Spring Lake Area Visitors Bureau (see below).

Grand Haven is a little slim in the accommodations department. (And if you're traveling with a dog, forget it.) Your best bets tend to be chain operations along US-31 like the newly renovated **Best Western Beacon Motel,** 1525 S. Beacon Blvd., 616/842-4720, for basic motel rooms with coffeemakers and free movies. Rates $100–150. Another choice is the **Days Inn,** 1500 S. Beacon Blvd., 616/842-1999, with an on-site restaurant/coffee shop. Rates $75–125.

For dining, try the **Kirby Grill,** 2 Washington St., 616/846-3299, for fresh fish in a historic building in the heart of downtown, and the **Stable Inn,** 11880 US-31, 616/846-8581, for steaks, seafood, and pretty good Mexican fare.

For more information on the Grand Haven area, contact the **Grand Haven/Spring Lake Area Visitors Bureau,** One South Harbor Drive, Grand Haven, 800/968-0892, website: www.grandhavenchamber.org.

## Whitehall/Montague

About 12 miles north of Muskegon, the sleepy twin towns of Whitehall and Montague are friendly rivals. Both sit on US-31 at the head of White Lake, both have weathervane manufacturers, drugstores with soda fountains, and two well-known bakeries (Riverview Cafe and Bakery in Whitehall; Robinson's in Montague, known for its Swedish-style breads and cookies), and both fill up with summer people during the high season. Friendly and unfussy, they're good places to wander in and out of nautical- and country-themed stores, watch the swans in the White River marsh, enjoy a root beer at the Dog 'N' Suds, and take in the sunsets and sailboats at the new marina that separates White Lake from the White River.

The **Hart-Montague Trail** stretches 22 miles along the former C&O Railroad right of way between Hart and Montague. The smooth paved surface is popular for hiking, biking, and in-line skating. It leads north from Montague, passing through high sandy hills and orchards between Muskegon and Ludington, and an area renowned as the United States' top producer of apples, tart cherries, and Christmas trees. Small towns along the trail have a rural 1940s feel; a map available at trailheads lists area restaurants, B&Bs, and bike rentals. For more information on the trail, contact Silver Lake State Park, 231/873-2817.

Famous as a logging river, the **White River** offers some wonderful paddling—the river feels more remote than many of the longer and better-known rivers farther north. On early morning and late afternoon floats, you'll share the waters with blue herons, sandhill cranes, and an occasional beaver. The narrow river winds between steep, forested banks, across marshy flats, and through the Manistee National Forest, a hardwood and conifer forest that hasn't seen a logger since the 19th century. Within the forest, the river has been designated a wild and scenic river, which means that timber on the floodplain can't be cut. Access points to the river can be hard to find; one of the easiest solutions is to arrange for a rental through the **Happy Mohawk Canoe Livery,** 735 Fruitvale Rd., 231/894-4209. The livery rents canoes, kayaks, inner tubes, and rafts. Happy Mohawk also owns the nearby **White River Campground,** 735 Fruitvale Rd. (off County B-86), 231/894-4708, in a heavily wooded valley near little Sand Creek. The facility includes 227 sites, along with camping cabins along the creek, a heated pool, and playground. Open May–Oct.

# North to Manistee

As you continue north up the Lake Michigan shoreline, towns grow sparser, summer crowds thin, and beaches climb into windswept dunes. If you're looking for a quiet beachwalk or mellow waterfront town without a full parade of activities and attractions, this may be the stretch of shore for you.

## PENTWATER AND SILVER LAKE

### Pentwater

Once considered a sleepy town along the Lake Michigan shore, the Victorian logging town of Pentwater ticks along at a pleasant—but not frantic—summer pace. On Hancock Street, Pentwater's main drag, visitors prowl through a growing number of antique shops, searching for turn-of-the-century treasures and nautical artifacts. A parade of pleasure boats purr through the boat channel that links Pentwater Lake and Lake Michigan, accompanied by folks strolling along the Channel Lane Park walkway. **Charles Mears State Park,** 231/869-2051, seems more like a city beach than a state park, right in town on the north side of the boat channel.

Get a taste of the gracious resort era at the grand old **Nickerson Inn,** 262 W. Lowell St., 231/869-6731. The 1914 home sits serenely atop an hilly emerald lawn just one block east of the state park. Rates $100–250. Another nice lodging choice is the **Pentwater Inn,** 231/869-5909, an 1860s gingerbread Victorian just a few minutes from the beach. Rates $75–150.

The **Nickerson Inn** also offers the best fine dining in town, with dishes like grilled salmon with cherry/chipotle chutney and cognac peppercorn duck. **Gull Landing,** 438 S. Hancock, 231/869-4215, has a kid-pleasing breakfast buffett and outside dining overlooking Pentwater Lake.

### Silver Lake

Between Silver Lake and Lake Michigan lie more than 2,000 acres of unspoiled and ever-shifting sand dunes, remnants of the glaciers that once scrubbed this landscape. They are one of the largest deposits of dunes on the shores of Lake Michigan, acre after acre of ridges and valleys of wind-blown sand that are void of trees, scrub, or in many places, even dune grass. Most of the dunes are protected at **Silver Lake State Park,** 231/873-3083, with hiking trails that climb high sand hills and weave through grasses and stunted trees. (You may wish to come early in the day—the northern portion of the park is open to off-road vehicles, which create a loud and obnoxious intrusion.) The park and dunes are located on one of the westernmost spots of the state's shoreline, a broad point that extends more than seven miles out from the main shore.

The Wood family once owned most this land, and sold it to the state in 1973. They retained the right to use about 700 acres at the park's south end to operate **Mac Wood's Dune Rides,** 231/873-2817. Visitor load into hybrid buggy/trucks for a seven-mile drive through the dunes, roaring up and down hills and splashing along the Lake Michigan surf line. While it's easy to question this kind of use of the dunes, the operation does make an effort to help visitors understand and appreciate the area ecology. Open daily mid-May through October; call for specific times. $12 adults, $8 children 11 and under.

# LUDINGTON AND VICINITY

Because of its mid-point position on Lake Michigan and its ample supply of lumber, Ludington enjoyed a boom as a busy port during the latter half of the 19th century. (Originally named Père Marquette in honor of the missionary explorer who died here in 1675, the city later changed it's name to reflect the influence of its more recent founder, James Ludington, a lumber baron.) Today visitors are drawn to its enormous expanse of sugar sand beach—or to the $50,000 prize in the **American Salmon Derby,** held each year late in August and early in September. As you'll see from the busy marina in the heart of town, fishing and boating are the pulse of this appealing community.

For more information on the Ludington area, contact the **Ludington Area Convention and Visitors Bureau,** 5827 W. US-10, 800/542-4600, website: www.ludingtoncvb.com.

## Lake Michigan Carferry

Ludington is also home to the Great Lakes' only trans-lake car ferry, offering sailings twice each day in summer between Ludington and Manitowoc, Wisconsin. This historic car ferry, the *S.S. Badger,* is the sole survivor of the fleet of auto/train/passenger ferries that once plowed across Lake Michigan. Ferries were to the Great Lakes what steamboats were to the Mississippi, linking Midwestern cities such as Chicago, Muskegon and Milwaukee. The first steamer, the *Pere Marquette,* was hailed as a "titan of size and power." These hard-working vessels were owned by the railroads, and were even equipped with rails in their holds, so they could load box cars, as well as automobiles and passengers.

The 410-foot Badger was built in 1952 and accommodates more than 600 passengers and 180 cars. The ship has public areas with chairs and tables, snack bars, staterooms, a gift shop, a maritime museum, a video game arcade, and a slew of cornball entertainment ranging from singalongs to bingo. But for most, the trip is entertainment enough, a chance to relax on deck, watch the water and peer over the blue horizon for that first glimpse of land.

The Badger operates daily from mid-May through mid-October. For specific times and rates, contact the Lake Michigan Carferry, 800/841-4243, website: www.ssbadger.com.

## Ludington State Park

Ludington State Park, 231/843-8671, is one of the state's finest outdoor playgrounds and the second largest state park in the Lower Peninsula. Attendance ranks in the top ten of all Michigan state parks, with good reason. The park encompasses more than 5,000 acres of beautiful beaches, almost six miles of Lake Michigan shoreline, dunes and forests that wrap around picnic areas, bike and hiking paths, three campgrounds, an interesting intrepretive center, an inland lake and a canoe trail.

The park occupies a wide strip of land between Lake Michigan and Hamlin Lake, straddling the Big Sable River, which connects them. The 11 trails that lace the park's interior are among the finest foot paths in the Lower Peninsula. They offer everything from a leisurely half-hour stroll to a rather strenuous six-mile round-trip trek to the 1867 Big Sable Point Light Station, painted in tiers of black and white, which stands guard over Au Sable Point. Trudging through sand is tiring on the calves, but the view from the top of the light tower ($2 fee) makes it all worth it.

At Hamlin Lake, a canoe pathway winds along the lakeshore and weaves through marshes and ponds. Canoe rentals ($6/hour, $30/day) are available at the park's Hamlin Lake concession area. Bring along a fishing rod—walleye, northern pike and panfish all thrive here.

## Lodging

**Snyder's Shoreline Inn,** 903 W. Ludington Ave., 231/845-1261, is Snyder's Shoreline Inn, Ludington, just steps from Lake Michigan and downtown. It offers a variety of rooms and cottages, with rates from $75–275. The **Lamplighter Bed and Breakfast,** 602 E. Ludington Ave., 231/843-9792, is a Victorian-inspired inn in a 100-year-old home, with five guest rooms, original paintings, lithographs and antiques througout. There's even a resident cocker spaniel. Rates $125–150.On Hamlin Lake, **Sauble Resort,** 231/843-8497, has housekeeping cottages overlooking the dunes and near the state park. Rates begin at $325 per week. A good economical choice is the **Four Seasons Motel,** 717 E. Ludington Ave., 231/843-3448, a smoke-free motel with nice garden patio. Rates $75–125.

## Camping

**Ludington State Park,** 231/843-8671, has nearly 400 sites to choose from in three campgrounds, as well as three rustic mini cabins. For reservations, call 800/44-PARKS; website: dnr.state.mi.us. **Mason County Campground and Picnic Area,** 5906 W. Chauvez Rd., Ludington, 231/845-7609, has 50 modern sites and a wooded picnic area set among tall trees. A paved path leads visitors to Vista Point, a scenic overlook above Lake Michigan.

## Good Eating

**Gibb's Country House Restaurant,** between Ludington and Scottville at 3951 W. US 10, 231/845-0311, has been a Ludington institution since 1947, known for their huge, home-baked sticky buns and all-you-can-eat dessert bar. Three large dining rooms have menus that change seasonally and are usually organized around a theme, including the spring Asparagus Festival and the autumn harvest. Reservations recommended. Entrees: $9–18. **House of Flavors,** 402 W. Ludington Ave., 231/845-5785, also has been around forever, serving up the best breakfast in town and the best ice cream too, homemade in more than 30 flavors.

**P.M. Steamers,** 502 W. Loomis, 231/843-9555, is a casual waterfront eatery across from the city marina with a great view and equally fine fare, including the famous "nutty walleye," turtle cheesecake and a well-known Sunday brunch. The restaurant has a tradition of ringing the Captain's bell each time a ferry arrives or departs, which can be a bit disconcerting if unexpected. Reservations recommended. Entrees: $11–22.

# MANISTEE AND VICINITY

## Manistee

Manistee's slogan is "Manistee: A Great Place to Be." While the city's downtown is a charming mix of historic logging buildings and ornate Victorian mansions, much of the credit for that claim goes to the wonderful Manistee National Forest (see below) that lies just outside the city limits. In fact, the national forest is such a part of Manistee's psyche that the city honors it with the annual **National Forest Festival** each July.

Manistee serves as a good base camp for exploring the forest, as well as an exceptionally lovely and untouched stretch of Lake Michigan shoreline. The **Best Western Manistee,** 200 Arthur St., 231/723-9949, has 72 regular rooms and four two-bedroom condos as well as a sauna, on-site restaurant and pool. Rates $50–100. The **Days Inn,** 1462 Manistee Hwy., 231/723-8385, has an indoor pool and spa, and a nice location at the south end of town near the scenic river walk. Rates $75–150. The mom-and-pop **Hillside Motel,** 1675 US-31 South, 231/723-2584, offers clean, simple rooms for $50–125.

For food, try **Four Forty West,** 440 W. River St., 231/723-7902, which has a great Sunday brunch, prime rib specials on Wednesday, fresh seafood in season, a salad bar and more in a casual, riverfront atmosphere. Entrees: $7–18.

For more information on the Manistee area, contact the **Manistee County Visitors and Convention Bureau,** 877/626-4783, website: www.visitmanistee.com.

## Manistee National Forest

Manistee National Forest stretches from Manistee south to Muskegon, almost a half-million acres of woods, beaches, dunes, and two fine paddling rivers, the Pine and Pere Marquette. Most notable of the national forest's many attractions is the **Nordhouse Dunes Wilderness Area,** a 3,450-acre swath of untouched dunes and dune forest. It is the only federally designated wilderness in Michigan's Lower Peninsula, and the only federal dune wilderness in the nation.

The wilderness area includes three miles of

isolated Lake Michigan beach, where dunes reaching more than 140 feet. From the beach, 10 miles of hiking trails spin inland. Because they are minimally signed, bring a map and compass, along with plenty of water. Back-country camping is permitted in the wilderness more than 200 feet from the waterline. The adjacent Nordhouse Dunes Recreation Area offers a modern camp-ground with potable water.

Hikers should seek out the **Manistee River Trail,** a 10-mile route that follows the east bank of the Manistee River. The trail offers plenty of diversity, scaling steep slopes, meandering through pine and hardwood for-est, dipping through ferny glades and crossing several creeks. It is open to foot traffic only. The north trailhead is near the south end of the Hodenpyl Dam, which is east of Manistee. (Got that?) Pick up a map at the ranger office.

For paddlers, the **Pine National Scenic River** serves up lots of twists and turns, and some Class II rapids, as well. There are four access sites within the national forest, each with toilets, water, grills and parking areas. Rent ca-noes from Horina Canoe and Kayak Rental, located on the Pine at 9889 M-37 in Wellston, 231/862-3470. The wonderfully clear **Pere Marquette River,** also a National Scenic River, is great for both canoeing and fishing, with healthy populations of brown trout, steelhead and salmon. The canoeable stretch within the national forest is more than 43 miles, with sev-eral access points.

For more information on the national forest, contact the **Cadillac-Manistee Ranger District,** 412 Red Apple Rd., Manistee, 231/723-2211,

*Nordhouse Dunes Wilderness Area— a 3,450-acre swath of untouched dunes and dune forest—is the only federally desig-nated wilderness in Michigan's Lower Peninsula and the only federal dune wilderness in the nation.*

## Cadillac

It may share a name with the luxury car maker, but snowmobiles, not Caddies, are the preferred means of transportation in the forest and lake country surrounding Cadillac. An intricate web of trails links the city with routes through the Man-istee National Forest. In summer, much of the same crowd turns to **fishing.** The city of 10,000 sits on the shore of large 1,150-acre Lake Cadillac, which is linked by canal to even larger Lake Mitchell. Both are known for excellent northern pike and walleye fish-ing. The canal was originally built by loggers, who grew tired of the twisting, shallow river that origi-nally traversed the wetlands be-tween the two lakes.

**William Mitchell State Park,** 6093 E. M-115 in Cadillac, 231/775-7911, is like a dream come true for an-glers and pleasure boaters, situated between two lakes. Some of its 215 modern campsites, in fact, are on the canal itself, where boats can be tied up right next to your tent or RV. The park main-tains a boat launch on Lake Cadillac, as well as swimming beaches on both Cadillac and Mitchell. There's a short nature trail skirting a wetlands area with an observation tower. Visit early in the morning to observe the active bird life here. Though pretty, be aware that this park and both its lakes tend to be extremely busy throughout the summer. Those looking for a peaceful retreat will likely be disappointed with the buzz of activity here.

For more information on other area attrac-tions and services, contact the **Cadillac Area Visitors Bureau,** 222 Lake St., 800/225-2537, website: www.cadillacmichigan.com.

# The Thumb

For a state that affectionately and commonly refers to the Lower Peninsula as "the Mitten," it seems only logical that the large and isolated protrusion of land in the southeastern corner of Michigan would come to be known as "the Thumb." The Thumb is shaped by Saginaw Bay to the west and Lake Huron to the east, two bodies of water that not only outline the Thumb but wrap the majority of it in rural isolation. Despite the presence of three of the state's largest cities (Flint, Saginaw, and Port Huron) on the region's periphery, the Thumb moves at a pace all its own.

The surrounding scenery along Lake Huron is pretty but flat—for most, no match for the sand dunes in the western part of the state, or the rolling hills and cherry orchards to the north. Development has been slow as

well. Once difficult to reach and misinterpreted as a poor-quality farming region, the area was bypassed by settlers. Even today, property turns over infrequently, and families keep country cottages for generations. Consequently, the Thumb still looks much as it did in the 1950s, with quiet fishing villages, lonely lighthouses, and solitary beaches.

The majority of the Thumb's tourist traffic comes from vacationers traveling north along I-75 and the masses heading to Frankenmuth. Those who venture out of the cities, off the interstate, and onto the backroads in this part of the state, however, are treated to a Michigan of prosperous farms and quiet small towns that they thought existed only in scrapbooks and postcards.

The area's sleepy personality belies its past as one of the most important lumber centers in the

Frankenmuth

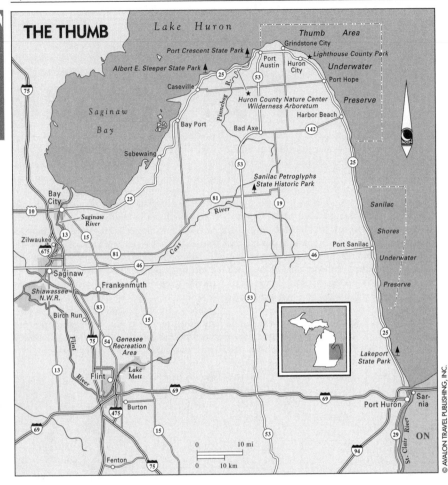

THE THUMB

Lake Huron

Thumb Area

Grindstone City

Port Crescent State Park ▲
Lighthouse County Park

Port
Austin
Huron
City
Underwater

Albert E. Sleeper State Park ▲

Port Hope

Caseville

Preserve

Huron County Nature Center
Wilderness Arboretum

Harbor Beach

Saginaw

Bay Port

Bad Axe

Bay

Sebewaing

Sanilac Petroglyphs
State Historic Park

Bay
City

Saginaw
River

Sanilac

Zilwaukee

Shores

Port Sanilac

Saginaw

Underwater

Frankenmuth

Shiawassee
N.W.R.

Preserve

Birch Run

Genesee
Recreation
Area

Flint

Lake
Mott

Lakeport
State Park

Flint

River

Burton

Port Huron
Sar-
nia

ON

Fenton

St. Clair River

0     10 mi
0     10 km

United States. Logs were floated by the millions down the Saginaw River to waiting mills in Saginaw and Bay City. The thriving timber industry generated great fortunes, many of which were later used to fund the establishment of the auto industry.

Like any natural commodity, however, lumber was limited. After the area was virtually stripped of all lumber, professors at the Michigan Agricultural College in East Lansing (now Michigan State University) encouraged area farmers to turn their attention to growing sugar

beets and dry beans. Today, the Thumb is predominantly a farm belt, its flat skyline punctuated now and then by bean silos and, in season, by colossal mounds of sugar beets. Huron County alone produces the largest number of navy beans per acre in the world—up to 65 percent of the U.S. supply.

The region's largest cities—Flint, Saginaw, and Bay City—all have their industrial roots in auto manufacturing. It's not unusual to see large transporter trucks laden with new automobile models on any of the area freeways bound for dealerships across the United States and around the world.

## Information

For more information on the Thumb area, contact the **Huron County Visitors Bureau,** 250 E. Huron Ave., Bad Axe, MI 48413, 800/35-

THUMB. Other information on this area, sometimes referred to by the tourism industry as Michigan's "Sunrise Side," is available from Michigan's Sunrise Side Travel Association, 1361 Fletcher St., National City, 800/424-3022, website: www.misunriseside.com.

## Flint

*Flint, Michigan. The Vehicle City. Greaseball Mecca. The birthplace of thud-rockers Grand Funk Railroad, game show geek Bob Eubanks, and a hobby shop called General Motors. A town where every infant twirls a set of channel locks in place of a rattle. . . . Beer Belly paradise. Gravy on your French fries. . . . The callus on the palm of the state shaped like a welder's mitt.*

—Ben Hamper,
Rivethead: Tales from the Assembly Line

Gritty Flint is now, and seems like it always has been, a worker's town. The city's economy has long been yoked to General Motors' plants. As long as the plants were booming, the city did well. By the mid-1980s, however, skyrocketing unemployment, corporate downsizing, and increased global competition had challenged the city's financial way of life forever. The city tried to launch an indoor theme park based on car culture, but AutoWorld, expected to boost the local economy and fuel tourism, was an embarrassing failure. Independent filmmaker and native son Michael Moore documented the city and its relationship with General Motors in the biting satire *Roger and Me,* filling Americans with images that are likely to haunt this weary town forever.

Despite its blue-collar image, Flint hides a rich cultural life. The abrasive Moore is just one of a long line of artists and activists native to the Flint area. Others include assembly line author Ben Hamper, whose book, *Rivethead,* topped the New York Times Best-Seller List for several weeks in 1991; novelist Ed Love, author of *Subways Are for Sleeping;* comedienne Sandra Bern-

hard, best known for her stint on the sitcom *Roseanne;* and 1960s activist and White Panther Party founder John Sinclair. The city's Institute of Music is one of only two locations nationwide chosen as the site of a workshop hosted by New York City's acclaimed Joffrey Ballet.

While most of Flint's attractions get little recognition outside the local area, many are well worth visiting, especially for those interested in labor relations or the evolution of the automobile.

## HISTORY

Long associated with transportation, the site now known as Flint was once an important river crossing on the Pontiac Trail, one trail associated with a network of Indian routes that crossed the wilderness, and a favorite rendezvous for the Ojibwa and Potawatomi Indians. In 1819, Jacob Smith, a Detroit fur trader, persuaded these tribes to renounce the British and surrender the lands of Saginaw County. Not long after, Smith became the first white man to settle on the site of the present city.

Other settlers soon followed. In 1837, when Michigan became a state, Flint was a village with a population of 300, one of just a handful in the state with a post office, bank, factory, sawmill, stores, doctors, a lawyer, and the U.S. land office.

In 1855 Flint was incorporated as a city. The explosion of the logging business created the need for katydids, two-wheeled vehicles used to haul logs, as well as carts and wagons—all of which were produced in Flint. By the 1890s, the city became known for producing road carts, which soon gave way to carriage manufacturers and, in 1904, to the birth of the Buick Motor Company, which marked the beginning of the city's organized auto manufacturing.

In 1937, Flint became the union town it is today after the first large-scale sit-down in Michigan resulted in an infamous strike involving riots, tear gas, guns, and the National Guard. When the rioting stopped, 16 strikers and 11 police officers were treated for injuries. Flint was later credited as the birthplace of the modern labor movement, ushering in an age of good wages and extensive benefits for thousands of autoworkers across the state and the nation.

For more information on the Flint area, contact the **Flint Convention and Visitors Bureau,** 400 N. Saginaw St., Flint, 800/25-FLINT, website: www.flint.org.

## SIGHTS AND RECREATION

### Museums and More

Perhaps Flint's most interesting attraction—and a good way to better understand the city's psyche—is the **GM Truck and Bus Flint Assembly Plant,** 810/236-0893, which offers tours. The workhorse plant was built in 1947 to make Chevrolets; it was the birthplace of the first Corvairs as well as generations of military vehicles from World War II to the Gulf War. More recently, it has churned out GMC and Chevy vans and full-size pickups. This is the plant where Ben Hamper, aka the Rivethead, worked from 1977 to 1987, but the infamous rivet line has since been replaced by robots. Automation and market forces have slashed the plant's employment from a high of 8,500 to about 3,000 workers today.

Veteran auto workers give 90-minute tours, which include a look at "gatekeeping," the dramatic part of assembly when the car's side panel is joined to the vehicle's floor; a visit to the ladder line, where the frame is riveted together; and the finishing line, where the final result is road-tested. Reservations are a must. Other tours are given at **Truck and Bus,** G-3100 Van Slyke, 810/236-4640. Call for more information.

After touring the city's modern factories, you'll gain a renewed appreciation for the hardships of the early Industrial Age. The often-hazardous working habits of the pre-industrial 19th century are the focus at the charming but truthful **Crossroads Village and Huckleberry Railroad,** 6140 Bray Rd., 810/736-7100. This restored village has more than 30 vintage buildings that show a variety of industries, complete with the era's authentic grit, noise, and pervasive smoke. An 1836 gristmill, sawmill, cider mill, print and blacksmith shop, and more give visitors an idea of the Genesee County in the mid-1800s. Numerous special weekend events are held throughout the year, including a Civil War weekend, colonial life weekend, and rail fans weekend. More unusual is February's ice harvesting weekend. Admission $7.50 adults; $5.50 children 4–12. Hours are Mon.–Fri. 10 A.M.–5:30 P.M., Sat.–Sun. 11 A.M.–6:30 P.M.

Flint's labor and manufacturing history is told with surprising candor in a 10,000-square-foot permanent exhibit on "Flint and the American Dream" at the city's **Alfred P. Sloan Museum,** 1221 E. Kearsley, 810/237-3450. The museum, which focuses on local history and culture, has an impressive collection of vintage automobiles, including the oldest production model Chevrolet in existence. This particular model is worth a look even if you're not a car buff. Exhibits trace the city from Native American hunting and gathering (check out the life-size teepee), through commercial fur trapping and logging, and finally to its identity as an auto manufacturing center. (A 1912 pennant promotes Good Roads Day with the slogan, No More Mud!) Other highlights include an exhibit on human anatomy and a new interactive science room unveiled in 1996. The museum is open Mon.–Fri. 10 A.M.–5 P.M., Sat.–Sun. noon–5 P.M.; admission $5 adults, $3 children 5–12.

Michigan's workers are memorialized at the **Labor Museum and Learning Center of Michigan,** 711 N. Saginaw, in the Walter Reuther Building on the Mott Community College Campus, 810/762-0200. United Auto Workers retirees, who offer unusually personal perspectives, give guided tours. You can also walk through well-planned exhibits that trace the evolution of labor from the small 19th-century shops to the 20th century's more impersonal style of mass production. Other areas look at work conditions in lumber mills, U.P. mines, and in the state's large manufacturing plants, which produced stoves, railroad cars, and the automobile. The story of the Flint sit-down strike is told in "up-to-the-minute" radio broadcasts circa 1930s. Still evolving, the museum ends just after World War II with the introduction of more women and minorities into the workforce. Admission is $2 adults, $1 seniors and children ages 12–17. Open Tues.–Fri. 10 A.M.–5 P.M.

Like Detroit, Flint benefited from the velvet-lined pockets of a number of wealthy auto industrialists. Generous donations from local citizens built the **Flint Institute of Arts (FIA)**, 1120 E. Kearsley, 810/234-1695, now the state's second largest museum of the arts. Dedicated to "making art available, accessible and appoachable," the permanent collection of 5,000 pieces is strong in areas that include contemporary paintings and sculpture, Asian art, and 19th-century French paintings (predominantly landscapes), including ever-popular works by the French Impressionists. The Bray Renaissance Gallery houses a fine array of European paintings and decorative art that ranges from the 15th to the 17th centuries. Special changing exhibits are more regionally motivated than most, with recent examples including "Painters of the Great Lakes Scene" and "Art from the Driver's Seat: Americans and Their Cars." Free admission. Open Tues.–Sat. 10 A.M.–5 P.M., Sun. 1–5 P.M.

Near the FIA in the expansive **DeWaters Art Center** is the **Mott Community College Fine Arts Gallery,** 810/762-0443. The gallery is often the site of one-person shows by prominent Michigan and national artists. In downtown Flint, the alternative **Buckham Gallery,** 134 W. 2nd, 810/239-6334, is dedicated to showing "contemporary cutting-edge art, with no censorship or interference," making for some interesting shows. The space is also often used for performance art and poetry readings.

The **Longway Planetarium,** 1310 E. Kearsley in the Cultural Center, 810/760-1181,

claims the state's largest sky screen. The huge, 60-foot domed screen used to reproduce the night sky is as large as those in New York and Chicago. Changing multimedia shows explore the skies, constellations, science fiction, and space travel. Laser shows are offered Friday and Saturday evenings. Call for a current schedule of programs.

## Recreation

The **Genesee Recreation Area,** 7004 N. Irish Rd., 810/736-7100, offers a pleasant contrast to Flint's urbanity. It covers more than 4,000 acres along the Flint River off of I-475, with beaches, bicycle paths, a boat launch, campground, fishing sites, hiking, and horse trails. The area hosts a popular laser light show from Memorial Day through Labor Day, which includes colored lights playing on Stepping Stone Falls, the spillway of the dam that impounds 600-acre Mott Lake.

In Flint, the 380-acre **For-Mar Nature Preserve and Arboretum,** 2142 N. Genesee Rd., Burton, 810/789-8567, includes a patchwork of woodlands, restored prairies, open fields, meadows, ponds, and Kearsley Creek, as well as an arboretum planted with specimen trees, shrubs, and vines. Seven miles of up-and-down hiking trails weave through a diverse habitat. Two trails are handicapped-accessible. A new interpretive center has a live bird-viewing area and several animal and reptile displays, including the Corydon E. Foote Bird Collection, which contains more than 600 stuffed and mounted specimens. This free park is open daily 8 A.M.–sunset.

## PRACTICALITIES

### Accommodations

The area has a number of chain hotels, including **Super 8,** 810/230-7888. Rates $50–75. For something a little different, **Pine Ridge,** N-10345 Old US-23 in Fenton, 810/629-8911, is one of the more unusual inns in the area and is well known as an adults-only retreat. Large rooms with canopied beds and in-room whirlpools overlook the surrounding woods. Rates $125–200.

## Camping

Within the Genesee Recreation Area, Genesee County operates the **Timber Wolf** and **Wolverine** campgrounds. Timber Wolf has 196 secluded campsites along the Flint River with modern restrooms and showers. Wolverine, located in the 2,000-acre Holloway Reservoir, has a nice setting in a pine forest, with 195 sites and a new shower and restroom building, a boat launch, and a guarded swimming beach. Rates range from $7 per night for tent sites. Reservations recommended. Contact the Genesee County Parks and Recreation Commission, 5045 Stanley Rd., Flint, 810/736-7100.

## Food

According to the *Flint Journal,* **Bill Thomas Halo Burger,** 810/238-1839, serves up the best burgers in town, with 10 locations in the Flint area. The most lively atmosphere, however, is at **Bubba's Roadside Inn,** 5311 Corunna Rd., 810/732-4600, which bills itself as "the last bastion of political incorrectness in Genesee County . . Bubba's for big food, cheap booze, and same-day service." Just off I-75 at the Miller Road exit, **Salvatore Scallopini,** 3227 Miller Rd., 810/732-1070, is part of a statewide chain known for its authentic Italian cuisine and seafood.

# Frankenmuth

It would be easy to dismiss Frankenmuth as the worst kind of overcommercialized kitsch. "Michigan's Little Bavaria" once was a quiet and undistinguished German farm town of just more than 4,000, but has since grown to become the state's top tourist attraction, with an estimated three million visitors each year.

Frankenmuth houses the world's largest Christmas store, a two-mile-long street of pseudo-Bavarian shops, and two huge restaurants that serve all-you-can-eat, family-style chicken dinners. Buoyed by the seemingly endless flow of visitors, the area recently added a new, 18-hole golf course and the state's largest outlet mall.

Despite the Bavarian image it relentlessly pushes today, much of Frankenmuth's history echoes that of other Saginaw Valley towns. A group of 15 young Lutherans from an area near Nuremberg founded the city in 1845 (Frankenmuth means "Courage of the Franconians"). This optimistic group followed the call to become missionaries in America, with hopes of tending to the growing Saginaw Valley German community and converting the local Ojibwa Indians to Christianity along the way.

The Indians stood steadfast and the mission the Franconians embarked on soon failed. Still, more and more Germans immigrated to the area, drawn by abundant opportunities for logging and a growing community. German, in fact, remained the community's principal language until well into the 1920s.

Once the forests were stripped by the logging business, settlers turned to farming. The chicken-dinner craze Frankenmuth enjoys today started as an attraction for traveling salesmen, but later became a staple of the Detroit Sunday drive set in the 1920s and 1930s. They had more reason to steer toward Frankenmuth in the 1950s, when signmaker Wally Bronner opened a Christmas decorating shop as a sideline to his regular business. By the 1970s, the city had been expanded into the Bavarian nerve center it is today.

For more information, contact the **Frankenmuth Convention and Visitors Bureau,** 635 S. Main St., Frankenmuth, 800/FUN-TOWN, website: www.frankenmuth.org.

## SIGHTS AND RECREATION

### Old Frankenmuth

Beneath the commercialism, however, is a genuine German community, where people are old-world friendly and everyone knows everyone else. Old Frankenmuth can still be found in a number of places in town, which are, not surprisingly, the places most tourists skip. **Satow's Drug Store,** 308 S. Main, has a lunch counter where locals hang out, soups are made from scratch, and prices are reminiscent of the 1950s.

The **Main Street Tavern,** 310 S. Main., 989/652-2222, is owned by a former baker from Zehnder's who makes all the fragrant bread and buns on the premises. His $2.50 cheeseburger is made from local beef and cheese; a house specialty is the square pizza made with Italian sausage from Willi's Sausage Haus next door. Wash it down with a once-locally made Carling's (50-cent taps on Wed. nights) or a Frankenmuth Pilsner for a delicious meal filled with old world flair at a reasonable price.

The **Frankenmuth Historical Museum,** 613 S. Main, 989/652-9701, traces the city's rich past through possessions and letters from the original settlers. Displays explore the city's connections to logging, Prohibition, the rise of the chicken-dinner phenomenon, and the Frankenmuth brewery. The museum shop is a pleasant surprise among all the cookie-cutter shops along Main Street, with vintage-style toys, surprisingly sophisticated crafts, and an excellent selection of books regarding the city and surrounding area. Hours are Mon.–Thurs. 10:30 A.M.–5 P.M., Fri. 10:30 A.M.–7 P.M., Sat. 10 A.M.–8 P.M., Sun. 11 A.M.–5 P.M. (shorter hours Jan.–April; call for information); admission is $1 adults, 50 cents children.

The 1880 **St. Lorenz Church** and the **Log Cabin Church,** Tuscola at Mayer, 989/652-6141, house the largest congregation east of the Mississippi of the conservative Missouri Synod of the Lutheran Church. Self-guided tours reveal scenes of Lutheran and Frankenmuth history, an early cemetery, and a reconstruction of the first settlers' original log church and parsonage.

## Twelve Months of December

Check any cynicism at the door when visiting **Bronners CHRISTmas Wonderland,** S. Main St., 800/ALL-YEAR, truly a phenomenon. Prepare yourself for a building that encompasses more than 200,000 square feet—that's more than four football fields—filled with more than 250 decorated Christmas trees, 800 animated figures, 500 styles of Nativity scenes from 75 countries, 6,000 kinds of glass ornaments, Bibles in more than 30 languages, Advent calendars, and nutcrackers… Many of the offerings are from Eastern

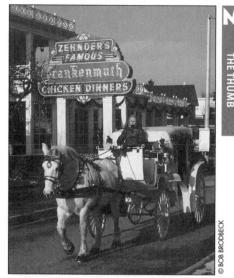

Frankenmuth is renowned for its chicken dinners.

Europe, but the staff has worked hard in recent years to add diversity to the store's offerings. These days you can find books on Hanukkah and Kwanzaa, as well as non-Caucasian Santas and Nativity characters. Hours are Mon.–Sat. 9 A.M.–9 P.M., Sun. noon–7 P.M.

**Zeesenagel Alpine Village,** 780 Mill, 989/652-2591, is the product of interior designers David Zeese and Don Nagel, who were so inspired by an 18th-century Nativity scene they saw in a European church that they decided to re-create one of their own. First displayed in a downtown Detroit bank, the two later moved it to Frankenmuth permanently, where it continues to charm visitors with richly evocative details and lively street scenes. Zeese and Nagel have created nearly a dozen scenes with over 550 figures, all one-sixth scale, and they add more every year. An eclectic gift shop sells international crafts and Christmas figures, including the popular Italian-style angels that are manufactured here. Admission is $2 adults, $1 children 12 and under; open daily noon–6 P.M. (winter hours may be shorter; call for information).

## Other Attractions

**St. Julian Wine Company,** 127 S. Main, 989/652-3281, the state's largest winery (based in Paw Paw), has a free tasting room here that showcases the company's many wines and sparkling juices. There's also a small winery on-site, where solera cream sherry is aged. Free tours; hours are Mon.–Sat. 10 A.M.–6 P.M., Sun. noon–6 P.M.

**Frankenmuth Woodcarving Studio,** 976 S. Main., 989/652-2975, is a small and personal workshop where visitors can watch noted German sculptor Georg Kielhofer work on commissions for churches and individual patrons. Kielhofer sells imported European carvings and offers woodcarving classes. Open Mon.–Sat. 9 A.M.–5 P.M.; free.

Once just an obscure village near Frankenmuth, **Birch Run** is now the state's discount shopping capital, with more than 200 stores currently and new ones are being added constantly. Plunder the offerings of Columbia Sportswear, Nike, Ann Taylor, Polo/Ralph Lauren, Laura Ashley, J. Crew, Eddie Bauer, Esprit, American Tourister, and more. Future plans for Birch Run include a new golf course, an indoor hockey and ice skating rink, a movie theater, and even more hotels and motels—a long list of development plans designed to make Birch Run a true weekend destination for the shopping set.

# PRACTICALITIES

## Accommodations

There is no shortage of chain hotels in Frankenmuth and nearby Birch Run, and it seems more are added almost daily. In downtown Frankenmuth, opt for the **Bavarian Inn Lodge,** 1 Covered Bridge Lane, 989/652-2651, set back behind the restaurant along the Cass River. The rooms are clean and bright, with balconies and Bavarian touches. Each is named in honor of one of the town's early inhabitants, complete with family pictures. The lodge is especially popular with kids, who flock here to hang out at the Family Fun Center, which includes indoor mini-golf, three pools (one with a waterfall), video games, and more. Rates $125–150.

## Food

Thousands of chicken dinners are sold annually at the vast **Bavarian Village Restaurant,** 713 S. Main St., 989/652-9941, which seats 1,200. If you'd rather skip the poultry, the Bavarian Village Restaurant also offers German specialties such as sauerbraten and strudel. Skip the restaurant itself if you like your food spicy, however; Frankenmuth caters to a largely senior citizen crowd, and many diners find the food bland at best.

A good alternative is the **Varsity Diner,** 11740 Gera Rd., Birch Run, 989/624-1355. It serves up daily blue-plate specials, burgers and fries, and other classic cuisine in a streamlined 1955 stainless steel diner moved to Frankenmuth from New York. You can spin a disc on the nostalgic jukebox for just a dime. **Satow's Drug Store,** 308 S. Main, has a lunch counter filled with locals, homemade soups and prices reminiscent of the 1950s.

Like any good tourist mecca, Frankenmuth and Birch Run have plenty of restaurants, including the usual rash of fast food places and chains. Across from Birch Run's discount mall, **Tony's,** 989/624-5860, is a long-standing local eatery that started in downtown Saginaw and is still known for its huge, overstuffed sandwiches and thick shakes. Lines can be long, so plan on a wait or visit during off-hours.

# Saginaw and Bay City

## SAGINAW

Saginaw, the industrial heart of east-central Michigan, stretches for four miles along both banks of the Saginaw River. Formerly a logging and agricultural center, all that remains of the city's logging era are scores of old wooden houses built with money gained from the felling of the city's forests.

Saginaw Bay appears variously on 17th- and 18th-century French maps as "Sikonam," "Sakonam," "Saaguinam," and "Saquinam." Southeastern Michigan was generally described as "Saquinam Country" as early as 1688. Later, when lumber camp raconteurs told of Paul Bunyan's legendary feat of "logging off the Saginaw Country," the reference included the entire Lower Peninsula.

Native Americans lived peacefully on these lands for centuries. The earliest whites to penetrate the Saginaw Valley were Canadians. In 1816, Louis Campau built a fur-trading post near downtown. Two years later, at the request of Governor Lewis Cass, he built a council house and helped Cass negotiate the Treaty of 1819 with the Ojibwa. Sensing growing friction, the white settlers stationed troops at Fort Saginaw in 1822. The following year, a harsh winter, disastrous floods, and a summer fever epidemic prompted the garrison's commander to inform the War Department that "nothing but Indians, muskrats, and bullfrogs could possibly exist here." To the delight of the area's Native Americans, the post was abandoned in 1823.

Although that early pessimism stalled the development of Saginaw, the white man didn't stay away long. By the 1850s, the lumberjacks moved in, bringing with them 14 busy, buzzing sawmills by 1857. Their prey: the heavily forested land around the city. That lasted until about the late 1880s, when timber was replaced by coal as the city's principal industry.

Remnants of those years can still be seen. One example is the stunning Montague Inn, which houses an elegant inn and restaurant in the Georgian-style mansion of a former sugar beet magnate.

For more information, contact the **Saginaw County Convention and Visitors Bureau,** 901 S. Washington, Saginaw, 800/444-9979, website: www.saginawcvb.org.

### Museums and Other Cultural Attractions

Easily dismissed as an aging industrial center, Saginaw is a city of surprises. One of the most delightful is **Awa Saginaw An,** 527 Ezra Rust Dr., 989/759-1648, an authentic Japanese teahouse and garden. The traditional 16th-century-style teahouse was built in 1986, designed to resemble a Zen monastery. It is one of the few places in the United States where visitors can see a formal Japanese tea ceremony performed in an authentic setting. Behind the teahouse, the Friendship

on display at the Marshal M. Fredericks Sculpture Gallery

Garden is a variation of a traditional Japanese garden, with delicate plantings and an arched footbridge over a stream. Many of the garden's trees, bridges, and stones came directly from Japan. Saginaw was chosen as the center's unlikely site because of its relationship with the city of Tokushima, Japan, Saginaw's sister city.

The serene formal tea ceremony, designed to promote inner tranquility, is performed once each month, at 2 P.M. on the second Saturday of the month. At other times, visitors can tour the teahouse and garden, learn more about the ancient Zen ritual of tea, and contemplate its importance in Japanese architecture, politics, and religion. The $6 tours include a cup of tea and a traditional Japanese sweet. Entrance to the garden is free.

Another surprise is the **Marshall M. Fredericks Sculpture Gallery** at Saginaw Valley State University, 2250 Pierce Rd., 989/790-5667. The Scandinavian-American artist who became one of the state's most renowned sculptors studied under famous Swedish artist Carl Milles and is best known for his elegant bronze gazelles in Detroit's Belle Isle conservatory and for the City-County Building's symbolic *Spirit of Detroit*. The gallery features original works, more than 200 original plaster models, photos of pieces installed around the world, a collection of bronze casts in the nearby sculpture garden, and original sketches. Open Tues.–Sun. 1–5 P.M., free admission.

The **Saginaw Art Museum**, 1126 N. Michigan Ave., 989/754-2491, features local and international artists, displaying

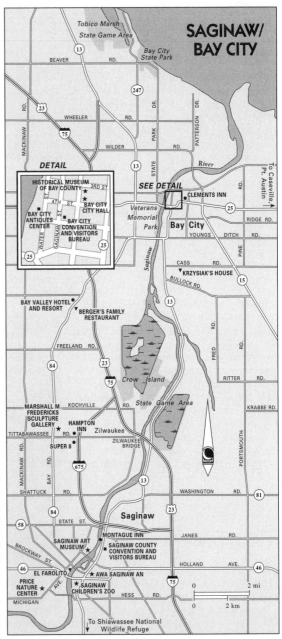

their works in a 1904 Georgian Revival mansion. Highlights include a hands-on gallery, fine collections of 19th- and 20th-century American art, and a garden restored to reflect the home's original plantings. Hours are Tues.–Sat. 10 A.M.–5 P.M., Sun. 1–5 P.M.

Saginaw is home to a large Hispanic community, many of whom initially settled here to work on the construction of the state's railroads. Many of their descendants stayed on to work at area sugar beet refineries. Saginaw and Bay City's sugar beet industry makes Michigan the fifth-largest sugar beet producer in the country. In May, the Saginaw area is home to the state's largest **Cinco de Mayo** festival, held on Ojibway Island behind the teahouse in Rust Park.

## Recreation

Nature takes center stage at the **Shiawassee National Wildlife Refuge,** 6975 Mower Rd., 989/777-5930, just southwest of Saginaw. The refuge and the nearby **Green Point Environmental Learning Center** share a location near the union of four rivers—the Flint, the Tittabawassee, the Cass, and the Shiawassee—all of which converge to form the Saginaw River.

Covering more than 9,000 acres, the refuge was established in 1953 as a wetland for migrating waterfowl, and is now widely regarded as one of the top 25 birding sites in the United States. A checklist available at the headquarters lists more than 250 species that frequent the refuge. In November, some 30,000 ducks and 25,000 geese converge on the area, as well as songbirds, wading birds, owls, hawks, and even bald eagles. About 500 tundra swans migrate through annually.

An observation deck and wheelchair-accessible blind are strategically placed for prime viewing. The refuge has more than 10 miles of hiking trails, open dawn to dusk, including a 3.5-mile Woodland Trail that loops through

*Awa Saginaw An, an authentic Japanese teahouse and garden, was designed to resemble a Zen monastery. Behind the teahouse, the Friendship Garden is a variation of a traditional Japanese garden, with delicate plantings and an arched footbridge over a stream. Many of the garden's trees, bridges, and stones came directly from Japan.*

bottomland hardwoods and skirts the Tittabawassee River. The adjacent 76-acre Green Point is operated under a co-op agreement with the U.S. Fish and Wildlife Service, with 76 acres of diverse habitat and an interpretive center. Because it lies in the floodplain of the Tittabawassee River, the Green Point trail system is often under water. It can be a magnet for mosquitoes, so be sure to bring repellent.

Each year, thousands drive over one of the state's best **birdwatching** areas without realizing it's there. The **Crow Island State Game Area** stretches along the Saginaw River from the foot of the Zilwaukee Bridge to Bay City and covers more than 1,000 acres. The area serves as a giant overflow basin for Michigan's largest watershed. M-13 runs along the Saginaw River's east bank and splits the preserve into east and west. It, too, is an excellent birdwatching area for waterfowl, ospreys, bald eagles, night herons, great egrets, and more.

The Saginaw County Parks and Recreation Commission manages the 170-acre **Price Nature Center,** 6685 Sheridan Rd., 989/790-5280. A good spot for day hikes, the center features a 200-year-old beech and maple forest and three main trail loops.

The **Saginaw Children's Zoo,** S. Washington Ave. and Ezra Rust Dr. in Celebration Square, 989/759-1657, is a bargain-priced zoo at a manageable size. It features more than 130 animals, most native to the region. The timber wolves and red-tailed hawks are especially popular with kids. Open Mon.–Sat. 10 A.M.–5 P.M., Sun. 11 A.M.–6 P.M. Admission is $1.50 adults, 75 cents children ages 3–12.

## BAY CITY

Lying three miles upstream from the point where the Saginaw River enters Saginaw Bay, Bay City today bears no resemblance to the rip-roaring mill town it was at the end of the 19th century. Little remains of the color and flavor of the days when bawdy Bay City attracted thousands of lumberjacks who came in with the spring log drives to work in the mills after months of toiling in the surrounding woods.

The first white settlers came here to trade with the Indians, founding Bay City in 1831. After 1860, however, the once-quiet community became the center of the area logging industry. By 1872 there were 36 mills buzzing along the banks of the river, some of which were among the largest in the country. The whine of saws biting into logs could be heard 10 hours each day, and the smell of fresh lumber was said to be strong enough to flavor food.

Logs waiting to be milled lined the banks of the river. With the logs came the lumberjacks who patronized the saloons along the city's Water Street looking for liquor and women. In about 1890, Bay City reached the height of its boom and the peak of its population—then declined about as quickly as it grew. The city's logging industry abruptly ceased after the stands of timber in Saginaw Valley were depleted and a Canadian export duty caused the abandonment of many mills. Bay City narrowly missed becoming one of the state's ghost towns by smartly developing industries revolving around soft-coal mining, commercial fishing, and beet sugar.

The last of the sawmills that once lined both banks of the Saginaw River were leveled in the late 1930s. Today, large freighters navigate the channel that was once filled with logs driven down from the river's upper reaches. The city's logging period is still reflected in the city's many wood-framed houses, as well as the opulent mansions built by the lumber barons.

More recently, Bay City gained notoriety as the birthplace of Madonna. The native daughter is persona non grata in these parts these days, though, after a few less-than-flattering comments about her hometown (referring to it as the "armpit" of the United States) that made their way into the national media.

For more information, contact the **Bay City Convention and Visitors Bureau,** 901 Saginaw St., Bay City, 888/BAY-TOWN, website: www.baycityarea.com.

## Sights

Bay City has other claims to fame besides the Material Girl. With more than 35,000 residents, it's the state's second largest port. Many of those residents can be found enjoying the city's well-maintained parks system, including the five-mile **Riverwalk,** which follows the river's banks, accessing an 820-foot pier and passing through Veterans Memorial Park and the Liberty Harbor Marina. Walkers, cyclists, in-line skaters, and passing freighters from all over the world make for a colorful scene.

On the east side of town, lumber magnates built grand homes along Center Avenue and the surrounding streets. Center Avenue is the heart of the historic district, with more than 250 homes listed on the national and state historic registers. A few, including the **Clements Inn,** 1712 Center Ave., have been opened to the public as bed and breakfasts.

Even more impressive than the grand homes is Bay City's **City Hall,** 301 Washington Ave., 989/894-8147, built in 1894 and listed on the National Register of Historic Places. A $3-million restoration in 1980 earned it mention by the Smithsonian Institution as one of the 10 most outstanding historic restorations in the United States. The Romanesque-style stone building dominates the city skyline with a 125-foot clock tower. Visitors are welcome to take a self-guided tour and climb the 68 steps in the clock tower, which offers impressive view of Bay City, the Saginaw River, and the surrounding countryside. Also take a look at the 31-foot tapestry that hangs in the council chambers. Depicting the community's historic buildings, it was woven with more than 500 colors by a young artist from Poland.

The **Historical Museum of Bay County,** 321 Washington Ave., 989/893-5733, traces the development of the county from pre-Columbian times through the 20th century. Displays include period rooms, Native American artifacts, and exhibits on the fur trade, logging, and shipbuilding. Hours are Mon.–Fri. 10

A.M.–5 P.M., Sat.–Sun. noon–4 P.M. Free admission; donations welcome.

Not surprising, the city also can be a fruitful spot for antiquing, with **Bay City Antiques Center** 1010 N. Water St., 989/893-1116, claiming the better part of a city block. It was named the state's best antique mall by readers of *Michigan Living* magazine. A large showroom includes more than 100 booths overflowing with furniture, kitchen items, and more. The century-old buildings on Midland Street, on the river's west side, also house some interesting antique shops.

### Recreation

The 2,800-acre **Bay City State Recreation Area,** 3582 State Park Dr., 989/667-0717, connects the Frank N. Anderson Nature Trail, the Bay City State Park, and the Tobico Marsh State Game Area. Together, they offer camping, a sand beach along Saginaw Bay, two 30-foot observation towers, a fishing pier, and a variety of trails.

The paved 1.6-mile Frank N. Anderson nature trail follows an abandoned rail grade to Tobico Marsh, a 1,700-acre refuge that is the largest coastal marsh on the Great Lakes. The Saginaw Bay Visitors Center contains permanent and changing exhibits depicting life in the wetlands, a 15-minute multimedia presentation on wetlands development, and a bird observation room and wet lab. Admission to the recreation area is $4 per car.

## SAGINAW/BAY CITY PRACTICALITIES

### Accommodations

Plenty of chain hotels can be found along the I-75 corridor and off of US-675, including the **Hampton Inn,** 989/792-7666, rates $75–100, and the **Super 8,** 989/791-3003, rates $50–75. But Saginaw's most distinctive lodging choice is the **Montague Inn,** 1581 S. Washington Ave., 989/752-3939, an elegantly restored two-story brick Georgian mansion with a library, sitting rooms, and a gracious dining room that is open to the public. All but one of the 17 guest rooms have private baths, and all are furnished with period pieces, including four-poster beds, wing chairs, and other antiques. Rates $75–200, including a lavish breakfast.

In Bay City, an 1886 lumber baron's mansion is now the **Clements Inn,** 1712 Center Ave. (M-25), 800/442-4605. It's been updated with plenty of modern comforts, including whirlpools. The candlelight breakfasts include fresh fruit, breads, and muffins. Rates $75–200.

The **Bay Valley Hotel and Resort,** 2470 Old Bridge Rd., 989/686-3500, offers nice grounds, a lobby full of antiques, and a championship Jack Nicklaus golf course. They'll help you arrange fishing charters in nearby Saginaw Bay. Rates $75–125.

### Food

In Bay City, try **Krzysiak's House,** 1605 S. Michigan Ave., 989/894-5531, for Polish dishes and a popular weekend seafood buffet. Four generations of Berger's have run **Berger's Family Restaurant,** 6519 Westside Saginaw Rd., 989/686-0224, a favorite for fish dishes and homemade pie. In Saginaw, you can enjoy authentic Mexican fare at the excellent **El Farolito** restaurant, 115 N. Hamilton, 989/799-8959.

# Skirting the Shore

## BAY CITY TO THE TIP OF THE THUMB

From Bay City, M-25 meanders east along Saginaw Bay until it joins Lake Huron. Along the way is a chain of small fishing ports, including Sebewaing, Bay Port, and Caseville, popular places for cottages but with little to stop those passing through. Caseville was once an important terminal for lake and rail shipping, with a prosperous salt well and ironworks. The area is remarkable only for its quiet, small towns, large, prosperous farms, and tabletop flat landscape punctuated by long stretches of blue water.

Between Caseville and Port Austin, south of M-25, is the **Huron County Nature Center Wilderness Arboretum,** 800/35-THUMB. This 280-acre nature center has rolling dune ridges and shallow, wet depressions known as swales that are traversed by an interpretive trail system. Trees, plants, vines, and wildflowers are protected here for educational and scientific purposes.

Also near Caseville, **Albert E. Sleeper State Park,** 6573 State Park Rd., 989/856-4411, draws most of its visitors because of its half-mile arc of wide sand beach on Saginaw Bay. Sleeper (named for the governor who created the state park system) is popular with suburbanites looking for that "up north" escape without the long drive. The 1,003-acre park is quite heavily wooded, mostly with oak and other hardwoods. Nearly five miles of trails wind through the lightly developed park, including the interpretive Ridges Nature Trail. Pick up a self-guiding brochure at the park office to identify native trees, shrubs, and wildflowers, and learn how Native Americans used them. Trails are groomed for skiing in winter.

The park's 280-site campground is quite popular on summer weekends. It's located on the south side of M-25, but there's a pedestrian bridge over the highway that safely links it to the beach. For campground reservations, call 800/44-PARKS; website: dnr.state.mi.us.

## Port Austin

Port Austin, population 1,500, is known as the "tip of the Thumb." Bob Talbert, a columnist for the *Detroit Free Press,* calls it "the best spot in Michigan to view the sunrise and sunset." Downtown Port Austin is a comfortable, simple place, full of old-fashioned dime stores, soda fountains, collectible shops, and halls run by local legions.

The city was first visited in 1837 by a fugitive of the Canadian Patriotic War, who found an excellent hiding place on this stretch of shore. Others soon followed, with a permanent settlement established not long after. Port Austin later became well known for Pointe Aux Barques, a point that extended north into Lake Huron that became a wealthy resort enclave of prominent Detroiters. The point is named for the large rocks offshore, many of which resemble the prows of ships. The 1848 Pointe Aux Barques lighthouse guards the point, surrounded by the pleasant **Lighthouse County Park,** with a campground, picnic area, beach, and small lighthouse museum. For information, call the Thumb Area Convention and Visitors Bureau, 800/35-THUMB.

Three miles of sugary sand beach and banks of dunes (unusual in this part of the state) are the highlights of **Port Crescent State Park,** 1775 Port Austin Rd., Port Austin, 989/738-8663. A three-mile trail winds through wooded dunes and above the banks of the Pinnebog River, climbing up to provide some great views of Saginaw Bay. The park's East side has a 181-unit modern campground near what was the village of Port Crescent, which disappeared in the 1930s. The stack from a sawmill is all that remains of this old industrial town; an interpretive display at

> *Port Austin was first visited in 1837 by a fugitive of the Canadian Patriotic War, who found an excellent hiding place on this stretch of shore.*

the site chronicles its rise and fall. The campground is very popular in summer—especially the sites right next to the beach. Make reservations by calling 800/44-PARKS; website: dnr.state.mi.us.

Quietwater **paddlers** can spend an entire day exploring the Pinnebog, a river that seems to tie itself in knots as it searches for an outlet to Saginaw Bay. Nearly four miles of river run through the state park and attract anglers for trout, walleye, salmon, and perch. A private livery, **Tip-A-Thumb Canoe Rental,** M-25 and Pinnebog River Bridge, 989/738-7656, rents canoes for leisurely paddles down the winding river.

## Fishing

"Deep-sea" fishing is popular throughout the Great Lakes, and the waters around the tip of the Thumb are considered some of the best. Charter boats operate out of many Thumb communities; the **Thumb Area Charter Captain's Association,** 989/738-5500, is a good clearinghouse of information about fishing opportunities in the area.

BOB RACE

lake trout

The larger **Miss Port Austin Perch Party Boat,** 989/738-5271, can handle up to 20 passengers for half-day fishing trips. It can be a bit of a circus atmosphere for serious anglers, but is less expensive than a charter and good fun for those who just want to get out on the water and give it a try. Trips depart from the Port Austin State Dock on Mon., Wed., Fri., Sat., and Sun. at 7:30 A.M. and 2:30 P.M., June–Labor Day. Weather permitting, they'll also run a reduced schedule in September. Rates are $30 per person; fishing rod rental is $2 extra. A valid state fishing license ($15) is required for anyone over 17.

## An Inland Detour

One of the state's great mysteries is the **Sanilac Petroglyphs State Historic Park,** a historic site about 13 miles south of Bad Axe via M-53 and Germania Road. The Michigan Archaeological Society raised private funds to purchase the 240-acre site and eventually transferred the land to the State of Michigan, which now maintains it.

The park holds the only known petroglyphs in the state. The petroglyphs are aboriginal rock carvings that were chipped into exposed sandstone up to 1,000 years ago. Fires that swept through the area in the late 1800s cleared the vegetation that once protected sandstone slabs near the Cass River. Once the fires burned out, astonished locals were surprised to discover newly exposed carvings of animals, animal tracks, birds, and hunters. Some claims that they were created as recordings of dreams, visions, or significant events done during hunting or religious rituals. Far off the beaten tourist path, they receive few visitors, which has undoubtedly helped protect these fragile treasures.

A 1.5-mile interpretive trail weaves through the park and educates visitors on its many historical facets, including the petroglyphs, Indian villages, and remains of Holbrook, a logging town that vanished nearly a century ago. This pleasant trail also cuts across the Cass River twice, weaving through woods and open meadows. The rest of the park is undeveloped with no staff or services. (That includes restrooms.) The site is open Memorial Day–Labor Day. In summer, it features a few special events revolving around Native American folklore and music. For information, call the Michigan Historical Museum in Lansing, 989/373-1979, or Port Crescent State Park, 989/738-8663.

## Accommodations and Food

In Port Austin, the 130-year-old **Garfield Inn,** 8544 Lake St., 989/738-5254, is named for President James Garfield, who once stayed in this home of a gentleman farmer and industrialist. Today, its elegant Victorian setting greets guests with six B&B-style rooms, an English-style pub, and an excellent restaurant. Featured on the menu: warm perch salad with pears, toasted almonds, and a ginger-chive vinaigrette; and a pan-fried Michigan walleye with almond dumplings in a roasted red pepper sauce. The

© BOB BRODBECK

**Port Austin's Victorian-era Garfield Inn, named after its famous guest**

inn is open generally from mid-April through January. Rates $100–125.

Also in Port Austin, **The Bank 1884,** 989/738-5353, is considered by many to offer the finest dining in the Thumb. The 1884 red-washed brick building, formerly a bank, opened as a restaurant in 1982, decorated with the original first-floor teller's cage, stained glass, and oversized historic photographs of Huron County. It has attracted a loyal crowd and high praise ever since, including a review from the *New York Times* speculating that The Bank "would give big city restaurants a run for the gold card." The menu changes regularly; one long-standing specialty has been the walleye prepared in a crabmeat dressing and baked in parchment paper. The restaurant is open Tues.–Sun. during the summer, weekends only in May, Sept., and Oct. Reservations recommended.

## GRINDSTONE CITY TO PORT HURON

### Grindstone City

For more than a century, this village took advantage of its plentiful supply of abrasive rock and produced some of the finest grindstones in the world, exporting them to England and other markets around the globe. Two factories operated until World War I, when the development of Carborundum quickly made grindstone quarrying unprofitable. Almost overnight, the town's greatest asset went from being highly prized to virtually worthless. Huge stones, many up to six feet in diameter, were left behind to litter the beach. Also left behind were old docks, stores, houses, mills, and office buildings. Many a grindstone can still be spotted as local lawn art.

You can probably pick up a little local history while you're eating one of the Thumb's best hamburgers at the **Grindstone Bar and Grill,** 3337 Pointe Aux Barques Rd., Grindstone City, 989/738-7665, near the public boat ramp. Hours are sporadic, but it's usually open for breakfast, lunch, and dinner from February to November.

### Huron City

Just south of Grindstone City lies the ghost of Huron City. Though not quite a ghost town, it certainly is a faded image of its past. Langdon Hubbard had big plans for Huron City when he arrived here from Connecticut in the 1870s, buying up thousands of acres of woodland and building sawmills that churned out thousands of feet of lumber a day. But his grand plans were dashed in 1881, when a huge fire—not uncommon in logging regions where dry clear-cut land easily ignited—roared across the Thumb and destroyed his young empire.

Huron City was partially rebuilt—Hubbard even contributed a public roller rink. But the area's water had been contaminated by salt-making, a secondary industry in the area. By 1884, the population had dwindled from 1,500 to about 15.

Huron City's quick demise makes its most dominant building all the more fascinating. The Italianate **House of Seven Gables,** 989/428-4123, was rebuilt by Langdon Hubbard after the 1881 fire. It later became the summer residence of Hubbard's son-in-law, William Lyon Phelps, a wildly popular Yale English teacher dubbed "America's favorite college professor" by *Life* magazine during the 1930s. The Hubbard family lived in the house from 1881 until 1987, when it was turned into an informal house museum. Open July–Aug. Thurs.–Mon. 10 A.M.–5 P.M.

As a result, the house offers an almost unparalleled glimpse into a past era, not someone's interpretation of what life must have been like. The family's books lie piled on tables, the ornate 1886 pool table looks ready for a match, the walls are lined with campy portraits of the beloved Hubbard dogs and cats, and the "state-of-the-art" 1915 kitchen even shows off its fancy and strange-looking dishwasher. Along with the House of Seven Gables, the public can visit the other remaining buildings of Historic Huron City, including the general store, inn, church, and school. Admission is $10, including mansion and village, $5 ages 10–15.

## Harbor Beach

From Huron City, M-25 curves south along Lake Huron. About 16 miles south lies the lakeshore town of Harbor Beach, home to the largest man-made freshwater harbor in the world. The need to improve on the natural harbor was prompted by Michigan's busy logging industry in the 1870s. More and more ships were plying the waters up and down the Lake Huron shore and across Saginaw Bay; in stormy weather, they needed a safe refuge from strong currents and heavy seas. The federal government began work on a harbor in 1873, and worked on the gargantuan project for more than two decades. When completed, the breakwall stretched 8,000 feet! It continues to do duty today, along with the 1881 Coast Guard Station and 1885 lighthouse.

Originally named Sand Beach, Harbor Beach was once notorious as the site of an illegal money factory. In the mid-19th century, counterfeit U.S. currency and Mexican dollars were made here and distributed throughout the Americas.

Frank Murphy ranks as Harbor Beach's most famous son, the Michigan governor who is best known for collective bargaining during the 1937 Flint sit-down strike, paving the way for the rise of the United Auto Workers (UAW). He went on to become U.S. Attorney General, and U.S. Supreme Court Justice. The 1910 **Frank Murphy Birthplace,** 142 S. Huron, 989/479-3363, serves as a repository for Murphy's personal memorabilia. While the contents prove interesting, the house itself is plain in comparison with the Hubbards' mansion. The museum is open daily from 9 A.M. to 4 P.M.

## Port Sanilac

Until the mid-1850s, the Port Sanilac area was known as Bark Shanty Point, a name that was heatedly defended in an issue of the village's alternative newspaper, the *Bark Shanty Times.* The *Times* was produced by placing a sheet of newsprint on the counter of the town's general store; townsfolk simply wrote news or commentary on a sheet of paper until it was filled up.

Port Sanilac's past is preserved at the **Sanilac County Historical Museum and Village,** 228 S. Ridge Rd., 810/622-9946. Housed in a nicely restored Victorian mansion, the 1872 Loop-Harrison House, the museum contains most of its original furnishings, as well as old-fashioned medical instruments, antique glassware, military and American Indian artifacts, and an original Bark Shanty post office stamp. The grounds also include a dairy museum, a restored late-19th-century cabin, general store, and a barn with exhibits relating to the fishing, logging, and blacksmithing trades. Admission is $6 adults; $5 children ages 5–12. Open mid-June–August, Tues.–Fri. 11 A.M.–4:30 P.M., Sat.–Sun. noon–4:30 P.M.

## Diving

Two of Michigan's excellent underwater preserves lie off this stretch of Lake Huron shoreline. Near Port Hope, 10 major shipwrecks lie within the 276-square-mile **Thumb Area Underwater Preserve.** Most sites are 100 feet deep or more, accessible only to advanced divers. An exception is the popular *Chickamauga,* a 322-foot turn-of-the-century schooner. Resting in just 35 feet of water, it's in a relatively protected area about a half-mile east of Harbor Beach. Farther south, the **Sanilac Shores Underwater Preserve** near Port Sanilac contains some recent shipwreck finds, including the 250-foot *Regina,* a freighter that sank in 1913 but wasn't discovered until 1986. Sanilac Shores shipwrecks tend to be in a little shallower water, and many are in excellent condition. For information on both preserves and a listing of dive shops and charters, contact the **Huron County Visitors Bureau,** 800/35-THUMB, or the **Michigan Underwater Preserves Council,** 800/338-6660.

## Lakeport State Park

About 20 miles south of Port Sanilac on M-25, Lakeport State Park, 810/327-6224, preserves more than a mile of fine sand beach on southern Lake Huron. The 556-acre park was established in 1936, one of Michigan's oldest state parks. A couple of miles to the north in a separate unit of the park, a popular campground offers 315 modern sites that are just a short walk from another beach and some lakeside bluffs. From the park's low bluffs, you can see distant views of freighter traffic heading in and out of the gateway to the upper Great Lakes. Other park amenities include a picnic shelter, beach house, and playground. For campground reservations, call 800/44-PARKS; website: dnr.state.mi.us.

## Accommodations and Food

Perched just 500 feet from Lake Huron in Port Sanilac, the **Raymond House Inn,** 111 S. Ridge Rd. (M-25), 810/622-8800, is an impressive 1871 home that's been converted to an inn. The inn has seven bedrooms on the second floor, an on-site fitness and pampering center, and bike rentals. Rates $75–125.

Across the street from the Raymond House Inn, the **Bellaire Motel,** 120 S. Ridge Rd., 810/622-9981, offers simple and inexpensive motel rooms and terrific eats—some claim it serves the best fish fry in the Thumb. Fish frys are a staple in many Michigan and Wisconsin towns, with fish fillets lightly breaded and pan- or deep-fried, and served with coleslaw and fries. The Douros family has been at it since 1945, serving perch and pickerel dinners, as well as tart lemon meringue pie.

# PORT HURON

At the southern end of M-25, Port Huron sits at the juncture of Lake Huron and the St. Clair River, which is part of a vital shipping route that links Lake Huron and Lake Erie. Port Huron stretches some eight miles along the lake and this international river boundary, opposite Sarnia, Ontario.

On any given day, visitors can watch as a steady procession of pleasure craft, oil tankers, and bulk freighters file past the city. The most dramatic vantage point is from the crest of the newly rebuilt **Blue Water International Bridge,** which rises 152 feet over the water and looks down to where Lake Huron meets the St. Clair River. Walk across for the best views.

Due to its strategic geographical position, Port Huron is one of the oldest settlements in Michigan and, in fact, one of the earliest outposts in the American interior. The French built Fort St. Joseph here in 1686, mainly to seal off the entranceway to the upper Great Lakes from the rival English. The first permanent settlement was established in 1790. In 1814, the Americans built Fort Gratiot on the Fort Joseph site, also an attempt to repel the British. The fort was occupied off and on after the Civil War when it served as a recruiting station.

In the late 1800s, four local villages—Peru, Desmond, Huron, and Gratiot—united to form

Port Huron and helped develop the area into a lumber center. When the big trees ran out, Port Huron weathered the industry's demise better than most Michigan cities, since it had already diversified into shipbuilding, railroading, and oil and natural gas distribution. Despite these early industries, the city rejected the bids of chemical companies to build plants here, fearing environmental and safety problems. The plants instead found a home on the Sarnia side of the river, and today make up the 20-mile long "chemical valley"—Canada's greatest concentration of chemical companies and the creator of most of the pollution in the lower St. Clair River.

For more information on Port Huron, contact the **Blue Water Convention and Visitors Bureau,** 520 Thomas Edison Pkwy., Port Huron, 800/852-4242, website: www.bluewater.org.

## Sights and Recreation

Port Huron's most famous resident was no doubt native son Thomas Alva Edison (1847–1931), who was born here and stayed until adulthood. He is honored at **Thomas Edison Park,** located under the enormous Blue Water Bridge. In the bridge's shadow is the restored **1858 Grand Trunk Depot,** where Edison boarded the Detroit-bound train daily to sell fruits, nuts, magazines, and newspapers. He used much of his earnings to buy chemicals for the small laboratory he had set up in the train's baggage car. The depot now houses the local visitors bureau as well as historical photos and displays, including artifacts excavated from the site of Edison's boyhood home.

Just north of the Blue Water Bridge, Michigan's oldest lighthouse, the **Fort Gratiot Light,** 800/852-4242, stands 86 feet tall over **Lighthouse Park.** The original tower was poorly constructed in 1825 and crumbled just four years later. It was replaced in 1829 by the much sturdier brick structure that stands today. That still makes it the state's oldest light and older than even Michigan itself, which wasn't admitted to the Union until 1837. The lighthouse was automated in 1933, and it continues to flash a warning to mariners coming south from Lake Huron. The lighthouse is occasionally open on Sundays for tours; call for information.

At nearby **Pine Grove Park,** you can take a self-guided tour of the 1921 *Huron Lightship,* 810/982-0891. This 97-foot vessel served as a floating lighthouse visible from 14 miles away. Retired in 1970, the *Huron Lightship* was the last to operate on the Great Lakes. The lightship is open Wed.–Sun. in July and August and weekends in May, June, and Sept. (Call for specific hours.) The park also offers a view of the bridge and passing boat traffic on the St. Clair River, and is an interesting place to watch fishermen with big nets scoop up walleye and steelhead.

You can check out more nautical history at the **Port Huron Museum of Arts and History,** 1115 6th St., 810/982-0891. Housed in a former library that dates to 1904, the museum's second-floor gallery includes a restored freighter pilothouse (you can even work the wheel, signal the alarm horn, and ring the engine bell), marine-related items, and objects recovered from Lake Huron shipwrecks. The museum has something for everyone, from Indian artifacts to contemporary paintings by local artists. One of the most interesting exhibits displays objects recovered from digs on the site of Edison's boyhood home, which include evidence of an early laboratory. The museum is open Wed.–Sat.; the $1.50 admission includes entry to the *Huron Lightship* in Pine Grove Park.

For a closer look at the St. Clair River, sign on for a trip on the *Huron Lady,* 810/984-1500, a 65-foot excursion boat that cruises under the Blue Water Bridge and heads out onto Lake Huron, where it treats passengers to views of giant freighters as they load and unload their cargo. The ship departs at 1 P.M. Tues.–Sat. and 7 P.M. Wed.–Sat. in season. Tickets are $11 adults, $6 children 5–12; call for reservations.

## Practicalities

Located just south of the Grand Trunk Depot and near the former Fort Gratiot site, the **Thomas Edison Inn,** 500 Thomas Edison Pkwy., 810/984-8000, is the city's nicest large hotel. It has some wonderful bridge and water views, which anyone can enjoy from the hotel's elegant dining room. Rates $100–125.

The **Fogcutter,** 511 Fort St., 810/987-3300, is another fine-dining restaurant with water views and a menu that features classic continental favorites and fresh fish. Other menu highlights include Hawaiian chicken, lobster, and duck à l'orange.

Be aware that Port Huron hosts its biggest event of the year in mid-July, the **Port Huron to Mackinac Race.** The race attracts some 300 sailboats for the trip up the Huron shore to Mackinac Island; in preceding days, sailors and spectators pack the area's restaurants and hotels. Don't plan to show up without reservations. Call the convention and visitors bureau for more information.

# Northeast Michigan

Northeast Michigan is the state's undervisited, underrated corner, land of commercial fishermen, lonely lighthouses, and large tracts of state and national forests. It's so lightly developed that this was the spot chosen by the state to reintroduce a herd of elk a few years ago; today it's the largest free-roaming herd east of the Mississippi.

In appearance, the area has come nearly full circle in less than 200 years. Its first inhabitants were the Native Americans who respected the land, leaving it much as they found it until the Europeans arrived in the 17th century. By the mid-1800s, logging companies who had exhausted the nation's eastern forests moved on to Michigan's fertile ground, making it the largest lumber-producing state in the country between 1850 and 1910, with an estimated 700 logging camps and more than 2,000 mills.

Before the rush of settlers to Michigan in the 1830s, more than 13 million of the state's 38 million acres were covered with white pine. These majestic trees thrived in sandy soil, grew up to 200 feet tall, and could live an incredible 500 years. By 1900, however, all that was left of these once awe-inspiring forests were stumps. Logging had devastated the land, leaving behind a wasteland.

In 1909, the federal government established the Huron National Forest, the first of many such preserves that sought to repair years of damage and regrow the land. Almost a century later, much of this region is once again forested, where it's possible to hike or backpack through towering pines and listen to their gentle whisper. While the impenetrable white pine forests that once characterized this part of the state are a thing of the past, one 49-acre stand of old-growth white pine in Hartwick Pines State Park near Grayling remains, a glimpse of the grandeur that once blanketed this landscape

## Getting There and Getting Information

Two main roads cut through the Huron shore region. US-23 hugs the coastline from Bay City (at the foot of Saginaw Bay) to the Straits of Mackinac, offering vistas and villages along the way. I-75 is

Grayling

the quicker, although decidedly less scenic, route, bisecting northeast Michigan before heading north through Grayling and Gaylord and arriving at the ever-popular Straits of Mackinac.

**Northwest Airlines,** 800/225-2525, offers service from Detroit to Midland/Bay City/Saginaw, and to Pellston, 20 miles southwest of Cheboygan. **United Airlines,** 800/241-6522, and **American Airlines/American Eagle,** 800 /433-7300, also serve Pellston. **Greyhound** serves Midland, Grayling, and Cheboygan.

Tourism folks market the Huron shore region as the state's "Sunrise Side." For information on the region, contact **Michigan's Sunrise Side Travel Association,** 1361 Fletcher St., National City, 800/424-3022, website: www.misunriseside.com.

## Midland

### SIGHTS AND RECREATION

When the lumbermen withdrew from Midland to follow the green frontier north, the city might have become just another ghost town if it weren't for Herbert H. Dow. In 1890, Dow began a series of experiments to extract chemicals from the common salt brine that was below the surface of most of central Michigan, eventually founding Dow Chemical Company.

Although the 24-year-old was called "Crazy Dow" by the locals when he arrived in town with little but a good idea, he was a surprisingly farsighted inventor and humanitarian who founded a well-planned city of neat streets and good architecture. Today, this city of 38,000 continues to benefit from Dow's influence, and many of the city's attractions—

from sports to cultural activities—bear his fingerprints.

For more information on the Midland area, contact the **Midland County Convention and Visitors Bureau,** 300 Rodd St., 888/464-3526, website: www.midlandcvb.org.

### The Legacy of Dow

**Dow Chemical,** 989/636-8659, offers one of the few remaining industrial tours in the state. (Many companies discontinued them due to corporate espionage and liability concerns.) The

impressive labyrinthine complex comprises 40 plants, labs, warehouses, and more. Stops include the Saran Wrap plant and a state-of-the-art analytical lab. The free tour lasts 2.5 hours. You can see more Dow products at the **Visitors Center,** 500 E. Lyon Rd., just east of downtown. Many of the 500 products made in Midland are on display here, including plastics, consumer products, personal care items, and pharmaceuticals. Also worth a stop is the **H. H. Dow Historical Museum,** 3200 Cook Rd., 989/832-5319, where Dow's influence can still be felt in the original buildings of Dow Chemical. The museum is owned and operated by the city's historical society and includes displays on the city at the turn of the century, an 1890s theater, and a 12-minute film on Dow's life and times. It's open Wed.–Sun.

Even if chemicals aren't your thing, Midland is worth a stop if only to visit the breathtaking Dow Gardens and the buildings designed by Alden Dow, Herbert's son. Alden Dow was one of Frank Lloyd Wright's original Taliesin fellows, and he had a long and distinguished architec-tural career. Like Wright, he tried to merge architecture and nature, insisting that "gardens never end and buildings never begin." Open Wed.–Sat. 10 A.M.–4 P.M., Sun. 1–5 P.M.

The **Alden Dow Home and Studio, 315 Post St.,** 989/839-2744, is one of the best places to experience Dow's work. It's open for tours Mon.–Sat. by appointment. Other Dow designs can be explored with a Midland Architectural Tour self-guided tape, which you can rent for $5 at the Midland Center for the Arts next to the Dow Gardens. The narrated tour takes you through the city's neighborhoods and points out noteworthy architecture ranging from 19th-century Victorians to a "futuristic" 1957 space-age dome, the latter insulated with Styrofoam made by Dow Chemical.

Alden Dow's studio and home looks out over the 100-acre **Dow Gardens,** 1809 Eastman Ave., 989/631-2677. Developed by Herbert and Alden Dow over the course of more than 70 years, this lovely landscape began as Herbert Dow's extended 10-acre backyard. When he arrived in Midland, the town was a barren landscape of

© TRAVEL MICHIGAN

**Dow Gardens**

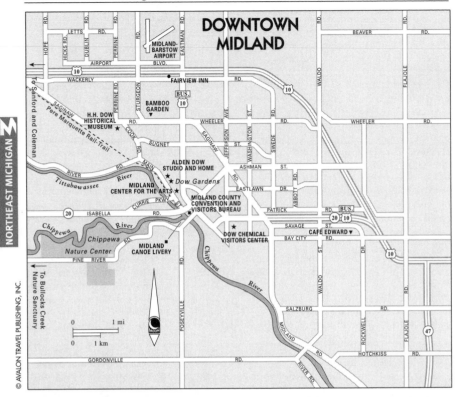

sad stumps left behind by the lumber industry. In 1899, Dow began to landscape the space around his house to show his fellow townsfolk what they could do with their yards. He took his hobby seriously, and corresponded with Luther Burbank and other leading horticulturists of his era. During his lifetime, Dow planted 5,000 fruit trees, including 40 varieties of plums.

Unlike other historic American gardens, which owe a design debt to the formal gardens of Europe, the Dow Gardens are original, an unusual place of unfolding environments often likened to Japanese or Oriental styles. Always an enthusiastic traveler, Dow traveled to Japan frequently and became friends with a noted designer of Tokyo parks.

Texture, form, and contrast are as important here as more obvious displays of blooms. The gardens were renovated in the 1970s by Alden

Dow as a retirement project, and more than a thousand trees and shrubs were added. Fantasy environments including a "jungle walk," a maze, and a "land sculpture" reveal Dow's gentle, playful spirit. Don't miss the handicapped-accessible sensory trail, the herb garden, the all-American display garden, and the extensive garden of perennials. Admission is $2. Open daily (except for holidays) 10 A.M.–dusk.

The **Midland Center for the Arts,** 1801 West St. Andrews, 989/631-5930, is another Alden Dow building. Inside the anthropomorphic, Guggenheim-style structure is a wide range of art and science displays, including changing exhibits on the fourth floor, a hands-on Hall of Ideas, and a ferocious-looking mastodon that's especially popular with kids. Admission is $3 adults, $8 for families of four or larger. Hours are daily 10 A.M.–6 P.M. The center is also the site of the popular 17-day **Matrix: Midland** festival held each June, a lively mix of dance, jazz, film, classical music, and science. For information, call 989/631-8250.

## Recreation

In Midland, **cyclists** favor the **Pere Marquette Rail-Trail,** a 22-mile-long, 14-foot-wide asphalt trail that's also a hit for those on foot, in-line skates, or with wheelchairs or strollers. It begins in downtown Midland near the **Tridge,** a three-way pedestrian footbridge spanning the confluence of the Tittabawassee and Chippewa Rivers. The Tridge is a local landmark, and a gathering spot for picnics, concerts, a farmer's market and more. From there, the rail trail follows Saginaw Road to Coleman, passing by the Dow Historical Museum before reaching the towns of Averill and Sanford. For information, call 989/832-6870.

**Paddlers** find three rivers to explore in the area: the Chippewa, Pine, and Tittabawassee. The **City of Midland Canoe Livery,** 989/832-8438, rents equipment from its location practically under the Tridge. If tubing's more your speed, the **Chippewa Valley Canoe Livery and Campground,** 13 miles west, rents tubes as well as canoes. Call 800/686-2447.

After a visit in the 1970s, the vice president of the National Audubon Society called the 1,000-acre **Chippewa Nature Center** "one of the finest—if not *the* finest—private nature centers in the world." More recently, the National Park Service cited the center for its outstanding educational accomplishments and designated it a National Environmental Study Area. Located at 400 S. Badour Rd., 989/631-0830, the Chippewa Nature Center sits along the Pine River and was designed (not surprisingly) by Alden Dow to merge with the living world around it. Its most striking feature is the River Overlook, a 60-foot-long, glass-walled room cantilevered over the Pine River, with great views

*The Chippewa Nature Center was designed (not surprisingly) by Alden Dow to merge with the living world around it. Its most striking feature is the River Overlook, a 60-foot-long, glass-walled room cantilevered over the Pine River, with great views of the center's wildlife.*

of the center's bird life and wildlife.

The center offers an unusually rich mix of things to see, including an authentic log homestead, items discovered from on-site archaeological digs, and a display that's a good all-around introduction to the area's natural history. Other highlights include an indoor wildlife observation area where visitors can sit for hours, and well-executed dioramas that show Michigan geology and scenes from the Saginaw Valley Indian culture. Despite the wide range of attractions, the center's hallmark is the seclusion, peace, and beauty of its surroundings. A map available at the visitors center guides visitors through the 14-mile trail system that parallels the Chippewa River. Popular with hikers and cross-country skiers, the trails include artificially created wetlands, begun in 1990 to compensate for a wetlands destroyed to build a nearby shopping mall. Admission is free but donations are welcome. Open Mon.–Fri. 8 A.M.–5 P.M., Sat. 9 A.M.–5 P.M., Sun. 1–5 P.M.

The **Pine Haven Recreation Area,** Maynard Rd., Midland, 989/687-5700, lies seven miles northwest of Midland in Sanford. Eight wooded trails—with intriguing names such as Logger's Flats, Mud Creek Loop, Riverside Ravine, and Oxbow Flats—cut through a dense, upland forest. Low sand ridges mark the flat landscape, following the shoreline of an ancient great lake and the floodplain valley of the nearby Salt River and Mud Creek, which flow through the park. Wide, well-marked trails range in length 0.7–2.3 miles, with wildflower carpets in spring, bright color in fall, and interesting contrasts in winter. Look for maps of the system posted at the trailhead. Each fall, the area hosts the **Mud Creek Crawl,** a footrace that *Runner's World* magazine lists as one of the nation's top 13 Out-of-the-Way races.

**Veterans Memorial Park,** Neiner Rd., Sanford, 989/687-2800, preserves one of only four known stands of virgin white pine in the Lower

Peninsula. Follow the half-mile Veterans Memorial Trail, which passes through a green canopy of trees, and the mile-long Upland Trail, which loops through the park's lower half past a pretty stream, through deep woods, and along low sand ridges that mark the shoreline of the prehistoric lake that preceded today's Lake Huron. **Hikers** looking for a little solitude should bushwhack into the park's completely undeveloped and unused northern half. **Paddlers** can launch on the Salt River, which crosses the park's eastern boundary and meets the Tittabawassee before meandering to downtown Midland. For more information, contact Midland County Parks and Recreation, 989/832-6870.

Along scenic Bullock Creek, the Michigan Nature Association protects an 80-acre parcel as **Bullock Creek Nature Sanctuary,** located off Five Mile Rd., 989/832-2081. No roads or groomed hiking trails scar the sanctuary, which remains completely undeveloped. Wildflowers here include Michigan lily, tufted loosestrife, trillium, bloodroot, buttercups, and cardinal flower. Tree cover is substantial, with burr oak, swamp white oak, hickory, basswood, cottonwood, red maple, black gum, white birch, and sassafras. It's a good **birding** area, frequented by grosbeaks, flycatchers, orioles, and warblers. A word of caution: The woods are quite thick with brush and prickly ash so heavy clothing is recommended. For more information, contact the Michigan Nature Association, P. O. Box 102, Avoca, MI 48006 (no telephone for information).

## PRACTICALITIES

### Accommodations

Nothing too original to report here, but you'll find a variety of dependable chain motels clustered near the intersection of Wackerly and Eastman, in the vicinity of the Midland Mall. Try the **Fairview Inn,** 2200 W. Wackerly, 989/631-0070, rates $75–100. For campers, **Black Creek Campground** in Midland offers rustic sites (no electricity or showers), at 220 W. Ellsworth, 989/832-6870. In nearby Sheperd, try **Chippewa River Campground,** 989/835-5657 or 832-2454, for sites with electricity, or **River Ridge Campground** in Breckenridge, 989/842-9911.

### Food

Not far from the hotel is **Café Edward,** 5010 Bay City Rd., 989/496-3012. The elegant family-owned restaurant does all its own baking and features an eclectic menu with everything from soup to nut-encrusted fish. Closed Sun. except Mother's and Father's Days. Entrees $15–25.

**Bamboo Garden,** 2600 N. Saginaw Rd., 989/832-7967, is a classy Chinese restaurant with a relaxing atmosphere and reliably good food, including sizzling steak, moo shu pork with Mandarin pancakes, and Buddha duck. Entrees $9–14.

# Grayling Area

From Midland, I-75 cuts across the northeast part of the state until it bisects the North Country near Grayling. Grayling, though, is River Country. Several clean, clear, and immensely popular rivers—most notably, the **Au Sable** and the **Manistee**—corkscrew their way through the area, making Grayling the hub of one of the Lower Peninsula's leading recreational areas.

First classified in 1884, the grayling once was the only game fish to inhabit the upper Au Sable system. Related to trout and salmon and characterized by a long, wavy dorsal fin, grayling were considered both a fine sporting fish and a delicious eating fish—a fatal combination. The thrill of landing one drew the attention of sportsmen near and far, who came by railroad to Grayling, which soon became a bustling center of fishing trips. With no regulations to speak of, anglers pulled grayling in from area rivers by the thousands. The wanton fishing, combined with the declining water quality caused by riverbank erosion from logging, put a quick end to the species. Grayling were rare in Grayling by 1900 and extinct by 1930.

Alas, the town's namesake fish may be gone, but we've learned a few lessons about protecting species and their habitat along the way. Today, Grayling offers some of the finest trout fishing in the Midwest—even the nation—and is a key destination for anglers, canoeists, hunters, cross-country skiing enthusiasts, and snowmobilers.

For more information, contact the **Grayling Area Visitors Council,** 213 N. James St., Grayling, 800/937-8837, website: www.grayling-mi.com.

## OUTDOOR RECREATION
### Paddling
Scenic streams crisscross the forests around Grayling. The Boardman, Manistee, Pine, Rifle, and Au Sable Rivers meander through wetlands, across dunes, and past tree-covered hills. **Canoeing** ranks among the area's most popular pastimes, with a number of liveries offering adventures on the Au Sable and other area rivers.

Even novice paddlers can handle the easygoing currents of these waterways as they scan the shoreline for deer, beaver, black bear, and winsome river otters.

The area's canoe liveries are concentrated in Grayling. For the popular Au Sable, **Penrod's Paddlesport Center,** 100 Maple St., 888/GO-RIVER, is one of the most well-run and amiable outfitters, with aluminum canoes and plastic kayaks for rent, and shuttle services that will retrieve you after a couple of hours or several days on the river.

Flowing east out of Grayling, the Au Sable coils through the **Au Sable State Forest,** 989/826-3211. Designated a state natural river with stretches of the main stream protected as a national wild and scenic river, the Au Sable flows past wooded islands and stretches of white sand. At night, weary paddlers can bed down at one of several state and national forest campgrounds along the river's shore. For day-trippers, the most popular takeouts are at Stephan Landing (about a four-hour leisurely paddle from Grayling) and Wakely Landing, a five-and-a-half-hour trip at a similar pace.

Recognized for its excellent trout fishing and often overlooked by paddlers, you can also launch a boat in the Au Sable's South Branch. You'll find landings at Chase Bridge on the south end and at Smith Bridge, 11 miles to the north.

The Au Sable can be a victim of its own success, though, with raucous crowds sometimes floating the river en masse on hot summer weekends. If you're looking for a party, this is the place, but be aware that local authorities watch for intoxication carefully and fine liberally. (Glass containers, kegs, and Styrofoam coolers are prohibited on the Au Sable to keep down the partying and the littering.) If you're looking for a more peaceful experience, avoid the party set by departing during the week or arranging to paddle a stretch farther outside Grayling, if you can talk an outfitter into it. Alternately, many paddlers find the Manistee River less of a scene. **Shel-Haven Canoe** in Grayling, 989/348-2158, has rentals on

# REBUILDING AMERICA: THE CIVILIAN CONSERVATION CORPS

By 1933, the United States was cracked deeply by the Great Depression. One after another, factories and businesses had shut down. Lines at soup kitchens straggled around city blocks. Nearly 14 million Americans were out of work.

Along with an economy in ruin, President Franklin D. Roosevelt saw an environment in ruin, as well. While virgin forests had once covered 800 million acres of the United States, old growth had dwindled to just 100 million acres. Erosion had ruined more than 100 million acres of the nation's tillable land, and more was eroding at an alarming rate.

In March 1933, President Roosevelt asked Congress for the power to create the Civilian Conservation Corps (CCC). A New Deal program, the proposed corps would recruit 250,000 unemployed young men to work on federal- and state-owned land for "the prevention of forest fires, floods, and soil erosion, plant, pest and disease control."

As proposed, the War Department would run the program, housing, clothing, and feeding the men in work camps, and paying them a monthly stipend of $30—$25 of which had to be sent home to their families. The Department of Agriculture and Interior planned the work projects, which included reforesting cutover land, fire prevention, developing state parks, and building dams, bridges, and roads. Along with the field work, education was a hallmark of the CCC. Camps helped members obtain their high school diplomas, and provided supplemental training in at least 30 different vocations.

The program was not without controversy. Some criticized the cost of the program; others balked at the idea of military control over labor, comparing it to fascism and Hitlerism. Still others contended young men should be with their families, or, as Michigan Congressman Fred Crawford suggested, at work in farm fields rather than in "some camp in the woods to participate in a face-lifting operation on Mother Earth."

But Roosevelt saw it differently. Through the CCC, he believed two invaluable and impoverished resources—the nation's young men and its land—could be brought together in an attempt to save both. In his message to Congress, Roosevelt declared that "We face a future of soil erosion and timber famine," and that the CCC would "conserve our precious national resources" and "pay dividends to the present and future generations."

The measure was easily passed, and so was Roosevelt's goal of 250,000 workers. On April 17, 1933, the nation's first CCC camp opened in the George Washington National Forest in Virginia. By July 1, 250,000 men were at work in more than 1,300 camps—the fastest large-scale mobilization of men (including World War I) in U.S. history. By 1935, "Roosevelt's Tree Army" had ballooned to more than 500,000 workers.

Evidence of the CCC's work remains apparent throughout the Great Lakes region. CCC workers eradicated white pine blister rust in Minnesota, built fire towers and fire roads in Wisconsin, and improved hundreds of miles of fishing streams in Michigan. They built park shelters in Ohio, campgrounds in Indiana, and trails in Illinois. They planted thousands of acres of trees and fought countless wildfires. They even moved moose from Isle Royale to the Upper Peninsula for wildlife studies.

By 1936, the CCC was above reproach, supported by more than 80 percent of Americans and even endorsed by Roosevelt's political opponents. With the bombing of Pearl Harbor in 1941, however, the nation soon had a more pressing duty for its young men. The nation's entry into World War II, along with an improving economy, meant the end of the CCC. But its legacy, like the trees it planted, continues to grow in our nation's parks and forests.

The Civilian Conservation Corps Museum in North Higgins Lake State Park tells the story of Michigan's CCC crews, and includes restored and replica CCC camp buildings. Open mid-June–Labor Day. (Adm. fee for park.) Contact North Higgins Lake State Park, 11252 N. Higgins Lake Dr., Roscommon, MI 48653; 989/821-6125.

the Manistee. For a complete list of liveries in the Grayling region, contact the Grayling Area Visitors Council at 800/937-8837.

As testament to its paddling popularity, Grayling is the site of one of the country's only canoeing festivals, the **Au Sable River Canoe Marathon.** Held in late July, the 120-mile route runs from Grayling to Oscoda on Lake Huron and ranks as North America's longest and most difficult nonstop canoe race. An estimated 30,000 fans turn out, many following the world-class athletes in the 120-mile nonstop race down the river, which requires some 55,000 paddle strokes and more than 14 hours to complete. It's worth going just to watch the thrilling 9 A.M. shotgun start, when more than 50 teams carrying canoes on their heads race through downtown Grayling to the launch site.

## Fishing

Fly fishermen from all over the country make the pilgrimage to the Au Sable, where the combination of spring-fed waters, clean gravel river bottoms, and all the right insect hatches make for

© BOB BRODBECK

trout fishing on the South Branch River

stellar trout fishing. "There are more than 100 miles of prime trout water in the Au Sable system," says Rusty Gates, who operates a simple lodge and Orvis-endorsed fly-fishing school, 989/348-8462. "If you designed a river to flyfish in, this would be it."

All along the area's rivers, you'll spot anglers plying their sport, standing midstream in hip waders, unfurling a long arc of lemon-colored line across the river with their fly rods, or casting from a flat-bottom Au Sable riverboat specifically designed for drifting these shallow waters. Many congregate just east of town in a 10-mile catch-and-release area known as "the holy waters."

While the Grayling Area Visitors Council will help you link up with fishing guides, you also can try your luck from shore. (Obtain a license—available at local shops and gas stations—and check fishing regulations first.) Both the Manistee and Au Sable pass through several miles of state and federal lands, so you won't have much trouble finding public access.

Farther southeast, the Rifle River and its upper tributaries have earned reputations for yielding good catches of brown, rainbow, and brook trout. Some steelhead and chinook salmon are caught on the river's upper reaches, and pike, bass, and panfish are pulled from the park's 10 lakes and ponds, many of which have public access sites.

## Mountain Biking

The rolling terrain of Crawford County makes for some great mountain biking, and even better, the local tourism council actually encourages it—a rare thing in the Midwest. The Grayling Area Visitors Council, 800/937-8837, recommends the following near Grayling: **Michigan Cross Country Cycle Trail,** a great technical single track that "goes for miles and miles." Access it where it crosses Military Road, 0.5 miles north of the North Higgins Lake State Park exit off US-27. Also check out **Hanson Hills,** a recreation area just outside Grayling, with challenging terrain that includes some sandy stretches, and **Wakely Lake,** with three loops of 4.5, five, and seven miles near this lovely lake.

# PARKS AND RECREATION AREAS

## Rifle River Recreation Area

Inner tubes seem to be the transportation option of choice on the slower-moving Rifle River, which meanders from the Rifle River Recreation Area, 989/473-2258, about 15 miles northeast of West Branch, to Saginaw Bay, some 90 miles south. Paddlers shouldn't overlook the Rifle, though, since it flows through Devoe Lake, one of five paddle-only lakes in this 5,000-acre preserve.

The 4,449 acres that now make up the Rifle River Recreation Area were once part of the private hunting preserve of H. M. Jewett, an early auto-industry tycoon. Today most of the visitors who are hoping to leave with a catch are bagging bass and other varieties of fish, not four-legged game. (See **Fishing,** above.)

The recreation area includes several miles of paved and packed dirt trails that travel across one-lane bridges, past forest-fringed lakes, and up several high hills that reveal vistas of tangled stands of cedar. For a great view, head for **Ridge Road,** a dirt track that passes over the park's highest elevations. Those who like to hike can follow 14 miles of picturesque trails that cut through some of the park's most breathtaking terrain.

Visitors can stay at a choice of **on-site accommodations,** including both rustic and modern campsites as well as five "frontier-style" cabins, all located in secluded areas far from campgrounds and day-trippers. They have vault toilets, hand pumps, and only basic furnishings. In winter, the park is a popular spot for cross-country skiing, ice fishing, and snowmobiling.

## Hartwick Pines State Park

The majestic white pine may be the state tree, but few virgin stands remain today. One of the last can be seen at the Hartwick Pines State Park, Route 3, Box 3840, Grayling, 989/348-7068, the largest state park in the Lower Peninsula and the fifth largest in the state. (To get there, take Exit 259 off I-75 just north of Grayling). A century ago, more than 13 million of the state's

---

# THE TINY BIRD WITH THE HUGE FOLLOWING

To call Kirtland's warbler endangered is an understatement—14 Michigan counties, especially the area around the Au Sable River between Grayling and Mio, are the only places in the world where the bird is known to breed today. The world population is estimated at less than 800 pairs.

A tiny blue-gray bird with a yellow breast, Kirtland's warbler winters in the Bahamas, then returns to the Au Sable River area, where it searches for the proper habitat to suit its picky nesting requirements: young stands of jack pine with small grassy clearings. It builds nests on the low-lying branches of jack pines between 5 and 20 feet high; when the trees get much higher, the warbler seeks out younger trees.

The birds' precarious plight is a classic case of habitat loss. When forest fires occur naturally, jack pines are one of the first trees to regenerate in burned areas. But decades of logging and fire suppression led to fewer forest fires, which in turn led to fewer young jack pines. To help the warbler, the U.S. Forest Service and other government agencies now do nature's job, cultivating, harvesting and replanting 2,500 acres of jack pines to keep an ample supply of young trees suitable for the warbler's nesting needs.

The bird's breeding grounds are off-limits to the public with the exception of guided tours led by the U.S. Forest Service (fee) and U.S. Fish and Wildlife Service (free) from May through early July. The Forest Service's 2- to 3-hour tour begins with a video about the warbler, then a visit to the nearby nesting grounds. The Forest Service estimates your chances of seeing one of these exceedingly rare warblers on the tour is near 90 percent. For information on the tours contact the Forest Service's Mio District Office (989/826-3252), or the U.S. Fish and Wildlife Service in Grayling (989/351-2555).

38 million acres were covered with the majestic trees, but by the early 1900s more than 160 billion board feet of timber had been harvested. By the 1920s these once majestic forests were denuded wastelands.

More than 250,000 visitors stroll through the pines annually, marveling at trees that have been here since before the Revolutionary War. Long a popular stop for vacationers heading north, the state park has recently been improved, with a superb new visitors center, a walkway to the pines that's accessible to both wheelchairs and strollers, and a steam sawmill that's part of an extensive logging museum area. The park is also the site of the **Hartwick Pines State Forest Festivals,** four different events held throughout the summer, including Sawdust Days, Wood Shaving Days, Black Iron Days, and Old Time Days.

The park's **Michigan Forest Visitors Center** boasts a 100-seat auditorium; a 14-minute audiovisual show on "The Forest: Michigan's Renewable Resource," which is presented every 30 minutes; and an exhibit hall that concentrates on forest management. Ironically, many of the displays were funded by forestry products companies, so don't expect to see explorations of the negative environmental effects of logging.

The 49-acre virgin tract of white and red pines is the main attraction. Reaching as high as nine or 10 stories, the majestic trees were slated for cutting in the mid-1890s. Fortunately for us, the logging company charged with felling the trees was forced to suspend operations due to economic problems. In 1927, the trees and the surrounding 8,000 acres were purchased from the lumber company and donated to the state for a park.

The self-guided **Old Growth Forest Trail** connects the pines with the visitors center, a 1.25-mile blacktopped path that weaves among the regal giants, including the Monarch. Once the tract's largest specimen at 155 feet, a windstorm destroyed the top 40 feet of the now-diseased and dying tree. Part of nature's cycle, several other immense white pines tower nearby, ready to take its place in the record books.

The pines and museums overshadow the rest of the park, but don't overlook it yourself. With more than 9,000 acres, it offers plenty to do be-

sides admire tall trees. Signs and other displays mark the eight-mile **Scenic Drive,** about two miles north of main entrance, encouraging visitors to explore the woods and natural world around them. **Hiking and biking trails** include 17 miles of easy trails open to mountain bikes in summer and cross-country skiers in winter. The Au Sable River Trail (no bikes) is one of the loveliest. It crosses the East Branch of the legendary river and passes a rare forest of virgin hemlock, saved from the saw by a sudden drop in the price of its bark, which was once used for tanning leather. The two-mile Mertz Grade Nature Trail loops through the park and past an old logging railroad grade before linking up with the Virgin Pines Trail behind the visitors center.

Open year-round, the park is especially popular in the spring, when wildflowers bloom, and in the early fall, when the colorful hardwoods explode in a riot of fiery reds, yellows, and oranges. Park admission is $4 per day or $20 per year.

## George Mason River Retreat Area

George Mason, an area industrialist, so loved this area that he bequeathed 1,500 acres to the state for its preservation in 1954. Located about 15 miles east of Grayling on Canoe Harbor Campground Rd., the George Mason River Retreat Area is considered part of the Au Sable State Forest, 989/826-3211. Subsequent land acquisitions have nearly doubled the size of this natural area, which provides ample opportunity to fish, canoe, or hike along a stretch of the South Branch of the Au Sable River.

## Michigan Shore-to-Shore Riding and Hiking Trail

Popular with equestrians, hikers, cross-country skiers, and snowshoers, this 220-mile trail traverses the entire Lower Peninsula. In this area, it skirts the north end of the George Mason River Retreat Area (see above), passing through pine plantations, stands of hardwood, and along the gentle Au Sable. Other good area access points include the McKinley Trail Camp in Oscoda and across from the Curtisville Store in Glennie.

For more information on the trail, contact the Huron National Forest Huron Shores Station, 989/739-0728.

## PRACTICALITIES
### Accommodations

The **Grayling Holiday Inn,** 2560 S. Business Loop (I-75), 989/348-7611, is a reliable family-oriented motel, with a pool, sauna, children's pool, and play area. The hotel's bar is often full of weary paddlers at the end of the day. Rates $75–175. For paddlers, you can't do better than **Penrod's Au Sable River Resort,** 100 Maple St., 888/467-4837, where tidy cabins line a peaceful bend in the river. Penrod's adjacent paddle-sport center rents canoes, kayaks, and mountain bikes, and offers shuttle service for river trips. Rates $50–100. If you care more about location than amenities and are coming to fish, **Gates Au Sable Lodge,** 471 Stephan Bridge Rd., 989/348-8462, has motel-style rooms with a perfect setting right on the banks of the Au Sable. Rates $75–100. Also right on the Au Sable, **Borcher's Au Sable Canoeing & Bed and Breakfast,** 101 Maple St., 800/762-8756, invites you to slow to the pace of the river on its wraparound porch. It offers convenient canoe rentals and moderate rates of $50–100.

### Camping

You'll find plenty of good and inexpensive public campgrounds in the Grayling area. **Hartwick Pines State Park** in Grayling offers clean, modern sites that fill up fast. Reserve one through the park reservation system, 800/44-PARKS; website: dnr.state.mi.us. You might find a little more solitude (and fewer RVs) at the **Au Sable State Forest,** Route 1, Box 146 in Mio, 989/826-3211, with 10 campgrounds and more than 260 campsites. The nearby **Huron National Forest,** has several campsites in the Grayling/Mio area. Contact the Ranger Station at 401 S. Court St., Mio, 989/826-3252 for more information. Many sites are on the Manistee and Au Sable Rivers and on nearby smaller lakes. The Grayling-area brochure lists a number of other public campgrounds in the area.

### Food

Hungry hunters, paddlers, and birders head for **Bear's Country Inn,** 608 McClellan, 989/348-5516. This cozy, family-style restaurant is known for its huge breakfasts (try the famous Grizzly: homemade sausages and gravy served over biscuits with two eggs on the side) and other comfort food. At dinner, entrees include chicken, batter-dipped cod, and prime rib. Be forewarned that they don't have a liquor license, in case you're craving a brew after a day on the river.

## Gaylord Area

North of Grayling on I-75, Gaylord was officially organized in 1875 as "Otsego," an Indian word that means "Beautiful Lake." Located at the north end of long and skinny Otsego Lake, Gaylord remains a basically rural village with a year-round population of less than 15,000. But its topography lures vacationers by the thousands.

Gaylord sits on the highest point in southern Michigan. For whatever reason, the town decided this was a good enough reason to morph itself into "the Alpine Village," with a Main Street decorated with balconies, window boxes, even a glockenspiel on the Glen's Market grocery store on W. Main Street. And while more Polish and German descendants reside here than Swiss, the townspeople happily don dirndls and lederhosen each July during the annual Alpenfest. Some visitors come for the kitsch, but Gaylord offers plenty of other attractions—from world-class golf to bugling elk—to make the area well worth a visit.

For more information on the Gaylord Area, contact the **Gaylord Area Convention and Tourism Bureau,** 101 W. Main St., Gaylord, MI 49735, 800/345-8621, website: www.gaylord-mich.com

## OUTDOOR RECREATION

### Paddling

Though not the mecca of Grayling, Gaylord is another popular gathering place for paddlers and anglers, since several rivers run through it (or nearby, anyway), including the Black, Manistee, Pigeon, Sturgeon, and the northern branch of the Au Sable. Unlike Grayling, however, liveries are practically nonexistent—bring your own boat.

### Golf

But Gaylord is best known for its golf, boasting the largest number of courses in the state: more than 20, with more on the drawing board all the time. The area around Gaylord, in fact, has emerged as one of the premier golf destinations in the country, with the thickest concentration of designer courses anywhere in the United States, including those by well-known designers such as Robert Trent Jones, Sr., Tom Fazio, and Al Watrous.

Skip the area if you're on a tight budget, however, or if you're not the golfing type. Many of the courses are located at posh, expensive resorts, like **Black Forest and Wilderness Valley Golf Resort,** 7519 Mancelona Rd., 989/585-7090. It was voted "Gaylord's best resort course combination" by the readers of *Golf Digest,* and its Black Forest course also made the list of *Golfweek Magazine's* "Best in America." Nearby, **Treetops Sylvan Resort,** 3962 Wilkinson Rd. also in Gaylord, 888/TREETOPS, lures golfers in with 81 holes (yes, 81) of championship golf featuring designs of Robert Trent Jones, Sr., Tom Fazio, and Rick Smith. Another Gaylord favorite is **Hidden Valley,**, 888/875-2954, with 54 holes on beautiful courses such as the Loon, the Lake, and the Classic.

Other well-known resort/golf combos include **Garland,** 30 miles from Gaylord at 700 N. Red Oak Road, Lewiston,877/4GARLAND, and **Marsh Ridge,** 4815 Old 27 South, 989/732-6794, a surprisingly secluded and serene place just off the freeway. For other top-notch courses, try **Black Bear,** the area's first and only 19-hole layout (the first hole is for warm-up); **Elk Ridge,** where elk sightings are common; and **The Natural,** a course designed by Michigan architect Jerry Mathews to appeal to golfers of all abilities, winding through some of the state's most scenic wetlands. Like elsewhere in the country, developing chemical-dependent golf courses amid natural areas often fuels debate, but the ever-growing popularity of golf continues to result in more courses.

For more on the individual golf courses in the Gaylord area, call the **Gaylord Convention and Visitors Bureau,** 800/345-8621, and ask for the annual *Golf Travel Planner.*

## PARKS AND RECREATION AREAS

### Pigeon River Country State Forest

With a shaggy chocolate mane and a crown of showy antlers, the eastern elk may be Michigan's most spectacular mammal, sometimes weighing in at close to 1,000 pounds. Elk are rare in the Midwest, but about 1,000 of them—the largest free-roaming elk herd east of the Mississippi River—populate this state forest and the surrounding countryside.

Although its primary draw is the opportunity to spot the elk herd, this 97,000-acre state forest north of Gaylord has miles of hiking trails, good fishing, and scenic rustic campgrounds. The **Shingle Mill Pathway** passes through deep woods and across rolling, hilly terrain. Keep an eye out for the forest's "other" wildlife, which includes bear, coyote, bobcat, beaver, otter, woodcock, turkey, bald eagle, osprey, loon, and blue heron. For more information on the state forest, stop by the Pigeon River forestry field office off Sturgeon Valley Road, 989/983-4101.

### High Country Pathway

The Shingle Mill Pathway links up with the High Country Pathway, an 80-mile route that snakes east through state land in four counties, passing through a wilderness of rolling hills and several creeks feeding the Black River. A side trail leads to Shoepac Lake and the Sinkholes

## MICHIGAN'S ELK

some of Michigan's nearly 1,000 elk

© BOB BRODBECK

Once a common sight in the Lower Peninsula, the eastern elk disappeared from Michigan in the late 1870s. Biologists made several attempts to reintroduce the animal to the state throughout the early 1900s, but it wasn't until the successful release of seven Rocky Mountain elk in 1918 that the mammals once again were seen regularly in northeastern Michigan.

Wildlife biologists today believe that the region's elk are descendants of those early animals. They roam a 600-square-mile area primarily east and north of Gaylord in Cheybogan, Montmorency, Otsego, and Presque Isle Counties. The heaviest concentration is north of Gaylord in the **Pigeon River Country Forest Area**, 9966 Twin Lakes Rd., Vanderbilt, 989/983-4101.

The best way to plan a visit is to stop by the Pigeon River forestry field office off Sturgeon Valley Road. Staff will provide maps and suggest good areas and times to view the elk. Fall rutting season proves most spectacular, when the bulls throw their heads back and fill the forests with an eerie whistlelike bugling, their distinctive mating call.

Pathway, where the land is pitted with dry sinkholes and sinkhole lakes, formed when underground limestone caves collapsed.

### Big Bear Lake Nature Pathway

Elk may be the main attraction at Pigeon River, but beavers bring visitors to the Big Bear Lake Nature Pathway, 17 miles east of Gaylord. Part of the Mackinaw State Forest trail, the pathway's two loops total just over two miles and lead through a variety of landscape and habitats home to deer, porcupine, woodcock, waterfowl, and beaver. The shorter, 0.8-mile Beaver Lodge Loop circles a pond with an active beaver colony. The longer Eagles Roost Trail carves a wide, two-mile loop that threads its way through upland hardwoods and through a dense stand of aspen and an open area carpeted with wildflowers in the summer. Both trails begin and end at a large state forest campground on the north shore of Big Bear Lake.

## PRACTICALITIES

### Accommodations

The Gaylord area is best known for its golf resorts, and they can offer some good package deals, especially for families. (See "Golf," earlier in this section.) Another fun resort-type choice is **El Rancho Stevens,** 2332 E. Dixon Lake, 989/732-5090. This ranch/resort sprawls over 40 acres and is perfect for horse lovers and those seeking a quiet, rural atmosphere. It's also great for families, with 29 rooms, as well as larger suites and cottages and a variety of organized children's programs. Rates are based on packages and vary widely.

If you want to splurge, you will not find "rustic elegance" handled anywhere better than at **Garland,** one of the few resorts in the Midwest that the AAA deemed worthy of a four-diamond rating. Encompassing 3,500 acres, Garland includes an enormous and appropriately burly log lodge, the largest one east of the Mississippi, with 160 hotel rooms, 30 condo/cottages, 72 holes of golf, tennis courts, an indoor pool, outstanding cross-country ski trails, a fine restaurant (even a private airstrip, to give you an idea of the clientele). Rates can be moderate to premium, but good package deals are available and, hey, the service and surroundings are top-notch. Garland is located 30 miles southeast of Gaylord on Hwy. 489 in Lewiston, 800/968-0042.

If you're just looking for a simple motel room, you'll find several of the usual chains—Super 8, Days Inn, Comfort Inn, etc.—near I-75.

## Camping
**Pigeon River State Forest,** 989/983-4101, offers 29 rustic sites in a nice secluded setting. For waterfront sites, try **Otsego Lake State Park,** 989/732-5485, with 206 sites on or near Otsego Lake and reliable state park quality, or **Circle S Campground,** 989/525-8300, in Wolverine, with modern sites on the Sturgeon River.

## Food
The same Greek-American family has been running the **Sugar Bowl,** 216 W. Main St., 989/732-5524, since 1919. Specialties include Lake Superior whitefish, scampi, Athenian chicken, and other favorite ethnic dishes, all prepared on an open hearth. Tip: They serve morel mushroom dishes in season, usually May. Don't miss the vintage photos of historic Gaylord on the walls. Entrees $8–18.

**Gobbler's Famous Turkey Dinners,** 900 S. Otsego, 989/732-9005, prepares more than 80,000 pounds of bird annually, all from scratch and served with mashed potatoes, biscuits, gravy, and dressing. The portion sizes are legendary. There are also hand-breaded fresh fish and barbecued ribs if you don't do turkey. Entrees $5–12.

A renovated house on a pretty private lake is the lovely setting for the **Blue Goose,** 900 Charles Brink Rd., 989/732-8254. The menu is a bit heavy on beef and veal, but also serves up fresh fish.

**NORTHEAST MICHIGAN**

# The Huron Shore

## CHEBOYGAN

With a population of 5,000, Cheboygan ranks as one of the largest cities along Lake Huron. But many boaters and anglers focus their gaze inland, where a 38-mile long waterway links Lake Huron with several large inland lakes, ending just shy of Lake Michigan's Little Traverse Bay. Cheboygan sits at the mouth of this popular waterway, welcoming boaters with open arms.

Hikers, birdwatchers, and other lovers of the outdoors will find plenty to interest them here, too. For more information on the area, contact the **Cheboygan Area Tourist Bureau,** 124 N. Main St., Cheboygan, 800/968-3302, website: www.cheboygan.com.

### Downtown
The **Cheboygan County Historical Museum,** 404 S. Huron, 231/627-9597, was built in 1882 and served as the county jail and local sheriff's home until 1969. The two-story brick structure houses a parlor, kitchen, schoolroom, and bedroom in period style, with an adjacent building that contains logging and marine displays. Admission is $1.

The city's **Opera House,** 403 N. Huron, 231/627-5432, once entertained the likes of Mary Pickford and Annie Oakley. Built in 1877 and later rebuilt after an 1888 fire, the Victorian-style theater serves as a stage for local entertainment and is open for tours in summer. Admission is $1.

From the boardwalk in Gordon Turner Park at the northern end of Huron Street, you can gaze out over one of the largest cattail marshes in the Great Lakes. A nesting ground for more than 50 species, it's a favorite of **birdwatchers.** From the boardwalk and nearby fisherman's walkway, you also can see the Mackinac Bridge and Round and Bois Blanc Islands.

## Parks and Preserves

Cheboygan's **Grass Bay Preserve** contains a rare find in the Great Lakes—one of the finest examples of an original interdunal wetland habitat, characterized by beach pools, marshes, flats, and wetlands, all separated by low dunes. Owned by the Nature Conservancy, this delicate ecosystem comprises a great diversity of plants, including more than 25 species of orchids and 11 types of conifers. Four of the species—dwarf lake iris, Lake Huron tansy, pitcher's thistle, and Houghton's goldenrod—grow only on the Lake Huron and Lake Michigan shores.

The Nature Conservancy considers Grass Bay its best property in Michigan. The preserve's original 80 acres have grown to more than 400, including a one-mile stretch of Lake Huron shore. From May to September, Grass Bay is noted for its carpet of wildflowers, including lady's slipper, Indian paintbrush, blue harebell, and sundews. The best way to take them all in is from one of the park's two short trails, which wander through an aspen/birch forest and across old shoreline ridges to the beach. Note, however, that this is private—and very fragile—land. Parking can be hard to find, too—most visitors use the lot at the Nordic Inn on US-23 (ask first). For more information, contact the Nature Conservancy's Michigan Chapter, 2840 E. Grand River Ave., Suite 5, East Lansing, MI 48823, 517/332-1741.

For hikers and cross-country skiers, the **Wildwood Hills Pathway** on Wildwood Road in nearby Indian River offers almost complete isolation. Three well-marked trails—ranging from four to nine miles in length—take visitors deep into the heart of a northern Michigan second-growth forest and cross high, rolling hills in the Mackinac State Forest just a few miles south of Burt Lake.

Two trailheads on Wildwood Road provide access to the pathway, leading into a dense forest of hardwoods and evergreens. Along the way, the only companion you'll likely have is the wind through the trees, an occasional bird call, and a curious chipmunk or two. Trail system maps are located at the trailheads and most major intersections. For more information, contact the Indian River Forest Area, 6984 M-68, Indian River, MI 49749, 231/238-4601.

The swift and turbulent Pigeon River, designated by the state as a wild scenic river, is the highlight of the **Agnes Andreae Nature Pre-**

a beach on Lake Huron

© THOMAS SCHNEIDER

serve. Located in Indian River, the beautifully secluded 27-acre preserve includes 2,000 feet of Pigeon River frontage. On the river's west side, a lowland stand of cedar bordering the riverbank rises to high bluffs covered with conifers and dense hardwoods. There are no designated trails, but hikers and cross-country skiers find well-worn tracks to follow and other trails that border the river. Like many other tracts in this undeveloped part of the state, the preserve is owned by the Little Traverse Conservancy.

## Accommodations and Food

There are several decent motels in the Cheboygan area, such as the **Best Western River Terrace Motel** on Main St., 231/627-5688, with most rooms overlooking the Cheboygan River. Rates $75–150. You can also find cabins and small mom-and-pop resorts inland along the waterway, including **Northwoods Lodge,** 2390 S. Straits Hwy., 231/238-7729, with 15 units for rent by the night or week. Camp at **Cheboygan State Park,** at one of 78 sites along Lake Huron's Duncan Bay. For campground reservations, contact the state park central reservation line, 800/44-PARKS; website: dnr.state.mi.us.

For good food served up with interesting history, try **The Boathouse,** 106 Pine St., 231/627-4316, the former boathouse of the infamous Purple Gang, part of Detroit's 1920s underworld; or the **Hack-Ma-Tack Inn,** 8131 Beebe Rd., 231/625-2919, housed in a rustic 1894 lodge overlooking the Cheboygan River. Whitefish is the specialty.

## THE INLAND WATERWAY

The geography of this region was kind to the early Indians and French voyageurs traversing the Lower Peninsula: a chain of lakes and rivers forms a 38-mile water route, very nearly linking Lakes Michigan and Huron. The route was safer and faster than traveling on the big lakes, and certainly beat the heck out of portaging. Today, the inland waterway remains extremely popular, mostly for fishing and recreational boating. Narrower portions are dredged to a depth of five feet and a width of 30 feet. Boats up to 30 feet

long can join in on what sometimes looks like a nautical parade.

If you want to participate, you can rent a pontoon or fishing boat from the **Indian River Marina,** 3020 Apple Blossom Lane in Indian River, 231/238-9373. You can paddle the route, too, but powerboat wakes can be a little hazardous, especially in large Burt and Mullett Lakes. The route passes through two locks. There are several marinas, boat launches, and put-ins along the way. Traveling west to east, the waterway begins at Crooked Lake about 2.5 miles east of Little Traverse Bay, then flows downstream on the Crooked River to Burt Lake, then the Indian River, Mullett Lake, and the Cheboygan River, which empties into Lake Huron at Cheboygan, 18 miles east of the Mackinac Bridge.

### Burt Lake State Park

Big Burt Lake is the focus of its namesake state park, 6635 State Dr., Indian River, MI 49749, 231/238-9392, located at the lake's southern end. Anglers flock to this 10-mile-long lake, known as one of the best fisheries in the state for walleye, panfish, and bass—but especially walleye. Swimmers seek it out, too, since a soft sand beach runs the entire length of the park. The park has two boat launches, one located next to a popular campground with 375 modern sites. The park offers little in the way of hiking, but does have a nifty observation tower that gives you a great view of the lake.

### Mullet Lake

Popular with anglers, Mullet Lake also has a lesser-known claim to fame: the origin of the term *kemosabe,* used by Tonto in *The Lone Ranger.* Yep, it's true—according to the diehard research of Cecil Adams, anyway, who authors "The Straight Dope," a quirky fact-finding column that began in the *Chicago Reader* and now appears in alternative weeklies around the country.

Here's what Cecil's research turned up: "The term *kemosabe. . .* seems to have been the contribution of Jim Jewell, who directed *The Lone Ranger* until 1938. In an interview, Jewell said he'd lifted the term from the name of a boys' camp at Mullet Lake, just south of Mackinac *(sic)*, Michigan, called Kamp Kee-Mo-Sah-Bee. The camp had been established in 1911 by Jewell's father-in-law, Charles Yeager, and operated until about 1940. Translation of kee-mo-sah-bee, according to Jewell: 'trusty scout.'" While Indian language experts scoff at the spelling, they agree that the pronunciation roughly jibes with the Ottawa word for scout. Now there's some trivia to throw out at your next party.

Speaking of name mysteries, no one really knows why a small town on the east end of Mullet Lake was originally named Aloha Depot. Today it's the site of **Aloha State Park,** 4347 3rd St. in Cheboygan, 231/625-2522, a small 100-acre state park that primarily consists of a boat launch and 295-site campground. Not particularly picturesque by Michigan standards, most sites sit in a relatively open setting, with just a handful directly on the water.

Along with neighboring Burt Lake, pretty Mullet Lake is one of the most popular and productive **fishing** lakes in the state. Anglers vie for walleye and northern pike, but larger stuff lurks down there as well: in 1974, Mullet produced a 193-pound sturgeon, a scaly, long-nosed creature that hasn't evolved much since prehistoric times. Think about that while you're taking a dip.

## ROGERS CITY AND VICINITY

Few travelers visit Rogers City, a quiet community on Lake Huron—a shame, since it is surrounded by beautiful Lake Huron beaches. The town of 4,000 is better known as home to the largest limestone quarry in the world.

The Huron shore's limestone was formed by ancient seas that once covered most of the state. Full of coral-forming organisms, they eventually created large limestone deposits, one of which approaches the earth's surface in Rogers City. In 1907, tests found that Rogers City limestone was unusually pure, an important factor in making steel and many chemicals. The Michigan Limestone and Chemical Company was formed a year later, then subsequently purchased by giant U.S. Steel. More than three miles long and nearly two miles wide, the quarry is expected to produce well into this century.

For more information, contact the **Rogers City Travelers Information,** 292 S. Bradley Hwy., 877/230-2840.

### Area Attractions

Learn area history at the **Presque Isle County Historical Museum,** 176 W. Michigan Ave., 989/734-4121. Built in 1914, this handsome bungalow once known as the Bradley House was occupied by Carl Bradley, the first president of Michigan Limestone and Chemical. Today it houses period furniture, local artifacts (including a beautiful Indian birchbark canoe), and a new maritime exhibit devoted to the mysterious 1958 sinking of the *Carl D. Bradley,* which left only two survivors. The display also explores the sinking of other ships, including the famous *Edmund Fitzgerald.* Open weekdays noon–4 P.M., June–Oct. Donations appreciated.

Travelers who find the Huron shore lacking in comparison with the state's Lake Michigan shore change their minds after a visit to the **Forty Mile Point Lighthouse.** Seven miles north of Rogers City on US-23, a limitless expanse of blue water sweeps in a 180-degree arc to the horizon. A gently sloping beach proves just right for wading, sandcastle building, and swimming. The lighthouse stands guard as a reminder that Huron can, and does, turn dangerous. Though not open to the public, it is a favorite of photographers.

Many rate **P. H. Hoeft State Park,** US-23 N, Rogers City, 989/734-2543, as the most beautiful state park along Michigan's Lake Huron shore. It's easy to see why. With a mile-long swath of soft, white sand, low rolling dunes, and a mixed hardwood/conifer forest, it offers a breathtaking, simple beauty. Surprisingly, it's also one of the least visited state parks in the Lower Peninsula. Even the 144-site modern campground, set against mature pines and hardwoods with lots of shade and privacy, sits half empty most of the time. Head directly for sites 1–33, located just a few steps from the beach. One cabin and four rent-a-tents are also available.

Behind the park's picnic area lies an almost totally undeveloped area, with dunes and woods that abound in wildlife and vegetation. Naturalists can search for the more than 40 species of wildflowers that grow here, including many orchids and irises rare in the state and North America. More than four miles of trails loop through the area for hikers and cross-country skiers.

From Rogers City, it's just 11 miles west on M-68 to the Lower Peninsula's only major waterfall. **Ocqueoc ("Sacred Water") Falls** cascades over a series of two- to six-foot drops. Though not on par with the Upper Peninsula's spectacular waterfalls, the picturesque site is a favorite of picnickers, sunbathers, and swimmers. A seven-mile trail for hikers and cross-country skiers starts next to the falls.

Just a few hundreds yards away, the **Bicentennial Pathway** (created in 1976) loops through the deep woods and over the gently rolling hills of the Mackinaw State Forest. The pathway's three loops measure three, four, and 6.5 miles and are well-used by area hikers. Bed down at the **Ocqueoc Falls State Forest Campground** across M-68.

Just north of Rogers City on US-23, **Seagull Point Park,** 193 E. Michigan Ave., Rogers City

(no telephone), draws visitors to its beautiful beach, curved like a scimitar. A wide band of soft sand and a gradual slope into Lake Huron create a perfect spot for beachcombers, sunbathers, and families. Behind the beach, a two-mile interpretive trail winds through a series of low dunes, with signs along the route that identify the area's natural history and accompanying flora and fauna. Near the park, the **Herman Vogler Conservation Area,** 240 W. Erie St., Rogers City, 989/734-4000, provides a quiet, car-free area on the Trout River. Five miles of nature trails are open to cross-country skiing in the winter.

One of Michigan's newest state parks, **Thompson's Harbor State Park,** 989/734-2543, features meadows, inland dunes, and rocky beaches. The state purchased the land with money left by Genevieve Gillette, ardent parks promoter and landscape architect. Still under development, the 158-acre park so far offers four miles of hiking trails.

## Presque Isle

It would be easy to pass the Presque Isle peninsula and never know it was there. Easy, but a mistake. This almost completely undiscovered resort area off the beaten path between Rogers City and Alpena features two of the jewels in the region's crown. Both are well worth driving out of the way to see.

On a map, the peninsula looks like a beckoning finger (*presqu'île* means "peninsula"— "almost an island"—in French). Two classic lighthouses perch at the tip of the strangely shaped peninsula, including the tallest lighthouse on the Great Lakes.

Inside the **Old Presque Isle Lighthouse Park,** Hwy. 405 between Alpena and Rogers City, 989/595-2787, exhibits and displays relate the history of Great Lakes shipping and lightkeeping, with artifacts and antiques that range from wooden doors from a shipwreck to an old pump organ that visitors can play. Built in 1840, the lighthouse was used for 30 years until it was replaced by a new light a mile north. But no automatic light can provide the view you'll get from the parapet surrounding the lantern room, reached by a trip up the two-story tower's winding steps.

the old Presque Isle lighthouse

The **Presque Isle Lighthouse and Museum,** 989/595-9917, dates to 1870. Trees had grown to obscure an older, shorter lighthouse; the "new" one stretches to 113 feet, the tallest on all the Great Lakes. Situated in the middle of 100-acre **Presque Isle Lighthouse Park,** the tower and restored lightkeeper's house look much as they did more than a century ago. Inside, a caretaker—a descendant of generations of Great Lakes sailors—plays the part of turn-of-the-century lightkeeper on special occasions. The museum and well-stocked gift shop is open May 1–Oct. 15 daily 9 A.M.–6 P.M. The tower is open to the public only on the Fourth of July and Labor Day.

The park's fine nature trails begin at the lighthouse and circle the peninsula's tip. The trails border rugged shoreline, then weave in and out of evergreens and hardwoods, before reaching the peninsula's tip and a sweeping view of Lake Huron from a rocky beach.

Presque Isle's **Besser-Bell Natural Area,** 989/734-2535, offers an intriguing mix of attractions: nearly a mile of wild, undeveloped Lake Huron shoreline, a ghost town, a sunken ship, and one of the few remaining stands of virgin white pine left in the state. Reach the 137-acre preserve from US-23 south of Grand Lake.

The boom-and-bust logging industry both created and destroyed the ghost town of Bell, which once included a school, sawmill, store, saloon, and several houses during the 1880s. A one-mile self-guided trail leads through a magnificent stand of virgin white pine and passes the ghost town and a tiny inland lagoon, the graveyard for an unnamed small vessel. Halfway along the trail, a plaque honors Jesse Besser, who donated this land to the state in 1966 as a memorial to Michigan's lumbermen. The trail continues through a dark cedar forest before emerging on Lake Huron's shore.

### Accommodations and Food

Accommodations are pretty limited in Rogers City. The best place in town (and the only place with an indoor pool) is the 43-room Driftwood Motel, 540 W. 3rd St., 989/734-4777. It overlooks Lake Huron, with rates ranging from $75 to $100. Adjacent to the motel, the **Buoy Restaurant,** 989/734-4747, serves up Lake Huron views and fish dishes.

## ALPENA

Protected by the deep curve of Thunder Bay, Alpena is the largest city north of Bay City on the Lake Huron shore, but it's always been tinged by a Rodney Dangerfield-esque lack of respect. When surveyed in 1839, a deed to the land was offered to anyone in the survey party in lieu of summer wages. . . but few took the offer. At the time, the area was considered mostly a desolate cedar swamp.

Not long after, however, the intrepid Daniel Carter arrived with his wife and young daughter and built a log cabin, becoming the town's first white settler. By 1857, a store and boardinghouse had popped up and, in 1859, Alpena became the site of the county's first steam sawmill. Before long, some 20 lumber and shingle mills buzzed life into the growing town.

Today, the town's economy relies on a large cement industry. But for visitors, it also offers the chance to enjoy the Great Lakes natural beauty without the trendy development and gentrification that have taken over so many of the old resort towns on the opposite side of the state.

Part of the reason visitors have overlooked Alpena is because it's not that easy to get to. More than 70 miles from the nearest interstate, it remains an unpretentious working-class town of corner bars and friendly residents. For decades, diversified industries including paper mills, cement plants and nearby Wurtsmith Air Force Base (now mothballed), meant that the area didn't have to seek out the tourist trade the way other areas—most notably, Mackinac and the Grand Traverse region—have.

But with its bread-and-butter industries gone or fading, Alpena has begun to promote its assets. And there's plenty worth promoting, including two lightly visited state parks with 14 miles of Lake Huron shoreline, a handsome marina, northern Michigan's only year-round professional theater, one of the state's most impressive museums, and a fascinating underwater preserve with more than 80 shipwrecks.

For more information, contact the **Alpena Convention and Visitors Bureau,** 235 W. Chisholm, 800/4-ALPENA.

## Sights and Recreation

The excellent **Jesse Besser Museum and Planetarium,** 491 Johnson, 989/356-2202, combines art, history, and science on two levels. The museum's highlight is the "Gallery of Early Man," a collection of Great Lakes Native American artifacts considered one of the finest in the country. To the probable dismay of archaeologists, the collection, which numbers more than 60,000 pieces, was gathered by Gerald Haltiner, a local state highway worker, and his museum-curator son, Robert.

The museum purchased the collection from the Haltiners in the 1970s and is working closely with local Native American tribes to review the collection with repatriation in mind. Some of its most intriguing artifacts are the copper items that date back more than 7,000 years, made by a people known only as the Copper Culture. The museum's Sky Theater Planetarium puts on changing shows, many with Native American themes, throughout the year.

**Negwegon State Park,** Sand Hills Rd., Harrisville, 989/739-9730, is the carefully guarded secret of a number of outdoor lovers. What exactly are they hiding? Some of the most beautiful and most isolated beaches on Lake Huron. The park's shoreline stretches more than six miles, a lovely string of bays and coves.

Named after Chippewa chief Negwegon, the park also offers three hiking trails named after Native American tribes: the Algonquin, Chippewa, and Potawatomi. The 10 miles of trails skirt the shoreline and loop through a heavily wooded interior. A serene retreat, this isolated park offers natural beauty to hikers and backpackers willing to trade conveniences for quiet, contemplative walks along eight miles of Lake Huron

*Negwegon State Park is the carefully guarded secret of a number of outdoor lovers. What exactly are they hiding? Some of the most beautiful and most isolated beaches on Lake Huron.*

shoreline. Note: There are no camping or picnic facilities here.

**Alpena Wildlife Sanctuary,** on US-23 within the Alpena city limits, has been a favorite sanctuary of hikers, paddlers, anglers, and nature lovers since it was established in 1938 by the Michigan Conservation Department. The 500-acre refuge bordering the Thunder Bay River contains a large expanse of wetlands, an island with fishing platforms, and a viewing platform that overlooks the river. According to the Thunder Bay Audubon Society, more than 130 different species of birds have been spotted here. Year-round residents include Canada geese and mute swans; spring migration brings others, including buffleheads, canvasbacks, whistling swans, and more.

**Divers** have their own sanctuary just off the Alpena shore. Here, the **Thunder Bay Underwater Preserve** thrills divers with its clear waters, interesting underwater limestone formations, and shipwrecks. Rocky islands and hazardous shoals proved treacherous for mariners; the preserve protects some 80 shipwrecks, 14 of which can be explored with the help of a wreck-diving charter. Among the most popular are the *Nordmeer,* a German steel steamer that sank in 1966, and the *Montana,* a 235-foot steamer that burned and sank in 1914. **Thunder Bay Divers,** 989/356-9336, offers charter diving services for about $44 per person, per day, departing from Alpena's city marina.

The state established the Thunder Bay Underwater Preserve—more than 288 protected miles in all—in 1981, largely to prohibit divers from removing artifacts from the site. In October 2000, the state preserve was also designated a national marine sanctuary, a status that grants it federal funding and additional resources for scientific and archaeological study.

## Accommodations and Food

Hotels and restaurants in Alpena have a funky, nostalgic flavor, as if you've been transported back to the 1950s or 1960s. Chief among them are the **40 Winks Motel,** 1021 State St., 989/354-5622, with simple rooms opposite Lake Huron for under $50, and the **Dew Drop Inn** (really), 2469 French Rd., 989/356-4414, also with rooms in the $50 range.

Restaurants include **Thunderbird Inn,** 1100 State Ave., 989/354-8900, an informal spot with fine views of the lake, specializing in steak and seafood, and the family-style **Hunan Chinese,** 1120 State Ave., 989/356-6461, which overlooks the public beach.

## OSCODA

Oscoda sits at the mouth of the Au Sable River, famed as a trout stream and navigable by canoe as far as Roscommon, and that waterway played a prominent part in the state's early pine-logging days. At its most populous, the city's population numbered more than 23,000, and the river was filled with pine logs on their way to the sawmills. While the logs were plentiful, Oscoda grew unchecked. With the depletion of the resource, though, its population began to shrink. Finally, nature put an abrupt end to the city's logging boom: a forest fire swept through in 1911, reducing the city's heyday to ashes. The current population is 12,000.

For more information on the area, contact the **Oscoda Area Convention and Visitors Bureau,** 4440 N. US-23, 800/235-4625, website: www.oscoda.com.

### Fishing Lake Huron

Today, Oscoda figures most prominently as a fishing village and a major sportfishing center for Lake Huron, with chinook salmon and lake and brown trout the main catches. For information on charters, contact the Charter Boat Skippers Association, 989/739-4982, which represents up to 15 charter captains.

### Other Water Diversions

Anglers also try their luck on the Au Sable, but **paddlers** may appreciate the river even more. The Au Sable River Canoe Marathon starts in Grayling and ends here. For **canoe rentals,** try Sunnyside Au Sable Canoe, 989/739-5239; Os-coda Canoe Rental, 989/739-9040; or Hunts Canoe, 989/739-4408.

Trips on the *Au Sable River Queen of Oscoda,* 989/739-7351, depart from Foote Dam daily in season. The tours are especially popular during fall color tours, and reservations are recommended. Tickets are $8.50 per person.

### Huron National Forest

Oscoda also is known as the gateway to the Huron National Forest, which covers most of the acreage between Oscoda to the east and Grayling to the west. (Together, the Manistee National Forest in the western part of the state and the Huron National Forest, 800/821-6263, cover more than 950,000 acres in the northern part of the Lower Peninsula.) The scenic Au Sable River flows through the Huron National Forest and was once used to float logs to the sawmills in East Tawas and Oscoda; now, of course, it's more popular with paddlers.

The national forest is popular with a wide range of outdoor lovers, including morel hunters who visit in the spring, backpackers, swimmers, and cross-country skiers. Trout fishing is a good bet in most lakes and streams, as well as in the legendary Au Sable River.

The forest's famous **River Road Scenic Byway** runs 22 miles along the southern bank of the Au Sable. The byway passes some of the most spectacular scenery in the eastern Lower Peninsula and provides stunning vistas of tree-banked reservoirs and views of wildlife that include everything from bald eagles to spawning salmon. Along the way you'll also pass the **Lumberman's Monument,** a nine-foot bronze statue that depicts the area's early loggers and overlooks the river valley 10 miles northwest of East Tawas. A visitors center here houses interpretive displays that explore the logging legacy. Just a short walk away, a cliff plummets in a near-vertical 160-foot drop to the Au Sable River below. It offers jaw-dropping views of the valley and marks the beginning of the **Stairway to Discovery,** an unusual interpretive nature trail that descends 260 steps to the river and earns distinction as the nation's only nature trail located entirely on a staircase.

Also in the national forest, the **Tuttle Marsh Wildlife Management Area,** about seven miles west of Au Sable, was created in the spring of 1990 as a cooperative effort by the U.S. Forest Service, the state Department of Natural Resources, and Ducks Unlimited. Once an area filled with sad-looking shrubs and scattered patches of grass, the wetlands now attract significant number of migrating waterfowl, shorebirds, and sandhill cranes, as well as muskrats, mink, beaver, and bald eagles.

**Backpackers** looking for a wilderness camping experience should try the **Hoist Lakes Trail System.** Backcountry camping is allowed just about anywhere in this large rugged area of more than 10,000 acres. Nearly 20 miles of trails (hiking only) wander through second-growth forest over gently rolling wooded terrain, around marshes, past beaver floodings, and across streams. The forest teems with deer, bear, coyote, fox, owls, hawks, and songbirds, along with turkey, woodcock, grouse, and other game birds. **Fishing** includes good numbers of bass and panfish. The 6.1-mile **Reid Lake Foot Travel Area** marks another great hiking area surrounded by some of the forest's most imposing hardwoods.

About 10 miles west of East Tawas, the **Corsair Trail System** bills itself as "Michigan's Cross-Country Ski Capital," but is equally popular with hikers and backpackers. Also part of the Huron National Forest, the well-marked trail system (groomed in winter) includes more than 15 loops totaling 44 miles. One writer described this sprawling complex as "a web spun by a spider high on LSD." Choose-your-own adventures range from a short jaunt along Silver Creek to a two-day trek through the entire system.

Full of rolling hills, deep glacial potholes, and a beautiful hardwood forest, the **Island Lake Recreation Area** offers a quiet and beautiful alternative to the more heavily used recreation areas. You'll find it seven miles north of Rose City via M-33 and CR-486. Out of the way and relatively small, it hides a swimming beach, a 17-site campground, and a 65-acre lake that supports perch, bluegills, and large- and smallmouth bass. A self-guiding nature trail explains

the area's natural history and notes points of interest along the way.

## Accommodations and Food

The **Redwood Motor Lodge,** 3111 US-23, 989/739-2021, offers both standard motel rooms as well as cottages near Lake Huron for $50–100. Also on Lake Huron, the **Rest-All Inn,** 4270 N. US-23, 989/739-8822, has clean motel rooms (some with microwaves and refrigerators), a beach, and playground. Rates $50–100.

The **Huron National Forest,** 989/739-0728, has rustic camping at several campgrounds throughout the region. Campers looking more for convenience than solitude can set up at **Acres & Trails KOA,** 3951 Forest Rd., 989/739-5115. Just two miles from downtown and 10 miles from East Tawas/Tawas City, it offers 12 miles of nature trails, housekeeping and "kamping kabins," shaded sites, pull-through sites, and a newly remodeled store and shower house. There's also a rec room, volleyball, hayrides, and a playground for the kids. Open year-round.

Order up a homemade brew at **Wiltse's Brew Pub and Family Restaurant,** 5606 N. F-41, 989/739-2231, to wash down the chicken dishes and steaks cut to order.

# TAWAS CITY/EAST TAWAS

"Tawas" derives from "Otawas," the name of an important Chippewa chief. He's honored in this stretch of Lake Huron shore many times over. The twin cities of Tawas and East Tawas straddle the Tawas River, which empties into Tawas Bay, which is formed by a crooked finger of a land called—you guessed it—Tawas Point.

Today, local festivals reveal the area's popularity with anglers: fishing and the Great Lake are honored at the **Tawas City Perch Festival** in February and the popular **MarinerFest** in July.

The 175 acres of **Tawas Point State Park,** on Route 2 in East Tawas, 989/362-5041, occupy the fishhook-shaped Tawas Point. It's a favorite of naturalists, as much for the ever-changing landscape created by wind and waves during annual winter storms as for the near-perfect model of

© BOB BRODBECK

**The 1876 Tawas Lighthouse guards Tawas Bay.**

interdunal wetlands and some of the best bird-watching in the state.

Opposite the large day-use beach on the shore of Tawas Bay, the 1876 **Tawas Light** is undoubtedly the park's most-photographed feature. While not open to the public (U.S. Coast Guard personnel still live there), it's a favorite among lovers of these classic lights. Not far away, **bird-**

**watchers** gather at the day-use area and nature trail. A checklist of birds spotted in the park lists more than 250, with 31 species of warblers and 17 species of waterfowl.

For more on the Tawas Area, contact the **Tawas Bay Tourist and Convention Bureau,** 402 E. Lake St., 877/TO-TAWAS, website: www.tawasbay.com.

## Accommodations and Food

The **Holiday Inn,** 300 E. Bay St., East Tawas, 989/362-8601, sits right on the beach. It caters to families, with paddleboats and other water sports diversions, as well as an indoor pool and sauna. Rates $100–150.

Michigan's state parks offer consistently good campgrounds. **Tawas Point State Park** is no exception, with 210 campsites and a large sand beach. For all state park camping reservations, call the central reservations line, 800/44-PARKS; website: dnr.state.mi.us. The **Huron National Forest,** 989/739-0728, has rustic campground scattered throughout the forest.

While you won't find any gourmet hideaways in the area, restaurants offer good, stick-to-the-ribs food in generous portions. They tend to be family-style, including **Genie's Fine Foods,** 601 W. Bay, 989/362-5913, a lakefront spot that serves up a country-style breakfast and a gluttonous evening buffet. **Champs Food and Spirits,** 444 W. Lake St., 989/362-8080, offers steaks, seafood, and lighter fare with fine views of Tawas Bay.

# Northwest Michigan:
## The Traverse Bays

Michigan clings tirelessly to that old cliché of the Lower Peninsula resembling a mitten, but in the northwest corner, it really looks more like a glove—its fingers splayed wide, every crack and crevice filled with Caribbean-hued bays, striped in shimmering bands of turquoise and teal.

Grand Traverse Bay dominates the region, a huge lobe of water that dives 30 miles inland, divided into two arms by the thin Mission Peninsula. A bit farther north, Little Traverse Bay burrows eastward to Petoskey. Throughout the region, large lakes pockmark the mainland, and large islands pepper the open waters of Lake Michigan, an intriguing jumble of green

and blue. It's all pretty breathtaking, and we haven't even mentioned one of the region's most striking features: Sleeping Bear Dunes National Lakeshore, great buff pyramids of sand that rise directly up from Lake Michigan to nearly 500 feet, the largest dunes in the Western world.

The remarkable region hasn't gone unnoticed by outsiders. Traverse City has been hosting visitors ever since the French explorers and fur traders passed through in the 1600s, soon spreading word of the treacherous canoe passage across the gaping mouth of the bay, *la grande traversée*. The Traverse region has attracted everyone from James Jesse Strang, a self-proclaimed king who set his sights on ruling Beaver Island, to a family called the Hemingways, who summered for decades on the shores of Walloon Lake.

Traverse City

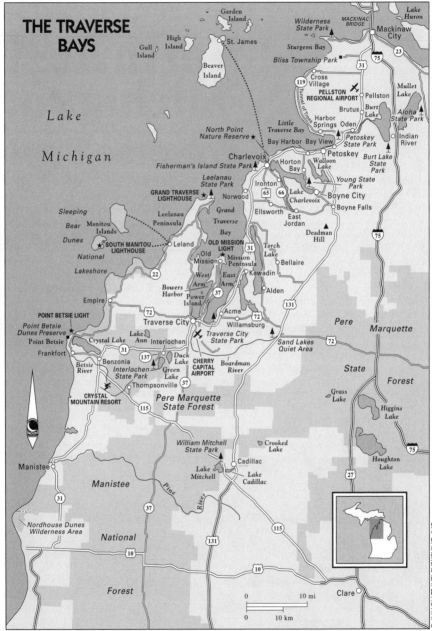

# THE TRAVERSE BAYS

But it was the Victorian "resorters" who left an indelible mark. Summer visitors began trickling in around the 1860s, escaping hot and sticky Midwestern cities for the lake's crisp breezes and gentle shores. Soon they were flooding into communities like Charlevoix and Petoskey, by steamship and by train. The Old Money of Chicago and Detroit and Cleveland built exclusive summer homes. The simply rich stayed in grand pastel-painted hotels. Good Christians came to the church-run camps, which soon evolved from canvas tents to frilly Victorian cottages that remain well preserved today. Decade after decade, they attended Sousa concerts in the park, sailed dinghies across the harbor, and sipped lemonade on verandas overlooking the beautiful blue-green bays.

Today, the two bays anchor one of the state's most popular vacation areas, where the air is still crisp and clean, and the waters are still clear and, for the most part, quite accessible. Like elsewhere, development is a hot-button issue here, as slick developments for urban visitors push aside the quaint cottages and small-town life that made everyone want to visit here in the first place.

The populations of lakeside Traverse City, Charlevoix, and Petoskey can grow several-fold on a good July weekend. Legions of "designer" golf resorts—some ranked among the best public courses in the nation—have drawn visitors in-

land, too. And the list of attractions grows each year: Visitors come for the blue-ribbon fly-fishing, the backroads cycling, some of the Midwest's largest ski resorts, the chic restaurants, the gallery hopping, the yachting, and parasailing and windsurfing.

But for all the new activities, the region's past still weaves into the scene—the lyrical French names, the proud old lighthouses, the industrialists' "cottages," a century-old family farm and its patchwork of cherry trees. It's like the great dunes that ignore park boundaries and drift across the newly paved park roads: past and present jumble together here, some parts planned, other parts as wild as the wind. And somehow the mix gives the whole region a unique sense of place.

## Getting There

Traverse City is 242 miles from Detroit and 305 miles from Chicago, via interstates and major highways. **Cherry Capital Airport** in Traverse City, 231/947-2250, offers service from Detroit and Minneapolis on Northwest Airlines and from Chicago on American Eagle and United Express. North of Petoskey in Pellston, **Pellston Regional Airport,** 231/539-8441, offers commuter service from Detroit and Minneapolis via Northwest Air Link, and from Chicago via United Express. All major rental car companies are available.

# Traverse City and Vicinity

Traverse City sits at the foot of Grand Traverse Bay, a body of water with incredible color and clarity. From blue to green to aquamarine, it shifts colors like a chameleon warming in the sun. The bay, not surprisingly, remains the top vacation draw in Traverse City. In summer months, the water hums with activity—filled with kayaks, fishing boats, jet skis, sailboards, cruising sailboats, and twin-masted tall ships—and the sand beaches fill up with sunbathers and volleyball players.

Though its population swells from 30,000 to nearly 300,000 in summer months, Traverse City has managed to accomplish what few "vacation

towns" have: it remains a real community, where services like hardware stores and quick-print shops still operate alongside the gift shops and galleries. Locals actually use their smart and pretty downtown, and peaceful neighborhoods still thrive just a few blocks away. Traverse City has style *and* substance. Oh, there's no doubt tourism drives the economy here. But Traverse City's strong sense of place makes it all the more appealing to residents and visitors alike.

The fancy **Traverse City Visitors Center,** 101 W. Grandview Pkwy., gives you an idea of tourism's muscle. Stop in to pick up maps and brochures, talk to a volunteer staffer about area activities, and check out rotating exhibits that feature the area's culture, history, and environment. For information ahead of time, contact the **Traverse City Convention and Visitors Bureau,** 800/TRAVERS, website: www.mytraversecity.com.

## TRAVERSE CITY
### Sights and Recreation

Traverse City's main east-west avenue, **Front Street,** is lined with dozens of cafés, galleries, and shops offering everything from nautical home furnishings to cherry pies. The 1892 red-brick **City Opera House,** 112 E. Front St., is being restored to its Victorian splendor and used for community events. Cobblestone **Union Street** marks Old Town, a growing area of arts and antiques.

Browse the **farmers market,** held every Saturday morning from spring through fall along the banks of the Boardman River, between Union and Cass Streets. Depending on the season, you'll find all manner of veggies, fruits (cherries!), flowers—and you can always count on the reliable muffin crop.

On the campus of Northwestern Michigan College, the **Dennos Museum Center,** 1701 E. Front St., 231/922-1055, is a wonderful find. It houses one of the nation's finest collections of Inuit art, along with interactive exhibits at the "Hands On Discovery Gallery" that combine art, science, and technology. Open Mon.–Sat. 10 A.M.–5 P.M., Sun. 1–5 P.M.; admission $2 adults, $1 children.

The **Music House,** 7377 US-31 N, Acme, 231/938-9300, is another surprise, showcasing a vast array of rare antique musical instruments. Its collection includes music boxes, jukeboxes, nickelodeons, pipe organs, and a hard-carved Belgian dance organ. The phonograph and radio galleries trace the history of sound reproduction. Open Mon.–Sat. 10 A.M.–4 P.M., Sun. 1–5 P.M. Admission is $6.50 adults, $2 ages 6–16, under six free.

### Water, Water Everywhere

The Mission Peninsula divides Grand Traverse Bay into two "arms." The West Arm (or West Bay) is the larger and deeper of the two, home to marinas, the bay's tall ship cruises, and a few commercial enterprises. The East Arm (or East Bay) is shallower, warmer, and ringed with sugary sand at its south end—prompting lodging and water sports ventures along its shores.

Along with all the wonderful beaches in the Leelanau Peninsula, Traverse City has several right downtown. Most popular is **Clinch Park Beach,** on West Bay at the foot of Union Street. It's a popular spot, next to the zoo and the park area known as the Open Space. A little farther west, at the foot of Division, **West End Beach** is the place to head for volleyball; pick-up games are common. On East Bay, **Bayside Park** has 600

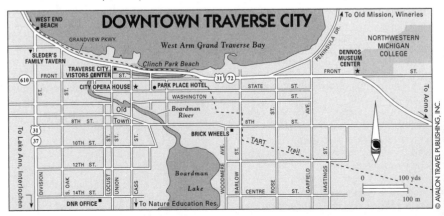

canoeing in the greater Traverse City area

feet of sand beach and a bathhouse, just off US-31 near the Acme turnoff.

The *Nauti-Cat,* 231/947-1730, offers 1.5–2-hour afternoon and sunset cruises on West Bay aboard a 47-foot catamaran. The open-deck arrangement allows for up to 40 guests. Prices range from $13 for a 90-minute kid's cruise, to $69 for a six-hour "island time" cruise with lunch buffett. Reservations recommended, but walk-ons are accepted if there's space. The *Nauti-Cat* docks behind the Holiday Inn, 615 E. Front Street. An authentic replica of an 18th-century wooden schooner, the *Tall Ship Manitou* sets sail three times daily in July and August, cruising West Bay. Call 800/678-0383, or stop by the Dockside Plaza, 13390 S. West Bay Shore Drive. Prices range from $25–39 for adults, $16–24 for children, depending on tour type and time of year.

Grand Traverse Bay isn't the only show in town. The beautiful **Boardman River** twists gently through Grand Traverse County before melting in the West Arm at Traverse City. The Boardman offers excellent fly-fishing and canoeing. Generally, its upper stretches run deeper and are better for paddling.

For information on area water activities—including fishing charters, boat rentals, parasail-ing, and other water sports—contact the Traverse City Convention and Visitors Bureau, 800/TRAVERS.

## Other Recreation

Here's the happy general rule about the Traverse Bays region: Downhill ski resorts seem to morph into golf resorts, and cross-country ski trails often become mountain bike trails (or vice versa, depending on your inclinations).

As proof, the **Pere Marquette State Forest** has a couple of "pathways" in the Traverse City area that double as **cross-country** and **mountain bike** trails. You may **hike** them, too, of course. Most widely known is the **North American VASA Trail,** a 25-kilometer loop that is the site of a popular Nordic race. The VASA (named after Swedish King Gustav Vasa) has challenging climbs and descents. Take US-31 toward Acme; turn right on Bunker Hill Rd.; follow it 1.5 miles, then turn right again on Bartlett to reach the trailhead.

The **Sand Lakes Quiet Area** is a classic northwoods area of small lakes, forest, and meadow about 10 miles east of Traverse City. Ten miles of trails loop through the 2,500 acres of terrain, which is moderately hilly—pleasant, but nothing extreme.

© TERRY W. PHIPPS

**Hobie Cats in the west arm of Greater Traverse Bay**

For more information on biking, hiking, and camping in the Pere Marquette State Forest, call or stop by the Department of Natural Resources office at 404 W. 14th St. in Traverse City, 231/922-5280.

For getting around Traverse City and to various trailheads on your bike, you can avoid busy US-31 by using the **TART** (Traverse Area Recreation Trail). The off-road path shares a railroad right-of-way. It currently extends from US-72 at the West Bay beach (providing good access to the country roads in the Leelanau Peninsula) to Traverse City State Park, with plans to continue expanding it eastward.

For road riding, the Traverse City area—the entire Traverse region, for that matter—offers fantastic backroad cycling. The **Cherry Capital Cycling Club,** 231/941-BIKE, has mapped out zillions of options on its *Bicycling Map of Grand Traverse Region of Michigan,* printed on coated stock that can take a lot of abuse. It's available for $5.95 at local bike shops like Brick Wheels, 736 E. 8th St., Traverse City, 231/947-4274. This good full-service shop has knowledgeable employees and rents road bikes, mountain bikes, and in-line skates.

A few miles south of Traverse City on Cass Road, the **Nature Education Reserve** preserves 370 acres along the Boardman River and the Sabin and Boardman Ponds. Though just outside of town, this surprisingly peaceful area includes seven miles of self-guided nature trails (no bikes) that wind along the river and cross through marshes and grasslands. The Traverse Bay region attracts particularly large populations of mute swans, and a pair frequently nests here, gliding gracefully across the glassy ponds. Farther upstream on the Boardman, large stands of oak crown a steep bluff climbing up from the river and another small flowage, **Brown Bridge Pond.** Stairs and trails lead out to observation platforms and down to water's edge.

Award-winning **golf courses** abound in the Traverse region, just a few minutes away from Traverse City. Just three miles from town, **Elmbrook Golf Course,** 231/946-9180, is an older course with less pretension than some of the new designer courses, with lots of hills and valleys and views of Grand Traverse Bay. The Grand Traverse Resort in Acme (five minutes east of Traverse City on US-31) features two signature courses: **The Bear,** a famously humbling course designed by Jack Nicklaus, with minute greens and deep, deep bunkers, and the newer **Wolverine,** a watery course with views of Grand Traverse Bay designed by Gary Player. Both tend to overshadow **Spruce Run,** the resort's other fine championship course. Contact Grand Traverse Resort, 100 Grand Traverse Village Blvd. in Acme, 800/748-0303, for more info. The rolling pine forests and old orchards of **High Pointe Golf Club** in Williamsburg, 800/753-PUTT, earned it a spot among *Golf* magazine's 100 favorites. The views of lovely Torch Lake add extra challenge to keeping your head down at **A-Ga-Ming,** 800/678-0122, north of Acme in Kewadin. For a complete list of area courses and package deals, contact the Traverse City Convention and Visitors Bureau, 800/TRAVERS.

What's that island in the West Arm, you ask? It's **Power Island,** a 200-acre nature preserve owned by the city, with beaches and five miles of hiking trails. For paddlers and other boaters, it's a fun destination for an afternoon picnic, but on weekends it often becomes a local party spot.

## Old Mission Peninsula

The Old Mission Peninsula pierces north from Traverse City, a narrow sliver of land that neatly divides Grand Traverse Bay in two. This whaleback ridge stretches 18 miles, a quiet agrarian landscape cross-hatched with cherry orchards and vineyards. Nowhere else on earth grows more cherries per acre than the Mission Peninsula, where the surrounding waters, insulating snows, and cool summer air form the perfect microclimate for raising fruit. Veer off M-37 onto almost any country road to wander past the pretty, peaceful orchards.

Grapes also thrive on the Mission Peninsula, creating a burgeoning **winemaking** industry. (Though locals like to tell you it's because the peninsula sits at the same latitude as Bordeaux, France, they really should thank the moderating effects of the lake.) Most wineries here offer tours and tastings, and visiting them brings an extra benefit: the ridgetop roads of

*Grapes thrive on the Mission Peninsula, creating a burgeoning winemaking industry.*

the Mission Peninsula come with incredible views that often take in both arms of Grand Traverse Bay.

**Chateau Grand Traverse,** located eight miles north of Traverse City on M-37, 231/223-7355, was a pioneer in bringing European vinifera wines to the Midwest. It has a beautiful tasting room, with wonderful bay views, for tasting its international-award-winning rieslings and chardonnays. It's open Memorial Day–Labor Day Mon.–Sat. 10 A.M.–7 P.M., Sun. noon–7 P.M.; off-season hours are Mon.–Sat. 10 A.M.–5 P.M., Sun. noon–5 P.M. **Bowers Harbor Vineyards,** 2896 Bowers Harbor Rd., just east of Bowers Harbor, 231/223-7615, is a small, friendly, family-run winery, with a tasting room open daily in summer months 11 A.M.–6 P.M., weekends Jan.–April. **Chateau Chantal,** 15900 Rue de Vin, 231/223-7355, includes both a tasting room and B&B in a French chateau–inspired winery high on a hill. Tours and tastings are offered daily noon–5 P.M., with longer hours in summer months. **Peninsula Cellars,** 18250 Mission Rd., 231/223-4310, is one of the peninsula's newest wineries, with a tasting room in the Village of Old Mission. Open in summer months Mon.–Sat. 10 A.M.–6 P.M., Sun. noon–6 P.M.

The peninsula was named for the mission first built near the tip of the peninsula in 1839 by a Presbyterian minister who came from Mackinac to convert the Ojibwa and Ottawa. The **Old Mission Church** on M-37 in Old Mission is a replica, but it houses the original bell. A few displays tell the peninsula's early history and evolution into a fruit-growing region. The 1842 **Old Mission House** nearby is the real thing. Curve east around Old Mission Harbor to **Haserot Beach,** a curve of sand near the small protected harbor.

The **Old Mission Light** stands sentinel over the point, a pretty structure dating to 1870, along with its white clapboard keeper's home (now privately owned). A plaque notes that the 45th Parallel crosses here. Curiously, this is a big claim to fame on the peninsula, as if it were the only place in America intersected by this line of

**NORTHWEST MICHIGAN**

latitude. The state has acquired several hundred acres around the lighthouse, including much of the rocky beach, land set aside for a possible future state park.

## PRACTICALITIES

### Accommodations

The Traverse City area has more than 5,000 rooms, everything from inexpensive motels to deluxe resorts. The **Traverse City Convention and Visitors Bureau,** 101 W. Grandview Pkwy., Traverse City, has a good directory and can help you narrow down your choices. In summer months, you'd be wise to show up with a reservation, so contact them ahead of time at 800/TRAVERS, website: www.mytraversecity.com.

Lots of mom-and-pop motels and chain operations line up on US-31 along East Bay, Traverse City's original tourist stretch, known as the "miracle mile." Some newer ones have nudged onto this desirable real estate, like the **Pointes North Inn,** 2211 US-31 N, 800/968-3422. It has 300 feet of private beach, a waterfront pool, balconies, and in-room mini-kitchens. Rates $150–250. You'll save money by staying on the other side of US-31, of course, and plenty of public beaches mean you can still get to the water easily enough. The **Traverse Bay Inn,** 2300 US-31 N, 800/968-2646, is a tidy and pleasant older motel, with an outdoor hot tub and pool, and some fancier new suites with kitchens and fireplaces. It gets bonus points for allowing dogs. Rates $50–125.

It's not on the water, but the upper floors of the **Park Place Hotel,** 300 E. State St., 800/748-0133, come with incredible views of Grand Traverse Bay. This 1870s downtown landmark was in sad disrepair in 1989, when the local Rotary club purchased it and poured $10 million into renovations. The Traverse City Rotary is believed to be the wealthiest in the nation, after it discovered oil on property it owned. The club did a fabulous job restoring the Park Place to its turn-of-the-century opulence. Rates $100–200.

Outside of town, the **Ellis Lake Resort,** 8440 US-31 S, Interlochen, 231/276-9502, has cute waterfront cabins and an outdoor hot tub just 10 minutes from Traverse City. Pets permitted, rates $50–100. **Ranch Rudolph,** 6841 Brown Bridge Rd., Traverse City, 231/947-9529, has motel units and a lodge with fireplace, but the draw here is the location: 12 miles from Traverse City in the Pere Marquette State Forest on the shores of the Boardman River. There's paddling and fly-fishing right outside the door. Rates $50–150.

### Camping

You won't find a quiet nature retreat, but if you're looking for clean and convenient camping, then **Traverse City State Park,** 1132 US-31, fits the bill. Just two miles east of downtown, the park has 344 modern sites in a suburbanish setting, grassy with shade trees. A pedestrian overpass will get you across busy US-31 to the main feature of the park: a grassy picnic area and a quarter-mile of beach on Grand Traverse Bay. Though pretty, the stretch of sand can quickly become unpleasantly jammed on a summer weekend. Camp here for convenience, maybe, but head elsewhere for a day at the beach—the region has plenty of better choices. For reservations, call 800/44-PARKS; website: dnr.state.mi.us.

You'll find more peace and seclusion at the many rustic campgrounds in the **Pere Marquette State Forest** just a few miles east of town. A couple to consider: **Arbutus Lake 4,** with 50 sites on a pretty chain of lakes. From US-31 near the state park, take Four Mile Road south to North Arbutus Road. **Guernsey Lake** has rustic sites on a small lake in the Sand Lakes Quiet Area. Follow CR-660 or 605 to Guernsey Lake Road (where it crosses the Boardman River for the second time). The Department of Natural Resources office, 404 W. 14th St. in Traverse City, 231/922-5280, can provide you with suggestions, maps, and directions.

### Food

Traverse City is thick with good restaurants, from simple to elegant. **Apache Trout Grill,** 13671 West Bay Shore, Traverse City, 231/947-7079, is a casual spot overlooking the West Arm, featuring "northern waters" fish specialties partnered with distinctive sauces. Entrees about $13. **Sleder's**

**Family Tavern,** 717 Randolph St., Traverse City, 231/947-9213, has been around since 1882, an institution known for its burgers, ribs, and its gorgeous original mahogany and cherry bar. Sandwiches about $5, entrees $11.

On the Mission Peninsula, the **Boathouse,** 14039 Peninsula Dr., 231/223-4030, is one of the region's newer and most highly touted restaurants, with fine, diverse cuisine in a nautical atmosphere overlooking the Bowers Harbor marina. Good vegetarian selections. Entrees about $18. The nearby **Bowers Harbor Inn,** 13512 Peninsula Dr., 231/223-4222, offers elegant dining in an 1880s mansion, complete with resident ghost. Specialties include Fish in a Bag and rack of lamb. Excellent wine list. Entrees about $32. The same restaurateurs operate the **Bowery,** 231/223-4333, in the home's servant's quarters. This more casual spot features great ribs, fish, pasta, and more than 50 different beers. Entrees about $12. Filled with the works of local artists, the **Old Mission Tavern,** 17015 Center Rd., 231/223-7280, incongruously features international cuisine from Poland, Greece, and Italy. Entrees about $18.

# SOUTH OF TRAVERSE CITY

## Interlochen

South of town, the summertime bustle of Traverse City quickly fades into rolling farmland and woodlots. Incongruously tucked in this rural landscape, the **Interlochen Center for the Arts,** 231/276-6230, operates a renowned school on a 1,200-acre campus under a tall canopy of pines. Each year, nearly 2,000 gifted students come to pursue music (and increasingly, dance, theater, and visual arts) at this acclaimed "summer camp."

Interlochen also presents its **Summer Arts Festival,** a three-month schedule of nightly concerts at its outdoor Kresge Auditorium. Its lineup of musicians and entertainers is diverse and impressive, ranging from Yo Yo Ma, Itzhak Perlman, and the Manhattan String Quartet to Ray Charles, the Neville Brothers, Judy Collins, and Vince Gill. Call for schedule and ticket information. Interlochen is located 14 miles

southwest of Traverse City on M-137, three miles south of US-31.

Nearby, **Interlochen State Park,** M-137, 231/276-9511, fans out between Green Lake and Duck Lake, preserving one of the area's few remaining stands of virgin white pine. Thanks to the park's location near Traverse City and Interlochen, its campsites are the main draw. They're very nice ones, too, clustered around the lakeshores with many nice lake views. The modern campground, with the bulk of the park's 490 campsites, is on Duck Lake. A couple of dozen rustic sites are across the park on Green Lake. Both fill up in summer, so reserve a site ahead by calling 800/44-PARKS; website: dnr.state.mi.us.

## Benzie County

Unspoiled Benzie County stretches from west of Traverse City to the Great Lakes port of Frankfort, a hilly region dotted with lakes and bisected by two pristine rivers, the Platte and the Betsie.

The six miles of trails in the **Lake Ann Pathway** offer plenty to see, taking you past Lake Ann, some smaller lakes, a stretch of the Platte River, bogs, and natural springs. The hilly terrain is pleasant for hiking, mountain biking, or cross-country skiing. Part of the Pere Marquette State Forest, 231/922-5280, it also has a very nice rustic campground with 30 shady, grass-covered sites and a swimming beach on Lake Ann. Follow US-31 west from Traverse City to Reynolds Road (4.5 miles past the turnoff to Interlochen). Turn right and drive four miles to the campground and trailheads.

The Betsie River wanders across Benzie County, eventually growing into a broad bay at Frankfort. Popular among anglers for trout and lake salmon, it also is a pretty paddling spot, a designated wild and scenic river. From a put-in at Grass Lake, it's a 44-mile float to Betsie Lake near the Lake Michigan shore, largely through undeveloped state forest. (You can camp on forest along the banks.) There are several other public launches for a shorter trip. Contact Pere Marquette State Forest, 231/922-5280, for maps and information.

West of Benzonia, the Betsie passes through the private wildlife sanctuary of **Gwen Frostic**

**Prints,** two miles west of US-31 on River Rd., 231/882-5505. Frostic's studio is an eclectic building of wood and stone and glass and cement, where a dozen old Heidelberg presses clank away, cranking out Frostic's woodblock prints and poetry. Frostic, who died in 2001, was a woman of bold spirit whose works paid homage to nature and independence. Aside from her riddling book titles like *The Caprice Immensity* and *Evolving Omnity,* Frostic's words are forthright, describing "the wondrous feeling that comes not from seeing but from being part of nature." This intriguing shop has note cards, gift wrap, books, and more.

At **Frankfort,** the Betsie River flows into Betsie Lake, which opens to Lake Michigan and forms a remarkably well-protected harbor. A crude wooden cross at the river's mouth marks the site of French explorer Père Jacques Marquette's death in 1677. Researchers now believe that the French voyageurs who wrote in their journals of the "Rivière du Père Marquette" were describing the Betsie.

North of Frankfort at Point Betsie, the 1876 **Point Betsie Light** perches atop a dune with waves practically lapping at its base, a tenuous but highly scenic setting. The lighthouse was automated in 1983, and still houses Coast Guard personnel who work in Frankfort. The **Point Betsie Dunes Preserve** stretches south from the lighthouse, 71 acres of wonderfully undeveloped duneland, with barren sand beach, scrubby pines, and low-lying dunes slowly marching inland.

West of Thompsonville on M-115, **Crystal Mountain Resort** began as a downhill **skiing** destination but has evolved into much more. While it still offers plenty of downhill—25 runs on two camel-humped slopes—it really shines in the cross-country department. Nordic skiers ride a chairlift from the Nordic Center to the top of the downhill slopes, where a trailhead leads to 30 kilometers of impeccably groomed cross-country terrain. And it's great stuff—a combination of gentle pathways and roller-coaster rides that weave all over the resort's 1,500 acres of land. Screaming Eagle, a 3.9-kilometer (3.2 mile) trail, actually qualifies as a double-black diamond. The network is truly one of the finest in the Midwest.

Crystal Mountain invested wisely in its architecture, with pretty villas and tasteful condos scattered all around the property. Rates begin at about $100, but vary widely depending on unit and time of visit. Ski or golf packages are usually your best deal. In summer, Crystal's 27 holes of **golf** are the main draw, but it also offers clay tennis courts, indoor and outdoor pools, and other resort amenities. Some of those great cross-country trails welcome mountain bikes in spring—more than 10 miles of intermediate and advanced terrain overlooking the Betsie River Valley, along with 13 more miles on nearby Department of Natural Resources land. For information and reservations, contact Crystal Mountain Resort, 12500 Crystal Mountain Dr., Thompsonville, MI 49683, 800/968-7686, website: www.crystalmountain.com.

# The Leelanau Peninsula

*I came home from New York City to a farmhouse at the base of Sleeping Bear Dunes. . . . It was in this farmhouse that I learned to love the peninsula I'd earlier left. The intense shadows on full moon nights. The sound of the grass. The early morning sun shining on the dunes behind the house, reflecting back pink and gold hammered air everywhere. . . .*

*So I'd moved back to the Leelanau Peninsula, into a little house on a little road. I needed land and country around me so I could feel I belonged to something bigger than myself. I needed birds and trees and the observable minutiae of seasons so I could feel my life as a stream of little movements. I needed huge hills and big lakes and that sense of panorama and distance that living on a peninsula gives one. I needed this place.*

—*Kathleen Stocking,*
**Letters from the Leelanau**

The Leelanau Peninsula has long held a grip on writers and artists (novelist Jim Harrison, among others, also makes his home here), a ragged land of hills and lakes and scribbled shoreline that straggles northward between Lake Michigan and Grand Traverse Bay. Maybe it's the dramatic dichotomy of the place. On its western shore, the oh-so-grand dunes, rising directly up from the lake's surface; inland, a soft and pretty landscape, a muted watercolor of red barns, white farmhouses, and Queen Anne's lace waving in the roadside ditches.

All kinds of people will tell you that Leelanau is an Indian word meaning "Land of Delights," a description that certainly fits this varied peninsula. Only problem is, the word never existed in the language of the area's Ottawa Indians; they never even used the letter L. Henry Schoolcraft, the white man who explored the Lake Michigan coast in the 1820s, most likely named it, giving it an "Indian-sounding" name. "Leelanau" can be anything you want it to be—just like your time here.

Leelanau County proper begins just west of Traverse City, and the county line stretches 30 miles straight west to the Sleeping Bear Dunes and Lake Michigan. Everything above that line is the Leelanau, a 28-mile-long peninsula that includes 98 miles of Great Lakes shoreline, 142 inland lakes and ponds, and 58 miles of streams. Roads twist along with the contours of the hills, luring you toward farm stands and onto dirt roads that can't possibly go anywhere you intended to go.

As local author Bill Mulligan notes, "The meandering expanse of water, woods, and sand of Leelanau is a nice counterweight to the exuberance of Traverse City." So meander.

## Information

The very capable **Traverse City Convention and Visitors Bureau,** 101 W. Grandview Pkwy., Traverse City, 800/TRAVERS, can give you all the information you need about the Leelanau Peninsula. For specific information on Sleeping Bear Dunes National Lakeshore, contact **Sleeping Bear Dunes National Lakeshore,** 9922 Front St. (M-72), 49630-0277 or 231/326-5134, website: www.nps.gov/slbe.

## SLEEPING BEAR DUNES NATIONAL LAKESHORE

Glaciers and a millennium of wind and water sculpted the Sleeping Bear Dunes, rimming this corner of Michigan with a crust of sand and gravel like salt on a margarita glass. "Beach dunes" line the southern part of the national seashore, the classic, low-lying hillocks of sand you might picture when you think of dunes, created by the prevailing west winds carrying sand to low-lying shores.

But it's the "perched dunes" that claim center stage here, immense pyramids of sand spiking up from the very edge of Lake Michigan and climbing at an impossible angle toward the sky. Glaciers first carried these mountains of sand and gravel to what is now the shoreline; nature con-

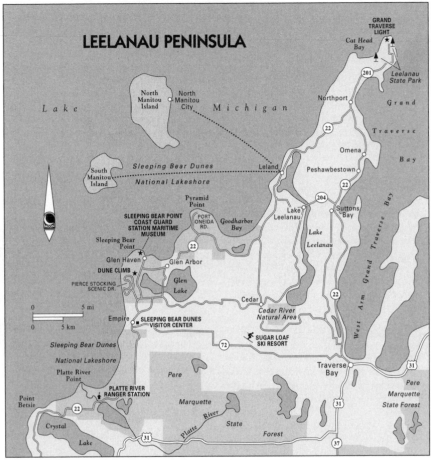

tinues the process, with waves eroding the great dunes and westerlies building them up again. At their highest, the perched dunes once topped out at about 600 feet. Today, Sleeping Bear measures about 460 feet, still believed to be the largest dune outside the Sahara Desert.

The Ojibwa named the Sleeping Bear Dunes. According to legend, a mother bear and her two cubs were driven from a raging forest fire in what is now Wisconsin, forced to swim across Lake Michigan. The mother reached the far shore and climbed to the top of a bluff to wait for her cubs, who had grown tired and lagged behind. "Sleeping Bear" is the largest dune, the mother bear lying in wait for her cubs. Alas, the cubs drowned, and they are the Manitou Islands that lie offshore.

To borrow an old cliché, words really *can't* describe the Sleeping Bear Dunes. They can be a sunny, friendly playground, with squealing children tumbling down the Dune Climb. They can be lunar-like and desolate, a bleak desert on a January day. They can be pale and white-hot at noon, then glow in peaches and pinks like white zinfandel at sunset.

But they are always spectacular. Today, the Sleeping Bear Dunes National Lakeshore en-

© TRAVEL MICHIGAN

Sleeping Bear Dunes, near Empire

compasses nearly 72,000 acres, including 31 miles of Lake Michigan shoreline, North and South Manitou Islands, lakes, rivers, beech and maple forest, waving dune grasses, clattering beach peas, and those unforgettable dunes. It's truly a magnificent landscape, unlike anything else on the continent.

## Empire and South

Start your visit to the Sleeping Bear Dunes National Lakeshore in Empire, where the **Philip A. Hart Visitors Center,** 9922 Front St., M-72, 231/326-5134, has an orientation slide program, displays on natural, maritime, and logging history; a ranger on duty; a good bookstore; and all kinds of maps and information. Open 9 A.M.–4 P.M. daily, until 6 P.M. in peak summer season. You can also pay your user fee here; Sleeping Bear was among the first crop of national parks to charge admission. Cost is $7 per vehicle, valid up to seven days, or $15 annually. You may also purchase passes at the Platte River Ranger Station, the Pierce Stocking Scenic Drive, the Dune Climb and the dock at Leland.

South of Empire, the **Empire Bluff Trail** winds through forest before erupting into a clearing for a dramatic vantage point of the big dunes some five miles north. In three-quarters of a mile, the trail dead-ends at a high bluff overlooking the water, so clear you can often see schools of big lake trout cruising by. Farther south, **Platte River Point** improves on a great day at the beach with a perfect setting, a sandy spit bordered by Lake Michigan and the mouth of the Platte River. Rent an inner tube from Riverside Canoe Trips, on M-22 at the Platte River Bridge, 231/325-5622, and join in on the popular sport of launching in the river and shooting out into the lake.

## Pierce Stocking Scenic Drive

"When I lived in Manhattan in the 1970s, I used to have a recurrent nightmare that there was a big highway across the top of the dunes and at the topmost point, a Holiday Inn," writes Kathleen Stocking in *Letters from the Leelanau.* "Now, except for the Holiday Inn, that prescient dream has materialized."

Ironically, the drive is named for Stocking's father, a lumberman who owned much of the land that is now national park. For those of us who didn't grow up with the dunes as our backyard, this 7.4-mile loop of pavement that winds through the woods and atop a stretch of dune is less offensive. In fact, it could be argued that it keeps people from traipsing over fragile dune plants for views. Either way, the extremely popular route *is* there, with scenic overlooks of Glen Lake, the dunes, and Lake Michigan.

The drive offers access to the **Cottonwood Trail,** a 1.5-mile sandy, self-guided walk through dunes that tells you about the ecology and diverse plant life in the dunes. The drive also leads you to the **Lake Michigan Overlook,** a platform 450 feet above the water with views stretching to Point Betsie, 15 miles south, and 54 miles across to Wisconsin. Though the park service discourages it—they've seen too many sprained ankles and broken arms and close cardiac calls—you can slide and tumble your way down the dune to the beach here. It is a steep, long, exhausting climb back up, though, about an hour's worth of crawling.

Which is why the park service points visitors instead to the **Dune Climb,** also accessible from Pierce Stocking Drive, a more manageable 130-foot dune that Mother Nature conveniently deposited on the lee side of the plateau. It's the perfect place to let kids run until exhaustion, and to climb yourself for a fine view of shimmering Glen Lake.

### Glen Haven Area

In sleepy Glen Haven, the Park Service operates a nifty museum in the old lifesaving station. In summer months, the **Sleeping Bear Point Coast Guard Station Maritime Museum** (whew) depicts the work of the U.S. Lifesaving Service, the forerunner of the U.S. Coast Guard. Exhibits include lifesaving boats and the cannon used to shoot lifelines out to the sinking vessels, while video programs illustrate the drill and the rigorous life the crews led. They got a regular workout: some 50 ships wrecked along this passage between the mainland and the nearby Manitou Islands, one of the busiest routes on the Great

Lakes in the mid-19th century, since it offered a convenient shortcut between Mackinac Island and Chicago. The station originally sat a few miles west at Sleeping Bear Point; it was moved here in 1931 when the ever-omnipotent dunes threatened to bury it. Open 10 A.M.–5 P.M. Memorial Day weekend–Labor Day weekend; free admission with park pass.

East on M-109, **Glen Arbor** occupies a small patch of private real estate completely surrounded by national park, Lake Michigan, and Glen Lake. It caters to the tourist trade with mostly tasteful galleries and craft shops, and also has a grocery for reloading the picnic supplies. Cherry lovers shouldn't miss **Cherry Republic,** 6026 S. Lake St., 231/334-3150, which bills itself as "the largest exclusive retailer of cherry products in the United States." You'll find cherry baked goods, cherry sodas, chocolate-covered cherries, cherry salsas, cherry jam… well, you get the idea.

Near Glen Arbor, the **Pyramid Point** hiking trail is a hilly 2.7-mile loop that leads to the park's northernmost point, with a high lookout over Lake Michigan and Sleeping Bear Bay. From Glen Arbor, take M-22 three miles east to Port Oneida Rd.

### North and South Manitou Islands

The Manitous lie about 17 miles off the mainland, 20,000 acres of once-developed land that has largely been reclaimed by nature and now is managed as part of Sleeping Bear Dunes National Lakeshore. South Manitou is the smaller (5,260 acres) and more accessible of the two, serviced by passenger ferry from Leland daily in summer months. The same ferry also stops at North Manitou five times a week in July and August, fewer times in spring and fall. The trip to either island takes about 90 minutes and costs $22 roundtrip adult, $13 children 12 and under. (No cars, bicycles, or pets permitted.) For schedule information and reservations, contact **Manitou Island Transit,** in Leland, 231/256-9061, website: www.leelanau.com/manitou. The islands have potable water at a very few locations, but no other services. Even day-hikers should pack a lunch.

**South Manitou** was first settled in the 1830s. Islanders made a living by farming and logging, supplying food and fuel to the wood-burning steamers that traveled through the busy Manitou Passage. Farming was exceptional on South Manitou. Isolated from alien pollens, it proved the perfect place to produce crops and experiment with hybrid seeds, and was soon highly respected in agricultural circles. A South Manitou rye crop won first prize in an international exposition in 1920; by the 1940s, most of Michigan's bean crop came from South Manitou seed. By the 1960s, though, the island had become mostly a summer cottage getaway and, a decade later, the National Park Service began condemning and buying up the land for national lakeshore.

Today, visitors can arrange for a **tour** through the ferry company, a 90-minute trip in an open-air truck that follows abandoned roads to farmsteads, a schoolhouse, and cemetery. Cost is $7 adults, $4 children. Near the ferry dock, a small **visitors center** in the old village post office has displays on island history. Nearby, the 1871 **South Manitou Lighthouse** is open on summer afternoons, allowing you to scale the 100-foot tower.

Hikers and backpackers will want to get farther afield, though. The island has 10 miles of marked hiking trails that lead to some interesting sights. Day-hikers will have to move right along, but they can make the six-mile roundtrip to check out the **wreck of the *Francisco Moran*** and still make it back in time for the afternoon ferry. Like many ships that failed to navigate the tricky Manitou Passage, in 1960 this Liberian freighter ran aground. Its battered skeleton lies largely above the water's surface just a few hundred yards offshore.

Nearby (check your time, day hikers!), a side trail winds through a grove of virgin cedars, some more than 500 years old. Deemed too isolated to log, the slow-growing trees are the largest of their kind left in North America, some measuring more than 15 feet around and nearly 90 feet tall. Another half mile west, the state's most remote dunes tower over the western shore, 300-foot perched dunes similar to those on the mainland.

To properly enjoy all the island has to offer, of course, you need to spend more than an afternoon. Camping is permitted only at three rustic campsites; reservations required.

Like South Manitou, **North Manitou Island** was once a farming and logging community, then a summer getaway. Acquired by the National Park Service in 1984, it still has some patches of private property. But otherwise, this large island is even less developed than its southern neighbor. Those who come here do so to camp, hike, and explore the abandoned homes and other buildings.

North Manitou receives far fewer visitors than South Manitou—until fall hunting season, anyway. Nine deer were introduced here in the 1920s in the hopes of developing a herd large enough to hunt. Boy, did that work! In 1981, more than 2,000 deer roamed the island, decimating the vegetation so much that the island's forests had an "open park-like appearance," according to the Park Service. Today, it manages the herd by issuing hunting permits.

North Manitou has only one water source and one small rustic campground near the ferry dock; backcountry camping is permitted throughout the island's public property. Backcountry permits are required but free.

For camping permits and more information on the Manitous, contact **Sleeping Bear Dunes National Lakeshore,** 231/326-5134, website: www.nps.gov/slbe.

## AROUND THE LEELANAU PENINSULA
### Leland

The restored **"Fishtown"** at Leland's harbor is probably one of the most photographed spots in all of Michigan, a collection of 19th-century weathered gray fish shanties lined up on the docks. Whether you find it charming or obnoxious pretty much pegs your feelings about development—or reveals you as a local who remembers what the harbor looked like before the gift shops came to town. For many Leelanau residents, slicked-up Leland is a sad commentary on how tourism is erasing a simpler lifestyle.

© TRAVEL MICHIGAN

**Fishtown, at Leland's Harbor**

Leland was a diverse industrial center in the mid-1800s, with two sawmills, a gristmill, an iron smelter, and a flourishing commercial fishing trade. By the early 1900s, eight fisheries were operating out of Leland. Where the Carp River spills into Lake Michigan, they built shanties along the docks, which they used to store ice, repair nets, and house equipment. Once common in ports all over the Great Lakes, most of these complexes completely disappeared when commercial fishing declined in the mid-1900s.

In Leland, the shanties happily remain, lined up on the docks right out of a historical photo. **Carlson's Fisheries,** 231/256-9801, still operates here, with its sturdy snub-nosed boats tied up to the pier and a shop that sells fresh fillets and smoked trout out of a long deli case. Most of the other shanties, though, now house gift shops and galleries, and the fishnets dry in the sun solely for the benefit of the summer tourist trade.

Though it's undeniably touristy, Leland is also undeniably attractive. The Carp River rolls by, where you can gaze down at the steelhead school-ing in the waters. And whether or not you care for the shops, appreciate the fact that no one tore down these neat old buildings. A couple of restaurants overlook the river and Fishtown, including **The Cove,** 231/256-9834, featuring seafood chowder, fish stew, and fresh fish specials. A block or two farther upstream, across M-22 (the main drag), the **Bluebird,** 231/256-9081, is a well-known dinner spot, with reasonably priced seafood dishes, homemade soups, and a good wine list. Entrees about $14. Next door, the same owners operate the **Early Bird,** 231/256-9656, a favorite breakfast spot among locals.

The company that operates the ferry service to the Manitou Islands also offers a 90-minute **sunset shoreline cruise** in July and August that travels south across Good Harbor Bay toward Sleeping Bear Dunes. It departs at 6:30 P.M. on Mon., Wed., Fri., and Sat. from Fishtown and costs $14 adults, $10 children 12 and under. For information and reservations, contact Manitou Island Transit, P. O. Box 591, Leland, MI 49654, 231/256-9061, website:

NORTHWEST MICHIGAN

www.leelanau.com/manitou, or stop by the ticket office in Fishtown.

## Western Shore Beaches

North of Leland, handsome **Peterson Park** sits high atop a bluff overlooking Lake Michigan, with picnic tables, a playground, and a great vantage point for the area's renowned sunsets. A steep staircase leads to a rocky beach, a good spot to hunt for Petoskey stones. Take M-201 to Peterson Park Road and turn left. For swimming, **Christmas Cove** offers a perfect arc of sugar-sand beach near the tip of the peninsula. To find it, follow M-201 north from Northport; just after it joins CR-640, turn left on Kilcherman Road, which leads to Christmas Cove Road.

## Leelanau State Park

Split into two units at the tip of the Leelanau Peninsula, this 1,250-acre state park is a wonderful surprise: while the northern unit, with its lighthouse and campground, is very popular, visitors seem to pretty much ignore its southern portion—which means you can often have its lovely beaches and trails all to yourself.

In the southern unit, low dunes and more than a mile of **sand beach** curve along Cathead Bay. It's a mile walk from the parking area through maple and beech forest to get to the water, so it rarely draws a crowd. The park's eight miles of **walking trails** radiate out from the same parking area. The **Mud Lake Tour** circles a wetland area and small lake, a good choice in spring and fall when waterfowl migrate through the area. The Lake Michigan Trail leads to the water, but don't skip the short side trail to the **overlook**—a stairway climbs up a dune for a breathtaking view of North Manitou Island. To reach the southern unit parking lot, follow CR-629 north and turn left just after Woolsey Airport. (The turn is marked with a state park sign.)

Five miles north, the **Grand Traverse Light** presides over the park's northern unit at the peninsula's tip. Built in 1858, the pretty white brick tower looks woefully small for the huge expanse of water that surrounds it. (The Coast Guard thought so, too; the light was decommissioned in 1972, replaced by a more pedes-

trian—but taller—steel tower churning away down on the beach.) Today the lighthouse is maintained by the Grand Traverse Lighthouse Foundation, and a son of one of its keepers serves as curator. You can climb the tower when the lighthouse is open, usually weekend afternoons in May, June, Sept., and Oct., and daily July–Aug. Call ahead for specific hours. Free admission, donations encouraged.

The rustic campground here has wonderful sites, 52 in all, with several right along the water and several more with water views. Though the campground is extremely popular in summer, most sites offer a fair amount of seclusion. Reservations are highly recommended; contact 800/44-PARKS; website: dnr.state.mi.us. For more information, contact Leelanau State Park, 15310 N. Lighthouse Point Rd., in Northport, 231/386-5422 (summer only) or 231/922-5270.

## Northport

With a fine horseshoe harbor in the protected waters of Grand Traverse Bay, it's not surprising that Northport was one of the first spots settled on the Leelanau. Catholic missionaries established a village there in 1849, bringing with them several area Ottawa families that they had successfully converted to Christianity. Within 20 years, Northport was the county seat, overseeing a population of 2,500, and had a thriving commercial fishing industry. At the turn of the century, it built a fancy resort hotel with room for 250 guests; within five years, the uninsured building burned to the ground. Today, Northport is popular with pleasure boaters, who still appreciate its snug harbor, and shoppers, who cruise its cute little downtown, a row of revamped 1860s buildings filled with eclectic antique and clothing shops.

## Peshawbestown

The Grand Traverse Band of the Ottawa and Ojibwa Indians owns tribal land around the bayside community of Peshawbestown and operates one of the region's most popular tourist attractions: the **Leelanau Sands Casino,** 800/938-2946. The complex on M-22 includes more than 600 slot machines, a full range of casino games, a lodge overlooking Grand Traverse Bay, and the Eagles Ridge restaurant.

## Suttons Bay

Once a town largely inhabited by immigrant laborers from the fruit orchards, Suttons Bay has gotten fancier and wealthier along with the rest of the Leelanau Peninsula. With mechanization, there simply aren't that many laborers anymore, and the desirable real estate—on Grand Traverse Bay, just 12 miles from Traverse City, with views of the cross-hatched orchards of the Mission Peninsula—was just too good to leave alone.

These days, Suttons Bay has almost become a suburb of Traverse City. Residents have worked hard to maintain the community's own personality, though, with colorfully painted storefronts and old-fashioned red telephone booths along St. Joseph's Avenue (M-22). Suttons Bay's downtown boasts a restored movie theater, all manner of galleries and boutiques, and some of the best restaurants in the Grand Traverse region.

**Cafe Bliss,** 420 St. Joseph Ave., 231/271-5000, offers the area's most extensive vegetarian menu and wide-ranging ethnic dishes in a comforting early 1900s home. Entrees about $14. Just a few blocks away, **Hattie's,** 111 St. Joseph Ave., 231/271-6222, has a particularly good wine list and an "upscale regional" menu that features knockouts like morel ravioli and grilled range hen with cherry barbecue sauce. Entrees about $20.

## Inland

Popular with anglers, Lake Leelanau is also a good spot for **paddlers,** especially at the **Cedar River Natural Area** along its southern shore, part of the Pere Marquette State Forest. Launch a canoe partway up the eastern shore, where Lake Leelanau Road intersects Bingham Road.

North of Cedar off CR-651, **Sugar Loaf ski resort** looms over Lake Michigan like the prow of a ship, with steep runs like Awful Awful and Sloot's Chute plunging off its tip. Sugar Loaf's 500-foot vertical and 23 runs make for a compact but diverse ski area with seemingly something for everyone. It's worked to create a great terrain park—you can even "bonk the bug," a buried

VW beetle—and a wild tubing run that careens down a banked path through the birches. Its best asset, though, is its view from the summit, overlooking Lake Michigan's cobalt waters and the forested Manitou islands.

Like most Michigan ski areas, Sugar Loaf becomes a primo **golf** resort in spring, home to an Arnold Palmer signature course opened in 1997. It also has terrific (and challenging) **mountain biking** terrain, on its 26 kilometers (16.2 miles) of cross-country trails and downhill runs. Motel-style rooms and villas available on site, some nicer than others. (Parts of Sugar Loaf are looking a bit tired.) For information, contact Sugar Loaf, 4500 Sugar Loaf Rd., 888/THE LOAF.

Northwest of Cedar on Little Traverse Lake, the **Leelanau Country Inn,** 231/228-5060, has won dozens of awards for its regional dishes like apple-stuffed chicken with cherry glaze and the ubiquitous northern Michigan whitefish. It's located in a renovated old country home, eight miles south of Leland on M-22. For more casual dining, excuse the silly name and try **Dick's Pour House,** 103 Philip, Lake Leelanau, 231/256-9912, for homemade soups, homemade pie, pizza, sandwiches, and a Friday fish fry.

## Wineries

As on the Mission Peninsula, the surrounding waters of Lake Michigan have a moderating effect on the Leelanau Peninsula, providing a surprisingly fruitful climate for growing cherries, apples, peaches, and, increasingly, wine grapes. Slow-changing lake temperatures keep things nice and cool during the growing season; come winter, they insulate the delicate trees and vines from killing deep freezes.

Michigan leads the nation in cherry production, and the Leelanau accounts for a quarter of that crop. And while Michigan's grape harvest isn't ready to challenge California's, a few of its wines have. Leelanau (and Mission Peninsula) wineries regularly produce award-winning vintages, especially rieslings, which do particularly well in this climate, and chardonnays. (No one yet has figured out a way to coax an exceptional full-bodied red out of Michigan soil.) Sure, you can still find some cheesy cherry wines and other sickly sweet creations. But serious vintners are letting their wines do the talking, and winning over new converts every year.

An ever-growing number of wineries on the Leelanau Peninsula—10 at last count—offer tours and tastings. The other key spot in the region for winery hopping is the Mission Peninsula (see **Traverse City and Vicinity,** earlier in this chapter).

**Leelanau Wine Cellars,** 12683 E. Tatch Rd., Omena, 231/386-5201, is the largest winery on the peninsula, producing 65,000 gallons of vinifera, hybrid, and fruit wines each year. Highest honors go to its Tall Ship Chardonnay. Open noon–5 P.M. daily, June–Oct.

**L. Mawby Vineyards,** 4519 Elm Valley Rd., Suttons Bay, 231/271-3522, on the other hand, is one of the region's smallest wineries—with a big reputation, especially for its sparkling wines and oak-barrel-fermented dry whites. Larry Mawby produces about 3,000 cases a year, with a goal to "keep things small enough to do what I want to do—make great wine with minimal intervention." He brings a creative flair to the winemaking business, evidenced in the artful wine labels designed by his wife, artist Peggy

Core. Open for tastings May–Oct. Thurs.–Sat. 1–6 P.M. From Suttons Bay, follow CR-633 south to Elm Valley Road.

**Boskydel Vineyard,** 7501 E. Otto Rd., Lake Leelanau, MI 49653, 231/256-7272, was the first vineyard in the Grand Traverse region, with French hybrid grapes first planted in 1964. Today, the winery produces about 2,500 cases a year—mostly semi-dry red and white table wines—from its vineyards sloping down toward Lake Michigan. Open for tastings 1–6 P.M. daily year-round. The winery is located two miles south of Lake Leelanau on CR-641.

Some consider Bruce Simpson's dry white chardonnays and pinots gris the finest wines to come out of the Traverse Bay region. An informative self-guided tour at **Good Harbor Vineyards,** three miles south of Leland on M-22, Route 1, Box 888, Lake Leelanau, MI 49653, 231/256-7165, explains how he's done it. After visiting the tasting room and purchasing a bottle, stop by the fine **Manitou Farm Market** next door to put together a perfect picnic lunch. Open for tours and tastings May–Nov. Mon.–Sat. 11 A.M.–5 P.M. and Sun. noon–5 P.M.

# Charlevoix and Vicinity

Situated between Grand Traverse Bay and Little Traverse Bay, Charlevoix (SHAR-luh-voy) was practically destined to become a vacation spot. Along with the inherent appeal of Lake Michigan, Charlevoix also sidles up against lovely Lake Charlevoix, a clean, clear, wishbone-shaped lake that draws anglers and pleasure boaters.

Inland, along the north arm of Lake Charlevoix toward Horton Bay, the land crumples like a fallen soufflé. This is lake country, river country, trout-fishing country, the boyhood backyard of a young Ernest Hemingway, whose family spent summers on nearby Walloon Lake. Just a few miles from the summer throngs that can descend on Charlevoix, much of Charlevoix County ticks along at a much mellower pace, the kind of place that inspires you to drift downstream in a canoe, make a few

casts from a quiet bank, or pedal the two lanes that twist through the region.

Or really get away from it all on Beaver Island, which you can reach by ferry or plane from Charlevoix. Originally settled by the Irish, it became a Mormon stronghold in the 1840s, ruled by a self-proclaimed king who was eventually assassinated by two of his followers. Things are considerably tamer on the island today, a sandy, wooded retreat with an Irish flavor and a decidedly somnolent air. Like much of the region, it's just the kind of place to spark creativity, maybe even inspire prose. Hey, it worked for Hemingway.

## CHARLEVOIX

Woodland Indians were probably the first to settle in present-day Charlevoix, summering along the Lake Michigan shores some 4,000 years ago. But it was a French missionary who gave the town its name. Pierre François-Xavier de Charlevoix traveled through the region in the early 1700s, surreptitiously searching for the fabled Northwest Passage without tipping off the British. They never found a passage, of course, but that hasn't stopped boats from gathering here, a yachter's paradise.

For more information, contact the **Charlevoix Area Convention and Visitors Bureau,** 408 Bridge St., Charlevoix, 800/367-8557, website: www.charlevoix.org/cvb.

## Downtown

"Charlevoix the Beautiful," they call this nautical town of 3,300, wedged on an isthmus between Lake Michigan and Round Lake, which opens to large Lake Charlevoix. With flowers flanking Bridge St. (US-31), a walkway along the Pine River linking the lakes, gleaming yachts with clanging halyards, screeching gulls, and yacht shops, Charlevoix *is* pretty beautiful.

Downtown Charlevoix also can be crammed on a summer weekend, so do yourself a favor: if you don't arrive by boat (many do), leave the car at your hotel or on the edge of town and walk. This is a town meant for strolling, and you can enjoy nearly all its sights on foot.

Bridge Street is Charlevoix's main drag, lined with 50,000 petunias (planted by volunteers each spring, watered by volunteers with a donated tank truck), restaurants, galleries, and gift shops. For a free directory, stop by the Charlevoix Area Convention and Visitors Bureau.

Toward the north end of the shopping district, a lift bridge rises on the half hour to allow tall-masted boats to travel the **Pine River Channel** from Lake Michigan to Round Lake, essentially a yacht basin that connects with much larger Lake Charlevoix. A lovely walkway lit with Victorian style lamps lines both sides of the channel between Bridge Street and Lake Michigan. Follow the north side to reach the long pier that extends far out into Lake Michigan. To your right, Michigan Avenue parallels the lakeshore, where stately old homes preside over the waterfront.

Follow the south side of the walkway to the **South Lighthouse** and **Michigan Beach,** with fine white sand, changing rooms, a playground, and picnic area. The woods behind the beach have some short walking trails. Cross the street that parallels the beach, Park Street, to check out the weird elfin architecture of **Earl Young** scattered throughout this pleasant neighborhood. Young, a local real estate agent and self-taught home designer, constructed or remodeled two dozen homes in the 1930s and 1940s, many in the triangular block bordered by Park, Clinton, and Grant. Young used natural materials like enormous lake boulders to build his odd mushroom-shaped homes, topping them with curved cedar shake roofs. Tucked amid Victorians, it looks like Smurfs have invaded the neighborhood.

Beauty must be in the eye of the beholder, because Young also was selected to design the Weathervane Terrace Hotel and Stafford's Weathervane restaurant along the channel. Rock walls and massive fireplaces characterize the designs; the restaurant's fireplace features a nine-ton keystone shaped like the state of Michigan. The local Convention and Visitors Bureau has a map that directs you to Charlevoix's Young homes.

On the east side of Bridge Street, **East Park** fronts the bustling marina and city docks on Round Lake. This is a fun spot to grab a sandwich and watch the comings and goings of all the boat business. Even better, pick up some smoked fish from **John Cross Fisheries,** 209 Belvedere, 231/547-2532. One of the last commercial fisheries left in the area, it sells fresh walleye, perch, lake trout, and whitefish, which it also supplies to local restaurants. You can also buy smoked whitefish or trout by the chunk.

The 85-foot schooner *Appledore,* 231/547-0024, docks near the end of Clinton Street, offering two-hour windjammer cruises down Lake Charlevoix's north arm. Three cruises are offered daily; call for information and reservations. The **U.S. Coast Guard cutter** *Acacia* also calls Round Lake its home port. It's often open to visitors if it will be around for a while; ask the seaman on duty for permission to come aboard.

## Charlevoix's Clubs

Around the southern end of Round Lake, the grounds of the century-old **Belvedere Club** spread across a high hill, overlooking both Round Lake and Lake Charlevoix. Founded by Baptists from Kalamazoo in the 1870s, the Belvedere Club was planned as a summer resort community, mirroring the Methodists' successful Bay View near Petoskey. Wealthy summer folk built homes in the opulent fashion of the day, with verandas, dormers, and gabled roofs. Today, many of the homes are occupied in summer by the grandchildren and great-grandchildren of the original owners. Though the streets through still-private Belvedere are closed in July and August, you can get a glimpse of the neighborhood from Ferry Avenue along Lake Charlevoix. Better yet, dine at the **Grey Gables Inn,** 308 Belvedere Ave., 231/547-9261, an old Victorian near the club's perimeter, which features locally caught fresh fish.

Inspired by the Belvedere Club, the First Congregational Church of Chicago formed a similar community on the north side of the Pine River Channel. As with the Belvedere, the **Chicago Club** is closed to the public. Check out its fancy Victorians from E. Dixon Avenue. As a bonus, this road also leads you to **Depot Beach,** a popular swimming beach, playground, and picnic area on Lake Charlevoix.

## Mt. McSauba and North Point

At the north end of Charlevoix (about a half mile north of the city pier), the city maintains the **Mt. McSauba Recreation Area,** 231/547-3252, an undeveloped 50-acre tract with high dunes rolling down to the Lake Michigan shoreline. Not surprisingly, it has a great sand beach; it also has pretty hiking/cross-country ski trails that wind through the woods behind the dunes. Nearby, a small downhill ski area runs a tow rope up one of the grass-covered dunes. Hike it for a great view of the big lake, all the way to Little Traverse Bay.

At its north end, Mt. McSauba shares a boundary with the **North Point Nature Preserve.** In the late 1980s, the Little Traverse Conservancy purchased the 28-acre parcel of woods and beach,

which was being eyed for a condo development. Today it offers some steep nature trails through hardwood forest and a pretty stretch of sand that's more secluded than the beach at popular Mt. McSauba. To reach the preserve, take US-31 north to Mercer and turn left; follow Mercer to Cedar and take another left. You'll see a small sign and parking area at the end of the road.

## Accommodations and Food

Don't plan on pulling into Charlevoix on a Friday afternoon in July and finding a great deal on a room—or even a crummy deal on a room. Make reservations, especially in July and August. Having said that, Charlevoix has loads of lodging possibilities, from basic motels on US-31 to swanky condos on the water. Check with the chamber of commerce for a complete listing. The **Edgewater Inn Condominium Hotel,** 100 Michigan Ave., 800/748-0424, has suites on Round Lake and amenities like an indoor/outdoor pool. Rates are rather steep at $200–300, but include full kitchen facilities, living areas, etc. The **Weathervane Terrace Hotel,** 111 Pie River Lane, 800/552-0025, sits right on the channel with views of Lake Michigan and Round Lake, with an outdoor pool and hot tub. Rates $50–150. The **Grey Gables Inn,** 308 Belvedere Ave., 231/547-9261, is a B&B with private baths and suites in a great location just a couple blocks from downtown. Rates $75–100. Charlevoix also has an array of newer franchise motels like the **Sleep Inn,** 801 Petoskey Ave. (US-31), 231/547-0300, with an indoor pool and location not far from Lake Charlevoix beaches. Rates $50–150.

Some of the area's best camping can be found in two nearby state parks, **Fisherman's Island** and **Young** (see **South of Charlevoix** and **Around Lake Charlevoix,** below). Almost directly across the north arm from Young State Park, **Whiting County Park** on Ironton Ferry Rd., 231/582-7040, has 35 rustic sites, a boat launch, and a sand beach. In East Jordan, **East Jordan Tourist Park,** 231/536-2561, has 114 modern sites adjacent to Lake Charlevoix.

Whether you find the weird Smurfy architecture of Earl Young intriguing or horrid, the

Young-designed **Stafford's Weathervane,** 106 Pine River Lane, 231/547-4311, is one of Charlevoix's best restaurants in terms of both food and location. Affiliated with the Stafford restaurants of Petoskey (a good barometer of quality), it specializes in planked whitefish and steaks, and overlooks the Pine River Channel. Outside seating available at lunch and dinner. **Terry's Place,** on Antrim near State, 231/547-2799, is known for its fresh walleye and whitefish.

Locals favor the home cooking at two downtown cafés: **Juilleret's Restaurant,** 1418 S. Bridge St., 231/547-9212, with great cinnamon rolls and homemade pies, and the fresh, innovative dishes at the **Acorn Cafe,** 101 Park Ave., 231/547-1835, proudly advertising that "Hemingway Never Ate Here." Both serve breakfast and lunch.

Outside of town, **Monte Bianco,** 02911 Boyne City Rd., 231/582-3341, specializes in updated San Francisco-style Italian cooking. The **Landing,** on M-66 next to the Ironton Ferry, has an eclectic menu that ranges from perch to fajitas to pizza, and a great deck that attracts fleets of Lake Charlevoix boaters.

## SOUTH OF CHARLEVOIX
### Fisherman's Island State Park
Five miles south of Charlevoix off US-31, this state park, 231/547-6641, does indeed encompass a little 10-acre offshore island, but most visitors come to enjoy its seven miles of Lake Michigan shoreline and wooded dunes. With long stretches of soft sand beach and exceptionally clear water, it's a particularly good spot at which to hunt for Petoskey stones.

There's evidence that Woodland Indians inhabited Fisherman's Island more than 1,000 years ago. In the early 1900s, one enterprising Charlevoix innkeeper planned a casino for the site. But those plans died with the property owner, and the state eventually acquired the island and nearby shoreline, naming it a state park in 1978. Today, the small island is inhabited only by birds and insects. Wading or swimming to it is not recommended, since a strong current often rushes between the island and mainland.

The park is nearly divided in two by a parcel of private property in its middle. The northern portion is the more popular of the two state park sections, with five miles of hiking trails, a pretty day use area, and 90 rustic campsites. Most are nice, private sites in the woods near the water; if you're really lucky, you'll snag one of the dozen or so sites right on the beach. Sites fill up in July and August, so consider reserving one ahead of time, 800/44-PARKS; website: dnr.state.mi.us.

To reach the day use area, hike the marked trail along the dune ridge, or drive south on the park road past the campgrounds. It has grills, picnic tables, outhouses, and a trail leading across bubbling Inwood Creek to the beach. On a clear day, you can see the tip of the Leelanau Peninsula from this fine stretch of beach, and you'll often be treated to a spectacular sunset. For real solitude, access the southern end of the park from the town of Norwood, 11 miles south on US-31. Follow signs to Norwood Township Park on the shoreline, then follow the double track into the state park. (Driving is not recommended if it's wet.) You're likely to have the beach and old truck trails all to yourself.

### Ellsworth
Eleven miles south of Charlevoix on CR-65, Ellsworth wouldn't be much more than a wide spot in the road but for a couple of very notable exceptions: The Rowe Inn and Tapawingo. These two restaurants have put unlikely Ellsworth on the map, with rave reviews in national publications like *Gourmet* and *Wine Spectator.*

With a warm farmhousey exterior and chic, modern interior, **Tapawingo,** 9502 Lake, 231/588-7971, features midwestern ingredients, like its renowned morel mushroom dishes, presented with a nouvelle artistic flair. It was named one of "America's Top Tables" by *Gourmet.* Entrees $25 plus.

A scant half mile away, the **Rowe Inn,** 6303 CR-48, 231/588-7531, has a more rustic decor and one-of-a-kind entrees like Duck Magret with Port Cinnamon Sauce. Its distinctive menu—thick with rich local ingredients like duck, veal, trout, morels, and fresh berries—along with the largest and most outstanding wine cellar in

Michigan have earned it a spot among the nation's top restaurants. Entrees $20–30.

## Shanty Creek

What happens when one company owns a huge swath of land anchored by two golf/downhill ski resorts? You get two resorts, and a fantastic trail network in between the two for cross-country skiers and mountain bikers. That's a real appeal of Shanty Creek, a 4,000-acre resort located a half hour south of Charlevoix near Bellaire.

**Ernest Hemingway preserves the region in his writing.**

BOB RACE

Shanty Creek encompasses two areas, Summit Village and Schuss Mountain. (They've toyed with the names over the years—Summit Slopes, Schuss Village—which has caused confusion, but no matter.) Summit Village is the more comprehensive of the two, with a large main lodge/conference center and loads of condominiums and villas scattered around it. The main draw here is golfing **The Legend,** designed by Arnold Palmer and named the best course in the Midwest by *Golf Digest.* Summit Village is also home to the more wide-open, traditional **Shanty Creek Course,** along with tennis courts, indoor and outdoor pools, shops, spa, and downhill ski area with three lifts, 11 runs, and a half-pipe.

Five minutes away, Schuss Mountain offers the more advanced skiing of the two, with 18 runs, terrain parks, and six lifts. Its Bavarian-style base area is smaller, with a couple of smaller inns and a scattering of villas. It, too, has tennis courts and a third golf course, the **Schuss Mountain Golf Club.** In between the two, 35 kilometers of groomed and tracked **cross-country** trails wind through hilly terrain and hardwood forest.

*Hemingway spent his childhood summers at the family cottage on nearby Walloon Lake, fished the waters of Lake Charlevoix, hunted on the point at Horton Bay, and once escaped a game warden by fleeing across the lake's north arm to the point between the arms, now known as Hemingway Point.*

In summer, many of those same trails become prime **mountain biking** terrain. Shanty Creek offers more than 19 miles of interconnected trails, along with the ski runs on Schuss Mountain that you can access by chairlift. About one-third is single track through the woods, and two-thirds is double track through woods and meadow. The network includes beginner to expert trails, some made even more difficult by the area's sandy terrain. A 5.2-mile championship course will get you gasping with a 783-foot climb each lap.

Shanty Creek's comprehensive trail network earned it a stop on the **National Off-Road Bicycling Association (NORBA) championship** series. It hosts the nation's top pros in late June and ranks as the state's largest mountain biking event. Trail passes ($5) and rentals are available at both Schuss Mountain and Summit Village.

For more information on lodging and activities, contact Shanty Creek at 800/678-4111, website: www.shantycreek.com.

## AROUND LAKE CHARLEVOIX

### Horton Bay

Several authors and artists have roots in northern Michigan, but none as celebrated as Ernest Hemingway. Hemingway spent his childhood summers at the family cottage on nearby Walloon Lake, fished the waters of Lake Charlevoix, hunted on the point at Horton Bay, and once escaped a game warden by fleeing across the lake's north arm to the point between the arms, now known as Hemingway Point.

The tiny town of Horton Bay, on Boyne City Road about 10 miles east of Charlevoix, played a special role in Hemingway's life. He whiled away summer afternoons on the front steps of the classic false-front, white-clapboard general store, which he describes in his short story "Up in Michigan." (He drew on many of his surroundings, in fact, for his Nick Adams short stories.) Later, he married his first wife, Hadley Richardson, at Horton Bay's Congregational church.

Today, the **Horton Bay General Store,** 231/582-7827, is preserved more as a shrine to Hemingway than a store—light on foodstuffs but heavy on Hemingway nostalgia. Built in 1876, the cavernous building is filled with Hemingway photos, novels, even a copy of his 1922 marriage certificate. There's a small lunch counter and a few assorted groceries. But it's the charming old building itself that draws you in. Steeped in literary history, its inviting front porch is still a great place to while away a summer afternoon.

## Young State Park

Situated at the inland end of Lake Charlevoix's north arm, the lake is the draw at Young State Park in Boyne City, 231/582-7523. Visitors fish or swim from its 1.5 miles of shoreline. Those with canoes or small fishing boats (under 16 feet) can launch from an unimproved but serviceable ramp.

Much of the park's shoreline area is campground with nearly 300 modern sites. Most appealing is the Oak Campground, with wooded, shady sites including several at water's edge. For reservations, call 800/44-PARKS; website: dnr.state.mi.us. In the park's interior, three miles of hiking trails loop through a wooded area that puts on an impressive wildflower show in spring.

## Boyne City

At the foot of Lake Charlevoix, pleasant and relaxing Boyne City was once a loud industrial town. In the 19th century, Boyne City thrived as a regional logging center, with 90 miles of railroad track and several hundred logging cars linking the town to the surrounding logging camps and feeding its hungry sawmills. Tanneries also became big business at the turn of the

century, using bark from the hemlock tree to tan leather. One Boyne City tannery produced six million pounds of shoe leather annually.

Boyne City has done a fine job preserving some of its historic buildings, with a main street that looks like it could be in the Wild West. The best example is the **Wolverine-Dillworth Inn,** 300 Water St., 231/582-7388, a 1911 brick hotel with big veranda, terrazzo tile lobby with fireplace, and saloon dining room. Open for dining and lodging.

## Everett Kircher and Boyne Mountain

Six miles southeast of Boyne City in Boyne Falls, Everett Kircher carved out his own piece of history at Boyne Mountain. A Studebaker dealer from the Detroit area, Kircher figured out in the 1940s that Detroit's booming auto industry would make for a lot of wealthy Michigan residents, many of whom would be looking for a place to vacation. He obtained some farmland near Boyne Falls and proceeded to develop the area's first downhill ski resort. Boyne Mountain opened in 1947.

Over the years, the visionary Kircher became known for "firsts"—the Midwest's first chairlift in 1948, the nation's first freestyle skiing exhibition in 1961, the world's first quad chairlift in 1967, the state's first high-speed quad in 1990, and the nation's first six-person chair in 1992. Kircher was the first to perfect artificial snowmaking, and Boyne's patented snowguns are used at resorts all over the world. Olympic ski planners still contact Boyne for snowmaking consultation.

Now in his 80s, Everett Kircher still comes to Boyne USA headquarters in Boyne Falls nearly every day, overseeing a privately held ski/golf enterprise that seems to grow exponentially every year. In the tightly consolidated ski industry, Boyne USA is a player: it owns Big Sky in Montana, Brighton Ski Bowl in Utah, Crystal Mountain in Washington, and Boyne Highlands and Boyne Mountain in Michigan. The company's not doing too badly in the golf industry department either, with its spectacular Bay Harbor development near Petoskey and another growing operation in Naples, Florida.

By those standards, Boyne Mountain seems almost quaint, but is an extremely popular resort in summer and winter. The **ski area** offers 40 runs, including the Disciples Ridge area, which features some of the steepest pitches in the state. The property also has 35 kilometers (22 miles) of groomed and tracked trails for cross-country skiing, which double as mountain biking trails. Come summer, two 18-hole **golf courses** help fill Boyne Mountain's 600-plus rooms (and its jumbo 30-person outdoor hot tub). For more information, contact 800/GO BOYNE, website: www.boyne.com.

## Jordan River

You'll better understand Ernest Hemingway's love for this land after passing a little time along the Jordan River, which empties into Lake Charlevoix's south arm. Look for the small wooden canoe signs that signify access points, like the one along Alba Road near the Charlevoix-Antrim county line. Here the Jordan rolls silently northward, the pale brown of hospital coffee, framed by weeping willows and grassy banks. Though anglers hate to advertise it, the Jordan is one of the finest trout streams in the state.

The Jordan River valley cuts a wide swath through the landscape south of Lake Charlevoix, and nowhere is the view more dramatic than from **Deadman Hill,** off US-131 south of Boyne Falls. Two miles south of M-32 west, watch for Deadman Hill Road; turn west and travel 1.5 miles or so to the end. Here, the flat country lane suddenly falls away to reveal a marvelous valley more than 1,000 feet below: the Jordan straggles through a woodland of pines interspersed with beech and maple, reaching out across the lowlands like spider veins.

The morbid name is in reference to Stanley Graczyk, a 21-year-old logger who, in 1910, mistakenly drove his team of horses up the hill and right over the edge. Whoops. Deadman Hill is also the trailhead for the **Jordan River Pathway,** which loops 18 miles through the valley floor. There's a marked three-mile loop, too. Maps are available at the trailhead.

## Ironton Ferry

Up M-66, a tiny ferry chugs its way from Ironton across the narrows of Lake Charlevoix's south arm to Hemingway Point—a distance of about 100 yards. The U.S. flag flies gallantly from the *Charlevoix*'s white steel pilothouse; a sign sternly warns auto passengers—all three of them—that "We will not be responsible for vehicles left unattended," a difficult task, considering you can't even open the car door wide enough to get out. The funky little ferry even made the Ripley's Believe It or Not newspaper feature, noting that its captain traveled more than 15,000 miles without ever being more than 1,000 feet from home.

It is efficient. The *Charlevoix* takes just two minutes to follow its cable to the far shore, and just a little over four minutes to unload, reload, and be back again—but saves a 15-mile trip around the south arm of the lake. People have found it to be a worthwhile service since 1876. Its "1884 Rates for Ferriage" are still posted: "Double Teams, .30; Single Teams, .20; Beast, .10 except sheep; Sheep, .10 up to 6, .05 over 6; footmen, .05 without beast." Today, one-way passage costs $1.50 for an auto and 25 cents for pedestrians. No reservations necessary; the ferry operates on demand mid-April–late Nov. daily 6:30 A.M.–10:30 P.M.; the captain can see if passengers are waiting on the other side.

## BEAVER ISLAND

Traveling to Beaver Island is kind of slow, rather expensive, and there isn't much to do when you get there. There is no must-see attraction and no particularly spectacular scenery on this flat, wooded island. Nope, Beaver Island ticks along at a rather sleepy, predictable pace: The bank opens every Tues. 9 A.M.–1 P.M. The ferry brings the mail. When Island Airways arrives from Charlevoix, everybody leaving pretty much knows everybody arriving.

If this sounds hopelessly dull, then don't go to Beaver Island. There is precious little in the way of formal entertainment on Beaver, save for some occasional Irish music and beer drinking at the Shamrock Bar. Though it ranks as the largest

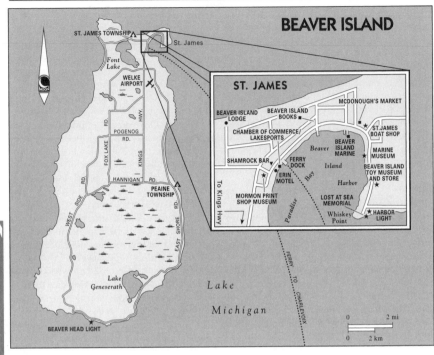

BEAVER ISLAND

ST. JAMES

MCDONOUGH'S MARKET

BEAVER ISLAND LODGE
BEAVER ISLAND BOOKS
ST.JAMES BOAT SHOP

CHAMBER OF COMMERCE/ LAKESPORTS
BEAVER ISLAND MARINE
MARINE MUSEUM

SHAMROCK BAR
FERRY DOCK
Beaver Island Harbor
BEAVER ISLAND TOY MUSEUM AND STORE

ERIN MOTEL

MORMON PRINT SHOP MUSEUM
LOST AT SEA MEMORIAL

To Kings Hwy
Paradise Bay
Whiskey Point
HARBOR LIGHT

ST. JAMES TOWNSHIP
St. James

Font Lake
WELKE AIRPORT

POGENOG RD.
FOX LAKE RD.
KINGS HWY
WEST SIDE RD.
HANNIGAN RD.
PEAINE TOWNSHIP
EAST SHORE RD.

Lake Geneserath

Lake Michigan

BEAVER HEAD LIGHT

FERRY TO CHARLEVOIX

0        2 mi
0        2 km

© AVALON TRAVEL PUBLISHING, INC.

NORTHWEST MICHIGAN

island in Michigan—13 miles long and six miles wide—you won't find any towns outside the port of St. James, just simple cottages and 100 miles of sandy roads.

On the other hand, if the inherent isolation and somnolent pace appeal to you, then by all means, go. Stranded 18 miles from the nearest Lower Peninsula shoreline, Beaver Island is the most remote inhabited island in the Great Lakes, offering what may be a quintessential glimpse of island life: unhurried, unbothered, unaffected by whim and fashion. You make your own entertainment here, and it can be delightful. Bike a quiet road to an even quieter beach. Explore the island's quirky history at a couple of terrific little museums. Buy a local a cup of coffee and talk island politics. Paddle a kayak to another island in the Beaver archipelago. Take off your watch.

For information on island services and lodging options, contact the **Beaver Island Chamber of Commerce,** 231/448-2505, website: www.beaverisland.net.

## History

Irish immigrants arrived here in the 1840s, fleeing the potato famine and looking for new opportunity. They built Beaver Island into one of the premier commercial fisheries on the Great Lakes, ringing the hooked harbor at St. James with docks, net sheds, and icehouses. The population soared to nearly 2,000 by the turn of the century.

A more bizarre history also was unfolding on the island in the 1840s. Jesse Strang, a New Yorker who challenged Brigham Young and claimed to be the leader of the Mormons, brought his faithful to Beaver Island, where he proclaimed himself king, took five wives, began a newspaper, pushed the Irish off their land, and eventually was assassinated by two of his followers. It goes down in the history books as the only kingdom to ever rule within the United States.

The Irish reclaimed their island, and today, more than a third of the island's 450 year-round residents are descendants of the original Irish immigrant families. There are, for example, 11 different Gallagher families on Beaver Island, so conversations with visiting relatives often begin something like, "You're a Gallagher? Which Gallaghers?" The island map is filled with names like "Hannigan's Orchard," "McCauley's Field" and "Paid Een Og Road." The St. Patrick's Day celebration lasts for the better part of a week.

The parasitic lamprey eel and overfishing pretty much ruined the commercial fishing trade, and the island's other main industry, logging, disappeared when ships converted from wood-burning engines to fossil fuels. Today, residents earn their living coaxing a few crops out of the rocky, sandy soil or, more commonly, by running service businesses that make a lion's share of their annual wages in July and August. By and large, residents encourage the summer tourist trade and the business visitors bring to the island. There's more of a battle when it comes to those who build summer cottages. While the building trades are a mainstay of the island economy and many welcome the jobs new construction provides, plenty of others oppose development. It's the universal controversy, fought in seasides, mountains, forests, and deserts all over the continent.

## St. James

Beaver Island activity centers around St. James on hook-shaped Beaver Harbor, which many locals still call by its 19th-century name, Paradise Bay. This is where the ferry lands, and where you'll find the sum of the island's commercial development. Everything in St. James is within walking distance.

You can pick up much of the island's colorful history and character without ever leaving the harbor. The **Shamrock Bar,** 231/448-2278, is the most popular spot in town for a burger, beer, and island news. **Beaver Island Books,** 231/448-2876, has a great selection of regional titles, including those, naturally, by owner Mary Blocksma. At the **St. James Boat Shop,** 231/448-2810, Bill Freese builds gorgeous wood-strip canoes and kayaks, along with beautiful handmade wooden buckets, gleaming through thick coats of varnish.

And do not miss the fun and funky **Beaver Island Toy Museum and Store,** 231/448-2480. Part penny candy store, dime store, and museum, owner Mary Scholl has stuffed an old house floor to ceiling with a jumble of rare antiques and contemporary dime-store toys, which she seems to enjoy with equal enthusiasm. Tin boats compete for space with glow-in-the-dark charms, cap guns, clay marbles, pig erasers, and pedal cars. Binders are filled with rare ornate valentines from the 1870s and colorful cigar labels from the 1880s. It's an amazing place, and upbeat Mary makes it all the more charming.

Few places chronicle their history as carefully and tirelessly as Beaver Island. The **Mormon Print Shop Museum,** 231/448-2254, on the west side of the harbor, does an excellent job of telling the story of King Strang and his Mormon followers. It's housed in the actual print shop where Strang published his newspaper. The **Marine Museum** on the harbor's east side, 231/448-2254, has lots of nifty displays about the Great Lakes commercial fishing industry, shipwrecks, and other nautical subjects. It currently is restoring the *Bob S,* one of the last wooden gillnet boats remaining on the Great Lakes, the kind widely used during the heyday of Beaver Island's fishery.

From the maritime museum, it's just a short walk to Whiskey Point, the **Lost at Sea memorial,** and the harbor light, marking the entrance to this well-protected natural harbor. The 19th-century light was "manned" for years by Beaver Island native Elizabeth Whitney Williams, the only woman lightkeeper on the Great Lakes. Her autobiography, *A Child of the Sea: Life Among the Mormons* is available at Beaver Island Books.

## Around the Island

You can have a great time poking around the island on your own, of course, or you can sign up for either a 90-minute tour ($20) or a three-and-a-half-hour tour ($30) to see area sights with **Beaver Island Classic Tours,** 231/448-2902.

The southern half of the island has far more public land than the north half, much of it a state wildlife research area. It has several small lakes, bogs, unimproved roads, and trails that are fun to explore, especially if you have a mountain bike. Fish in **Lake Geneserath,** swim at several sandy beaches on the southern shore, or check out **Beaver Head Light** near the island's southern tip, a pretty cream-brick house and tower built in 1851, the third oldest on all the Great Lakes. Back in the 1920s, thrillseekers from Charlevoix drove across the thick lake ice, headed for Beaver Island. When a thick fog left them completely disoriented, the keeper guided them to safety with the light's fog signal.

If you plan to explore Beaver Island on your own, pick up two maps in St. James first: the comprehensive island map available for $4.25 at McDonough's Market, and a small photocopied history map, available at the chamber of commerce. It points out several noteworthy attractions that you can seek out on your own.

## Paddling the Outer Islands

Eleven other islands scatter around Beaver's northern half, an inviting archipelago for sea kayakers. The islands range in distance from Garden (two miles away) to Gull (11 miles). Garden, practically due north from St. James, is probably the most intriguing for paddlers, with several protected bays and inlets. High Island, four miles west, has bluffs along the western shore rising to 240 feet. Most of High and Garden are public land, part of the **Beaver Island State Wildlife Research Area.** Some of the smaller islands are privately owned or otherwise off-limits to preserve nesting sites.

The **Inland Seas School of Kayaking** 231/448-2221, offers instruction and guided tours. If you have the skills to go it alone, **Island Hopper Charters,** 231/448-2309, offers water-taxi and freight service to outer islands. If you plan to do any inter-island paddling, observe all the usual safety precautions, watch the weather, and make sure you have a good nautical chart. The open waters of the Great Lakes are not for amateurs.

## Practicalities

Commercial transportation to Beaver Island is available only from Charlevoix, 32 miles away. The **Beaver Island Boat Company,** 102 Bridge St., 231/547-2311, makes scheduled trips April–Dec., with two trips daily most of the summer. It takes a little over two hours each way, and the 100-foot *Beaver Islander* can be a bit of a rough ride in choppy waters. It costs $32 roundtrip for adults, $16.50 for children ages 5–12, $14 for a bike, $114 for a car. Reservations recommended for passengers and required for autos. If you take the first ferry in the morning, you can make Beaver Island a day trip of six hours or so, returning on the late afternoon ferry. Of course, the time constraints will limit you to exploring just a small portion of the island.

**Island Airways,** 800/524-6895, provides daily air service from Charlevoix in a little 10-seater. It takes about 20 minutes and costs $62 roundtrip adults, $31 children under nine. Reservations required; call for specific schedule.

Do you need a car on Beaver Island? Probably not. Though the island is quite large and has more than 100 miles of roads, it's ideal for walking and biking, and is there really anywhere you *have* to go? Many accommodations provide transportation from the dock or airport; if there's something specific you want to see (the lighthouse on the southern shore, for example), you can hire a taxi/tour guide for a lot less than $98. A few rental cars are also available from **Beaver Island Marine Rentals,** 231/448-2300. Reserve ahead of time.

**Lakesports,** 231/448-2166, on the harbor near the ferry dock, rents mountain bikes, sea kayaks, canoes, tents, and more. It also keeps rental rowboats on inland lakes for fishing and exploring. If you're bringing your own bike, be aware that roads are quite sandy on a lot of the island, so wide tires are mandatory.

There are several motels, lodges, B&Bs, and cabins for rent on the island. Near the ferry dock, the **Erin Motel,** 231/448-2240, overlooks the water with a sand beach. Rates $50–75. The **Beaver Island Lodge,** 231/448-2396, sits along a secluded stretch of beach west of town with nice rooms and an on-site restaurant. Rates $75–100.

The island has two rustic **campgrounds** (with pit toilets and water), both on the lakeshore. The St. James Township Campground is on the north side of the island one mile from town, and has 12 sites. The Peaine Township Campground, with 22 sites, is along the east shore, seven miles south of town. Both are $7 per night, no reservations. There are two grocery stores and a handful of restaurants on the island.

# Little Traverse Bay

North of the Leelanau Peninsula and just a half hour south of the Straits of Mackinac, Little Traverse Bay delves due east nine miles, forming a picture-perfect bay ringed by bluffs, fine sand, and well-protected harbors. Well-known Petoskey, with its historic downtown Gaslight District, sits at the foot of the bay, justifiably drawing many of the area's visitors. But golfers, skiers, anglers, and wanderers will find plenty to enjoy in this appealing and compact region, too.

The well-run and helpful **Boyne Country Visitors Bureau** promotes a 30-mile corridor along US-131 stretching from Harbor Springs south to Boyne Falls. You'll find it in downtown Petoskey at 401 E. Mitchell, 800/845-2828, website: www.boynecountry.com.

## PETOSKEY AND VICINITY

Petoskey (puh-TOS-kee) was originally settled by the Ottawa Indians in the 1700s and takes its name from a local Indian, Petosega. With bountiful fishing and hunting, the region was a desirable place to live, and Ottawa and Ojibwa tribes thrived here. In the 1800s, the federal government negotiated more equitably with local tribes than it did elsewhere in the young nation; Indians were given the first choice of land (albeit their land!) until 1875.

White settlers began arriving in the 1850s, establishing logging operations along the Bear River, the name the town used until 1873. With a sawmill, lime quarry, and other enterprises along the river and bayfront, Bear River quickly became an industrial town of buzzing saws and belching smoke.

But the town began changing with the arrival of the railroad in 1873. Lured north by the beautiful Lake Michigan waters and cool northern air, residents from southern Great Lakes cities like Chicago and Detroit began migrating to Petoskey, gradually converting its industrial squalor to an elegant summer getaway. The artesian springs that bubbled throughout town and their "health-giving waters" only encouraged Petoskey's growth.

By the turn of the century, Petoskey's downtown was filled with fine shops and 13 grand resort hotels like the Arlington, with its imposing columns, dance hall, and 24-foot-wide veranda. At its heyday in 1900, three trains a day stopped at the Arlington, which could sleep 800—surpassed only by the rival Grand Hotel on Mackinac Island.

The Arlington burned to the ground in 1915, the same fate that met almost every single one of Petoskey's grand resorts—The Jewel, The Imperial, the City Hotel. Only the Perry Hotel, made of expensive brick, still stands.

Thankfully, plenty of other historical buildings still stand in the Petoskey area, a city that wisely realized early the value of protecting them. From its well-preserved Gaslight District to the entire Victorian neighborhood of Bay View, Petoskey maintains the charm of the grand resort era, along with the natural resources that brought summer visitors here in the first place.

Time and resolve will determine if it will last. In 1996, the National Trust for Historic Preservation listed Petoskey as one of 10 national historic treasures most worthy of fighting for, warning that "retail, roadway, and residential sprawl threaten the town's historic character and pastoral setting."

### Downtown

Though growth indeed threatens Petoskey—busy US-31 slices right between downtown and the bayfront—it remains a charming city for vacationers, with a downtown made for strolling. The **Gaslight District** anchors the downtown, an eight-block area of well-preserved Victorian brick storefronts filled with shops and restaurants that has drawn shoppers since the early 1900s. A low-interest loan program sponsored by the regional chamber of commerce encourages their preservation and renovation. Centered around Lake and Howard Streets, the district mixes high-brow boutiques (ever notice how many chic shops list locations like "Petoskey and Palm Beach"?) with bookstores, galleries, antique haunts, and home-grown souvenir shops. Pick up a handy *What's in Store* brochure from the visitors bureau to help plan a shopping excursion.

Near the intersection of Petoskey and Bay Streets, follow the pedestrian tunnel under US-31 to **Bayfront Park,** which merges with **Sunset Park** to the east, offering a vast greenspace along the waterfront. Once the center of Petoskey's sawmill operations, now this beautifully renovated area comprises a marina, a walkway along the Bear River, one of the area's historic mineral springs, and the fine **Little Traverse History Museum,** 231/347-2620, in the restored rail depot.

The museum is crammed full of interesting displays, including a photo collection of Petoskey's old hotels and an exhibit detailing the sad tale of the passenger pigeon, which migrated to the Little Traverse Bay area by the billions (yes, *billions*) in the 1870s. Accounts tell of the skies blackening when the birds were in flight, with individual flocks stretching for miles and miles. Alas, the nesting habits and docile nature of the pigeons made them easy to hunt by simply clubbing them to death in their nests. Entrepreneurs did so with glee, since their meat was considered a delicacy. By the 1870s, entire steamships were loaded with pigeons for delivery to urban restaurants in the southern Great Lakes. In less than 25 years, the passenger pigeon had completely disappeared from the region; by 1914, it became officially extinct.

Probably the museum's most popular display is the collection of Ernest Hemingway memorabilia. Hemingway's family began vacationing on nearby Walloon Lake when Hemingway was just a boy, and the family still owns a couple of acres of land there. After he was injured in World War I, Hemingway recuperated in Petoskey, living in a rooming house at the corner of State and Woodland Streets in 1919–1920. Here he gathered material and began drafting *Torrents of Spring,* which alludes to several Petoskey locations. The museum's display includes first editions of that classic novel as well as *For Whom the Bell Tolls* and *A Farewell to Arms.*

Hemingway overshadows Petoskey's other famous author, Bruce Catton, who won a Pulitzer Prize in 1954 for his Civil War account *A Stillness at Appomattox.* The Little Traverse History Museum gives him his due. The museum is open May–Nov. Tues.–Sat. and Memorial Day–Labor Day Mon.–Sat.; $1 donation.

## PETOSKEY STONES

Michigan's official state stone isn't really a stone at all, but a chunk of fossilized coral more than 300 million years old. Coral reefs once thrived in the warm-water seas that covered northern Michigan from Grand Traverse Bay across to about Alpena on present-day Lake Huron. They are characterized by a small, distinct ringlike pattern that covers them. Petoskey stones are common enough that they don't have much real value, but are prized nonetheless by rockhounds and anyone looking for a true local souvenir.

When dry, Petoskey stones often look like, well, stones. Usually sort of a dusty gray-brown color, their pattern becomes more apparent when wet and especially when polished. The stones are quite soft; locals recommend polishing them by hand with 180–220 grit wet sandpaper, then finishing with 400 grit. Rock tumblers are not recommended.

Hunt for Petoskey stones along public beaches almost anywhere in the Traverse Bay region. Some of the more productive spots include Fisherman's Island State Park south of Charlevoix and Magnus Park in Petoskey. You also can find Petoskey stones at gift shops throughout northwestern Michigan, polished up and often carved into shapes and crafted into jewelry.

Near the museum, you can pick up the **Top of Michigan trail,** a 15-mile paved, off-road path that stretches from Bay Harbor through Petoskey to Harbor Springs. Several other trails radiate off this route, creating a network of 180 miles of multi-use recreation pathways trails between Charlevoix to Mackinaw City. Trails maps are available at the Boyne Country Visitors Bureau.

## Practicalities

Petoskey offers an enormous array of lodging, from basic motels along US-31 to resort complexes to condo units that are especially convenient for families or groups. The visitors bureau, 800/845-2828, can help you sort through the choices.

Unless you're on a tight budget, opt for a stay at the lemon-chiffon-colored **Stafford's Perry Hotel,** Bay at Lewis, 231/347-4000, which overlooks Little Traverse Bay and dates back to 1899. Today, it's run by successful local innkeeper/restaurateur Stafford Smith, who has done a wonderful job of updating the venerable old building while retaining every bit of its charm. Rates are reasonable for such a treasure, $75–225.

You can also enjoy the Perry Hotel's old-world ambience and killer bay views from its **bayfront dining room,** which serves excellent and reasonably priced meals all day long. Lunch entrees about $7, dinner entrees about $17. The **Roast & Toast,** 309 E. Lake St., 231/347-7767, is part coffeehouse (they roast beans on the premises) and part restaurant. It serves three meals a day, but is above all a great soup and sandwich kind of place, with fresh bread and good variety. Entrees are a bargain at about $5.

For picnic supplies, head directly for **Symon's General Store,** 401. E. Lake, 231/347-2438. This wonderfully creaky old store with wood floors and tin ceilings offers up all kinds of gourmet groceries including fresh baked goods, imported cheeses, olives, vinegars, and old-fashioned penny candy. A deli counter in back serves great carryout sandwiches.

A few doors down, **American Spoon Foods,** 411 E. Lake, 231/347-1739, is well worth a noshing stop. A Michigan success story, Justin Rashid

began making and selling fresh fruit preserves and "spoon food" (fruit preserves sweetened only with fruit juices, no sugar) using local crops like cherries and blueberries. A top seller: Sour Cherry Spoon Fruit. He's since expanded into all sorts of fruit butters, dried fruits, salsas, vinaigrettes, grilling sauces, and more, in partnership with acclaimed chef Larry Forgione. You can taste your way through many of their offerings at this retail shop, where sampling is welcome. Guaranteed you won't make it out the door without at least one purchase. The Petoskey store was American Spoon Foods' first operation; it now has eight locations in Michigan, Indiana, and Maryland, as well as a burgeoning mail-order business. Gift boxes and baskets make a great gift for that neighbor taking care of your cat while you hang out in northern Michigan. For a catalog, contact American Spoon Foods at 800/647-2512 or website: www.spoon.com.

## Bay Harbor

A couple of miles west of downtown Petoskey, Bay Harbor represents the nation's largest land reclamation project, a stunning example of what foresight and $100 million can accomplish. Stretching five miles along the shore of Little Traverse Bay and encompassing more than 1,100 acres, this beautiful chunk of real estate spent its last life as, of all things, a cement plant. When the plant closed in 1981, it left behind a scarred, barren landscape that sat untouched for a decade.

But from industrial squalor comes impressive luxury. With the combined resources of CMS Energy (the Jackson, Michigan, parent company of a large utility) and ski-industry giant Boyne USA, Bay Harbor is shaping up to become one of the nation's most spectacular resort communities. The **Bay Harbor Yacht Club,** with little touches like a compass rose made of inlaid cherrywood, overlooks a deepwater port (the old quarry) with nearly 500 slips, including 120 for public transient use. An equestrian club entertains the horsy set. Multimillion-dollar homes dot the property, at a low density that maintains a breezy, resort feel. Public parks buffer Bay Harbor on both sides.

Acclaimed golf designer Arthur Hills has created **The Links, The Preserve, and The Quarry golf courses,** 27 holes that ramble atop 160-foot bluffs, over natural sand dunes and along the shoreline for more than two miles. Eight holes hug the water—more, Boyne USA developers like to tell you, than at Pebble Beach. Completed in 1998, it was almost immediately named the eighth-best public course in the nation by *Golf Magazine*. Microsoft has even chosen Bay Harbor as one of two U.S. courses it features in its latest golf computer game.

The centerpiece of the development is the **Inn at Bay Harbor,** an impressive 180-suite hotel with turrets and other Victorian architectural detailing that echoes the Hotel del Coronado in San Diego. It includes a fitness center, conference facilities, a pool, spa, and lakefront restaurant. **Marina Village,** a 45,000-square-foot mixed-use development of condos, restaurants, and retail space rounded out the development.

For information on any of the facilities, contact Bay Harbor at 800/GOBOYNE or website: www.innatbayharbor.com.

## Bay View

Adjacent to Petoskey on the east side of town, Bay View looks like a Hollywood set for a Victorian romance. This amazing community includes 430 Victorian homes, most built before 1900s, a riot of gingerbread trim, and cotton-candy colors. All are on the National Historic Register, and represent the largest single collection of historic homes in the country.

Bay View was founded by the Methodist Church in 1875, a summer-only religious retreat that took some inspiration from the Chautaqua movement in the East. Summers at Bay View were filled with lectures, recitals, craft classes, and religious programs. Over the years, speakers included such notable names as Booker T. Washington, Helen Keller, and William Jennings Bryan.

Originally a tent community, Bay View's canvas lodgings were slowly replaced by Victorian cottages, many with grand views of Little Traverse Bay. Bay View residents were not an extremely wealthy lot; the homes come in all shapes and sizes, lined up in tidy rows in a shady, park-like campus. Residents own their cottages but lease the land from the Methodist Church.

Today, Bay View remains a quiet enclave, still hosting a full roster of courses and concerts and other events. While many residents are descendants of Bay View's founding families, the strict religious focus has been diluted. The biggest emphasis now, it seems, is on carefully preserving Bay View's slice of history. (Even minor renovations require approval by the Bay View Association.) Plan a stroll or a bike ride through this calm, gentle place for a taste of truly another era.

**Stafford's Bay View Inn,** 2011 Woodland Ave., 231/347-2771, is a matronly Victorian on US-31, right between Bay View's homes and the bayfront itself. The Stafford inns and restaurants in the Little Traverse region are consistently excellent, and the Bay View is no exception. It combines Victorian pleasures like warm furnishings, a wide porch, and pretty bayfront grounds and gardens, with modern amenities like whirlpool tubs and air conditioning. Open May–Oct. The inn also has a very nice restaurant, with an especially popular Sunday brunch.

In the heart of Bay View, the **Terrace Inn,** 1549 Glendale,800/530-9898, gives you a chance to experience this unique community firsthand. The serene, almost austere inn is virtually unchanged from 1910, still without televisions and telephones in the guest rooms. Instead, guests gather around the fireplace or on the large front porch. Each of the 44 rooms, all with private baths, contains original period furniture. Rates $50–100.

The Terrace Inn's restaurant is a find, featuring local dishes like whitefish, walleye, and a delicious chicken salad with dried cherries. Entrees about $13. Pick a warm night and hold out for a table on the porch. Open for dinners only Mon.–Sat. May–Oct.

## Petoskey State Park

Just beyond Bay View, Petoskey State Park, 2475 M-119, Petoskey, 231/347-2311, bends along the east end of Little Traverse Bay. Though quite small at 300 acres, the park nonetheless offers a nice dose of nature right smack between the summertime bustle of Petoskey and Harbor Springs. Its main attraction is its **mile-long beach,** with soft sand and enough rocks to keep people on the hunt for Petoskey stones. (The coral pattern appears most clearly when wet, so dip a promising-looking stone in the water.) Try to look up occasionally; the beach has great views of Petoskey and Harbor Springs, and can serve up some terrific sunsets.

Climb the 0.7-mile **Old Baldy Trail** for an even better view from the top of a dune. The park's only other hiking trail, the **Portage Trail,** is an easy 2.8-mile loop that winds south to a little inland lake. It's groomed in winter for cross-country skiing.

Nearly 200 modern campsites are tucked behind some small dunes, mostly wooded sites with good privacy. Sites along the southern loop are closer to the bay, with a few prime (though more public) sites right on the water. In July and August, the campground fills daily; make a reservation by calling 800/44-PARKS; website: dnr.state.mi.us.

## Area Golf

While the grand new courses at Bay Harbor are getting a lot of the current ink (see **Bay Harbor,** above), the Petoskey/Harbor Springs area has no shortage of great golf. Several lodgings in the area offer packages and will reserve tee times. For more information, contact the Boyne Country Visitors Bureau golf line, 888/31-NORTH.

Best known are the four courses at Boyne Highlands, a ski/golf resort a few miles north of Harbor Springs: **The Moor, the Donald Ross Memorial, The Heather,** and the new **Arthur Hills.** *Golf Digest* considers The Heather course, designed by Robert Trent Jones, Sr., the best of all Michigan resort courses, with lots of sculpted bunkers and water hazards (and cool global positioning systems on the carts to feed you yardage information). The Ross Memorial course is a perennial favorite. It re-creates several of the most famous holes throughout the world designed by Ross, considered by many to be the "father of golf course architecture." Courses start from either the Boyne Highlands main lodge or the fancy Country Club of Boyne clubhouse nearby. For information, call 800/GO BOYNE, website: www.boyne.com.

Boyne also operates the **Crooked Tree Golf Club,** 800/GO-BOYNE, a British-style course overlooking Little Traverse Bay near Petoskey. In Harbor Springs, the **Harbor Point Golf Course,** 231/526-2951, had been an exclusive private club since 1896; it's now open to the public and named one of *Golf Digest's* favorite walking courses. Near Burt Lake in Brutus, **Hidden River Golf and Casting Club,** 800/325-GOLF, offers classic "up north" scenery, with tall stands of pine and hardwoods and the meandering Maple River.

## Area Skiing

Before it was a big player in the ski industry, Boyne USA operated two resorts in northern Michigan: Boyne Highlands, near Harbor Springs, and Boyne Mountain, about a half hour south in Boyne Falls. Now the privately held company also owns large resorts out west, including Big Sky in Montana, Brighton in Utah, and Crystal Mountain in Washington. It hasn't forgotten its flagship properties, though. **Boyne Highlands,** 800/GO BOYNE, website: www.boyne.com, is one of the best full-service resorts in the Midwest, with 42 runs, a 550-foot vertical drop, and base accommodations for more than 1,200, much of it ski-in/ski-out lodging. Intermediate skiers will be happiest here, as well as snowboarders-Highlands has an admirable half-pipe and terrain park. FYI, everyone toasts to après ski at the resort's Zoo Bar.

Just a few miles east, **Nub's Nob,** 231/526-2131, often gets overshadowed by the Boynes, but has its own loyal following. The well-protected, wooded slopes (read, blocked from cold winter winds) are best known for short and steep faces like Twilight Zone and Scarface, but its 23 trails and 427-foot vertical drop have plenty of beginner and intermediate terrain, too. If Boyne Highlands gets crowded, this is the place to escape.

# UP THE SHORELINE

Just before Petoskey State Park, US-31 veers inland toward Mackinaw City and the Straits. To stay along the water, turn west on M-119, which follows the curve of Little Traverse Bay and traces the Lower Peninsula's final stretch of Lake Michigan shoreline.

## Harbor Springs

If you were to imagine the quintessential summer resort getaway, it might look a lot like genteel Harbor Springs on the north side of Little Traverse Bay: a deep clear harbor tucked against a high, wooded bluff, ringed with grand estates and white church spires and, for good measure, gleaming yachts bobbing at anchor.

Harbor Springs, in fact, has the deepest natural harbor on all of the Great Lakes, which made it a natural stopping point for the large passenger steamers in the early 1900s. Several artesian wells added to its appeal, making it a popular destination for those seeking healthful air and water. Families like the Fords and the Gambles (of "Proctor and" fame) decided Harbor Springs looked pretty good and helped create exclusive resort communities like Harbor Point and Wequetonsing, where crisp white mansions line up across crisp emerald lawns.

Those Old-Money communities still thrive, now inhabited largely by younger generations of Fords and Gambles. Harbor Point remains the more exclusive of the two, with homes topping $10 million hidden away behind gates. The only way in and out is by foot or carriage; even cars are banned from the point. You can walk, bike, or drive through Wequetonsing (WEE-kwee to the locals), where homes have wonderfully nostalgic names like Summer Set and Brookside, and long lines of Adirondack chairs line up on porches, just in case 10 or 12 friends drop by for gin and tonics.

It all makes for an interesting diversity, where ultrawealthy Old Guard, younger trust funders, vacationing families, and hired help all commingle easily in the delightfully tidy downtown. No one begrudges the wealthy their lot in life (Old Money, after all, always has exhibited finer manners than the nouveau riche), and everyone seems to appreciate the civility and gentle grace that is Harbor Springs—a welcoming enclave of continuity in a world that seems so hellbent on change. Of course Harbor Springs has no strip malls, no sprawl, no ugly franchise signs. Of course Thursday is "Maid's Day Out." It *always* has been.

Shopping is a popular sport in Harbor Springs, which hosts an appealing mix of galleries, tony boutiques, and distinctive handmade crafts. Start your exploring at Main and State. Also check out the **Andrew Blackbird Museum,** 368 E. Main, 231/526-7731, named for an Ottawa chief who lived here in the mid-1800s. The town's first postmaster, Blackbird wrote books about Indian language, legends, and adapting to white civilization. Run by the local Ottawa tribe, the museum shares Indian history and artifacts like elaborate birchbark quill boxes. Open daily Memorial Day–Labor Day.

The harborfront is a natural for strolling, with ample benches and a swimming beach at Zorn Park near the west end. (Hardy bathers only—the harbor's water is *cold.*) For a more natural beach, the **Thorne Swift Nature Preserve** offers a quiet 300-foot sand beach and dune observation deck with a wonderful bay view. Other trails wind through cedar lowlands, with trees canted and curved at crazy angles, and are marked with interpretive signs. A protected holding of the very active Little Traverse Conservancy, Thorne Swift has a naturalist on duty daily from Memorial Day to Labor Day. Pick a breezy day to visit, since bugs can be zealous here in summer months. The preserve is off M-119 on Lower Shore Dr., just west of downtown.

> *If you were to imagine the quintessential summer resort getaway, it might look a lot like genteel Harbor Springs on the north side of Little Traverse Bay: a deep clear harbor tucked against a high, wooded bluff, ringed with grand estates and white church spires, and, for good measure, gleaming yachts bobbing at anchor.*

## Tunnel of Trees

The stretch of M-119 from Harbor Springs to Cross Village is considered one of the prettiest drives in Michigan, and deserves the distinction. The narrow lane twists and turns as it follows Lake Michigan from high atop a bluff, with furtive views of the water and the Beaver Island archipelago. Yet it is the trees that take top billing, arching overhead to form a sun-dappled tunnel. The effect is spectacular on autumn afternoons, when the fiery oranges and bronzes glow in the angled sunlight like hot coals.

In spring, trilliums form a blanket of white on the forest floor. Spring also offers a few more deep blue glimpses of the lake, since the trees usually are not fully leafed out until late May. And any season is a good time to spot wildlife. One trip up the corkscrewy road tallied five deer, 15 wild turkeys, and countless grouse.

Try to bike or drive this road during the week, or at least early or late in the day, when traffic should be lighter. The combination of narrow blacktop, blind curves, no shoulders, and lots of wildlife means you'll need to keep a close eye on the road. The more cars there are, the less scenery you can enjoy.

## Legs Inn

Even if you've traveled far and wide, it's doubtful you've ever encountered anything like the Legs Inn. Part ethnic restaurant, part eclectic folk art display, this is a weird and fascinating place to explore. Outside is strange enough, a roadside building with a facade of fieldstones, accented with bizarre-looking totems and carved wooden legs spiking up from the roof (hence, the "legs" name).

But that's nothing compared with the interior, where the bar is a dark and mysterious den crammed with twisted driftwood, roots, and stumps-turned-cocktail tables. Seemingly every square inch has been carved into fanciful shapes, weird faces, and indescribable animals—and more and more seem to appear as your eyes adjust to the darkness. The theme carries through to the dining rooms, though not with such intensity. These areas are brighter and warmer, with picture windows overlooking gardens and distant views of Lake Michigan.

Legs Inn was created by Stanley Smolak, a Polish immigrant who moved to Cross Village from Chicago in the 1920s. He became enamored with the local land and its native people. He befriended the local Ottawa tribes, still thriving here in the 1920s, and was accepted enough into their culture that they gave him an Indian name, Chief White Cloud. Inspired by their art, he began carving. Soon, word of his restaurant and his relations with the Indians made Smolak a celebrity back in Poland.

With its eccentric decor, it's almost easy to overlook the food at the Legs Inn, but you shouldn't. It offers a wonderful array of Polish cooking, with rich soups, thick stews, and popular Polish specialties like pierogis. Even the drink menu offers Polish vodkas and Polish meads, made from honey and fruit juices. This is authentic stuff—many of the cook staff are immigrants themselves. They'll smile and nod and feed you like long lost relatives. Entrees about $11.

## Sturgeon Bay

M-119 ends at Cross Village, but continue northeast on Scenic Route 1 along Sturgeon Bay to reach **Bliss Township Park,** with low dunes and a pretty sand beach, great for swimming and sunsets. Far enough away from Petoskey and the Straits, it rarely draws a crowd.

Sturgeon Bay also offers the best big-water **windsurfing** in the area, with easy shorebreak and generally warmer water than Little Traverse Bay. Bliss Township Park is a wonderful launch in southwest through north winds. A second launch is about a mile north of the township beach, just where the road makes a hard right. Watch for poison ivy. Advanced sailors looking for big waves should check out the boat launch in Cross Village. Good in west through north winds.

## Wilderness State Park

North of Cross Village near the top of the "mitten," Waugoshance Point stretches west out into Lake Michigan and dribbles off into a series of islands. This is the spectacular setting for Wilderness State Park, Carp Lake, 231/436-

5381, the second largest state park in the Lower Peninsula. Aptly named, it occupies more than 7,500 acres of largely undeveloped land, including more than 26 miles of shoreline. Considering that it sits just 15 minutes away from the Straits of Mackinac, it offers remarkable solitude.

As proof, this is one of the nesting sites of the endangered piping plover. (When the birds are nesting in late spring and early summer, part of the point is closed to visitors.) About 100 other bird species also nest or migrate through Wilderness State Park, making it a favorite of **birders. Anglers** also gather here, with notable bass fishing especially in the grassy beds along the southern shore of the point. The park has a boat launch near the campgrounds and day-use area.

The park offers a wide range of topography, with sandy beaches and rocky limestone ledges along the shore. Inland, 12 miles of trails (mostly old truck trails) wind through cedars, pines, and birches. A gravel road leads toward the end of the point, open to autos. To hike there, you can follow the northern shoreline for two miles, unless the endangered piping plovers are nesting. Depending on weather conditions and water depths, it's often possible to wade to Temperance Island—a fun mini-adventure.

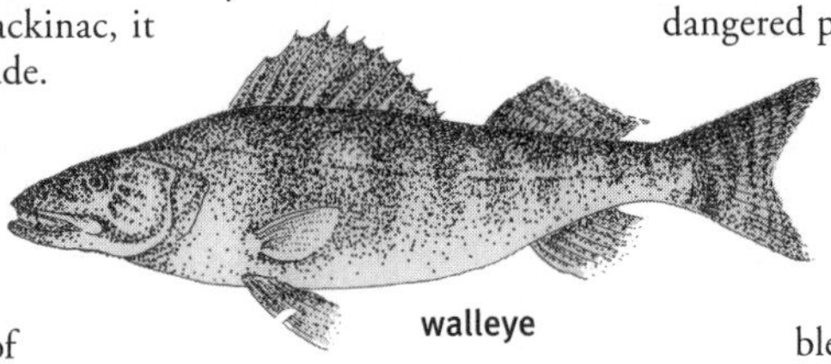

**walleye**

BOB RACE

Wilderness State Park has two large campgrounds with 250 sites. The Lakeshore Campground sits on Big Stone Bay in an open, grassy setting, with several sites right along the water. Just across the park road, the Pines Campground has more shaded, private sites in the, uh, pines. Both fill up in summer, so reserve a site by calling 800/44-PARKS; website: dnr.state.mi.us.

NORTHWEST MICHIGAN

# The Upper Peninsula

Rugged. Isolated. Utterly wild. They're not words one usually associates with the Midwest, but they aptly describe the Upper Peninsula, Michigan's sparsely populated and thickly forested northern half. Sprawling more than 300 miles along the southern shore of Lake Superior, the U.P. harbors a staggering mother lode of natural resources—rushing rivers, deep gorges, crashing waterfalls, desolate beaches, and forests so immense that it's one of the few places in the Midwest that can claim true wilderness.

The U.P. has a long and colorful history of settlement, though, from highly industrialized mining operations to roaring logging camps. Fascinating historical treasures abound—ghost towns, shipwrecks, lumber baron mansions—but nature is slowly erasing many of those human footprints. Wilderness wins out over civilization here; turns out, no one's really tamed the U.P. yet.

Traverse the U.P. by highway, and it may all look pretty much the same, a classic northwoods panorama of lake-dotted pine forests. You need to get off the highway to see the rumpled landscape of the Porcupine Mountains in the northwestern corner, the past glories of the copper boom in the Keweenaw Peninsula, the pristine backcountry of the wild Huron Mountains, the rich mining stories in towns like Iron River, Negaunee, and dozens of others. Continuing east, the attractions grow more and more well known—Pictured Rocks National Lakeshore, the Soo Locks, Tahquamenon Falls, forever charming Mackinac Island—all of them proof that you've drawn closer to population centers in the Lower Peninsula, whose residents justly view the U.P. as prime vacation territory.

But don't worry. If you're seeking solitude, you'll find plenty in the Upper Peninsula. Though large enough to contain Massachusetts, Connecticut, Delaware, and Rhode Island within its borders, the U.P. is home to just 300,000 people—barely three percent of the state's population. Its largest city, Marquette, has just 23,000 people. Head into the backwoods and you're far more likely to see deer, bear, bald eagle—maybe even a moose or wolf—than another human being. The U.P.'s wildlife population vastly outnumbers its human one.

But this suits UPers, or "Yoopers," just fine. Like Alaskans, they revel in their isolationism, their independence. And like Alaskans, they know they inhabit one of the most breathtaking, best-kept secrets around.

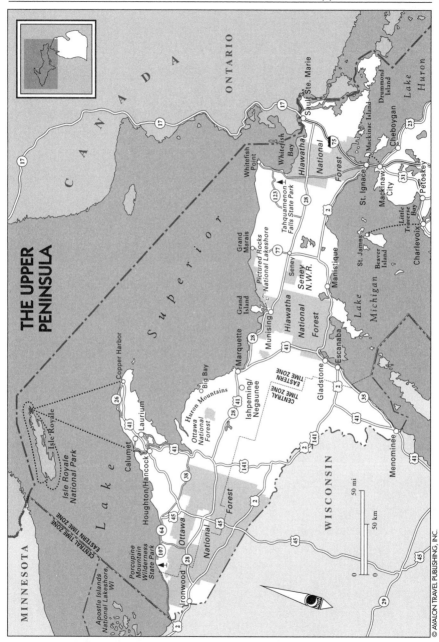

THE UPPER PENINSULA

© AVALON TRAVEL PUBLISHING, INC.

# The Western U.P.

The Keweenaw Peninsula has its roots in veins of copper, but much of the rest of the western Upper Peninsula traces its heritage to iron. You can read it in the town names—Iron Mountain, Iron River, Ironwood, National Mine, Mineral Hills—and see it on the faces of the residents, an ethnically diverse mix descended from the melting pot of immigrant mine workers.

The U.P.'s iron industry stretched from the western border east some 150 miles to the Lake Superior port of Marquette and the Lake Michigan port of Escanaba. It comprised three major ranges: the Gogebic Range, with operations centered around Ironwood; the Menominee Range, based largely around the Iron River and Iron Mountain areas; and the Marquette Range, encompassing Marquette and the Ishpeming/Negaunee area.

Federal surveyors first discovered iron ore in 1844, near present-day Iron River. As workers systematically surveyed this strange landmass recently acquired by Michigan, their compasses swung wildly near Negaunee, where iron ore was so plentiful it was visible even on the surface, intertwined in the roots of a fallen tree. The tree is the official symbol of the city of Negaunee, which itself became completely intertwined with the rise and fall of the iron industry.

Aside from a handful of small mining operations, the unfathomable wealth of the Upper Peninsula's iron remained largely untapped for several decades, until the ever-expanding web of railroad lines reached the area. In the 1870s, the arrival of the railroad prompted the development of the first major mines in the Menominee Range. A few years later, the Gogebic Range opened. Many of the early mines were open-pit affairs, but soon the need for iron ore drove miners deeper and deeper underground. Today communities like Ishpeming sit atop a Swiss-cheese patch of earth riddled with mine shafts and adits; occasionally, tracts of land sink, leaving behind tilted and abandoned houses. Near Iron Mountain, the entire town of Norway was moved—twice—when the streets kept caving in.

World War II and its insatiable demand for iron drove area mines to peak production, eventually depleting some of them. By the 1960s and 1970s, the western U.P. iron ranges grew quiet after shipping out nearly two billion tons of ore. All underground iron mines in the U.P. closed by 1978, hurt by foreign steelmakers and the use of

Lake of the Clouds, Ontonagon County

more and more plastics in manufacturing. Only a few open-pit mines remain in operation; you can see one in Republic, where a small viewing platform (free) overlooks a gargantuan crater in the earth. Republic is located just off M-95 about six miles south of US-41 in Marquette County.

Today outdoor pursuits dominate the western U.P., a region liberally dotted with lakes, stitched with rivers, and sculpted with ancient mountains jutting skyward from Lake Superior. While folks from other parts of the country may scoff at the Midwest's idea of mountains, the altitudes in this part of the U.P. rise to downright unmidwestern-ly heights: Mt. Arvon, deep in the Huron Mountains due east of L'Anse, measures 1,979 feet.

The western U.P.'s surprising terrain matches its surprising variety. It is a land of popular downhill ski resorts and private old-world enclaves of the super-wealthy. A place to explore remote paddling lakes and excellent museums. Home to derelict towns with strip joints, and the smart and pretty city of Marquette, the U.P.'s largest. Did we say city? Travel a half hour west, and you can hike through remote terrain that's home to the state's largest moose herd. Wolves roam undisturbed just a few counties south. The iron ore may lie deep underground, but the western Upper Peninsula offers plenty of magnetic attractions up on the surface, too.

## Time Zones

The four counties bordering Wisconsin—Gogebic, Iron, Dickinson, and Menominee—are in the central time zone, while the rest of the Upper Peninsula, like the Lower Peninsula, is in the eastern time zone.

## Getting There

From Wisconsin, US-51 leads to Ironwood, US-45 to Watersmeet, US-141 to Iron Mountain, and US-41 to Menominee. From Duluth/Superior, US-2 travels east across the northwestern corner of Wisconsin to Ironwood. US-2 continues east along the southern boundary of the peninsula all the way to the Mackinac Bridge. For a more northerly route through the U.P., M-28 splits off from US-2 at Wakefield in Gogebic County, linking Marquette, Munising, and Sault Ste. Marie.

Greyhound, 800/231-2222, website: www .greyhound.com, offers service via Ironwood. The area's primary airport is in Marquette, served by Northwest Airlines, 800/225-2525, website: www.nwa.com, American Airlines, 800/433-7300, website: www.aa.com, and Skyway Airlines, the shuttle partner for Midwest Express Airlines, 800/452-2022, website: www.midwestexpress.com.

# Gogebic and Ontonagon Counties

Squeezed between Lake Superior and the Wisconsin border, these westernmost Upper Peninsula counties perhaps best explain why many Yoopers feel little affinity with urban areas like Detroit and Lansing in lower Michigan: The two regions are 600 miles and a lifetime apart. Life here revolves around outdoor recreation—fishing, hunting, hiking, paddling, skiing, snowmobiling—which largely fuels the local economy. Residents of Detroit could sooner drive to New York City than Ironwood—and would probably feel more at home when they got there.

Gogebic (go-GIB-ic) is derived from a lyrical Ottawa word describing the rings in the water made by trout as they rise to the surface to feed.

It's a lovely and appropriate moniker, since fishing is a favorite pastime and important tourism draw. Lake Gogebic, stretching 13 miles from north to south, ranks as the U.P.'s largest inland lake, known for walleye, smallmouth bass, northern pike, and perch. Dozens of smaller lakes also dot the landscape in the two counties, many within the vast boundaries of the Ottawa National Forest.

Come November, Lake Superior snows inundate the region, marketed to downhill skiers throughout the Midwest as "Big Snow Country." Many visitors never get past the area's well-known downhill resorts and the homely stretch of US-2 that links them. Their loss, because when the snow melts, a beautiful landscape emerges of inland lakes and rivers for fishing and paddling, and hundreds of miles of national forest trails for hiking and biking. After all, even in Big Snow Country it stops snowing—for a few months, anyway.

While many of the area's small communities have chambers of commerce that can help with lodgings and other services, the area's most comprehensive source of visitor information is the **Western Upper Peninsula Convention and Visitors Bureau**, 137 E. Cloverland Dr., P. O. Box 706, Ironwood, MI 49938, 906/932-4850, website: www.westernup.com

## IRONWOOD AREA

With mammoth Lake Superior providing the requisite moisture, the northwestern corner of the U.P. isn't exaggerating when it markets itself as "Big Snow Country." Cool air moving across the warmer waters of Lake Superior create lake effect snows when they hit land, generating an average of 200 inches per season. This combines nicely with the area's rugged hills and Midwestern mountains, home to many of the Midwest's largest downhill ski resorts. As a result, the western U.P., especially around Ironwood, is one of the Upper Peninsula's more heavily marketed tourism areas, luring sizable crowds of skiers up I-39/US-51 every weekend from Wisconsin and the Chicago area.

Cross-country skiers and, increasingly, snowshoers also take advantage of the abundant snows. Gogebic County has more dedicated Nordic skiing resorts than you'll find elsewhere in the Upper Peninsula. And the Ottawa National Forest offers a dizzying array of terrain for those seeking solitude. The U.P. never overlooks snowmobiling, though, and you'll see plenty of trucks pulling snowmobiles; snowmobile routes radiating out from Lake Gogebic seem especially popular. To avoid them, ask state park/national forest officials about the proximity of snowmobiling trails where you plan to set out.

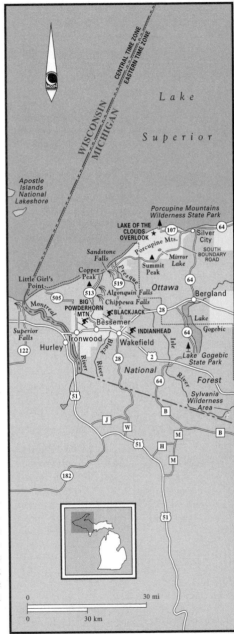

# THE WESTERN U.P.

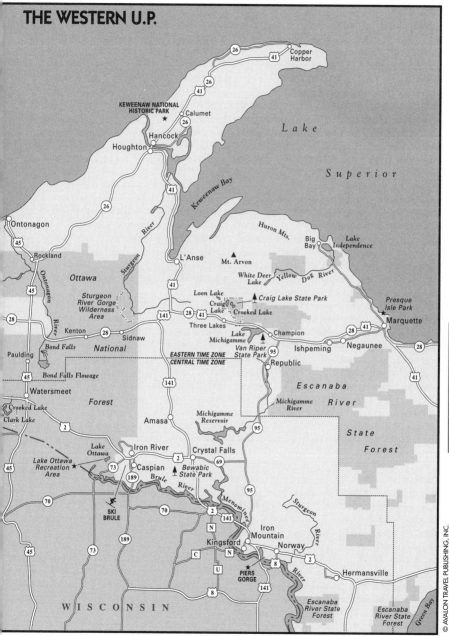

Copper Harbor

KEWEENAW NATIONAL HISTORIC PARK

Calumet

Hancock

Houghton

Keweenaw Bay

L a k e

S u p e r i o r

Ontonagon

Rockland

Ottawa

L'Anse

Mt. Arvon

Huron Mts.

Big Bay

Lake Independence

White Deer Lake

Yellow Dog River

Sturgeon River Gorge Wilderness Area

Loon Lake

Craig Lake State Park

Presque Isle Park

Marquette

Craig Lake

Crooked Lake

Kenton

Sidnaw

Three Lakes

Champion

Ishpeming

Negaunee

Bond Falls

National

Lake Michigamme

Van Riper State Park

Paulding

EASTERN TIME ZONE
CENTRAL TIME ZONE

Republic

Watersmeet

Bond Falls Flowage

Escanaba

Crooked Lake

Clark Lake

Forest

Michigamme Reservoir

Michigamme River

River

Amasa

Lake Ottawa

Iron River

Crystal Falls

State

Lake Ottawa Recreation Area

Caspian

Bewabic State Park

Forest

SKI BRULE

Brule River

Sturgeon River

Menominee

Kingsford

Iron Mountain

Norway

Hermansville

W I S C O N S I N

PIERS GORGE

Escanaba River State Forest

Escanaba River State Forest

Green Bay

## Ironwood

Ironwood hugs the border and merges with its sister city of Hurley, Wisconsin, once the center of civilization for the iron miners of the Gogebic Range. Ironwood had the stores and services, Hurley had the bars and brothels. (Strip joints remain a key business.) At the peak of iron mining—from the early 1900s to about 1930—the population topped 15,000. But mining grew less economically viable and, unlike the riches generated by copper in the Keweenaw, the millions made from iron left the region, without leaving behind opulent mansions and other monuments of wealth.

Consequently, Ironwood today is a tattered town that hardly hints at its past. Still, locals are pleasantly friendly, and they would probably agree that Ironwood isn't the tourist attraction—the natural beauty of the surrounding area is.

Ironwood is a worthwhile stop for goods and services, with a large grocery store, some quality restaurants, and the like. You'll find most services along US-2 north and east of town. **Hobby Wheel,** 1435 E. Cloverland (US-2), 906/932-3332, sells a full line of cycling and ski gear, has a knowledgeable staff, and rents snowshoes and cross-country ski equipment. **Trek & Trail,** 1310 E. Cloverland, 906/932-5858, offers a good selection of cross-country skiing, mountain-biking, and fly-fishing equipment. Plenty of packs and clothing, too. East on US-2 in Bessemer, **Big Sno Outfitters,** 906/663-4646, is another excellent source for ski and snowboard rentals and sales.

## Outside of Town

Just minutes from the strip-mall world of US-2, the real UP awaits. Follow M-505 north from Ironwood to reach **Little Girl's Point,** an area favorite. Perched high on a bluff over Lake Superior, this county park features a sand beach, a boat launch, picnic tables, grills, and fantastic views—the Porcupine Mountains to the east, the Apostle Islands to the west.

From Little Girl's Point, continue west on M-505 to reach **Superior Falls.** The rushing Montreal River puts on its final spectacular show here, plummeting more than 40 feet, then squeezing

through a narrow gorge before spilling into Lake Superior a short distance away. You can also reach it by taking US-2 about 11 miles west from Ironwood and turning north on W-122. (You'll travel through Wisconsin and back into Michigan in the process.) In about 4.8 miles, watch for a small brown sign that directs you west into a small parking area near a Northern States Power substation. From here, it's a short walk to the falls. You also can continue down the path past the falls to Lake Superior, a fine sunset spot.

Old Highway 2, which runs south of the current one, links together several interesting old mining towns filled with quirky and unexpected finds. A good example is Ramsay, just east of Bessemer. Though it's now little more than a sleepy collection of miner's homes (many refurbished as weekend ski getaways), check out the **keystone bridge** that spans the Black River. Built in 1891, the 57-foot-high bridge was made out of limestone blocks without an ounce of mortar.

## Downhill Ski Resorts

With the exception of the ski area in the Porcupine Mountains Wilderness State Park (see below), the area's downhill ski resorts line up conveniently along a short stretch of US-2 just east of Ironwood. All welcome downhill skiers and snowboarders. Ticket prices vary with age and time of the year. Package rates with lodging usually bring the best deals. For those who want to explore all the area's terrain, ask about the interchangeable lift ticket (available at each participating resort) good on weekdays only at the area's four major resorts: Powderhorn, Blackjack, Indianhead, and Whitecap Mountain (located just over the border in Wisconsin).

Heading east from Ironwood, the first resort you'll reach is **Big Powderhorn Mountain,** 906/932-4838, website: www.bigpowderhorn.net, in Bessemer. Powderhorn oozes an early 1970s feel, and the giant fiberglass skier at its entrance—complete with red and blue vintage '70s skiwear—says it all. Its 25 downhill runs wrap across two faces, with 700 feet of vertical drop and nine double chairlifts. Perhaps more than the others, Big Powderhorn Mountain caters to families with affordable lift tickets, mostly tame runs, and plen-

© TRAVEL MICHIGAN

**Cross-country skiing is a great way to enjoy the outdoors.**

ty of ski-in/ski-out lodging bordering its slopes. The main lodge at the base houses a cafeteria, ski rental and repair, ski school, bar, and other services. Resort open daily.

Also in Bessemer, the smaller, family-run **Blackjack Ski Resort,** 888/906-9835, website: www.skiblackjack.com, carves out a niche in the market by making the most of its terrain. Cameron Run and Spillway often are left ungroomed and offer up good bump skiing, and it's arguably the best resort around for snowboarders, with the area's best half-pipe (served by its own rope tow) and a great terrain park on Broad Ax. Look to Blackjack for a variety of snowboard events, including camps and competitions. It's also a good place to avoid the weekend crowds that can plague Powderhorn and Indianhead. Blackjack offers 16 runs, four double chairlifts, and 465 feet of vertical. A day lodge at the base has food service, rental, and repair; some limited condo accommodations line the slopes. Its Loggers Lounge upstairs hosts the area's liveliest après-ski scene. Blackjack has been open daily only during high season, closed on

Tues. and Wed. other times. Call or check the website for a current schedule.

A few more miles down the road bring you to Wakefield and **Indianhead Ski Resort,** 800/3-INDIAN, website: www.indianheadmtn.com, the area's largest resort with 638 feet of vertical, five chairlifts, two T-bars, and 22 runs. Indianhead offers some of the region's most challenging (although overly groomed) skiing, and pleasant runs that wind for more than a mile through the woods. Indianhead's lodging and skier services (sales, rentals, and repairs) sit at the top of the resort and offer more choices than the other area resorts. The day lodge even comes with great views of the Ottawa National Forest, spilling out across the valley beyond the slopes. Open daily.

## Cross-Country Skiing
**Active Backwoods Retreats** (ABR for short), E5299 W. Pioneer Rd. in Ironwood, 906/932-3502, grooms 40 kilometers (25 miles) of trails for skating and striding, on hundreds of acres of private land three miles south of Ironwood. Fee is $4. Open daily, as well as some nights for lighted

skiing or moonlight skiing. Warming hut, lessons, and rentals available.

South of Wakefield, **Milje Cross Country Ski Trail,** 906/229-5267, has 11 kilometers (6.8 miles) of groomed trails winding through the woods, along with a warming hut, rentals, and more. This is an easygoing kind of place; trails open when Rollie Milijevich can get the parking lot plowed open. No fee, but be sure to make a donation so Rollie can buy new snow tires. To find Milje's, turn south off US-2 at Sunday Lake St. (the stoplight) and drive about 2.5 miles.

Between Ironwood and Bessemer, take Section 12 Road north from US-2 to reach **Wolverine Nordic Trails.** Situated on private land and maintained by volunteers, its 15 kilometers (9.3 miles) of groomed trails wind through the hilly country south of the Big Powderhorn ski area. You can, in fact, ride one of Powderhorn's chairlifts ($2 per ride) to access the network. Otherwise, begin at the lot with the warming hut on Sunset Road off Section 12 Road. Donation requested.

If solitude is more important to you than track-set trails, don't overlook the vast terrain available in the 982,895-acre Ottawa National Forest. The U.S. Forest Service office, 2100 E. Cloverland in Ironwood, 906/932-1330, has national forest maps and can suggest trails to try.

## Accommodations

You'll find a large selection of mom-and-pop motels along US-2, many of which offer great deals and clean, comfortable, if simple, rooms. A couple of good choices are the **Sandpiper Motel,** 1200 Cloverland (US-2), 906/932-2000, and the **Crestview Cozy Inn,** west end of US-2, 906/932-4845. Both $25–75; rates may be higher in peak ski season.

The larger area ski resorts have slopeside (or near-slopeside) accommodations that range from dormitories to simple motel rooms to deluxe condominiums. (This ain't Aspen, so forgive the occasional bad paneling.) Prices range wide enough to fit almost every budget, and they can be a good value in non-skiing months. Try Indianhead reservations, 800/3-INDIAN, or Big Powderhorn Mountain and Lodging, 800/222-

3131, for plenty of choices. Ask about package deals with lift tickets if you're traveling in winter. The handy **Big Snow Country lodging referral service,** 906/932-4850, can fill you in on even more lodging options throughout the region—not just those near downhill ski resorts—from the Wisconsin border to just east of the Porcupine Mountains.

For something a little more intimate, you can't beat the **Bear Track Inn,** N15325 Black River Rd., Ironwood, MI 49938, 906/932-2144. National forest land practically surrounds the inn's three log cabins, with a great location one mile from Lake Superior's Black River Harbor and near loads of hiking/biking/ski trails. Each cabin has a full kitchen and use of the Finnish sauna.

Finally, chain motels cluster near the US-2/W-51 interchange, like the **Days Inn** in Hurley, 715/561-3500, with indoor pool; some rooms have microwaves and refrigerators. Rates $50–100.

## Camping

The **Ottawa National Forest** maintains 27 auto-accessible campgrounds, all with tent pads, fire grates, and some sort of toilet facilities. Many are located along rivers and lakes. Most tend to be quite rustic and secluded, with the exception of Black River Harbor, Sylvania, and Bobcat Lake. A few, like Black River Harbor, require a fee and allow reservations through a central reservation system, 800/280-CAMP or 283-CAMP. For more information on a specific campground, contact a district ranger station or the Ottawa National Forest Headquarters in Ironwood at 2100 E. Cloverland Dr., 906/932-1330 or 800/562-1201 (U.P. only).

True to Michigan state park form, **Lake Gogebic State Park** offers a fine modern campground, with large (but rather open) sites on the western shore of Lake Gogebic. A boat launch, small sand beach, and nice picnic area are nearby. Lake Gogebic is known for great walleye and perch fishing, so pack a rod even if you don't come with a boat. Though reservations are rarely needed, you can obtain one through the state park central reservation system, 800/44-PARKS; website: dnr.state.mi.us.

## Food

Yep, it looks like a classic corner tavern, but **Don & GG's,** on US-2 in Ironwood, 906/932-2312, might surprise you with its vegetarian dishes and smoked trout salad. Don't worry—you can still get burgers and chicken dinners, too. Okay, so the **Kimball Inn,** 715/561-4095, is actually in Wisconsin. It's worth the extra four mile drive west on US-2 from the Michigan/Wisconsin border to sample its smoked barbecue, charbroiled steaks, grinders (Italian sandwiches) and more. Closed Mon. Also in Wisconsin, **Petrusha's Supper Club** in downtown Hurley, 715/561-9888, serves up good Italian and classic supper-club fare like prime rib and seafood. Some interesting Austrian dishes, too, like the filet with chicken livers and cognac sauce. Back in Ironwood, the **Royal Bakery,** at the corner of Cloverland (US-2) and Douglas, 906/932-1931, is a good bet for fresh homemade pasties, as well as basic doughnuts and pastries.

# PORCUPINE MOUNTAINS WILDERNESS STATE PARK

Anchored along the Lake Superior shore in the northwest corner of the U.P., Porcupine Mountains Wilderness State Park covers 60,000 acres, the largest in Michigan's excellent state park system. The Porcupine Mountains were considered as a national park site in the 1940s, but were quickly preserved as a state park in 1945 when loggers threatened to get to work on their virgin timber before the federal government took action.

Someone once decided that this rumpled landscape of low mountains and tall pines looked like the silhouette of a porcupine. Hmm. But the name stuck, endearingly dubbed "the Porkies." It is a mecca for casual hikers and hardcore backpackers alike, home to 90-plus miles of well-marked, well-maintained trails—more than you'll find in many national parks, and certainly more than you'll find in most of the Great Lakes region.

And in this case, bigger also means better. The park preserves vast stands of virgin hemlock, pine, and hardwoods—the largest tract of virgin hardwoods between the Rockies and Adirondacks, in fact—secluded lakes, wild rivers, and some of the Midwest's highest peaks. (Summit Peak tops out at 1,958 feet.) Unlike most state parks, the Porkies are large enough to provide a sense of wilderness and serenity, an escape from the civilized world.

## Getting There and Getting Information

Two roads lead to Porcupine Mountains Wilderness State Park, located 65 miles northeast of Ironwood. From Wakefield, M-519 leads to the park's western edge and the Presque Isle campground. From Bergland, M-64 heads north to Lake Superior, where it meets up with M-107 for a quick jog west to the park's eastern boundary. The South Boundary Road connects both roads along—you guessed it—the south end of the park.

Start your visit at the park's **visitors center** at the junction of M-107 and South Boundary Road. Rangers on duty can provide you with maps and suggest trails. A gift shop has topo maps and a good selection of nature guidebooks.

For more information, contact **Porcupine Mountains Wilderness State Park,** 412 South Boundary Rd, 906/885-5275.

## Hiking Trails

Many park visitors head immediately for the justly famous **Lake of the Clouds Overlook.** From the parking lot at the end of M-107, it's just a few steps to the overlook, where the placid lake slices a long sliver of blue through a thick mat of jade forest hundreds of feet below. The view is the stuff postcards are made of and is probably the most photographed scene in the U.P.

The overlook also serves as the trailhead for some of the park's most rugged and scenic routes. To properly soak in the Lake of the Clouds view, hike the aptly named **Escarpment Trail,** which winds east and skims over Cloud Peak and Cuyahoga Peak. Bordered by a sheer cliff, the four-mile trail is considered by many to be the most beautiful in the park. Allow ample time to stop and enjoy the shimmering lake and valley floor spreading out around you.

© TRAVEL MICHIGAN

**Porcupine Mountain scenic view**

At its eastern trailhead, the Escarpment Trail links up with the 7.5-mile **Government Peak Trail.** This secluded route drops south over the Upper Carp River and past Trap Falls, then swings west and scales Government Peak. As quickly as it rises, the trail drops down to quiet Mirror Lake, a perfect spot to soak weary feet after a full day of hiking.

From Mirror Lake, the dull and heavily wooded **Correction Line Trail** heads west, where it meets the **Big Carp River Trail,** another good choice. Running nine miles from Lake Superior to the Lake of the Clouds Overlook, this fine route leads hikers along a shaded river valley of hemlocks and ferns, past the park's highest waterfall (25-foot Shining Cloud Falls), and along a dry ridgetop with more dramatic peeks at Lake of the Clouds.

Several miles south, visitors get another soaring view from the **Summit Peak observation tower.** At 1,958 feet, Summit Peak grows even taller with a 40-foot observation tower at its crest. It's an inspiring panorama, a vast landscape unscarred by humans. In fact, the only

sign of civilization is the spindly ski jump 18 miles away, rising above the treeline like a circus clown on stilts. On a clear day, scour the horizon for a glimpse of Lake Superior's Apostle Islands, nearly 40 miles to the west.

One of the park's most spectacular trails is probably its most accessible: the **East and West River Trail** parallels the wild and turbulent Presque Isle River. From the Presque Isle Campground at the park's west end, you can follow the Presque Isle one mile upriver and back down the other bank as it roils and boils through narrow rock walls and tumbles into Lake Superior. Keep a tight hold on children and pets along this trail, and don't think about wading in—the current is swift and dangerous. To dangle your toes or let Fido take a swim, there's a wonderfully deep, clear, and placid backwater pool just east of the main channel right near Lake Superior.

Long before the Porcupine Mountains were preserved for their virgin timber and natural beauty, miners harvested the rich minerals buried in their bedrock. At the east end of the park, the **Union Mine Trail** provides a glimpse into the

1840s, when the Porkies pulsed with the excitement of the area's copper rush. Marked with white mine shovels to indicate points of interest, this self-guided interpretive trail forms a mile loop along the spring-fed Union River and the site of an old copper mine, now largely swallowed by nature. In the shadow of lofty hemlocks, you'll see how miners tunneled shafts into the riverbank and learn about their life in the wilderness—a wilderness still untamed today.

### Winter in the Porkies

Downhill skiers are surprised to find a state-run **downhill ski area** within the park, and even more surprised to find it offers a 640-foot vertical and 14 runs. Runs range in difficulty from bunny to advanced, spanning a north-facing flank, served by two chairlifts, one T-bar, and a rope tow. A day lodge at the base has food service, rentals, and a small ski shop. Sure, the lifts are old and creaky, but the terrain is great, the snow is reliable (annual average tops 175 inches), and the views of Lake Superior from the top are phenomenal. For all its charms, though, it's not a good choice on a day when a strong north wind is blowing—you'll feel the windchill all the way from Canada.

Located just west of the park headquarters on M-107, the ski area is open 9:30 A.M.–5:30 P.M. weekdays, 10 A.M.–5 P.M. weekends. Call the park headquarters, 906/885-5275, for information on ticket prices and snow conditions.

The same chalet and base area serves cross-country skiers, who can access a terrific network of trails. The park service grooms and tracks 23 kilometers (14.2 miles) of the park's hiking trails, which wind through the eastern end of the park. Some skirt the Lake Superior shoreline, where snow and ice sculptures form. Others scale the hilly terrain in the interior of the park and can be reached via one of the downhill ski area lifts. Skiing is free, but there is a charge for lift service and park admission. Call the park headquarters for more information.

### Camping

Campers have their choice of two modern campgrounds, both with a number of sites overlooking Lake Superior: Union Bay (full hook-ups) at the east end of the park or Presque Isle (no hookups) near the mouth of the Presque Isle River on the park's western edge. Both offer flush toilets and showers. In addition, three rustic campgrounds (called "outposts") with three to 11 sites each are located off the South Boundary Road, accessible by car, but with no facilities. They tend to offer more privacy than the modern campgrounds. Reservations for all campsites are recommended in summer, 800/44-PARKS; website: dnr.state.mi.us.

As another option, the park offers 16 hike-in rustic cabins. These are great retreats after a day on the trail. They come with two to eight bunks, mattresses, a woodstove, basic utensils, and protection from the elements, but no electricity or running water. Bring your own stove for cooking. Cabins situated on inland lakes even come with a rowboat, so you can finish the day with a lazy drift across the water. Reserve one as much as a year in advance by calling 906/885-5275.

Two more options for backpackers: three hike-in Adirondack shelters with sleeping platforms (available only on a first-come, first-served basis) and backcountry camping. Trailside camping is permitted throughout the backcountry, as long as you stay a quarter mile or more from cabins, shelters, scenic areas, and roads. All backpackers must register at the visitors center before setting out.

## ONTONAGON AND ENVIRONS

The Ontonagon Boulder was pried from its namesake riverbank a few miles upstream from the Lake Superior shoreline community of **Ontonagon.** Today the two-ton mass of native copper resides at the Smithsonian, and Ontonagon's mining heritage today thrives only in museums—especially since the nearby copper mine and smelter in White Pine closed in 1995. (White Pine now is little more than a creepy ghost town of 1950s tract housing.) Check out Ontonagon's happier heyday at the worthwhile Ontonagon County Historical Museum, a lavender building on US-41/M-38, downtown's main street. The Historical Society's biggest project these days is restoring the 1866 Ontonagon Lighthouse, which replaced one of Lake Superior's first lighthouses, built in 1853. Contact the Ontonagon County Historical Society, 906/884-6165, to learn more on restoration efforts and public tours.

Originally established by copper miners in the 1840s, the tiny town of **Rockland** was nearly leveled by a fire in 1890. It was rebuilt in the popular Victorian style of the day, and several Victorian facades still decorate this small community in the Ontonagon River valley, 14 miles south of Ontonagon on US-45. From downtown Rockland, follow Victoria Dam Road southwest two miles to **Old Victoria,** 906/886-2617, a cluster of miners' log homes huddled around a once-lucrative copper-mine shaft. Locals have scratched to save this preservation work-in-progress; its new designation as a Keweenaw National Historic Park cooperating site may funnel new attention and needed funds. The homes are open on most summer afternoons when a guide is on hand to offer tours. Donations needed and appreciated. You can wander the grounds at any time. Continue past Old Victoria to the **Victoria Dam,** a power company hydroelectric facility and surprisingly pretty spot, popular with local anglers.

## Accommodations

You'll find a string of motels along M-64 between Silver City (two miles east of park headquarters) to Ontonagon. Many are plain, somewhat tired mom-and-pop-type places, but they work just fine after a long day outdoors. **Tomlinson's Rainbow Lodging,** two 2900 M-64, 906/885-5348, offers motel rooms and cottages on the shores of Lake Superior, with a private sand beach. Somes units have whirlpools and kitchen facilities. Pets okay. Rates average $75–150. **Mountain View Lodges,** 906/885-5256, features two-bedroom cottages on Lake Superior with amenities like fireplaces and fully equipped kitchens. Rates $100–150. The **Best Western Porcupine Mountain Lodge** in Silver City, 906/885-5311, offers the full array of motel services, including indoor pool, sauna, meeting rooms, and a dining room. Rates $75–150. For other options, contact the Ontonagon Chamber of Commerce, 906/884-4735.

## Food

**Paul's Restaurant,** 906/885-5311, in Silver City's Porcupine Mountain Lodge, gets high marks for fish and other supper-club fare. In Ontonagon, **Syl's,** 713 River, 906/884-2522, is a classic small-town café, with some of the best pasties around. Fifteen minutes south of Ontonagon on US-45, **Henry's Never Inn** in Rockland, 906/886-9910, draws 'em in far and wide for its enormous buffets ($8), with various fish dishes on Friday night and Italian on Saturday. Soups and sandwiches are great, too, but it's really the spirited locals that add flavor to this old mining haunt.

If you're camping in the Porkies, your closest full-service grocery is in Ontonagon, 17 miles east of the park. For last-minute supplies, try the **Silver City General Store,** 906/885-5885, on M-107. It has basic camping and fishing supplies, and picnic staples like cheese and bread.

# OTTAWA NATIONAL FOREST

Sprawling across nearly a million acres, the Ottawa National Forest blankets much of the western peninsula from the Wisconsin border to US-141, which runs north from Iron River. Unlike a national park with a contiguous boundary, the Ottawa National Forest is a patchwork of protected lands, pieced together around towns, private property, and various state parks and forests.

Named for the Ottawa Indians who lived and traded in this region (though they actually populated the eastern half of the U.P. in greater numbers), the Ottawa National Forest encompasses more than 400 lakes, seven major river systems, some of the U.P.'s most outstanding waterfalls, 27 campgrounds, and three wilderness areas: Sylvania, the Sturgeon River Gorge, and the McCormick Tract.

## Information

To make sense of the what the Ottawa has to offer, start with a map. You can pick up a small brochure (free) or large topo map ($4) at **National Forest Headquarters** in Ironwood, 2100 E. Cloverland Dr., 906/932-1330, or at the **Watersmeet Ranger District** office at the intersection of US-2 and US-45 in Watersmeet, 906/358-4551. Other district offices, in Bessemer, Bergland, and Ontonagon, may have maps and brochures, but budget cuts have forced them to curtail other visitor services.

Several of the Ottawa's key attractions lie within Gogebic County, described above. For further information on other areas to visit within the national forest, see the **Menominee Range** and **Huron Mountains** sections of this chapter.

## Black River Road National Scenic Byway

Gogebic County tourism folks heavily promote this 15-mile stretch of M-513 from Bessemer north to Lake Superior, and for good reason. The two-lane road itself is pleasant enough, a wooded drive that twists in tandem with the Black River, hidden away in the forest just off the road's eastern shoulder. But even better, it links together several notable attractions.

You'll see the first long before you reach it. About nine miles north of Bessemer, the rocky outcrop of **Copper Peak** rises 364 feet above the surrounding countryside, crowned by the 421-foot **Copper Peak Ski Flying Hill,** 906/932-3500. Ski flying is similar to ski jumping but uses different equipment to launch—believe it or not—*farther* distances. (The current record is 512 feet.) Copper Peak, built in 1970, is the only ski flying hill in the western hemisphere, and the highest artificial jump in the world. It periodically holds sanctioned events for the sport, which is very popular in Europe.

From Memorial Day to Labor Day (and weekends through mid-October) a chairlift, elevator, and steps (fee) will bring you to the top for a heart-thumping skier's-eye view of the chute. This is not a trip for the faint of heart. But if you can get over a little knee-knocking, you'll be wowed by the panorama of the surrounding countryside, with views stretching across the undulating green of the national forest, the serpentine Black River, and the blue, blue horizon of Lake Superior. The Copper Peak complex also offers 12 miles of mountain biking trails.

The Black River rolls and tumbles over seven magnificent waterfalls north of Bessemer be-

fore rushing into Lake Superior, believed to be the largest concentration of waterfalls in the state. The first two, **Chippewa Falls** and **Algonquin Falls,** 9.5 and 9 miles north of Bessemer, are a little tough to find without a topo map, since they don't lie along well-marked trails. The next five are a different story. The national forest has marked and mapped a good trail network, beginning from a parking lot off M-513, about 13 miles north of Bessemer. From this lot you can hike, from south to north, to **Great Conglomerate, Potawatomi, Gorge, Sandstone,** and **Rainbow Falls.** Only strong hikers and waterfall junkies should try to cover them all in one 10-mile outing—it's a lot of steps and a lot of waterfalls.

Like babies and sunsets, each waterfall is beautiful in a different way, and it's impossible to name the "best." Potawatomi is the closest—just a few minutes' walk from the lot—and accessible by wheelchair. And it is lovely, a delicate fretwork of foam cascading over remnants of an ancient lava flow. The last falls, Rainbow, is the largest of the group, cascading 40 feet. The resulting spray sometimes creates a rainbow effect, which gives the falls its name. The best view of this falls is from the east side of the river, which you can access from a suspended foot bridge near the river's mouth at **Black River Harbor.**

The end of the road for M-513, Black River Harbor is a popular national forest campground on Lake Superior, with a large day-use area, sand beach, and boat launch. You can also pick up North Country Scenic Trail here. For campground reservations, call the national forest central reservation system, 800/280-CAMP or 283-CAMP.

## Pines and Mines

This marked and mapped trail system gives a glimpse of the tantalizing **mountain biking** opportunities in the western Upper Peninsula. A joint effort of local tourism/economic development groups, the Ottawa National Forest, and TRALE UP (a local trail-access organization), it comprises some 200 miles of trails in three networks. Routes range from tame gravel roads to single-track trails deep in the woods. As a bonus, many link up with waterfalls, remote lakes, and historical features.

Near Marinesco in Gogebic County, the **Pomeroy/Henry Lake network** offers 100 miles of gentle rides on wide gravel roads around a national forest area peppered with small lakes. It's a good choice for families. The **Ehlco network,** just south of the Porcupine Mountains Wilderness State Park, includes more single track deep in the forest, on grass or dirt paths. (This area can be wet thanks to some lowlands and the work of local beavers, so avoid it after a rain.) Arguably the best of the three is the one located outside the national forest: the Iron Co. (Wisc.) system. Trails radiating out of Hurley lead you past waterfalls, large flowages, and old mining relics like the Plummer headframe near Pence. Good interpretive signs help make sense of historic sites. Routes in this system range from gravel roads to terrific single track, though it's not clear from the map which is which. (Single-track trails 6 and 13 are recommended.)

While the Pines and Mines trails are great, the map is mediocre; it's best to bring a topo map, and before you set out, get a little local advice from national forest rangers, local bike shops (Trek and Trail in Ironwood, 906/932-5858), or the Pines and Mines organizers. Pick up a map at the Wisconsin or Michigan state information centers (both on US-2 near the border), local bike shops, or the Ottawa National Forest office in Ironwood.

## National Forest Rivers

Seven major river systems flow within the forest, a staggering 1,000 miles of navigable waters for **paddlers.** Congress has designated more than 300 of those miles as wild and scenic or recreational rivers, leaving them largely in a pristine state. In general, rivers like the Ontonagon and Presque Isle offer quiet water in their southern reaches, winding through relatively flat woodlands. North of M-28, they begin a more rugged descent through hills and bluffs, requiring higher skills and boats appropriate for whitewater. For strong paddlers with good whitewater skills, these rivers offer some of the finest paddling in the Midwest.

Of course, all of this can change depending on rainfall and the time of the year. Rivers that normally flow gently can be torrents in the spring. Always check with national forest officials before setting out. Also, the Forest Service publishes an extensive *River Digest* (free) that outlines navigable rivers, launch areas, liveries, and high flow/low flow times. Pick one up at a district ranger office.

The three branches of the mighty Ontonagon spread across the western U.P. like a spiderweb; at times it seems every road you travel crosses one branch or another. While many parts of the river system are worth exploring, one spot gets particular attention: the upper reaches of the middle branch of the Ontonagon, where **Bond Falls** cascades down a series of black boulders. Some consider it one of the most spectacular falls in the Upper Peninsula—a mighty big claim—while others feel the setting is far too developed with walkways and viewing platforms.

To decide for yourself, head for Paulding on US-45 in Ontonagon County. Bond Falls is three miles east on Bond Falls Road, well-marked by signs. Though virtually surrounded by national forest land, the falls themselves sit on power company property, just below a power company dam that forms the adjacent **Bond Falls Flowage,** a popular area for fishing, swimming, and camping. To view the falls, follow the trail down the west side of the river, ignoring the spillway, cement retaining wall, and other power company additions. Once you begin descending the stairs, the falls come into your view to the right, close enough to touch. Continue down the path to a footbridge that spans the base of the falls for an in-your-face view. Water gushes down a 50-foot face of chiseled rocks, so perfectly dramatic it almost looks like a Disney creation.

## Sylvania Wilderness Area and Recreation Area

Sylvania protects its assets well—36 crystalline glacial lakes hidden among thick stands of massive, old-growth trees. For anglers who dream of landing (and then releasing) that once-in-a-lifetime smallmouth bass, for paddlers who yearn to glide across deep, quiet waters and along untrammeled shoreline, for hikers who wish to travel under a towering canopy of trees and hear nothing more than the haunting whistle of a loon, Sylvania can be a truly magical place.

One of three wilderness areas within the national forest, Sylvania stretches across 18,000 acres near Watersmeet, an area roughly bordered by US-2 to the north, US-45 to the east, and the Wisconsin border to the south. The adjacent **Sylvania Recreation Area** acts as a buffer, an additional 3,000 acres of lakes and woodlands with a few developed services like a drive-in campground, nice beach, flush toilets, and running water.

Once viewed as just another tract of good timber, Sylvania's fate turned in the late 1890s, when a lumberman who purchased 80 acres near the south end of Clark Lake decided it was too lovely to cut, and instead kept it as his personal fishing retreat. He invited his wealthy buddies—some of them executives of U.S. Steel—who also were captivated by the land. Together, they purchased several thousand additional acres and formed the private Sylvania Club.

Like other upscale U.P. "great camps," the Sylvania Club soon had grand log lodges along its shores, guards to keep trespassing anglers away from its bountiful lakes, and caretakers to squelch forest fires as they cropped up. Ownership changed a few times over the decades, eventually ending up in the hands of Lawrence Fisher of Fisher Auto Body. When he died, his heirs sold the property to the federal government for $5.7 million. It was operated as a recreation area from the late 1960s to 1987, when the bulk of it was converted to wilderness status.

We can partly thank Old Money for the condition of the land today. With the public previously barred from fishing here, Sylvania's lakes now provide some epic fishing, especially for bass. Its waters remain pristine, thanks to the lack of development and powerboat access, as well as the area's topography—Sylvania lies on the divide between Lake Superior and the Mississippi, so it doesn't suffer from runoff of nearby lands. And whatever your thoughts on fire management, Sylvania's decades of fire protection means that visitors today can marvel at a virgin forest of white pine and hardwoods—hemlocks, maples, and basswood trees more than 200 years old.

*Once viewed as just another tract of good timber, Sylvania's fate began in the late 1890s, when a lumberman who purchased 80 acres near the south end of Clark Lake decided it was too lovely to cut, and instead kept it as his personal fishing retreat.*

Begin a trip to Sylvania with a call or visit to the Watersmeet Visitors Center, at the intersection of US-2 and US-45, 906/358-4724. The staff can help you with maps, regulations, campsite reservations, and other information. Sylvania's rules can be quite unique—especially fishing regulations—so take time to ask questions and read through the materials rangers provide. To reach Sylvania itself, follow US-2 west about four miles from the visitors center and turn south on Thousand Island Lake Road. Travel about four miles, following signs to reach the entrance building. All visitors are required to register upon arrival.

The entrance sits in the recreation area, near the drive-in campground on Clark Lake. If you intend to travel into the wilderness area, plan on treating your own water; you'll find water pumps only in the recreation area. Cookstoves are highly encouraged, too, to lessen the number of feet tramping through the forest in search of dead wood. During summer months, make sure you also have ample bug dope or, better yet, a head net to combat mosquitoes and black flies.

Like the Boundary Waters Canoe Area in Minnesota, **paddling** is the best way to explore the Sylvania Wilderness. Most lakes are linked by water or by relatively easy portages (though there are a couple of grunt portages of two miles or more). Many campsites are accessible only by water. Motors and other "mechanized equipment" are forbidden—that even includes sailboats. The one exception is Crooked Lake, which allows electric motors of 4hp or less.

From the entrance road, you can park your vehicle and put in at Clark Lake or Crooked Lake. According to a ranger, Clark (the largest lake), Crooked, and Loon are the three busiest lakes. Some of the smaller lakes—like Mountain and High, both accessible from Crooked—see less traffic and are just a short portage away. One ranger recommends bringing snorkel gear—the crystal-clear waters provide great visibility for viewing monster fish. Rent canoes and kayaks from **Sylvania Outfitters,** 23423 US-2 in Watersmeet, 906/358-4766, website: www.sylvaniaoutfitters.com. You can outfit your entire trip—boat, food, fishing gear, maps—at this helpful spot, and even arrange to have the stuff delivered and picked up from water's edge.

For **hikers,** Sylvania maintains 15 miles of trails, including a seven-mile trail (marked with blue blazes) around Clark Lake. It provides access to campsites and trails to other lakes. Most of Sylvania's trails are old roads left over from its fishing-camp days; though not always well-marked, they are quite easy to follow. These same roads become a great **cross-country ski** network in winter months. The national forest grooms 15 miles of trails within Sylvania.

# The Menominee Range

The Menominee Range is an anomaly in the Upper Peninsula, the only area not within rock-tossing distance of one of the Great Lakes. Roughly encompassing Iron, Dickinson, and Menominee Counties (all in the central time zone), as well as the southern reaches of Baraga County, it is a land of deep forests and literally thousands of inland lakes.

Tourists tend to pass right though the region, which admittedly doesn't look like much from US-2, the main thoroughfare. But that thin strip of development masks an astounding amount of untrammeled wilderness. As proof, wolves thrive here (without any human assistance), because the region provides exactly the habitat wolves need: large tracts of land not sliced up by roads where they can avoid civilization, and plenty of large prey in the form of the region's abundant white-tailed deer. Large-scale development isn't likely, either, since huge amounts of land fall under the auspices of the Ottawa National Forest and Copper Country State Forest. Mead Paper owns thousands more acres, which it holds as commercial reserve land and uses for only sporadic logging operations.

The cities and towns, too, hold pleasant surprises. The region's productive iron mines drew large immigrant populations here in the 1800s; their descendants today spice the region with a colorful mix of Italian, Lebanese, Polish, and Cornish cooking and culture (as well as a half dozen other ethnic groups).

## OTTAWA NATIONAL FOREST

Covering nearly a million acres in all, the Ottawa National Forest blankets large tracts of land north and west of Iron River. For specific information on camping, trails, lake access, and other attractions, contact the district ranger office at 990 Lalley Rd. in Iron River, 906/265-5139, or on M-28 in Kenton, 906/852-3500.

### Sturgeon River Gorge Wilderness Area

The Sturgeon River, a federally designated "Wild and Scenic River," travels a circuitous route through much of Baraga County before bleeding into Portage Lake near Chassell. One of the three wilderness areas within the national forest, the Sturgeon River Gorge Wilderness protects 14,000 acres that surround this river and its tributaries. The highlight is west of US-41 and south of M-38, where the river cuts and tumbles through a magnificent 300-foot-high gorge. To reach it, follow Forest Road 2200 north from Sidnaw. Follow signs onto Forest Road 2270 to reach a parking area and foot trail that winds down about a half mile or so to a falls and the river. Continue west from the parking area on Forest Road 2270 to reach Silver Mountain, with stone steps that lead to a remarkable valley view. Come in fall for a fiery display by the abundant maple forest.

The U.S. Forest Service has marked few trails within the wilderness area which, of course, is its appeal for those who love the backcountry. Several grown-over logging roads wind through the area for hikers who want to explore on their own. (A topo map is an absolute necessity.) No-trace **camping** is permitted throughout the wilderness, and you can find some pretty choice spots out there. If you'd like a few more services (water and pit toilets), the Forest Service maintains a rustic campground on Forest Road 2200, with nine appealing sites on a bend in the river. Cost is $5 a night.

BOB RACE

**Henry Ford, founder of an empire**

### Lake Ottawa Recreation Area

Nearly 15 miles of marked hiking/ski trails loop around crystal-clear Lake Ottawa and Hagerman Lake in the Lake Ottawa Recreation Area west of Iron River. Trails pass through hardwood forest and over hilly terrain, with some nice views. There often aren't any trail maps at the trailhead, so pick up one at the ranger station in Iron River. Facilities at Lake Ottawa include a small swimming beach, handsome CCC log lodge, and 32-site lakefront campground ($7 per night). To reach it, follow US-2 west to M-73 south; follow it less than a mile to Forest Road 101 and travel west about five miles to the recreation area.

## IRON RIVER AND VICINITY

Iron County's population centers around Iron River, an iron mining center, and Crystal Falls, the picturesque county seat 15 miles to the east. Both retain their small-town charm.

### Sights and Attractions

You won't find a lot of dramatic lighting and fancy display cases at the **Iron County Historical Museum,** two miles south of US-2 off M-189 in Caspian, 906/265-2617, website: www.iron-countymuseum.com. What you will find is an in-

teresting, appealing, and eclectic blend of local history and culture at this rambling, funky, and homegrown museum. Located on the site of the productive Caspian iron mine—whose rusting headframe still looms over the complex—it runs largely on donated money and donated time. In the main museum building, displays cover everything from Native American history to logging, mining, and sporting equipment and kitchenware from the early 1900s. The perennial favorite display is the mechanized iron mine and railroad model: for five cents, a miniature ore skip hauls rocks to the surface and loads them on the railroad.

Other displays not to miss: the Mining Memorial, with a computer database of area mines and miners and a video of life in the mines; a Plexiglas 3-D mine diagram that shows the depths of the mine, where ore has been mined and where it remains; a 50-foot-long diorama of a logging camp, complete with hundreds of folk-art figures by local artist William Monogal; newspaper clippings on Iron River's 1920 "rum rebellion," when federal agents from Chicago stormed the house of the priest (discovering eight barrels of rum), only to by defied by the state's attorney; and a history of the local labor movement, which helped boost miners' earnings from $365 per year in 1931 to $1,886 per year a decade later.

Outside, several relocated buildings occupy the grounds, including a streetcar barn and the streetcar that once traveled between the mines in Caspian and Iron River. The museum is open daily mid-May–October. Small admission.

Much of the U.P. is dotted with ghost towns, but **Triangle Ranch** may be its only ghost farm. In the 1920s, one developer had grand plans for some of Iron County's clear-cut logging land. He purchased nearly 10,000 acres, built pens, corrals, barns, and a rancher's home, intent on raising beef cattle. The idea went bust after just one year—it proved too costly to care for the animals over the long U.P. winter. Most of the land was sold back to a pulp/paper company (and has since been reforested), but the skeletons of the operation remain. Triangle Ranch remains on the Michigan state map; from Crystal Falls, take US-141 north about 15 miles to the marked Triangle Ranch Road (a few miles north of Amasa). Follow the road east about a mile to the remains of the ranch.

## Outdoor Recreation

A small but pleasant chain of lakes is the highlight of **Bewabic State Park,** 1933 US-2, 906/875-3324, located five miles west of Crystal Falls. Boaters can put in at the first of the Fortune Lakes and make their way to Fourth Lake, an easy day's paddling adventure. Though First Lake can be somewhat frenetic on summer weekends, the waters get quieter and downright pristine as you proceed down the chain. Most of the shoreline is dotted with cottages, though you can camp on state-owned land bordering Third Lake. **Fishing** for perch and bass is best on First Lake, the largest (192 acres) and deepest (72 feet). **Paddlers** can escape fishing boats by darting under the low US-2 bridge to Mud Lake. The park itself has a modern 144-site campground with good privacy, a small stretch of sandy beach, tennis courts, and other amenities. For camping reservations (though they're rarely needed), con-

tact the state park reservation line, 800/44-PARKS; website: dnr.state.mi.us.

Without the benefit of the "Big Snow Country" marketing muscle that serves the ski resorts of Gogebic County, **Ski Brule** is left to its own devices to market this appealing ski area six miles south of Iron River. Its gimmick is a "first to open, last to close" motto, which translates to about six months of skiing. Brule is reliably open for downhill skiing by mid-November and continues through April. The terrain is nice, too, with 500 feet of vertical, eight chairs and T-bars, and a decent half-pipe for snowboarders. Nordic skiers can check out 23 kilometers (14.2 miles) of groomed and tracked trails, some of which wind along the Brule River. (Because they aren't covered by the resort's snowmaking, the Nordic trails don't always open as soon as the downhill area.) Contact Ski Brule, 800/362-7853, website: www.skibrule.com, for information on lift rates, rentals, and resort lodging.

North of Crystal Falls, the amoeba-shaped **Michigamme Reservoir** draws attention because of its size and crooked shoreline. Not to be confused with Lake Michigamme (that's farther north, in Marquette County), the reservoir is an impoundment of the Michigamme River, regulated by Wisconsin Energy Corp. for hydroelectric power. These impoundments—also called "ponds"—are open to the public for fishing and for camping along their shores. Sites are rustic but very peaceful; boat launches provided. Along with Michigamme, similar facilities are located on Peavy Pond. For specifics, pick up the power company's *Wilderness Shores* brochure from the **Iron County Tourism Council,** 50 E. Genesee St. in Iron River, 800/TRY-IRON, website: www.tryiron.com

## Accommodations and Food

The **Lakeshore Motel,** 1257 Lalley Rd., 906/265-3611, sits on the edge of spring-fed Ice Lake in Iron River (just east of downtown on US-2), with tidy motel rooms, some with kitchenette units, going for $50–75 per night. A great find, complete with sand beach and boat launch. Iron River also has an **AmericInn** franchise, 906/265-9100, on US-2 just east of downtown, with a nice indoor pool, whirlpool, and sauna. Suites available. Rates $100–150.

The namesake of **Alice's** produces Italian specialties just as her immigrant mother did in Iron River before her, with homemade ravioli and other pasta dishes, gnocchi (Italian dumplings), and soups. Entrees about $10. For picnics, pick up supplies at **Angeli's Foods,** in Riverside Plaza on US-2 E, 906/265-5107. An ordinary-looking modern supermarket from the outside, inside it surprises with a superb bakery, produce department, and deli. The family-run operation also has a store in Menominee.

## Information

For more information on the Iron River area and Iron County, contact the **Iron County Tourism Council,** 50 E. Genesee St. in Iron River, 800/TRY-IRON, website: www.try-iron.org. All of Iron County is in the central time zone.

## IRON MOUNTAIN AND VICINITY

Iron Mountain was first settled in about 1880 and reached its heyday soon after, when vast deposits of iron were discovered underfoot. The Chapin Mine—located near present-day US-2 and Kent Avenue on the north end of downtown—helped boost the town's population to almost 8,000 by 1890. Italian immigrants led the melting-pot mix working at the Chapin Mine, and Italian neighborhoods still thrive around the old mine on Iron Mountain's north side—as evidenced by a mouthwatering supply of Italian restaurants and corner markets.

The long-abandoned Chapin Mine still serves an important role, this time as a magnet for brown bats. An estimated two million bats winter in the shaft, protected from predators yet able to enter and exit freely, thanks to bat-friendly grates installed at the mine entrance. As the weather turns cool (usually sometime in September), the bats congregate all around Iron Mountain before retreating to the mine, an amazing sight.

While iron mining seems to dominate the city's psyche, Henry Ford added to the economic mix in the 1920s, when he bought up huge tracts of nearby forest and built his first company sawmill on land southwest of town, which he dubbed Kingsford (named for Iron Mountain's Ford dealer, Edward Kingsford). Soon Ford's Kingsford empire included the main plant for making floorboards for the Model T, residential developments for workers, an airport, a refinery, even a plant to make newfangled charcoal briquettes. All of it eventually closed or was sold off, including the briquette plant, which relocated to Oakland, California, and still manufactures the ever-popular Kingsford charcoal briquettes.

## Sights and Attractions

A lot of museums bill themselves as a "step back in time," but you truly feel it at the **IXL Museum,** 906/498-2498, in downtown Hermansville, 28 miles east of Iron Mountain. For more than a century, this wood-frame building served as the northern office of the Wisconsin Land & Lumber Co., which got its start in the 1860s building doors and window sashes in central Wisconsin. After the Great Chicago Fire of 1871, founder C. J. L. Meyer moved north to tap into the vast pine reserves of the Upper Peninsula. He built the Hermansville office and adjacent sawmill in 1881. "IXL" stands for "I excel," and was used as a logo on all the company's products.

Today, the perfectly preserved IXL building is a time warp, one of the most fascinating museums in the Upper Peninsula. The dictaphones, the mimeograph machines, the payroll records… it's all still here, in place, just like you popped into the office on a weekend when everyone was off duty. The second floor, originally used as apartments for Meyer and his family, now displays a variety of machinery from logging days. When Meyer expanded the business north, he came up with a clever little innovation: tongue-and-groove flooring, precision-milled in one operation. The Hermansville operation quickly became the largest flooring plant in the country, crafting the floors for the Mormon Temple in Salt Lake City and Yellowstone National Park's main lodge, among other notable clients. At its peak, it held 30 million board-feet of lumber in its yards and operated three railroads to keep the supply coming. The museum is open Memorial Day weekend–Labor Day 12:30–4 P.M. Small admission fee.

Iron Mountain's Chapin Mine once led Menominee Range mining production, but was also one of the wettest mines ever worked. In 1893, an immense steam-operated pump was put to work, a 54-foot-high, 725-ton behemoth—the largest in the world at the time. Though electric pumps replaced it just 20 years later, the pump survives intact at the **Cornish Pump and Mining Museum,** one block east of US-2 in downtown Iron Mountain, 906/774-1086. Along with the impressive pump, this comprehensive museum includes a good-sized collection of mining equipment, photos, and clothing; a small theater; and, arguably the most compelling display of all, the story of the World War II gliders built by Henry Ford's nearby Kingsford plant, used to quietly deploy troops behind enemy lines. Open mid-May through mid-October Mon.–Sat. 9 A.M.–5 P.M., Sun. noon–4 P.M.

## Outdoor Recreation

Where the U.P. isn't bordered by lakes, it's bordered by rivers: the grand Menominee rambles from near Iron Mountain all the way to Lake Michigan's Green Bay, forming nearly half the boundary between Wisconsin and the Upper Peninsula. Just south of Norway, it narrows through **Piers Gorge,** a pretty run of frothing whitewater and waterfalls. In the mid-1800s, loggers relied on the Menominee to float logs to the river's mouth; they cursed this stretch of river for the logjams it caused, and built a series of wooden piers here in an attempt to slow the current and channel the flow—hence the name. To view it, follow US-8 south from Norway and turn right on Piers Gorge Road just before you cross the river into Wisconsin. Follow the road about a half mile until it ends at a trail. Along this mile-long trail, you'll be treated to several views of the gorge (from as high as 70 feet above) and several side trails of varying safety, some of which

wind down to the river itself. This is not a good choice for those with small children, since steep drop-offs abound.

Only experienced whitewater kayakers who can handle class III and IV rapids should consider running the Menominee. For an easy **paddle** on the nearby Brule or Pine Rivers, though, contact **Northwoods Wilderness Outfitters,** N4088 Pine Mountain Rd. in Iron Mountain, 906/774-9009, website: www.northwoodsoutfitters.com. This excellent shop will set you up for an afternoon or an extended trip, with canoe and kayak rentals as well as drop-off/pickup service. Northwoods also rents winter gear like snowshoes and cross-country skis, and organizes **ski, dogsled, and snowshoe outings.**

## Accommodations and Food

The **Pine Mountain Resort,** N3332 Pine Mountain Rd., 877/553-7463, anchors a full-service ski and golf resort on the northwest side of town, complete with dining room, indoor pool, outdoor pool, sauna, tennis courts, hiking/mountain biking trails, etc. Choose from standard lodge rooms ($50–100) or condominiums ($125–200). Just off US-2, the **Edgewater Resort,** 4128 N. US-2, 800/236-6244, makes the most of its fine setting overlooking the Menominee River, with 10 log cabins scattered across its grounds, along with a picnic area, playground, volleyball court, canoes and fishing boats for rent, and more. Two- and three-bedroom cabins with kitchens rent by the week (daily if available at the last minute), $300–500 per week. Pets permitted. Two miles north of Iron River, the mom-and-pop **Woodlands Motel,** N3957 US-2, 906/774-6106, offers standard motel rooms with small kitchenettes. Rates $50–75. Look for standard chain motels in downtown Iron Mountain.

Italian is the way to go if you're eating out in Iron Mountain. Homemade ravioli, slow-roasted pork, Italian sausage, Roma red sauce. . . you'll find it all in Iron Mountain's unassuming Italian eateries. For authentic pizza pie, try **Bruttomesso's,** 305 N. Stephenson (US-2), 906/774-0801. **Bimbo's Wine Press,** 314 E. Main,

906/774-8420, dishes out mouthwatering Italian sandwiches like porketta for incredibly reasonable prices ($5 on average). More upscale is **Fontana's Supper Club,** 115 S. Stephenson, 906/774-0044, for steaks and, yes, Italian specialties. Save room for cheesecake. Dinner entrees average $15.

## Information

For information on Iron Mountain and the surrounding area, contact the **Tourism Association of Dickinson County,** 600 S. Stephenson Ave., 800/236-2447, website: www.ironmountain.org. Also remember that Iron Mountain is on central time.

## Marquette and Vicinity

## MARQUETTE

With 23,000 hardy year-round souls, Marquette ranks as the largest city in the Upper Peninsula. Tucked in a well-protected natural harbor nearly midway across the U.P.'s northern shore, it grew and thrives largely because of its location—an important Lake Superior port for the iron industry, and a rather central location that has helped it evolve into the U.P.'s center of commerce and government.

Don't be dissuaded by the strip mall blight along US-41. Head toward the water, where you'll discover a thriving downtown rich in architecture, a U.S. Olympic Training Center, Northern Michigan University (home to 8,000 students), and a beautiful setting along a high, rocky shoreline of Lake Superior. Marquette has never really billed itself much as a tourist destination, but it's actually a terrific spot to unpack your bags: lodging and good restaurants are plentiful, the downtown and lakefront are ideal for strolling, and the U.P.'s blue ribbon attractions—rugged hills, waterfalls, wildlife, wild rivers—await you barely outside the city limits.

For information on the region, contact the **Marquette Country Convention and Visitors Bureau,** 2552 US-41 W, Suite 300, 800/544-4321, website: www.marquettecountry.org.

## Downtown

Third Street, running north-south, and Washington, running east-west, represent Marquette's main cross streets and where they meet is a good area to begin an exploration of the downtown. This puts you in the heart of the shopping and historic district. Buildings like the 1902 Marquette County Courthouse, at 3rd and Baraga, and the 1927 MFC First National Bank, at 101 W. Washington, showcase the city's affinity for **Beaux Arts architecture**. Step inside the courthouse for a better look, and also to check out a display about Michigan Supreme Court Justice and author John Voelker. Better known by his pen name, Robert Traver, the Ishpeming native wrote *Anatomy of a Murder,* among other works. Scenes from the popular 1959 movie starring Jimmy Stewart were filmed here, as well as in nearby Big Bay, where the actual murder occurred. The **Marquette County Historical Society,** 213 N. Front St., 906/226-3571, offers a walking tour brochure ($1). Open Mon.–Fri. 10 A.M. –5 P.M. open until 9 P.M. on the third Thursday of the month.

Downtown Marquette is home to some distinctive shops worth a little browsing time. **Bookworld,** 36 W. Washington, and **Snowbound Books,** 118 N. 3rd, offer a good selection of local and regional titles. Follow Main down to the waterfront, where **Thill's Fish House,** 906/226-9851, sells fresh catch and smoked whitefish spread from a little shop at the marina, in the shadow of the old wooden ore dock. (See the end of this chapter for more dining suggestions.)

The U.P.'s Scandinavian heritage looms large in Marquette. **Scandinavian Gifts,** 1025 N. 3rd, 906/225-1993, showcases the sleek and simple lines of classic Scandinavian design in its selection of glassware and silver (lots of Norwegian sweaters, too). Back on the highway, **Touch of Finland,** US-41 across from Kmart, 906/226-

2567, has a little bit of everything in its 4,000-square-foot store, including housewares, textiles, and a complete sauna department.

The old red brick waterworks building at 300 Lakeshore Boulevard now houses the **Marquette Maritime Museum,** 906/226-2006, open daily 10 A.M.–5 P.M., May 1–Oct. 31. This worthwhile stop includes exhibits on everything from Native American birchbark canoes to Great Lakes shipwrecks, lighthouses, an interactive display of a freighter's pilot house and working submarine periscope. Open daily May–Oct. Admission $3. The **Marquette County Historical Museum,** 213 Front Street, 906/226-3571, features excellent Native American exhibits, as well as lots of mining and logging photographs and a large collection of old maps. Good bookstore, too. Open weekdays year-round. $3 adults, $1children over 12. If you've got kids in tow, head for the **UP Children's Museum,** 123 W. Baraga St., 906/226-3911, where they can climb into a tree habitat to learn about its root system, crawl into a replica wasp nest, or explore life in the aquifer under a pond. Open Mon.–Thurs. 10 A.M. –6 P.M., Friday 10 A.M. –8 P.M., Saturday 10 A.M. –6 P.M., Sunday 12 P.M–5 P.M.. Small admission fee.

Where else would you expect to find the world's largest wooden dome? In the heart of logging country, of course, and along Lake Superior, where changing weather regularly foils outdoor sporting events. In 1991, Northern Michigan University completed the 8,000-seat **Superior Dome,** 1401 Presque Isle Ave., 906/227-2850, affectionately known as the "Yooper Dome." Encompassing some five acres, the dome is fashioned from a framework of 781 huge fir beams, strong enough to withstand substantial snows. Along with hosting a variety of school sporting events and practices, the dome is open to the public for walking and running on weekday mornings. Call or stop by for specific times.

The **UP 200** is a sled-dog race held in mid-February that begins and ends in Marquette and loops all the way down to Escanaba on the Lake Michigan shore. An estimated 30,000 watch the annual race, which has quickly grown into one of the U.P.'s most beloved spectator events. The start and finish are the big draws, but the race has prompted a week-long calendar of activities, from broomball tournaments (think hockey with boots instead of skates, balls instead of pucks and brooms instead of sticks) to fireworks. For information and upcoming dates, visit website: www.up200.org, or contact the Marquette Country Convention and Visitors Bureau, 800/544-4321.

## Outdoor Recreation

A thumb of land thrust out into the big lake, **Presque Isle Park,** about four miles north of downtown off Lakeshore Boulevard, is a microcosm of the area's beauty: rocky red bluffs, tall pines, and lovely Lake Superior vistas. You can drive through the 323-acre park, but you'd do better to get out and stroll or ski along its many trails. Watch for albino deer (white-tailed deer lacking pigment), which survive in this protected setting. Near the park's entrance, there's a playground, picnic area, tennis courts, and marina, and a good spot from which to watch the huge 800-foot freighters arrive at the towering **railroad ore dock.** Trains carrying taconite pellets (an iron/clay mixture) from one of the nearby open-pit iron mines chug out onto the 70-foot-high elevated track, where they empty their loads into the hold below. Chutes transfer the taconite into the bellies of the ore freighters, which transport the shipment to the industrial centers in the southern Great Lakes. Also at the entrance of the park, you can pick up the **Marquette Bicycle Path,** a paved route that hugs the shoreline all the way to Harvey, offering access to downtown and the Northern Michigan University campus.

Among skiers and snowboarders, **Marquette Mountain,** 906/225-1155, gets the thumbs-up for its 600-foot vertical drop, one of the highest in the state. The 23 trails may not be exceptionally long, but they offer good variety—including bumps and tree runs—and the halfpipe and terrain park grow and improve every year. Located just three miles south of town on CR-553, it's popular all week long among local residents and college students. Night skiing is offered Tues.–Sun. in season, which usually runs from about mid-November to early April. Lift rates $15–30, rental equipment available.

For Nordic skiing, continue heading south on CR-553 to the **Blueberry Ridge Ski Trails.** Fifteen miles of groomed and tracked trails loop through the Escanaba River State Forest, including one lighted 1.7-mile circuit. Free. Another option is the **Anderson Lake Pathway,** five miles south of Gwinn on CR-557, with four hilly loops ranging from 2 to 4.3 miles in length. Both networks are open to mountain bikes in summer months.

As CR-550 heads north out of Marquette toward Big Bay, you've traveled just six miles when the sign and parking area for **Sugar Loaf Mountain** lures you to pull over. Heed your instincts; for a relatively easy 15-minute hike (a stairway makes for a gradual ascent up the rock), you'll be rewarded with a sweeping view of Lake Superior to the north, the city of Marquette to the east, and the rumpled-blanket landscape of the wild Huron Mountains stretching all the way to the western horizon.

There's great **hiking and mountain biking** in the surrounding terrain, much of it part of the **Little Presque Isle State Forest Recreation Area.** Several miles of trails wind around nearby Harlow Lake, up Hogsback Mountain, and along the Lake Superior shore. Park at the unmarked lot on the west side of CR-550 near an old gravel pit, about a mile north of the Sugar Loaf Mountain lot. First, though, pick up the free *Marquette Region Hike and Bike Trail Guide* from the Marquette Country Convention and Visitors Bureau, 2552 US-41 W, Suite 300, or local shops. Better yet, enlist the knowledge of the guides at **Great Northern Adventures.** See Outfitters under the Practicalities section at the end of this chapter.

## THE HURON MOUNTAINS

Ask 10 people where the Huron Mountains begin and end, and you're likely to get 10 different answers. But everyone will agree that they fall within the fuzzy boundaries of Lake Superior to the north and east, and US-41 to the south and west. That's a swath of land some 50 miles wide by 25 miles long, where the terrain rises into rugged

hills and, yes, even mountains. Mt. Arvon, about 15 miles due east of L'Anse, tops out at 1,979 feet, the highest point in the state.

Look at a map, and you'll see it's an intriguing parcel of land, virtually devoid of towns and roads. What the Huron Mountains do have, however, includes washboard peaks and valleys, virgin white pine forests, hundreds of lakes, the headwaters of a half dozen classic wilderness rivers, dazzling waterfalls, far more wildlife than people, and utter silence. Even by U.P. standards, it's a rugged, remarkable place.

The preservation wasn't the result of happy accident; beginning around the 1880s, the Huron Mountains became the wilderness retreat of choice for several millionaire industrialists. Cyrus McCormick, head of the lucrative farm implement company that would become International Harvester, amassed a huge wilderness estate around White Deer Lake, now part of the Ottawa National Forest's McCormick Tract Wilderness Area. Frederick Miller of Miller Brewing owned his piece of wilderness at Craig Lake, now a wilderness state park. Dozens of others owned "camps" at the Huron Mountain Club, an organization so exclusive, even Henry Ford was turned downed for membership when he first applied. The members easily had enough clout to stop construction of a road that was to link L'Anse with Big Bay—CR-550 abruptly ends west of Big Bay at a gate and security guard house.

Today, the 25,000-acre enclave is shared mostly by the descendants of those original members, who quietly protect and preserve this spectacular landholding. Though locals grumble about the lack of access onto the property (remember, trespassing is considered a right here), no one can argue that the Huron Mountain Club has proved to be an exceptional steward of the land. It kept away the loggers, the miners, and the developers, leaving what some consider the most magnificent wilderness remaining in the state, maybe even all of the Midwest. Within its boundaries lie towering virgin pines, blue-ribbon trout streams, pristine lakes, and waterfalls that don't even appear on maps. If the club should ever come up for sale, government officials admit (albeit off the record) that they would clamor to turn to it into a state or national park.

In the meantime, the rest of us have to be content simply knowing that such wonderful natural beauty is there, and lovingly protected. Besides, there's plenty of Huron Mountain wilderness open to the public—more than enough to go around for those who are fortunate and smart enough to explore this special place.

## Big Bay Area

Many people approach the Huron Mountains from the east, where CR-550 climbs 30 miles out of Marquette to the tiny town of **Big Bay,** population 260. Sited above Lake Independence and within minutes of Lake Superior, Big Bay is a scrappy little place, where residents take pride in their simple life on the fringes of wilderness. The town has swung from prosperity to near-ghost-town status more than once, first as a bustling logging outpost, then one of Henry Ford's company towns, home to busy sawmills. More recently, residents joke about how the local bank, well aware of the town's volatile economy, was loathe to loan money to Big Bay businesses; while the town's 20 businesses are thriving, the bank closed down. Folks now frequent Big Bay for its Huron Mountains access, Lake Superior harbor, Lake Independence fishing, and unique lodgings (see Practicalities, below).

*Wildlife sightings can be excellent here—the state's largest moose herd roams in the McCormick Wilderness, which in turn has attracted predators like the elusive gray wolf. You're not likely to see a wolf, but you may be treated to its hollow wail at your camp some evening.*

From Big Bay, your best bets for venturing into the backcountry are CR-510, which branches off CR-550 on the southeast edge of town (and continues south all the way to US-41 west of Marquette), and the Triple A Truck Trail, which branches off of CR-510. Both are usually well-maintained dirt/gravel roads, though be aware that wet or snowy weather can quickly render them impassable. Dozens of old logging roads and single tracks branch off of these main routes. To find your way around, you'll want a topo map or a very good local map (sometimes called the "waterfall map") available free from the Marquette Country Convention and Visitors Bureau.

The waterfall map will indeed point you toward many of the region's wealth of falls. Some of the finest and/or most accessible include Big and Little Garlic Falls, Hills Falls, and Big Pup Falls. The latter two are part of the Yellow Dog River, a beautiful river that splashes and tumbles over cliffs and through canyons from the Yellow Dog Plains north to Lake Independence. Pack a fly rod if you enjoy casting for trout—fishing can be great here.

The Commercial Forest Reserve Act gives property owners a tax break in exchange for allowing others access onto their property, so trespassing isn't really an issue as you explore the Huron Mountains. As a result, you have near limitless possibilities for hiking and mountain biking on old logging roads and various foot trails. Two spots worth exploring are **Gobbler's Knob,** a rock outcrop off CR-510 that overlooks Lake Independence and Lake Superior; and the **Elliott Donnelley Wilderness Area** off CR550, where a four-mile trail winds along the Little Garlic River and past Little Garlic Falls.

Keep in mind that the Huron Mountains can be a confusing place. You can drive yourself crazy heading down one dead-end logging road after another, or worse, get hopelessly lost on one of hundreds of unmapped, unmarked trails. Before you head off into the woods, make sure you're comfortable and competent with a map and compass. Otherwise, you're best off hooking up with a local guide who can show you around on foot, mountain bike, or snowshoe.

## McCormick Wilderness

Once the private wilderness retreat of Cyrus McCormick, whose father invented the reaping machine, this 27-square-mile tract of wilderness was willed to the U.S. Forest Service by the Mc-Cormick family in 1967. Today it remains in pristine wilderness condition—remote, undeveloped, and largely unused. In other words, perfect for backcountry hiking and camping. No-trace camping is permitted throughout the wilderness area. For more information, contact the Ottawa National Forest Ranger District, 4810 E. M-28, Kenton, MI 49943, 906/852-3500.

To access the McCormick Tract, follow US-41/M-28 west from Marquette about 50 miles to Champion. Just after you cross the Peshekee River, follow the first paved road north. This is CR-607, also called the Peshekee Grade or the Huron Bay Grade. In about 10 miles, you'll see a sign for Arfelin Lake; take the next road to your right and watch for a sign and small parking area.

Once you've arrived, you'll be pretty much on your own to explore this rugged terrain of high hills, rivers, muskeg, and bedrock outcroppings. Don't expect marked and maintained hiking trails. This tract is wild, so with the exception of a well-worn path to White Deer Lake (where the McCormicks' lodge once stood), you'll mostly be traveling cross-country. A compass and topo map are absolute necessities. Wildlife sightings can be excellent—the state's largest moose herd roams here, which in turn has attracted predators like the elusive gray wolf. You're not likely to see a wolf, but may be treated to its hollow wail at your camp some evening.

## Craig Lake State Park

Craig Lake is probably unlike any state park you've ever visited. For starters, the entrance is nearly seven miles down a rugged truck trail that often requires four-wheel drive and is periodically "improved" with sharp old mining rock that has the nasty knack of inflicting lethal wounds in your tires. Once you arrive at the Craig Lake parking area, you access the 7,000-acre park on foot or, with a short portage, by canoe or kayak. No wheeled vehicles or boat motors are permitted anywhere within the park.

For **hikers,** a seven-mile trail loops around Craig Lake, the park's largest body of water, a beautiful wild lake dotted with rocky islands. Side trail portages lead to small Clair Lake at the north end and Crooked Lake to the east. **Paddlers** will enjoy the serenity of any of the park's six lakes, though Crooked is perhaps the most appealing, with lots of interesting bays and inlets. To reach it, paddle across the southeastern corner of Craig Lake and follow the half-mile portage east. Wildlife sightings in the park include bear, deer, loons, moose, and the occasional wolf. **Fishing** can be great here, especially for trophy muskie (catch-and-release only). Several special regulations apply, so be sure to check with park officials. For maps, regulations, and other information, contact nearby Van Riper State Park (on US-41, just west of Champion), P. O. Box 66, Champion, MI 49814, 906/339-4461.

## Van Riper State Park

Though it's situated right on busy US-41, Van Riper State Park is worthy of mention for several reasons. For one, it offers a good, rarely full modern campground on the eastern shore of Lake Michigamme, where you'll find a boat launch, good walleye fishing, and a fine swimming beach with unusually warm water and a sand bottom. Two, many campers overlook the park property on the north side of the road, its largest and most appealing acreage. It includes a rustic campground on the Peshekee River and four miles of hiking trails. Climb the Overlook Trail, a loop that climbs up a rocky outcrop for a great view of the rolling forestland and Lake Michigamme. What's more, Van Riper is less than a dozen miles from the gated entrance of the McCormick Tract—so you can take advantage of modern comforts (hot showers!) while spending your days in the rugged backcountry that begins just across the highway.

Van Riper State Park is perhaps best known for its Moose Information Center, a kiosk that tells the story of the U.P.'s successful **moose reintroduction program.** Though moose were once common in the U.P., hunting and disease nearly devastated the herd in past decades. Two "moose lifts" in the 1980s transported 59 of the giant mammals from Algonquin Provincial Park in Ontario to the lightly traveled wilderness along the Peshekee Grade, near the McCormick Tract. It was quite a project: wildlife biologists captured each moose, then airlifted them one by one in a sling, dangling beneath a helicopter, to a base camp where they were trucked 600 miles to the Huron Mountains.

Today, the region's moose population has climbed to 200 or 300. You may see them anywhere in this region, but your chances are best at dawn or dusk, and in wet, swampy areas. The Marquette Country Convention and Visitors Bureau also publishes a *Moose Locator Guide,* detailing six backroad tours that lead you through areas frequented by moose, including the Peshekee Grade and Wolf Lake Road, east of Champion. For more information, contact Van Riper State Park, 906/339-4461.

# ISHPEMING/NEGAUNEE

In many ways, these twin towns 15 miles west of Marquette represent the heart of the iron range. One of the Upper Peninsula's earliest iron mines, the Jackson Mine, opened here in 1847; the nearby Empire and Tilden Mines mark the end of the era, the last operating iron mines in the range.

Ishpeming and Negaunee pretty much faded right along with the glory days of mining. The economy never quite recovered from the closing of the area mines in the 1960s, and the once-vital downtowns were further displaced by the commercial strips along US-41, which passes just north of town. But anyone who enjoys tidbits of history will find these towns intriguing, with their leftover ornate storefronts, ramshackle an-

tique shops, and fenced-off "cave-in" areas—where the land once and for all has succumbed to its mining heritage.

## Sights and Attractions

One of the finest museums in the Upper Peninsula, the state-run **Iron Industry Museum,** 73 Forge Rd. in Negaunee, 906/475-7857, is well worth the short detour off US-41 to its picturesque location along the Carp River. The spot wasn't chosen for its scenery; it marks the site of one of the area's earliest iron forges, built in 1848. This small facility packs a lot of information and well-done displays into a single exhibit hall. It tells the story of Michigan's $48-billion iron mining and smelting industry, which dwarfed the California Gold Rush ($955 million), Michigan's lucrative logging industry ($4.4 billion), and even Michigan's venerable copper mining empire ($9.6 billion). You'll learn how iron prompted the development of dozens of port towns and the giant 1,000-foot ore freighters that now ply the Great Lakes. The "Technology Timeline" traces the advancements of exploration, working conditions, and mining methods. Open May 1–Oct. 31 daily 9:30 A.M.–4:30 P.M. Free.

Few people think of Ishpeming as the center of the U.S. ski industry, but a lot of those big resorts in the Rockies can trace America's interest in the sport to Michigan. Michigan residents—many of them Scandinavian immigrants—established the Ishpeming Ski Club in 1887, one of the oldest continuously operating clubs in the nation, and organized the country's first ski jumping competition in 1888. Everett

the pioneer furnace in Negaunee, circa 1880

BOB RACE

Kircher, visionary founder of Michigan's Boyne Mountain resort, invented the first successful snowmaking machine. Hence, Ishpeming was chosen as the site of the **U.S. National Ski Hall of Fame and Ski Museum,** the "official" hall of fame, just like the Football Hall of Fame in Canton, Ohio, and the Baseball Hall of Fame in Cooperstown, New York.

The museum, on US-41 between 2nd and 3rd Streets, 906/485-6323, covers the sport from *way* back, beginning with a replica of a 4,000-year-old ski and pole found in Sweden. Most interesting are the displays of early ski equipment (including early poles which "often doubled as weapons"), the evolution of chairlifts, and an account of the skiing soldiers of the 10th Mountain Division, who played an important role in the mountains of Italy during World War II. The Hall of Fame plaques offer insightful short biographies of those who shaped the sport, from racers to resort owners to, ahem, orthopedic surgeons. Open year-round Mon.–Sat., 10 A.M.–5 P.M. Admission is $3 adults, $1 students, children under 10 free.

Lovers of kitsch absolutely must stop at **Da Yoopers Tourist Trap,** 906/485-5595, a self-mocking gift shop on US-41, just west of Ishpeming. (The "world's largest chainsaw" draws you in from the highway.) The singing group Da Yoopers—the U.P.-ers, get it?—from Ishpeming have earned a cult following with their U.P. parodies like "Smelting USA" and "The Second Week of Deer Camp." Some find their humor crude, but others love the inside jokes about beer, bullet-ridden highway signs, ice fishing, and jabs at the Lower Peninsula. The shop features a goofy array of paraphernalia like beer gut T-shirts and silly bumper stickers, but also surprises with some neat old historic photo prints and local crafts/folk art. Open year-round.

### Outdoor Recreation

You'd hardly guess that the 300-acre **Al Quaal Recreation Area,** on the north shore of Ishpeming's Teal Lake, is a city park. To get there, take Deer Lake Road north from US-41. You can make a winter day of it, with a few downhill runs served by a rope tow, a three-kilometer (1.9 mile) cross-country loop, outdoor ice rink, and especially the 1,200-foot iced toboggan run where a small hourly fee includes rental toboggan. Open daily except downhill runs, which are open only on weekend afternoons. Call 906/486-8301 for specific fees and hours.

Nordic skiers looking for a challenge should head for the ominous-sounding **Suicide Bowl** trail network between Ishpeming and Negaunee. Groomed for skating and diagonal stride, it offers 30-plus kilometers (18.6 miles) of trails, and a map dotted with phrases like "hairpin curve," "bad downhill," and "very difficult trail." Parking area is south of Business M-28 (follow it past downtown Ishpeming) on Cliff Drive. This area is also the site of **Suicide Hill,** a ski jump used in international competitions.

Ski jumping not wild enough? How about luge? Just south of Negaunee on M-35, **Lucy Hill** meets International Luge Federation standards as an official luge track, dropping 300 feet with 29 turns. Open to the public most weekend afternoons, with instruction and equipment available. For information, call 906/475-LUGE.

In summer, the entire area is part of the comprehensive **Range Mountain Bike Trail System,** with more than 25 miles of trails stretching from Teal Lake to Lake Sally, south of Suicide Bowl. Routes are covered in the *Marquette Region Hike and Bike Trail Guide,* available from the Marquette Country Convention and Visitors Bureau, 2552 US-41 W, Suite 300, or local shops.

## PRACTICALITIES

### Outfitters and Sports Shops

Want to find the best spots among the vast woods and waters around Marquette? Want to kayak or mountain bike or snowshoe without having to lug (or buy) all the gear? Then hook up with Rah Trost and **Great Northern Adventures.** Rah and her staff know the area from Marquette to Pictured Rocks National Lakeshore inside and out. Great Northern offers a wide variety of outdoor trips in the region, ranging from one to 10 days, including hiking, biking, kayaking, snowshoeing, cross-country skiing and dogsled adventures. Contact Great Northern Adventures at 906/225-TOUR, website: www.greatnorthernadventures.com.

Jeff TenEyck of **Huron Mountain Outfitters,** 906/345-9265, grew up with the Hurons as his boyhood backyard. He can lead you to more hidden waterfalls and mountain vistas than you could ever hope to find on your own, on day trips or overnight backpacking tours. He's also darned colorful and entertaining, regaling guests with poetry and childhood stories along the way.

If you arrive in winter, try your hand at mushing. **Triple Creek Sled Dog Kennels,** 800/DOG-SLED, offers trips ranging from two hours to five days powered by a team of eager huskies. Owner Bob Johnson was instrumental in bringing dogsled racing to the Upper Peninsula, and is one of the most experienced mushers around. Package tours include a stay at Johnson's Buck Sporting Lodge, a solar-powered wilderness lodge north of Rapid River.

**Down Wind Sports,** 514 N. 3rd St. in Marquette, 906/226-7112, is a great local source for information on mountain biking, whitewater kayaking, sea kayaking, rock climbing, and more. The shop also hosts weekly climbing outings, mountain bike rides and river trips in summer months. Down Wind sells a full line of sporting equipment, including kayaks, skis, and snowshoes, and has rentals available. In nearby Ishpeming, **Maple Lane Sports,** 1015 Country Lane, 906/485-1636, is another good mountain bike/ski/snowshoe shop, with rentals available.

## Accommodations

The best spot in Marquette is easily the **Landmark Inn,** 230 N. Front St., 888/752-6362. Built in the 1930s as the Northland Hotel, it hosted such luminaries as Amelia Earhart and Abott and Costello. After falling into disrepair and eventually closing in the 1980s, it now has been beautifully remodeled and reopened as the Landmark. For not much more than you'd pay for a basic franchise motel room, you get a taste of history, a touch of elegance and a primo location:

Lake Superior on one side, downtown Marquette on the other. Rates $100–150.

For a pet-friendly spot overlooking Lake Superior and rooms with mini-kitchens (some with balconies), try the **Birchmont Motel,** 2090 US-41, 906/228-7494. Rates $25–50. The **Tiroler Hof Inn,** 1880 US-41, 906/226-7516, offers tidy Austrian-style buildings on spacious, landscaped grounds overlooking Lake Superior. Small pets permitted. Rates $50–75. Many of the major hotel/motel franchises are represented in Marquette, especially along the US-41/M-28 strip.

There's also a surprisingly good and varied choice of lodgings in tiny Big Bay. Probably the best known is the **Big Bay Point Lighthouse Bed and Breakfast,** 3 Lighthouse Rd., 906/345-9957, website: www.lighthousebandb.com. Being a lighthouse, it naturally occupies a dramatic position on a rocky point just a few miles from the town of Big Bay. The red-brick lighthouse keeper's home, attached to the 1896 light, has been restored and retrofitted with seven very comfortable guest rooms, all with private baths. Five have Lake Superior views. The inn has extensive grounds, more than 43 acres and a half mile of shoreline, set far back from busy roads and hustle and bustle. Guests are welcome to use the sauna, climb the light tower, or relax in the living room, where owners Linda and Jeff Gamble have collected loads of lighthouse lore and history. Rates $100–200, including full breakfast. Reserve well in advance.

The wonderful **Thunder Bay Inn,** 400 Bensinger St., 906/345-9376, also has plenty of history to share. Originally built in 1911 as a warehouse and office for the area's thriving lumber industry, Henry Ford purchased the large clapboard building in "downtown" Big Bay in 1940 for use as an executive retreat, adding an immense two-story porch in the process. The location was a natural—it overlooks Lake Independence and a sawmill that produced the panels for the Ford "Woody." Later, the inn's restaurant was the setting for the Jimmy Stewart movie *Anatomy of a Murder,* based on a crime that took place at the Lumberjack Tavern a block away. Current owners Darryl and Eileen Small have restored the inn and filled it with movie memorabilia, as well as artifacts chronicling Ford's significant U.P. influence. Darryl's a history buff and a great source of Henry Ford knowledge. Twelve guest rooms all have private toilets/sinks; some require showering down the hall. Rates $50–100, including continental breakfast.

Two more choices with good locations in Big Bay and rates in the $50–75 range: The **Big Bay Depot,** 906/345-9350, occupies an old freight depot overlooking Lake Independence. Large rooms include full kitchens. Pets welcome. The mom-and-pop **Picture Bay Motel,** 906/345-9820, is neat as a pin. Two units have basic cooking facilities.

## Camping

Backcountry campers will find nearly unlimited options in the **Huron Mountains** and **McCormick Wilderness.** Respect private property rights, observe backcountry camping principles, and travel with a map, compass, and other backcountry essentials. If you're not experienced in the backcountry, it might be wise to plan your first trip with the company of a local guide like Great Northern Adventures, 906/225-TOUR, or Jeff TenEyck of Huron Mountain Outfitters, 906/345-9265.

Straddling the highway, **Van Riper State Park** offers easily accessible modern and rustic campsites, although within earshot of US-41. The park also rents out three rustic cabins, two near the modern campground ($32) and one north of the highway on the Peshekee River ($45). Reserve well in advance by calling 800/44-PARKS; website: dnr.state.mi.us.

At 7,000-acre **Craig Lake State Park,** you essentially get an organized campsite tucked in the backcountry wilderness. A rough seven-mile drive and one- or two-mile hike will bring you to lovely—and often empty—sites. Choose from sites that sit on a bed of pine needles above the east shore of Craig Lake, or follow the portage trail east to sites on a small peninsula sticking out into Crooked Lake. No reservations; pay the $6 nightly fee at the park-

ing area. If you're smart, you called in January and booked one of the rustic cabins on the northwestern shore of Craig Lake. Originally built by Frederick Miller of Miller Brewing fame, these barebones cabins offer bunks for your sleeping bag, some utilitarian furniture, and protection from bugs and cold. The larger of the two boasts a huge gathering room with stone fireplace and sleeps 14 ($45). The other ($35) sleeps six. Both have a water pump, firewood, and a rowboat. For maps and information, contact Van Riper State Park, 906/339-4461.

## Food

For a city its size, Marquette has a very good selection of quality, locally owned restaurants. The **Vierling Saloon,** 119 S. Front St., 906/228-3533, stands out for its consistently good food, century-old decor, and interesting views of Marquette Harbor ore docks. (Ask for a table near the large windows in back.) The menu offers lot of variety, including vegetarian dishes and whitefish served five ways. Excellent breakfasts, soups, and sandwiches, too. Dinner entrees start at $9. A couple years ago, the owners added a microbrewery downstairs, featuring British-style ales and stouts. Closed Sun.

Marquette's newest dining addition is **Upfront and Company,** 102 E. Main St., 906/228-5200. Renovated with wood from the city's old ore dock, it's not only beautiful to look at, it features great wood-fired pizza. Frequent live music is turning Upfront into Marquette's most popular nightspot, too. For organic, natural food dishes, you can't do better than the **Sweet Water Cafe,** 517 N. 3rd St., 906/226-7009. Locals give its tofu scramble and pancakes with whipped maple butter extra high marks. Good smoothies, too. Locals will also point you to the **Panini Grill,** 1125 N. 3rd St., 906/226-9000, for good sandwiches, wraps, and soups; and the no-frills **Border Grill,** 180 S. McClellan Ave., 906/228-5228, for yummy Tex-Mex with fresh salsa.

A bit farther afield, the aptly named **Northwoods Supper Club,** 906/228-4343, offers exactly what its name implies: great supper club fare (read: steaks and seafood, a salad bar) in a rustic, northwoodsy log building. Particularly good prime rib and lake trout. Entrees start at about $10. Follow US-41 three miles west of Marquette and turn south on Northwoods Drive (watch for signs). In Big Bay, the piney pub at the **Thunder Bay Inn,** 800/732-0714, has a large following of regulars who come for the great sandwiches, burgers, pizza, homemade soups, and popular nightly specials like steaks and whitefish. Dinner entrees start at about $9.

## Information

Contact the **Marquette Country Convention and Visitors Bureau,** 2552 US-41 W, 800/544-4321. Marquette and its surrounding areas are in the eastern time zone.

# Copper Country:
## The Keweenaw
# Peninsula and Isle Royale

## Introduction

Raking off the back of the Upper Peninsula like a ragged dorsal fin, the Keweenaw Peninsula (KEE-wuh-naw) was quickly shunned by early European immigrants of the Michigan Territories: Hopelessly remote. Nearly engulfed by Lake Superior. Smothered in snows half the year. Blanketed by impenetrable forests, which grew out of untillable rock and infertile sand. They dismissed it as nothing more than a wasteland, even more so than the rest of the Upper Peninsula.

But then in 1840, state geologist Douglass Houghton confirmed the presence of copper. Vast deposits of pure, native copper, much of it right near the surface, there for the taking. The young United States had an insatiable appetite for the metal, first for new industrial machinery, and later, for Civil War hardware, electrical wiring, and other innovations. Houghton's find was as good as gold. Actually, it was even better than gold.

The Copper Rush began almost overnight, first with prospectors, then large mining enterprises flooding the "wasteland" of the Keweenaw. It was the nation's first mineral rush. Copper employed thousands of immigrant laborers, built cities, made millionaires, and prompted extravagant luxuries like opera houses and "copper baron" mansions. Before it was over, King Copper generated more than $9.6 billion—10 times more money than the California Gold Rush.

The Keweenaw's copper legacy still looms large, but in the form of abandoned mines, ghost towns buried in the forest, and the odd juxtaposition of lavish buildings in almost-forgotten towns. Neglected for most of the 20th century, a slow pull finally began in the

Isle Royale

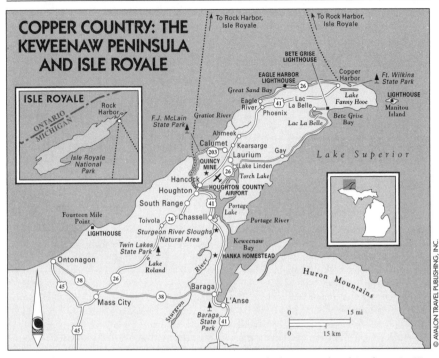

COPPER COUNTRY: THE KEWEENAW PENINSULA AND ISLE ROYALE

ISLE ROYALE

© AVALON TRAVEL PUBLISHING, INC.

1970s to preserve the Keweenaw's copper heritage. The result is the Keweenaw National Historic Park, established in 1992 (and still very much in development). To be sure, a lot of rich history has been demolished, thrown away, or crushed under the weight of winter snows. But an astounding amount remains, too. While cheesy chain restaurants across the United States line their walls with fake tools and other "junque," here you'll find the real thing: piles and piles of mining artifacts decorating restaurants, front porches, and anywhere else they can think to put the century-old stuff.

Today, the Keweenaw's wealth is measured not in copper but in its incredible natural beauty—a mother lode of wild rivers, hidden waterfalls, and lonely Lake Superior beaches. Some 48 miles north (and also part of Michigan), Isle Royale National Park lies stranded in Lake Superior, a wild, craggy, roadless archipelago of lakes and forests and moose and hiking trails. It remains the least-visited park in the entire National Park Service system.

The remote Keweenaw has never had the tourist appeal—and subsequent amenities—of say, a Traverse City. That is just how many people like it, of course. But it's beginning to happen anyway. The national park will bring them, more museums and other attractions are opening, and more people every year discover its unspoiled beauty. Some locals seem almost uneasy (or maybe unsure?) about how to handle the growing tourism interest. The backcountry is filled with amazing hiking and mountain biking trails, which lead to waterfalls and other gems—but you'll find little guidance in where to go or how to get them.

Yet for those who crave a little adventure and solitude, the Keweenaw Peninsula and Isle Royale offer it up in spades. As it was for those early copper miners, the Keweenaw remains a remarkable land of discovery.

# HISTORY

## The First Miners

The Anishinabe gave the Keweenaw its name, calling it Ke-wai-wo-na, which has been paradoxically translated from Ojibwa as both "The Place We Go Around" and "Portage." But no matter. Truth is, many Native Americans didn't just portage across the peninsula or paddle around its tip. They summered here, mining the native copper as their ancestors had.

We know that natives were the Keweenaw's first copper miners, dating back to the Copper Culture Indians of about 5000–500 B.C. These prehistoric miners dug pits to expose the chunks of native copper layered in the basalt, built fires against the bedrock to get it hot, then splashed the rock with water to help loosen and break it up to extract the copper.

The Copper Culture Indians left behind evidence of remarkable engineering skills. They dug thousands of mining pits, some as deep as 80 feet. (Many of these ancient pits are still visible, best preserved on Isle Royale.) They used copper extensively, trading it and pounding it into fishhooks and tools. Archaeologists believe they were the first fabricators of metal tools in the Americas, and perhaps in the entire world.

> *The Anishinabe gave the Keweenaw its name, calling it Ke-wai-wo-na, which has been paradoxically translated from Ojibwa as both "The Place We Go Around" and "Portage." Truth is, many Native Americans didn't just portage across the peninsula or paddle around its tip. They summered here, mining the native copper as their ancestors had.*

## The Prospectors of the Copper Rush

The Indians extracted only a minuscule portion of the Keweenaw's copper over the centuries, though, and its vast riches were left nearly untouched until 1840. That's when Douglass Houghton—a medical doctor, naturalist, the mayor of Detroit, and the new state geologist—returned from an expedition surveying the Keweenaw's mineral resources. The land, he noted, held incredible promise of vast native copper deposits. Mineral wealth was even obvious right at the surface.

Houghton's careful report of the region instantly ignited copper fever. "While I am fully satisfied that the mineral district of our state will prove a source of eventual and steady increasing wealth to our people," he wrote in the report, "I cannot fail to have before me the fear that it may prove the ruin of hundreds of adventurers who will visit it with expectations never to be realized."

Houghton guessed right. The United States acquired the western half of the U.P.—and its mineral rights—from the Ojibwa in 1842, as prospectors began flooding toward the wild and remote Keweenaw. Lucky ones secured deck space on Great Lakes vessels, sailing up Lakes Huron and Michigan, then along the southern shore of Superior. But hundreds of others straggled through the roadless wilderness, trudging overland through northern Wisconsin by snowshoe, or following rivers through thick forests to reach the fabled riches.

Few struck it rich. Most prospecting centered around Houghton, Eagle River, and Ontonagon, but with limited success. Though the areas would later reveal large amounts of copper, the early prospectors didn't have the knowledge or equipment to find it, much less extract it. Most eventually stumbled southward again, despondent and destitute.

## Big Mines, Big Money

But there were exceptions. A pharmacist from Philadelphia hooked up with a local prospector, financing his explorations near what is today US-41 south of Phoenix. Soon he had convinced a few other Pittsburgh associates to help finance mining in this promising area. In 1849, the Cliff Mine became the first copper mine in the Keweenaw to produce a dividend for its investors. And it continued to do so handsomely: by 1871, it had spawned a town and paid out more than $2.2 million.

The stab-in-the-dark prospectors were quickly replaced by more sophisticated mining operations, with financial backing to build tools and dig shafts. The Quincy Mining Co. opened a mine above Hancock in 1856, hitting almost instant success. With its profits it built schools, homes, and a hospital, and kept expanding a mine that eventually burrowed underground nearly 10,000 feet. You could stack six of Chicago's Sears Tower in the hole.

© TRAVEL MICHIGAN

**The occasional moose is seen around the Keweenaw Peninsula.**

The entire nation turned to the Keweenaw for its copper. From 1845 to 1895, the peninsula produced 75 percent of U.S. copper; during the Civil War, it produced 90 percent. More than 400 mining companies operated in the Keweenaw over the course of the 19th century, and the resulting demand for labor drew immigrants from more than 30 countries—most notably, the British Isles and Scandinavia. With multiple cultures sharing the same mine shafts and communities, the Copper Country served as one of the nation's first true melting pots.

But virtually all the big mines—the Cliff, Calumet, Phoenix, Delaware, Central—disappeared one by one in the mid-1900s, sealed up by economic conditions, leaving behind tattered houses and empty streets. They had extracted the easiest-to-reach copper; soon newer mines in the southwestern U.S. and South America proved more cost-effective.

### The Keweenaw, A.C. (After Copper)

The loss of copper mining decimated the economy of the Keweenaw. Today, the peninsula is peppered with the remains of ghost towns and "historic townsites" (the local jargon for a deserted town where a few residents remain), when townspeople, unable to make a living, simply walked away from homes and went elsewhere for work. Cities like Calumet

and Houghton plummeted in population; even now, they're just shadows of their former selves, with fewer than a quarter of the residents they once had.

Logging, some small manufacturing, and, increasingly, tourism, have come in to fill the void. Since logging never played the huge role in the Keweenaw in the late 1800s the way it did in other parts of Michigan, the forests that remain fuel much of the local economy. Lumber and paper companies own thousands of acres of land in the Keweenaw today, and the whine of saws and rumble of logging trucks are common sounds in the woods.

And copper mining may return some day. The Keweenaw still holds massive quantities of copper deep underground, some of the world's purest. Modern extraction techniques, along with the eventual depletion of other sources of copper, may once again cast a spotlight on the Keweenaw.

## THE LAND
### A Geological Bonanza

The Keweenaw is home to some of the Midwest's most distinctive geology and oldest exposed rock. Part of the Precambrian Canadian

Shield, the peninsula was created more than two billion years ago by spewing volcanoes and colliding continents. Much later, about 1.2 billion years ago, the hardened crust broke apart. More lava began seeping out through fissures, forming bedrock called basalt. For hundreds of years, the basalt piled up thicker and thicker; groundwater percolated in, too, filling the bubbles and cracks with minerals, creating the Keweenaw's vast deposits of pure copper.

Eventually the basalt layers sank, forming a basin surrounded by tilted, uplifted rock. These high spots today are visible as the Keweenaw Mountain Range, the spine that runs the length of the peninsula and across Isle Royale. Consequently, the basalt found throughout the Keweenaw is believed to be among the oldest—perhaps *the* oldest—exposed volcanic rock on earth.

Though the Keweenaw's variety of minerals is not particularly vast, it contains some unusual gemstones in substantial quantity. Rockhounds seek out three in particular: porcelaneous datolite, mohawkite, and chlorastrolite. Chlorastrolite is more commonly known as the Isle Royale greenstone, a tortoiseshell-patterned rock rarely found elsewhere in the world. The peninsula's beaches are also a good place to hunt for agates, thomsonite, epidote, zeolites, red feldspar, and others. Area mineral shops are excellent sources for guidebooks and hunting tips.

### Flora and Fauna

While Isle Royale is known for its unusual wolf/moose relationship, the Keweenaw Peninsula mirrors the rest of the Upper Peninsula in terms of animal life. The more common mammals include white-tailed deer, black bears, raccoons, squirrels, snowshoe hares, red foxes, coyotes, and bobcats. A few moose have been seen in the area, wandering north from the Huron Mountains, but they are not regular residents of the area—and heavy snows will probably prevent them from becoming one.

Birders find good habitat and a variety of northern species, including red and white-winged crossbills, Canada geese, hawks, peregrine falcons, bald eagles, and an estimated 20 species of warblers are frequently spotted.

Plant life, too, is similar to the surrounding U.P., with both deciduous and coniferous forests bringing a broad mix of hardwoods, birch, cedar, tamarack, and the ubiquitous pine. Estivant Pines, near Copper Harbor, protects a stand of virgin white pine, some scraping the sky 10 stories above. Sharing the deep forests are various ferns, mushrooms, berries, trilliums, 30-plus species of orchids, and other wildflowers.

## A NEW NATIONAL PARK

The **Keweenaw National Historic Park** is not so much a place on a map but a place in time. One of the nation's newest national parks, it was established in 1992 "to commemorate the heritage of copper mining on the Keweenaw Peninsula—its mines, its machinery, and its people."

Rather than a park with simply defined boundaries, the Keweenaw National Historic Park consists of historic attractions throughout the Keweenaw. Two units anchor the park—the Quincy Unit at the Quincy Mine in Hancock and the Calumet Unit in historic downtown Calumet—but some of this land remains in private ownership. The National Park Service will own outright just a limited amount of land to preserve key sites and conduct interpretive activities. In addition, the park has designated "cooperating sites" throughout the peninsula, including mine tours and museums that will also remain in private ownership, but will benefit from increased visibility and federal monies.

The park will continue to be under development for several years, busy preserving buildings, creating interpretive displays, and developing educational programs. The National Park headquarters in Calumet currently operates with just a skeleton administrative staff. For visitor information, contact the Keweenaw Tourism Council, 56638 Calumet Ave., 800/338-7982, website: www.keweenaw.org.

## RECREATION

Folks may just be beginning to appreciate the Keweenaw's history, but those in the know have appreciated its vast natural resources for a long time. "Hook and bullet" sports remain prevalent, but anglers and hunters increasingly find themselves sharing the backwoods and waters with hikers, mountain bikers, and paddlers.

## Paddling

Rivers in the Keweenaw tend to be pretty bony, so whitewater kayaking is limited (though this varies with the year's precipitation). Sea kayaking, on the other hand, is outstanding, the perfect way to access bluffs, caves, sea stacks and rocky islands all along the Lake Superior shoreline. The Keweenaw Water Trail, still under development, guides small craft around the peninsula and through the Portage Waterway. Isle Royale makes for an excellent paddling destination, too, and the ferries will transport kayaks and canoes for an additional fee. Canoeing is popular on inland lakes, but open boats are not recommended on Lake Superior. See individual areas below for more information.

## Mountain Biking

Mountain bikers new to the area can hardly believe the wealth of terrific trails in the Keweenaw, literally hundreds of miles of old mining and logging roads, overgrown double-track routes, and technical single track. They loop through towering pines to backwoods waterfalls, to otherwise inaccessible Lake Superior shorelines, even past ghost towns now buried deep in the woods. (Consider it fair warning that many trails also peter out and stop in the middle of nowhere.)

Vast tracts of land in the Keweenaw are privately owned by large corporations—some mining firms, but mostly paper companies. In exchange for a break in state taxes, the companies allow public use of the land for recreation, including hiking, fishing, and mountain biking. Still, for liability reasons, some outfitters and bike shops are loathe to hand out maps or "endorse" these lands for riding. If you ask, though, most bike shops tend to be quite helpful about suggesting trails, especially the Keweenaw Adventure Company (906/289-4303) in Copper Harbor. If you're going on your own, snowmobile

maps make decent trail guides. Cross-reference them with a topo map, though—snowmobile trails often cross frozen lowlands that are impassable in summer months.

And use common sense. Don't venture out without a map and compass, and the skill to use them. Stay away from active logging areas, usually marked by signs and the audible presence of buzzing logging equipment. If you hear a logging truck coming, don't just move to the side, get completely off the trail. Logging trucks are wide and heavy, and they can blaze down logging roads at surprising speeds. They aren't expecting to see you and probably couldn't stop in time even if they did.

## Winter Sports

A giant snow gauge on US-41 south of Phoenix proudly marks the Keweenaw's record snowfall, a staggering 390.4 inches in the winter of 1977–78. It wasn't an aberration; the surrounding waters of Lake Superior routinely generate colossal lake effect snows, often averaging over 300 inches. That reliable snowfall, combined with the remarkable local terrain, makes the Keweenaw a haven for snowmobilers.

Thankfully, skiers and snowshoers will find there's enough wilderness to go around. Many towns have developed Nordic ski trail systems. For backcountry skiing and snowshoeing, pick up a snowmobile map and steer clear of marked trails. Also note that some accommodations located on signed and groomed trails cater to snowmobilers, and the roar can get pretty deafening. Don't be afraid to ask about the presence of "sleds" before booking lodging in winter months.

Downhill skiers can check out Michigan's most challenging terrain at **Mt. Bohemia,** 888/937-2411, website: www.mtbohemia.com, near Lac La Belle. New in the 2000–2001 season, Mt. Bohemia offers the Midwest's highest vertical drop (900 feet), with some steep pitches, rock outcrops and gladed terrain that may make you think you're somewhere in the Rockies. Mont Ripley near Houghton/Hancock (owned and operated by Michigan Technological University), 906/487-2340, website:

www.aux.mtu.edu/ski, also offers some decent downhill runs and is lit for night skiing.

## FESTIVALS AND EVENTS

Leave it to those engineering students at Michigan Tech to design and build elaborate snow sculptures at the university's **Winter Carnival** in January. Houghton also hosts the **Bridge Fest and Seafood Fest** in June, with food and music on a parking deck overlooking the Portage Lift Bridge. Chassell's **Strawberry Fest** is held the second week in July, just in time for the sweet and juicy harvest. Copper Harbor hosts the peninsula's best **Fourth of July** fireworks show, and Sam Raymond, owner of Copper Harbor's Keweenaw Adventure Company, puts on a growing **Fat Tire Festival** the day before Labor Day. For more information on all area festivals and celebrations, contact the Keweenaw Tourism Council, 800/338-7982.

## PRACTICALITIES

The twin towns of Houghton/Hancock represent the area's largest population center, where you'll find the lion's share of area services, like medical care and public transportation. They also serve as the unofficial gateway to the Keweenaw, even though they sit halfway up the peninsula.

### Getting There

Bus service is spotty in the U.P. in general, and in the Keweenaw in particular. Northwest Airlines, 800/225-2525, offers the only commercial airline service, with flights to the Houghton County Airport in Hancock. For those traveling by car, US-41 and M-26 are the main routes to the peninsula. Many secondary roads in the Keweenaw are dirt or gravel. For old logging roads and other questionable routes, a four-wheel-drive vehicle is highly recommended.

### Information

With offices in both Houghton and Calumet, the **Keweenaw Tourism Council,** 800/338-7982, website: www.keweenaw.org, serves as an excellent one-stop source for attractions and lodging information. Until the Keweenaw National Historic Park gets more funding and more bodies, the council also handles park inquiries. If you're stopping in, the staff seems better informed in the downtown Houghton office, located at 326 Sheldon Ave. The Calumet office is on US-41 at the south end of town, at 1197 Calumet Avenue.

## South of Houghton/Hancock

Geographically speaking, the Keweenaw Peninsula merges with the rest of the U.P. at about Ontonagon on its western shore and L'Anse to the east—an imaginary line traced neatly by M-38. Between this highway and the Portage Waterway, the southern Keweenaw is quiet and sparsely populated. It's quite a change from the turn of the century, when the Copper Range Company operated successful mines across this whaleback of a peninsula. Like elsewhere in the Keweenaw, the tall skeletons of mining shaft houses occasionally lurch skyward out of the pines, dying relics of the copper rush.

Here, too, logging came in to fill the void. Today, a sawmill operated by Mead Paper in South Range (south of Houghton on M-26) ranks as one of the area's largest employers, milling the rare and prized bird's-eye maple that grows just north of here. Still, the economy struggles, and the locals have made few attempts—so far, anyway—to fill the void with tourism dollars.

### SIGHTS AND RECREATION

#### Bill Nichols Rail-Trail

The old Copper Range Railroad grade bisects the southern Keweenaw from Houghton south to Mass City, a distance of more than 41 miles. Throughout the state, the Department of Natural Resources has purchased many of these old grades, removed the rails, and maintains them as "multi-use" trails. In the U.P., that usually means snowmobiles and ATVs, but the Bill Nichols Rail-Trail from Houghton to Mass City provides good access for mountain bikes, too. (The trail is too rocky and rough for narrow-tire bikes.) Near the intersection of M-26 and M-38 at Lake Mine, the trail spans the Firesteel River on three bridges 65, 75, and 85 feet high. Snowmobile trails and old double-track roads spin off various points of the trail. Stop at the Keweenaw Tourism Council in Houghton or the Department of Natural Resources office in Baraga for a map of the rail-trail that shows access points. Where the trail crosses roads, look for a yellow-and-black snowmobile crossing sign on the highway and/or a DNR ATV wooden trail sign on the trail itself.

## Baraga and L'Anse

At the foot of Keweenaw Bay between Baraga (BARE-a-ga) and L'Anse (LAHNTS), the enormous wooden statue *Shrine of the Snowshoe Priest* looms 35 feet above Red Rock Bluff. It commemorates the life of Bishop Frederic Baraga, a Catholic missionary from Slovenia who gained recognition for his work with local Ojibwa, traveling by snowshoe to reach distant communities in the mid-1800s. Unlike most missionaries in his day, it's believed Baraga worked in support of Indian rights, helping them gain title to their land—not too popular with the local European fur traders and government Indian agents. Baraga spoke the native language fluently, and his guide to the Ojibwa vocabulary and grammar is still consulted today.

While Baraga and L'Anse suffer from stuttering economies, the Keweenaw Bay Indian Community economy is on the upswing. Ojibwa tribal leaders here were among the first to profit from treaty rights that allow them to establish gaming on tribal lands along Keweenaw Bay. Today the popular **Ojibwa Casino and Resort** generates millions of dollars in revenues and feeds much-needed tax dollars into the local economy. Other tribes have followed suit and opened successful casinos throughout the U.P. and the northern Lower Peninsula. Consequently, tribal governments now wield consid-

erable influence in the region.

On a more traditional note, the tribe also hosts a colorful powwow each July, a traditional celebration of dancing and drumming. On the eastern shore of Keweenaw Bay, north of L'Anse, you can visit an Ojibwa burial ground from the mid-1800s, with spirit houses marking graves. These small shelters held offerings of food, provisions to help sustain the soul on its journey to the afterlife.

A few miles south of L'Anse on US-41, a white clapboard lumber mill marks your arrival in **Alberta.** In 1935, Henry Ford built the mill, dammed nearby Plumbago Creek for the mill's water supply, and added a few streets' worth of homes to house the mill's workers. It's a classic example of a "company town," one that has not changed much since operations shut down in the early 1950s. Today it is operated by Michigan Technological University as a forestry research center. The grounds, including a small museum, are open to the public.

Just south of the company town, watch the west side of the road for a rest stop. Not just your run-of-the-mill rest stop of picnic tables and restrooms, this one includes a lovely short hike along the **Sturgeon River** to two cascades, Canyon Falls and Upper Falls.

## Hanka Homestead

Hidden away in the creases of the landscape above Keweenaw Bay between Baraga and Houghton, the Finnish Hanka family established this farmstead in 1896, building a log house, barn, milk house (built over a spring for natural refrigeration!), and, of course, a sauna. The self-sufficient Hankas raised dairy cows and chickens, grew vegetables and grains, tanned hides, and did pretty much whatever else it took to scrape out a living to get them through the harsh winters. What they didn't do much was modernize. Even though the last Hanka, Jalmar, lived here until the mid-1960s, the Hanka Homestead remains frozen in time at about 1920, complete with the Hankas' belongings filling the home and its nine outbuildings. Guides offer comprehensive tours, and the homestead is a cooperating site of the Keweenaw National Historic Park. Hours are somewhat spotty, currently Memorial Day weekend–mid-October Tues., Thurs., Sat., and Sun. noon–4 P.M. Best to call ahead, 906/353-7116, before you make the drive. To find it, head north about 10 miles on US-41 from Baraga, turn west on Arnheim Rd., and follow the small wooden signs (many of which refer to it as the Finnish Homestead Museum).

## Sturgeon River Sloughs Natural Area

Just north of the Hanka Homestead, the Sturgeon River bleeds across the lowlands before emptying into Portage Lake, forming sloughs that attract migrating waterfowl. For the best access, stop at the Sturgeon River Sloughs Natural Area, marked by an observation tower along US-41 near Chassell. The 1.5-mile De Vriendt Nature Trail follows a series of dikes and boardwalks back into the slough, with interpretive signs about the herons, osprey, eagles, kestrels, ducks, and dozens of other species that frequent the area.

## ACCOMMODATIONS

### Motels and Inns

The **Lake Shore Motel** on US-41 north of Baraga, 906/353-6256, has clean, inexpensive ($25–50) rooms with a view of Keweenaw Bay, and it gets bonus points for allowing your pooch ($5 extra). Baraga also has a few chain motels, including **Super 8**, 906/353-6680, and **Best Western Baraga Lakeside Inn**, 906/353-7123. Rates for both $50–100. After a visit to Hanka Homestead, you can sample a stay at a Finnish farm at **Palosaari's Rolling Acres,** 906/523-4947. A tidy dairy farm near Chassell, it offers three simple rooms, a shared bath, sauna, a nearby swimming beach, and big country breakfast for $50/night. Four miles south of Chassell, take North Entry Road east 1.3 miles.

### Camping

At Toivola, head 6.2 miles west on Misery Bay Road, then north and west on Agate Beach Road for 4 miles to **Agate Beach Park,** 906/288-3644, a rather unknown little spot on Lake Superior. No modern plumbing, but an empty curve of sand beach, Lake Superior sunsets, and $5 tent fee ($7 for sites with electricity) make up for it. The campground at **Baraga State Park,** 906/353-6558, pretty much is the state park. Most come for its modern sites (more than 100, with electricity and showers) with a convenient location just off US-41 a mile south of the town of Baraga. Reservations usually not necessary. Across the highway, a day-use area offers a sand beach and bathhouse. The Bill Nichols Rail-Trail passes through **Twin Lakes State Park,** 906/288-3321, in the southern Keweenaw. Though also right along the highway, many of its modern sites sit on the shores of Lake Roland, which someone once determined was "the warmest lake in the Upper Peninsula." For campsite reservations at any Michigan state park, call 800/44-PARKS; website: dnr.state .mi.us. To rent rustic cabins or walled tents, contact the parks directly.

## Houghton/Hancock

When the hip outdoor sporting magazine *Outside* listed Houghton (Hoe-ton) among America's "next wave of dream towns," you knew times were a-changin'. Ho-where? Well, turns out *Outside* may have something here. Houghton—and the adjacent city of Hancock—not only offers great sporting diversions, it boasts a quirky ethnic flair, streets lined with beautifully preserved early-1900 buildings, and a university to add a dollop of culture and liveliness. If you find old mining ruins intriguing instead of ugly, then Houghton/Hancock is downright pretty, too.

Houghton (population 7,500) and Hancock (population 4,500) face each other across the Portage Waterway, with homes and churches tumbling down steep 500-foot bluffs. (Especially on the Hancock side, streets can be downright unnerving, rivaling those in San Francisco for pitch.) The Portage Waterway effectively slices the Keweenaw in two, a 21-

mile passage that saves boaters the 100-mile-trip around the peninsula.

Natives had used the route for centuries to cross the peninsula, traveling from Keweenaw Bay across Portage Lake and along the ancient Portage River, then crossing over land the rest of the way to the shores of Lake Superior. In the late 1800s, a dredged canal eliminated the need for the west-end portage. Commercial traffic plied the waterway, largely to serve the smelters, stamping plants, and vibrant cities of the burgeoning copper trade.

A unique lift bridge spans the waterway to link Houghton and Hancock, its huge center section rising like an elevator to let water traffic pass. Today the Portage Waterway largely serves pleasure boaters and the 125-foot *Ranger III,* the ferry that transports hikers to Isle Royale National Park, 70 miles northwest. Houghton and Hancock are considered the gateways to the Keweenaw and to Isle Royale—but visitors just whizzing through will miss an appealing slice of the region.

## SIGHTS AND RECREATION

### Downtown

You can conduct your own historic walking tour of Houghton by strolling down Shelden Ave., the city's main street. Tall facades of red brick and red sandstone line the street, like the **Douglass House Hotel,** 517 Shelden, built in 1860 as a luxury hotel and dining establishment for travelers through the Portage Waterway. An addition in 1899 provided the lavish building you see today. Inside, the **Douglass House Saloon,** 906/482-2003, still shows off those genteel days, with original Tiffany chandeliers, leaded glass windows, and frilly trim.

On the east end of town, **Michigan Technological University** stretches out along the Portage Waterway. Nearly 6,300 students attend Michigan Tech, about three-quarters of them in some type of engineering program. Not surprisingly, geology, mining, and interestingly, "industrial archaeology" are some of the school's most notable fields of study. Students interested in mining management get real-life experience here, actually

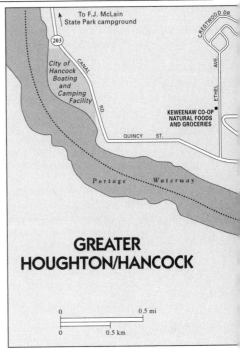

## GREATER HOUGHTON/HANCOCK

learning hands-on mining practices deep inside the nearby Quincy Mine.

Michigan Tech is home to the highly regarded **A. E. Seaman Mineral Museum,** 906/487-2572, the official mineralogical museum of the state of Michigan. The Keweenaw is considered one of the most geologically rich and fascinating regions in the world, and the Seaman Museum holds the premier collection of area minerals and gemstones, including crystallized copper, silver, datolites, greenstones, and agates. Don't miss the nifty exhibit of an iron mine and glowing fluorescent minerals. The museum also houses an impressive collection of minerals from around the world. All in all, its collection numbers more than 30,000 specimens. Open weekdays 9 A.M.–4:30 P.M., as well as Sat. noon–4 P.M. in summer months, by appointment only Nov.–Feb. The museum is on the fifth floor of the Electric Energy Resource Center (EERC) Building, behind the J. R. Van Pelt Library. Obtain a parking pass by stopping at the Hamar House, a few

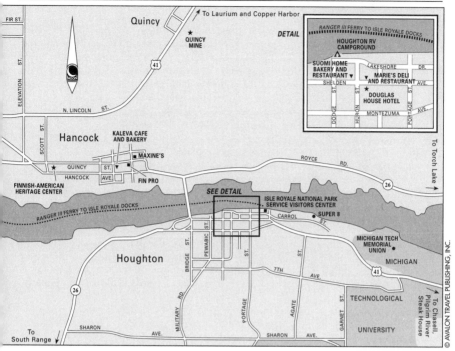

buildings to the east of the library. Admission is $3 for adults, 12 and under free

Michigan Tech isn't the only show in town. Well technically, yes. But across the waterway sits **Finlandia University,** which began as a Finnish academy in 1896 to serve the area's ever-growing number of immigrant miners' families. Today, enrollment hovers around 400. The institution's **Finnish-American Heritage Center** at 601 Quincy St., 906/487-7367, maintains a gallery open to the public that features Finnish artists, as well as archives of the area's Finnish settlement.

Even nonshoppers might be drawn into some of Hancock's stores, with their emphasis on unusual Finnish products. Where else do you shop for sauna supplies but **Fin Pro,** 208 Quincy St., 906/482-9202? The shop owners, who retired here from Helsinki, also carry an excellent selection of Finnish textiles, glassware, books, and music. You'll also find a good array of Finnish glassware and gifts at **Maxine's,** 119 Quincy St., 906/482-5101.

## Quincy Mine

Just north of Hancock, the mammoth shaft house of the Quincy Mine dominates the skyline. The Quincy ranked as one of the world's richest copper mines in the late 1800s, producing over a billion pounds of copper. Today, a few of its buildings still stand, and the land beneath it remains stitched with the shafts (vertical tunnels) and adits (horizontal tunnels) of the mammoth mine, which stretched more than a mile and a half deep—92 levels!—and two miles wide.

The Quincy Mine is a key site in the Keweenaw National Historic Park, and it offers a fascinating tour that takes you through the historic buildings and deep into the mine itself. Many of the tour guides are mining students at nearby Michigan Tech, so they can handle just about any mining or engineering question you can toss at them. The tour begins with a look at the much-ballyhooed steam hoist, the world's largest. A giant spool of sorts, it powered the steel pulleys that hauled the miners and mine cars loaded with

COPPER COUNTRY

© TRAVEL MICHIGAN

**shaft house at the Quincy Mine**

copper in and out of the mine. It's nearly twice the size of other steam hoists, since the mine was so much deeper than most.

As interesting as the hoist is the building itself. In an era when miners made $1 a day (considered quite a good wage), the Quincy Mining Co. built its hoist house of poured concrete, then decorated it with lovely arched windows, lined the walls with imported Italian tile, and topped it off with green tiles imported from Spain. Thanks to all that concrete, the immense room remains in pretty good shape. It also houses plenty of artifacts and photos, including bilingual safety instructions posted next to the machinery—an indication of the predominance of Finnish miners.

From the hoist house, the tour continues with a rather dramatic ride in a glass-enclosed tram down the side of a steep hill. Views of Houghton/Hancock are terrific as the tram descends to an entrance to the mine, an adit at Level 7. A tractor carries you a couple thousand feet into the mine, where guides demonstrate mining techniques and give you a feel for what it was like to work deep inside the earth, in a drippy, damp environment with only hand tools and candles. Two-hour tours are offered May–Oct., with more

frequent tours in summer months. Contact the Quincy Mine Hoist Association, 906/482-3101, website: www.quincymine.com, for tour times and other information. Hoist and mine tour is $12.50 adults, $7 children 6–12, children under six free. Surface tour and tram mine costs $7.50 adults, $2.50 children.

## Outdoor Recreation

Backpacking into the wilderness is on the minds of thousands of visitors to Houghton each year, here to board a ferry or seaplane for Isle Royale National Park. If you're intrigued by this wild archipelago in northern Lake Superior, stop by the **Isle Royale National Park Service Visitors Center** in Houghton, 906/482-0984, website: www.nps.gov/isro. You'll find it down the hill from Shelden Ave., on the waterway at 800 E. Lakeshore. Park rangers on duty can give you a good feel for the park, its trails, campsites, climate, and transportation options to help you plan a future trip. The center's shop includes a good selection of relevant books (including some particularly good titles on Native American history). Open weekdays 8 A.M.–6 P.M., Sat. 8 A.M.–5 P.M.

The *Ranger III* docks just outside, departing twice a week for the six-and-a-half-hour trip to Isle Royale. On Thursday evenings from June to September, it does easier duty on a sunset **Waterway Cruise.** The pleasant trip runs 6:00–8:30 P.M. and costs $13 for adults, $5 for children.

For paddlers, the **Keweenaw Water Trail** provides a mapped passageway of more than 100 miles through the Portage Waterway and along the Lake Superior shore, indicating accommodations, campgrounds, launches, and more. For more information and to purchase a water trail map, contact the Keweenaw Tourism Council at 800/338-7982. For whitewater boaters, Down Wind Sports, 308 Shelden Ave. in Houghton, 906/482-2500, is your best source for local information on river conditions.

Old railroad grades threading across the northern Keweenaw have been converted to public multi-use trails, intended for snowmobiles, ATVs, and, perhaps to a lesser extent, mountain bikes. For cyclists not comfortable venturing deep into the woods, they're a nice way to get off the road. The **Jack Stevens Rail-Trail** runs 14 miles from Hancock north to Calumet on the former Soo Line grade. Somewhat less appealing, because it parallels M-26 for a lengthy stretch, is the **Keweenaw Rail-Trail,** an 18-mile route from Hancock along Torch Lake, also ending in Calumet. Note that surfaces can be a rough collection of rock, gravel, wood, and sand— whatever happened to be there when they ripped up the rails—so they're not appropriate for narrow-tire bikes. For more information and a map listing access points, contact the Keweenaw Tourism Council at 800/338-7982.

## ACCOMMODATIONS AND FOOD

### Accommodations

For such a small metropolitan area, Houghton accommodations run a bit on the pricey side. The following all fall in the $50–100 range: Tucked below downtown Houghton along the Portage Waterway, **Super 8,** 1200 E. Lakeshore, 906/482-2240, offers one of the best locations in town, on the water and the bike path, with an indoor pool and free continental breakfast. A good mom-and-pop operation is the **Downtowner Motel,** 110 Shelden Ave., 906/482-4421. Dog owners, try the slightly dog-eared but comfortable **Best Western Kings Inn,** 215 Shelden Ave., 906/482-5000.

### Camping

Sunsets get top billing at **F. J. McLain State Park,** 906/482-0278, where the sky often glows in peaches and pinks before the sun melts into Lake Superior. Like most Michigan state parks, the campsites are fine, too, and many come with those waterfront views. The 103 modern sites go for $14; rustic mini-cabins sleep six for $32. Follow M-203 seven miles north of Hancock. For reservations, call 800/44-PARKS; website: dnr.state.mi.us. The **City of Houghton** maintains an RV-only campground on West Lakeshore Drive, 906/482-8745, $15 per night, with every site near the water. No pets allowed. Tent campers should head instead for the **Hancock Recre-** ation Area, 906/482-7413, on the Portage Waterway. Follow M-203 a mile from downtown. The 45 primitive sites ($7) are situated in a quieter area apart from the 50 modern RV ones ($14) that are so modern they even include—yikes!—cable TV. Showers, washer and dryer on premises.

### Food

Combine a college town with a large ethnic population, and you come up with good range of eating options in the Houghton/Hancock area. Houghton offers a number of fine places to eat. At 518 Shelden downtown, **Marie's Deli & Restaurant,** 906/482-8650, is a terrific find—homemade breads, soups, sandwiches, salads, and lots of Middle Eastern dishes like kibbie and spinach pies, reflecting the Lebanese heritage of its cheery owner. Plenty of vegetarian options on the menu, too. A good value at breakfast, lunch, and dinner. The **Library** probably ranks as the most popular spot in town, with homemade brews, good salads, pizzas, pastas, and lots of sandwich choices. It's at 62 North Isle Royal, 906/487-5882. The **Pilgrim River Steak House,** on US-41 on the southeast end of Houghton, 906/482-8595, is *the* place to go for beef of all sorts, especially prime rib. Along with your basic eggs-and-hash-browns fare, **Suomi Home Bakery and Restaurant,** 906/482-3220, tosses a few Finnish specialties on the menu. Try the *pannukakku,* billed as a "Finnish pancake" (but more like deep-dish custard pie) topped with raspberry sauce. Most breakfasts come with *nisu,* a Finnish yeast bread spiced with cardamom. The restaurant is tucked under Houghton's covered walkway at 54 Huron, a block down the hill from Shelden.

On Hancock's main street, the **Kaleva Cafe and Bakery** at 234 Quincy St., 906/482-1230, draws the locals for its baked goods, including its self-proclaimed "famous" whipped cream cakes. Kaleva makes a good pasty, a pot-pie creation of beef, potatoes, onions, and rutabagas—just the kind of hearty, self-contained meal that miners could take with them deep underground. You'll find them at coffee shops and grocery store deli counters throughout the Upper Peninsula.

Though you'll find plenty of traditional grocery stores along M-26 south of town and US-41 north, opt instead for the **Keweenaw Co-op Natural Foods and Groceries,** 906/482-2030, in Hancock. A friendly staff, excellent organic produce, and plenty of reasonably priced staples make this a great option for picnic supplies. As you head up the hill on US-41, veer left onto Ethel when the highway swings hard right. (Watch for the colorful wooden sign.) The co-op is a couple blocks ahead on your right.

## Calumet, Laurium, and Vicinity

At the height of the Keweenaw's copper mining glory, the Calumet and Hecla Consolidated Copper Co., operating largely in Calumet, proved the grandest operation of all. At the turn of the century, C&H employed some 11,000 workers, who extracted more than 1.5 billion tons of copper from a web of mines tunneled out under Calumet and the adjacent Laurium. A surface plant in town, considered the most efficient in the nation, roared and whistled with the sound of 50 steam engines at work.

C&H generated more than $72 million in revenues. It built low-cost housing for its miners, more than 1,000 dwellings lined up like chess pieces in towns with colorful names like Swedetown and Limerick to reflect the miners' homelands. Most of all, it spawned the city of Calumet—known then as "Red Jacket," a booming metropolitan area of more than 60,000. Striking red sandstone buildings with false fronts and cornices lined the 12-square-block downtown, filled with elegant shops, soaring churches, some 70 saloons, even a lavish

theater that attracted the nation's leading vaudeville stars. The city buzzed day and night both above—and belowground.

After mining died, no one ever bothered to "modernize" Calumet—the economy was lousy and the land wasn't worth enough—and those sturdy sandstone buildings survived years of neglect pretty well. As a result, downtown Calumet is a marvel of architecture in the early 1900s, and was a deciding factor in the area earning national park status. "We are fortunate that this area has been little disturbed since those glory days," lobbied park supporters. "Few modern intrusions have marred the area's scale and the feeling of its mining heritage." Today, Calumet (pop. 800) anchors the new Keweenaw National Historic Park, one of the park's two key units and a designated historic site.

## HISTORICAL ATTRACTIONS
### Downtown Calumet

Thanks to the new national park and renewed civic pride, downtown Calumet looks more like a movie set everyday. Ugly 1960s facades are coming down off the elegant sandstone and brick buildings, and new money is coming in to further restore and preserve them. To appreciate this architectural bonanza, stop by the Keweenaw Tourism Council, 1197 Calumet Ave., 906/482-2388, to pick up a walking tour guide. A few stops of particular note: The **Union Building,** at 5th and Red Jacket, was home of one of the area's first banks in 1888 and remains in excellent shape, with a decorative metal cornice. **Shute's Bar,** 322 6th St., doesn't look that special on the outside, but inside preserves ornate plaster ceilings and

The Calumet's theater's opening was "the greatest social event ever known in Copperdom's metropolis."

© BOB BRODBECK

COPPER COUNTRY

a magnificent back bar with a stained-glass canopy. Across the street, the **Red Jacket Fire Station** typifies the Romanesque style favored for public buildings and churches at the time. At 340 Sixth Street, the **Red Jacket Town Hall and Opera House,** now called the **Historic Calumet Theater,** 906/337-2610, was the pride of the community. The theater portion, added in 1898 as the first municipally owned theater in the country, was a showy extravagance of plaster rococo in cream, crimson, green, and gilt. It even had electric lights! Referred to as "the greatest social event ever known in copperdom's metropolis" when it opened in 1900, the theater attracted first-run celebrities including John Philip Sousa, Houdini, Douglas Fairbanks, Jr., and Sarah Bernhardt. Today, you'll need to pony up $4 ($1.50 for children ages 6–12) to see the interior on a worthwhile 45-minute tour. Tours run from early June–mid-October. In the off-season except for the month of January, you can take a self-guided tour for $2.

## C&H Industrial Core

One of Calumet and Hecla's mines was located right in town, an area bisected by Red Jacket Road, just west of US-41. Beginning at the Coppertown USA museum, a self-guided "industrial core" walking tour takes you past a drill shop, powder house, machine shop, and several other mining buildings in various states of preservation. The park service is adding interpretive signs to guide you along and share mining information, but you'll also want an information sheet that maps the route, available from the Keweenaw Tourism Council, Park Service headquarters, or the Coppertown USA museum.

## Coppertown USA

The mine's pattern shop, where wooden patterns were made as molds for machine parts, now serves as the home of Coppertown USA, a privately run museum (and national park cooperating site) that traces the region's copper industry. It includes loads of artifacts, a display of area minerals, replica of a mining captain's office, diorama of Native American mining, and more,

with all the exhibits close enough to really examine. Don't miss the pattern shop area, which still houses thousands of patterns, lined up on shelves like they haven't been touched for 50 years. (Some have been relocated to the Smithsonian.) Another interesting exhibit is a 1976 scale model that shows elaborate plans for Calumet, including a cultural center, festival plaza, and products exhibit center. Coppertown USA, 906/337-4354, is open mid-June–mid-October Mon.–Sat. 10 A.M.–5 P.M., as well as Sun. 12:30 P.M.–4 P.M. July–Aug. $3 adults, $1 children 12–18. It's located near the intersection of US-41 and Red Jacket Rd.

## Downtown Laurium

Just across US-41 from Calumet, Laurium was largely a residential district for the area mines. The west end of town (closest to Calumet) has a few streets of plain company homes remaining, looking rough and dilapidated—like much of Laurium. But a few blocks farther east, around Pewabic and 3rd, mining management built their homes, and today it remains a quiet and stately neighborhood worth visiting. Pick up a *Laurium Walking Tour* guide from the Keweenaw Tourism Council, 1197 Calumet Ave. It will direct you to impressive homes like the one at 305 Tamarack, where a wise mining investor made enough to create this grand home with seven fireplaces, a third-floor ballroom, and carriage house.

But the finest home belonged to Capt. Thomas Hoatson, founder of the Calumet and Arizona Mining Co., who built his dream mansion at 320 Tamarack. Today it operates as the **Laurium Manor Inn.** 906/337-2549, which means the public can enjoy a glimpse of this remarkable place. Sprawling across 13,000 square feet, the 45-room mansion includes ceilings covered in silver leaf, elephant-hide wallcoverings, a triple staircase of hand-carved oak, and a turntable in the carriage house so carriages could be rotated to face forward. The inn is open year-round, with most rates $50–100. For nonguests, the inn offers guided tours in summer noon–3 P.M. Adults $4, children $2. In winter, you can take a self-guided tour 11 A.M.–5 P.M. for $3 adults, $2 children.

Football or cinema fans may want to view the decidedly less dramatic home at 432 Hecla. Laurium's most famous citizen was born here— **George Gipp,** the Notre Dame football star. "The Gipper" gave Ronald Reagan his most famous role—until he became president, anyway. A George Gipp Memorial decorates the corner of Tamarack and M-26.

## IN THE AREA
### Hiking and Mountain Biking

Like much of the Keweenaw, the forests around Calumet are filled with hundreds of miles of trails for hiking and mountain biking. If you're handy with a map and compass, some fine single track winds down along the **Gratiot River** about five miles north of town. As a bonus, you can check out the little-visited Upper and Lower Gratiot Falls as the river rolls and tumbles its way to Lake Superior. For other ideas, check in at **Cross Country Sports,** 506 Oak St. in Calumet, 906/337-4520. Most of the staff, in fact, are willing to divulge at least a couple of their favorite trails.

For something a little less adventurous, pedal the **Swedetown Trails,** a cross-country trail network on the southwest edge of Calumet. (From 6th St. near St. Ann's church, pick up Oceola Road and follow it south.) It has about 25 kilometers of trails over rolling hills and through woods, and all are great for biking except the northernmost loop (the Red Trail), which is too wet. From this small network, you can veer off onto seemingly endless trails beyond, too. In winter, the network obviously offers great Nordic skiing, along with a warming chalet open noon–5 P.M. For information, contact the Keweenaw Tourism Council, 800/338-7982 or 906/337-4579.

### Ghost Towns

Ghost towns litter the Keweenaw, faded testament to the boom-and-bust days of copper. The ruins of old mines and stamping plants (facilities that separated copper from rock) line M-26 between Hancock and Calumet. The gray piles of residue are mine tailings or stamping plant leftovers called "stamp sand." Several bona fide ghost

towns hide in the woods, too, especially between Calumet and Copper Harbor. At **Central** (watch for the small brown sign on US-41 about 11 miles north of Mohawk), an exceptionally rich mine produced nearly $10 million by 1898; the surrounding town grew to 1,200. Today, nature has all but reclaimed Central, with just a few clapboard houses creaking in the breeze. Turn right near the top of the hill for a look at the mine ruins and rows of house foundations. (Watch where you're walking.)

Just south of Copper Harbor on US-41, another sign announces your "arrival" in **Mandan,** directing you down a dirt road disappearing into birches. Follow it south for about 50 yards and homes suddenly erupt out of the woods, lined up in a tidy row. Welcome to Mandan, the last stop on a trolley line from Hancock.

### East of Calumet

One of the Keweenaw's prettiest drives begins east of Calumet in Gay. Heading north, the only blacktop road dips through forest before emerging along the shores of Keweenaw Bay on the peninsula's eastern shore. The road hugs the water, with great views of the Huron Mountains across the bay. Stop at Burnette Bay Park for a chilly dip or wade. Just before you reach Bete Grise Bay, the road swings inland the Lac La Belle. At a roadside picnic area, Haven Falls drops 20 feet over a sheer wall of rock. Beyond Lac La Belle, the road to the right brings you to more sand beaches on Bete Grise Bay.

## ACCOMMODATIONS AND FOOD
### Motels and Inns

The **AmericInn Motel and Suites,** 5101 6th St. in Calumet, 906/337-6463, is the area's only full service motel with indoor pool and other amenities. Rates $75–100. The **Wonderland Motel and Cabins** at 787 Lake Linden Ave. in Laurium, 906/337-4511, offers good budget accommodations, $50–75, with kitchens in cabins. At the other end of the spectrum, stay in an opulent copper baron mansion at the **Laurium Manor Inn,** 320 Tamarack in Laurium, 906/337-2549. Rates average $50–100; examine the rooms for yourself at website: www.lauri-ummanorinn.com. Across the street, the owners have also restored the 1906 brick **Victorian Hall** (same telephone number). Most rooms have private baths. Another mining executive lived in what is now **Belknap's Garnet Haus,** 906/337-5607, on US-41 in Kearsarge. The well-restored home features five rooms with mostly shared baths, with rates from $50–100. The **Sand Hills Lighthouse Inn,** 906/337-1744, may not be cheap—rooms run $125 to $185—but with a 90-foot tower to climb and rooms with balconies overlooking Lake Superior, you can justify the cost. Owner Bill Frabotta has restored the 1919 lighthouse, filled it with antiques, and decorated it in a lavish Victorian decor. Great breakfast, too. Take M-26 west out of Ahmeek to Five Mile Point Road.

### Camping

West of Ahmeek on Five Mile Point Rd, **Sunset Bay Campground,** 906/337-2494, indeed offers a fine view of the sunset from your tent flap. Ten of its 15 primitive sites ($15) sit on Lake Superior. RV sites available for $20–25.

Keep in mind that many locals simply head out into the woods on weekends and set up camp near a favorite stretch of beach or river. If you choose to do the same, respect "no trespassing" signs and observe all backcountry camping practices (bury waste, hang packs, stay back 50 feet from water, etc.).

### Food

In downtown Calumet at 315 5th St., **Thurner Bakery,** 906/337-3711, churns out hearty pasties, soups, and baked goods. You can also find similar homemade coffee shop fare—and Finnish bakery items like saffron bread—at Toni's Country Kitchen, 79 Third St., Laurium, 906/337-0611. In Ahmeek on US-41, **Streetcar Station,** 906/337-0350, serves up sandwiches in, yes, an old streetcar station from the copper glory days. Don't leave without a malt or, in season, a wild blueberry sundae. At the **Lindell Chocolate Shop,** 300 Calumet in Lake Linden, 906/296-0793, visitors come to ooh and aah over this untouched 1920s shop, gleaming with golden oak, stained glass, and marble. Locals, though, come for the food, especially breakfasts and a Friday night fish fry.

## Copper Harbor and Vicinity

Wedged between Lake Superior to the north and long and lovely Lake Fanny Hooe to the south, Copper Harbor has always been an outpost in the wilderness—for the copper prospectors who came in the mid-1880s, for the military who built a stockaded fort to keep the miners and Indians at peace, and today, for those who come for its water and its woods.

Copper Harbor marks the end of the road in the Keweenaw Peninsula. Literally. Even US-41 peters out here, circling in a loop some 1,990 miles from its other terminus in Miami. The tip of the peninsula probably draws people precisely because it is the end of the road. And when they get there, they discover one of the Upper Peninsula's most scenic natural areas and one of its most appealing little towns.

## COPPER HARBOR ACTIVITIES

### Downtown

Tiny Copper Harbor, population 30, offers more than you might expect from its size. If shopping is your thing, check out the Finnish pottery at Sataman Ruukku, 906/289-4636, a shedlike storefront on US-41, and the artwork and gifts at the Laughing Loon, 906/289-4813. (No one has—or needs—a street address in a town just a few blocks long.) Rockhounds will like the Keweenaw Agate Shop, 906/353-7285, and Swede's Gift Shop, 906/289-4596, both with a good selection of local minerals and, as the Keweenaw Agate Shop advertises, "advice and stories."

The **Thunderbird Shop** at the **Minnetonka Resort,** 906/289-4449, is a terrific source for books on mining, shipwrecks and other histori-

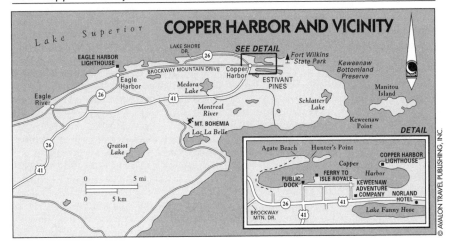

**COPPER HARBOR AND VICINITY**

DETAIL

© AVALON TRAVEL PUBLISHING, INC.

cal subjects. The shop also has a lot of interesting artifacts, like miner's lanterns and clay pipes left behind by miners, for sale at very reasonable prices. The motel's adjacent **Astor House Antique Doll and Indian Artifact Museum** is well worth a visit, too.

You won't find a full-service grocery store in Copper Harbor, so load up in Houghton or Calumet if you're planning a campout or cabin stay. However, the exceptionally friendly Gas Lite General Store, 906/289-4652, has all the basics, and also happens to be the spot to catch up on local news. (What you don't learn there, you'll hear about at the Pines across the street.) For fresh or smoked fish, head to the ferry dock and Jamsen's Fish Market, 906/289-4285, run by the last commercial fishing family to pull a living out of the local waters.

### Around Town

You can enjoy a couple of nice walks just a few blocks from downtown. From the parking lot of the municipal marina at the west end of town (farther west than the ferry dock), a 3.2-mile round-trip trail winds through the woods and over twisted roots to Hunter's Point. This point helps form the protected waters of the harbor; on the open Lake Superior side, Agate Beach is a good spot to look for the namesake banded rocks. Downtown, a sign will point you south toward

**Estivant Pines,** a 377-acre sanctuary of virgin white pines just a few miles south of town. As recently as the 1970s, local conservationists like Jim Rooks saved the magnificent trees, some towering nearly 10 stories high and dating back nearly 1,000 years, from loggers' saws. At first the pines seem hidden by the maturing oaks and maples. But just look up, up, up.

You can easily follow the well-marked trail yourself, but for some insight into the area, you might want to hook up with one of Rooks' **Keweenaw Bear Track Tours,** 906/289-4813. Rooks delights in the little things in nature, so be warned that his tours are often slow-going. But you'll return with Rooks as a friend, along with tidbits of history and sightings of wildflowers or insects you probably would have otherwise missed. Call about tour destinations and times, which are rather flexible.

### Fort Wilkins State Park

The history of Fort Wilkins reads like one of those overblown military spending stories of the 20th century. With miners pouring north during the Copper Rush, the federal government feared fighting would surely erupt between miners and the local Indian tribes, and ordered the construction of a garrisoned fort. In 1844, they sent troops of more than 100 men, who built barracks, a mess hall, hospital,

COPPER COUNTRY

and other buildings behind a tall stockade fence, then hunkered down to fend off the fighting. Only no fighting ever erupted, and winters proved long, cold, and desolate. By the following year, half the troops were pulled out and sent south, where the country faced the threat of war with Mexico. By 1846, the rest were gone.

Today, Fort Wilkins stands as one of the only wooden forts remaining east of the Mississippi, with 16 whitewashed buildings wonderfully restored and filled with exhibits of life on the northern frontier. From mid-June to late August, costumed "inhabitants" even re-create military life. Along with the fort, the state park includes rocky and scenic Lake Superior frontage, a few short hiking trails, the 1866 Copper Harbor Lighthouse (accessible only by boat—see below), and an excellent campground on Lake Fanny Hooe. The park's telephone is 906/289-4215; for campsite reservations, call 800/44-PARKS; website: dnr.state.mi.us.

### Boat Trips and Tours

You can't reach the **Copper Harbor Lighthouse** by land since adjacent property owners refuse to grant right-of-way, so the Park Service has arranged for boat tours of the light and keeper's house, which contains a worthwhile small museum. Originally built in 1849, the stone lighthouse is the oldest operating light on Lake Superior. (An adjacent tall steel tower now does duty, however.) Just wandering around the lovely rocky point is worth the trip. It was on this point, by the way, where Douglass Houghton first spotted a thick green stripe in the rock indicating the presence of copper, a discovery that unleashed the Keweenaw's copper boom. The 90-minute tour leaves from the municipal marina several times daily Memorial Day–early September. Call 906/289-4966 for specific times and reservations, adults $12, children 12 and under $6. Also ask about sunset cruises.

The Kilpela family who runs the Isle Royale ferry service also offers sunset cruises on the *Isle Royale Queen III* every evening at 9 P.M. from July 4 to Labor Day. From mid-May through the end of September, the *Queen* earns her keep

by ferrying passengers from Copper Harbor to Isle Royale National Park, a four-and-a-half-hour trip. Call 906/289-4437 for reservations and to check the schedule, which varies throughout the summer. Roundtrip cost is $84 adults, $42 children 12 and under. Canoes and kayaks are an additional $40. See **Isle Royale** for more information on the national park and transportation options.

### Kayaking

This growing sport is at its finest in the Keweenaw, where you have plenty of islands, rock formations, and wilderness coastlines to explore. **Keweenaw Adventure Company,** 906/289-4303, website: www.keweenawadventure.com, rents kayaks, guides trips, and offers lessons. Beginners should try the two-and-a-half-hour introductory paddle, which includes novice dry-land instruction and a fine little trip around the harbor and along the Lake Superior shoreline. Keweenaw Adventure Company also offers some day-long trips around the peninsula—to Horseshoe Harbor, Agate Harbor and the mouth of the Montreal River—as scheduling permits. Check the website or give them a call for specifics.

If you have your own boat, don't overlook the peninsula's inland waters. Fanny Hooe, Medora, and other nearby lakes offer classic northwoods peace and scenery, often with the company of bobbing loons or shoreline black bears.

### Diving

The cold, gin-clear freshwater of Lake Superior offers outstanding visibility for divers. Though there isn't much to look at in the way of plant and animal life—the cold waters make for a pretty sterile-looking environment—the waters provide plenty of entertainment in the form of interesting underwater geologic formations and shipwrecks.

Ships have been running aground for well over a hundred years around the Keweenaw Peninsula, a navigational hazard if there ever was one. Within the 103-square-mile **Keweenaw Bottomland Preserve,** divers can explore the *Tioga*, a freighter that ran aground near Eagle River in 1919, and the *City of St. Joseph,* which met its fate north of Eagle Harbor in 1942. Both ships lie in less than 40 feet of water, with large sections of the hull, deck machinery, and other artifacts clearly visible.

One of the Upper Peninsula's oldest shipwrecks, the *John Jacob Astor,* lies just offshore from Copper Harbor, near the Fort Wilkins State Park Lighthouse Overlook. An Underwater Trail marks the location of the rudder, anchor, and other remnants of the *Astor,* which sank in 1844, and another ship. Before the Keweenaw Bottomland Preserve was established in 1989, rumor has it that locals learned of a couple salvage divers who were planning on retrieving one of the anchors. Without the legal protection of an underwater preserve, local divers took the matter into their own hands: they hauled up the anchor themselves and hid it in nearby Lake Fanny Hooe, where it remained until a few years ago when it was safely returned to its original wreck site. Today, disturbing or removing any artifact is a felony under Michigan law.

The U.S. Coast Guard has to be more than a little humiliated over the preserve's most popular dive site, the Coast Guard cutter *Mesquite.* In 1989, the 180-foot *Mesquite* ran aground on a reef off Keweenaw Point while tending to a navigational buoy. Efforts to free her failed and winter winds battered her so badly, the Coast Guard later decided to sink her as a dive site rather than pay the costs of retrieving and repairing the aging vessel. It sits in 110 feet of water in Keystone Bay with virtually all equipment on deck. Experienced divers can explore the *Mesquite*'s interior. For dive services, contact **A Superior Diver's Center** in Copper Harbor, 906/289-DIVE.

## THE TIP OF THE PENINSULA

Copper Harbor lies at the top of the Keweenaw Peninsula, but it doesn't lie at the end. The tip of the peninsula curves to the east and continues about 10 more miles beyond town, leaving about a 60-square-mile tract to the east and south of Copper Harbor with no pavement, development or attractions—unless you like to hike, mountain bike, fish, or just get out alone in the woods.

## Information and Unwritten Rules

Probably more than 100 miles of trails crisscross the tip of the peninsula; no one's ever bothered to count. They range from deer trails to tight single track to wide gravel-and-dirt roads used by logging trucks and snowmobiles. Aside from a few tracts held by the state and the Nature Conservancy, the vast majority of the land is owned by International Paper, which uses it for logging purposes. The paper company has put the land in what is called "Commercial Forest Reserve." CFR lands, common throughout the U.P. give tax breaks to companies that agree to keep the land open to the public for recreation. That means you are free to hike, bike, and otherwise explore this area. Avoid any active logging areas and follow the same guidelines you would on any lands: respect "no trespassing" signs and pack out what you pack in.

## Hiking and Biking Trails

You'll need a map to make sense of the area. A snowmobile map (available through local shops and the Keweenaw Tourism Council) is decent for major routes, the *DeLorme Atlas and Gazetteer* includes a few more, and a topo map is best—though no map yet shows even half the trails in the area. Sam Raymond, owner of the **Keweenaw Adventure Company** in Copper Harbor, 906/289-4303, has mapped and signed (although the signs keep disappearing) dozens of miles of mountain biking routes. He's also clearing and maintaining the trails with only the help of a few friends. It's a huge undertaking for minimal return, so show Sam your appreciation by giving him your business. Keweenaw Adventure Company rents and services mountain bikes, and sells those helpful maps for a nominal fee.

Not surprisingly, Keweenaw Adventure Company is your best source for trail suggestions in the area. The **Red Trail** is the region's classic route, a single-track trail with plenty of technical twists and turns. It runs roughly from the gravel **Burma Road Trail,** past the south end of the Keweenaw Mountain Lodge golf course and the north shore of Lake Manganese, where you can pick up **Paul's Plunge** back to Lake Fanny

Hooe. Another good loop is the two-track **Surprise Valley Trail,** which hooks up with the **Kamikaze Trail** that traces the southern side of Lake Fanny Hooe.

In the same general area, the **Clark Mine Trail,** drops south out of Copper Harbor at the south end of Lake Fanny Hooe. Just outside town, brown and white signs will direct you to **Manganese Falls,** a pleasant walk down into a ferny oasis; **Manganese Lake,** a popular fishing and swimming hole; and the **Clark Mine,** where the old brick furnace chimney still stands against a backdrop of mine tailings. Where the Clark Mine Trail swings east, make your way south to meet up with the Montreal River if you're interested in a little trout fishing.

In addition to the trails south of Copper Harbor, here are a few other destinations to consider: From the end of US-41, the road continues east as a wide dirt-and-gravel road. Follow it for about a mile to the first main left branch, which winds north and east to the Lake Superior shore and **Horseshoe Harbor,** a fine place to spend an afternoon scrambling around the rock ledges and beaches. This picturesque sliver of a harbor is owned by the Nature Conservancy, so keep mountain bikes off the property as requested. Backtracking to the main road, continue east about three miles to another left (northeast) turnoff, which skirts **Schlatter Lake** and continues on to **High Rock Bay** at the tip of the peninsula. Don't be surprised to see a camp or two set up here.

The Montreal tumbles over some beautiful **waterfalls** before joining Lake Superior just to the southeast, but they're difficult to reach from here. An easier approach is from Bete Grise (bay-duh GREE). Just before you reach Bete Grise Bay, you'll see two dirt routes heading east into the woods. One reads, "This is not the road to Smith Fisheries." Take the other one. It will indeed lead you around Bear Bluff to this old commercial fishing enterprise (now private property). Continue on the smaller trail behind the fishery, a terrific path that traces the steep bluffs of the bayshore. It's about another 1.5 miles to the mouth of the Montreal and its fine waterfalls.

# WEST OF COPPER HARBOR

## Brockway Mountain Drive

Dubbed "the most beautiful road in Michigan," this 10-mile route traces the spine of a high ridge between Copper Harbor and Eagle Harbor. Rising 735 feet above Lake Superior, it is the highest paved road between the Rockies and Allegheny Mountains. A parking area midway allows you to stop and soak in the panorama of Lake Superior and the rolling forests of the Keweenaw, an incredible vista no matter how many times you've seen it. Watch for ravens, bald eagles, and peregrine falcons—which sometimes soar below you. Traveling west to east, the end of the drive is marked by a picture-postcard shot of Copper Harbor, tucked between Lake Superior and Lake Fanny Hooe.

## Scenic Lakeshore Drive

This stretch of M-26 between Copper Harbor and Eagle River lives up to its name: Lake Superior looms just alongside the road, studded with rocky islands and swelling dunes. Unfortunately, you miss about 10 miles of the route if you take Brockway Mountain Drive. Plan to do both on your trip to Copper Harbor—Brockway is better headed east, this drive better headed west.

About five miles south of Copper Harbor, **Hebard Park** is a good picnic, sunset, or agate-hunting spot. Where M-26 and Brockway Mountain Drive meet, watch for the small sign marking **Silver Falls.** It's a short downhill walk to this pretty little falls, splashing and pooling in the forest.

West of Eagle Harbor, the road climbs above **Great Sand Bay** toward Eagle River. From this high vantage point, you can sometimes see huge 1,000-foot lake carriers out in the shipping lanes, which squeeze close to shore to round Keweenaw Point. Inland, beach peas, sand cherries, and wild roses cling to windswept, volatile mounds of sand. Like beach grasses, the plants' spreading root systems help trap sand, stabilizing and building dunes.

The Keweenaw's tilted fault line is particularly pronounced in this part of the peninsula. To the south rises the exposed basalt face of the Cliff Range, while to the north, the fault line

COPPER COUNTRY

drops away so quickly that Great Sand Bay plummets to depths of more than 1,000 feet. In between, deep ridges allow microclimates to thrive. Along the south side of the road, watch for faintly marked **Michigan Nature Association trails** that dip into dark, deep forests, where lichen drapes from the pines and deep cushions of moss cover the rocky path.

### Eagle Harbor

One of the Keweenaw's most charming little towns, Eagle Harbor has a sleepy, comfortable feel to it, with a wonderfully protected natural harbor, perfect crescent of beach, even a historic lighthouse and observation deck out on the rocky point. In short, a classic summer getaway. "Everybody in Copper Harbor is trying to make money," noted one local. "Everybody in Eagle Harbor has already made it."

The red-brick **Eagle Harbor Lighthouse,** built in 1861, is one of the area's prettiest. Its outbuildings contain a small museum filled with information on shipwrecks, mining, and commercial fishing. Open mid-June–mid-September; $3 admission. The one-room schoolhouse in Eagle Harbor (two blocks west of the harbor on Center St.) was the birthplace of the odd **Knights of Pythias,** a secret fraternal society known for its elaborate rituals and fanciful costumes.

### Eagle River

Today a lonely-looking village, Eagle River bustled in the mid-1800s as a busy shipping port for the nearby Cliff and Phoenix Mines. It became the Keweenaw county seat in 1861 (and remains so today) as well as a rollicking social center for area miners, with two breweries and 32 saloons. The town's Phoenix Hotel was considered the finest north of Detroit, and hosted President James Garfield, newspaperman Horace Greeley, and other dignitaries. Douglass Houghton, the state geologist who first spread word of the Keweenaw's riches, was at least partly responsible for the town's success. Ironically, he drowned just offshore in 1845 at age 37, while traveling by canoe on another survey expedition.

BOB RACE

the Eagle Harbor Lighthouse

## ACCOMMODATIONS AND FOOD

### Motels and Inns

Located high on a ridge above Copper Harbor, the log lodge and cabins of the **Keweenaw Mountain Lodge,** 906/289-4403, were built as a public works project in the 1930s. Reservations here can be tough, but shoot for a cabin rather than an uninspired motel room (added much later than the other buildings). Motel rooms $50–75, cabins $75–100. At the northern boundary of Fort Wilkins State Park and just a short bike ride from town, the **Norland Motel,** 906/289-4815, is the kind of find you almost hate to share. Mom-and-pop motel rooms are made special with knotty pine paneling, a wonderful setting on Lake Fanny Hooe, extras like canoes and in-room refrigerators (great for picnic lunches), and prices that don't top $50.

Though not as good a deal, the no-frills rooms at the **King Copper Motel,** 906/289-4214, come with great views of the harbor and are just a few steps from the ferry dock—perfect for a warm shower and real bed after a week on Isle Royale. Rates $50–100.

Between Copper Harbor and Eagle Harbor on M-26, **Eagle Lodge,** 888/558-4441, offers simple housekeeping cabins perched on Lake Superior's shore. Rates $50–100. In Eagle River, the **Eagle River Inn,** 800/352-9228, offers motel-style accommodations with a similar outstanding setting, right at water's edge and flanked by a long sand beach. All rooms come with lake views. Rates $50–100.

## Camping

**Fort Wilkins State Park,** 906/289-4215, has 165 modern sites in two campgrounds, both on Lake Fanny Hooe. Many sites back up to the water and offer decent privacy. To reserve a spot (but not a specific site), call the Michigan state parks central reservation line, 800/44-PARKS; website: dnr.state.mi.us. **Lake Fanny Hooe Resort and Campground,** 800/426-4451, offers uninteresting sites in an open grassy area, but with a decent location near town and the south shore of Lake Fanny Hooe. As another option, many simply head off into the woods and set up camp. If you choose to follow suit, hang your packs and follow other backcountry practices—you'll be sharing the woods with plenty of black bears.

## Food

The **Pines,** a small café in downtown Copper Harbor, 906/289-4222, is great for rainy-day breakfasts, with its homemade cinnamon rolls and crackling fireplace. Delicious soups, sandwiches, and local fish specialties keep folks coming all day. The adjacent **Zik's Bar** is the hangout for Copper Harbor locals. The **Harbor Haus** in Copper Harbor, 906/289-4502, offers top-notch dining overlooking the harbor—the staff drops what they're doing to rush outside and perform the can-can when the *Isle Royale Queen III* passes by. Though the ever-changing menu highlights some excellent German specials, you can't do better than the whitefish or lake trout. Another good choice for whitefish is the **Mariner North,** 906/289-4637, featuring steaks and seafood. This Copper Harbor institution lost some of its spirit when the original log building burned to the ground several years ago, but it remains a popular gathering place.

In Eagle Harbor, the **Shoreline Restaurant,** 906/289-4441, draws 'em in for homemade pies, but there's plenty of other home-style cooking—like soups, sandwiches and well-prepared fresh lake trout—to make it worth the stop.

In the Eagle River Inn, **Fitzgerald's Restaurant,** 906/337-0666, offers upscale dining overlooking Lake Superior. The menu features Black Angus steaks, fresh fish and seafood, inventive vegetarian dishes and a comprehensive wine list.

# Isle Royale

Stranded in the vast waters of Lake Superior, Isle Royale is perhaps the model of what a national park is supposed to be—wild, rugged, and remote. No roads touch the 45-mile-long island, and its only contact with the outside world remains ship-to-shore radio. The least-visited park in the National Park Service system, Isle Royale attracts just 18,000 visitors a year—fewer visitors than elbow into Yosemite in a single weekend.

Civilization on Isle Royale (pronounce it "ROY-al," like it didn't have an "e") is concentrated in two small developments at opposite ends of the island. Windigo, on the southwest end, includes a National Park Service information center, camp store, and marina. Rock Harbor, near the east end, offers the same, plus a no-frills lodge and restaurant across from the ferry dock, and a handful of cabins overlooking finger-like Tobin Harbor. The rest of the island is backcountry, 210 square miles of forested foot trails, rocky bluffs, quiet lakes, and wilderness campsites.

Those who make the trek by boat or seaplane to Isle Royale come primarily to hike its 165 miles of trails, fish its 46 inland lakes, and paddle its saw-toothed shoreline. Wildlife viewing is popular, too, especially for the moose that swam across from Ontario several decades back, and the eastern timber wolves that later followed their prey across on the pack ice. Though the wolves are notoriously elusive, you can pretty much bet that your wildlife sightings will outnumber your human ones on Isle Royale.

## THE LAND

### A Washboard of an Island

Backpackers may sense Isle Royale's distinctive topography as they traverse the long, narrow island, which runs southwest to northeast, less than nine miles across at its widest point. A series of ridges and valleys fall away from the park's high interior backbone, the Greenstone Ridge, creating a washboard of forest and rock. Mt. Desor marks the highest point on the island, rising from the Greenstone Ridge to 1,394 feet.

The same Precambrian lava flows that formed the Keweenaw Peninsula more than one billion years ago also formed Isle Royale. After each lava flow, wind and rain carried sand and other sediments into the area, producing slabs of softer rock sandwiched between the hard layers of basalt, and creating the island's characteristic ridge-and-trough pattern. Hikers crossing the width of the island will feel this layout in their quads, as the trail continually rises and falls with each ridge. The topography becomes most obvious on the park's northeastern edge, where it meets Lake Superior: the ridges become long rocky fingers, and the valleys become narrow slivers of water wedged between the rocky points.

When the center of the Superior Basin began to subside, it thrust the layers of rock on Isle Royale upward at an angle, giving the island a northwest side of steep ridges and bluffs, and a southeastern shore that slopes gradually to the water and includes lowlands and bogs. The northern Keweenaw Peninsula is a near mirror image of Isle Royale, with a gradual northern shore and more steeply angled southern side.

The geography of Isle Royale is inseparable from the water that surrounds it. Along with its namesake island—the largest in Lake Superior—Isle Royale National Park actually consists of an archipelago of some 400 islands, all of them remnants of the same landmass. More than 80 percent of the national park lies underwater, beneath shallow ponds, bogs, inland lakes, and the

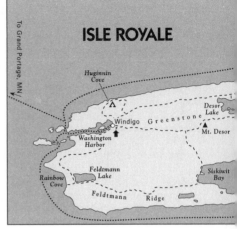

clear, cold water of Lake Superior. And here's some trivia to toss out at a backpacker you may pass on the trail: Ryan Island, located on Isle Royale's Siskiwit Lake, is the largest island in the largest lake on the largest island in the largest freshwater lake in the world.

### Climate

Isle Royale is the perfect escape from hot, sticky summers. With its water temperature rarely exceeding about 45° F, Lake Superior does a fine job as North America's largest air conditioner. It also has a significant modifying effect on the island: summers are generally a little cooler than on the mainland, with daytime temperatures from mid-May to mid-August ranging from about 65–75° F. Nights are northwoods cool, often dipping into the 40s and even 30s. Clouds obscure the sun more than half the time in summer. And be aware that fog can strike at anytime; more than one disappointed backpacker has returned from Isle Royale without any memories of the island's lovely vistas.

Lake Superior's modifying effect works in winter, too—winters on Isle Royale are a little warmer than the mainland, though that can be

*Ryan Island, located on Isle Royale's Siskiwit Lake, is the largest island in the largest lake on the largest island in the largest freshwater lake in the world.*

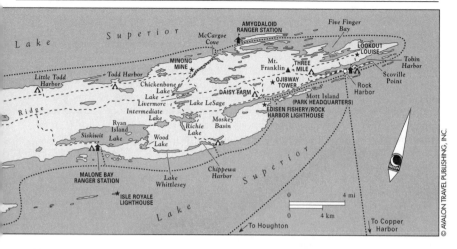

© AVALON TRAVEL PUBLISHING, INC.

small consolation in this part of the world. Once Lake Superior turns from cobalt to dark gray in late autumn and its infamous winter storms begin churning, the island becomes shrouded in fog, whipped by wind, and buried under several feet of snow.

Besides, isolation isn't the only reason Isle Royale has low visitor numbers. Come mid-October, it shuts up tight like a summer resort, the only national park to do so. The ferries stop running, the concessionaires in Rock Harbor close down, and the rangers head for Houghton or take seasonal work in warmer climes. Only the wildlife researchers are in their glory, able to track free-roaming wolves and moose by air.

## FLORA AND FAUNA

Isolated from the effects of civilization, Isle Royale acts as a living laboratory, a study of how plants and animals interrelate with each other in the ebb and flow of nature's cycles. Because of these unique natural qualities, in fact, the United Nations declared the park an International Biosphere Reserve in 1980.

### The Island's Most Famous Mammals

The island's **moose** provide the best example. Naturalists believe moose first came to Isle Royale in the early 1900s, several of them swimming the 15 miles from mainland Ontario. With ample vegetation for food and no natural predators, the moose multiplied rapidly, their numbers soaring to somewhere between 1,000 and 3,000 by the late 1920s. But soon they had ravaged their food sources. Starvation, combined with some particularly harsh winters, killed off hundreds of the huge mammals in the 1930s. A fire in 1936 prompted a lush regrowth of vegetation; thanks to revived food sources, the moose population skyrocketed again, followed by another round of starvation.

The seesaw pattern might have continued for decades, but nature intervened in the form of the eastern **timber wolf** (also known as the gray wolf). During the exceptionally cold winter of 1948–1949, the lake iced over between Ontario and Isle Royale, and a small pack of wolves made its way to the island. They found a bountiful food source in the local moose and multiplied, reaching a peak population of about 50 animals in 1970.

Since then, the wolves and moose, fenced in by the waters of Lake Superior, have provided scientists with a fascinating study of the predator/prey relationship. With a large moose herd, wolves cull the sick, the old, and the young, preventing overpopulation. But a smaller, stronger moose herd means more difficult hunting, which, in turn, reduces wolf breeding.

Populations for both animals have fluctuated rather dramatically over the decades. Today, the moose population hovers around a healthy 850. Hikers have an excellent chance of spotting these 1,000-pound mammals, which often feed in ponds and lowlands or along inland lakeshores. Hidden Lake, across Tobin Harbor south of Lookout Louise, is an exceptionally good spot, since moose have a taste for its mineral licks. If you're lucky enough to come upon a moose, give it very, very wide berth. Although they look cartoonish and friendly, moose can be exceptionally dangerous if approached too closely—especially cows with calves or males during the fall rutting season—capable of inflicting lethal blows with their hooves.

For reasons not clearly understood, Isle Royale's wolf population plummeted in the 1990s. By 1998, just 14 wolves roamed the island in three packs, and biologists feared a lack of genetic diversity might mean the demise of the island's wolves. But now they've rebounded again. The winter 2000 count recorded 29 wolves, and a realignment in territories, from three packs to just two. Whether the wolves will continue to thrive remains one of the most compelling questions this living laboratory has yet to answer.

The wolves tend to hide out largely in the remote southwestern corner of the island, but lately have been migrating east, where moose populations are higher. Only the rare backpacker ever spots one of the shy and stealthy creatures, and many a wolf howl heard at night is probably the haunting call of a loon. But the notion that wolves are there, somewhere—perhaps even watching from deep in the forest—is compelling enough for most, especially those lucky enough to spot a pawprint across the trail.

## Other Animals

Some of the other large mammals common in the northern Great Lakes region are notably absent from the island. Black bears never made it here, and white-tailed deer introduced for hunting purposes vanished early in the century. Likewise, caribou and lynx, present in the 19th century, also disappeared. Instead, hikers may spot red foxes (which love to scavenge around campsites, so hang your pack), beavers, muskrats, hare, red squirrels, otter, and mink.

**Birdwatchers** will enjoy scouring the water's surface for the common loon—which is indeed common here—along with the Canada goose, bufflehead, black duck, merganser, and mallard. Smaller birds frequenting the island include warblers, chickadees, thrushes, woodpeckers, and kingfishers.

None of Isle Royale's inland lakes can be reached by car or motorized boat, and many of them require serious effort to reach by foot—a combination that makes for great **fishing.** While sportfishing boats ply the Lake Superior waters around Isle Royale for lake trout, it is the island's inland waters—nearly all of them!—that offer some top-notch fishing. Northern pike is considered the prime fish in these parts for its fighting spirit and can be found in almost any of the local lakes. Hungry hikers will be pleased to know walleye, perch, and trout abound, too. Wise backpackers tote along a pack rod to fish with from shore; many lakes, like Feldtmann, Desor, Siskiwit, Richie, and Chickenbone have foot trails leading directly to them. (Other more remote lakes are open to fishing but require good backcountry skills to reach.) No license is needed to fish Isle Royale's inland lakes, though Michigan regulations apply; if you plan to drop a line in Lake Superior, you'll need a Michigan license, sold at the island's two camp stores.

A discussion of Isle Royale's animal life is not complete with mention of the island's insects. Like much of the Upper Peninsula—and many other wilderness areas—Isle Royale provides a fine home for **mosquitoes** and **black flies,** especially in low-lying areas. From mid-June to mid-August or so, keep insect repellent close at hand. In general, insects are less of a problem on higher trails, which often catch a lake breeze.

Spruce, firs, and jack pines share the island with beech and maple forests. But numerous varieties of wildflowers take center stage in June and July. Forests can be dotted with yellow lady slipper and American starflower; lowlands are brightened by wild iris, calla lilies, and yellow pond lilies. July and August are the months to

watch for berries; look for blueberries, thimble-
berries, and red raspberries, especially in the sun-
nier, rockier high areas.

## FROM CIVILIZATION TO WILDERNESS

Signs of the first human visitors to Isle Royale are
still visible today: shallow pits pockmarked in
the rock near McCargoe Cove on the island's
north shore are remnants of the island's earliest
copper mines. Archaeologists estimate that by
7000 B.C. humans had migrated to the north
shore of Lake Superior, where the hazy outline of
Isle Royale can be seen in the distance. It's less certain exactly when and why they made the first
crossing to Isle Royale, a 15-mile trip from its
closest point, the tip of Ontario's Sibley Peninsula.

Thanks to radiocarbon dating of artifacts found
in the mining pits, we do know that by 2000 B.C.
they were mining the rich veins of copper, pounding the raw ore with stones and fashioning it into
knives and ornaments. The rewards must have
been worth the treacherous trip across the open
lake. Indians actively mined on Isle Royale for
more than 1,000 years and traded their Isle Royale
copper wares as far away as New York and Mexico. They came only in summer, however, and left
few other signs of their inhabitation.

Word of the Indians' copper riches eventually
spread to French voyageurs, prompting them to
strike out for Lake Superior. They, too, began
trading the island's copper riches in the 1600s,
and gave the island its name. Even Benjamin
Franklin may have gotten into the act. Franklin
was instrumental in negotiating the 1783 Treaty
of Paris, which delineated the boundary between
the United States and Canada. If Franklin knew
of the island's copper, some historians reason,
he may have persuaded the British to draw the
line north of Isle Royale.

Many other historians dispute this theory,
claiming it wasn't Franklin's shrewd diplomacy
but mapmaker error that gave Isle Royale to the
United States. Early maps do, in fact, show the island much farther south than its actual location.
Either way, it belonged to the United States and
became part of Michigan when the state joined

the Union in 1837.

Fishermen also began discovering the rich
fishing grounds of Isle Royale, and by the
1830s, several fishing camps sprouted up
around the island, mostly to feed the area's fur
traders. The American Fur Company used gill
nets to take whitefish, lake trout, and herring.
The once plentiful whitefish suffered a serious decline later in the century, though, and
most commercial fisheries had closed by the
1880s. Today, the Park Service maintains a reconstructed fishery on the south end of the
island at the mouth of Moskey Basin. Sportfishing remains extremely popular for Lake
Superior trout and the resurgent whitefish;
angling on inland lakes for walleye, trout, and
northern pike can be epic.

Tourism to the inland began with a trickle in
the late 1800s and flourished at the turn of the
century with the growth of Midwestern cities.
Great Lakes steamers and excursion boats fer-
ried hundreds to the archipelago, where they
would picnic on the rocky shores or opt for
longer stays at exclusive clubs and resorts. The
Singer Resort on Washington Island (off Windigo) featured a dance hall and bowling alley; another on Belle Isle, just north of Isle Royale,
lured guests with its fine dining, shuffleboard,
and pitch-and-putt golf.

Visitors began to buy plots of land, many
of which had been owned by fisheries or cop-
per-mining enterprises. Summer homes grew
up mostly on the east end of Isle Royale, especially near lovely Tobin Harbor, just over the
ridge from Rock Harbor. In 1920, the island's
residents, especially Detroit newspaperman Albert Stoll, began the drive for national park
protection. Congress passed legislation to fold
the island into the National Park Service system
in 1931 "to conserve a prime example of
Northwoods Wilderness" and began acquiring
land parcels. Isle Royale National Park was
dedicated in 1946.

## THE NATIONAL PARK

While many national parks struggle with their
fate as islands of wilderness surrounded by a

© TRAVEL MICHIGAN

**Isle Royale Tour Boat Ranger**

more developed world, Isle Royale has the advantage of a much larger buffer zone protecting it from outside encroachment and influence. As a result, it is one of the most closely managed holdings in the national park system. That's good or bad depending on your opinion of the Park Service, but it does present some unique opportunities for protecting the wilderness. For starters, it is one of the few parks that already regulates the number of visitors who pass through its "gates." Though logistics have done a sufficient job of keeping numbers down thus far, the National Park Service need only cut back on ferry service or campsites to slow the flow.

Limited access also allows the Park Service to enforce rules more effectively. Dogs, for example, are not allowed on the island for fear they might bring rabies and other diseases to the island's wolf pack. Arrive with a poodle on your powerboat—even if it never sets paw on the dock—and you will be quickly waved off the island. Thumbs-down also to wheeled vehicles like mountain bikes or canoe carts. (Exceptions are made for wheelchairs.) The Park Service also takes great pains to preserve its backcountry solitude, with a park brochure reminding hikers to "refrain from loud conversation," "avoid

songfests," and "select equipment of subtle natural tones rather than conspicuous colorful gear."

## Information

For general information on the park, camping, transportation options, and more, contact Isle Royale National Park, 906/482-0984, website: www.nps.gov/isro.

Isle Royale was one of the first national parks to charge a "park user fee." Daily fees are $4 per person per day. If you're traveling to the island by ferry or seaplane, the concessionaire will collect your fee. If you're traveling by private boat, you can pay at the ranger station at Windigo or Rock Harbor, or at the Houghton Visitors Center prior to your departure.

The National Park Service had long talked about implementing admission fees to national parks as a way to compensate for shortfalls in federal funding. In the past, the incentive wasn't there, since all gate fees were fed back into the federal government's general treasury. With the new user fee program, however, 80 percent of the monies gathered will be spent at the collecting park. (The remaining 20 percent will be spent at national parks with priority maintenance projects.) In Isle Royale's case, that means hundreds of thousands of dollars that will be spent maintaining trails, and repairing or replacing docks. So hand over your cash willingly.

## Getting There

If getting there is half the fun, you'll be positively giddy by the time you arrive at Isle Royale. Travel to the island is not particularly convenient or cheap, which probably accounts for "average visitor stays" that are considerably longer than most other national park destinations. The average visit to Rocky Mountain National Park is a few hours; to Isle Royale, three days. (And that's counting the day-trippers who flow off the ferry, wander around the harbor for a few hours and hop back on that afternoon.)

Many, however, come to appreciate even the trip to and from Isle Royale, a mental decompression chamber of sorts that eases the passage between island wilderness and real world.

Your options to Isle Royale are seaplane, ferry, or personal boat. The National Park Service operates the largest ferry, the 165-foot *Ranger III*. It departs from Houghton twice a week from the end of May through mid-September for the six-and-a-half-hour passage to Rock Harbor. Roundtrip cost is $96 adults, $48 children under 12. Canoes and kayaks are an additional $40. Make reservations through the national park, 906/482-0984, website: www.nps.gov/isro.

If you'd rather see more of the Keweenaw and spend less time on the ferry, drive another hour up the peninsula to Copper Harbor, where you can catch the *Isle Royale Queen III* for a four-and-a-half-hour trip to Rock Harbor. It operates mid-May through the end of September, with a varying schedule throughout the summer (adding additional departures as needed in July and August). Roundtrip cost is $84 adults, $42 children 12 and under. Canoes and kayaks are an additional $40. The *Queen* is notoriously reliable and has happily surprised weary backpackers when it shows up to retrieve them even on the stormiest of days. But it hasn't earned the nickname "the Queasy" for nothing; in heavy seas, its 81-foot hull can rock and roll at a pretty good pitch. To check the schedule and make reserva-

tions, contact the Royale Line, 906/289-4437, website: www.isleroyale.com.

A third and fourth ferry run from Grand Portage, Minnesota. The 65-foot *Wenonah* makes the three-hour passage to Windigo, on the island's west end, daily from mid-June to mid-September. Roundtrip cost is $68 adults, $34 children under 12. If you're departing and returning the same day—essentially, just a boat ride since you'll have less than three hours on the island—the cost is $40 adults, $20 children under 12. Canoes and kayaks are an additional $56. Reserve a spot through Grand Portage-Isle Royale Transportation Line, 715/392-2100, website: www.grand-isle-royale.com.

A faster but more expensive boat, the 63-foot *Voyageur II,* travels to Windigo in two hours, then continues on to Rock Harbor. On its way to Rock Harbor, it circumnavigates the island, offering drop-off and pick-up service along the way. (This makes for a slow but interesting trip.) Roundtrip cost to Windigo is $98; call for prices to other locations. It also can carry canoes and kayaks for an additional $56. Again, make arrangements through Grand Portage-Isle Royale Transportation Line.

Seaplane service from Houghton is the most expensive but quickest way to the island—usually. The 45-minute flight is often delayed by wind and fog. The plane flies on demand (except Sunday) and can carry up to five passengers for $221 roundtrip per person ($154 one way). The plane cannot carry stove fuel, but you can purchase it on the island at the park store. Contact Isle Royale Seaplane Service, 906/482-8850 in season, 715/526-5103 off-season.

Arriving by private boat is also popular in midsummer—a little too popular for many who resent the whine of powerboats jarring the silence. The Rock Harbor and Windigo marinas offer docking and refueling for powerboats and sailboats; boats also are permitted to drop an anchor in a secluded bay overnight and save the marina fee. Protected harbors are plentiful on the east end of the island (though most remain exposed on an east wind) but are nonexistent on the west end. Every boat arriving at the island must first stop at a ranger station in

Windigo or Rock Harbor to obtain a permit and pay the park user fee.

Those with boats under 20 feet are strongly urged not to attempt a Lake Superior crossing. Even if you have a larger vessel, consider the passage only if you possess strong navigation skills and a good marine radio. Think ocean, not lake. Remember, these are the waters that sank the 729-foot *Edmund Fitzgerald* like it was a cheap rowboat.

## Accommodations and Food

Those just looking for a quiet island stay and some swell day hikes can set up a base in comfort at the **Rock Harbor Lodge,** 906/337-4993 May–Sept., 502/773-2191 Oct.–April. Lodge rooms are pretty much your basic motel-style accommodations, but they sit right at the water's edge with a glorious view of nearby islands and the open waters of Lake Superior. You'll pay for this little slice of civilization in the wilderness: Rates average $150–200 per night, including three meals at the lodge dining room. (Dinner often features fresh lake trout from the restored Edisen Fishery.) Guests also have use of an adjacent day lodge with a comfy wood-burning fireplace. Nearby housekeeping cottages include small kitchens, one double bed, and two bunk beds. Rates average $150–200 per night, without meals. Reservations are a must.

The Rock Harbor Lodge dining room is open to the public, and its meals taste like a gourmet feast after a week of freeze-dried fare. The Marina Store in Rock Harbor carries a good supply of food, camping supplies, film, fuel... pretty much anything important you forgot to pack. Windigo doesn't have any sort of lodging but offers an equally well-equipped camp store. Both stores also offer shower and laundry facilities.

If you want to see more of the island, **camping** is the way to do it. Rustic campsites are located throughout the island, with three types of sites available: tent sites for one to three tents, group sites for parties of 7–10 campers, and three-sided shelters that hold up to six people. You must obtain a free camping permit from the ranger station outlining your itinerary, but you can't obtain a reservation. All sites are

on a first-come, first-served basis. Should you reach a site at the end of the day and find it full (this can happen, especially in August, especially sites a day's hike from Rock Harbor), the unwritten rules say double up. No one expects you to hike off into the dwindling light to the next campsite.

Come prepared. The camp stores, though very well supplied, are not the places to outfit your trip. Carry a stove and fuel, since many sites do not permit fires, and dead wood is limited anyway. A water filter is another good idea, unless you plan to boil everything. Potable water is only available in Rock Harbor or Windigo, and chemical purifiers like Halizone tablets will not kill the hydatid tapeworm that can be found in Isle Royale waters.

## Boat Tours

The Park Service shuttles visitors to various island attractions on its 25-passenger *Sandy*. For information on destinations, schedules, and fares, contact the Park Service, 906/482-0984, website: www.nps.gov/isro. Twice a week, the *Sandy* makes the short trip across the mouth of Moskey Basin to the historic fishery of Peter and Laura Edisen, restored to show what life was like for the commercial fisheries that once thrived on the island. From Edisen Fishery, it's a short quarter-mile walk to the stout and simple Rock Harbor Lighthouse, a white edifice built in 1855 to guide ships to Isle Royale's then-busy copper ports.

The *Sandy* also cruises once a week to the Minong Mine, site of the island's largest copper mining operation in the 1870s. The boat excursion alone is worth the trip, rounding Blake Point and cruising past Five Finger Bay and Belle Harbor, one of the park's most scenic areas. Once at the mine, you can examine ancient copper mining pits dug by natives that still pockmark the area, which probably tipped off the later miners to the area's underground wealth. Relics like ore cars and rails remain visible, too. Hikers can view the remnants of another mine on the Island Mine Trail. A wagon road, old powder house, and mine tailings are about all that's left of the island's second-largest mining operation. Around all mine areas, watch the ground carefully—shafts and pits remain, but are obscured by undergrowth.

# HIKING THE ISLAND
## Day Hikes from Rock Harbor

Several day hikes are doable if you choose to "motel camp" in Rock Harbor. Don't miss **Scoville Point,** a 4.2-mile loop with interpretive signs that traces a rocky finger of land east of Rock Harbor. Another popular short hike (3.8 miles) is the loop to Suzy's Cave, formed by the wave action of a once much-deeper Lake Superior. **Lookout Louise,** north of Tobin Harbor, offers one of the island's most spectacular views, looking out over its ragged northeastern shoreline. If you've got a canoe, it's a short paddle and short two-mile hike. Without a canoe, it's a fine hike along lovely Tobin Harbor and the eastern end of the Greenstone Ridge, but you'll have to retrace your steps to return to Rock Harbor, about a 20-mile trek in all.

For another all-day hike, follow the Lake Superior shoreline to the Daisy Farm campground and the Ojibway Trail, which heads north and brings you to the **Ojibway Tower,** an air-monitoring station. The tower marks the highest spot on the eastern end of the island, and you can climb its steps (but not enter the tower room) for an unmatched view of the island's interior lakes and bays on both the north and south sides of the island. Travel back via the Greenstone Ridge and along Tobin Harbor for a varied 18-mile hike that will take you through blueberry patches, wildflower meadows, and serene shorelines. For a similar but shorter hike of about 10 miles, turn north at the Three Mile campground to ascend Mt. Franklin, another high point on the Greenstone Ridge.

## Day Hikes from Windigo

If you'd prefer not to haul your possessions on your back, it's possible—but a little more difficult—to do day hikes out of Windigo. Because fewer trails exist here, most hikes will be the out-and-back variety. The best loop option is to **Huginnin Cove,** a 9.7-mile route that passes through prime moose habitat before emerging onto the Lake Superior shore. (There's a campground here if you choose to make it an overnighter.) The east side of the trail passes an old mine, last active in 1892. Another excellent option is the **Feldtmann Lake Trail,** which winds along Washington Harbor before heading inland to one of the island's least-visited lakes. You can hike the 17-mile route out and back in a day, but you'll be sorry if you don't plan it as an overnight. Set up camp here and you'll likely be treated to moose sightings, dynamite fishing, and maybe, just maybe, the howl of a distant wolf. Plus, if you stay overnight, you'll have the time and energy for the short side trip to Lake Superior's pretty Rainbow Cove.

## Longer Hikes

With 165 miles of trail, it's impossible to outline all of Isle Royale's outstanding hiking options here. Consider a comprehensive guide like Jim DuFresne's excellent *Isle Royale National Park: Foot Trails and Water Routes,* published by The Mountaineers, Seattle, Washington. If you prefer to avoid the more bottlenecked areas of Windigo and Rock Harbor, consider arranging for the *Voyageur II* ferry, 715/392-2100, or the island's water-taxi service, 906/337-4993, to drop you off and pick you up at another location.

In general, the **Greenstone Ridge** is the main route to traverse the island, a 42-mile trail of mostly high and dry terrain. It also is the most popular, though crowds are a relative thing on Isle Royale.

The park's second-longest trail, the 26-mile **Minong Ridge Trail,** easily ranks as its most challenging. Traversing the north end of the island from near Windigo to McCargoe Cove, the rough and lightly used trail hobbyhorses over a rocky ridge and disappears through bogs. If you like primitive and peaceful, and don't get nervous about some poorly marked stretches that may lead you astray, this trail is for you. Wildlife sightings, especially moose, are likely here. Though campgrounds are far apart on this trail, they're worth the effort—Little Todd Harbor and Todd Harbor are some of the nicest on the island.

BOB RACE

sea kayak

Finally, the **Feldtmann Ridge Trail** loops along the southwestern shore, a well-marked but also lightly used route of 22 miles. The trail offers outstanding variety, from the shoreline of Washington Harbor, through gentle bogs, up the high Feldtmann Ridge itself, and finally to the open wildflower meadows and waters of Siskiwit Bay.

## PADDLING THE ISLAND

For paddlers, Isle Royale is a dream destination, a nook-and-cranny wilderness of rocky islands, secluded coves, and quiet bays interrupted only by the low call of a loon. For first-time visitors, you can't do better than the **Five Fingers,** the collection of fjord-like harbors and rocky promontories on the east end of the island. Not only is it well-protected (except from northeasterlies), it offers some of the finest and most characteristic Isle Royale scenery and solitude. Though Isle Royale is generally better suited to kayaks, open canoes can handle these waters in calm weather.

For kayaks, the entire island offers paddling opportunities, though some areas require long stretches of paddling without good shoreline access. Note that open-water passages on Lake Superior should be attempted by experienced paddlers only, and are not at all recommended in an open boat like a canoe. Capsizing in Lake Superior is not an unfortunate experience, it is a life-threatening one. With waters rarely exceeding temperatures in the 40s, hypothermia can occur in a matter of minutes.

You can avoid open-water passages and still explore other areas of the island by making use of the *Voyageur II* ferry or the island's water-taxi service, which will transport you and your boat to various docks on the northeastern half of the island. For more information and rates, call the *Voyageur II,* 715/392-2100, or the water taxi, 906/337-4993.

Ferries can transport your boat (see **Getting There,** above), provided it is less than 20 feet long. You also can rent canoes, 14-foot fishing boats, and outboard motors at Windigo and Rock Harbor. For rental information, call 906/337-4993. For Rock Harbor visitors, a wonderful day can be spent exploring Tobin Harbor, where rental canoes await.

Exploring inland lakes is a remarkable experience on Isle Royale. Fishing is often superb, and moose often loiter near the shore, unaware of your presence. Plan your routes carefully, though, to avoid grueling portages. Again, your best bet is to arrange for the water taxi or the *Voyageur II* ferry to drop you and your boat at a mid-island spot like Malone Bay, Chippewa Harbor, or McCargoe Cove. From there you have manageable (and even easy) portages to more than a half dozen lakes, including Siskiwit, Wood, Whittlesey, Intermediate, Richie, LeSage, Livermore, and Chickenbone. And there's nothing quite like drifting across a wilderness lake in the middle of a wilderness island.

# The Central U.P.

The Upper Peninsula, local tourism officials like to tell you, encompasses huge quantities of public property—all told, some four million acres of protected state and federal forestland. In both quantity and quality, the central U.P. may hold more than its fair share. From Marquette east about 100 miles to the plumb line of M-77, this tidy patch of the peninsula offers up Pictured Rocks National Lakeshore, Grand Island National Recreation Area, Seney National Wildlife Refuge, the huge Hiawatha National Forest, a half dozen state parks, and a bunch more county parks, but who's counting? Suffice it to say there's plenty to see and plenty of places to spread out.

The central U.P. is also a tale of two shores. Like a woman girdled into a Victorian dress, the giant peninsula cinches in its waist here, squeezed tight between Lake Superior to the north and Lake Michigan to the south. Along both shores, you'll find history—from restored towns to protected shipwrecks—the deep curve of protected bays, winking lighthouses, and ribbons of sand that unfurl mile after blissfully deserted mile.

## The Lake Michigan Shore

Four factors created the logging legacy that once dominated the southern reaches of the U.P.: vast stands of timber, wide rivers for transporting logs, well-protected harbors, and a building frenzy that began in southern Great

Lake Michigan Sand Dunes

© TRAVEL MICHIGAN

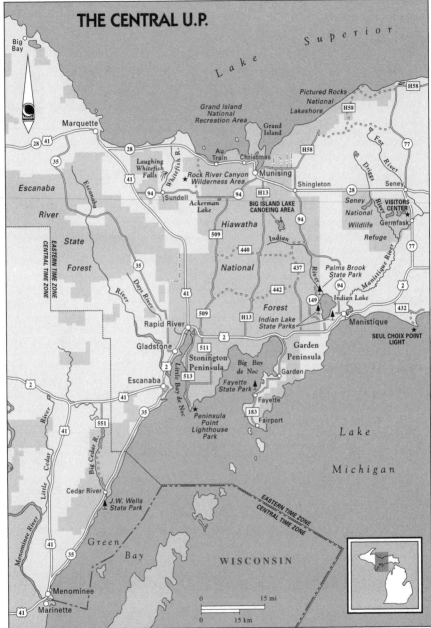

# THE CENTRAL U.P.

*Lake Superior*

Big Bay

Marquette

28 41

Escanaba

28

35

*Escanaba*

*River*

*State*

35

*Forest*

EASTERN TIME ZONE
CENTRAL TIME ZONE

41

35

*Days River*

Rapid River

Gladstone

2

Escanaba

41

511

Stonington
Peninsula

513

35

551

*Little Bay de Noc*

*Peninsula
Point
Lighthouse Park*

Cedar River

J.W. Wells
State Park

*Big Cedar R.*

*Menominee River*

*Little Cedar River*

41

Green Bay

Menominee

Marinette

41

Laughing
Whitefish
Falls

41

Rock River Canyon
Wilderness Area

94

Sundell

*Whitefish R.*

Ackerman
Lake

509

*Hiawatha*

440

*National*

509

H13

*Forest*

Au
Train

Christmas

94

Munising

H13

BIG ISLAND LAKE
CANOEING AREA

*Indian*

437

442

149

Grand Island
National
Recreation Area

Grand
Island

*Pictured Rocks
National
Lakeshore*

H58

H58

H58

H58

Shingleton

28

*Driggs River*

*For*

*River*

77

Seney

Seney
National
Wildlife
Refuge

VISITORS
CENTER

Germfask

77

432

2

*Manistique River*

94

Palms Brook
State Park

*River*

Indian Lake

Indian Lake
State Parks

Manistique

SEUL CHOIX POINT
LIGHT

*Garden
Peninsula*

*Big Bay
de Noc*

Garden

Fayette
State Park

Fayette

183

Fairport

*Lake*

*Michigan*

EASTERN TIME ZONE
CENTRAL TIME ZONE

WISCONSIN

0          15 mi

0          15 km

© AVALON TRAVEL PUBLISHING, INC.

Lakes ports like Chicago and stretched west across the treeless prairie.

Devastating clear-cuts and diminished demand pretty much ended the region's logging boom by the early 20th century. Those well-protected ports and deep harbors still serve the area well, though, as busy shipping centers and enviable fishing waters.

## Information and Time Zones

For information, your best source is the large and comprehensive **Michigan Welcome Center,** 906/863-6496. The picturesque log building is located on US-41 near the state line (just north of the bridge), providing ample local and statewide visitor information. Open daily year-round. For information on Menominee and the surrounding area, contact the **Menominee Area Chamber of Commerce,** 1005 10th Ave., Menominee, 906/863-2679. For information on Escanaba/Gladstone and the nearby peninsulas and bays, contact the **Delta County Area Chamber of Commerce,** 230 Ludington St., Escanaba, 888/335-8264, website: www.deltami.org, or the **Bays de Noc Convention and Visitors Bureau,** 2401 12th Ave. N., Escanaba, 800/533-4FUN, website: www.deltafun.com.

Menominee County is in the central time zone, like neighboring Wisconsin, but when you cross the line into Delta County, just north of Fox County Park, you're back on eastern time.

## MENOMINEE TO ESCANABA

Spiking south like a canine tooth between Wisconsin and the waters of Green Bay, the triangle of land comprising Menominee County and southern Delta County has been dubbed the peninsula's "banana belt." Well, it does have the U.P.'s most temperate climate, thanks to the warm (okay, relatively warm) waters of protected Green Bay, and the lightest snowfall in the entire Upper Peninsula—just 50 inches a year on average, a quarter of what typically falls on the rest of the U.P.

Locals take advantage of this quirk of nature not for growing bananas, but raising dairy cattle and crops like corn and soybeans. Farms dot the countryside here, many on land long ago clear-cut by loggers. The longtime logging industry still echoes through the region, too, in the historic waterfront district of Menominee and the mammoth Mead Paper plant near Escanaba—a key factor in the area's stable economy. Many visitors, though, have a tough time getting past the big lake always looming on the eastern horizon. The lapping waters of Green Bay are infinitely enticing and easily accessible here.

## Menominee

The Menominee River spills into Green Bay between the twin cities of Marinette, Wisconsin, and Menominee, Michigan, once the region's richest lumber port. The bustling business district centered on 1st Street along the waterfront. Happily, most of the late-19th-century brick and sandstone buildings have survived intact, and renovation and restoration is underway on many of them. You can explore the **historic district,** guided by a walking tour brochure available at the Spies Public Library, 940 1st Street. Its 1905 Beaux Arts facade happens to be one of the tour's most handsome buildings. A growing number of shops and restaurants along 1st Street are adding new life to this pleasant area.

The waterfront district is also home to bayside parks, easily accessible on foot. **Victory Park** stretches along the water between 6th and 10th Avenues, flanked by a new marina and a band shell that hosts summer concerts on Tuesday and Thursday evenings. For a longer walk or bike ride, head south along the water to the **Tourist Park** swimming beach. Farther south, the **North Pier Light** marks the entrance to Menominee Harbor with a beacon at the end of a rocky breakwater.

Menominee's most popular park is a bit farther afield. Located at the north end of town off M-35, **Henes Park** (HEN-iss), 906/863-2656, occupies a 50-acre point that juts out into Green Bay. Designed by noted landscape architect Ossian Simonds, this unusual park combines tracts of virgin hemlock and pine with the more-expected park amenities like walking trails, swimming beaches, and playgrounds.

Lodging choices are pretty much limited to a few franchise motels in both Menominee and neighboring Marinette, Wisconsin. Two of the better values: **Howard Johnson's Express,** 2516 10th St, Menominee, 906/863-4431, which has rooms overlooking the bay. Rates $50–75. In Wisconsin, **Best Western Riverfront Inn,** 1821 Riverside Ave., Marinette, WI 54143, 715/732-1000, is just west of US-41 at the river. Rates $75–100.

Dining in Menominee runs along classic super-club fare, with an emphasis on fish from the local waters. The **Landing,** 450 1st St., 906/863-8034, offers terrific views of Green Bay and good, reliable steaks, seafood, and chicken dishes. Locals will likely point you toward **Schloegel's,** 906/863-7888, right on US-41, for daily home-made pies, generous sandwiches, and ethnic menu items like Swedish pancakes. Good view of Green Bay, too.

## Along M-35

As you head north out of Menominee, you're al-most immediately treated to a lovely drive as M-35 hugs the shoreline of Green Bay. In the 55 miles between Menominee and Escanaba, sever-al parks and beaches lure you off the highway. About 13 miles north of Menominee, **Bailey Park** is a favorite swimming beach of the locals, with fine sand and low dunes on a point that stretches away from the highway. Just north, **Kleinke Park** is more exposed to M-35, but of-fers campsites overlooking the bay, as well as a sand beach.

**J. W. Wells State Park,** 906/863-9747, about 25 miles south of Escanaba on M-35, is the most extensive park along this route. Flanking both sides of M-35, the 800-acre park is known for its three-mile stretch of rocky beach and large mod-ern campground; many overlook its seven miles of ski and hiking trails. The Timber Trail fol-lows the lakeshore north. Watch for wildflow-ers (and mosquitoes) in the sandy lowland areas, and virgin white pine towering above. The pines prompted the park, donated by the children of J. W. Wells, who was a successful area lumberman and mayor of Menominee. The Cedar River Trail winds north to the mouth of the Cedar River, the park's northern boundary and a very popular fishing launch. Put in a boat at the river to fish for

northern pike, walleye, and bass, or surf cast for trout along the bayshore.

The park's modern campground doesn't offer much privacy, but all 178 sites are near the beach, and 30 back up right on the water. All sites often fill on summer weekends. If you've planned well ahead, you might be able to score one of the park's six rustic cabins, stone and log buildings built as a CCC project in the 1930s and tucked in seclud-ed woods near the water. They sleep 8–16 and feature barrel stoves for warmth and cooking. For cabin or campsite reservations, contact 800/44-PARKS, website: www.dnr.state.mi.us

At the Cedar River, the **Escanaba River State Forest,** 906/786-2351, offers a quiet, rustic campground ($6) right on the banks of the river just a few miles upstream from the mouth. No reservations. From M-35 at the village of Cedar River, follow CR-551 west for eight miles. A network of hiking/mountain biking trails begins here, too, with four loops ranging from two to seven miles that travel over hilly terrain sculpted by Ice Age glaciers.

Before you reach Escanaba, two more coun-ty parks offer beaches and campgrounds. **Fox Park,** 906/753-4582, seven miles north of Cedar River, has a 25-site primitive campground ($7) that rarely fills, and a nice sand beach. The more popular **Fuller Park,** 906/786-1020, nine miles north, has 25 modern sites ($11), a sand beach, bathhouse, boat launch, and access to the Bark River.

## Escanaba and Gladstone

A metropolis for these parts, Escanaba and neighboring Gladstone (just a few miles north) are home to some 20,000 people, serving as the industrial and commercial center for the south-central Upper Peninsula. The natural deepwater port gave Escanaba its start back in the Civil War days, when a hastily built rail line linked the iron mines in Negaunee with the port, to bring coveted raw materials to the weapons-makers and railroad builders of the Union Army. Today Escanaba's modern ore port still ships iron, now in the form of iron/clay taconite pellets, to steelmakers in In-diana and Ohio.

Downtown Escanaba focuses on Ludington Street, an east/west route that runs from M-35 to the waterfront. Here's where you'll find most of the town's restaurants, shops, and a growing local arts presence. The town's landmark is the **House of Ludington,** 223 Ludington St., a grand old Queen Anne resort hotel built in 1865. After enjoying a second heyday in the 1940s and '50s, the old hotel has stuttered and stumbled with some shoddy interior remodeling and mismanagement. The most recent owners have reopened the hotel's restaurant with an upscale menu, and the building's imposing facade continues to anchor the downtown.

At the foot of Ludington Street, lovely **Ludington Park** offers paved pathways along the water and to a small island (in-line skates permitted), interpretive signs explaining local history, a band shell that hosts concerts on Wednesday evenings in summer, a playground, beach, tennis courts, and boat launch. One of the park's most popular attractions is the **Sand Point Lighthouse,** 906/786-3763, an 1868 brick light that was restored and reopened in 1990 by the Delta County Historical Society. It was a big job: in the 1940s, the Coast Guard remodeled the obsolete light for staff housing, removing the lantern room and lopping off the top ten feet of the tower. For a couple of bucks, you can climb the tower and take a look at the restored keeper's house.

The light's first keeper, by the way, was Mary Terry, one of the nation's first woman lightkeepers. Open June 1–Sept. 30, daily 9 A.M.–5 P.M. (after 1 P.M. in Sept.). Just to the south, the **Delta County Historical Society,** 906/786-3763, has interesting and informative displays on local logging and maritime history. Free admission, same hours as the lighthouse.

Heading north on M-35 toward Gladstone, you'll pass the **UP State Fair Grounds.** As further evidence that the U.P. often feels little affinity with its Lower Peninsula counterpart, Michigan hosts two state fairs. The UP fair is held the third week of August. For events information, contact the Delta County Tourism and Convention Bureau, 230 Ludington St., Escanaba, 888/335-8264, website: www.deltami.org.

Gladstone's most unique attraction certainly must be the **Hoegh Pet Casket Company,** 317 Delta Ave., 906/428-2151. "You've read about it, you've seen it on television," proclaims one advertisement. "Now tour the only model pet cemetery in the world and see the world's largest pet casket manufacturing operation." Indeed, Hoegh offers tours of the pet casket manufacturing line and explains the "pet burial phenomenon." Open Mon.–Fri. 8 A.M.–4 P.M.; free tours are available except 11:30 A.M.–12:30 P.M.

Just three miles north of Gladstone, the Escanaba River State Forest maintains the **Days River Pathway,** a fine nine-mile hiking trail that loops through forest and along the scenic Days River, which cuts a deep gorge near the trailhead. This is a good stream for brook trout, so bring along a fly rod. Toss in binoculars, too, since the area is thick with warblers and other songbirds. To reach the trailhead, follow US-2 east of Gladstone three miles, then turn left onto Days River Road. For more information, contact the Escanaba River State Forest, 906/786-2351.

The typical sprawl of chain motels runs along M-35 between Escanaba and Gladstone, but some nice family-owned operations are still holding their own along the waterfront, with rates in the $50–100 range. The **Terrace Bay Resort,** 906/786-7554, on Little Bay de Noc between Escanaba and Gladstone, has nice, clean motel rooms with great bay views. The 200-acre resort complex includes an 18-hole golf course, indoor and outdoor pools, tennis courts, game room, and more. To find Terrace Bay, watch for the signs on US-41 south of Gladstone. About six miles south of Escanaba on M-35, **Fishery Pointe Beach Cottages,** E5041 M-35, 906/786-1852, and **Sandy Shores Resort,** E4717 M-35, 906/786-3625, offer housekeeping cottages on a nice stretch of sand beach.

You'll find your best dining options in downtown Escanaba. The hottest spot in town is **Hereford and Hops,** 614 Ludington St., 906/786-1945, a cook-your-own-steak place and microbrewery in the 1914 Delta Hotel. For homemade soups, sandwiches, and wonderful Finnish baked goods, don't miss the

**Drury Lane Bakery and Cafe,** 906 Ludington St., 906/786-0808.

## GLADSTONE TO MANISTIQUE

At Green Bay's northern end, two large peninsulas—Stonington and Garden—hang down from the U.P., forming Little Bay de Noc and Big Bay de Noc. More than 200 miles of wonderfully protected and undulating shoreline, combined with the region's temperate climate, make for outstanding **fishing** for northern pike, perch, lake salmon, rainbow trout, smallmouth bass, and especially tasty walleye. *USA Today*, in fact, named the Bays de Noc one of the top 10 walleye spots in the country. For area information, contact the **Bays de Noc Convention and Visitors Bureau,** 2401 12th Ave. N., Escanaba, 800/533-4FUN, website: www.deltafun.com.

### Hiawatha National Forest

The 860,000-acre Hiawatha National Forest spans much of the central U.P., with its western unit stretching all the way from the Lake Michigan shoreline of the Stonington Peninsula to the Lake Superior shore near Munising. (See the **Eastern U.P.** chapter for more on the forest's eastern unit.) For information on hiking trails, campgrounds, canoe routes, and other attractions, stop at the **Visitor Information Station,** 906/474-6442, just east of Rapid River on US-2. You can talk with rangers and pick up a wide selection of maps and handouts. It also includes interpretive displays and a small bookshop. Open Mon.–Fri. 7:30 A.M.–4 P.M.

The national forest's 40-mile **Bay de Noc/Grand Island Trail** follows an old Ojibwa portage route, used to carry canoes and supplies between Lakes Michigan and Superior. Today it runs just short of both lakes, beginning just northeast of Rapid River and ending 10 miles shy of Lake Superior at Ackerman Lake. The trail parallels the Whitefish River about one-half to two miles away, tracing its eastern bluff and often affording high, sweeping views of the forested river valley. It hopscotches over several streams and passes several lakes. Because of the preponderance of hardwoods, the route is particularly beautiful in fall color season.

Horses and mountain bikes are allowed on the Bay de Noc/Grand Island Trail, but no motorized vehicles. Primitive camping is permitted throughout the national forest (no permit required). One established campground, Haymeadow, lies about one-fourth of the way up the trail. It includes 15 rustic sites, water, and outhouses. There are no other drinking water outlets along the trail, so carry in your own or bring a purification system. You may want to pack in a fishing rod, too; trout fishing can be quite good in several of the small streams. To find the trailhead, follow US-2 east from Rapid River two miles, then turn left on CR-509 and drive another 1.5 miles. You'll see a parking area on the west side of the road.

In winter, this same area is the stomping grounds for the sled dogs of **Triple Creek Sled Dog Kennels,** 800/DOG-SLED. Owner Bob Johnson, one of the U.P.'s most experienced mushers, offers a variety of two-hour to five-day dogsled trips in the region around the Bay de Noc/Grand Island Trail. Package tours include a stay at **Johnson's Buck Sporting Lodge,** his solar-powered wilderness lodge north of Rapid River.

A few miles east of the Forest Service Visitor Information Station, turn north off US-2 onto H-13 to reach the great hiking and mountain biking trails of **Pine Marten Run.** The trail network lies between the Indian River to the north, CR-440 to the south, Forest Road 2258 to the west, and CR-437 to the east. This newly signed area includes 26 miles of rolling single track and overgrown double track. Various loops wind through huge hemlocks and white pines, around a dozen lakes, and along the pretty Indian River. From H-13, turn right on CR-440, and watch for the Forest Service sign directing you to Iron Jaw Lake. Alternately, head north from CR-440 on Forest Road 2258, where you'll find another trailhead just before the road crosses the Indian River. Get maps and more information from the Hiawatha National Forest Visitor Information Station (see above).

Just north of Pine Marten Run and the Indian River, the **Big Island Lake Canoeing Area** offers paddlers a quiet chain of nine lakes. Since there are few launches for powerboats, the lakes usually remain peaceful and pristine even in the height of summer. Again, obtain directions, maps, and more information from the Visitor Information Station.

## Stonington Peninsula

The quiet Stonington Peninsula is largely ignored by tourists, lacking accessible sand beaches or commercial attractions. It is a soft and peaceful place, with smooth slabs of bedrock shoreline and sunny meadows that have reclaimed abandoned farmland. To explore the 15-mile-long peninsula, follow US-2 east of Gladstone and turn south on CR-513 or CR-511. The Hiawatha National Forest manages a nice **stretch of shoreline** along the peninsula's west side, with a couple of campgrounds and hiking trails. Watch for forest service signs south of Garth Point.

The peninsula preserves several stands of old-growth hemlocks, hardwoods, and pines. One of the most notable examples is now protected as the **Squaw Creek Old Growth Area,** part of the Hiawatha National Forest. Though not virgin timber, loggers in the 19th century practiced selective cutting (quite unusual in those days) and left behind several large trees, now huge. Trails are few—just a couple of abandoned logging roads open only to foot traffic. Walking is easy, however, since the high shade canopy created by the trees crowds out the underbrush usually found in the woods. (Do take a compass.)

The southern part of the 65-acre tract is particularly scenic, with the clear, tea-colored waters of Squaw Creek slaloming between the fat trunks. You'll find the largest hemlocks south of the creek and huge hardwoods just to the north. Squaw Creek is not marked by a sign and shows up on few maps. To find it, drive south on CR-513 nine miles; just before and after the road crosses the creek, you'll see pull-offs on the east side of the road and old roads leading inland.

At the tip of the Stonington Peninsula, **Peninsula Point Lighthouse Park** is the perfect place

to sprawl out on a sunny day: an open meadow, grassy picnic area, great beachcombing shoreline, and—the main attraction—an 1865 lighthouse. Climb the spiral stairway for one of the most expansive views around: a 270-degree survey of the long and leggy Green Bay, even Wisconsin's Door County on a clear day. The lighthouse was abandoned in the 1930s, replaced by a more effective shoal light several miles offshore. Local volunteers restored and reopened the old light, which was subsequently ravaged by fire in 1959. While the keeper's home was destroyed, the tower withstood the blaze.

This is also an excellent spot for **birders,** since the Stonington is a favorite migration stopping point for songbirds. Watch the water's edge for the great blue herons, who have a rookery nearby. These grand birds stand stick-straight and motionless in the water for several minutes, then quickly snatch unsuspecting fish out of the shallows.

## Garden Peninsula

Like the Stonington Peninsula, the Garden Peninsula is a quiet, peaceful point of land, filled with little-used blacktopped roads perfect for cycling, and a handful of sleepy farms and orchards. Sleepy unless the narcotics agents are at work, anyway: It seems that marijuana growers have reclaimed some of the area's sleepy farmland themselves, taking advantage of the peninsula's solitude and moderate climate. Locals can fill you in on the stories of drug enforcement officers buzzing the place with helicopters and busting down doors. You decide where truth meets fiction.

The main road down the peninsula is CR-183, accessed off US-2. In late summer or fall, stop at **Garden Orchards,** 906/644-2140, for juicy apricots and apples. As it traces the east shore of Big Bay de Noc, CR-183 passes through the tiny hamlet of **Garden.** Along with a few shops, it's home to a commercial fishery at the end of Little Harbor Road, where you can buy some fresh catch.

By far the peninsula's most notable attraction—and rightly so—is **Fayette State Park,** 13700 13.25 Lane, 906/644-2603. If you make time for just one stop in this part of the U.P., make it this outstanding state park. Once the site of a large smelting operation, Fayette's limestone furnaces converted raw iron ore from U.P. mines into pig iron that was loaded onto barges bound for Escanaba. In the 1880s, stinky and industrial Fayette boasted a population of 500, and its loud, hot blast furnaces cranked away seven days a week. By 1891, nearby forests that fueled the furnace were all but depleted, and more efficient steelmaking methods came into vogue. The furnace shut down, and the town died with it.

Nearly a century later, Fayette was reborn as a wonderfully restored historic site and state park. Today, Fayette is surely one of the nation's most scenic ghost towns, its dozen limestone buildings tucked along the sheer white bluffs and deep, clear waters of Snail Shell Harbor. Start at the visitors center, which gives a good historical overview and features a helpful scale model of the village. You can wander in and out of the hotel, opera house, homes, and other buildings, some intact, some more decayed. Horse-drawn carriage rides around the grounds and boat tours are available Memorial Day–Labor Day. The visitors center and buildings are open late April–Oct. daily 9 A.M.–6 P.M. You're welcome to explore the grounds anytime. In fact, a very early morning or off-season visit can add to the ghostly appeal of the place.

With the historic townsite acting like a magnet for visitors, the rest of the 750-acre park is often overlooked. It includes a semimodern campground (electricity but no modern restrooms or showers) and seven miles of hiking trails, including one that swings north along the bluffs above Snail Shell Harbor.

One of the finest ways to explore the Garden Peninsula and its chalky white limestone bluffs is from the seat of a sea kayak. **Great Northern Adventures,** an excellent guide service out of Marquette, offers two- and three-day kayak tours along the peninsula's bluffs, caves, and beaches. Contact Great Northern at 906/225-TOUR, website: www.greatnorthernadventures.com, for dates and prices.

If commercial fishing interests you, continue down CR-513 to **Fairport** near the tip of the peninsula, where a commercial fleet still operates. There's not much else in this simple town, but it's fun to watch the comings and goings of the fishing boats, especially in midafternoon, when they usually return with the day's catch.

## Indian Lake

The Upper Peninsula's fourth-largest lake, Indian Lake is well known among anglers and RV campers. (Be warned that jet skiers have discovered it, too.) The anglers come for the perch, walleye, and muskie that thrive in its warm and quite shallow waters. The RVers come for its convenient location—just north of US-2 and the Garden Peninsula, with plenty of campsites and sand beaches.

Best known is **Indian Lake State Park,** Route 2, Manistique, MI 49854, 906/341-2355, with two units, one on the south shore and a second unit three miles away on the west shore. Each offers a modern campground and a boat launch. (The lake is the focus here, so hiking is limited.) The western unit sites, while not on the water, tend to be less busy. If you're aiming for a waterfront site in the southern unit, plan to come midweek or off season, and keep your fingers crossed. To reach Indian Lake State Park, take US-2 to Thompson, then go north on M-149 and east on CR-442. To reach the west unit, stay on M-149.

Farther up Indian Lake's western shore, **Palms Brook State Park,** Route 2, Manistique, 906/341-2355, guards one of the U.P.'s more remarkable natural attractions. Kitch-Iti-Kipi, or "Big Spring," looks like a deep, dark pool tucked away in a grove of cedars—until you get up close. Then you discover it's an enormous spring, where gin-clear water bubbles out of the earth at a staggering 10,000–16,000 gallons per *minute.*

The park maintains a nifty raft, so you can propel yourself across the 200-foot-long spring with the help of a hand-powered cable. It's an amazing view, peering 45 feet down into its eerie emerald waters and erupting sand bottom, where lunker brown trout glide among the skeletons of downed trees. The spring is a popular attraction, so come in early morning or, better yet, midwinter. (The spring never freezes over.) You'll have to hike 100 yards or so up the park's gated and unplowed entrance road, but Kitch-Iti-Kipi is the kind of magical place best appreciated in solitude.

## Manistique

The wildly corkscrewing Manistique River pours through the sloughs of the Lake Superior State Forest then empties into Lake Michigan at Manistique, a community of 6,000. Its name comes from a derivative of the Ojibwa word for vermilion, in reference to the color of the river. The town loves to talk about its **siphon bridge,** which crosses the Manistique River. A strange engineering feat, the 1919 bridge is partially supported by the water underneath it; the roadway actually sits four feet below water level. Its construction was prompted by a paper mill just upstream, which needed to dam the river for its water needs, thus raising the river. Also interesting is the adjacent **water tower,** a fancy brick neoclassical structure, and the town's landmark.

Good **swimming beaches** can be found all along the Lake Michigan shore, such as those at Town Beach near the East Breakwater Light, and at Township Park just east of Manistique (turn right on Township Park Road). For information on other attractions, contact the **Schoolcraft County Chamber of Commerce,** 1000 W. Lakeshore Dr. (US-2 just west of downtown), 906/341-5010.

## Practicalities

Several nice mom-and-pop motels are managing to hang on along US-2, though they're getting more and more competition from chains. Let's hope places like the **Star Motel,** 906/341-5363, continue to fend off the big boys. Located a mile

or two east of Manistique on US-2, this tidy, vintage 1950s motel has large rooms, rates in the $50 range, meticulous owners and a nice setting on the lake. It allows well-behaved dogs, too. What more could you ask? Another good non-chain option is the **Beachcomber Motel,** 906/341-2567, across from the lake one mile east of Manistique on US-2.

Between the Stonington and Garden Peninsulas, the 1915 **Nahma Hotel,** 906/644-2486, is one of the last vestiges of the town of Nahma, a lumber company that was sold part-and-parcel to a corporation that had plans for a big resort. It never materialized, and today the Nahma Hotel sits amid a ghost town on Main Street. The hotel is terrific, a former lumber baron home with 15 ample, nicely decorated rooms for$50–100. The mouth of the Sturgeon River and Big Bay de Noc are just out the back door. Lots of **chain motels** are represented along US-2, especially near Manistique.

**Camping** is readily available at dozens of rustic campgrounds within the Hiawatha National Forest (see above) and in the Lake Superior State Forest, 906/452-6227. A particularly nice one is the very secluded—and difficult to reach—Portage Bay campground on the Garden Peninsula's eastern shore. It's southeast of Garden, at the end of Portage Bay Road. For modern campsites, your best bets are often state parks like Indian Lake or Fayette (see above). For campsite reservations at any Michigan state park, call 800/44-PARKS; website: dnr.state.mi.us.

It seems everyone who drives along US-2 stops for a bite at the **Sunny Shores Restaurant,** on US-2 in Manistique, 906/341-5582. It's known for breakfast, but serves all day long. Also in Manistique, the **Harbor Inn** 238 Cedar St., 906/341-8393, has good whitefish dinners, a bountiful salad bar, and a neat old tavern perfect for a beer after a day of mountain biking or beachcombing.

# Munising and Vicinity

## MUNISING

When it comes to enticing visitors, nature dealt Munising a royal flush. The town of 2,700 curves around the belly of protected Munising Bay. The Grand Island National Recreation Area looms just offshore. Pictured Rocks National Lakeshore begins at the edge of town and stretches for 40-plus miles. The Hiawatha National Forest spills across the forests to the south and west. If you're looking for outdoor activities, Munising's got all the right cards.

M-28 leads you right to the heart of town, where you'll find most restaurants, mom-and-pop motels, and the ferry dock for cruises to Pictured Rocks. For more information on Munising services, contact the **Munising Visitors Bureau,** 422 E. Munising Ave., 906/387-2138, website: www.munising.org.

### Accommodations

**The Sunset Resort Motel,** 1315 E. Bay, 906/387-4574, has a great location right on Munising Bay at the east end of town. Some rooms have kitchenettes. It's a great find, with great rates, too: $50–75 in high season. Unlike most commercial strips, the one along M-28 on Munising's near east side is still within walking distance of downtown and the waterfront. It has some nice and tidy small motels like the **Star-Lite Motel,** 500 E. M-28, 906/387-2291 (rates $25–50), as well as chain offerings like the **Days Inn,** 906/387-2493, the best of the chains with a close-in location and indoor pool. Rates $50–75.

### Camping

For ultimate convenience but with a sense of seclusion, the Hiawatha National Forest's **Bay Furnace** is a good choice. Just west of Munising north of M-28, it offers 50 rustic sites with a very nice setting next to Lake Superior and overlooking Grand Island. Some sites almost have their own private stretch of beach, and a short cross-country ski trail at the campground's north end gives campers a little extra breathing room.

Near the day-use area you can check out the remains of the old charcoal furnace that produced 20 tons of iron a day in the 1870s. In its heyday, as many as eight steamers at a time would line up at docks here, bringing wood to fuel the furnace and hauling away iron. Camping fee is $8, no reservation accepted. Take M-28 west from Munising to Christmas and turn north at the Forest Service campground sign.

The Hiawatha National Forest has several other designated campgrounds nearby. Contact the Hiawatha Visitors Center, 400 E. Munising Ave., 906/387-3700, for more information and directions.

Families gravitate to the **Wandering Wheels Campground,** 906/387-3315, on M-28 three miles east of Munising, with 89 sites in a nice wooded setting. What you lose in wilderness you gain in kid-friendly amenities like an outdoor pool, basketball courts, and recreational room.

### Food

For a town on the edge of a national park that presumably gets a fair amount of tourist traffic, Munising has surprisingly little in the way of dining. Try **Sydney's,** on M-28 downtown, 906/387-4067, for fresh whitefish and lake trout, as well as steaks and a Friday seafood buffet, served with an Australian touch. **Muldoon's Pasties,** 1246 West M-28, 906/387-5880, is the best spot in town for a fresh, authentic taste of this pot-pie-type meal, a U.P. classic. If you're willing to take a little drive, one of the better restaurants in the Upper Peninsula is about 15 miles west in Au Train. Along the curve of Lake Superior's Au Train Bay on M-28, the **Brownstone Inn,** 906/892-8332, serves up original and ever-changing dishes, including delicious versions of the ubiquitous Lake Superior whitefish. Good vegetarian options and an excellent Friday night fish fry, too.

© TRAVEL MICHIGAN

**Munising Falls**

## OUTSIDE OF TOWN

### Waterfalls

The Munising area is thick with waterfalls, and many are easy to reach. (There also are plenty that are difficult to reach, but well worth it, like Rock River Falls in the Rock River Canyon Wilderness—see below.) The **Munising Visitors Bureau,** 422 E. Munising Ave., 906/387-2138, prints a waterfall map that will direct you to most of them. Nearby Pictured Rocks National Lakeshore also has several notable falls.

The Tannery Creek spills over **Memorial Falls** and **Olson Falls** just on the northeast edge of town. Follow H-58 (Washington Street) northeast out of town, and watch for a small wooden staircase on the right side of the road, across from the road to Sand Point and the National Park Service headquarters. (If you've come by car, note that you can't park alongside the road here.) Climb the stairs and follow the trail through a small canyon to Tannery Falls. To reach Memo-

rial Falls, it's easiest to return to H-58, turn right on Nestor St., and follow the signs.

Right on the outskirts of town, M-28 east leads to **Horseshoe Falls** (turn east on Prospect Street) and **Alger Falls,** which spills down along the highway. The impressive **Wagner Falls** is right in the same area, just off M-94 near the junction of M-94 and M-28. It's a well-marked spot, operated by the state park system as a scenic site. Though it feels secluded, 20-foot Wagner Falls is just a few minutes' walk from the parking area. Continue up the streamside trail past the main falls to a second cascade. About 20 miles west of Munising, wonderful **Laughing Whitefish Falls** has also been protected as a state park scenic site. Here, water plunges 30 feet over hard dolomite rock ledges, then continues rolling and frothing at least twice that far to the bottom of a gorge. To reach Laughing Whitefish Falls, follow M-94 west from Munising to Sundell, then go north on Dorsey Road for 2.5 miles.

### Hiawatha National Forest

A huge swath of the massive 860,000-acre Hiawatha National Forest sprawls out to the south of Munising, stretching all the way to Lake Michigan. It offers almost endless opportunities for hiking, mountain biking, and camping. Your best bet for gathering information is the **Hiawatha National Forest Visitors Center,** 906/387-3700, which shares a building and staff with the Pictured Rocks National Lakeshore at 400 E. Munising Ave., Munising, MI 49862.

Another option for exploring this vast area is to hook up with an outfitter like **Great Northern Adventures** in Marquette, 906/225-TOUR. Along with an established roster of hiking, paddling, and mountain biking trips in the Marquette and Munising areas, owner Rah Trost can also suggest and customize trips to a number of destinations within the national forest.

One of Trost's favorite spots is the **Rock River Canyon Wilderness Area.** In this undisturbed corner of the national forest about 12 miles west of Munising, the Rock River and Silver Creek have carved deep crevices in the sandstone, forming dark and narrow canyons. Adding to the area's wild beauty is **Rock River Falls,** which pours 20 feet over a sandstone ledge. Though there are few developed hiking trails in the area, you can make your way along old logging roads and railroad grades. The canyons themselves require some scrambling for the adventurous. If you plan to explore the area, be sure to bring a compass and topo map; maps are available from the visitors center (see address above). To reach the wilderness area, take M-28 west from Munising. About five miles west of Au Train, watch for Rock River Road on your left (also called H01). Follow it to Forest Road 2276 and turn right (west). Within four miles, you'll arrive at Forest Road 2293; turn south and travel another three-quarters of a mile to a small parking area; a short trail leads down to the canyon and falls.

## GRAND ISLAND NATIONAL RECREATION AREA

Though it's just a 10-minute ferry ride from Munising, the surrounding Lake Superior waters effectively isolate Grand Island. Owned since 1901 by the Cleveland Cliffs Iron Co., the 13,000-acre, largely wooded island was maintained for decades as a private hunting playground for the firm's executives and stockholders. In 1989, the Hiawatha National Forest purchased all but 40 acres of Grand Island and proclaimed it a national recreation area. Except for those few patches of private property, you have the entire island—roughly the size of Manhattan—for hiking, beachcombing, mountain biking, and camping.

With its status as a national recreation area, Grand Island will likely see more development than the rest of the Hiawatha National Forest. Since 1989, the Forest Service has generated mountains of paperwork developing various management plans and putting them out for public comment. Ideas range from leaving the island in its natural state to developing roads, lodges, and other visitor amenities.

So far, a few compromises have been reached. Autos are not allowed on the island except with special permission or those rare few owned by island landholders. Van tours now operate under special permit, bumping along few dirt roads on

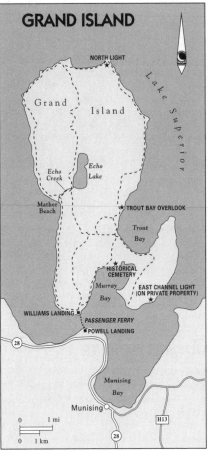

the island's southern half. ATVs are allowed Oct. 1–April 15; mountain bikes are permitted anytime on all public-land trails. Pets are allowed on leash. Note that drinking water is not available anywhere on the island. There is a $2 daily user fee for visiting the island, collected by the ferry service. For more information, contact the Hiawatha National Forest, Munising Ranger District, 400 E. Munising Ave., 906/387-3700, website: www.fs.fed.us/r9/hiawatha/grand.htm.

### Exploring Grand Island

About 50 miles of trails crisscross Grand Island, mostly old roadbeds. If you're just visiting for a day, a mountain bike is the only way you'll have time to see the entire island: it's about a 23-mile trip around the perimeter. In fact, it's probably one of the best mountain bike routes in the U.P. for the nontechnical rider, with wide grassy paths cutting through hardwood forests, passing under towering pines, shinnying up against Lake Superior shorelines, and rewarding you with grand views of wilderness bays and the distant Pictured Rocks.

Both hikers and bikers can reach **Murray Bay,** about two miles from the ferry dock at the southern end of the island. Murray Bay has a nice day-use area and sand beach nestled in a grove of pines. There also are two campsites here, but the location near the ferry dock means you'll have less privacy than elsewhere on the island.

Don't miss the nearby **historic cemetery,** where you can pick up a little history and examine the gravestones of various shipwreck victims and the island's first white settlers. Grand Island had long been a summering ground for the Ojibwa when Abraham Williams arrived in the 1840s to establish a trading post. He raised a family and died on the island in 1873 at the rather amazing age of 81. Today, only the descendants of Williams and their spouses can be buried here.

North of Murray Bay, the island sprouts a tombolo off its southeastern corner known as "the thumb." This landmass wraps north and forms **Trout Bay,** a lovely spot ringed with honey-hued beaches and sandstone cliffs. Watch for the low profile of loons bobbing in calm waters. Trout Bay is home to the island's four other developed campsites, and you could camp a long time before finding another site this pretty.

Most of the island's private property is on the thumb, including the unique **East Channel Light,** an 1867 wooden lighthouse made of hand-hewn timbers. Sadly, the light has deteriorated badly from vandalism and neglect. Its piecemeal ownership—some 20 landholders own a piece of the lighthouse—leaves its future uncertain. Note that you cannot visit the lighthouse by land, since it's surrounded by private property. You can view it at a distance from Sand Point

on the mainland, near the western end of Pictured Rocks National Lakeshore.

Farther north, the island's most interesting trails follow the eastern and western shorelines. The **eastern shore** climbs high above lake level, offering occasional outstanding views of Pictured Rocks and the Grand Sable Dunes. The **western shore** provides ample opportunities to reach the fine sand beaches that line much of this side of the island. The island's interior trails are largely wooded and somewhat less interesting, unless you're hoping to glimpse a black bear—they're plentiful here.

**Echo Lake** lies near the center of Grand Island. Though it offers great bass and northern fishing for anyone with a Michigan fishing license, access can be a little tricky, since it is largely ringed with marshy grasses. The remote northern end of the island is perhaps its most outstanding parcel, with high cliffs, creeks, and untouched beaches. In recent years, peregrine falcons have nested nearby. On North Point, the **North Light** has just a 25-foot tower, but since it rises up from a 175-foot cliff, it earns the honor as the highest lighthouse above sea level. The 1867 building is now a well-cared-for summer residence; please respect the owner's privacy and stay off the property.

## Van Tours

Altran Bus Service offers two- to three-hour van tours of Grand Island, from June through early October. The tour makes six stops on the southern end of the island, including Echo Lake, the Trout Bay Overlook, and Mather Beach, an excellent swimming beach where Echo Creek empties into Lake Superior. Unless you have limited mobility, though, outdoor types likely will grow frustrated with the amount of time spent inside a vehicle. Tours cost $16 for adults, $8 for children, including the ferry fee (but not the $2 recreation area user fee). For schedule information, contact Altran Bus Service, 906/387-4845.

## Camping

There are no reservations, fees, or permits required for camping on Grand Island. The island has two designated campgrounds at Murray Bay (two sites) and Trout Bay (four sites), offering the relative luxury of pit toilets and fire rings. Backcountry camping is permitted throughout the island as long as you stay off the tombolo, off private property and at least 100 feet away from lakes, streams, cliffs, trails, roads, and natural research areas. No ground fires permitted. And remember, there is no drinking water anywhere on the island, so come prepared.

### Getting There

A **passenger ferry** travels from Munising to Grand Island daily Memorial Day weekend–early October. The cost is $10 adults, $5 children, under age five free. There's a $3 additional charge for bicycles. Call 906/387-3503 for a current schedule. The ferry's departure point is about two miles west of downtown near Powell Point. Follow M-28 west and watch for the signs. Even if you're planning a just a day trip, you'd be wise to pack some warm clothing and a method for purifying water. Rough weather can cancel ferry service at any time; similarly, probably more than one hiker or biker has lost track of time and missed the last ferry. There is a ship-to-shore radio at Williams Landing in the event of an emergency.

**Private boats** may be pulled ashore at Williams Landing and Trout Bay, and moored offshore in Murray Bay and Trout Bay. Paddlers in particular will enjoy Trout Bay, which features some sea caves along its eastern shore and interesting paddling around the thumb. It's a full two-day paddle around the entire island—a trip you'll long remember. It's an outstanding way to experience an outstanding parcel of the Upper Peninsula.

## ALGER UNDERWATER PRESERVE

When loggers were felling the vast stands of pine across the central Upper Peninsula in the 1800s, Munising grew into a busy port, with schooners carrying loads of timber to the growing cities of the southern Great Lakes and iron ore to an ever-growing number of factories. Yet the narrow and shoaly passage between the mainland and Grand Island, and along the Pictured Rocks shoreline, was the downfall of many ships; their skeletons litter the lake floor here.

The Alger Underwater Preserve covers 113 square miles, from just west of Grand Island to

diving in Alger Underwater Preserve

Au Sable Point near the east end of Pictured Rocks National Lakeshore. Nearly a dozen ships lie here, well preserved in Lake Superior's cold, fresh water. Some wrecks, like the 19th-century *Bermuda* and the 145-foot *Smith Moore,* lie upright and nearly intact. The Alger Underwater Preserve marks many of the dive sites with buoys and helps ensure that they will be protected from poachers—it's a felony to remove or disturb artifacts within any Great Lakes underwater preserve.

## Diving

Several factors combine to make the Alger Underwater Preserve one of the finest sport diving locations in the Midwest: there are several wrecks concentrated in one area; the cold, fresh water keeps them from deteriorating; many wrecks are in very shallow water, as little as 20 feet deep; visibility is excellent, usually a minimum of 25 feet and sometimes twice that; and Grand Island helps moderate the cold water temperatures. "It's one of the best wreck diving sites for beginners that I can imagine," notes Pete Lindquist, who operates a dive charter in Munising.

Just offshore from the Munising High School, an **underwater museum** among dock ruins includes underwater signs that interpret large maritime artifacts. The Alger Underwater Preserve also attracts divers for its **sea caves** in about 20 feet of water, where sandstone cliffs have been eroded by wave action.

*If you do just one thing in the Munising area, make it this marvelous two-hour glass-bottom boat tour. Pete Lindquist, an experienced local who also operates a dive charter, came up with the idea of installing viewing wells in the hulls of a couple of tour boats, so even nondivers can marvel at the area's shallow-water shipwrecks.*

To arrange a dive charter, contact Lindquist's **Shipwreck Dive Tours,** 1204 Commercial St. in Munising, 906/387-4477.

## Glass-Bottom Boat Shipwreck Tours

If you do just one thing in the Munising area, make it this marvelous two-hour tour. Pete Lindquist, an experienced local who also operates a dive charter, came up with the idea of installing viewing wells in the hulls of a couple of tour boats, so even nondivers can marvel at the area's shallow-water shipwrecks.

The view through the 8- to 10-foot-long windows is truly remarkable. The boat glides directly over shipwrecks, some in as little as 28 feet of water. They fill the viewing windows like historic paintings, perfectly visible in the clear water and looking close enough to touch. On the *Bermuda,* you can easily make out deck lines, hatches, even piles of iron ore lying on the deck. Weather permitting, the tour visits three shipwrecks, dating from 1860 to 1926. Along the way, Lindquist's knowledgeable crew also shares history and points out features (including the wooden East Channel Light) along the shore of Grand Island. Tours $20 adults, $8.50 12 and under, operate June–Sept. Reservations recommended. Contact Grand Island Shipwreck Tours, 1204 Commercial St. in Munising, 906/387-4477, website: www.shipwrecktours.com.

# Pictured Rocks National Lakeshore

Lake Superior takes center stage at this national park, just three miles wide but stretching 40 miles along this magnificent lake from Munising to Grand Marais. Pictured Rocks derives its name from the sandstone bluffs that rise 200 feet directly up from the water's surface, washed in shades of pink, red, and green from the mineral-rich water that seeps from the rock. These famous bluffs stretch for more than 15 miles, in places sculpted into crazy castle-like turrets, caves, and arches. The national lakeshore also features a lesser known, but equally spectacular, stretch of shoreline called the Grand Sable Banks, where 200-foot sand dunes are hemmed by a 12-mile ribbon of sand and pebble beach. If that's not enough, you'll also find lakes, forest trails, waterfalls, a lighthouse, and other historic attractions—enough to put Pictured Rocks at the top of the list for anyone visiting the Upper Peninsula.

For general information, contact the National Lakeshore at 906/387-3700, website: www.nps.gov/piro. Pictured Rocks also operates two visitors centers; see Practicalities at the end of this section.

Miners Castle

## MUNISING TO BEAVER LAKE
### Pictured Rocks from the Water

To really see the namesake bluffs, you need to get out on the water. **Pictured Rocks Boat Cruises** offers three-hour trips up the shoreline from Munising, practically sidling up close enough to touch the rock formations. It gives you the perspective you need to appreciate turreted shapes like Miners Castle. Though trips are offered up to seven times a day, plan for a late-afternoon cruise, when the sinking sun shows off the multicolored sandstone in its best light. The boats operate from the Friday before Memorial Day through mid-October, weather permitting, and depart from the Munising City Pier. Rates are $24 adults, $10 for children 6–12, under five free. For more information, contact Pictured Rocks Cruises, 906/387-2379, website: www.picturedrocks.com.

For paddlers, an even better alternative is a **sea kayak.** You avoid somewhat cheesy narration and really experience the grandeur of this shoreline. Safety warnings cannot be overemphasized, however. Only experienced paddlers should venture out on their own, and only in a closed cockpit (i.e., no canoes) and after scrupulously monitoring weather conditions. Paddlers can get themselves into serious trouble along Pictured Rocks, caught in sudden summer squalls along the 15-mile rock wall with nowhere to hide. Having said that, sea kayaking along Pictured Rocks ranks as one of the finest paddles on all the Great Lakes.

If you're unsure of your abilities, hook up with **Northern Waters,** 1200 Commercial Street, Munising, 906/387-2323, website: www.northernwaters.com. The company offers outstanding day-long guided trips ($85 adult, $65 age 16 and under), ferrying guests and boats to a departure point at Miners Castle. Beginners are welcome, since the day includes some basic instruction and you'll be traveling with an experienced guide.

© RAYMOND J. MALACE

## PICTURED ROCKS NATIONAL LAKESHORE

H58

WOODLAND PARK △
Sable Falls ⚲
Grand Marais
GRAND SABLE VISITOR CENTER (SUMMER ONLY) ■
Grand Sable Banks
Grand Sable Lake
77
LOG SLIDE OVERLOOK ★
Au Sable Point ★
Grand Sable Dunes
AU SABLE LIGHT STATION
HURRICANE RIVER △
Hurricane River

*Lake Superior State Forest*

TWELVEMILE BEACH △

*Alger*

*Underwater*
Twelvemile
Beach

△ KINGSTON LAKE

Lakeshore Trail

H58

*Preserve*
Beaver Beach
Lake
Little Beaver Lake
LITTLE BEAVER LAKE △
Spray Falls ⚲ ⟍Spray Creek
Chapel Beach
Grand Portal Point
Chapel Lake
Chapel Falls
CHAPEL ROAD
Mosquito River
Melstrand

Mosquito Falls ⚲

*Lake Superior State Forest*

*Alger Underwater Preserve*
Miners Castle
Miners Falls
MINERS CASTLE ROAD
Miners Creek
H58
28

Grand Island
Sand Point
■ NATIONAL LAKESHORE HEADQUARTERS
28

Munising Falls ⚲
Munising ●
Bay
■ MUNISING FALLS INTERPRETIVE CENTER
■ MUNISING INFORMATION CENTER
Munising
⚲ Alger Falls

28

0        4 mi
0        4 km
94

*Hiawatha National Forest*

© AVALON TRAVEL PUBLISHING, INC.

N
THE CENTRAL U.P.

Kayak rentals (and longer trips to Grand Island and Isle Royale) are also available. **Great Northern Adventures** of Marquette, 906/225-TOUR, website: www .greatnorthern adventures.com, also offers guided paddling trips, from one-day excursions along Pictured Rocks ($85) to multi-day trips that combine kayaking with hiking and mountain biking on nearby Grand Island.

## Munising Falls Area

Just inside the park's western boundary, a short trail leads to 50-foot Munising Falls, which spills into a narrow gorge before emptying into Lake Superior's Munising Bay. The highlight of this spot used to be the trail that led hikers behind the falls, but erosion problems prompted its closure. It's still worth a stop here, though, for the falls and the adjacent **interpretive center,** which offers a glimpse of this peaceful area's history, home to a belching pig iron furnace in the 1860s. Munising Falls also marks the west trailhead for the **Lakeshore Trail,** a 43-mile segment of the North Country Trail that spans seven states from New York to North Dakota. The Lakeshore Trail runs the length of the Pictured Rocks National Lakeshore—predictably, never far from the water's edge. The park's eastern trailhead lies near Sable Falls.

Past Munising Falls, the paved access road ends at **Sand Point,** home of the national lakeshore headquarters. While the headquarters primarily houses offices (not visitor services), it displays some interesting Coast Guard and shipwreck artifacts on its grounds. Sand Point has a small beach and a boat ramp, a good spot to launch a small craft for exploring nearby Grand Island.

## Miners Castle

For whatever reason, we love to attach manmade descriptions to natural creations. Thus, the sandstone cliffs five miles northeast of Munising Falls are known as Miners Castle, for the turretlike shapes caused by wind and wave erosion. The nine-story-high rock formation is impressive and ranks as one of the park's most popular attractions. Boardwalks and steps lead you to two viewing platforms out on the rock, where you can peer down into the gloriously clear waters of Lake Superior. If that entices you to do a little beachcombing and wading, a nearby trail leads down some steps through the pines to inviting **Miners Beach.**

To reach Miners Castle, follow H-58 east from Munising to the well-marked turnoff for Miners Castle Road. Before you reach the Miners Castle formation itself, you'll see another sign on Miners Castle Road directing you to Miners Falls. It's a one-mile walk to this pleasant falls, where Miners Creek tumbles 40 feet over a rocky escarpment.

## Chapel Basin Area

Continuing northeast on H-58, the next auto-accessible route into the heart of the park is at Melstrand, where the gravel/dirt Chapel Road bumps six miles toward the shore and another park highlight, the Chapel Basin area. Park your car here and you'll find plenty to entertain you during a long day hike or a weekend: three waterfalls, a deep inland lake, Superior beaches, and a good loop hiking trail.

Chapel Falls is the key attraction, as evidenced by the wide paved pathway that leads 1.5 miles to the falls. Amid a pale birch forest, frothing water drops like a horsetail some 90 feet into a deep gorge and Chapel Lake below. Continue past the falls to reach Chapel Beach in another 1.75 miles, where you'll find a backcountry campground. From here, you can turn right to Chapel Rock and follow the Lakeshore

Trail 1.5 miles to Spray Falls, one of the least visited and loveliest waterfalls in the park, where Spray Creek drops over the sandstone cliffs right into Lake Superior.

If you turn left instead of right at Chapel Beach, you can make a 10-mile loop around Chapel Basin. Along the way, you'll pass Grand Portal Point—another significant Pictured Rocks landmark—before returning to the parking area. Don't leave Chapel Basin without a visit to Mosquito Falls, a little farther inland off Chapel Road. The Mosquito River spills over a series of ledges, creating an accessible and calm enough waterfall for wading and soaking fatigued hiking feet. A trail leads to various sections of the falls and links up with the Lakeshore Trail.

## Beaver Lake

Located near the center of the park, 800-acre Beaver Lake is the largest inland lake in Pictured Rocks. Anglers are drawn to the lake and the tributaries that feed it, especially for trout. Little Beaver Lake, connected by a small channel, has a boat launch. Boats are limited to 10 hp or less, making this a pleasant waterway for paddlers. Little Beaver has one of the park's three auto-accessible campgrounds, with eight sites available on a first-come, first-served basis. Be aware that wetlands cover much of the land between Beaver Lake and Lake Superior, so bugs can be a problem here especially in June and early July.

Two good hiking trails leave from the campground. The short and pleasant 0.7-mile **White Pine Trail** is a self-guided nature trail that circles through a 300-year-old pine forest. The five-mile **Beaver Basin Loop Trail** makes a lap around Little Beaver and Big Beaver Lakes, then follows the Lake Superior shore past sea caves cut by the lake's pounding waves. Boardwalks skirt the wetlands before returning you to the trailhead.

# BEAVER BASIN TO GRAND MARAIS
## Lake Superior State Forest

Traveling east from Beaver Basin, several dirt roads spiral south off the H-58 into the woods.

These lead into the Lake Superior State Forest, part of the "buffer zone" protecting Pictured Rocks. They offer plenty of inland lakes, hiking and biking trails, and rustic campgrounds, and are largely ignored by the summer visitors to the national lakeshore. For more information on the state forest, contact the Michigan Department of Natural Resources, P. O. Box 30028, Lansing, MI 48909, 517/373-1275. Topo maps ($4) of the area are available at the visitors center in Munising.

## Twelvemile Beach

An icon near the Twelvemile Beach campground says it all: indicating that this is a permitted beach area, it shows a swimmer not in the usual "crawl" position, but with water lapping at the ankles. In other words, the water here is damn *cold*. Swim if you dare, but wading is really more realistic.

Which is what keeps Twelvemile Beach the pristine, stunning ribbon of sand that it is. After all, if such a perfect beach boasted 75° water, it would be overrun with boomboxes, jet skis, and zinc oxide. Instead, it's a beach where you can stroll for hours with only the company of peregrine falcons, bald eagles, deer wandering down for a drink, even the occasional black bear snorting around in the sand.

The **Twelvemile Beach campground** is easy to reach, just a short drive off H-58 through a pretty birch forest. Many of the 37 campsites string out along a bluff over the beach—come midweek (or early on Saturday, often a turnover day) for one of the choice spots. Some are larger than the average house lot and undoubtedly have a better view. Well-placed stairs deposit campers and picnickers at lake level. The campground also has a nice **day-use area** at its east end.

Just about five miles farther up the beach (or H-58) lies the auto-accessible **Hurricane River campground,** where the Hurricane River spills into Lake Superior. This is also an exceptionally scenic campground, with 21 sites and a good location near the water and Au Sable Point.

## Au Sable Point

It's a 1.5-mile walk along the Lakeshore Trail from the Hurricane River campground to the

**Au Sable Light Station** at Au Sable Point. Built in 1874, the 87-foot brick light and its keepers did yeoman's duty for decades—warning ships away from the rock shoals that extend out for nearly a mile and create shallows of just six to 30 feet. Nonetheless, at least 10 steamers were wrecked here. As you walk the trail from the campground, look for parts of the **shipwrecks** just offshore, often poking out of the sand bottom and easily visible in the gin-clear water. The light was automated in 1958.

Several restoration projects are currently underway at the lighthouse, including renovating the lightkeeper's quarters and installing a photovoltaic (solar power) system to power the site. Once work is completed in Summer 2002, free tours of the light station will resume in high season, probably July and August.

## Grand Sable Dunes

Just east of Au Sable Point, the **Log Slide Overlook** marks the spot of a once-busy logging operation. In the late 1800s, loggers used this high point—some 300 feet above Lake Superior—to send freshly cut logs down to the water's edge where they were loaded on Great Lakes schooners. Today, you can stand on a platform and simply marvel at the view, with the lighthouse to your left, the great dunes to your right, and the brilliant blue of the big lake filling the horizon. If you're in the mood for some exercise, the two-mile stretch of the **North Country Trail** from the Log Slide to the Au Sable Light Station is one of the park's most scenic hikes.

The **Grand Sable Banks and Dunes** (*grand sable* is French for "big sands") stretch for nearly five miles from the overlook, glacial banks of gravel supporting the huge mounds of sand. They are magnificent when viewed from a distance, glowing gold and rising up abruptly from the cobalt waters of Lake Superior. In many areas, especially near the overlook, the dunes are free of grasses and plants, so you can play around on them without fear of damaging fragile plant life or causing erosion. Though park officials discourage it for safety reasons, no one will stop you from flopping on your butt and rocketing down the slope.

Be aware, though, that the climb back up takes a lot longer!

Most people, however, choose to explore the dunes from the eastern end. Near the Grand Sable Visitors Center, a trail winds across the top of the dunes, where marram grass, beach pea, and sand cherry cling to the sand for dear life. (Be careful to stay on the trail here.) Interpretive signs discuss the plants' tenuous hold on the environment. The trail to **Sable Falls** also leaves from the visitors center, a half-mile walk largely composed of steps. As you work your way downhill, you'll be treated to several views of this exceptionally pretty falls, which drops in tiers through a narrow canyon and out to a rocky Lake Superior beach. Across H-58, the sandy shores and often warm waters of **Grand Sable Lake** make this a wonderful spot for a swim or picnic.

## Grand Marais

Though not part of Pictured Rocks National Lakeshore, sweet little Grand Marais marks the park's western boundary and is an excellent jumping-off point for a visit to the national lakeshore. This sleepy New Englandy village is worth a visit of its own for its simple windswept beauty. With an outstanding natural harbor—rather rare on Lake Superior's southern shore—Grand Marais was originally settled by fishermen. Loggers soon followed, when sawmills were built here in the 1860s and 1870s to handle the logging that went on just south of here.

Today, commercial fishing remains an economic factor (though an increasingly difficult way to make a living), but a little bit of tourism is what keeps the town slowly ticking along. The downtown huddles around the harbor, which, incidentally is a good spot for kayakers to play in the surf on a north to east wind. The few stores here offer some arts-and-crafts shops and a handful of clean, inexpensive motels and restaurants. **Alverson Motel,** 906/494-2681, has large rooms, each with a view of the water. A block east of H-77 on Randolph, it's within walking distance to everything in town. Rates $50–75. East of H-77 on Wilson Street, **Voyageur's Motel,** 906/494-2389, sits atop a ridge overlooking Grand Marais Harbor. Nice new rooms with

mini-fridge and sauna/whirlpool facility make this a good choice. Rates $50–100.

Grand Marais has a couple of good finds in the food department, both right downtown on H-77. The **Sportsman's Restaurant** 906/494-2671, is more distinctive than its name suggests, with good fish dishes, salads, and homemade soups, as well as plenty of burgers and steaks. Visit for breakfast, too—how many places can you find "two eggs and pan-fried whitefish" on the menu? Down the street, **Lake Superior Brewing Company,** 906/494-BEER, does the microbrewery tradition proud, with homemade brews like Sandstone Pale Ale and Granite Brown, as well as sandwiches, soups, and great homemade pizzas. For a summer treat, stop in the time-warpy **Superior Hotel** on the corner of Lake and Randolph, where a soda fountain still sells phosphates and penny candy. For fresh and smoked fish, head two miles east of town to **Bugg's Fish Market.** You can't do better for a Lake Superior beach picnic.

Follow the bay around to its western point to reach the pier (popular with anglers) and a small volunteer-run **maritime museum,** 906/494-2660, in the former Coast Guard Station. Hours vary, so call ahead. The adjacent Lake Superior shoreline offers a nice sand-and-pebble beach, sometimes closed if endangered piping plovers are nesting. Rockhounds should continue west along the beach, past the Woodland Park city campground, to reach a good spot for **hunting agates.** With an excellent location just outside the national lakeshore boundary, **Woodland Park** has more than 100 sites; opt for the more secluded ones that require you to hoof it up the beach a bit. Open May 15–Oct. 15.

## PRACTICALITIES

Pictured Rocks' tourist season is short—most of the park's 300,000 or so visitors come in July and August when they're most likely to enjoy summerlike weather and daytime temperatures in the 70s. Visit in June and you'll share the park with fewer people, but the black flies and mosquitoes often aren't worth the trade-off. May and September may be the park's finest months.

No matter when you go, pack plenty of warm clothing along with the shorts. Even at the height of summer, evenings are almost always cool, dipping into the 50s. And the giant refrigerator of Lake Superior—where the water temperature rarely climbs out of the 40s—can put a chill in the air near the shoreline. In fact, a Lake Superior beach on a sweltering August afternoon may just be the most refreshing place on earth.

## Information

You'll find visitors centers at both ends of the national lakeshore—one in Munising, the other inside the park at the Grand Sable Dunes, just a few miles from Grand Marais. Be sure to stop at one of these centers before beginning your trip—they have rangers on duty, and very good maps (at the very least, pick up a free general park map), displays, and historical information that will enhance your visit. Both have small but very good bookstores, too. The **Munising Information Center,** serving both the Pictured Rocks National Lakeshore and the Hiawatha National Forest, 906/387-3700, is open year-round, daily in "peak season" (which seems to change from year to year) 8 A.M.–6 P.M., otherwise Mon.–Sat. 9 A.M.–5 P.M. It's located at 400 E. Munising Ave. in Munising. The **Grand Sable Visitors Center,** 906/494-2660, is open from mid-May to mid-October only, 9 A.M.–6 P.M.

## Getting There

H-58 provides access to the park, winding roughly along the park's southern boundary and linking Munising and Grand Marais. A large stretch of the road—from Beaver Lake to the Grand Sable Dunes—is unpaved and can deteriorate into washboard rough enough to jar your dental work loose. Leave the '55 T-bird at home and plan your time accordingly—it's about a 90-minute trip from one end to the other.

As a linear park, Pictured Rocks perennially struggles with auto accessibility versus invasiveness. There have been stop-and-start discussions for decades about a "Beaver Basin Rim Road" that would weave through the park nearer Lake Superior, offering easier auto access to park attractions but undeniably changing the spirit and peace of largely road-free preserve. For now, consider a superb compromise: the **Altran Shuttle,** a county bus that makes regular runs three times a week during the high season to Munising Falls and Grand Marais, and will drop off hikers at any point along H-58. It's the perfect way for backpackers to enjoy the park without contributing to the growing vehicle problem. Call Altran, 906/387-4845, for updated schedules, rates, or to make a reservation. Call at least a day in advance to book a spot.

## Camping

Having made the case for leaving the car behind, you should also know that Pictured Rocks has three auto-accessible campgrounds—Beaver Lake, Twelvemile Beach, and Hurricane River—with water and pit toilets. No reservations are accepted, and fees are $10 per night. **Backcountry camping** is permitted only at designated hike-in sites, mostly along the Lakeshore Trail. A $15 permit is required, good for one to six campers, and for any number of nights. Most sites do not have water or toilets. Camping is also available in Munising, Grand Marais, and the Lake Superior State Forest, which borders Pictured Rocks to the south.

# Seney and Vicinity

*The train went up the track and out of sight, around one of the hills of burnt timber. Nick sat down on the bundle of canvas and bedding the baggage man had pitched out of the door of the baggage car. There was no town, nothing but the rails and the burnt-over country. The thirteen saloons that had once lined the one street of Seney had not left a trace.*

—Ernest Hemingway,
"Big Two-Hearted River"

Well, not exactly. Seney still exists, a small dot on the map at the crossroads of M-77 and M-28. But by the time Hemingway—rather, his Nick Adams character—was tramping through the central U.P., the town of Seney was indeed just a shadow of its former self.

"Helltown in the Pine!" loggers once called it, the new center of a logging trade that had crept northward into the U.P. after depleting the lucrative stands of red and white pine in the northern Lower Peninsula. Seney was the center of action in the 1880s, both in and out of the woods. Situated along a railroad siding and the shores of the Fox River—used to transport the logs—it became an important transit point. Turns out, the local economy also revolved around drinking, whoring, and gambling. Seney didn't lack for local color: legendary (and mythical?) characters included P. K. "Snap Jaw" Small, who entertained barroom crowds and earned drinks by biting the heads off live toads and birds, and "Protestant" Bob McGuire, who sharpened his thumbnails into miniature bowie knives. Seney was sensationalized in the national press, right along with Tombstone and other wild towns in the Wild West.

Problem was, Seney never had the huge fertile forests so common elsewhere in Michigan. Glaciers scrubbed this swath of the central U.P. flat, creating a patchwork of rivers, wetlands, and rocky, sandy soil. The red and white pines that

did grow here were leveled in just a few short years; soon loggers were settling for the less valuable hardwoods and small conifers, burning the scrub as they went. Shortly after the turn of the century they moved on, leaving behind the denuded land and vast "stump prairies."

Optimistic farmers followed the quickly departed loggers. They burned the brush and went to great lengths to drain the wetlands, digging miles of 20-foot ditches. Yet their hopes were quickly buried by the area's poor soils and they, too, departed almost as quickly as they came. But the fires had a more lasting effect, scarring the fragile soil deeply.

Finally, humans are trying to help instead of harm this beleaguered land. The immense Seney National Wildlife Refuge now manages and protects 150 square miles immediately west of M-77, restoring the wetlands with an intricate series of dikes and control ponds in what began as a Civilian Conservation Corps project in the 1930s. Today it serves as an important sanctuary and nesting place for a rich variety of waterfowl.

The area's rivers remain a wonderful resource, too—the Fox, the Manistique, and the Driggs all twist through the land, along with countless creeks and lesser branches. Henry Ford, Calvin Coolidge, and Ernest Hemingway fished these legendary trout waters, as anglers continue to do today. Here, too, Hemingway used a little literary license: it was really the Fox that he so eloquently chronicled in his Nick Adams stories—he merely borrowed the name of the more romantic sounding Big Two-Hearted River, which flows just east of here.

## SENEY NATIONAL WILDLIFE REFUGE

The Seney National Wildlife Refuge occupies a huge swath of land west of M-77 and south of M-28. It is an intensely managed 95,000-acre parcel, with dikes and control structures used to artificially raise and lower the water levels in 21 major pools, thus simulating a natural wetlands cycle.

The system impounds more than 7,000 acres of water in these pools, and natural wetlands sprawl beyond that. While humans on foot or bicycle can access much of this preserve via an extensive network of maintenance roads, the refuge offers true refuge and plenty of seclusion for its inhabitants. More than 200 species of birds and nearly 50 species of mammals have been recorded here, including bald eagles, trumpeter swans, loons, even the occasional—though not likely to be spotted—moose or wolf. Whether you're a dedicated and experienced birder or a casual observer, Seney is a wonderful place to get in and among a fascinating array of wildlife.

For information, contact Seney National Wildlife Refuge, HCR 2, Box 1, Seney, MI 49883, 906/586-9851.

## Visitors Center and Marshland Drive

Start your visit at the excellent National Wildlife Refuge Visitors Center, five miles south of the town of Seney on M-77. A 15-minute audiovisual program, very good displays, and printed materials give you a good overview of what you can expect (or at least look for) in the refuge. Some of the handouts will increase your chances of spotting bird life, pinpointing things like eagle nests and ponds frequented by loons. Sightings are often best in early morning and evening. The center is open May 15–Oct. 15 daily 9 A.M.–5 P.M.

The **Pine Ridge Nature Trail** departs from the visitors center and allows for a quick 1.4-mile foray into wetland habitat. The self-guided trail circles a pool, and a stretch of boardwalk spans a marshy area.

The one-way **Marshland Wildlife Drive** also departs from the visitors center and forms a seven-mile loop through the refuge, with several interpretive signs placed along the way. The route includes three observation decks, equipped with spotting scopes. You can also borrow binoculars

*Strangmoors, or string bogs, are fingerlike bogs alternating with sand ridges that are relics from ancient beaches. They are typically found only in arctic and subarctic regions, and Seney's bog is one of the southernmost examples in North America.*

from the visitors center. An eagle's nest is visible from the road, as are several pools frequented by herons and swans. Trumpeter swans were hand-raised and released here, and are now seen regularly. Tundra swans also migrate through in spring and fall. An adjacent three-mile **fishing loop** accesses a fishing platform and is also open to autos.

## Hiking/Biking Trails

Many visitors to Seney never get out of their cars and beyond the Marshland Drive, which is a shame. A bicycle is really the way to experience Seney. Bikes are welcome on more than 100 miles of gravel and dirt maintenance roads, which are closed to all motorized traffic except refuge vehicles. Though you won't find any exciting or technical rides—the land is *flat*—a bicycle allows you to cover far more ground than you could hiking and is quiet enough not to spook much of the wildlife. Besides, there's something magical about spinning down a gravel road amid chirping, twittering, and honking, with nothing but waving grasses and glinting ponds surrounding you for miles.

Easy terrain, easy access, and well-marked trails make Seney a great choice for families or less active cyclists. You will want a mountain bike or hybrid bike, since the gravel can be tough to navigate with skinny tires. No off-road riding is permitted in the refuge.

There are three main access points into the refuge. One is at the visitors center on M-77, where trails sprout off the Marshland Drive. Though this area is the most heavily visited, trails here weave between many pools, so riding is interesting, and waterfowl sightings can be particularly good. Note: Loops 1 and 2 are part of the Marshland Drive and are open to motor vehicles.

A second access point is about three miles south of the visitors center, near the Grace Lutheran Church. Turn west at the sign for the Northern Hardwoods cross-country ski area. (This area is called Smith Farm by lo-

## A DYNASTY OF PINE

In the mid-1800s, a young and growing United States suddenly had an insatiable appetite for lumber. Settlers were moving west, into the treeless plains, and needed lumber to build their new towns. Burgeoning cities needed lumber to build more homes and businesses. Railroads needed lumber as they laid mile after mile of track to connect it all.

Michigan's natural resources proved the perfect mix to fuel a hungry nation. Immense white pines and other conifers grew thick and tall across the Upper Peninsula and more than half of the Lower Peninsula. Rivers honeycombed through these vast forests, providing a route to the Great Lakes, which in turn connected the northern wilderness to Chicago, Detroit, and other railroad centers in the south. Mother Nature had created the perfect delivery system for the logging industry.

Around 1850, logging camps began springing up deep in the woods, from the western U.P. to the shores of Lake Huron. Young men streamed north, some of them farm laborers looking for winter wages, others newly arrived immigrants looking to gain a foothold in their new homeland. It was not easy work. The lumberjacks worked by hand, with ax and saw, tree after tree, acre after acre. With a shout of "timber!" the old pines came down with an earth-shaking thud, some of them as much as 20 feet in circumference and 100 feet tall.

The logging camps operated primarily in the winter months, when it was easier to transport the huge logs. With horses and sleighs, workers hauled the logs from the woods to the river's edge, branded the ends with the lumber company's mark, and stacked them there until spring, when they were floated downriver to waiting sawmills on the Great Lakes.

In spring, when the ice melted the colorful and chaotic log drives began. Thousands of logs were shoved into northwoods rivers, guided downstream by daredevil workers known as "river pigs," who danced across the dangerous mass of moving wood, using hooks, poles and sometimes dynamite to dislodge log jams. It was the most dangerous job in the trade; with one misstep, river pigs ended up crushed between tons of logs or trapped underwater.

Once at the mills, the jumble of logs was sorted according to the millowner's mark, and floated into mill storage ponds. From there, buzzing sawmills sliced it into lumber and loaded it onto lumber schooners—and later, barges and steamers—headed primarily to Chicago, the nation's

---

cals.) You'll soon reach a small parking area and gate across the road; the trail begins just a few hundred yards west. This is a more lightly visited area of the refuge. From here, Loop 5 makes a 12.2-mile circle, including a stretch paralleling the Driggs River.

If you stay on the trail that follows the Driggs (rather than swinging back east to complete Loop 5), in about nine miles you'll emerge onto M-28, eight miles west of the town of Seney. This is your third access point, called Driggs River Road. (It is indeed a road for the first mile and a half south of M-28, until it arrives at the refuge boundary.)

### Paddling and Fishing

Paddling is an excellent way to explore the western reaches of the refuge, and it just so happens that the Manistique is a wonderful canoeing river, easily navigable with a sand bottom and just enough twists and turns to keep things interesting. It can be popular at the height of summer, though, so go off-season or early in the day if your goal is solitude and wildlife watching. Put in at the roadside park on M-77 a mile south of Germfask, or arrange a trip through Northland Outfitters (see below). If you've got your own boat, you can opt for the lightly traveled Driggs or Creighton. Both cross M-28 west of Seney. Paddling is not permitted on any refuge pools or marshes.

The refuge allows some fishing within its boundaries; pick up information on its unique regulations at the visitors center. Perch and northern pike are most common. Fishing can be quite

largest lumber market and railroad hub.

In its heyday, the logging industry generated billions of board feet of lumber and billions of dollars, the actual numbers almost incalculable. Lumber companies made all sorts of proclamations: Michigan mills claimed they produced enough lumber to lay an inch-thick plank across the state.

Success stories were everywhere. A sawmill in Hermansville, Michigan, came up with the idea of tongue-and-groove flooring, and quickly became the largest flooring plant in the country, crafting the floors for the Mormon Temple in Salt Lake City and the main lodge in Yellowstone National Park. Timber baron homes were marvels of hand-carved mahogany, gold-leaf inlay, and cut-crystal chandeliers.

But the era that everyone thought would last forever lasted less than 50 years. By 1900, nearly all the big trees were gone, a scorched, denuded landscape of stump prairies left in their place. When farmers were able to convert some of the southernmost pineries into useful crop land, ambitious entrepreneurs sought to do the same in the north. A newspaper publisher in Menominee, Michigan, extolled the virtues of Upper Peninsula cutover land for farming or ranching. "No matter where the first Garden of Eden was located," he proclaimed, "the present one is in the Upper Peninsula."

Thousands of hard-working folks were lured north by the promise of cheap land in exchange for the back-breaking labor of removing pine stumps and tilling soil. But by the late 1920s, their work proved futile. Nearly half the U.P. was tax-delinquent cutover land. Ranches had failed. Most farms had failed. The stock market had crashed, and the nation's economy was in shambles.

The federal government took a different approach. In 1911, it established the first national forests in Michigan and Wisconsin, setting aside land and creating tree nurseries as a first step in reestablishing the Midwest's great forests. The Civilian Conservation Corps, established in 1933, continued the reforestation efforts, planting trees, fighting fires, and slowly nursing the remaining great forests back to health.

Although we can never recreate the magnificent old-growth forests of yesteryear, pines once again stretch skyward across Michigan. Logging continues, too, though with sophisticated forest management and reforestation practices that help ensure the livelihood of the state's important lumber and paper industries. And a few stands of virgin old-growth timber remain, giving us an awe-inspiring glimpse of a lost Michigan landscape.

good on area rivers, especially for bass, northerns, and walleye. You'll need to head for the upper reaches if you're after trout.

**Northland Outfitters,** 906/586-9801, is located on M-77 in Germfask, just south of the refuge entrance. The company rents mountain bikes, camping gear, and canoes and kayaks, and offers paddling trips on the Manistique.

## Strangmoor Bog

One of Seney's most unusual features, Strangmoor Bog lies deep in the wetlands near its western boundary (and not very accessible to visitors). Strangmoors, or string bogs, are fingerlike bogs alternating with sand ridges that are relics from ancient beaches. They are typically found only in arctic and subarctic re-gions, and Seney's bog is one of the southernmost examples in North America.

## IN THE AREA
### Iverson Snowshoe Company

Aluminum snowshoes now dominate the sport, but for beauty and tradition, they simply can't match white-ash-and-rawhide snowshoes. In Shingleton, 25 miles west of Seney on M-28, Anita Hulse and her two sons operate this wonderful factory, where workers hand-shape strips of local ash into those classic snowshoe frames.

Visitors are welcome to visit Iverson Snowshoe, one of just two wooden snowshoe manufacturers left in the country. You can watch workers shave and saw strips of ash, steam them, bend them around a form, and send them to a drying kiln overnight. Finished frames are laced with gummy strips of rawhide, or newer-style neoprene. All of this happens in a small building, and visitors practically lean over the shoulders of the workers.

Iverson manufactures about 11,000 snow-shoes a year, about a third of which go to L. L. Bean. Other customers include REI, the Nor-wegian army, park rangers, and utility work-ers. Iverson also makes rustic chairs and tables by order only. Iverson Snowshoe, 906/452-6370, is open Mon.–Fri. 8 A.M.–3:30 P.M. It doesn't hurt to call ahead if you're interested in a tour. (Groups of more than five or six should definitely call.) To find it, turn north on Maple Street (just west of the stoplight) in Shingleton.

## The Fox River

In 1919, Ernest Hemingway stepped off a train in Seney, asked for directions to a good trout stream, and was directed up an old railroad grade to the east branch of the Fox. Where truth meets fiction we'll never know, but Heming-way's U.P. travels resulted in "Big Two-Hearted River," his Nick Adams tale about fishing what was really the Fox. (The more lyrical Big Two-Hearted actually flows about 25 miles to the northeast.) Consequently, the Fox has always carried a special cachet in the U.P. and among trout fishermen.

Of course, Michigan has dozens of superb **trout fishing** streams, but most anglers seem to agree that the Fox indeed belongs on the A-list. According to Jerry Dennis, author of sever-al Michigan fishing books, it has produced some gargantuan brookies: "The Fox even today has a reputation for brook trout of a size rarely en-countered elsewhere in the United States. Fish fifteen to twenty inches long are taken with fair regularity," he writes. The east branch still is considered the river's prime stretch, partly be-cause it's more difficult to reach. (You can hike in from M-77 north of Seney where it flows just west of the road. A state forest campground eight miles up M-77 from Seney offers public ac-cess.) Many locals simply cast near the bridge

at Seney, where the main river flows under M-28. Because of the Fox's allure, the Department of Natural Resources is considering instituting special fishing regulations; check with authorities before heading out.

The **Fox River Pathway** was no doubt prompted by perennial interest in Hemingway's river. The route stretches 27 miles from Seney north to just shy of Pictured Rocks National Lakeshore, and by U.P. standards, is really noth-ing that special. Its most appealing stretch—es-pecially for anglers looking for fishing access—is the southern end, where the trail parallels the main river for 10 miles. Farther north it follows the Little Fox and the west branch. Heading north, the trail traverses the Kingston Plains, where loggers left behind "stump prairies." Mark-ers along the route provide information about the area's logging history.

Because it passes through a lot of cutover land, the trail can be extremely hot and dry. If you plan to hike it, be sure to carry a water purifica-tion system. You'll find rustic campgrounds at both trailheads, and just one along the route, six miles from the southern end.

For hikers, another option (albeit much short-er) is the trail that heads north from the Fox River Pathway's northern terminus at Kingston Lake Campground. Not considered part of the pathway, this trail winds through pines and hard-woods in the Lake Superior State Forest for four miles before spilling out onto a particularly de-serted and delightful stretch of Twelvemile Beach on Lake Superior, part of the Pictured Rocks National Lakeshore.

## Blaney Park

Blaney Park today is more a historical anecdote than a town, located 10 miles south of Germfask on M-77. Once a turn-of-the-century logging town, the entire townsite and some 30,000 acres of surrounding land were sold to the Earle fam-ily in 1909, who continued to log it until the 1920s. When the lumber ran out, the family converted the land to a rather comprehensive resort, complete with golf course, tennis courts, riding stable, backcountry hunting, and fish-ing, even a private airstrip. A lumber baron's

BOB RACE

the Seul Choix Point Light, built in 1895

fine out-of-the-way relaxation spot, or a good base for day trips to Pictured Rocks National Lakeshore, Seney National Wildlife Refuge, Lake Michigan beaches, and more. You're welcome to explore the inn's grounds, which cover 85 acres and include a small lake, beaver ponds, woods, and meadows. A hoard of hummingbirds frequenting the backyard birdfeeders practically guarantees a wildlife encounter. Rates $50–100, including breakfast. The **Blaney Inn,** is open, too, filled with old photos and resort-era artifacts, and serving up good whitefish, chicken, steaks, and soups. The adjacent **Historic Blaney Lodge Bed and Breakfast,** 906/283-3883, is another Blaney Park lodging option, with rates from $25–75, including breakfast.

## Seul Choix Point Light

Ten miles south of Blaney Park at Gulliver, a road leads you down a point to this 1895 light, a worthwhile detour. Pronounced "sul SHWA"—French for "Only Choice"—it sits at the end of a finger of land that offers boaters the "only choice" for hiding from storms along this stretch of Lake Michigan shoreline. The township of Gulliver has done a splendid job restoring the light and creating a maritime museum in the fog signal building. (It includes an admirable scale model of the lighthouse, made by hand with thousands of miniature bricks.) Climb the tower (small fee/donation) for great views of much of northern Lake Michigan. You have a good chance of seeing ship traffic, since Port Inland, just to the east, is an important commercial port. The lighthouse is open daily Memorial Day weekend–mid-September, 10 A.M.–4 P.M. From US-2 at Gulliver, go southeast on CR-432 about four miles. Turn right on CR-431 (a gravel road) and travel another four miles to the light.

home became a fancy hotel, a boardinghouse became more lodging, and the Blaney Inn was built in the 1930s to supply a grand dining experience, with stone fireplaces, knotty pine paneling, and seating for hundreds. Considering the Great Depression plaguing the nation, it all seemed quite extravagant.

The Blaney Park Resort bustled until the early 1960s, then slowly declined until the land and buildings were eventually auctioned off in 1985. Many folks blame good roads for the resort's demise—it simply became too easy to hopscotch around the U.P., to beaches and waterfalls and sightseeing attractions, rather than settle down in an quiet spot like Blaney Park for a week or more.

But Blaney Park appears to be resurgent. The gracious **Celibeth House Bed & Breakfast,** 906/283-3409, once a lumber baron's home, is a

# The Eastern U.P. and the Straits of Mackinac

Perhaps more than anywhere else in the state, the eastern Upper Peninsula offers up a landscape of remarkable contrasts. The swath of land stretching from Grand Marais east to Whitefish Point remains some of the most inaccessible and lightly traveled in all of the Midwest, a long-ago pine forest reduced to sandy or marshy cutover land by late 19th-century loggers. Travel can be slow-going here, whether on foot or in a vehicle. (Beyond the area's few county and state highways, view any other "roads" as an adventure.) Much of the eastern end of the peninsula will remain undeveloped, too, with

thousands of acres from Lake Superior to Lake Michigan protected as a unit of the Hiawatha National Forest, and hundreds more managed by the Lake Superior State Forest.

Adding to the allure of this remote terrain are the rivers twisting through the region—clear, spring-fed waters like the Two-Hearted and the Tahquamenon, prized by anglers and paddlers who know that the extra effort required to reach these banks will be well rewarded. And of course,

Sugarloaf Rock, Mackinac Island

© TRAVEL MICHIGAN

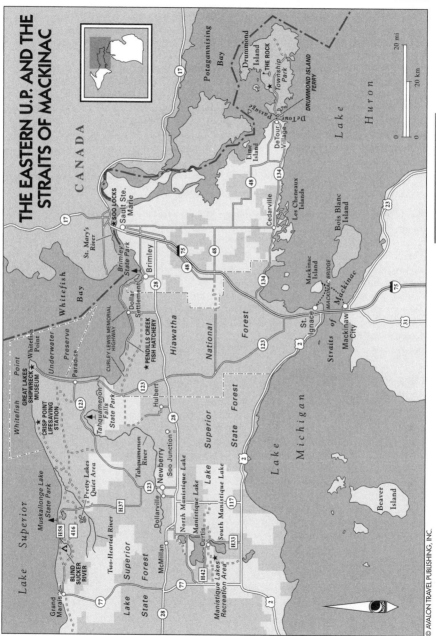

THE EASTERN U.P. AND THE STRAITS OF MACKINAC

CANADA

Potagannissing Bay

Drummond Island

THE ROCK

Township Park

DRUMMOND ISLAND FERRY

DeTour Passage

DeTour Village

Lime Island

Lake Huron

20 mi

20 km

SOO LOCKS

Sault Ste. Marie

17

48

134

Cedarville

Les Cheneaux Islands

Bois Blanc Island

23

St. Mary's River

Brimley State Park

Brimley

75

48

Dollar Settlement

28

48

134

Mackinac Island

MACKINAC BRIDGE

St. Ignace

Mackinaw City

Whitefish Bay

Whitefish Point

GREAT LAKES SHIPWRECK MUSEUM

Underwater Preserve

Paradise

CURLEY LEWIS MEMORIAL HIGHWAY

PENDILLS CREEK FISH HATCHERY

Hiawatha National Forest

123

Straits of Mackinac

75

31

Whitefish Point

CRISP POINT LIFESAVING STATION

123

Tahquamenon Falls State Park

Hulbert

28

Lake Superior State Forest

2

Lake Michigan

Muskallonge Lake State Park

H58

416

Pretty Lakes Quiet Area

Tahquamenon River

Newberry

Soo Junction

123

H37

Dollarville

North Manistique Lake

Manistique Lake

117

Beaver Island

Lake Superior

Two-Hearted River

McMillan

Curtis

South Manistique Lake

H33

BLIND SUCKER RIVER

Grand Marais

77

Lake Superior State Forest

28

H42

Manistique Lakes Recreation Area

77

2

© AVALON TRAVEL PUBLISHING, INC.

THE EASTERN U.P.

N

there's Lake Superior, dominating the northern horizon, a stretch of shoreline known as the "Graveyard of the Great Lakes." More than 300 ships have foundered here, including the 729-foot *Edmund Fitzgerald,* which disappeared off radar in a November 1975 storm, just 17 miles northwest of Whitefish Point.

Yet by contrast, the eastern U.P. also holds such popular attractions as Tahquamenon Falls, one of the largest waterfalls east of the Mississippi (and with impressive crowds to match on summer weekends); Manistique Lakes, abuzz with powerboats; the busy shipping traffic of the Soo Locks; and the granddaddy of all Michigan tourism, magical Mackinac Island. In such an eclectic corner of the state, it seems only fitting that the Victorian fairy tale of Mackinac Island should sit in the shadow of a modern engineering marvel, the Mackinac Bridge. After all, this is where the two disparate halves of Michigan are forced to meet, if only by the tenuous tether of a manmade bridge.

## The Land of Hiawatha

"By the shores of Gitche Gumee, by the shining big sea water," Henry Wadsworth Longfellow wrote of Lake Superior in *Song of Hiawatha.* Though it's highly doubtful Mr. Longfellow himself ever visited the U.P., he based his celebrated poem about this region on Ojibwa writings and legends, also making reference to "the rushing Tahquamenew." Just as Longfellow's words remain with us, so does much of the area's natural beauty, rolling east of M-77 between two "big sea waters," Lakes Superior and Michigan.

### NEAR THE LAKE SUPERIOR SHORE

Traveling east from Pictured Rocks National Lakeshore, you leave behind the grand bluffs and dunes and the well-marked attractions for the unknown. Like many Upper Peninsula roads, the sometimes paved, often gravel H-58 winds along through the trees, giving few clues as to what lies beyond the pines and hardwoods.

The land flattens out here—a far less dramatic landscape than the nearby Pictured Rocks area—so many visitors just pass on by. That's good news for those looking for simple solitude, since these woods hide little-used hiking trails, undeveloped stretches of Lake Superior shoreline, and all kinds of secluded lakes and campsites known only by regulars.

### Lake Superior State Forest

H-58 passes largely through state forest land,

which encompasses much of the Lake Superior shoreline and extends six or seven miles inland in many places. Several other "truck trails" spin off gravel H-58, sandy roads that are *usually* well-marked at intersections and quite navigable. They can be confusing, however, so venture off onto them with a good map or at least a good sense of direction.

About 11 miles east of Grand Marais on H-58, you'll reach the **Blind Sucker River** campground, an incredibly horrid name for an appealing place to set up camp. (You'll cross the river once or twice before that.) There are three state forest campgrounds in this area, along the Blind Sucker River, the Blind Sucker Flooding, and near Lake Superior. (If you choose to camp along Superior, be prepared for cold nights, even in August.)

Even more attractive may be the state forest's **Pretty Lakes Quiet Area,** about eight miles to the southeast. Here you'll find five small and clear lakes, ringed with sand, linked together by short portages. There are canoe campsites on Beaverhouse, Camp Eight, and Long Lakes, along with an 18-unit rustic campground near the approach road at Pretty Lake. No motors are allowed on Pretty, Brush, Beaverhouse, or Long Lakes. This is indeed a pretty, secluded spot where you'll listen to loons and other wildlife rather than the whine of powerboats and automobiles. To reach it, it's easiest to stay on H-58, which becomes H-37/CR-407 when it swings south at Muskallonge Lake State Park. About five miles south, turn west on CR-416 and follow it 2.5 miles to the campground. (If you have a good map, you can also follow CR-416 from the Blind Sucker area.)

There are dozens of other lakes and campsites in the Lake Superior State Forest. Pick up a good topo map and/or contact the state forest office, 906/293-5131, for more information.

## Muskallonge Lake State Park

Wedged on a quarter-mile strip of land between Lake Superior and Muskallonge Lake, Muskallonge Lake State Park, 906/658-3338, occupies the site of the old Deer Park township, once home to a sawmill, hotel, and no doubt a saloon or two. Today, a couple of fishing resorts represent the only commerce in this remote area 18 miles east of Grand Marais.

Water is the draw here. The park's two miles of Lake Superior frontage is wonderfully secluded, with low, grass-covered dunes stretching off to the east and west, and no visible development in either direction. It offers peace, quiet, and good **rockhounding,** especially for agates. Muskallonge Lake is stocked by the Department of Natural Resources and produces good **fishing** opportunities for northern pike, walleye, smallmouth bass, and perch. Because the lake is relatively shallow, it warms up enough for comfortable swimming—a rarity in much of the U.P., which accounts for this park's somewhat surprising popularity in summer. A modern campground has several sites overlooking the water. Sites are usually available even in summer, but you can always reserve one by calling 800/44-PARKS; website: dnr.state.mi.us.

## Paddling the Two-Hearted

The Two-Hearted is a fine canoeing river, clean and clear and usually quite mellow—except in spring when, depending on snowmelt, it can crank out some pretty serious whitewater. A state-designated wilderness river, the Two-Hearted winds through pine and hardwood forest; the only signs of civilization you're likely to see are a handful of cottages at the river's mouth. It offers plenty of low banks and sandbars, so picnic spots are easy to find. The Two-Hearted is also a widely regarded blue-ribbon trout stream, so be prepared for plenty of anglers when the season opens in April.

Put in at the High Bridge state forest campground on CR-407 for a 23-mile trip to the mouth. (You'll find two state forest campgrounds and other camping sites along the route.) Alternately, you can hook up with **Two Hearted Canoe Trips,** 906/658-3357, a livery based out of the Rainbow Lodge at the river's mouth. It operates trips ranging from a couple of hours to three days. A popular half-day trip departs from the Reed and Green Bridge (east of Muskallonge Lake State Park on CR-410) and takes out at Lake Superior.

## Crisp Point Life Saving Station

If lighthouses are your thing, here's a truly obscure one to add to the list. The 58-foot Crisp Point Light sits on a tiny arc of land 14 miles west of Whitefish Point, an isolated, unbroken stretch of Lake Superior shoreline. Though an automated light took over duty decades ago, the handsome 1904 tower and adjacent home still stand. The buildings definitely need work, but the tower was recently painted, so there's some movement afoot for their preservation. You'll need a map or the *DeLorme Gazetteer* to find the light—and a four-wheel-drive vehicle wouldn't hurt either. (Don't attempt the last couple of miles if the ground is wet.) The light is about nine miles east of the mouth of the Two-Hearted. Reach it from the west on CR-412, or from the east via the Farm Truck Road truck trail off M-123.

# WHITEFISH POINT

"The searchers all say they'd have made Whitefish Bay if they put 15 more miles behind her..." Singer/songwriter Gordon Lightfoot immortalized the ill-fated ore carrier *Edmund Fitzgerald* for the masses, but locals here need no reminders. Less than 20 miles from Whitefish Point and the safety of Whitefish Bay, the huge laker and all 29 hands on board were swallowed up in mere minutes by a fierce November squall in 1975.

On Lake Superior—the largest and fiercest of the Great Lakes—northwest storms can build

# THE MEMORY, THE MYSTERY OF THE EDMUND FITZGERALD

*...Superior they said never gives up her dead*
*When the gales of November come early...*

*—Gordon Lightfoot,*
*"The Wreck of the Edmund Fitzgerald"*

In early November 1975, the 729-foot lake carrier *Edmund Fitzgerald* departed Superior, Wisconsin, loaded with 26,000 tons of taconite pellets, bound for the port of Detroit and area steel mills. Launched in 1958, the *Fitzgerald* had a long and profitable record for the Columbia Line, the ship's Milwaukee-based owner. This was to be one of the last trips across Lake Superior before the shipping lanes and Soo Locks shut down for the season.

The *Fitzgerald* had rounded the Keweenaw Peninsula when, at dusk on November 10, one of the worst storms in 30 years screamed across Lake Superior. Winds howled at 90 miles an hour, whipping the immense lake into 30-foot seas. The *Fitzgerald* was prepared for bad weather from the northeast; Superior was notorious for her November gales. Like the captain of the 767-foot *Arthur M. Anderson* traveling nearby, the captain of the *Fitzgerald* had chosen to follow a more protected route across the lake, some 20 to 40 miles farther north than usual.

Just 10 miles apart, the two captains had been in intermittent visual and radio contact, discussing the perilous weather, which had dangerously shifted from northeast to northwest. At 7:10 P.M., the Fitzgerald captain radioed, "We are holding our

over 200 miles of cold, open water. They unleash their full fury on the 80-mile stretch of water from Grand Marais to Whitefish Point (hence the nickname, the "Graveyard of the Great Lakes"). Whitefish Point has long served as a beacon for mariners, a narrow finger of land reaching toward Ontario and forming the protected waters of Whitefish Bay, one of the few safe havens on the big lake.

## Great Lakes Shipwreck Museum

To commemorate the many ships that failed to round that point of safety, Whitefish Point is now the proper home of the Great Lakes Shipwreck Museum. With dim lighting and appropriately haunting music, this fine, compact museum traces the history of Great Lakes commerce and the disasters that sometimes accompanied it. Several shipwrecks are chronicled here, each with a scale model, photos or drawings, artifacts from the wreck, and a description of how and why it went down. Most compelling is the *Edmund Fitzgerald* display, complete with a life preserver and the ship's huge bell, recovered in a 1994 expedition led by museum founder Tom

Farnquist, an accomplished diver and underwater photographer.

Housed in the former Coast Guard Station, the museum also includes the restored lightkeeper's home, a theater showing an excellent short film about the Fitzgerald dive, and an interesting gift shop with nautical charts, prints, books, and more. The Great Lakes Shipwreck Museum, 877/SHIPWRECK, is open mid-May–mid-October daily 10 A.M.–6 P.M. Prices are $7.50 adults, $4.50 for 12 and under, $21.50 family. To reach it, take M-123 to Paradise and follow Whitefish Point Road 11 miles north. The museum alone makes this out-of-the-way point a worthy detour.

## Whitefish Point Light

Whitefish Point first beamed a warning light in 1849, and has done so ever since, making it the oldest operating light station on all of Lake Superior. Marking the bay's entry, the Whitefish Point Light is a utilitarian-looking 80-foot steel structure supported by a framework of steel girders. Though it looks relatively modern, the light actually dates to 1902. The beefy design was considered an extraordinary engi-

own." Then abruptly at 7:15, radio contact was lost. Turning to his radar, the captain of the Anderson stared in disbelief: the *Fitzgerald* had completely disappeared off the screen. A 729-foot lake carrier and all 29 hands simply vanished, without a single distress call, without a trace.

When the storm cleared, the wreck of the *Edmund Fitzgerald* was found in 530 feet of water, just 17 miles from the shelter of Whitefish Bay. She lay at the bottom in two pieces, 170 feet apart, with debris scattered over three acres—evidence of the force with which the massive hull hit bottom. Many believe the *Fitzgerald* torpedoed bow first, which would have meant nearly 200 feet of the ship was towering above the water's surface at impact.

But even after almost 30 years, an exhaustive Coast Guard investigation, and several dives to the site, no one really knows what happened. Theories abound, of course. The Coast Guard's best deduction is that the ship took on water through leaking hatches, then developed a list and was swamped by the storm's huge waves. Others believe that, outside the normal shipping lane, she scraped bottom on uncharted shoals. Still others believe the warm taconite pellets weakened the structure of the ship, causing it to snap in two when caught between two particularly enormous waves. No doubt books will continue to be written and new theories put forth.

Meanwhile, the *Edmund Fitzgerald* remains in its grave at the bottom of the lake, along with all its victims, whose bodies were never recovered. It ranks as the worst modern-day disaster on the Great Lakes, a constant reminder of the power of these inland seas.

neering experiment at the time, but one deemed necessary to withstand the gales that frequently batter this exposed landscape. It was automated in 1970 and continues to do yeoman's duty.

## Whitefish Point Underwater Preserve
For experienced divers, this preserve offers a fantastic array of wrecks—18 steamers and schooners littered all around the point. (The *Edmund Fitzgerald* is not among them.) Good visibility is a hallmark of this 376-acre preserve. Most wrecks lie in deep water, though—anywhere from 40 to 270 feet—and in an area with few protected harbors. Needless to say, only very experienced divers and boaters should consider this spot. Contact the **Paradise Area Tourism Council,** 906/492-3927, for information on area dive services.

## Birds and Beaches
A needed resting spot for birds migrating across Lake Superior, Whitefish Point is a birdwatcher's dream. Beginning with the hawk migration in April through late fall, the point attracts an amazing variety of birds. Eagles, loons (by the *thousands!*), songbirds, waterbirds, owls,

**Whitefish Point Lighthouse**

© TOM BUCHKOE

some unusual arctic species like arctic loons and arctic terns, and more all pass through, some 300 species in all. Even if you're not a birder, plan to spend some time at this lovely point, where you can wander the sand beaches, watch the birds, and keep an eye out for the big lakers that pass quite close to shore as they round the point. Bring along binoculars and an extra jacket.

## TAHQUAMENON FALLS

West of Newberry, the headwaters of the Tahquamenon bubble up from underground and begin a gentle roll through stands of pine and vast wetlands. Rambling and twisting northeast through Luce County, the river grows wide and majestic by the time it enters its namesake state park. Then, with the roar of a freight train and the power of a fire hose, it suddenly plummets over a 50-foot drop, creating a golden fountain of water 200 feet wide.

As much as 50,000 gallons of water per second gushes over the Upper Tahquamenon, making it the second largest falls (by volume) east of the Mississippi, outdone only by Niagara. Adding to Tahquamenon's majesty are its distinctive colors—bronze headwaters from the tannic acid of decaying cedars and hemlocks that line its banks, and bright white foam from the water's high salt content.

### Tahquamenon Falls State Park

Accessing Tahquamenon Falls is easy, since both the Upper Falls and Lower Falls lie within Tahquamenon Falls State Park, 41382 W. M-123, 906/492-3415, which has provided short, well-marked paths to prime viewing sites. At the Upper Falls, follow the trail to the right and down the 74 steps to an observation deck, which brings you so close you can feel the fall's thundering power and its cool mist on your face. The view provides a dual glimpse of the placid waters above and the furious frothing below. Four miles downstream, the Lower Falls plunges over a series of cascades. The best vantage point is from a small island midriver; a state park concessionaire obliges visitors by renting canoes and rowboats to make the short crossing.

With the dramatic centerpiece of Tahquamenon Falls, it's easy to overlook the rest of this 40,000-acre state park, Michigan's second largest. In sharp contrast to the often frenzied crowds at the falls (more than half a million people per year, the greatest of any U.P. state park), the vast majority of the park remains peaceful, etched with 25 miles of little-used **hiking trails.** From the Upper Falls, the Giant Pines Loop passes through a stand of white pines before crossing M-123. Once on the north side of the highway,

Tahquamenon Falls

© TRAVEL MICHIGAN

link up with the Clark Lake Loop, a 5.6-mile hike that traces the southern shoreline of the shallow lake.

The final 16 miles of the Tahquamenon River wind through the park, spilling into Lake Superior's Whitefish Bay at its eastern end. **Fishing** for muskie and walleye is usually quite good in the pools below the Lower Falls. Also consider joining the fleet of runabouts and anglers in waders near the mouth of the river, where trout often school.

It's possible to **paddle** nearly all 94 miles of the Tahquamenon. A popular put-in is off CR-415 north of McMillan, but you'll start off through several buggy miles of wetlands. A better choice is about 10 miles downstream, off CR-405 at Dollarville, where you'll also avoid portaging around the Dollarville Dam. Beyond Newberry, you'll be treated to a pristine paddle, since no roads come anywhere near the river. Watch the banks for bear, deer, and other wildlife. Naturally, you'll have to portage around the falls, but then can follow the river to its mouth without any other interruptions.

You can **camp** pretty much anywhere along the banks of the Tahquamenon. Past Newberry, you'll find a rustic campground at Sixteen Creek in the Lake Superior State Forest. The state park has four campgrounds: near the Lower Falls, the Riverbend and Overlook campgrounds have nearly 200 sites, including some fronting the river itself. Near the mouth of the river, there's a smaller modern campground with 76 sites and a rustic 60-site campground just upstream. None are particularly quiet; the Lower Falls campsites are close the activity of the falls and its requisite parking area, while the Rivermouth sites are within earshot of M-123. Nonetheless, all are extremely popular in summer months, so consider making a reservation, 800/44-PARKS; website: dnr.state.mi.us, or pitching your tent elsewhere.

### Taq Falls Tours

For another look at the river and falls, you may want to plan a day for the **Toonerville Trolley and Riverboat,** 888/778-7246. It's much more appealing than its cheesy name suggests, and a

good way to experience a remote stretch of the river. Departing from Soo Junction near Newberry (watch for sign on M-28), a narrow-gauge train chugs its way five miles along an old logging route, through roadless spruce and maple forest, tamarack lowlands and peat bogs. In about a half-hour, the train sighs to a stop deep in the woods at the Tahquamenon's banks. Here you'll transfer to a large tour boat and cruise downstream nearly two hours toward the falls. Just as the river begins roil and boil, the boat docks on the river's south shore, and guests walk the last half mile to the falls. It's a nifty trip, one that has been in operation since long before there was a state park providing easy access to the falls. Originally, the tour operator—the grandfather of present-day owner Kris Stewart—used a Model T truck with train wheels to reach the river. The six-and-a-half-hour trip costs $24 adults, $12 children 6–15, under six free. You can also opt for just the train trip to the river bank and back, a 1.75-hour trip, $12 adults, $6 children 6–15. The Toonerville Trolley operates daily mid-June–mid-October. Show up by 10 A.M.; reservations recommended.

## CURLEY LEWIS MEMORIAL HIGHWAY

This twisting, scenic road (also called Lakeshore Drive) follows the curve of Lake Superior's Whitefish Bay from M-123 east 20 miles or so to Sault Ste. Marie. It's almost an attraction in itself, passing through the Hiawatha National Forest, offering up plenty of water views and a handful of worthwhile stops.

### Pendills Creek National Fish Hatchery

Four miles west of tiny Dollar Settlement, this federally run fish hatchery, 906/437-5231, raises thousands of lake trout that grow up to tempt anglers in Lakes Superior, Michigan, and Huron. Visitors can wander around the tanks to peer down at the hundreds of wriggling trout fry (the raceways are covered to keep birds and other predators from helping themselves to a free lunch) and the breeder trout that weigh in at 15 pounds or more. Open weekdays; call for current hours. Outdoor areas are also accessible on weekends. Free.

### Big Pine Picnic Grounds

Just beyond the Bay View campground (see Practicalities, below), this day-use area in the Hiawatha National Forest is a wonderful spot to take a break. It offers a pleasant shaded area under a canopy of huge white pines, and a pretty sand/pebble beach along Whitefish Bay.

### Point Iroquois Light Station and Museum

Continuing east, don't miss a chance to climb the tower at the Point Iroquois Light, where Whitefish Bay narrows into the St. Mary's River. Since 1855, a beacon here has helped guide ships through this extremely difficult passage, where reefs lurk near the Canadian shore and the rock walls of Point Iroquois threaten on the Michigan side. In 1870, the original wooden light tower was replaced with the present one, a classic white-painted brick structure. A keeper's home was added in 1902.

With fewer and fewer lighthouses open to the public, it's fun to climb the iron spiral staircase for a freighter-captain's view of the river, the bay, and frequent shipping traffic. Stop in the adjacent lightkeeper's home, too, where the local historical society has restored some rooms to illustrate the life of a lightkeeper; other rooms feature displays and old photos. The lighthouse and adjacent beach are now part of the Hiawatha National Forest, which should help ensure continued protection. The complex is open Memorial Day weekend–October 15, daily 10 A.M.–5 P.M., and also from 7 P.M.–9 P.M. Fri.–Sun. Call 906/437-5272 for more information.

### Mission Hill Overlook

This is the kind of road where every view is better than the last. As the highway curves south, watch for the turnoff to the west marking this terrific overlook. Drive up the sand and gravel road for grand, sweeping views of the river and bay,

Ontario's Laurentian mountains, the cityscape of Sault Ste. Marie, freighters that look like toy ships, the Point Iroquois light, and just below, Spectacle Lake.

## MANISTIQUE LAKES

At the intersection of H-32 and H-42, the town of Curtis serves as base camp for the Manistique Lakes Recreation Area. Three lakes— North Manistique, Big Manistique, and Little Manistique—combine to offer 15,000 acres of shallow, warm waters that are extremely popular with boaters, swimmers, and anglers. Big Manistique, one of the largest lakes in the U.P., is just 5–10 feet deep, and best known for its perch and bass fishing.

### Accommodations, Camping, Food

Cottages and resorts line the lakes. Your best bet is to contact the **Manistique Lake Area Tourism Bureau,** 906/586-3678, website: www.curtismi.com, for resort information and a list of vacancies. For a little history (like much of the U.P., this area was once a logging and railroad center), try the **Helmer House Inn,** 906/586-3204, an 1880s home overlooking Big Manistique, or **Chamberlin's Ole Forest Inn,** 906/586-6000, built in the late 1800s as a hotel next to the train depot, and moved to this site on Big Manistique in 1924. Both have moderate rates. Both also are the best spots around for dining, with steaks and whitefish reliably on the menu. The Helmer House is located on H-33 just north of Helmer; Chamberlin's Ole Forest Inn is also on H-33, one mile north of Curtis.

Campers can find a relatively quiet spot at the **Lake Superior State Forest campground,** 906/293-5131, on the west shore of South Manistique Lake, with most sites right on the water's edge. The **Log Cabin Resort and Campground,** 906/586-9732, on the southern shore of Big Manistique, is geared more to RVs, with open, grassy sites, a sand beach, boat launch/marina, laundry facilities, game room, and more.

# Sault Ste. Marie

Compared to much of the eastern U.P., Sault Ste. Marie is urban, the U.P.'s second-largest city with a population of 15,000. This historical city is well worth a visit, especially to view the boat traffic through the famous Soo Locks that link Lakes Superior and Huron. But don't overlook the area to the south and east, where the lovely blue-green waters of Lake Huron wrap around the end of the peninsula, a scalloped shoreline of quiet bays and a scatter of islands.

## THE SOO

At the foot of Whitefish Bay, grand Lake Superior narrows to a close at the St. Mary's River, the sole waterway that links it to Lake Huron and the other three Great Lakes. With Superior 21 feet higher than the other lakes, the St. Mary's

naturally erupted in a series of falls and rapids near Sault Ste. Marie. Sault, pronounced "Soo" (and often spelled that way as a city nickname), means "Falling Water," a name given by early French explorers.

## History

The Ojibwa were the first settlers of the area, migrating here in the 1500s. They discovered a rich supply of whitefish in the area's turbulent waters, and established a permanent settlement at the edge of the rapids, making it one of the oldest continuously settled areas in the Midwest. *Addik-kim-maig*, the Ojibwa called the whitefish—"deer of the waters," a reference to its importance as a food source. The Ojibwa lived here off the river's riches for more than 300 years. But in a sad and repetitive tale, the white

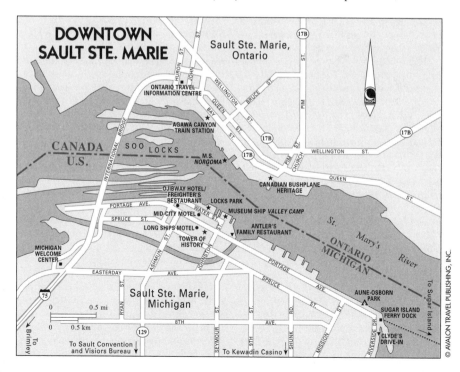

man and progress put an end to the Ojibwa way of life and took away this important fishing ground. The combination of warring Iroquois—forced west by European immigrants taking over their homeland—and new European settlement in the Soo eventually drove the Ojibwa out of the region.

The French, too, had lived off the area's riches for many years, establishing a major fur trading post here in the mid-1600s, then a Jesuit mission. By the early 1800s, Michigan's northern reaches were increasingly being settled, and people were discovering the bounty of natural resources—copper, iron, lumber, grain—ringing the shores of Lake Superior.

The only problem was those rapids. For decades, ship cargo had to be unloaded by hand, portaged around the rapids by horses and mules pulling carts, then reloaded onto another boat. In 1839, the American Fur Company built a short railroad line, which eased the job, but it remained backbreaking and exceedingly slow. While Great Lakes shipping was booming on the lower Great Lakes, Superior remained largely isolated, its cargo backed up by the rapids.

Eastern industrialists began lobbying for government funded locks. The portaging business was the lifeblood of Sault Ste. Marie's economy, though, so the community opposed such a project. Locals managed to stave off the inevitable for more than a decade until 1852, when President Millard Fillmore signed a bill authorizing the first lock at Sault Ste. Marie.

In 1855, the State Lock opened, a system of two locks, each 350 feet long. They were an instant success. In the first year, nearly 12,000 tons of iron ore passed through the locks; within a decade, that figure grew to more than 120,000 tons. By World War I, the nation's hunger for iron and copper, coupled with the opening of vast iron mines in Minnesota's Mesabi Range, made the Soo Locks the busiest shipping canal in the world. Even today, the freight transported across Lake Superior and through the Soo Locks exceeds that of the Panama and Suez Canals put together.

Soon after the completion of the State Lock, the burgeoning commercial traffic made it clear more locks were needed. The 515-foot Weitzel Lock opened in 1881. Since then, a succession of locks have been built, both to handle the traffic and the growing size of Great Lakes ships. Today, three U.S. locks are in operation (there's a fourth smaller lock on the Canadian side), including the 1,200-foot Poe Lock built in 1968 to accommodate the huge lakers now common on the Great Lakes.

The oldest city in Michigan, Sault Ste. Marie is inseparable from the locks that shaped its past and continue to define it today. A linchpin for the economy of the entire Great Lakes, the city's own economy has been rather stagnant. The Ojibwa-owned Kewadin Casino and a prison complex south of town rank as the area's largest employers. Some state government administrative jobs and the small Lake Superior State University help, too. But tourism remains a staple of the economy—with many of those visitors coming specifically to see the parade of commerce that incessantly passes through town.

## Soo Locks

Nearly every visitor to the Soo makes a pilgrimage to the locks, right in the heart of downtown at the end of Ashmun Street (Business I-75). The city has smartly dressed up this area beautifully, with lovely **Locks Park.** Blue freighter signs mark the **Locks Park Walkway,** which wanders along Water Street and is dotted with interpretive plaques that share the city's history.

In the heart of the rather formal park, the U.S. Army Corps of Engineers manages the locks and a **visitors center,** next to a raised **viewing platform** that lets you peer down on the action. Start at the visitors center to make sense of what's going on. Here, a moving model shows how the locks raise and lower ships by opening and closing the gates of a lock chamber and allowing water to rush in or rush out. No pumps are required; the water simply seeks its own level. Other displays explain the construction of the locks. A knowledgeable staff with a P.A. system, along with video cameras upriver, notify you about approaching vessels. In summer months, you can usually count on a ship coming through every hour or so. You can also call the visitors center, 906/932-1472, to get the day's shipping schedule, but be aware that times can change depending on weather conditions and other factors. For more information consult the website: huron.lre.usace.army.mil/SOO/soohmpg.

It's easy to while away an hour or two watching the ships as they slither into the locks with seemingly just inches to spare. Summer evenings are especially pleasant, when you'll likely have the platform to yourself to watch the illuminated ships. If you're lucky, you might see a "saltie," an ocean-going vessel that's likely hauling grain to foreign ports. Overall, the three most plentiful Great Lakes shipments are iron ore (for steelmaking), limestone (a purifying agent for steelmaking, also used in construction and papermaking), and coal (for power plants).

The locks and viewing platform are open throughout the Great Lakes shipping season, which runs March 25–January 15. Those are the official dates when the locks cease operation for maintenance; ice build-up on Superior sometimes affects the length of the shipping season,

too. The visitors center is open from mid-May–mid-November daily 7 A.M.–11 P.M.

## Soo Locks Boat Tours

After viewing the locks, you can "lock through" yourself on one of these extremely popular tours. The two-hour trip ($17 adults, $14.50 children 8–13, $7.50 children 5–12) takes you through both the American and Canadian locks and travels along both cities' waterfronts. At busy times, you'll be in the midst of freighter traffic, dwarfed by their enormous steel hulls. The large passenger boats have both heated and open deck areas. Boats depart daily from early May to mid-October beginning at 9 A.M., from two docks on Portage Avenue. Contact Soo Locks Boat Tours at 800/432-6301, website: www.soolocks.com, for a current schedule.

## Other Downtown Attractions

After watching the big Great Lakes boats, the **Museum Ship Valley Camp,** 906/632-3658, gives you a chance to see what it was like to live and work aboard a giant steamer. This 550-foot

Soo Locks

© TRAVEL MICHIGAN

THE EASTERN U.P.

steamship logged more than a million miles on the Great Lakes, hauling ore, coal, and stone on the Great Lakes from 1907 to the mid-1970s. Now it's permanently docked five blocks east of the Soo Locks. Visitors can tour the pilothouse, engine room, main deck, crew quarters, coal bunker, and more. Throughout, the ship has a number of aquariums and maritime displays, some better than others. Most popular: a display on the sinking of the *Edmund Fitzgerald*, including two tattered lifeboats found empty and drifting on the lake. All in all, it's well worth a couple of hours. It's open mid-May–mid-October 10 A.M.–6 P.M.; longer hours in July and August. Admission is $7 adults, $3.50 children 6–16. Make sure to stop at the museum shop, housed in a separate building next to the parking lot. It has an excellent selection of maritime books and videos. Open daily 10 A.M.–6 P.M.

Like most observation towers, the **Tower of History,** four blocks east of the Soo Locks at 326 Portage, 906/632-3658, is sort of an ugly blight on the landscape—a 21-story stark concrete monolith—but with a wonderful 360-degree view of the twin Soos, the St. Mary's, Lake Superior, and forests rolling off in the distance. Rather than being stuck behind windows, you get to enjoy the views from an open-air deck. (Bring a jacket!) The tower also includes a few small exhibit areas and a theater showing documentary videos. Yes, there is an elevator to the top. Curiously, the tower was originally built as a bell tower for the neighboring church—a project that went, uh, slightly over budget. Open mid-May–mid-October daily 10 A.M.–6 P.M. Admission is $3.25 adults, $1.75 children 6–16.

The **River of History Museum,** 209 E. Portage, 906/632-1999, uses St. Mary's River as the framework for telling the story of the region's history. Life-sized dioramas depict things like Native Americans spearfishing in the rapids and a French fur trapper's cabin (the French were the first white settlers in the region). The museum incorporates lots of sound in its displays: dripping ice from melting glaciers, roaring rapids, Ojibwa elders passing down legends. One hopes this relatively new museum (founded in 1992) will keep building on this idea.

Open mid-May–mid-October Mon.–Sat. 10 A.M.–5 P.M., Sun. noon–5 P.M. Admission is $2.50 adults, $1.25 children 5–16.

## The Soo's Canadian Sister

Just across the International Bridge lies the Soo's sister city in Ontario, also named Sault Ste. Marie. With a population of 84,000, it's the larger of the two cities, home to a huge steel plant and paper company. But along with these industries, Sault Ste. Marie, Ontario, also has a lot to offer visitors. Downtown, a lovely **boardwalk** rambles along the river for a mile or so, beginning at the bridge and extending east past fishing platforms, shops, and the MS *Norgoma,* the last passenger cruise ship built for the Great Lakes, now a museum. On Wednesday and Saturday, there's a farmers market near the tented pavilion.

One of the most advertised and popular visitor attractions is the **Agawa Canyon Train Tour,** 800/242-9287, a seven-hour roundtrip through the scenic wooded gorge of the Agawa Canyon. The day-long tour includes a two-hour stopover in the canyon, where you can hike to lookouts, visit waterfalls, wander along the river, or just hang out in the grassy picnic area. The train trip is even more popular (and $15 more expensive) in the fall color season, which usually runs mid-September–mid-October, and in winter when it is known as the "Snow Train." (The two-hour layover is eliminated in the winter trip). Tours depart at 8 A.M. from the station at 129 Bay Street. Trains run once daily from early June–mid-October and weekends Jan.–March. Reservations recommended. Round-trip fares in summer are C$49 for adults, C$18 children five and older, C$8.25 children under five.

Like in Alaska, bush planes are an integral part of life in the wilds of the Canadian interior. A small plane with pontoons can get you where no auto can, since almost any remote lake can serve as a landing strip. The **Canadian Bushplane Heritage Centre,** near Pim and Bay Streets on the waterfront, 705/945-6242, chronicles the history of Canada's bush planes, which began in the Soo with the Ontario Air Service in the 1920s, established to fight forest fires. Others besides aviation buffs will enjoy this unique museum, housed the Air Service's old waterfront hangar. Open daily year-round. Admission is C$5 for adults, children 12 and under free.

Reach Ontario via the three-mile-long **International Bridge** (one way costs US$1.50 for autos, 75 cents for bikes). U.S. citizens do not have to have a passport, but need a photo I.D. like a driver's license. You can exchange money and pick up maps and other useful area information at the **Ontario Travel Information Centre** at the foot of the bridge, 705/945-6941.

## Practicalities

For more information on the Sault Ste. Marie area, contact the **Sault Convention and Visitors Bureau,** 2581 I-75 Business Spur, 800/647-2858, website: www.saultstemarie.com. For regional information and maps, stop by the **Michigan Welcome Center,** 906/632-8242, near the International Bridge.

Now part of the Ramada chain, the rather plush **Ojibway Hotel,** 240 W. Portage Ave., 906/632-4100, has the nicest accommodations in town, and the best location, too, overlooking the St. Mary's River and the locks. Ask for an upper-level north-facing room. The elegant 1928 building has been well restored, with large rooms, an indoor pool, whirlpool, and Freighters restaurant (see below). Rates average $125–175, but ask about packages for a better deal.

For the same good location but for less money, try the **Long Ships Motel,** 427 W. Portage Ave., 888/690-2422, a clean and comfortable mom-and-pop-style motel with a fine spot across from Locks Park. Rates $50–75. A little farther east, but still within walking distance of the river and downtown is the **Mid-City Motel,** 304 E. Portage Ave., 906/632-6832. Rates $50–75. There are plenty of chain hotels near I-75, but they are nowhere near the locks or other downtown walking attractions.

Right in Sault Ste. Marie, there's a modern, 65-site **municipal campground** at Aune-Osborn Park, on the St. Mary's River near the Sugar Island ferry dock. Just east of Brimley, **Brimley State Park,** 906/248-3422, offers about a mile of sandy Lake Superior beach, a large modern campground, and not a whole lot else. Still, it's a good choice for anyone looking for an easy place to set up camp to enjoy the Soo and other nearby attractions. This is a popular park, so consider making reservations, 800/44-PARKS; website: dnr.state.mi.us, if you're aiming for a summer weekend. For a little more seclusion, head farther west to the **Hiawatha National Forest.** Within a half-hour drive of the Soo, you can find pretty and private tent sites next to the Lake Superior shore at Bay View, or on a good fishing lake at Monocle Lake. No reservations. For information, contact the Hiawatha National Forest, 906/635-5311.

Start your day at **Cup of the Day,** 406 Ashmun, 906/635-7272, for good coffee drinks, a juice bar, and sandwiches and salads at lunchtime. In the Ojibway Hotel, 240 Portage Ave., **Freighters,** 906/632-4211, offers a wall of glass overlooking the locks and a very nice menu featuring steaks and seafood, especially local fish. This is a great spot for a good breakfast, too. For an old-fashioned service-at-your-car burger joint, cruise on over to **Clyde's Drive In,** 1425 Riverside Dr. at the Sugar Island ferry dock, 906/632-2581, for the great grilled hamburgers they've been making since 1949. Inside seating and a menu of other fried items are available, too. **Antler's Family Restaurant,** 804 E. Portage Ave., 906/632-3571, serves up burgers, ribs, fresh fish, Mexican-style dishes, and such in a taxidermist-gone-mad setting with more than 300 mounts and who knows how many antlers. Don't go when you have a headache—they have the wacky habit of setting off sirens and whistles for no particular reason. Kids love this place, naturally.

## LAKE HURON WATERS

East of I-75, the Upper Peninsula narrows and dribbles off into a series of peninsulas, points, and Lake Huron islands. The area has a simple, pretty feel, the kind of place where casual cycling, beachcombing, and picnicking set the pace for a summer day. While there's plenty to explore for the casual putterer, there are few true "destinations." In fact, the whole area is often overlooked by guidebooks—which is just fine with the locals and summer cottage owners. So don't get too excited about sightseeing. Just pack a lunch, put on a pair of comfortable shoes, and wile away the day along a rocky shoreline.

## The Huron Shore

Traveling south from the Soo, stop-and-start roads make it difficult to hug the waterfront—a shame, since the frequent shipping traffic on the St. Mary's River always makes for an interesting parade. But M-134 between I-75 and Drummond Island is another story. This pretty and unusually peaceful road skims along the Lake Huron shore, past rocky bays and pine-studded islands, close enough for the water to practically lap at the pavement. It's hard to overcome the urge to stop and explore, which is okay. There's plenty of public property along the way. The best is just a few miles east of M-48. On land that was formerly a state park, the **Lake Superior State Forest,** 906/293-5131, still manages a campground and public beach hidden away behind the pines.

**DeTour Village** marks the end of the road and the end of the Upper Peninsula mainland. This small village has long served an important navigational role for ships heading up and down the St. Mary's. Many ships squeeze through De-Tour Passage here, the narrow waterway between the point and Drummond Island. They make a turn, or detour, to chart a course from the St. Mary's River to the Straits of Mackinac. When Detroit was still a blank spot on the map, DeTour Village was busy guiding ships, with a navigational light as far back as 1848. It remains a pleasant place to watch the ship traffic, from public parks and gardens along M-134.

Nearby Lime Island marks the centerpiece of the **Island Explorer Water Trail,** a boater's route that travels from Lime to Mackinac Island along a linked network of islands. For more information, contact the **DeTour Area Chamber of Commerce,** 104 Elizabeth St., 906/297-5987. You can also stay at cabins and cottages on state forest land on Lime Island. For more information on rates and availability, contact the Sault Ste. Marie Forest Management Unit, 906/635-5281.

The **Drummond Island ferry,** 906/297-8851, departs from DeTour Village year-round. From

April to December, it departs hourly; from January through March, two to four times a day. Extra passages may be added during peak summer months. Fare is $11.25 for a vehicle and driver, $2 for each additional passenger.

## Drummond Island

Here's a trivia question: What's the largest U.S. island in the Great Lakes?

Probably few would guess Drummond, a low-key place if there ever was one. Some 65 percent of Drummond Island is state-owned land; the rest is largely owned by summer residents, who swell the island's population to about 5,000 in July and August. You'd never know it—life in this fishing-oriented place is concentrated along the shorelines, which you can rarely see from the island's few roads.

With rocky shorelines, inland lakes, marshy lowlands, hardwood forests, and open meadows, Drummond Island boasts remarkably diverse animal and plant habitat. More than 24 different kinds of orchids grow wild on the island. Loons, bobcats, moose, and a pack of wolves all roam here, along with more common species.

Drummond and its neighboring islands are humps of limestone, part of the Niagara escarpment that stretches from Door County, Wisconsin and across northern Lake Michigan. In an area called the Maxton Plains at the island's north end, this slab of limestone bedrock lies right near the surface, covered by just a thin layer of alkaline soil. This unusual combination supports one of the world's foremost examples of alvar grassland, a rare mix of Arctic tundra and Great Plains plants, including Hill's thistle, false pennyroyal, and prairie dropseed. The Nature Conservancy owns more than 800 acres of the Maxton Plains. The preserve is open to the public, so you can explore this lunar-like landscape where large boulders of conglomerate flecked with red jasper—called "puddingstone"—punctuate the barren expanses of limestone bedrock.

A mountain bike is a fun way to explore the island, since M-134 dissolves into a variety of double tracks and, eventually, single track. (Don't expect technical riding—the island is quite flat.) A canoe or kayak is even better. The fjord-like bays and 150 miles of ragged shoreline make this a magical place to paddle.

For such a mellow place, you might be surprised to run across **The Rock,** 906/493-1006, a spectacular "designer" golf course completed in 1990 by then-owner Tom Monaghan, owner of the Domino's Pizza chain. The first-rate course makes fine use of the natural environment, its holes weaving through woods and limestone outcroppings.

For more information on Drummond Island, call the **Drummond Island Tourism Association,** 800/737-8666, website: www.drummond-island.com.

## Les Cheneaux

"The Snows," everyone calls them, though the real name for these islands is Les Cheneaux (lay shen-O), French for "The Channels." And there are channels aplenty. Like shards of glass, 36 long and narrow islands lie splintered just off the U.P.'s southeastern shore, forming a maze of calm channels and protected bays in northern Lake Huron just 35 miles from the Mackinac Bridge. Not surprisingly, it is a delight for boaters. Tall sailboats, small runabouts, classic cabin cruisers, and simple canoes all share these waters, as they have for more than a century.

Les Cheneaux islands first attracted boaters in the 1880s, drawn here from nearby Mackinac Island—already a popular vacation getaway for the wealthy—for the area's renowned fishing. At first, resorters from Mackinac came on day-long excursions. Before long, they were building their own cottages, reveling in the solitude not found in the other established Great Lakes resort areas. Though its summer guests were, by and large, wealthy industrialists from southern Michigan, Indiana, Illinois, and Iowa, Les Cheneaux quickly developed a tactful, understated style. Cottages were elegant, but not ostentatious; boats were sleek, but not showy.

Les Cheneaux still maintains that genteel, yet simple, air. If you're the kind of person who doesn't need (or even like) to "be entertained," then you'll enjoy this charming area, free of in-your-face tourism. Boating remains king here, and in proper Les Cheneaux style, it rarely is expressed in macho powerboat posturing or screaming jet skis. No, boating here is best defined by the amazing array of classic wooden craft you'll see puttering and purring through the channels. The nation's first (and now, oldest) Criss Craft franchise was founded in Hessel in 1926. Many of those early boats survive today, thanks to the area's clean freshwater, short boating season, and careful maintenance, which help preserve the somewhat tender wooden hulls.

Les Cheneaux's love affair with classic boats is put on parade each summer at the annual **Les Cheneaux Antique Boat Festival** at the Hessel docks. Held the second Saturday in August, it is believed to be the largest such show in the country, featuring more than a hundred wood-hulled vessels. For information, contact the Les Cheneaux Historical Association, 906/484-2821.

The best way to see Les Cheneaux, of course, is to get out on the water. Aside from the pretty wooded islands themselves, part of the fun is eyeing the beautiful old boathouses that dot the shorelines, especially on Marquette Island. If you've got your own craft, you'll find launches in Hessel and Cedarville, the only two towns in the area. Though the waters are protected and normally quite safe, be sure to bring a chart, or at least a map provided by local businesses. The various bays and channels and points can get pretty confusing to a newcomer. Many cottages rent boats or include them in their rates.

For information on the Les Cheneaux area, contact **Les Cheneaux Islands Area Tourist Association,** 906/484-3935.

## Accommodations and Camping

On Drummond Island, stay in luxury at **Woodmoor,** 800/999-6343, the grandiose retreat with handsome log lodge rooms dreamed up by pizza magnate Tom Monaghan. Guests have access to all resort facilities, including an outdoor pool, tennis courts, bowling, even sporting clays. Rates $100–200 in summer months, with many package deals available. You can also rent some Frank Lloyd Wright-style cottages, many overlooking Potagannissing Bay, for varying rates. Another good lodging choice is **Drummond Island Yacht Haven,** 906/493-5232, with large cabins overlooking island-studded Potagannissing Bay. The larger three-bedroom cabins have limestone fireplaces. The property also boasts sand beaches, boat rentals, and other amenities. Rates $100–300 per night; weekly rates available. Contact the Drummond Island Tourism Association, 800/737-8666, website: www.drummond-island.com, for more choices.

The island's best camping is at **Township Park,** just north of M-134 not far from the ferry dock. This rustic campground (no showers) has pretty sites tucked in the woods on Potagannissing Bay. Sand beach and boat launch. No reservations; $8 for sites without electricity; $9.25 for sites with electricity.

Along the Lake Huron shore near Cedarville, the **Spring Lodge Cottages,** 906/484-2282, has a wonderful location in the heart of Les Cheneaux, right on the Snows Channel. Large and well-kept grounds house cottages, most overlooking the water. Boat rentals on-site. For nicer-than-average motel rooms and an indoor pool, try the **Comfort Inn** on M-134 in Cedarville, 906/484-2266. Rates for both $100–150.

Camp along the Lake Huron shore and under the pines in a former state park now managed by the Lake Superior State Forest, 906/293-5131. The marked beach/picnic area is on M-134, six miles west of DeTour Village. For more seclusion, boaters should head for Government Island, the only publicly owned island in Les Cheneaux. Once a Coast Guard Station, it's now part of the Hiawatha National Forest, 906/643-7900. Outhouses and picnic tables are available at a couple of primitive sites on the northeastern and southern ends of the small island; no-trace camping is permitted anywhere on the island.

## Mackinac Island and the Straits

Linking Lakes Huron and Michigan, the Straits of Mackinac have been a crossroads of the Great Lakes for hundreds of years, a key waterway for hunting, fishing, trading, and transportation.

The four-mile-wide Straits also sever the Michigan in two, a break that is emotional as well as geographical. Until the 1950s, the only way across was by ferry, effectively stymieing the development of the Upper Peninsula and creating half-day backups at the ferry dock during prime hunting and fishing season.

Today the magnificent five-mile-long Mackinac Bridge stitches the state together, allowing a free flow between the Upper and Lower Peninsulas. But the Straits, now a key vacation area for much of the Midwest, continue to stop people. Many come specifically for Mackinac Island. Others take advantage of the area's abundant lodging as a base for visiting U.P. sights like Tahquamenon Falls or the Soo Locks (easy day trips) or Lower Peninsula destinations like Petoskey.

To slow down visitors and keep them from viewing their towns only as pass-through points, St. Ignace and Mackinaw City, each at the foot of the bridge, have developed attractions and events of their own. They include some excellent historic parks and popular festivals like the Straits Area Auto Show, which draws more than 100,000 car buffs from around the country each June.

Before you go, there's one thing you must know. Whether it's spelled Mackinaw (the original British spelling) or Mackinac (the original French spelling), it's always, *always* pronounced "MAK-i-naw." It's never correct to say "MAK-i-nak." Okay? Okay.

### HISTORY

The Ojibwa and Ottawa peoples called Mackinac Island Michilimackinac, "The Great Turtle," which pretty accurately describes the hump of limestone that is the island. The area near Sugar Loaf Rock on the island's interior was a sacred place, the birthplace of the "tree of knowledge," the white pine. The Indians summered here and on nearby Bois Blanc Island, hunting and fishing in the incredibly productive area, and trading some of their catch for grains and vegetables with tribes to the south.

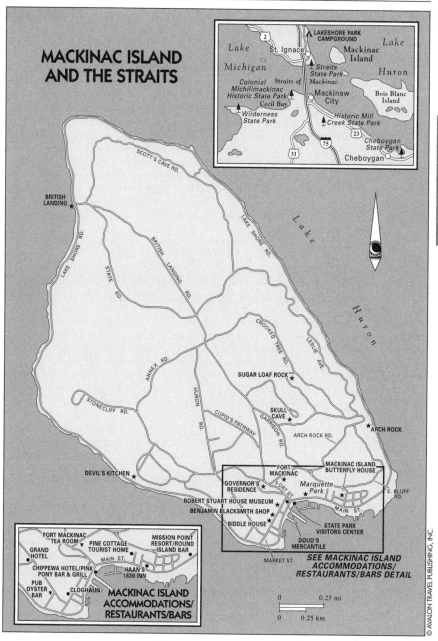

# MACKINAC ISLAND AND THE STRAITS

**THE EASTERN U.P.**

SCOTT'S CAVE RD.

BRITISH LANDING

LAKE SHORE RD.

STATE RD.

BRITISH LANDING RD.

LAKE SHORE RD.

*Lake*

*Huron*

ANNEX RD.

CROOKED TREE RD.

LESLIE AVE.

STONECLIFF RD.

SUGAR LOAF ROCK ★

HURON RD.

SKULL CAVE ★

GARRISON RD.

CUPID'S PATHWAY

ARCH ROCK RD.

★ ARCH ROCK

DEVIL'S KITCHEN ★

FORT MACKINAC

MACKINAC ISLAND BUTTERFLY HOUSE

GOVERNOR'S RESIDENCE ★

FORT ST.

*Marquette Park*

E. BLUFF RD.

ROBERT STUART HOUSE MUSEUM ★

BENJAMIN BLACKSMITH SHOP ★

MAIN ST.

BIDDLE HOUSE ★

STATE PARK VISITORS CENTER

DOUD'S MERCANTILE

MARKET ST.

**SEE MACKINAC ISLAND ACCOMMODATIONS/ RESTAURANTS/BARS DETAIL**

### Inset (top right)

LAKESHORE PARK CAMPGROUND

2

St. Ignace

*Lake Michigan*

*Lake Huron*

Mackinac Island

Straits State Park Mackinac

Colonial Michilimackinac Historic State Park

Straits of Mackinac

Cecil Bay

Mackinaw City

Bois Blanc Island

Wilderness State Park

Historic Mill Creek State Park

23

31

75

Cheboygan State Park

Cheboygan

### Inset (bottom left): MACKINAC ISLAND ACCOMMODATIONS/RESTAURANTS/BARS

FORT MACKINAC TEA ROOM

MISSION POINT RESORT/ROUND ISLAND BAR

PINE COTTAGE TOURIST HOME

GRAND HOTEL

MAIN ST.

CHIPPEWA HOTEL/PINK PONY BAR & GRILL

HAAN'S 1830 INN

PUB OYSTER BAR

CLOGHAUN

**MACKINAC ISLAND ACCOMMODATIONS/ RESTAURANTS/BARS**

0        0.25 mi

0        0.25 km

**THE EASTERN U.P.**

## The Feuding French and British

French Jesuit missionaries were the first Europeans to settle in the area, establishing a mission in nearby St. Ignace in 1671, with the obvious goal of converting the Indians. The French were also the first whites to exploit the rich fur harvest, establishing a trading post in St. Ignace in the late 1600s. They established Fort Michilimackinac, in Mackinaw City, in 1715, today a state park. (See **Mackinaw City,** below.)

The British, meanwhile, were also eager to expand their land development in the area. They regularly skirmished with the French, and Fort Michilimackinac traded hands more than once. That was ended by the 1763 Treaty of Paris, which gave all French land east of the Mississippi to Great Britain.

## Americans Enter the Fray

Alas, upstart colonists quickly became the new enemy. The British commander abandoned Fort Michilimackinac in favor of Mackinac Island in 1780, where the high limestone bluffs offered better protection from attack. Though American troops never came, they won the fort anyway, gaining title to the northern territory after the American Revolution. Still, the stubborn British refused to turn over the fort until 1796.

Did we say stubborn? During the War of 1812, British troops landed at the northern end of the island in early morning darkness, dragged a couple of cannon up the bluff and aimed them at Fort Mackinac below. The surprised Americans surrendered without firing a single shot. The British once again controlled Fort Mackinac until 1814, when the Treaty of Ghent passed the land back to the United States once and for all.

The first American to benefit was John Jacob Astor. He set up the headquarters of the American Fur Company here in 1817, bartering with the Indians for beaver pelts and storing them in warehouses on the island. Until overhunting decimated the fur industry and commercial fishing became the area's mainstay, Astor ranked as the richest man in the United States.

## The Gilded Age

By the second half of the 19th century, Mackinac Island had evolved from a battleground to a gracious getaway. Egged on by railroads and steamer lines looking to build business, wealthy Midwesterners began summering on Mackinac, having heard about its lovely waters and clean, pollen-free air. "The air up here is so healthy, you have to go somewhere else to die," an American soldier stationed at the fort recorded in his journal.

They came by lake steamer from Detroit, Chicago, and Montreal; as word spread of this gracious spot, others came from farther afield, traveling by railroad to a Great Lakes port. Hotels and boardinghouses sprang up, often housing guests for the entire summer. By the 1890s, private homes began appearing along the east and west bluffs, Victorian "cottages" that grew to 30 rooms or more, with elaborate carriage houses and stables and rooms for servants.

The automobile was banned from Mackinac Island as quickly as it arrived, as unusually wise and forward-thinking islanders quickly realized the destructive impact it would have on the tiny island. Today, more than 600 horses are stabled on the island in summer, used for hauling freight, pulling carriages, and private transportation and recreation. Most horses winter on the mainland (now, that would be a ferry trip worth seeing!), while a couple of dozen remain on the island to provide service for the island's 600 or so year-round residents.

The horses, carts, and carriages, the fleets of bicycles, and the well-preserved Victorians lined up across the bluffs all combine to give Mackinac the magical, frozen-in-time feel that has turned it into one of the most popular vacation destinations in the Midwest.

## ST. IGNACE

The St. Ignace (IG-nus) economy benefits from two groups of tourists: those stopping by on their way to Upper Peninsula destinations, and those using it as a base for Mackinac Island day trips and area exploration. Along with a large supply of lodgings, restaurants, and services, the city at the north end of the Mackinac Bridge has a few attractions of its own.

# JACQUES MARQUETTE

A Roman Catholic missionary and explorer from France, Jacques Marquette (1637–1675) established a mission among the Ottawa at St. Ignace. He, along with Louis Joliet, was probably the first white man to explore much of the Great Lakes region and the Upper Mississippi.

Born in Laon, France, Marquette joined the Jesuit order in 1656 and spent the next 10 years studying and teaching in France. In 1666, Jesuit priests sent him to the New France (present-day Quebec) as a missionary. Like many Jesuits, he lived among the Indians and studied their languages. In 1671, he was appointed missionary to the Ottawa tribe, and established the St. Ignace mission on the north shore of the Straits of Mackinac.

In 1672, French explorer Louis Joliet arrived at the mission, sent by the governor of New France, Comte de Frontenac, to search for a trade route to the Far East. They had heard from the Indians about a great waterway, Missi Sipi ("Big River"), that they thought might flow into the Pacific Ocean. Marquette, with his knowledge of Indian languages, was to accompany Joliet.

Marquette, Joliet, and five other Frenchmen set out in canoes across the northern shore of Lake Michigan in May 1673. They traveled down Green Bay and up the Fox River in present-day Wisconsin, where local Indians led them to a portage to the Wisconsin River. The team followed the Wisconsin to its confluence with the Mississippi and explored the Mississippi all the way to the Arkansas River. They grew alarmed by both the swiftness of the water and word from the Indians about white men downstream. Fearing they would be attacked by Spaniards and deducing that the southerly flow of the river would not lead to the Pacific, the explorers turned back. They paddled the Illinois River to the Chicago River, then followed the western shore of Lake Michigan to Green Bay—a staggering journey of more than 2,900 miles. Along the way, they peaceably communicated with dozens of Indian tribes.

An ailing Marquette spent the winter at a mission in Wisconsin, returning to Illinois the following spring to work with Indians he had met along his voyage. In 1765, he died on Lake Michigan near present-day Ludington, Michigan, en route back to Sault Ste. Marie. Marquette and Joliet's exploration added greatly to the white man's knowledge of North American geography. The Indians who treated him so well would later suffer when that new knowledge spurred increasing European settlement.

## Father Marquette National Memorial and New France Discovery Center

High above the Straits of Mackinac, this largely open-air site commemorates French explorer and Jesuit missionary Jacques Marquette. In the 1660s and 1670s, Marquette paddled through the Great Lakes, founding dozens of cities—including Sault Ste. Marie and St. Ignace—along the way. Next, Marquette linked up with Louis Joliet and paddled another several thousand miles, thus becoming the first white explorers of the Mississippi.

Walking trails feature interpretive signs that discuss Marquette's Great Lakes travels and the impact the area geography had on the area's settlement. A small museum (open Memorial Day–Labor Day only) includes displays and artifacts, including an intriguing replica of Marquette's journal, in which he describes his Mississippi River excursion. Little emphasis is given to the impact Marquette's missionary work had on Native Americans, thousands of whom Marquette converted to Christianity.

The memorial is on the grounds of Straits State Park, west of I-75 and south of US-2. Park sticker required for entry. For information on the memorial and current museum hours, call 906/643-9394.

## Museum of Ojibwa Culture

In contrast to the Father Marquette memorial, this excellent museum at 500 N. State in downtown St. Ignace, 906/643-9161, tells the story of the Ojibwa and the effect the European explorers had on their culture. Ironically, the museum is on the presumed site of Father Marquette's grave and the site of his Jesuit mission.

Displays housed in a former Catholic church include artifacts from archaeological digs on the grounds (some dating to 6000 B.C.), explanations of how the Ojibwa adapted and survived in the area's sometimes harsh climate, and a discussion of how they allied with the French fur traders, though it greatly diminished their traditional way of life. The Huron boardwalk follows the shoreline, with interpretive signs explaining the role of the bay in the area's settlement.

One of the best ways to learn about Michigan's Native Americans is to attend a powwow. Powwows celebrate a tribe's heritage, through colorful dancing, feasting, ancient stories, and ceremonies. Many are open to the public and are a wonderful learning experience. One of the most elaborate powwows is held in St. Ignace each Labor Day weekend. You may also want to plan a visit around the **Festival of Native American Culture,** held the third weekend in August.

> *St. Ignace's claim to fame is its **Straits Area Auto Show,** which draws some 3,000 cars and 100,000 spectators the last weekend of June.*

Understand that powwows and many other Native American cultural events have a spiritual element to them. Halter tops, bare chests, pets, drinking, smoking, and other behavior is out of place here. Look around and see how others are acting and dressing, or ask questions of tribal representatives.

Don't miss the museum's adjacent gift shop, featuring authentic, locally made crafts such as black ash baskets, quill jewelry, and more. It also offers an excellent selection of books on both Indian and French Straits history.

### Auto Shows

St. Ignace's claim to fame is its **Straits Area Auto Show,** which draws some 3,000 cars and 100,000 spectators the last weekend of June. Most tend to be 1950s and '60s muscle cars, which cruise the streets à la *American Graffiti.* Based on the success of this auto show, St. Ignace added a variety of other automotive shows throughout the summer, featuring antiques, classics, trucks and whatever else with wheels they can come up with. Contact the St. Ignace Tourist Association (see

telephone and website information below) for specific dates, and book a room early.

### Practicalities

The St. Ignace area offers plenty of lodging, from simple motels to full-service resorts. For information, contact the **St. Ignace Area Tourist Association,** 800/338-6660, website: www.stignace.com.

The St. Ignace area gives campers lots of options, especially if you want to stay somewhere with a little seclusion but still be close to the area's many attractions. Just a couple miles west of the bridge, the **Lakeshore Park Campground,** 416 Pointe La Barbe, 906/643-9522, has RV and tent sites and access to Lake Michigan. **Straits State Park,** 906/643-8620, may not be particularly peaceful, but modern sites are clean and convenient. Of the four modern campgrounds, aim for East Loop or West Loop, which have nicely wooded sites right on the Straits with great views of the bridge. To reach the park, take I-75 to US-2 and exit at Church St., then follow Church south for a half mile.

A little farther afield, **Hog Island Point State Forest** has nice and often little-used rustic sites on the Lake Michigan shore. There are lots of sandy beaches and rest stops along this pretty stretch of road between St. Ignace and Naubinway. Follow US-2 west of Epoufette and watch for the brown sign marking the turnoff for the campground. Self-registration.

## MACKINAC ISLAND

No place name in Michigan conjures up as much history, as much attention, and as much affection as the tiny parcel known as Mackinac Island. Over the centuries, the 2,200-acre island has been a sacred ground for the Native Americans who summered here, an important base for French fur trappers, a fort for British soldiers, and a gilded summer retreat for the wealthiest of Victorian-era industrialists.

It is the Victorian era that Mackinac chose to preserve, from the exquisite 1887 Grand Hotel, with its 660-foot-long porch stretching across the hillside, to the clopping of the horse-drawn carriages down the vehicle-free streets. Yes, it can seem touristy at first blush. Yes, it can be crowded. But Mackinac Island can also be irrepressibly charming, all buffed up and neatly packaged, the state's heirloom jewel.

Some of the criticism lobbed at Mackinac is based on misconception, anyway. For starters, Mackinac is more than the tangle of fudge shops and cheap souvenirs that greet you at the ferry dock. A full 82 percent of the island is state park, comprising a restored 18th-century fort and largely undeveloped woodlands, crisscrossed with hiking and biking trails, and sprinkled with rare wildflowers and sculpted limestone outcroppings.

Secondly, Mackinac Island has far more lodging choices than the famous—and spendy—Grand Hotel. Many are moderately priced. Plan to spend at least one night, so you have a little time to wander around and get past the cliché. Mackinac doesn't lend itself well to a cursory glance. (Isn't that the joy of islands in the first place?) Like those wealthy resorters knew, Mackinac is the place to relax and retreat from the pulls of the real world.

## Downtown

Everyone wants to wander among the four blocks of shops and restaurants on Main Street. The ferry docks themselves are particularly interesting. At the Arnold Line dock, you can sneak a peek at the day-to-day grunt work of Mackinac, like workers unloading carton after carton of vegetables from the ferry and reloading them by hand onto drays (wagons) for horse-drawn delivery to area restaurants. Even the UPS man does his route on bicycle, pulling a cart loaded with packages.

Once you've done the Main Street stroll and nibbled your requisite hunk of fudge (there's a reason tourists are known as "fudgies"), make the most of your visit by getting off the main drag. You can get a good taste of what the island has to offer on a carriage tour with **Mackinac Island**

**Carriage Tours,** 906/847-3307, located across from the Arnold Line ferry dock next to the chamber of commerce. The pleasant narrated tour takes about two hours, rambling along at a relaxing pace past the Grand Hotel, Arch Rock, Skull Cave, Fort Mackinac, and most of the island's other key sights. This locally owned business is the world's largest horse and buggy livery, with more than 300 horses, mostly crosses of beefy Percherons, Belgians, and Clydesdales. Rates are $15 adults, $7.50 children 4–11.

One block inland from Main, some of Mackinac's original residences line up on **Market Street.** Much quieter than frenetic Main, Market has several interesting stops for visitors. The headquarters of the American Fur Co., John Jacob Astor's empire, is now the **Robert Stuart House Museum.** The 1817 building retains much of its original decor, including fur company ledgers, fur weighing scales, and other artifacts. The museum is operated by the City of Mackinac Island and is open daily June–Sept.

A block west, knowledgeable interpreters demonstrate spinning at **Biddle House** and smithing at the **Benjamin Blacksmith Shop.** These and other historic buildings are part of the state park, and are included with the admission ticket to Fort Mackinac. They have shorter hours than the fort, though, open from 11 A.M.–4 or 5 P.M. For current information, stop by the park visitors center across from Marquette Park on Huron Street, or contact Mackinac State Historic Parks, 213/436-4100, website: www.mackinacparks.com.

From Marquette Park, follow Fort Street up the hill to the **Governor's Residence** at the corner of Fort and East Bluff Road. The state purchased the "cottage" in the 1940s. It is the official summer residence of the governor, though the amount of time actually spent here varies from governor to governor. The house is open for tours on Wednesday mornings.

Some of the island's more impressive "cottages" line up along **East Bluff.** Wander east from the governor's mansion to see some of these Victorian marvels. Happily, most survived the Depression era—when they could be purchased for pennies on the dollar, of course. Today, they're

the Grand Hotel

well cared for and worth $1 million plus. (And remember, most are summer homes only!)

Work your way down one of the sets of public steps to the lakefront. Main Street has become Huron Street here. Continue your walk east, passing smaller but no less appealing cottages and homes. Many are skirted with geraniums and lilacs, the island's signature flowers. Behind Ste. Anne's Catholic Church, seek out the **Mackinac Island Butterfly House,** 906/847-3972, tucked away on McGulpin Street.

Owner Doug Beardsley used to use his greenhouses to grow thousands of geraniums for the Grand Hotel and others. He relied on biodynamic growing methods, releasing beneficial insects to care for his plants rather than chemical sprays. When economics made his small greenhouse less viable, he stuck with his insects. After hearing about a butterfly house in Europe, Beardsley added some different host plants and began ordering pupa from around the world. Now hundreds of butterflies fly freely in his greenhouse/atrium, some nearly six inches long. You can observe them up close on walls and plants, or sit still long enough and they'll land on you.

The engaging Beardsley hopes his attraction will help convince gardeners to wean themselves off herbicides and pesticides. He sells helpful insects to control garden pests like aphids and will give you ideas for attracting butterflies to your own garden. (Host plants like milkweed and cabbage, where butterflies like to lay their eggs, will work best. "Think of it as planting a caterpillar garden, not a butterfly garden," he says.) Admission is $5 adults, $2 children 6–12.

## Grand Hotel

The Grand Hotel has become practically synonymous with Mackinac Island, a gracious edifice built on a truly grand scale. It is the largest summer resort in the world, operating from early May through late October. Its famous 660-foot-long covered front porch gets decked out each spring with 2,000 geraniums planted in seven *tons* of potting soil. Its 11 restaurants and bars serve as many as 4,000 meals a day. Its impeccable grounds offer guests every amenity, from saddle horses to designer golf to bocci ball to swimming in the outdoor pool made famous by the 1940s swimming actress Esther Williams, who filmed *This Time for Keeps* here.

But opulence is what the railroads and steamships were after when they formed a consortium and built the Grand Hotel in 1887, dragging construction materials across the frozen waters by horse and mule. The wealthiest of all Mackinac Island visitors stayed here, of course, high on the hill.

Yet unlike other turn-of-the-century resorts that burned to the ground or grew dog-eared and faded, the Grand Hotel has managed to maintain its grace and dignity over the years. It still hosts all manner of celebrities and politicians—five U.S. presidents to date—and still offers a sip of the Gilded Age, with high tea in the parlor each afternoon and demitasse served after dinner each evening. Room rates still include a five-course dinner in the soaring main dining room, and jacket/ties and skirts/dresses are still the required attire.

The Grand Hotel's time-capsule setting prompted director Jeannot Szwarc to choose it as the location for the 1980 film *Somewhere in Time,* starring Christopher Reeve, Jane Seymour, and Christopher Plummer. For whatever reason, the movie has developed a huge following; its fan club reunites at the hotel each year in late October.

While room rates can get outright absurd ($650-plus per night), doubles start at $350, including breakfast and dinner, and perhaps can be considered a worthwhile splurge if you enjoy this kind of thing. What the heck—take tea, loll in the beautifully landscaped pool, or dance to the swing orchestra in the Terrace Room. Nonguests can sneak a peek at the hotel's public areas and grounds for a not-unreasonable $7. (It's needed to

thin the sightseers more than anything.) Highly recommended are a stroll through the grounds, filled with Victorian gardens—24,000 tulips in spring!—and a visit to the snazzy Cupola Bar, with views halfway to Wisconsin.

For availability and rates, contact Grand Hotel, 800/33-GRAND, website: www.grandhotel.com.

## Fort Mackinac

Located at the crest of the bluff, whitewashed Fort Mackinac is worth a visit for the views alone, presiding over—as forts do—the downtown, the marina, and Lake Huron. But there's also plenty to see at this military outpost, which the British and Americans haggled over for nearly 40 years (see **History,** above).

Along with peering over the parapets, you can wander in and out of 14 buildings within the fort. The barracks, officers' quarters, post hospital, and others are filled with interpretive displays and decorated in period decor. Costumed guides lead all sorts of reenactments, including musket firings and cannon salutes. A short audiovisual presentation, "The Heritage of Mackinac," does a good job of presenting basic history.

Admission to the fort is $8 adults, $5 children 6–17, and also includes admission to several other historic buildings on the island. If you're planning on visiting Colonial Michilimackinac or Historic Mill Creek State Park on the mainland, the combination ticket is your best deal, giving you unlimited seasonal admission to all three parks for $17 adult, $10 children 6–17. The fort is open early May through mid-October—June 15–Labor Day 9:30 A.M.–5 P.M., with reduced hours in early and late season. For information, stop by the park visitors center across from Marquette Park on Huron Street, or contact Mackinac State Historic Parks, 213/436-4100, website: www.mackinacparks.com.

## Natural Mackinac

Often overshadowed by other visitor attractions, Mackinac Island's natural history has attracted scientific observation for nearly 200 years. In the early 19th century, botanists discovered several species completely new to science, including the dwarf lake iris, still found only in the Straits of Mackinac region.

Early scientists also marveled at the island's distinctive geology, mostly brecciated limestone that has been sculpted by eons of wind and waves. The result is some dramatic rock formations, like the giant inland slab of limestone called Sugar Loaf Rock, the lakeside caves of Devil's Kitchen, and impressive Arch Rock, which rises nearly 150 feet above the eastern shore and spans some 50 feet.

In recognition of the park's distinctive "natural curiosities" and growing tourism, the U.S. government created Mackinac National Park in 1875—following Yellowstone as the nation's second national park. Twenty years later, it was returned to Michigan and became Mackinac Island State Park, Michigan's first state park.

### Exploring the Rest of the Island

Walk, run, or bike, but make sure you get out of downtown to really see Mackinac Island. You'll be surprised how quickly you can leave any crowds behind as you set out on the paved eight-mile path that circles the island. The trail never wanders far from the pleasant shoreline and passes many of the island's natural features, which are well marked. Traveling clockwise, the first you'll reach is Devil's Kitchen; heading in the opposite direction, you'll arrive first at Arch Rock, the most dramatic of all Mackinac limestone oddities.

About halfway around, on the island's northwestern side lies **British Landing,** where British soldiers sneaked onto the island in 1812. They hiked across Mackinac's interior, totally surprising the American garrison stationed at the fort (and apparently looking the other way), and recaptured the island. Today, the landing is a good spot for a picnic or short break (water and restrooms available). There's a small **nature center** here, staffed in summer months by a helpful naturalist. Hike the short **nature trail,** which has several interpretive signs as it weaves up a bluff.

British Landing is also a good spot from which to head inland and explore the island's interior. British Landing Road bisects the island

**Arch Rock**

© TRAVEL MICHIGAN

and links up with Garrison Road near Skull Cave, leading to the fort. It's a hilly, three-mile trip from shore to shore. British Landing Road is considered a "major road" by Mackinac standards, meaning you'll share it with carriages. On bike or foot, you'll have endless other options—at last count, Mackinac had some 140 miles of trails and footpaths.

Pick up a free *Mackinac Island Map,* available all over town, and venture off. The map marks the location of old cemeteries, rock formations, and such, but it's even more appealing to just explore the smaller trails on your own and discover pretty, peaceful Mackinac. Everything's well marked, and you can't really get lost anyway—you're on a small island, after all.

### Accommodations

Along with the Grand Hotel (see above), there are plenty of grand and graceful places to stay on Mackinac Island. Yes, rates can be high, and as you'll see below, the range of prices can be astounding wide even within one particular property. (You'll pay dearly for a water view.) But don't dismiss staying on Mackinac; you can find reasonable rates at smaller B&Bs and apartments, the latter of which often have good deals for weeklong stays. The options below tip both ends of the scale. For information on more island accommodations, including rates and photos, visit website: www.mackinac.com/lodging.

The **Chippewa Hotel,** 800/241-3341, is a venerable old Mackinac Hotel that had a $3 million renovation a few years back. The result is a classy and comfortable place to stay, with a location in the heart of the island, on Main St. overlooking the marina. The 24-person lakeside hot tub alone may be worth the stay. Rates $100–300.

The **Mission Point Resort,** 906/847-3312, may have the island's very best location, spread across 18 acres at the island's southeastern tip. Though not Victorian era—it was built in the 1950s by the Moral Rearmament Movement, a post-World War II patriotic group—the sprawling, bright-white resort is attractive and well-kept, with beautiful lawns lined with Adirondack chairs. Amenities include an outdoor pool, tennis and volleyball courts, and loads of kids' activities. ("No Nintendo to be found," its brochure announces.) Rates $125–500.

**Cloghaun** (CLA-hahn), 906/847-3885, was built in 1884 by Thomas and Bridgette Donnelly, who left their Irish homeland during the great potato famine and followed a relative to Mackinac Island. Today, this grand Victorian with large grounds is still owned by their descendants. It's located on Market Street, next to some of the island's historic attractions and just one block from Main. Eight rooms have private baths; two others share. Rates $110–175, including breakfast.

Below East Bluff near Ste. Anne's Church, **Haan's 1830 Inn,** 906/847-6244, is a Greek Revival built by Colonel Preston, one of the last officers to preside over Fort Mackinac. Just try to drag yourself out of the wicker chairs on the big front porch. Four of the seven rooms have private baths; one suite includes a full kitchen. Rates $125–175, including continental breakfast.

The **Pine Cottage Tourist Home,** just three blocks from Main Street, 906/847-3820, offers one of the island's most economical lodging op-

tions, with inexpensive double occupancy rates starting at $50.

There is **no camping** on Mackinac Island. See **St. Ignace** and **Mackinaw City** for nearby campgrounds on the mainland.

## Food

One of the best dining deals on the island is the **Fort Mackinac Tea Room,** located in the lower level of the Officer's Stone Quarters within the fort. Surrounded by thick masonry walls, the tearoom serves up both a great atmosphere and great food, with good soups, salads, and sandwiches prepared by Grand Hotel chefs. Entrees are a reasonable $7. Opt for a spot on the terrace since the high setting is outstanding, and forts were not exactly designed for expansive views.

Everyone has to hit the **Pink Pony Bar & Grill,** 906/847-3341, at least sometime during a Mackinac visit. Located in the Chippewa Hotel overlooking the marina, this is *the* party place following the famed Chicago-to-Mac yacht race. The food's great, too, with good burgers, whitefish sandwiches and such on the lunch menu, and steaks, seafood, and ribs for dinner. Dinner entrees average about $17. Outdoor patio dining in season.

The **Round Island Bar,** 906/847-3312, at the Mission Point Resort, has sandwiches and salads in a casual setting overlooking the Straits and neighboring Round Island. The **Pub Oyster Bar,** 906/847-3454, on Main just a few doors west of the chamber of commerce, serves all day long in its appealing 1890s saloon setting.

Sooner or later, you'll succumb to **fudge.** A visitor treat since Victorian tourism days, shops line Main Street. Two of the oldest, Murdick's and Ryba's, both have three Main Street locations. You can buy a sizable slab to take or mail home, or just a small sliver to nibble. (A little goes a long way—it's very rich stuff.) Pick up picnic fixings at **Doud's Mercantile,** 906/847-3551, at the corner of Main and Fort Streets.

## Getting There and Getting Around

A million people visit Mackinac Island every year, so getting there isn't a problem. Three **ferry services** can zip you across to Mackinac in less than

20 minutes. They operate several times a day and are virtually nonstop June–Aug. Ferries run from late April through late October, when the island pretty much shuts down for the winter. (More and more lodges, though, are reopening for the holidays to accommodate a growing population of snowmobilers and cross-country skiers.)

All three ferry lines depart from docks—essentially next to one another—at both St. Ignace on the north end of the bridge and Mackinaw City on the south end. Roundtrip prices for all three are also comparable: $15.50 adults, $7.50 children 5–13. Pick up the omnipresent brochures to find one with the most convenient departure times. The **Arnold Line,** 800/542-8528, is the granddaddy of them all, operating since 1878. Also contact **Shepler's Mackinac Island Ferry,** 800/828-6157, and **Star Line,** 800/638-9892, for current rates and schedules.

No matter which ferry you choose, it will deposit you at the southern end of the island, in the heart of the hotels and shops lined up along Main Street, which follows the curve of the waterfront. It's a wild scene: dock workers load luggage onto pull-carts and carriages, flocks of bicycles dodge horse-drawn buggies, pedestrians stream up and down the road eating fudge and window shopping.

**Horse-drawn "taxis"** are available 24 hours a day from organizations like Carriage Tours Taxi Service, 906/847-3323. If you enjoy walking and hiking, you can get around Mackinac on foot; the island is about eight miles in circumference. Mackinac is a wonderful place for casual strolls and all-day hikes. The island also is a great place to cycle. **Bicycle rentals** are available all over downtown, for about $5/hour or $20/day. Equipment varies, so look before you pay. If you plan to do much cycling, you'll be happier with your own bike, since you can transport it on the ferry for about $6.50 roundtrip. You'll want a hybrid or mountain bike to negotiate most interior trails. Bring your own helmet.

### Information

The tiny but helpful **Mackinac Island Chamber of Commerce** is located across Main from the Arnold Line ferry dock. For help with accommodations and other information ahead of time, contact the office at 800/454-5227, website: www.mackinac.com/Touristinfo.

## MACKINAW CITY

Unless you're a fan of strip malls and souvenir shopping, there's not a lot to recommend in hyper-developed Mackinaw City, with a few very notable exceptions. Two of Michigan's excellent historic parks are here—and, of course, the always-beautiful Great Lakes views.

### Colonial Michilimackinac Historic State Park

Believed to be the nation's longest-running archaeological dig, archaeologists have been uncovering treasures since 1959 on the site of this 18th-century fur-trading post. Long a well-traveled Indian hunting and trading ground, the French built a post here in 1715. The French exploited the Indians, bribing them with gifts and alcohol, and encouraging them to work in the fur trade. Though the unfortunate relationship led many Indians to abandon their traditional way of life, the two groups rarely fought. Instead, the

**Historic Mill Creek State Park**

French feuded with the British, who sought to expand their landholdings in the region. For the next 65 years, the fort along the Straits alternately fell under French and British control.

The fort's most violent episode occurred while it was under British rule. In 1763, Pontiac, the Ottawa war chief, ordered an attack on British posts all over Michigan, an attempt to drive the growing British population out of their native land. While Pontiac laid siege to Detroit, local Ojibwa stormed the fort, killing all but 13 soldiers. In the end, though, it was the feisty colonists who sent the British fleeing from Fort Michilimackinac. They dismantled what they could and burned the rest to the ground in 1780, opting for a new, more-defensible post on nearby Mackinac Island.

Today, Colonial Michilimackinac State Park portrays the lives of both the Indians and European settlers, with costumed interpreters reenacting daily life at an Indian encampment and a stockaded fort. Displays include many of the artifacts unearthed by archaeologists. Interpreters demonstrate various crafts and skills, from cooking and weaving to cleaning weapons. Interpreters are quite knowledgeable and able to answer most visitors' questions. Don't miss the underground archaeological tunnel exhibit, "Treasures from the Sand." The park also includes an often-overlooked maritime museum at the nearby Old Mackinac Point lighthouse.

Admission to Colonial Michilimackinac is $8 adults, $5 children 6–17. If you're planning on visiting nearby Historic Mill Creek State Park or Fort Mackinac on Mackinac Island, buy a combination ticket, which gives you unlimited seasonal admission to all three parks for $17 adult, $10 children 6–17.

The park is open early May through mid-October, June 15–Labor Day 9 A.M.–5 P.M., until 6 P.M. from mid-June to mid-August. It's located just west of the Mackinac Bridge in Mackinaw City. For information, contact Mackinac State Historic Parks, 213/436-4100, website: www.mackinacparks.com.

## Historic Mill Creek State Park

Today, this exceptionally pretty glen and rushing stream create a pleasant oasis for visitors, but it once was an innovative industrial site. When the British made plans to move from Fort Michilimackinac to Mackinac Island, Scotsman Robert Campbell recognized their imminent need for lumber. He purchased 640 acres of the land around the only waterway in the area with enough flow to power a sawmill. He built the mill in 1790 and later added a blacksmith shop and gristmill.

The site was no longer profitable when the fort ceased operation, so it was abandoned in the mid-1800s. Since the 1970s, archaeologists and historians have worked together to re-create the water-powered sawmill on its original site. Today, visitors can see the splashing waterwheel in action and visit the Orientation Center, which has an audiovisual presentation and displays on other artifacts uncovered during the dig. Make sure to walk the park's 1.5 miles of trails, which wind along the creek and mill pond, rising up to scenic overlooks with views of the Straits and Mackinac Island.

Mill Creek is located just southeast of Mackinaw City on US-23. Mill Creek has the same schedule and information contacts as Colonial Michilimackinac Historic State Park (see above). Admission is $6.75 adults, $4 children 6–17. It also participates in the combination ticket package, as described in the Colonial Michilimackinac Historic State Park listing.

## Mackinac Bridge Museum

It's not slick or fancy, but this small museum above Mama Mia's Pizza at 231 E. Central, 231/436-8751, is loaded with tidbits and artifacts on the construction of the $100 million Mackinac Bridge. A very well-done video doc-

**THE EASTERN U.P.**

## THE BUILDING OF "BIG MAC"

A bridge across the Straits of Mackinac, connecting the Lower and Upper Peninsulas of Michigan, was first proposed in 1884. It remained a point of debate for decades. Detractors believed that such a structure—required to span nearly five miles of open water—was an impossible feat. But "the people of Michigan built the world's greatest bridge," wrote bridge designer David B. Steinman. "They built it in the face of discouragement, of faintheartedness on the part of many of their leaders, of warnings that the rocks in the Straits were too soft, the ice too thick, the winds too strong, the rates of interest on the bonds too high, and the whole concept too big."

Steinman and his supporters proved the detractors wrong. After three years of construction and $99 million, the Mackinac Bridge opened on November 1, 1957. It was, and is, an engineering marvel, the world's longest total suspension bridge. Some 33 underwater foundations support the four-mile-long steel structure. It is designed to withstand anything Mother Nature can dish out, including winds up to 600 miles per hour!

© DAVE MICHIGAN

Not everyone appreciates the engineering show; bridge workers take over the wheel about 3,000 times a year for drivers too terrified to cross the bridge themselves.

But for most, the Mackinac Bridge is Michigan's pride and joy. Not only do hotel rooms with bridge views command premium rates, the bridge opened up the Upper Peninsula to the hundreds of cars that used to form a huge snarl waiting for the ferry. (Especially during fall hunting season, the wait to cross the Straits could

It can be unnerving to drive across the Mackinac Bridge, which visibly bows as much as 30 feet in strong crosswinds. The 552-foot-high towers are designed to give, too, swaying as much as 15 feet.

stretch to six hours or more.) Today, it's just a matter of handing over $1.50 and keeping both hands on the wheel—and all of Michigan is yours to explore, linked together as one.

uments the bridge's design and construction. Free admission.

## Old Mackinac Point Light

Located on a point just east of the Mackinac Bridge, this 1892 cream-brick light guided ships through the busy Straits of Mackinac for nearly 70 years. When the Mackinac Bridge was completed in 1957, it became obsolete, since vessels could range on the bridge's high lights instead of the diminutive 40-foot tower. Today this charming lighthouse, topped with a cherry-red roof, houses a maritime museum, part of Colonial Michilimackinac State Park. A schooner and other ships are docked and on display. The lighthouse grounds serve as their own delightful little park, with impressive views of the Mackinac Bridge as well as picnic tables scattered around a tidy lawn.

## Beaches

About four miles west of Mackinaw City on Wilderness Park Road, Lake Michigan curves into Cecil Bay, with sandy shores and shallow water. Public restrooms available.

## Practicalities

With the Straits a major tourism draw, Mackinaw City alone has more than 3,000 rooms. For lodging and other information, contact the Mackinaw Area Tourist Bureau, 800/666-0160, website: www.mackinawcity.com.

The nearest state campground is 12 miles west at wonderful Wilderness State Park, 898 Wilderness Park Dr., 231/436-5381, situated at the end of a point. It offers 26 miles of Lake Michigan shoreline and 16 miles of hiking trails. The park has two campgrounds, one on the lakeshore and another tucked away in a grove of mature pines. It also has five rustic cabins and three larger, 24-bunk lodges for rent.

Twenty miles east of Mackinaw City, Cheboygan State Park, 4490 Beach Rd., 616/627-2811, has modern sites near Lake Huron's Duncan Bay. (None are directly on the water.) The area is a favorite among anglers, but there's not much in the way of swimming at the campground; instead, head for the park's day-use area, four miles away, which has a sandy beach and bathhouse.

# Resources

# Suggested Reading

Barnes, Burton, and Wagner, Warren. *Michigan Trees.* Ann Arbor: University of Michigan, 1981. Field guide written by two University of Michigan professors of forestry and botany, respectively.

Blacklock, Craig. *The Lake Superior Images.* Moose Lake, MN: Blacklock Nature Photography, 1993. Blacklock, son of famous nature photographer Les Blacklock, circumnavigated Lake Superior by kayak to capture images for this award-winning book that belongs on every northern coffee table.

Catton, Bruce. *Waiting for the Morning Train: An American Boyhood.* Detroit: Wayne State University Press, 1987. Pulitzer prize–winning Catton wrote this book reflecting on his boyhood in Benzonia, southwest of Traverse City. A beguiling look at boyhood memories that segues into more serious discussions about the impact of technology on our society.

Clifton, James, McClurken, James, and Cornell, George. *People of the Three Fires.* Grand Rapids: Grand Rapids Inner-Tribal Council, 1986. An excellent introduction to the Ottawa, Potawatomi, and Ojibwa cultures, with an emphasis on history and traditions, but also a good discussion of modern Indian issues.

DuFresne, Jim. *Isle Royale National Park: Foot Trails and Water Routes.* Seattle: The Mountaineers, 1984. The definitive guide to Isle Royale, filled with practical information about campsites, portages, fishing spots, and more. Small enough to carry along, and you should.

DuFresne, Jim. *Michigan State Parks: A Complete Recreation Guide for Campers, Boaters, Anglers, Hikers, and Skiers.* Seattle: The Mountaineers, 1989. Michigan outdoor writer DuFresne worked with the Michigan Department of Natural Resources to compile this handy guide, which devotes a couple of pages to each of Michigan's state parks.

Emerick, Lon L. *The Superior Peninsula: Seasons in the Upper Peninsula of Michigan.* Skandia, MI: North Country, 1996. A collection of essays and "love letters" about the big lake, categorized by seasons.

Hemingway, Ernest. *The Complete Short Stories.* New York: Simon & Schuster, 1987. Hemingway's works have been packaged and repackaged, of course, but this volume includes his finest Michigan-based short stories: "Up in Michigan," set in Horton's Bay, and numerous Nick Adams tales, including "Big Two-Hearted River," about fishing in the Upper Peninsula.

Huber, N. King. *The Geologic Story of Isle Royale National Park.* Washington, D.C.: U.S. Department of the Interior Geological Survey, 1996. For a government publication, this is a rather colorfully written study of Isle Royale's distinctive topography. Understanding even a little makes an Isle Royale backpacking trip all the more memorable.

Michigan Department of Natural Resources. *A Most Superior Land.* Lansing: Two Peninsula Press, 1983. A wonderful series of short essays and anecdotal tales about the history of the Upper Peninsula. Loaded with great historical photos, too.

Rydholm, C. Fred. *Superior Heartland: A Backwoods History.* Marquette: (published privately), 1989. These two enormous volumes comprise hundreds of short chapters of U.P. history, the kind of thing you don't have to read chronologically. Exhaustively researched, it's filled with all kinds of quirky stories and character studies you won't find elsewhere.

Smith, Helen V. *Michigan Wildflowers*. Bloomfield Hills, MI: Cranbrook Institute of Science, 1979. Field guide written by University of Michigan professor of paleobotany.

Stocking, Kathleen. *Lake Country*. Ann Arbor: University of Michigan Press, 1994. Another series of essays from this talented local writer, this time expanding her observations beyond the Leelanau to other areas of Michigan.

Stocking, Kathleen. *Letters from the Leelanau*. Ann Arbor: University of Michigan Press, 1990. Poignant personal essays about the people and places of Stocking's native Leelanau Peninsula.

Stonehouse, Frederick. *The Wreck of the Edmund Fitzgerald*. Marquette: Lake Superior Press, 1997. The definitive (if there can be such a thing) discussion on the events leading up to this famous shipwreck and the various theories that caused its demise.

Traver, Robert. *Anatomy of a Murder*. New York: St. Martins Press, 1983. The popular novel-turned-movie was penned by local state Supreme Court Justice John Voelker (a.k.a. Robert Traver), about a lover's-triangle murder that took place in nearby Big Bay.

Traver, Robert. *Trout Madness*. West Bloomfield, MI: Northmont Publishing, 1992. As the introduction reads, "Being a dissertation on the symptoms and pathology of this incurable disease by one of its victims."

Traver, Robert. *Trout Magic*. West Bloomfield, MI: Northmont Publishing, 1992. Another trout essay by the prolific Michigan author and judge.

# Welcome Centers

## In the Lower Peninsula:

Clare: US-27 just north of town
Coldwater: I-69, six miles north of the state line
Dundee, US-23, six miles north of the state line
Mackinaw City: M-108 in town
Monroe: I-75, 10 miles north of the state line
New Buffalo: I-94 at the state line
Port Huron: Off I-94 at 2260 Water St.

## In the Upper Peninsula:

Iron Mountain: US-2, two miles north of the state line
Ironwood: US-2 at the state line
Marquette: 2201 S. US-41
Menominee: US-41 at the state line
Sault Ste. Marie: I-75, south of the International Bridge
St. Ignace: I-75, north of the Mackinac Bridge

# Index

## Camping/Campgrounds

## Canoeing/Kayaking

## Historic Homes And Buildings/Architectural Sights

## Lighthouses

### M

## Nature And Conservation Areas

## Parks

## Trails

# Acknowledgements

This would be longer and duller than an Academy Awards speech if I tried to thank all the people who contributed to this book. As I traveled around the state, the people of Michigan were unfailingly generous and helpful, directing me to wonderful hiking trails, hidden waterfalls, good whitefish dinners, and other favorite spots. I hope I've done you justice and not given away too many secrets. As for the staff at Avalon Travel Publishing—well, there's a reason these guidebooks turn out so well, and it ain't necessarily the authors. Thank you, Erin and other Avalon editors, for your support, guidance, patience, and ability to feign calm as deadlines loomed.

Khristi Zimmeth gets special mention, a Michigan native and veteran travel writer who originally researched and wrote nearly everything you'll read in this book about the southern half of the Lower Peninsula. I could've pounded the pavement for years and still would not know Detroit and environs as well as Khristi. Thanks also to Leslie Cowan, a smart and capable high-school student who helped update the Thumb chapter.

And of course, thanks to the dozens of outfitters, park and forest service rangers, and convention and visitors bureau staffers who pointed me in all the right directions, and then put up with endless follow-up questions to boot. They often come and go too fast, moving on to different jobs before I can ever thank them properly.

Thank you to my magazine editors, who were more than generous about letting deadlines slide as I hit the home stretch with Avalon. (You're every writer's dream editor, Lois Anne!) And thanks to my office mates at Acme Illustration and ZD Studios, who encouraged me to tackle this project in the first place, and to my friends, who listened to a lot of whining.

A proverbial pat on the head goes to Brunswick, my charming yellow Lab, who galloped hundreds of miles of hiking trails, paddled in countless lakes and rivers, snuck politely into several motels, never complained about long car trips, and provided endless companionship. No, they didn't name the Yellow Dog River after him, but he doesn't know that.

And lastly, thanks to you, the reader. May you find Michigan as magical as I have.

# U.S.~METRIC CONVERSION

| | |
|---|---|
| 1 inch | = 2.54 centimeters (cm) |
| 1 foot | = .304 meters (m) |
| 1 yard | = 0.914 meters |
| 1 mile | = 1.6093 kilometers (km) |
| 1 km | = .6214 miles |
| 1 fathom | = 1.8288 m |
| 1 chain | = 20.1168 m |
| 1 furlong | = 201.168 m |
| 1 acre | = .4047 hectares |
| 1 sq km | = 100 hectares |
| 1 sq mile | = 2.59 square km |
| 1 ounce | = 28.35 grams |
| 1 pound | = .4536 kilograms |
| 1 short ton | = .90718 metric ton |
| 1 short ton | = 2000 pounds |
| 1 long ton | = 1.016 metric tons |
| 1 long ton | = 2240 pounds |
| 1 metric ton | = 1000 kilograms |
| 1 quart | = .94635 liters |
| 1 US gallon | = 3.7854 liters |
| 1 Imperial gallon | = 4.5459 liters |
| 1 nautical mile | = 1.852 km |

To compute celsius temperatures, subtract 32 from Fahrenheit and divide by 1.8. To go the other way, multiply celsius by 1.8 and add 32.

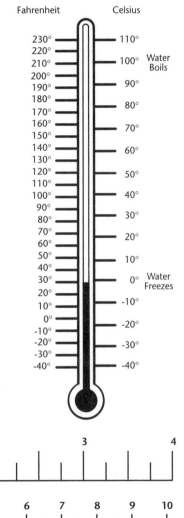

**AVALON**
**TRAVEL**
p u b l i s h i n g

How far will our travel guides take you? As far as you want.

Discover a rhumba-fueled nightspot in Old Havana, explore prehistoric tombs in Ireland, hike beneath California's centuries-old redwoods, or embark on a classic road trip along Route 66. Our guidebooks deliver solidly researched, trip-tested information—minus any generic froth—to help globetrotters or weekend warriors create an adventure uniquely their own.

And we're not just about the printed page. Public television viewers are tuning in to Rick Steves' new travel series, *Rick Steves' Europe*. On the Web, readers can cruise the virtual black top with *Road Trip USA* author Jamie Jensen and learn travel industry secrets from Edward Hasbrouck of *The Practical Nomad*.

In print. On TV. On the Internet.

We supply the information. The rest is up to you.

Avalon Travel Publishing

Something for everyone

# www.travelmatters.com

Avalon Travel Publishing guides are available at your favorite book or travel store.

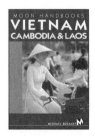

# MOON HANDBOOKS provide comprehensive

coverage of a region's arts, history, land, people, and social issues in addition to detailed practical listings for accommodations, food, outdoor recreation, and entertainment. Moon Handbooks allow complete immersion in a region's culture—ideal for travelers who want to combine sightseeing with insight for an extraordinary travel experience in destinations throughout North America, Hawaii, Latin America, the Caribbean, Asia, and the Pacific.

## WWW.MOON.COM

*Rick Steves* shows you where to travel and how to travel— all while getting the most value for your dollar. His Back Door travel philosophy is about making friends, having fun, and avoiding tourist rip-offs.

*Rick* has been traveling to Europe for more than 25 years and is the author of 22 guidebooks, which have sold more than a million copies. He also hosts the award-winning public television series *Rick Steves' Europe*.

## WWW.RICKSTEVES.COM

# ROAD TRIP USA

Getting there is half the fun, and Road Trip USA guides are your ticket to driving adventure. Taking you off the interstates and onto less-traveled, two-lane highways, each guide is filled with fascinating trivia, historical information, photographs, facts about regional writers, and details on where to sleep and eat—all contributing to your exploration of the American road.

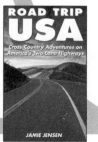

*"[Books] so full of the pleasures of the American road, you can smell the upholstery."*
~BBC radio

## WWW.ROADTRIPUSA.COM

**FOGHORN OUTDOORS** guides are for campers, hikers, boaters, anglers, bikers, and golfers of all levels of daring and skill. Each guide focuses on a specific U.S. region and contains site descriptions and ratings, driving directions, facilities and fees information, and easy-to-read maps that leave only the task of deciding where to go.

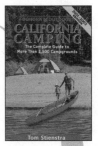

*"Foghorn Outdoors has established an ecological conservation standard unmatched by any other publisher."*
**~Sierra Club**

**WWW.FOGHORN.COM**

**TRAVEL SMART** guidebooks are accessible, route-based driving guides focusing on regions throughout the United States and Canada. Special interest tours provide the most practical routes for family fun, outdoor activities, or regional history for a trip of anywhere from two to 22 days. Travel Smarts take the guesswork out of planning a trip by recommending only the most interesting places to eat, stay, and visit.

*"One of the few travel series that rates sightseeing attractions. That's a handy feature. It helps to have some guidance so that every minute counts."*
**~San Diego Union-Tribune**

**CiTY·SMaRT™** guides are written by local authors with hometown perspectives who have personally selected the best places to eat, shop, sightsee, and simply hang out. The honest, lively, and opinionated advice is perfect for business travelers looking to relax with the locals or for longtime residents looking for something new to do Saturday night.

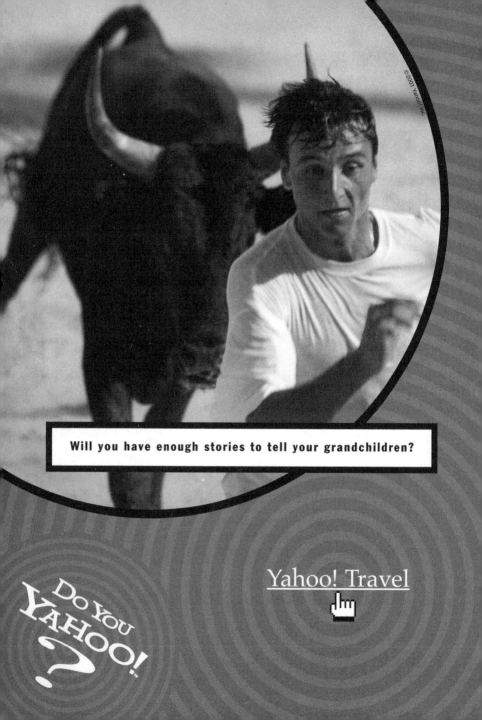